Mastering the Art of French Cooking

Illustrations by Sidonie Coryn

Mastering the Art of
FRENCH COOKING

by

Julia Child

Louisette Bertholle

Simone Beck

NEW YORK

Alfred · A · Knopf

2 0 0 9

THIS IS A BORZOI BOOK
PUBLISHED BY ALFRED A. KNOPF

Copyright © 1961, 1983, 2001 by Alfred A. Knopf
All rights reserved under International and Pan-American Copyright Conventions.
Published in the United States by Alfred A. Knopf, a division of Random House, Inc.,
New York, and simultaneously in Canada by Random House of Canada Limited,
Toronto. Distributed by Random House, Inc., New York.
www.aaknopf.com
Knopf, Borzoi Books, and the colophon are registered trademarks
of Random House, Inc.

Library of Congress Cataloging-in-Publication Data
Child, Julia. Mastering the art of French cooking.
Rev. ed. of: Mastering the art of French cooking / Simone Beck,
Louisette Bertholle, Julia Child.
Vol. 2 by Julia Child and Simone Beck.
Includes index.
1. Cookery, French. I. Bertholle, Louisette.
II. Beck, Simone.   III. Beck, Simone. Mastering the art
of French cooking. IV. Title.
TX719.C454   1983   641.5944   83-48113
ISBN 0-394-40178-6 (set)
ISBN 0-394-72114-4 (pbk.: set)
ISBN 0-394-53399-2 (v. 1)
ISBN 0-394-72178-0 (pbk.: v. 1, 40th ann. ed.)
ISBN 0-394-40152-2 (v. 2)
ISBN 0-394-72177-2 (pbk.: v. 2)
ISBN 0-375-41340-5 (v. 1, 40th ann. ed.)

Manufactured in the United States of America
PUBLISHED OCTOBER 16, 1961
REPRINTED FROM NEW PLATES, OCTOBER 1971
THIRTY-FOURTH PRINTING (REVISED), SEPTEMBER 1983
FORTIETH ANNIVERSARY HARDCOVER EDITION, OCTOBER 16, 2001
FIFTEENTH PRINTING, OCTOBER 2009
FIRST FORTIETH ANNIVERSARY PAPERBACK EDITION, OCTOBER 2004
EIGHTH PRINTING, OCTOBER 2009

TO

La Belle France

WHOSE PEASANTS, FISHERMEN, HOUSEWIVES,

AND PRINCES — NOT TO MENTION HER CHEFS —

THROUGH GENERATIONS OF INVENTIVE AND

LOVING CONCENTRATION HAVE CREATED ONE

OF THE WORLD'S GREAT ARTS

INTRODUCTION TO
THE ANNIVERSARY EDITION
by Julia Child

WHAT WAS AMERICAN food like forty years ago when this book first appeared? It's hard for me to remember since the "now" is so much with me. I grew up in Southern California, in a comfortable family, with a New England background since my mother was from Massachusetts. We ate in the typically middle-class WASP American way of the teens and twenties—a big prime-rib roast of beef for the traditional family Sunday lunch of twelve to fourteen people. If not beef we might have a fine, big, well-aged leg of lamb—always cooked medium gray, never pinky-red rare, and always served with mint sauce as well as gravy. Or there would be a fat roasted chicken with creamed onions and mashed potatoes. Always an enthusiastic carnivore, I particularly remember the beef, not only rib roasts but also magnificent big well-marbled porterhouse steaks. They were full of real beefy flavor in those days, and they were juicy. Of course, that was the happy era when emphasis was on the quality of the beef, not the fat content. Our family cooking was essentially simple and straightforward, and since it was California we always had plenty of fresh fruits and vegetables.

As to specifics, I remember aspics. Jellied madrilene was a favorite fancy soup of the period, a beef consommé flavored with fresh tomato and topped with a splash of whipped cream—that was before sour cream came upon us. Melba toast was a standard accompaniment to the soup at ladies' luncheons—and there were many of them then because running a household rather than having a career gave many women the leisure time. These carefully orchestrated meals often featured a large molded ring of tomato aspic, its center filled with chicken, crab, or lobster salad.

I cannot forget one ladies' lunch back in the 1950s. Our hostess proudly led us to our seats around a nicely appointed table where we each sat down to a pretty china plate upon which stood an upright, somewhat phallic-shaped molded aspic holding in suspension diced green grapes, diced marshmallows, and diced bananas. Surrounded lavishly but neatly with squirts of whipped cream, this lovingly constructed edifice rested on several leaves of iceberg lettuce far too small to hide anything under. After the main course, and grandly brought in to the acclaim of the guests, was a very large and high coconut cake, almost certainly made from a cake mix and, again, constructed with utmost care. That was a quite typical, dressy example of the period, created earnestly and with the most generous intentions.

When Paul and I married in the mid 1940s I had very little kitchen experience, but since his mother was a fine cook and he had lived in France, I went into it seriously with *Gourmet* magazine and *Joy of Cooking* as my guides. It took hours to get dinner on the table, but he was encouraging. A year or so after our marriage he was offered a position at the American embassy in Paris.

It was a dream fulfilled. I had always yearned to know France, and Paul, having lived there for several years as a penniless young man, dreamed of returning. He had a gift for languages and spoke beautiful French. As for me, although I had taken French all during my school years, it was taught in that useless old-fashioned way where you rarely heard the spoken language but you knew the declensions of all the verbs. Thus, I could neither speak French nor understand it. We were fortunate indeed to rent the top floor of a fine old Louis XVI–style private house, and as soon as we settled ourselves I enrolled in the Berlitz school of languages for two hours every day. Then, when I had a foot on the language, I enrolled in the Cordon Bleu cooking school. With Paul's help plus the Berlitz, and especially being at the Cordon Bleu where at that time all the lessons were in French, conversation was slowly beginning to come.

Nobody I knew, either American or French, seemed at all interested in *la cuisine française*. My American colleagues had little *femmes de ménage* who did the housekeeping, shopping, and cooking, and I was considered more than a little odd because I did all the cooking and marketing—such fun!—as well as the serving when we had company. Then one day a friend in the embassy introduced me to Simone Beck

Fischbacher—a tall, blond, vivacious Frenchwoman, known as Simca. She was passionate about cooking, had grown up in a household of fine food, and had taken many lessons with the Cordon Bleu school's master chef, Henri Pellaprat. We took to each other at once, and she introduced me to Le Cercle des Gourmettes, a French ladies' gastronomical club that met every other Tuesday to cook and eat lunch in the kitchens of the electric company.

The members of Les Gourmettes were mostly in their sixties and seventies and came just for the luncheon. Simca's friend and colleague Louisette Bertholle was also a member, and the three of us made a point of arriving at 9:00 a.m. so that we could work with the chef. We helped in the preparation of wonderfully elaborate dishes such as stuffed pheasants, poached oysters served in classic wine sauces, and beautifully molded desserts. What a marvelous opportunity it was for me, a foreigner, to be accepted in a totally French atmosphere and to be witness to and participant in the preparation of the most stylish type of *la cuisine bourgeoise.* My several Paris years with them gave me an invaluable experience and background.

During this period some American friends of mine asked Louisette, Simca, and me to give them cooking lessons. They wanted a real introduction, from *cuisine ménagère,* such as how to boil a potato, on up to *pâtés en croûte.* They didn't speak the language and preferred us to a school. Simca, always the enthusiast, agreed, and L'Ecole des 3 Gourmandes—School of the 3 Happy Eaters—was born in 1950. We not only conducted the classes ourselves, but we also enlisted the professional help of my favorite Cordon Bleu teacher, Chef Max Bugnard.

Chef Bugnard had begun as a young apprentice in his family's restaurant kitchen, then did classic *"stages"* in Paris, on several luxurious transatlantic steamers of the period, as well as at the Ritz in London, where he worked briefly under the great Escoffier. Before World War II Chef Bugnard had had his own restaurant in Bruxelles, Le Petit Vatel, but was forced to flee before the occupying Germans. When I became one of his pupils, he had retired from restaurant life and was teaching.

We raided the Cordon Bleu again in soliciting the services of its excellent pastry chef and teacher Claude Thilmont. As a younger man Chef Thilmont had been the *pâtissier* at the Café de Paris, during which period he also worked with the author herself in the writing of her seminal book for the French home cook, *Le Livre de Cuisine de Mme. E. Saint-Ange.*

You may well wonder how we were able to acquire such real treasures in our modest classes. I think that in their later years many chefs of the old school welcomed teaching. They were adored by their pupils, their work hours were civilized, and the pay was undoubtedly superior to what they could make in restaurant kitchens. We three teachers were thus being subsidized by our own pupils—not a bad idea!

For several years before we met one another, Simca and Louisette had been involved in writing a book on French cooking for Americans. They needed an American collaborator, and I was delighted to join. Because we had to write up all the recipes for our school, the basis for our book slowly took shape. We gave especially full directions for all the dishes we cooked in class, and we also wanted to discuss in detail hows and whys and basic techniques. In general our aim was to take out the mystique and to make French cooking make sense. As the work progressed Paul and I were transferred from Paris to Marseilles, and then to Germany. Our last post was in Norway, where he finally left the diplomatic service. We then settled in our big, old, gray-clapboard three-story house in Cambridge, Massachusetts. During this separation, voluminous recipes and discussions flew back and forth.

When at last our book was published the Kennedys were in the White House and whatever they did was news, including how they lived and even what they ate. They had a talented French chef in residence, René Verdon, and one read frequently about their spectacular dinners. In 1961 Americans were beginning to go to Europe almost by droves, taking but a few hours for the voyage by plane rather than almost a week by boat. People were interested in more adventurous foods, and serving those meals at home was becoming a matter of pride.

Simca came from Paris to help launch the book—her first visit to America. Although she spoke English, she did so in a delightfully French way, and was in every aspect very French indeed. In fact Paul and I always called her *"La Super Française."* The cooking classes that she had been conducting for Americans in Paris during the years before the book came out meant that she had friends and former students in various cities here. It was she who suggested we go out and drum up some sales. Book tours were something of a novelty then even for well-known authors, and certainly unusual for writers of cookbooks. I don't know how we had the chutzpah, but off we went, Simca and Paul and I. We had announced to our friends that we were coming and asked them to provide us with opportunities.

Our first stop was in Chicago, where Simca and I both had friends, and we did interviews and cooking demonstrations in private houses and for the *Chicago Tribune*. Then we went on to Detroit, and when in San Francisco we were asked to do a demonstration at one of the big department stores. The wife of the owner, in a fit of exuberance, had purchased dozens of madeleine pans—the kind you use for those shell-shaped little French cakes made famous by Marcel Proust in *Remembrance of Things Past*. But nobody there was familiar with them. Simca, of course, knew all about madeleines, so we made them by the score during our demonstrations, the audiences gobbled them, and the store sold so many pans it had to order more.

The demonstration in my hometown of Pasadena, California, was in the theater of a private club where there were no cooking facilities. However, we had managed to procure a portable stove and cooktop, buckets for water, and a six-foot demonstration table, and were able to produce a quite complicated menu. We started out with Roquefort quiche, an exotic dish at that time, which you'll find here on page 148. Then we demonstrated a handsome fish mousse baked in a ring mold, an example of which is on page 562, and we finished with Simca's signature Queen of Sheba chocolate almond cake, page 677, and my all-time favorite. Looking back on the menu, I am amazed that we managed such sophisticated food in such minimal conditions.

The morning went off very well, but then we were to repeat the performance for the afternoon demonstration. While Simca and I had to stay onstage signing cookbooks and receiving the audience, my Paul, who always volunteered to do anything that was needed, was left alone to clean up—a sticky, fishy, chocolatey mess. And where did he wash the dishes? He took over the tiny closet-size ladies' room with its little sink and soap dispenser, and he cleaned up every plate, utensil, and platter. I often marvel at this valiant and uncomplaining contribution to our cause by a former diplomat and cultural attaché.

Our tour ended in New York, with a dinner at the restaurant of Dione Lucas, the country's most revered and well-known teacher of French cooking. When Simca had arrived in New York before our tour, Judith Jones, our young editor at Knopf, asked us whom we would especially like to meet. I had always wanted to know James Beard, and Simca wanted to see Dione Lucas, since they had mutual friends in Normandy. A date was made in Dione's restaurant, where we sat up at her counter and talked while she made us her famous omelets for lunch. She and Simca had immediately started an animated conversation about Normandy, and finally Dione said to Simca, "I want to give you a dinner party!" What unheard-of generosity! We fixed a date in December, when we were to have finished our tour.

We had numerous telephone calls with Dione during our trip, and one endless conversation between Simca and our future hostess involved a pay telephone at Disneyland, and multiple quarters supplied by Paul. The menu was finally agreed upon. Dione was to prepare the first course, her renowned filets of sole in a splendid classical white wine sauce, and the dessert. We were to furnish the main course, Epaule d'Agneau Viroflay—the boned shoulder of lamb on page 335, but with a spinach and mushroom stuffing. We were to provide the wines—fortunately, Simca had a cousin in the business. We were also to supply the guest list.

The three of us professional neophytes, however, had no friends in the New York food establishment, although we knew some of the names. So we turned to nice James Beard, who entered into the project with his usual enthusiasm. Under his guidance we invited all the "who's-a-whoms" we could think of, and surprisingly almost all of them accepted—some thirty or so people.

On the day of the dinner, while Simca and I were closeted with our lamb in my niece's tiny fourth-floor walk-up apartment way off on New York's east side, Paul took over the front of the house. He found a printer to produce the menus in record time. He made out the place cards, arranged the seating, and even opened the wine just before the guests arrived. Kind James Beard got there early and introduced us and our Knopf friends, Judith Jones and Bill Koshland, to all the guests as they arrived. It was a wonderful dinner, everyone had a good time, and no one left until after midnight.

That was our beginning. We had received a marvelously favorable review from Craig Claiborne, the influential food editor of the *New York Times,* and we even appeared on NBC-TV's morning *Today* show. A few months later, while Public Television was still "Educational Television," our local Boston station decided to enlarge its programming from almost exclusively academic "talking heads" to a more diverse menu. They inaugurated an art program and a science program, and I was asked about trying out a cooking session. I had already done a book review with them, which involved, besides talk, the then highly unusual methods of making a tossed French omelet and the beating of egg whites in a big copper bowl. We agreed to try out three pilot programs, which appeared in the summer of 1962.

The station put us in the charge of Russell Morash, then a young producer of science programs, now the well-known master of *This Old House, The Victory Garden,* and other successful series. They also gave me Ruth Lockwood as associate producer—she had been with the Eleanor Roosevelt series. Ruthie and I worked closely together, with Paul in attendance, to block out three half-hour shows. They were on *coq au vin,* that famous chicken stew in red wine, see page 263, a noncollapsible cheese soufflé, titled as an unmolded soufflé, page 171, and French omelets, fully described and illustrated, see page 126.

The first was shown on a Monday in July, at 8:00 p.m. The evening was so hot and humid, and we had no air-conditioning, that we set the television out in the garden, turned on a large fan, and watched while dining with friends. Our other two shows in succeeding weeks gathered an appreciable audience even for that time of year. Although Dione Lucas had hosted the first full television cooking series, she had been off the air for several seasons, and we had the only one at that time. The station asked us if we would do thirteen more—a year's fifty-two weeks, by the way, are divided into four thirteen-week sessions. We agreed, and *The French Chef* was launched, following the general ideas in this book.

Why *The French Chef,* since I am neither the one nor the other? The first reason was that I always hoped we would have some real French chefs on the shows. We never managed that until later on. The second and more important reason: The title was short, it described the shows as real French cooking, and, of equal significance, it fit on a single line in the TV guides. It seemed that a goodly number of people wanted to know about *la cuisine française,* and it was an almost immediate success. At first we were on only in the Boston area, then Pittsburgh took us up, then San Francisco, finally New York—and I felt we were made! WGBH-Boston asked us to do thirteen more, we continued on, and the television shows certainly helped the book. We even made the cover of *Time* magazine at one point.

This fortieth anniversary edition is essentially the same book that first came out in 1961, which was reedited in 1983 to bring it up to date, especially because the food processor had appeared in American kitchens. Before the arrival of that incomparable machine, we did have the electric blender and heavy duty mixer, but the food processor revolutionized many otherwise almost hopelessly onerous tasks such as the making of fish mousses and quenelles. It simplified such often tricky procedures as pie doughs, and made fast work of routine dog work like mushroom dicing, cheese grating, bread crumbing, and onion slicing.

Mastering the Art of French Cooking is just what the title says. It is how to produce really wonderful food—food that tastes good, looks good, and is a delight to eat. That doesn't mean it has to be fancy cooking, although it can be as elaborate as you wish. It simply means careful cooking, *la cuisine soignée,* by people who know what they are doing. According to me, if you are thoroughly skilled in French techniques, because the repertoire is so vast, you have the background for almost any type of cuisine. In other words, and at the risk of creating mayhem in some circles, I think you are better as an Italian, Mexican, or even Chinese cook when you have a solid French foundation.

There is certainly nothing particularly difficult about the basics. It is a question of getting started, and of learning how to pick the best and freshest ingredients, and of knowing, reading, seeing, or being shown how to hold the knife, chop the onion, peel the asparagus, make the butter and flour *roux,* and above all of taking it seriously. If you are not used to slicing potatoes by hand or peeling, seeding, and juicing tomatoes you will be slow and a little clumsy at first. However, once you decide you are really going to do it right, you will find that with surprisingly little practice you are mastering the techniques.

The recipes here are thoroughly detailed since this is a teaching book. How about eight pages on making a simple omelet? You've got all the directions and if you can read, you can cook. You are learning by doing, and if the dish is to turn out as it should, no essential direction can be left out. How far, for instance, should the chicken be from the heat element when you are broiling it? Five to six inches. Or how fast should the oil be beaten in when you are making the garlic-and-mustard coating for a roast leg of lamb? Drop by drop. Every detail takes up space, making some actually quite simple recipes look long.

Certainly one of the important requirements for learning how to cook is that you also learn how to eat. If you don't know how an especially fine dish is supposed to taste, how can you produce it? Just like becoming an expert in wine—you learn by drinking it, the best you can afford—you learn about great food by finding the best there is, whether simple or luxurious. Then you savor it, analyze it, and discuss it with your companions, and you compare it with other experiences.

In the 1950s, when this book was conceived, and on into the 1980s, we in this country pretty well ate as we liked with little or no attention paid to lashings of the best butter and the heaviest cream. You will note this indulgence here, especially in sauces, where you reduce them with cream or where you swirl in fresh butter a generous tablespoon at a time to render them smooth, shining, and luscious. I have not changed any of these original proportions or directions, because this is the way the dishes were conceived. However, do use your own judgment as to how much or how little of the enrichments you care to use, since the amounts will not interfere with the basic recipe. In my case, for instance, I have been known to substitute a modest teaspoon for the generous tablespoon.

Finally, I do think the way to a full and healthy life is to adopt the sensible system of "small helpings, no seconds, no snacking, and a little bit of everything." Above all—have a good time!

What a happy task you have set for yourself! The pleasures of the table are infinite. *Toujours bon appétit!*

THE STORY OF "MASTERING" AT KNOPF

by Judith Jones

In June of 1960 a hefty manuscript—a treatise on French cooking by an American woman, Julia Child, and two French ladies, Simone Beck and Louisette Bertholle—landed on my desk. I had been an editor at Knopf for about three years, working primarily on translations of French books. But it was no secret that I had a passion for French cooking, so I was the logical person to read it.

The manuscript had been sent down from Cambridge by Avis

de Voto, who worked as a scout for the Knopfs. She was the wife of the historian and writer Bernard de Voto, who had had a lively transatlantic correspondence with Julia on the subject of knives as a result of a piece he had done in *The Atlantic Monthly*. Avis soon became involved when she heard that Julia was working on a cookbook in Paris with Mesdames Beck and Bertholle, and she offered to try to find an American publisher. Her first submission met rejection, the publisher's comment being, Why would any American want to know this much about French cooking?

Well, it so happened that I did. As I turned the pages of this manuscript, I felt that my prayers had been answered. I had lived in Paris for three and a half years—at just about the same time the Childs were there, although our paths had never crossed—and most of what I learned then about cooking I absorbed from the butcher, the baker, the greengrocer, and the fishmonger. I would ask questions of them all, and then back in my tiny kitchen I would try to remember what the butcher's wife had told me about making *frites* or the *poissonière* about sautéing a *dorade*.

When I returned to the States, I realized how totally inadequate the few books that dealt with French food really were. They were simply compendiums of shorthand recipes and there was no effort to instruct the home cook. Techniques were not explained, proper ingredients were not discussed, and there was no indication in a recipe of what to expect and how to rectify mistakes. So the home cook, particularly an American home cook, was flying blind.

Yet here were all the answers. I pored over the recipe, for instance, for a beef stew and learned the right cuts of meat for braising, the correct fat to use (one that would not burn), the importance of drying the meat and browning it in batches, the secret of the herb bouquet, the value of sautéing the garnish of onions and mushrooms separately. I ran home to make the recipe—and my first bite told me that I had finally produced an authentic *French boeuf bourguignon*—as good as one I could get in Paris. This, I was convinced, was a revolutionary cookbook, and if I was so smitten, certainly others would be.

Below is the report I wrote at the time on "The French Cookbook," which I hoped would convince the Knopfs that this book would be a credit to their imprint. I also enlisted the help of a senior colleague, Angus Cameron. He had been an editor at Bobbs-Merrill when *Joy of Cooking* was published and he loved to say that he had enough larceny in his soul to know just how to pitch a book. So his report, I'm convinced, did the trick (also included is his final paragraph).

The rest is history. In the fall of 1961 we published *Mastering the Art of French Cooking* (incidentally, Alfred Knopf, when I told him the title we had settled on, said if anyone would buy a book by that title, he would eat his hat), and after Craig Claiborne pronounced the book a classic, the book went into a second printing before Christmas. Of course, when Julia went on television the following summer as the French Chef all of America fell in love with her. But everything she taught on camera was grounded in this seminal book—understand what you are cooking, do it with care, use the right ingredients and the proper equipment, and, above all, enjoy yourself.

My Report on French Cookbook by Julia Child, Simone Beck, and Louisette Bertholle

I've had this French cookbook for Americans for almost two months now, have read it through, tried innumerable recipes, some simple and some challenging, and I think it's not only first-rate but unique. I don't know of another book that succeeds so well in defining and translating for Americans the secrets of French cuisine. The reason? Because the authors emphasize technique—not the number of recipes they can cram into a volume, nor the exotic nature of the dishes. Reading and studying this book seems to me as good as taking a basic course at the Cordon Bleu. Actually it's better than that because the authors' whole focus is on how to translate the tricks learned to the problems that confront you at home (i.e., the differences in meat cuts, utensils, materials). It is not a book for the lazy but for the cook who wants to improve, to take that giant step from fair-to-good accomplishment to that subtle perfection that makes French cooking an art. I swear that I learned something from this manuscript every few pages.

As to recipes, they have very intelligently selected the dishes that are really the backbone of the classic cuisine. (Attached is the table of contents.) The approach is to introduce the general subject first: what to look for in buying, best utensil to use, timing, testing for doneness, tricks to improve. Then there is usually a master recipe, presented in painstaking detail, followed by variations, different choices of sauces for embellishing the same dish. There is a good deal of text devoted not to cuisine lore but to practical detail; you are seldom directed to do something without being told *why*. The authors are perfectionists, opinionated, and culinary snobs in the best sense—that is, they will approve of a frozen short cut, when time demands it, but they tell you how to add some tastiness to the packaged good. They also give of themselves; their dos and don'ts are not arbitrary but they stress that their method is one that they have arrived at through experimentation.

Finally, I do not believe that this book will in any way hurt others, such as Donon's *Classic French Cuisine,* on our list. The fact is that it enhances other French cookery books because one can apply techniques learned in it in order to use effectively the recipes offered so sketchily, by comparison, in all the other books, and it should be so promoted. I think this book will become a classic.

From Angus Cameron's Report

This manuscript is an astonishing achievement and there is simply nothing like it. Cooks will know this by word of mouth very soon, I'm sure. I think we should have this confidence and venture it with the knowledge that others will have to look to their laurels when this one is available.

THE RECEPTION OF THE BOOK IN 1961

"Probably the most comprehensive, laudable, and monumental work on [French cuisine] was published this week, and it will probably remain as the definitive work for nonprofessionals . . . [It is] a masterpiece."

— Craig Claiborne's review in the *New York Times* when *Mastering the Art of French Cooking* was first published on October 16, 1961

"I only wish that I had written it myself."

—James Beard

THE INFLUENCE OF "MASTERING" OVER THE LAST FORTY YEARS

"Julia Child paved the way for Chez Panisse and so many others by demystifying French food and by reconnecting pleasure and delight with cooking and eating at the table. She brought forth a culture of American ingredients and gave us all the confidence to cook with them in the pursuit of flavor."

—Alice Waters, Chez Panisse

"It's hard to believe that forty years have passed since wonderful Julia freed the American public from their fears of cooking French. By doing so, she greatly expanded the audience for all serious food writers. Her demystification prepared that public for the rest of us. I believe that the television shows based on that landmark book did even more to encourage reluctant cooks to try their hands . . . much to our benefit."

—Mimi Sheraton

"Julia Child was the opposite of the mid-western, mid-American, mid-century, middlebrow food I grew up on. She was also the antithesis of the women I saw cooking, all of whom had serious June Lockhart aspirations. Julia, on the other hand, turned imperfection into a hoot and a holler. She seemed to teach cooking, but she was really celebrating the human, with all its flaws and appetites. I was a goner the first time I heard her voice, which happened to be while I was a cook in a feminist restaurant that served nonviolent cuisine. If it weren't for Julia Child, I might never have moved past brown rice and tofu. Worse, I might still be afraid of being less than perfect. Cooking through *Mastering the Art of French Cooking*, I learned how to cook without fear because I got over fearing failure. Julia Child gave an entire generation this gift—and dinner, too."

—Molly O'Neill

"The more I have come to know Julia over the years, the more I realize that Julia, the friend, the author, the TV superstar, are one and the same. *Mastering the Art of French Cooking* was one of the most influential books in twentieth-century America. It was the book, more than any other, that, combined with her television shows, taught Americans how to cook simple and not-so-simple classic French dishes. Like Julia herself, the book is a classic, a catalyst in the refinement of American culture. My own copy of Volume One (a 1975 edition) is so worn that the duct tape holding it together looks natural. Although this book wasn't intended for professionals, I knew a few young American chefs who, like me, referred to it often because Julia was a trusted secret mentor, and her recipes were clear-cut and dependable. They still are."

—Jasper White, Summer Shack

"The recipes in *Mastering the Art of French Cooking* are classics—dishes that taste so good because the ingredients work together with no need for gimmicks. Julia's opening sentence in the foreword to the '83 edition couldn't be more true: 'This is a book for the American cook who can be unconcerned *on occasion* with budgets, waistlines, time schedules . . . or anything else which might interfere with the enjoyment of something *wonderful* to eat [emphasis mine].'

I remember the excitement and pride I felt when I first served Julia's Veal Orloff. The Soubise, on its own, that glorious mixture of melting onion and rice, has never left my repertoire. But mostly my old Volume One wears its badge of use with all those errant chocolate fingerprints wandering across its torn cover as I make Julia's Le Marquis or Soufflé au Chocolat.

This book will teach you to cook, show you How and tell you Why!"

—Lydia Shire, Biba

"I remember it was in the early 1970s when I first began to pour through *Mastering the Art of French Cooking*. I was in heaven. All this technique that I knew nothing about all laid out in English! It was all very meticulous and the descriptions were so detailed and that's just what I needed because I had no experience as a cook. I told my mother what I was reading and she said, 'Oh that crazy woman? She's way too complicated for me and the way I cook.' I never listened much to my mother back then and just kept on reading. Today, JULIA, as I call it, remains the book I turn to when I need to know how to do something."

—Gordon Hamersley, Hamersley's Bistro

"Long before there was a TV Food Network or Celebrity Chefs, there was Julia Child. The first cookbook my mother purchased for our home was *Mastering the Art of French Cooking*. It was this book, along with Julia's first television series and her obvious joy for cooking, that helped influence me to enter the culinary field. Always warm and gracious, still working hard sharing her knowledge and love of life, Julia continues to be an inspiration to all who are privileged to know her and choose to be part of this profession. She is and will always be the 'Grand Lady of Cooking.' Thank you, Julia, for your encouragement and friendship."

—David Cecchini, Wine Cask

"*Mastering the Art of French Cooking* was one of my first introductions to my foundation of understanding the art of French cooking. The combination of reading Julia's book, working in the kitchen, and watching her television shows helped lead me to my beginnings in serious cuisine. Julia is a dear friend and a great cook—the grande dame of cooking, who has touched all of our lives with her immense respect and appreciation of cuisine."

—Emeril Lagasse, Emeril's Restaurant

"Julia has slowly but surely altered our way of thinking about food.
She has taken the fear out of the term 'haute cuisine.' She has

increased gastronomic awareness a thousandfold by stressing the importance of good foundation and technique, and she has elevated our consciousness to the refined pleasures of dining. Through the years her shows have kept me in rapt attention, and her humor has kept me in stitches.

She is a national treasure, a culinary trendsetter, and a born educator beloved by all."

—Thomas Keller, The French Laundry

"1961 was the year that gave us three important and enjoyable events:
- Picasso painted his *Still Life with a Lamp;*
- *Breakfast at Tiffanys* had its premier with Audrey Hepburn;
- *Mastering the Art of French Cooking* was published by Knopf, starring our very own Julia Child.

Trying to avoid the current fashion for exaggeration, let me just say that this volume not only clarified what real French food is, but simply taught us to cook."

—George Lang, Café des Artistes

"1961 A.D. Julia Child's *Mastering the Art of French Cooking* is published. Her black-and-white TV show on WGBH in Boston soon follows. Child is one of the great teachers of the millennium: She is intelligent and charismatic, and her undistinguished manual skills are not daunting to her viewers. An entire generation of ambitious American home cooks is instantly born."

—Jeffrey Steingarten, conferring the Vogue Millennial
Food and Drink Awards on "those events and persons who
have most advanced the joys and beauties of mealtime
over the previous thousand years"

FOREWORD

TO THE

1983 EDITION

THE FIRST EDITION of *Mastering* was conceived and written in the late 1950s, and many changes, particularly in kitchen equipment, have taken place since then. Probably the most significant has been the appearance of the electric food processor, which has made amazingly light work out of many formerly long and arduous cooking procedures like the mincing of mushrooms and onions, the slicing of potatoes, the making of mayonnaise, pie doughs, many yeast doughs, as well as purées and mousses. We have redone numerous recipes here to include the processor, but had it been around when we began, we would have had a host of dishes created because of it. No-stick pans were not available then. All-purpose flour needed sifting, and that required a cumbersome measuring system, which we have eliminated here. Chocolate has changed character, and that gave rise to a different melting technique as well as a new chocolate soufflé recipe. Rice is now enriched and takes shorter cooking, and we have revised a number of meat-thermometer readings. Little details here and there wanted fixing, little remarks now and then needed updating, and a few drawings have been added or improved.

On the whole, however, it is the same book, written for those who love to cook—it is a primer of classical French cuisine. And no wonder that cuisine has always been and will always remain so popular, said a friend of ours; it just makes such wonderfully good eating!

S. B. and J. C.

Bramafam and Santa Barbara
February 1983

FOREWORD

This is a book for the servantless American cook who can be unconcerned on occasion with budgets, waistlines, time schedules, children's meals, the parent–chauffeur–den-mother syndrome, or anything else which might interfere with the enjoyment of producing something wonderful to eat. Written for those who love to cook, the recipes are as detailed as we have felt they should be so the reader will know exactly what is involved and how to go about it. This makes them a bit longer than usual, and some of the recipes are quite long indeed. No out-of-the-ordinary ingredients are called for. In fact the book could well be titled "French Cooking from the American Supermarket," for the excellence of French cooking, and of good cooking in general, is due more to cooking techniques than to anything else. And these techniques can be applied wherever good basic materials are available. We have purposely omitted cobwebbed bottles, the *patron* in his white cap bustling among his sauces, anecdotes about charming little restaurants with gleaming napery, and so forth. Such romantic interludes, it seems to us, put French cooking into a never-never land instead of the Here, where happily it is available to everybody. Anyone can cook in the French manner anywhere, with the right instruction. Our hope is that this book will be helpful in giving that instruction.

Cooking techniques include such fundamentals as how to sauté a piece of meat so that it browns without losing its juices, how to fold beaten egg whites into a cake batter to retain their maximum volume, how to add egg yolks to a hot sauce so they will not curdle, where to put the tart in the oven so it will puff and brown, and how to chop an onion quickly. Although you will perform with different ingredients for different dishes, the same general processes are repeated over and over again. As you enlarge your repertoire, you will find that the seemingly endless babble of recipes begins to fall rather neatly into groups of theme and variations; that *homard à l'américaine* has many technical aspects in common with *coq au vin,* that *coq au vin* in turn is almost identical in technique to *boeuf bourguignon;* all of them are types of fricassees, so follow the fricassee pattern. In the sauce realm, the cream and egg-yolk sauce for a *blanquette* of veal is the same type as that for a sole in white-wine sauce, or for a *gratin* of scallops. Eventually you will rarely need recipes at all, except as reminders of ingredients you may have forgotten.

All of the techniques employed in French cooking are aimed at one goal: how does it taste? The French are seldom interested in unusual combinations or surprise presentations. With an enormous background of traditional dishes to choose from (*1000 Ways to Prepare and Serve Eggs* is the title of one French book on the subject) the Frenchman takes his greatest pleasure from a well-known dish impeccably cooked and served. A perfect *navarin* of lamb, for instance, requires a number of operations including brownings, simmerings, strainings, skimmings, and flavorings. Each of the several steps in the process, though simple to accomplish, plays a critical role, and if any is eliminated or combined with another, the texture and taste of the *navarin* suffer. One of the main reasons that pseudo-French cooking, with which we are all too familiar, falls far below good French cooking is just this matter of elimination of steps, combination of processes, or skimping on ingredients such as butter, cream—and time. "Too much trouble," "Too expensive," or "Who will know the difference" are death knells for good food.

Cooking is not a particularly difficult art, and the more you cook and learn about cooking, the more sense it makes. But like any art it requires practice and experience. The most important ingredient you can bring to it is love of cooking for its own sake.

SCOPE

A complete treatise on French cooking following the detailed method we have adopted would be about the size of an unabridged dictionary; even printed on Bible paper, it would have to be placed on a stand. To produce a book of convenient size, we have made an arbitrary selection of recipes that we particularly like, and which we hope will interest our readers. Many splendid creations are not included, and there are tremendous omissions. One may well ask: "Why is there no *pâte feuilletée?* Where are the *croissants?"* These are the kinds of recipes, in our opinion, which should be demonstrated in the kitchen, as each requires a sense of touch which can only be learned through personal practice and observation. Why only five cakes and no *petits fours?* No boiled, souffléed, or mashed potatoes? No zucchini? No tripe? No *poulet à la Marengo?* No green salads? No pressed duck or *sauce rouennaise?* No room!

A NOTE ON THE RECIPES

All of the master recipes and most of the subrecipes in this book are in two-column form. On the left are the ingredients, often including some special piece of equipment needed; on the right is a paragraph of instruction. Thus what to cook and how to cook it, at each step in the proceedings, are always brought together in one sweep of the eye. Master recipes are headed in large, bold type; a special sign, $*$, precedes those which are followed by variations. Most of the recipes contain this sign, (*), in the body of the text, indicating up to what point a dish may be prepared in advance. Wine and vegetable suggestions are included with all master recipes for main-course dishes.

Our primary purpose in this book is to teach you how to cook, so that you will understand the fundamental techniques and gradually be able to divorce yourself from a dependence on recipes. We have therefore divided each category of food into related groups or sections, and each recipe in one section belongs to one family of techniques. Fish *filets* poached in white wine, starting on page 208, are a good example, or the chicken fricassees starting on page 258, or the group of *quiches* on pages 146 to 153. It is our hope that you will read the introductory pages preceding each chapter and section before you start in on a recipe, as you will then understand what we are about. For the casual reader, we have tried to make every recipe stand on its own. Cross references are always a problem. If there are not enough, you may miss an important point, and if there are too many you will become enraged. Yet if every technique is explained every time it comes up, a short recipe is long, and a long one forbidding.

QUANTITIES

Most of the recipes in this book are calculated to serve six people with reasonably good appetites in an American-style menu of three courses. The amounts called for are generally twice what would be considered sufficient for a typical French menu comprising hors d'oeuvre, soup, main course, salad, cheese, and dessert. We hope that we have arrived at quantities which will be correct for most of our readers. If a recipe states that the ingredients listed will serve 4 to 6 people, this means the dish should be sufficient for 4 people if the rest of your menu is small, and for 6 if it is large.

SOME WORDS OF ADVICE

Our years of teaching cookery have impressed upon us the fact that all too often a debutant cook will start in enthusiastically on a new dish without ever reading the recipe first. Suddenly an ingredient, or a process, or a time sequence will turn up, and there is astonishment, frustration, and even disaster. We therefore urge you, however much you have cooked, always to read the recipe first, even if the dish is familiar to you. Visualize each step so you will know exactly what techniques, ingredients, time, and equipment are required and you will encounter no surprises. Recipe language is always a sort of short-hand in which a lot of information is packed, and you will have to read carefully if you are not to miss small but important points. Then, to build up your over-all knowledge of cooking, compare the recipe mentally to others you are familiar with, and note where one recipe or technique fits into the larger picture of theme and variations.

We have not given estimates for the time of preparation, as some people take half an hour to slice three pounds of mushrooms while others take five minutes.

Pay close attention to what you are doing while you work, for precision in small details can make the difference between passable cooking and fine food. If a recipe says, "cover casserole and regulate heat so liquid simmers very slowly," "heat the butter until its foam begins to subside," or "beat the hot sauce into the egg yolks by driblets," follow it. You may be slow and clumsy at first, but with practice you will pick up speed and style.

Allow yourself plenty of time. Most dishes can be assembled, or started, or partially cooked in advance. If you are not an old campaigner, do not plan more than one long or complicated recipe for a meal or you will wear yourself out and derive no pleasure from your efforts.

If food is to be baked or broiled, be sure your oven is hot before the dish goes in. Otherwise soufflés will not rise, piecrusts will collapse, and *gratinéed* dishes will overcook before they brown.

A pot saver is a self-hampering cook. Use all the pans, bowls, and equipment you need, but soak them in water as soon as you are through with them. Clean up after yourself frequently to avoid confusion.

Train yourself to use your hands and fingers; they are wonderful instruments. Train yourself also to handle hot foods; this will save time. Keep your knives sharp.

Above all, have a good time.

S. B., L. B., J. C.

July 1961

Acknowledgments

OUR FRIENDS, students, families, and husbands who have gracefully and often courageously acted as guinea pigs for years are owed a special thank you from the authors. But there are others toward whom we feel particular gratitude because of help of a different kind. The Agricultural Research Service of the U.S. Department of Agriculture has been one of our greatest sources of assistance and has unfailingly and generously answered all sorts of technical questions ranging from food to plastic bowls. The Meat Institute of Chicago, the National Livestock and Meat Board, and the Poultry and Egg National Board have answered floods of inquiries with prompt and precise information. Wonderfully helpful also have been the Fish and Wildlife Service of the Department of the Interior, and the California Department of Fish and Game. Sessions with *L'École Professionelle de la Boucherie de Paris* and with the *Office Scientifique et Technique de la Pêche Maritime* have been invaluable in our research on French meat cuts and French fish. During our years of practical kitchen-training in Paris, *Chef de Cuisine* Max Bugnard and *Chef Pâtissier* Claude Thillmont have been our beloved teachers. More recently we have also had the good fortune to work with Mme Aimée Cassiot, whose long years as a professional *cordon bleu* in Paris have given her a vast store of working knowledge which she has willingly shared with us. We are also greatly indebted to *Le Cercle des Gourmettes* whose bi-monthly cooking sessions in Paris have often been our proving grounds, and whose culinary ideas we have freely used. We give heartfelt thanks to our editors whose enthusiasm and hard work transformed our manuscript-in-search-of-a-publisher into this book. Finally there is Avis DeVoto, our foster mother, wet nurse, guide, and mentor. She provided encouragement for our first steps, some ten years ago, as we came tottering out of the kitchen with the gleam of authorship lighting our innocent faces.

CONTENTS

Illustrations

Mastering the Art of French Cooking

*	THIS SYMBOL preceding a recipe title indicates that variations follow.

(*)	WHEREVER you see this symbol in the body of recipe texts you may prepare the dish ahead of time up to that point, then complete the recipe later.

KITCHEN EQUIPMENT

Batterie de Cuisine

THEORETICALLY A GOOD COOK should be able to perform under any circumstances, but cooking is much easier, pleasanter, and more efficient if you have the right tools. Good equipment which will last for years does not seem outrageously expensive when you realize that a big, enameled-iron casserole costs no more than a 6-rib roast, that a large enameled skillet can be bought for the price of a leg of lamb, and that a fine paring knife may cost less than two small lamb chops. One of the best places to shop for reasonably priced kitchenware is in a hotel- and restaurant-supply house where objects are sturdy, professional, and made for hard use.

STOVES AND OVENS

For top-of-stove cooking you want to switch from very high indeed to very low heat with gradations in between, which a restaurant gas range can provide if you have the space and gas pressure for one. Otherwise a good modern electric cooktop is far better than weak domestic gas burners.

Electric ovens give more even heat for pastry baking (especially meringues) than gas, which has surges of heat. Gas is desirable for broiling, but electricity does well especially if you have a rheostat heat control setting. One of each is ideal!

POTS, PANS, AND CASSEROLES

Pots, pans, and casseroles should be heavy-bottomed so they will not tip over, and good heat conductors so that foods will not stick and scorch. With the exception of heavy tin-lined copper (expensive to maintain), enameled iron or stainless-steel-lined heavy aluminum is our choice. The smooth surface does not discolor foods, and it is easy to clean. Stainless steel with a wash of copper on the bottom for looks is a poor heat conductor—the copper bottom should be ⅛ inch thick to be of any value. Stainless steel with a cast aluminum bottom, on the other hand, is good, as the thick aluminum spreads the heat. Glazed earthenware is all right as long as it has not developed cracks where old cooking grease collects and exudes whenever foods are cooked in it. Pyrex and heatproof porcelain are fine but fragile. Thick aluminum and iron, though good heat conductors, will discolor foods containing white wine or egg yolks. Because of the discoloration problem, we shall specify an enameled saucepan in some recipes to indicate that any nonstaining material is to be used, from enamel to stainless steel, lined copper, pyrex, glazed pottery, or porcelain.

A Note on Copper Pots

Copper pots are the most satisfactory of all to cook in, as they hold and spread the heat well, and their tin lining does not discolor foods. A great many tourist or decorative types are currently sold; these are thin and glittering, and have shiny brass handles. To get the full benefit out of cooking in copper, the metal must be ⅛ inch thick, and the handle should be of heavy iron. The interior of the pot is lined with a wash of tin, which must be renewed every several years when it wears off and the copper begins to show through. A copper pot can still be used when this happens if it is scrubbed just before you cook with it, and if the food is removed as soon as it is done. If cooked food remains in a poorly lined pot, some kind of a toxic chemical reaction can take place. It is thus best to have the pot re-tinned promptly.

In addition to re-tinning, there is the cleaning problem, as copper tarnishes quickly. There are fast modern copper cleaners available. A good homemade mixture is half a cup of white vinegar, and ¼ cup each of table salt and scouring powder. Rub the mixture over the copper, using steel wool if the pot is badly tarnished, then rinse in hot water. The tin lining is cleaned with steel wool and scouring powder, but do not expect it ever to glitter brightly again once you have used the pot for cooking. (All cleaning, alas, removes infinitesimal bits of the tin lining.)

Never let a copper pot sit empty over heat, or the tin lining will melt. For the same reason, watch your heat when browning meats in copper. If the tin begins to glisten brightly in places, lower your heat.

No-stick Pots and Pans

Since our first edition, pans with no-stick surfaces have appeared everywhere, and modern improvements have made their surfaces increasingly more resistant. We are enthusiastic about no-stick cookie sheets, cake pans, muffin tins, and especially no-stick frying pans. What a particular blessing they are for omelettes, sautéed potatoes, and hash. Treat no-stick surfaces with care, however: use wooden or plastic utensils, hide your pans from kooks and non-cooks, and don't expect the surface to last forever.

Any of the following items come in enameled cast iron:

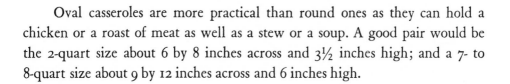

Oval Casseroles

Oval casseroles are more practical than round ones as they can hold a chicken or a roast of meat as well as a stew or a soup. A good pair would be the 2-quart size about 6 by 8 inches across and 3½ inches high; and a 7- to 8-quart size about 9 by 12 inches across and 6 inches high.

Baking Dishes

Round and oval baking dishes can be used for roasting chicken, duck, or meats, or can double as *gratin* dishes.

Saucepans

Saucepans in a range of sizes are essential. One with a metal handle can also be set in the oven.

Chef's Skillet and
Sauté Pan

A chef's skillet, *poêle,* has sloping sides and is used for browning and tossing small pieces of food like mushrooms or chicken livers; the long handle makes it easy to toss rather than turn the food. A sauté pan, *sautoir,* has straight sides and is used for sautéing small steaks, liver, or veal scallops, or foods like chicken that are browned then covered to finish their cooking in the sauté pan.

Besides the usual array of pots, roasters, vegetable peelers, spoons, and spatulas, here are some useful objects which make cooking easier:

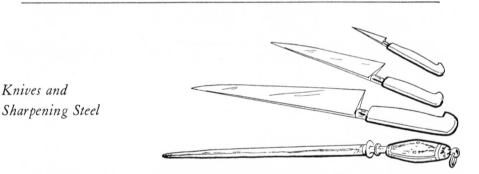

Knives and
Sharpening Steel

A knife should be as sharp as a razor or it mashes and bruises food rather than chopping or cutting it. It can be considered sharp if just the weight of it, drawn across a tomato, slits the skin. No knife will hold a razor-edge for long. The essential point is that it take an edge, and quickly. Plain rustable steel is the easiest to sharpen but discoloration is an annoying problem. Good stainless steel knives are available in cookware and cutlery shops, and probably the best way to test their quality is to buy a small one and try it out. The French chef's knives, pictured here, are the most useful general-purpose shapes for chopping, mincing, and paring. If you cannot find good knives, consult your butcher or a professionally trained chef.

Knives should be washed separately and by hand as soon as you have finished using them. Tarnished blades are cleaned easily with steel wool and scouring powder. A magnetic holder screwed to the wall is a practical way of keeping knives always within reach and isolated from other objects that could dull and dent the blades by knocking against them.

Wooden Spatulas and Rubber Scrapers

A wooden spatula is more practical for stirring than a wooden spoon; its flat surfaces are easily scraped off on the side of a pan or bowl. You will usually find wooden spatulas only at stores specializing in French imports. The rubber spatula, which can be bought almost anywhere, is indispensable for scraping sauces out of bowls and pans, for stirring, folding, creaming, and smearing.

Wire Whips or Whisks

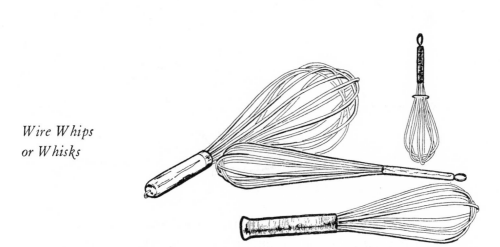

Wire whips, or whisks, are wonderful for beating eggs, sauces, canned soups, and for general mixing. They are easier than the rotary egg beater because you use one hand only. Whisks range from minute to gigantic, and the best selections are in restaurant-supply houses. You should have several sizes including the balloon whip for beating egg whites at the far left; its use is illustrated on page 159.

Bulb Baster and
Poultry Shears

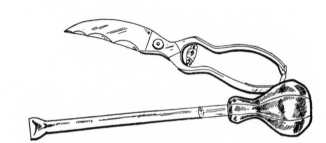

The bulb baster is particularly good for basting meats or vegetables in a casserole, and for degreasing roasts as well as basting them. Some plastic models collapse in very hot fat; a metal tube-end is usually more satisfactory. Poultry shears are a great help in disjointing broilers and fryers; regular steel is more practical than stainless, as the shears can be sharpened more satisfactorily.

Drum Sieve and Pestle

The drum sieve, *tamis,* is used in France when one is instructed to force food through a sieve. The ingredients, such as pounded lobster shells and butter, are placed on the screen and rubbed through it with the pestle. An ordinary sieve placed over a bowl or a food mill can take the place of a *tamis.*

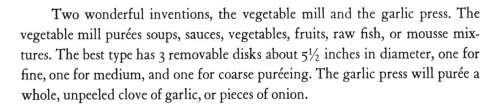

*The Vegetable Mill
(or Food Mill) and
Garlic Press*

Two wonderful inventions, the vegetable mill and the garlic press. The vegetable mill purées soups, sauces, vegetables, fruits, raw fish, or mousse mixtures. The best type has 3 removable disks about 5½ inches in diameter, one for fine, one for medium, and one for coarse puréeing. The garlic press will purée a whole, unpeeled clove of garlic, or pieces of onion.

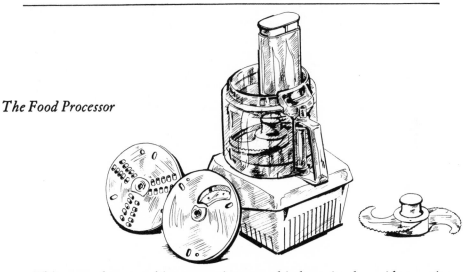

The Food Processor

This marvelous machine came into our kitchens in the mid-seventies—fifteen years after the first edition of this book! The processor has revolutionized cooking, making child's play of some of the most complicated dishes of the *haute cuisine*—mousses in minutes. Besides all kinds of rapid slicing, chopping, puréeing, and the like, it makes a fine pie crust dough, mayonnaise, and many of the yeast doughs. No serious cook should be without a food processor, especially since respectable budget models can be bought very reasonably.

Mortar and Pestle

Small mortars of wood or porcelain are useful for grinding herbs, pounding nuts, and the like. The large mortars are of marble, and are used for pounding or puréeing shellfish, forcemeats, and so on. The electric blender, meat grinder, and food mill take the place of a mortar and pestle in many instances.

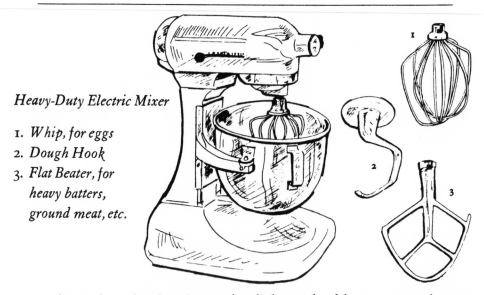

Heavy-Duty Electric Mixer

1. *Whip, for eggs*
2. *Dough Hook*
3. *Flat Beater, for heavy batters, ground meat, etc.*

A heavy-duty electric mixer makes light work of heavy meat mixtures, fruit cake batters, and yeast doughs as well as beating egg whites beautifully and effortlessly. Its efficient whip not only revolves about itself, but circulates around the properly designed bowl, keeping all of the mass of egg whites in motion all of the time. Other useful attachments include a meat grinder with sausage-stuffing horn and a hot-water jack which attaches to the bottom of the stainless steel bowl. It's expensive, but solidly built and a life-long aid to anyone who does lots of cooking.

DEFINITIONS

W<small>E HAVE TRIED</small>, in this book, to use ordinary American cooking terms familiar to anyone who has been around a kitchen, but we list a few definitions here to avoid possible misunderstanding.

BASTE, *arroser* To spoon melted butter, fat, or liquid over foods.

BEAT, *fouetter* To mix foods or liquids thoroughly and vigorously with a spoon, fork, or whip, or an electric beater. When you beat, train yourself to use your lower-arm and wrist muscles; if you beat from your shoulder you will tire quickly.

BLANCH, *blanchir* To plunge food into boiling water and to boil it until it has softened, or wilted, or is partially or fully cooked. Food is also blanched to remove too strong a taste, such as for cabbage or onions, or for the removal of the salty, smoky taste of bacon.

BLEND, *mélanger* To mix foods together in a less vigorous way than by beating, usually with a fork, spoon, or spatula.

BOIL, *bouillir* Liquid is technically at the boil when it is seething, rolling, and sending up bubbles. But in practice there are slow, medium, and fast boils. A very slow boil, when the liquid is hardly moving except for a bubble at one point, is called to simmer, *mijoter*. An even slower boil with no bubble, only the barest movement on the surface of the liquid, is called "to shiver," *frémir*, and is used for poaching fish or other delicate foods.

BRAISE, *braiser* To brown foods in fat, then cook them in a covered casserole with a small amount of liquid. We have also used the term for vegetables cooked in butter in a covered casserole, as there is no English equivalent for *étuver*.

COAT A SPOON, *napper la cuillère* This term is used to indicate the thickness of a sauce, and it seems the only way to describe it. A spoon dipped into a cream soup and withdrawn would be coated with a thin film of soup. Dipped into a sauce destined to cover food, the spoon would emerge with a fairly thick coating.

DEGLAZE, *déglacer* After meat has been roasted or sautéed, and the pan degreased, liquid is poured into the pan and all the flavorful coagulated cooking juices are scraped into it as it simmers. This is an important step in the preparation of all meat sauces from the simplest to the most elaborate, for the deglaze becomes part of the sauce, incorporating into it some of the flavor of the meat. Thus sauce and meat are a logical complement to each other.

DEGREASE, *dégraisser* To remove accumulated fat from the surface of hot liquids.

Sauces, Soups, and Stocks

To remove accumulated fat from the surface of a sauce, soup, or stock which is simmering, use a long-handled spoon and draw it over the surface, dipping up a thin layer of fat. It is not necessary to remove all the fat at this time.

When the cooking is done, remove all the fat. If the liquid is still hot, let it settle for 5 minutes so the fat will rise to the surface. Then spoon it off, tipping the pot or kettle so that a heavier fat deposit will collect at one side and can more easily be removed. When you have taken up as much as you can—it is never a quick process—draw strips of paper towels over the surface until the last floating fat globules have been blotted up.

It is easier, of course, to chill the liquid, for then the fat congeals on the surface and can be scraped off.

Roasts

To remove fat from a pan while the meat is still roasting, tilt the pan and scoop out the fat which collects in the corner. Use a bulb baster or a big spoon. It is never necessary to remove all the fat at this time, just the excess. This degreasing should be done quickly, so your oven will not cool. If you take a long time over it, add a few extra minutes to your total roasting figure.

After the roast has been taken from the pan, tilt the pan, then with a spoon or a bulb baster remove the fat that collects in one corner, but do not take up the browned juices, as these will go into your sauce. Usually a tablespoon or two of fat is left in the pan; it will give body and flavor to the sauce.

Another method—and this can be useful if you have lots of juice—is to place a trayful of ice cubes in a sieve lined with 2 or 3 thicknesses of damp cheesecloth and set over a saucepan. Pour the fat and juices over the ice cubes; most of the fat will collect and congeal on the ice. As some of the ice will melt into the saucepan, rapidly boil down the juices to concentrate their flavor.

Casseroles

For stews, *daubes,* and other foods which cook in a casserole, tip the casserole and the fat will collect at one side. Spoon it off, or suck it up with a bulb baster. Or strain off all the sauce into a pan, by placing the casserole cover askew and holding the casserole in both hands with your thumbs clamped to the cover while you pour out the liquid. Then degrease the sauce in the pan, and return the sauce to the casserole.

New Edition Note: An efficient degreasing pitcher now exists: pour in the hot meat juices and let the fat rise to the surface. Pour out clear juices—the spout opening is at the bottom of the pitcher; stop when fat appears in the spout.

DICE, *couper en dés* To cut food into cubes the shape of dice, usually about ⅛ inch in size as illustrated on page 29.

FOLD, *incorporer* To blend a fragile mixture, such as beaten egg whites, delicately into a heavier mixture, such as a soufflé base. This is described and illustrated in the Soufflé section on page 161. To fold also means to mix delicately without breaking or mashing, such as folding cooked artichoke hearts or brains into a sauce.

GRATINÉ To brown the top of a sauced dish, usually under a hot broiler. A sprinkling of bread crumbs or grated cheese, and dots of butter, help to form a light brown covering (*gratin*) over the sauce.

MACERATE, *macérer;* **MARINATE,** *mariner* To place foods in a liquid so they will absorb flavor, give off flavor, or become more tender. Macerate is the term usually reserved for fruits, such as: cherries macerated in sugar and alcohol. Marinate is used for meats: beef marinated in red wine. A marinade is a pickle, brine, or souse, or a mixture of wine or vinegar, oil, and condiments.

MINCE, *hacher* To chop foods very fine, as illustrated on page 27.

NAP, *napper* To cover food with a sauce which is thick enough to adhere, but supple enough so that the outlines of the food are preserved.

POACH, *pocher* Food submerged and cooked in a liquid that is barely simmering or shivering. The term can also be used poetically for such things as "chicken breasts poached in butter."

PURÉE, *réduire en purée* To render solid foods into a mash, such as applesauce or mashed potatoes. This may be done in a mortar, a meat grinder, a food mill, an electric blender, or through a sieve.

REDUCE, *réduire* To boil down a liquid, reducing it in quantity, and concentrating its taste. This is a most important step in saucemaking.

REFRESH, *rafraîchir* To plunge hot food into cold water in order to cool it quickly and stop the cooking process, or to wash it off.

SAUTÉ, *sauter* To cook and brown food in a very small quantity of very hot fat, usually in an open skillet. You may sauté food merely to brown it, as you brown the beef for a stew. Or you may sauté until the food is cooked through, as for slices of liver. Sautéing is one of the most important of the primary cooking techniques, and it is often badly done because one of the following points has not been observed:

1) The sautéing fat must be very hot, almost smoking, before the food goes into the pan, otherwise there will be no sealing-in of juices, and no browning. The sautéing medium may be fat, oil, or butter and oil. Plain butter cannot be heated to the required temperature without burning, so it must either be fortified with oil or be clarified—rid of its milky residue as described on page 15.

2) The food must be absolutely dry. If it is damp, a layer of steam develops between the food and the fat preventing the browning and searing process.

3) The pan must not be crowded. Enough air space must be left between each piece of food or it will steam rather than brown, and its juices will escape and burn in the pan.

TOSS, *faire sauter* Instead of turning food with a spoon or a spatula, you can make it flip over by tossing the pan. The classic example is tossing a pancake so it flips over in mid-air. But tossing is also a useful technique for cooking vegetables, as a toss is often less bruising than a turn. If you are cooking in a covered casserole, grasp it in both hands with your thumbs clamped to the cover. Toss the pan with an up-and-down, slightly jerky, circular motion. The contents will flip over and change cooking levels. For an open saucepan use the same movement, holding the handle with both hands, thumbs up. A back-and-forth slide is used for a skillet. Give it a very slight upward jerk just as you draw it back toward you.

INGREDIENTS

Except for wines and spirits, and possibly *foie gras* and truffles, all the ingredients called for in this book are available in the average American grocery store. The following list is an explanation of the use of some items:

BACON, *lard de poitrine fumé* The kind of bacon used in French recipes is fresh, unsalted, and unsmoked, *lard de poitrine frais*. As this is difficult to find in America, we have specified smoked bacon; its taste is usually fresher than that of salt pork. It is always blanched in simmering water to remove its smoky taste. If this were not done, the whole dish would taste of bacon.

Blanched Bacon

Place the bacon strips in a pan of cold water, about 1 quart for each 4 ounces. Bring to the simmer and simmer 10 minutes. Drain the bacon and rinse it thoroughly in fresh cold water, then dry it on paper towels.

BUTTER, *beurre* French butter is made from matured cream rather than from sweet cream, is unsalted, and has a special almost nutty flavor. Except for cake frostings and certain desserts for which we have specified unsalted butter, American salted butter and French butter are interchangeable in cooking. (*Note:* It has recently become a habit in America to call unsalted butter, "sweet butter"; there is an attractive ring to it. But technically any butter, salted or not, which is made from sweet, unmatured cream is sweet butter.)

Clarified Butter, beurre clarifié

When ordinary butter is heated until it liquefies, a milky residue sinks to the bottom of the saucepan. The clear, yellow liquid above it is clarified butter. It burns less easily than ordinary butter, as it is the milky particles in ordinary butter which blacken first when butter is heated. Clarified butter is used for sautéing the rounds of white bread used for canapés, or such delicate items as boned and skinned chicken breasts. It is also the base for brown butter sauce, and is used rather than fat in the brown *roux* for particularly fine brown sauces. To clarify butter, cut it into pieces and place it in a saucepan over moderate heat. When the butter has melted, skim off the foam, and strain the clear yellow liquid into a bowl, leaving the milky residue in the bottom of the pan. The residue may be stirred into soups and sauces to serve as an enrichment.

Butter Temperatures, Butter Foam

Whenever you are heating butter for an omelette or butter and oil for a sauté your recipe will direct you to wait until the butter foam looks a certain way. This is because the condition of the foam is a sure indication of how hot the butter is. As it begins to melt, the butter will foam hardly at all, and is not hot enough to brown anything. But as the heat increases, the liquids in the butter evaporate and cause the butter to foam up. During this full-foaming period the butter is still not very hot, only around 212 degrees. When the liquids have almost evaporated, you can see the foam subsiding. And when you see practically no foam, you will also observe the butter begin to turn light brown, then dark brown, and finally a burnt black. Butter fortified with oil will heat to a higher temperature before browning and burning than will plain butter, but the observable signs are the same. Thus the point at which you add your eggs to the omelette pan or your meat to the skillet is when the butter is very hot but not browning, and that is easy to see when you look at the butter. If it is still foaming up, wait a few seconds; when you see the foam begin to subside, the butter is hot enough for you to begin.

CHEESE, *fromage* The two cheeses most commonly used in French cooking are Swiss and Parmesan. Imported Swiss cheese is of two types, either of which may be used: the true *Gruyère* with small holes, and the *Emmenthal* which is fatter, less salty, and has large holes. Wisconsin "Swiss" may be substituted for imported Swiss. *Petit suisse,* a cream cheese that is sometimes called for in French recipes, is analogous to Philadelphia cream cheese.

CREAM, *crème fraîche, crème double* French cream is matured cream, that is, lactic acids and natural ferments have been allowed to work in it until the cream has thickened and taken on a nutty flavor. It is not sour. Commercially made sour cream with a butterfat content of only 18 to 20 per cent is no substitute; furthermore, it cannot be boiled without curdling. French cream has a butterfat content of at least 30 per cent. American whipping cream with its comparable butterfat content may be used in any French recipe calling for *crème fraîche*. If it is allowed to thicken with a little buttermilk, it will taste quite a bit like French cream, can be boiled without curdling, and will keep for 10 days or more under refrigeration; use it on fruits or desserts, or in cooking.

1 tsp commercial buttermilk   Stir the buttermilk into the cream and heat to luke-
1 cup whipping cream   warm—not over 85 degrees. Pour the mixture into a

loosely covered jar and let it stand at a temperature of not over 85 degrees nor under 60 degrees until it has thickened. This will take 5 to 8 hours on a hot day, 24 to 36 hours at a low temperature. Stir, cover, and refrigerate.

[NOTE: French unmatured or sweet cream is called *fleurette*]

FLOUR, *farine* Regular French household flour is made from soft wheat, while most American flour is made from hard wheat; in addition, French flour is usually unbleached. This makes a difference in cooking quality, especially when you are translating French recipes for yeast doughs and pastries. We have found that a reasonable approximation of French flour, if you need one, is 3 parts American all-purpose unbleached flour to 1 part plain bleached cake flour.

Be accurate when you measure flour or you will run into cake and pastry problems. Although a scale is ideal, and essential when you are cooking in large quantities, cups and spoons are accurate enough for home cooking when you use the scoop-and-level system illustrated here.

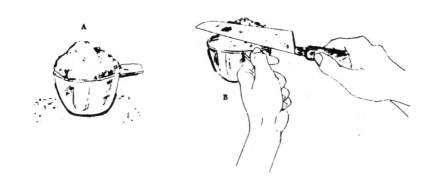

For all flour measurements in this volume, scoop the dry-measure cup directly into your flour container and fill the cup to overflowing (A); do not shake the cup or pack down the flour. Sweep off excess so that flour is even with the lip of the cup, using a straight edge of some sort (B). Sift only after measuring.

In first edition copies of this volume all flour had to be sifted, and we advised that our flour be sifted directly into the cup; cake flour weighed less per cup than all-purpose flour, and it was a cumbersome system all around. The scoop-and-level is far easier, and just as reliable. See next page for a chart of weights and measures for flour measured this way.

FLOUR WEIGHTS: Approximate Equivalents (scoop-and-level method)

3½ cups of flour	1 pound	454 grams
1 cup	5 ounces	140 grams
¾ cup	3½ ounces	105 grams
⅔ cup	3¼ ounces	90 grams
½ cup	2½ ounces	70 grams
⅓ cup	1½ ounces	50 grams
1 Tb	¼ ounce	8¾ grams
3¾ cups	17½ ounces	500 grams or ½ kilo

NOTE: *1 cuillère de farine* in a French recipe usually means 1 heaping French tablespoon, or 15 to 20 grams—the equivalent of 2 level American Tb.

GLACÉED FRUITS, CANDIED FRUITS, *fruits confits*   These are fruits such as cherries, orange peel, citron, apricots, and angelica, which have undergone a preserving process in sugar. They are sometimes coated with sugar so they are not sticky; at other times they *are* sticky, depending on the specific process they have been through. Glacéed fruits are called for in a number of the dessert recipes; most groceries carry selections or mixtures in jars or packages.

HERBS, *herbes*   Classical French cooking uses far fewer herbs than most Americans would suspect. Parsley, thyme, bay, and tarragon are the stand-bys, plus fresh chives and chervil in season. A mixture of fresh parsley, chives, tarragon, and chervil is called *fines herbes*. Mediterranean France adds to the general list basil, fennel, oregano, sage, and saffron. The French feeling about herbs is that they should be an accent and a complement, but never a domination over the essential flavors of the main ingredients. Fresh herbs are, of course, ideal; and some varieties of herbs freeze well. Excellent also are most of the dried herbs now available. Be sure any dried or frozen herbs you use retain most of their original taste and fragrance.

A Note on Bay Leaves
American bay is stronger and a bit different in taste than European bay. We suggest you buy imported bay leaves; they are bottled by several of the well-known American spice firms.

HERB BOUQUET, *bouquet garni*   This term means a combination of parsley, thyme, and bay leaf for flavoring soups, stews, sauces, and braised meat and vegetables. If the herbs are fresh and in sprigs or leaf, the parsley is folded around them and they are tied together with string. If the herbs are dried, they are wrapped in a piece of washed cheesecloth and tied. A bundle is made so the herbs will not disperse themselves into the liquid or be skimmed off it, and so that they can be removed easily. Celery, garlic, fennel, or other items may be included in the packet, but are always specifically mentioned, such as "a medium herb bouquet with celery stalk." A small herb bouquet should contain 2 parsley sprigs, ⅓ of a bay leaf, and 1 sprig or ⅛ teaspoon of thyme.

MARROW, *moelle*   The fatty filling of beef leg-bones, marrow is poached and used in sauces, garnitures, and on canapés. It is prepared as follows:

A beef marrowbone about 5 inches long	Stand the bone on one end and split it with a cleaver. Remove the marrow in one piece if possible. Slice or dice it with a knife dipped in hot water.
Boiling bouillon or boiling salted water	Shortly before using, drop the marrow into the hot liquid. Set aside for 3 to 5 minutes until the marrow has softened. Drain, and it is ready to use.

OIL, *huile*   Classical French cooking uses almost exclusively odorless, tasteless vegetable oils for cooking and salads. These are made from peanuts, corn, cottonseed, sesame seed, poppy seed, or other analogous ingredients. Olive oil, which dominates Mediterranean cooking, has too much character for the subtle flavors of a delicate dish. In recipes where it makes no difference which you use, we have just specified "oil."

SHALLOTS, *échalotes*   Shallots with their delicate flavor and slightest hint of garlic are small members of the onion family. They are used in sauces, stuffings, and general cooking to give a mild onion taste. The minced white part of green onions (spring onions, scallions, *ciboules*) may take the place of shallots. If you can find neither, substitute very finely minced onion dropped for one minute in boiling water, rinsed, and drained. Or omit them altogether.

TRUFFLES, *truffes*   Truffles are round, pungent, wrinkled, black fungi usually an inch or two in diameter which are dug up in certain regions of France and Italy from about the first of December to the end of January. They are always expensive. If you have ever been in France during this season, you will never forget the exciting smell of fresh truffles. Canned truffles, good as they are, give only a suggestion of their original glory. But their flavor can be much enhanced if a spoonful or two of Madeira is poured into the can half an hour before the truffles are to be employed. Truffles are used in decorations, with scrambled eggs and omelettes, in meat stuffings and *pâtés,* and in sauces. The juice from the can is added to sauces and stuffings for additional truffle flavor. A partially used can of truffles may be frozen.

MEASURES

A PINT'S A POUND the world around except in England where a pint of water weighs a pound and a quarter, and all measurements in this book are level. The following table is for those who wish to translate French measurements into the nearest convenient American equivalent and vice versa:

AMERICAN SPOONS AND CUPS	FRENCH EQUIVALENTS	LIQUID OUNCES	LIQUID GRAMS
1 tsp (teaspoon)	1 *cuillère à café*	⅙	5
1 Tb (tablespoon)	1 *cuillère à soupe, cuillère à bouche* or *verre à liqueur*	½	15
1 cup (16 Tb)	¼ *litre* less 2 Tb	8	227
2 cups (1 pint)	½ *litre* less ½ *décilitre*	16 (1 pound)	454
4 cups (1 quart)	9/10 *litre*	32	907
6⅔ Tb	1 *décilitre* 1 *demi-verre*	3½	100
1 cup plus 1 Tb	¼ *litre*	8½	250
4⅓ cups	1 *litre*	2.2 pounds	1000 (1 kilogram)

A pinch, *une pincée* The amount of any ingredient you can take up between your thumb and forefinger. There are big and little pinches.

BRITISH MEASURES

British dry measures for ounces and pounds and linear measures for inches and feet are the same as American measures. However, the British liquid ounce is .96 times the American ounce; the British pint contains 20 British ounces; and the quart, 40 ounces. A gill is 5 ounces, or about ⅔ of an American cup.

CONVERSION FORMULAS American, British, Metric

To Convert	Multiply	By
Ounces to grams	The ounces	28.35
Grams to ounces	The grams	0.035
Liters to U.S. quarts	The liters	0.95
Liters to British quarts	The liters	0.88
U.S. quarts to liters	The quarts	1.057
British quarts to liters	The quarts	1.14
Inches to centimeters	The inches	2.54
Centimeters to inches	The centimeters	0.39

CUP–DECILITER EQUIVALENTS 1 deciliter equals 6⅔ tablespoons

Cups	Deciliters	Cups	Deciliters
¼	0.56	1¼	2.83
⅓	0.75	1⅓	3.0
½	1.13	1½	3.4
⅔	1.5	1⅔	3.75
¾	1.68	1¾	4.0
1	2.27	2	4.5

GRAM–OUNCE EQUIVALENTS

Grams	Ounces	Grams	Ounces	Grams	Ounces
25	0.87	75	2.63	100	3.5
30	1.0	80	2.8	125	4.4
50	1.75	85	3.0	150	5.25

MISCELLANEOUS MEASURES

We have used the following measurements and equivalents throughout.

ALMONDS

4 ounces of whole shelled, powdered, or slivered almonds equal about ¾ cup.

APPLES

3 pounds of whole apples yield about 8 cups of sliced apples, and 3½ cups of applesauce.

BACON

2 ounces of diced raw bacon yield about ⅓ cup.

BREAD CRUMBS

2 ounces of lightly packed fresh bread crumbs make about 1 cup; 2 ounces of dry bread crumbs make about ¾ cup.

BUTTER

1 pound of butter equals 16 ounces, 2 cups, or 32 tablespoons. A ¼-pound stick of butter is 4 ounces, ½ cup, or 8 tablespoons. For easy measurement of butter in tablespoons, mark a ¼-pound stick with the edge of a knife into 8 equal portions; each portion is 1 tablespoon.

CABBAGE

½ pound of minced or sliced cabbage, pressed down, equals about 3 cups.

CARROTS

1 medium carrot equals 2½ to 3 ounces; 1 pound of sliced or diced carrots equals 3½ to 4 cups.

CELERY STALK

1 celery stalk of medium size weighs 1½ to 2 ounces; 2 sliced celery stalks equal ¾ to 1 cup.

CHEESE

2 ounces of lightly packed grated cheese equal about ½ cup.

EGGS

1 U.S. large graded egg weighs about 2 ounces.

1 U.S. large egg white equals 1 ounce or 2 tablespoons.

1 U.S. large egg yolk equals ½ ounce or 1 tablespoon.

FLOUR

See table of equivalents and measuring directions, pages 17, 18.

GARLIC

1 medium clove of garlic equals $\frac{1}{16}$ ounce or ⅛ teaspoon. To remove the smell of garlic from your hands, rinse them in cold water, rub with table salt, rinse again in cold water, then wash with soap and warm water. Repeat if necessary.

MUSHROOMS

½ pound of sliced fresh mushrooms equals about 2½ cups.

½ pound of diced fresh mushrooms equals about 2 cups.

ONIONS

1 medium onion equals 2½ to 3 ounces.

1 pound of sliced or diced onions yields 3½ to 4 cups.

See the note on garlic about how to remove the smell of onions from your hands.

POTATOES

1 medium potato equals 3½ to 4 ounces.

1 pound of sliced or diced potatoes yields 3½ to 4 cups.

1 pound of unpeeled raw potatoes yields about 2 cups of mashed potatoes.

RICE

½ pound of raw rice equals about 1 cup; and 1 cup of raw rice yields about 3 cups of cooked rice.

SALT

Use 1 to 1½ teaspoons of salt per quart of liquid for the boiling of vegetables and the flavoring of unsalted soups and sauces. Also use 1 to 1½ teaspoons of salt per pound of boneless raw meat. If you have oversalted a sauce or a soup, you can remove some of the saltiness by grating in raw potatoes. Simmer the potatoes in the liquid for 7 to 8 minutes, then strain the liquid; the potatoes will have absorbed quite a bit of the excess salt.

SHALLOTS

1 medium shallot equals ½ ounce or 1 tablespoon when minced.

SUGAR, GRANULATED

1 cup equals 6½ ounces or 190 grams.
1 pound equals 2½ cups or 454 grams.
100 grams equals 3½ ounces or ½ cup.

SUGAR, POWDERED

1 cup equals 2¾ ounces or 80 grams.

TOMATOES

1 tomato equals 4 to 5 ounces; 1 pound of fresh tomatoes peeled, seeded, juiced, and chopped as illustrated on page 505 will yield about 1½ cups of tomato pulp.

TEMPERATURES

Fahrenheit and Centigrade

TO CONVERT FAHRENHEIT INTO CENTIGRADE, subtract 32, multiply by 5, divide by 9.

Example: 212 (Fahrenheit) minus 32 equals 180
180 multiplied by 5 equals 900
900 divided by 9 equals 100, or the temperature of boiling water in centigrade

TO CONVERT CENTIGRADE INTO FAHRENHEIT, multiply by 9, divide by 5, add 32.

Example: 100 (centigrade) multiplied by 9 equals 900
900 divided by 5 equals 180
180 plus 32 equals 212, or the temperature of boiling water in Fahrenheit

TEMPERATURE CONVERSION TABLE

American—French—British

FAHRENHEIT DEGREES (AMERICAN AND BRITISH)	CENTI-GRADE DEGREES	AMERICAN OVEN TEMPERATURE TERMS	FRENCH OVEN TEMPERATURE TERMS, AND FAIRLY STANDARD THERMOSTAT SETTINGS	BRITISH "REGULO" OVEN THERMOSTAT SETTINGS
160	71		#1	
170	77			
200	93		*Très Doux; Étuve*	
212	100			
221	105		#2	
225	107	Very Slow	*Doux*	
230	110		#3	#¼ (241 F)
250	121			
275	135			#½ (266 F)
284	140	Slow	*Moyen; Modéré*	#1 (291 F)
300	149			
302	150		#4	
320	160			#2 (313 F)
325	163			
				#3 (336 F)
350	177	Moderate	*Assez Chaud; Bon Four*	
356	180			#4 (358 F)
375	190		#5	
390	200			#5 (379 F)
400	205			#6 (403 F)
410	210	Hot	*Chaud*	
425	218		#6	#7 (424 F)
428	220			
437	225			
450	232			#8 (446 F)
475	246	Very Hot	*Très Chaud; Vif*	#9 (469 F)
500	260		#7	
525	274		#8	
550	288		#9	

CUTTING

Chopping, Slicing, Dicing, and Mincing

FRENCH COOKING requires a good deal of slicing, dicing, mincing, and fancy cutting, and if you have not learned to wield a knife rapidly a recipe calling for 2 cups of finely diced vegetables and 2 pounds of sliced mushroom caps is often too discouraging to attempt. It takes several weeks of off-and-on practice to master the various knife techniques, but once learned they are never forgotten. You can save a tremendous amount of time, and also derive a modest pride, in learning how to use a knife professionally.

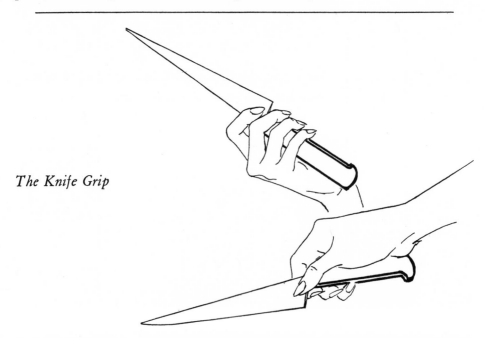

The Knife Grip

For cutting and slicing, hold the knife with your thumb and index finger gripping the top of the blade, and wrap your other fingers around the handle.

Chopping

For chopping, hold the knife blade by both ends and chop with rapid up-and-down movements, brushing the ingredients repeatedly into a heap again with the knife.

Slicing Round Objects (a)

To slice potatoes or other round or oval objects, cut the potato in half and lay it cut-side down on the chopping board. Use the thumb of your left hand as a pusher, and grip the sides of the potato with your fingers, pointing your fingernails back toward your thumb so you will not cut them.

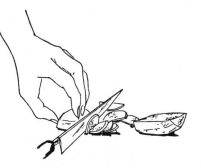

Slicing Round Objects (b)

Cut straight down, at a right angle to board, with a quick stroke of the knife blade, pushing the potato slice away from the potato as you hit the board.

The knuckles of your left hand act as a guide for the next slice. This goes slowly at first, but after a bit of practice, 2 pounds of potatoes can be sliced in less than 5 minutes.

Slicing Long Objects Like Carrots

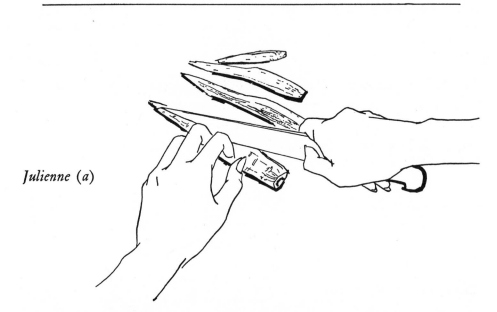

To slice long objects like carrots, cut a thin strip off one side so the carrot will lie flat on the board. Then cut crosswise slices as for the potatoes in the preceding paragraph.

Julienne (a)

To cut vegetables such as carrots or potatoes into julienne matchsticks, remove a thin strip off one side of the carrot and lay the carrot on the board. Then cut it into lengthwise slices $\frac{1}{8}$ inch thick.

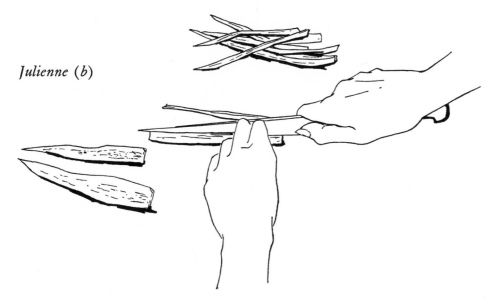

Julienne (b)

Two at a time, cut the slices into strips ⅛ inch across, and the strips into whatever lengths you wish.

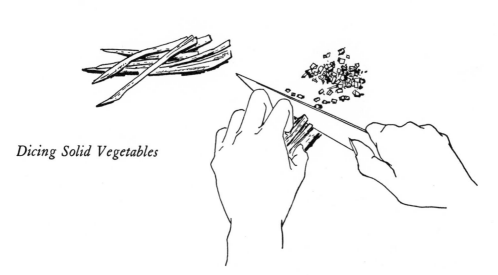

Dicing Solid Vegetables

Proceed as for the julienne, but cut the strips, a handful at a time, cross-wise into dice.

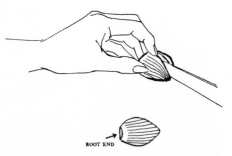

Dicing Onions and Shallots (a)

Once mastered, this method of dicing onions or shallots goes like light-ning. Cut the onion in half through the root. Lay one half cut-side down, its root-end to your left. Cut vertical slices from one side to the other, coming just to the root but leaving the slices attached to it, thus the onion will not fall apart.

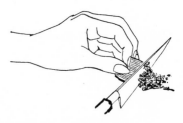

Dicing Onions and Shallots (b)

Then make horizontal slices from bottom to top, still leaving them at-tached to the root of the onion.

Dicing Onions and Shallots (c)

Finally, make downward cuts and the onion falls into dice.

Mushrooms

Various methods for cutting mushrooms are illustrated on page 509.

WINES

I · *Cooking with Wine*

Food, like the people who eat it, can be stimulated by wine or spirits. And, as with people, it can also be spoiled. The quality in a white or red wine, vermouth, Madeira, or brandy which heightens the character of cooking is not the alcohol content, which is usually evaporated, but the flavor. Therefore any wine or spirit used in cooking must be a good one. If it is excessively fruity, sour, or unsavory in any way, these tastes will only be emphasized by the cooking, which ordinarily reduces volume and concentrates flavor. If you have not a good wine to use, it is far better to omit it, for a poor one can spoil a simple dish and utterly debase a noble one.

WHITE WINE

White wine for cooking should be strong and dry, but never sour or fruity. A most satisfactory choice is white Mâcon, made from the Pinot Blanc or the Chardonnay grape. It has all the right qualities and, in France, is not expensive. As the right white wine is not as reasonable to acquire in America, we have found that a good, dry, white vermouth is an excellent substitute, and much better than the wrong kind of white wine.

RED WINE

A good, young, full-bodied red wine is the type you should use for cooking. In France you would pick a Mâcon, one of the lesser Burgundies, one of the more full-bodied regional Bordeaux such as St.-Émilion, or a good local wine having these qualities.

FORTIFIED WINES, SPIRITS, AND LIQUEURS

Fortified wines, spirits, and liqueurs are used principally for final flavorings. As they must be of excellent quality they are always expensive; but usually only a small quantity is called for, so your supply should last quite a while. Here, particularly, if you do not want to spend the money for a good bottle, omit the ingredient or pick another recipe.

RUM and LIQUEURS are called for in desserts. Dark Jamaican rum is the best type to use here, to get a full rum flavor. Among liqueurs, orange is most frequently specified; good imported brands as touchstones for flavor are Cointreau, Grand Marnier, and curaçao.

MADEIRA and PORT are often the final flavor-fillip for sauces, as in a brown Madeira sauce for ham, or chicken in port wine. These wines should be the genuine imported article of a medium-dry type, but can be the more moderately priced examples from a good firm.

SHERRY and MARSALA are rare in French cooking. If used in place of port or Madeira they tend to give an un-French flavor to most French recipes.

BRANDY is the most ubiquitous spirit in French cooking from desserts to sauces, consommés, aspics, and *flambées*. Because there are dreadful concoctions bottled under the label of brandy, we have specified cognac whenever brandy is required in a recipe, as a reminder that you use a good brand. You do not have to buy Three-star or V.S.O.P, but whatever you use should compare favorably in taste with a good cognac.

II · *Wine and Food*

Tʜᴇ ᴡᴏɴᴅᴇʀꜰᴜʟ ᴛʜɪɴɢ about French wines is that they go so well with food. And there is always that enjoyable problem of just which of the many possible choices you should use for a particular occasion. If you are a neophyte wine drinker, the point to keep in mind in learning about which wine to serve with which dish is that the wine should complement the food and the food should accentuate and blend with the qualities of the wine. A robust wine overpowers the taste of a delicate dish, while a highly spiced dish will kill the flavor of a light wine. A dry wine tastes sour if drunk with a sweet dessert, and a red wine often takes on a fishy taste if served with fish. Great combinations of wine and food are unforgettable: kidneys and one of the great red Burgundies, where each rings reminiscent changes on the characteristics of the other; sole in one of the rich white wine sauces and a fine white Burgundy; *soufflé à la liqueur* and a Château d' Yquem. And then there are the more simple pleasures of a stout red wine and a strong cheese, white wine and oysters, red wine and a beef stew, chilled *rosé* and a platter of cold meats. Knowledge of wines is a lifetime hobby, and the only way to learn is to start in drinking and enjoying them, comparing types, vintages, and good marriages of certain wines with certain foods.

Wine suggestions go with all the master recipes for main courses. Here is a list of generally accepted concordances to reverse the process. As this is a book on French cooking, we have concentrated on French wines.

SWEET WHITE WINES (*not champagnes*)

The best known of these are probably the Sauternes, the greatest of which is Château d' Yquem. They may range from noble and full bodied to relatively light, depending on the vineyard and vintage.

Sweet white wines are too often neglected. Those of good quality can be magnificent with dessert mousses, creams, soufflés, and cakes. And a fine Sauternes is delicious with foie gras *or a* pâté *of chicken livers. In the old days sweet wines were drunk with oysters.*

LIGHT, DRY, WHITE WINES

Typical examples are Alsatian Riesling, Muscadet, Sancerre, and usually Pouilly-Fumé, Pouilly-Fuissé, and Chablis. Local wines, *vins du pays,* often fall into this category.

Serve with oysters, cold shellfish, boiled shellfish, broiled fish, cold meats, egg dishes, and entrées.

FULL-BODIED DRY, WHITE WINES

White Burgundy, Côtes du Rhône, and the dry Graves are examples.

Serve with fish, poultry, and veal in cream sauces. White Burgundy can also be drunk with foie gras, *and it is not unheard of to serve a Meursault with Roquefort cheese.*

ROSÉS

Rosés *can be served with anything, but are usually reserved for cold dishes,* pâtés, *eggs, and pork.*

LIGHT-BODIED RED WINES

These are typically Bordeaux from the Médoc or Graves districts. Many of the regional wines and local *vins du pays* can also be included here.

Serve Bordeaux with roast chicken, turkey, veal, or lamb; also with filet of beef, ham, liver, quail, pheasant, foie gras, *and soft fermented cheese like camembert. Regional wines and* vins du pays *go especially well with informal dishes such as beef or lamb stew,* daubes, *bouillabaisse, hamburgers, steaks, and pâtés.*

FULL-BODIED RED WINES

All of the great Burgundies and Rhônes fall into this category; the full bodied Bordeaux from St. Émilion may be included also.

Serve with duck, goose, kidneys, well-hung game, meats marinated in red wine, and authoritative cheeses such as Roquefort. They are called for wherever strong-flavored foods must meet strong-flavored wines.

CHAMPAGNE
Brut

Serve as an apéritif, *or at the end of an evening. Or it may accompany the whole meal.*

Dry, Sec

Serve as an apéritif, *or with crustaceans, or* foie gras, *or with nuts and dried fruits.*

Sweet, Doux, Demi-sec

Sweet champagne is another neglected wine, yet is the only kind to serve with desserts and pastries.

III · *The Storage and Serving of Wine*

Except for champagne, which has sugar added to it to produce the bubbles, great French wines are the unadulterated, fermented juice from the pressings of one type of grape originating in one vineyard during one harvest season. Lesser wines, which can be very good, may also be unadulterated. On the other hand, they may be fortified with sugar during a lean year to build up their alcoholic strength, or they may be blended with wines from other vineyards or localities to give them more body or uniformity of taste. The quality of a wine is due to the variety of grape it is made from, the locality in which it is grown, and the climate during the wine-growing year. In exceptional years such as 1929 and 1947, even lesser wines can be great, and the great ones become priceless. Vintage charts, which you can pick up from your wine merchant, evaluate the various wines by region for each year.

Fine wine is a living liquid containing no preservatives. Its life comprises youth, maturity, old age, and death. When not treated with reasonable respect it will sicken and die. If it is left standing upright for a length of time, the cork will dry out, air will enter the bottle, and the wine will spoil. Shaking and joggling are damaging to it, as are extreme fluctuations of heat and cold. If it is to be laid down to grow into maturity, it should rest on its side in a dark, well-ventilated place at a temperature of around 50 degrees Fahrenheit. If it is to be kept only for a year or two, it can be laid in any dark and quiet corner as long as the temperature remains fairly constant and is neither below 50 degrees nor over 65.

Even the most modest wine will improve if allowed to rest for several days before it is drunk. This allows the wine to reconstitute itself after its journey from shop to home. Great wines, particularly the red ones, benefit from a rest of at least two to three weeks.

TEMPERATURE AT WHICH WINE SHOULD BE SERVED

Red wines, unless they are very young and light, are generally served at a normal room temperature of around 65 degrees Fahrenheit. At lower temperatures they do not show off their full qualities. At least four hours in the dining room are required to bring them slowly up from the temperature of a 50-degree cellar. Never warm a wine artificially; an old wine can be ruined if the bottle is heated. It is better to pour it out too cold, and let it warm in the glass.

White wines, champagnes, and *rosés* are served chilled. As a rule, the sweeter the wine, the colder it should be. A Sauterness or sweet champagne will take four to five hours in the refrigerator. For other white wines, two to three hours are sufficient; if they are too cold, they lose much of their taste.

UNCORKING

White wines, rosés, and many red wines, particularly young reds, are uncorked just before serving, but there is no set rule; this applies especially to the Bordeaux reds and other cabernets. Many authorities recommend that these be uncorked and poured at once, then one waits upon them in the glass, tasting them as they develop. Some fine old reds fade within a few minutes of opening, while other wines are utterly wasted if drunk before they have had time to bloom forth in the glass. If you know your particular bottles from previous tastings, you can, of course, judge the pouring and drinking of them accordingly. Therein lies the science of the experienced wine connoisseur— the more you drink (and think upon it), the more you'll know.

WINE BASKETS, DECANTERS, AND GLASSES

Old red wines that throw a deposit in the bottom of the bottle must be handled so as not to disturb the deposit and circulate it through the wine. Either pour the wine into a decanter leaving the deposit behind, or serve it from a wine basket where it will remain in a prone position. When serving from a basket, pour very smoothly so the wine does not slop back into the bottle and agitate the sediment.

Young red wines, white wines, *rosés,* and champagnes throw no deposit, so the use of a wine basket is silly. The bottle is stood upright after the wine is poured.

The bigger the wine, the bigger the glass. A small glass gives no room for the bouquet to develop, nor for the drinker to swirl. A good all-purpose glass is tulip-shaped and holds ¾ to 1 cup. It should be filled to just below the halfway mark.

CHAPTER ONE

SOUP

Potages et Soupes

An EXCELLENT LUNCH or light supper need be no more than a good soup, a salad, cheese and fruit. And combined according to your own taste, a good homemade soup in these days of the can opener is almost a unique and always a satisfying experience. Most soups are uncomplicated to make, and the major portion of them can be prepared several hours before serving. Here is a varied handful of good recipes.

A NOTE ON BLENDERS, PROCESSORS, AND PRESSURE COOKERS

Although we are enthusiastic supporters of blenders and food processors, we almost invariably prefer a vegetable mill when soups are to be puréed. Blenders and processors chop up and serve forth tough woody vegetable bits, while a vegetable mill holds them back to give you a fiber-free brew.

A pressure cooker can save time, but the vegetables for a long-simmered soup should have only 5 minutes under 15 pounds pressure; more gives them a pressure-cooker taste. Then the pressure should be released and the soup simmered for 15 to 20 minutes so it will develop its full flavor.

✳ *POTAGE PARMENTIER*

[Leek or Onion and Potato Soup]

Leek and potato soup smells good, tastes good, and is simplicity itself to make. It is also versatile as a soup base; add water cress and you have a water-cress soup, or stir in cream and chill it for a *vichyssoise*. To change the formula a bit, add carrots, string beans, cauliflower, broccoli, or anything else you think would go with it, and vary the proportions as you wish.

For about 2 quarts serving 6 to 8 people

A 3- to 4-quart saucepan or pressure cooker 3 to 4 cups or 1 lb. peeled potatoes, sliced or diced 3 cups or 1 lb. thinly sliced leeks including the tender green; or yellow onions 2 quarts of water 1 Tb salt	Either simmer the vegetables, water, and salt together, partially covered, for 40 to 50 minutes until the vegetables are tender; or cook under 15 pounds pressure for 5 minutes, release pressure, and simmer uncovered for 15 minutes.
	Mash the vegetables in the soup with a fork, or pass the soup through a food mill. Correct seasoning. (*) Set aside uncovered until just before serving, then reheat to the simmer.
4 to 6 Tb whipping cream or 2 to 3 Tb softened butter 2 to 3 Tb minced parsley or chives	Off heat and just before serving, stir in the cream or butter by spoonfuls. Pour into a tureen or soup cups and decorate with the herbs.

VARIATIONS

Potage au Cresson

[Water-cress Soup]

This simple version of water-cress soup is very good. See also the more elaborate recipe on page 41.

For 6 to 8 people

Ingredients for the leek and potato soup, omitting cream or butter enrichment until later ¼ lb. or about 1 packed cup of water-cress leaves and tender stems	Follow the preceding master recipe, but before puréeing the soup, stir in the water cress and simmer for 5 minutes. Then purée in a food mill and correct seasoning.

4 to 6 Tb whipping cream or 2 to 3 Tb softened butter	Off heat and just before serving, stir in the cream or butter by spoonfuls. Decorate with the optional water-cress leaves.
Optional: a small handful of water-cress leaves boiled ½ minute in water, rinsed in cold water, and drained	

Cold Water-cress Soup

Use the following *vichyssoise* recipe, adding water cress to simmer for 5 minutes before puréeing the soup.

Vichyssoise

[Cold Leek and Potato Soup]

This is an American invention based on the leek and potato soup in the preceding master recipe.

For 6 to 8 people

3 cups peeled, sliced potatoes	Simmer the vegetables in stock or broth instead of water as described in the master recipe. Purée the soup either in the electric blender, or through a food mill and then through a fine sieve.
3 cups sliced white of leek	
1½ quarts of white stock, chicken stock, or canned chicken broth	
Salt to taste	
½ to 1 cup whipping cream	Stir in the cream. Season to taste, oversalting very slightly as salt loses savor in a cold dish. Chill.
Salt and white pepper	
Chilled soup cups	Serve in chilled soup cups and decorate with minced chives.
2 to 3 Tb minced chives	

OTHER VARIATIONS on Leek and Potato Soup

Using the master recipe for leek and potato soup on page 37, a cup or two of one or a combination of the following vegetables may be added as indicated. Proportions are not important here, and you can use your imagination to the full. Many of the delicious soups you eat in French homes and little restaurants are made just this way, with a leek-and-potato base to which left-over vegetables or sauces and a few fresh items are added. You can also experiment on your own combinations for cold soups, by stirring a cup or more of heavy cream into the cooked soup, chilling it, then sprinkling on fresh herbs just before serving. You may find you have invented a marvelous concoction, which you can keep as a secret of the house.

To be simmered or cooked in the pressure cooker with the potatoes and leeks or onions at the start

Sliced or diced carrots or turnips

Peeled, seeded, and chopped tomatoes, page 505; or strained canned tomatoes

Half-cooked dried beans, peas, or lentils, including their cooking liquid

To be simmered for 10 to 15 minutes with the soup after it has been puréed

Fresh or frozen diced cauliflower, cucumbers, broccoli, Lima beans, peas, string beans, okra, or zucchini

Shredded lettuce, spinach, sorrel, or cabbage

To be heated in the soup just before serving

Diced, cooked leftovers of any of the preceding vegetables

Tomatoes, peeled, seeded, juiced, and diced, page 505.

POTAGE VELOUTÉ AUX CHAMPIGNONS

[Cream of Mushroom Soup]

Here is a fine, rich, mushroom soup either for grand occasions or as the main course for a Sunday supper.

For 6 to 8 people

A 2½-quart, heavy-bottomed enameled saucepan ¼ cup minced onions 3 Tb butter	Cook the onions slowly in the butter for 8 to 10 minutes, until they are tender but not browned.
3 Tb flour	Add the flour and stir over moderate heat for 3 minutes without browning.
6 cups boiling white stock or chicken stock; or canned chicken broth and	Off heat, beat in the boiling stock or broth and blend it thoroughly with the flour. Season to taste. Stir in the mushroom stems, and simmer partially covered

2 parsley sprigs, ⅓ bay
leaf, and ⅛ tsp thyme
Salt and pepper to taste
The chopped stems from ¾
to 1 lb. fresh mushrooms

for 20 minutes or more, skimming occasionally. Strain, pressing juices out of mushroom stems. Return the soup to the pan.

2 Tb butter
An enameled saucepan
The thinly sliced caps from
¾ to 1 lb. fresh mush-
rooms
¼ tsp salt
1 tsp lemon juice

Melt the butter in a separate saucepan. When it is foaming, toss in the mushrooms, salt, and lemon juice. Cover and cook slowly for 5 minutes.

Pour the mushrooms and their cooking juices into the strained soup base. Simmer for 10 minutes.
(*) If not to be served immediately, set aside un-covered, and film surface with a spoonful of cream or milk. Reheat to simmer just before proceeding to the step below, which will take 2 or 3 minutes.

2 egg yolks
½ to ¾ cup whipping
cream
A 3-quart mixing bowl
A wire whip
A wooden spoon

Beat the egg yolks and cream in the mixing bowl. Then beat in hot soup by spoonfuls until a cup has been added. Gradually stir in the rest. Correct season-ing. Return the soup to the pan and stir over moderate heat for a minute or two to poach the egg yolks, but do not let the soup come near the simmer.

1 to 3 Tb softened butter
Optional: 6 to 8 fluted
mushroom caps, page 510,
cooked in butter and
lemon juice; and/or 2 or
3 Tb minced fresh chervil
or parsley

Off heat, stir in the butter by tablespoons. Pour the soup into a tureen or soup cups, and decorate with optional mushrooms and herbs.

* *POTAGE CRÈME DE CRESSON*

[Cream of Water-cress Soup]

This is a lovely soup, and a perfect one for an important dinner.
For 6 servings

⅓ cup minced green on-
  ions, or yellow onions
3 Tb butter
A heavy-bottomed, 2½-
  quart saucepan

Cook the onions slowly in the butter in a covered
saucepan for 5 to 10 minutes, until tender and translucent but not browned.

3 to 4 packed cups of fresh
  water cress leaves and
  tender stems, washed, and
  dried in a towel
½ tsp salt

Stir in the water cress and salt, cover, and cook slowly
for about 5 minutes or until the leaves are tender and
wilted.

3 Tb flour

Sprinkle in the flour and stir over moderate heat for
3 minutes.

5½ cups boiling white stock
  or canned chicken broth

Off heat, beat in the boiling stock. Simmer for 5
minutes, then purée through a food mill. Return to
saucepan and correct seasoning.
(*) If not to be served immediately, set aside uncovered. Reheat to simmer before proceeding.

2 egg yolks
½ cup whipping cream
A 3-quart mixing bowl
A wire whip
1 to 2 Tb softened butter

Blend the yolks and cream in the mixing bowl. Beat
a cupful of hot soup into them by driblets. Gradually
beat in the rest of the soup in a thin stream. Return
soup to saucepan and stir over moderate heat for a
minute or two to poach the egg yolks, but do not
bring the soup to the simmer. Off heat, stir in the
enrichment butter a tablespoon at a time.

A handful of water-cress
  leaves dropped for ½
  minute in boiling water,
  refreshed in cold water,
  and drained

Pour the soup into a tureen or soup cups and decorate
with optional water-cress leaves.

TO SERVE COLD: Omit final butter enrichment and chill. If too thick,
stir in more cream before serving.

VARIATIONS

Potage Crème d'Oseille or Potage Germiny

[Cream of Sorrel Soup]

Potage Crème d'Épinards

[Cream of Spinach Soup]

Follow the recipe for the preceding *crème de cresson,* using sorrel or spinach leaves instead of water cress, but cut the leaves into chiffonade (thin slices or shreds). Do not purée the soup.

✳ *SOUPE À L'OIGNON*

[Onion Soup]

The onions for an onion soup need a long, slow cooking in butter and oil, then a long, slow simmering in stock for them to develop the deep, rich flavor which characterizes a perfect brew. You should therefore count on 2½ hours at least from start to finish. Though the preliminary cooking in butter requires some watching, the actual simmering can proceed almost unattended.

For 6 to 8 servings

1½ lbs. or about 5 cups of thinly sliced yellow onions
3 Tb butter
1 Tb oil
A heavy-bottomed, 4-quart covered saucepan

Cook the onions slowly with the butter and oil in the covered saucepan for 15 minutes.

1 tsp salt
¼ tsp sugar (helps the onions to brown)

Uncover, raise heat to moderate, and stir in the salt and sugar. Cook for 30 to 40 minutes stirring frequently, until the onions have turned an even, deep, golden brown.

3 Tb flour

Sprinkle in the flour and stir for 3 minutes.

2 quarts boiling brown stock, canned beef bouillon, or 1 quart of boiling water and 1 quart of stock or bouillon
½ cup dry white wine or dry white vermouth
Salt and pepper to taste

Off heat, blend in the boiling liquid. Add the wine, and season to taste. Simmer partially covered for 30 to 40 minutes or more, skimming occasionally. Correct seasoning.
(*) Set aside uncovered until ready to serve. Then reheat to the simmer.

3 Tb cognac
Rounds of hard-toasted French bread (see recipe following)
1 to 2 cups grated Swiss or Parmesan cheese

Just before serving, stir in the cognac. Pour into a soup tureen or soup cups over the rounds of bread, and pass the cheese separately.

GARNISHINGS FOR ONION SOUP

Croûtes – hard-toasted French bread

12 to 16 slices of French bread cut ¾ to 1 inch thick

Place the bread in one layer in a roasting pan and bake in a preheated 325-degree oven for about half an hour, until it is thoroughly dried out and lightly browned.

Olive oil or beef drippings
A cut clove of garlic

Halfway through the baking, each side may be basted with a teaspoon of olive oil or beef drippings; and after baking, each piece may be rubbed with cut garlic.

Croûtes au Fromage – cheese *croûtes*

Grated Swiss or Parmesan cheese
Olive oil or beef drippings

Spread one side of each *croûte* with grated cheese and sprinkle with drops of olive oil or beef drippings. Brown under a hot broiler before serving.

VARIATIONS

Soupe à l'Oignon Gratinée

[Onion Soup *Gratinéed* with Cheese]

The preceding onion soup
A fireproof tureen or casserole or individual onion soup pots
2 ounces Swiss cheese cut into very thin slivers
1 Tb grated raw onion
12 to 16 rounds of hard-toasted French bread

Preheat oven to 325 degrees.

Bring the soup to the boil and pour into the tureen or soup pots. Stir in the slivered cheese and grated onion. Float the rounds of toast on top of the soup, and spread the grated cheese over it. Sprinkle with the oil or butter. Bake for 20 minutes in the oven, then set for a minute or two under a preheated broiler to brown the top lightly. Serve immediately.

1½ cups grated Swiss, or
Swiss and Parmesan
cheese
1 Tb olive oil or melted
butter

Soupe Gratinée des Trois Gourmandes

[Onion Soup *Gratinéed de Luxe*]

A final fillip to the preceding onion soup may be accomplished in the kitchen just before serving or by the server at the table.

A 2-quart bowl	Beat the cornstarch into the egg yolk, then the Worces-
1 tsp cornstarch	tershire and the cognac.
1 egg yolk	
1 tsp Worcestershire sauce	
3 Tb cognac	

The preceding onion soup	Just before serving the soup, lift up an edge of the
A soup ladle	crust with a fork and remove a ladleful of soup. In a
A serving fork	thin stream of droplets, beat the soup into the egg
	yolk mixture with a fork. Gradually beat in two more
	ladlefuls, which may be added more rapidly.
	Again lifting up the crust, pour the mixture back into
	the soup. Then reach in under the crust with the ladle
	and stir gently to blend the mixture into the rest of
	the soup. Serve.

SOUPE AU PISTOU

[Provençal Vegetable Soup with Garlic, Basil and Herbs]

Early summer is the Mediterranean season for *soupe au pistou,* when fresh basil, fresh white beans, and broad *mange-tout* beans are all suddenly available, and the market women shout in the streets, *"Mesdames, faites le bon piste, faites le pistou!"* The *pistou* itself, like the Italian *pesta,* is a sauce made of garlic, basil, tomato and cheese, and is just as good on spaghetti as it is in this rich vegetable soup. Fortunately, this soup is not confined to summer and fresh vegetables, for you can use canned navy beans or kidney beans, fresh or frozen string beans, and a fragrant dried basil. Other vegetables in season may be added with the green beans as you wish, such as peas, diced zucchini, and green or red bell peppers.

For 6 to 8 servings

3 quarts water

2 cups each: diced carrots, diced boiling potatoes, diced white of leek or onions

1 Tb salt

(If available, 2 cups fresh white beans, and omit the navy beans farther on)

Either boil the water, vegetables, and salt slowly in a 6-quart kettle for 40 minutes; or pressure-cook for 5 minutes, release pressure, and simmer uncovered for 15 to 20 minutes. Correct seasoning.

2 cups diced green beans or 1 package frozen "cut" beans

2 cups cooked or canned navy beans or kidney beans

⅓ cup broken spaghetti or vermicelli

1 slice stale white bread, crumbled

⅛ tsp pepper

Pinch of saffron

Twenty minutes before serving, so the green vegetables will retain their freshness, add the beans, spaghetti or vermicelli, bread and seasonings to the boiling soup. Boil slowly for about 15 minutes, or until the green beans are just cooked through. Correct seasoning again.

4 cloves mashed garlic

6 Tb fresh tomato purée, page 78, or 4 Tb tomato paste

¼ cup chopped fresh basil or 1½ Tb fragrant dried basil

½ cup grated Parmesan cheese

¼ to ½ cup fruity olive oil

Prepare the following *pistou* while the soup is cooking: place the garlic, tomato purée or paste, basil, and cheese in the soup tureen and blend to a paste with a wooden spoon; then, drop by drop, beat in the olive oil. When the soup is ready for serving, beat a cup gradually into the *pistou*. Pour in the rest of the soup. Serve with hot French bread, or hard-toasted bread rounds basted with olive oil, page 44.

---

* *AÏGO BOUÏDO*

[Garlic Soup]

Enjoying your first bowl of garlic soup, you might never suspect what it is made of. Because the garlic is boiled, its after-effects are at a minimum, and its flavor becomes exquisite, aromatic, and almost undefinable. Along the Mediterranean, an *aïgo bouïdo* is considered to be very good indeed for the liver, blood circulation, general physical tone, and spiritual health. A head of garlic is not at all too much for 2 quarts of soup. For some addicts, it is not even enough.

For 6 to 8 people

1 separated head or about 16 cloves whole, unpeeled garlic

Drop garlic cloves in boiling water and boil 30 seconds. Drain, run cold water over them, and peel.

2 quarts water
2 tsp salt
Pinch of pepper
2 cloves
¼ tsp sage
¼ tsp thyme
½ bay leaf
4 parsley sprigs
3 Tb olive oil
A 3-quart saucepan

Place the garlic and the rest of the ingredients in the saucepan and boil slowly for 30 minutes. Correct seasoning.

A wire whip
3 egg yolks
A soup tureen
3 to 4 Tb olive oil

Beat the egg yolks in the soup tureen for a minute until they are thick and sticky. Drop by drop, beat in the olive oil as for making a mayonnaise.

A strainer
Rounds of hard-toasted French bread, page 44
1 cup of grated Swiss or Parmesan cheese

Just before serving, beat a ladleful of hot soup into the egg mixture by droplets. Gradually strain in the rest, beating, and pressing the juice out of the garlic. Serve immediately, accompanied by the bread and cheese.

VARIATIONS

Soupe à l'Oeuf, Provençale

[Garlic Soup with Poached Eggs]

The preceding garlic soup, omitting the egg yolk and olive oil liaison
6 very fresh eggs

After the soup has been simmered for half an hour, strain it into a wide, shallow saucepan. Correct seasoning and bring to a simmer. Following directions on page 116, poach the eggs in the soup.

6 to 8 rounds of hard-toasted French bread, page 44

2 to 3 Tb chopped parsley

1 cup grated Swiss or Parmesan cheese

Place a round of bread in each soup plate and top with a poached egg. Pour in the soup and decorate with parsley. Pass the cheese separately.

Soupe à l'Ail aux Pommes de Terre

[Saffron-flavored Garlic Soup with Potatoes]

Ingredients for garlic soup, omitting the egg yolk and olive oil liaison

3 cups diced "boiling" potatoes

Pinch of saffron

After the garlic soup has simmered for 30 minutes, strain it and return it to the saucepan. Simmer the potatoes in the soup with the saffron for about 20 minutes or until tender. Correct seasoning. Serve with French bread and grated Swiss or Parmesan cheese.

SOUPE AUX CHOUX – GARBURE

[Main-course Cabbage Soup]

This fine and uncomplicated peasant soup is a comforting dish for a cold winter day. In the Basque country, a good cabbage soup must always include a chunk of *lard rance,* their slightly rancid and much appreciated salt pork; otherwise, the dish is considered to lack distinction. In neighboring Béarn, *confit d'oie*—preserved goose—is added to the pot to warm up in the soup at the end of its cooking.

For about 8 people

3½ quarts water

3 to 4 cups peeled, quartered "boiling" potatoes

A 1½-pound chunk of lean salt pork, lean bacon, or smoked, unprocessed ham

Place the water, potatoes, and meat in the kettle and bring it to the boil.

2 pounds or 3 quarts of roughly sliced cabbage

8 crushed peppercorns or a

Add the cabbage and all the other ingredients. Simmer partially covered for 1½ to 2 hours or until the meat is tender. Discard parsley bundle. Remove the

big pinch of ground chili
peppers

Salt as necessary, added near
the end

6 parsley sprigs tied with 1
bay leaf

½ tsp marjoram

½ tsp thyme

4 cloves mashed garlic

2 medium onions studded
with 2 cloves

2 peeled, quartered carrots

Optional additions:

2 to 4 peeled, quartered
turnips

2 to 3 sliced celery stalks

1 to 2 cups fresh white
beans, or half-cooked navy
beans, or add canned
white or red beans to soup
10 to 15 minutes before
end of simmering

meat, slice it into serving pieces, and return it to the
kettle. Correct seasoning. Skim off accumulated fat.
(*) If not to be served immediately, set aside uncovered. Reheat to simmer before serving.

Rounds of hard-toasted
French bread, page 44

Serve in a tureen or soup plates, accompanied by the
bread.

TWO MEDITERRANEAN FISH SOUPS

How to make a real Mediterranean fish soup is always a subject of lively
and utterly dogmatic discussion among French experts; and if you do not
happen to live on the Mediterranean, you cannot obtain the particular rockfish,
gurnards, mullets, weavers, sea eels, wrasses, and breams which they consider
absolutely essential. But you can make an extremely good fish soup even if you
have only frozen fish and canned clam juice to work with because the other
essential flavorings of tomatoes, onions or leeks, garlic, herbs, and olive oil are
always available.

FISH TO USE

Fish soups are usually made from lean fish. The flavor of the soup is
more interesting if as many varieties of fish are included as possible, and the

soup has more body if a proportion of gelatinous fish such as halibut, eel, and some of the firmer-fleshed flounder types are used. Here are some suggestions:

Rock, Calico, or Sea Bass	Pollock or Boston Bluefish
Cod or Lingcod	Porgy or Scup
Conger or Sea Eel	Redfish or Red Drum
Flounder	Rockfish or Sculpin
Grouper	Scrod
Grunt	Red or Gray Snapper
Haddock	Spot
Hake or Whiting	Fresh-water Trout; Sea Trout or
Halibut	Weakfish
Lemon Sole	Shellfish—Clams, Scallops, Mus-
Perch	sels, Crab, Lobster

To prepare the fish for cooking, have them cleaned and scaled. Discard the gills. Save heads and trimmings for fish stock. Cut large fish into crosswise slices 2 inches wide. Scrub clams. Scrub and soak the mussels, page 226. Wash scallops. If using live crab or lobster, split them just before cooking. Remove the sand sack and intestinal tube from lobsters.

SOUPE DE POISSON

[Strained Fish Soup]

Soupe de poisson has the same taste as bouillabaisse, but the soup is strained and *pasta* is cooked in it to give a light liaison. If you are making the soup on the Mediterranean, you will come home with dozens of tiny, freshly caught fish all colors of the rainbow. Elsewhere, use whole fish, fish heads, bones, and trimmings, shellfish carcasses, or just bottled clam juice.

For 6 to 8 people

A soup kettle	Cook the onions and leeks slowly in olive oil for 5
1 cup minced onions	minutes or until almost tender but not browned.
¾ cup of minced leek, or ½	
cup more onions	
½ cup olive oil	

4 cloves mashed garlic	Stir in the garlic and tomatoes. Raise heat to moderate
1 lb. of ripe, red tomatoes	and cook 5 minutes more.
roughly chopped, or 1½	

cups drained canned to-
matoes, or ¼ cup tomato
paste

2½ quarts water
6 parsley sprigs
1 bay leaf
½ tsp thyme or basil
⅛ tsp fennel
2 big pinches of saffron
A 2-inch piece or ½ tsp
dried orange peel
⅛ tsp pepper
1 Tb salt (none if clam juice
is used)
3 to 4 lbs. lean fish, fish
heads, bones, and trim-
mings, shellfish remains,
or frozen fish from the
list, page 50. Or, 1 quart
clam juice, 1½ quarts of
water, and no salt

Add the water, herbs, seasonings, and fish to the kettle and cook uncovered at a moderate boil for 30 to 40
minutes.

½ cup to ⅔ cup spaghetti
or vermicelli broken into
2-inch pieces
A 3-quart saucepan

Strain the soup into the saucepan, pressing juices out
of ingredients. Correct seasoning, adding a bit more
saffron if you feel it necessary. Stir in the *pasta* and
boil for 10 to 12 minutes or until tender. Correct
seasoning again.

Rounds of hard-toasted
French bread, page 44
1 to 2 cups grated Swiss or
Parmesan cheese and
rouille (following recipe)

Pour the soup into a tureen or soup plates over the
bread rounds, and pass the cheese and *rouille* separately.

VARIATION

Substitute 3 or 4 cups of diced "boiling" potatoes for the *pasta,* or poach
eggs in the soup as for the garlic soup on page 47.

Rouille

[Garlic, Pimiento, and Chili Pepper Sauce]

The following strong sauce is passed separately with fish soup or bouillabaisse; each guest helps himself and stirs it into the soup.

For about 1 cup

¼ cup chopped red bell pepper simmered for several minutes in salted water and drained, or canned pimiento

A small chili pepper boiled until tender, or drops of Tabasco sauce

1 medium potato cooked in the soup

4 cloves mashed garlic

1 tsp basil, thyme, or savory

Pound all ingredients in a bowl or mortar for several minutes to form a very smooth, sticky paste.

4 to 6 Tb fruity olive oil
Salt and pepper

Drop by drop, pound or beat in the olive oil as for making a mayonnaise. Season to taste.

2 or 3 Tb hot soup

Just before serving, beat in the hot soup by driblets. Pour into a sauceboat.

BOUILLABAISSE

[Bouillabaisse]

You can make as dramatic a production as you want out of a bouillabaisse, but remember it originated as a simple, Mediterranean fisherman's soup, made from the day's catch or its unsalable leftovers, and flavored with the typical condiments of the region—olive oil, garlic, leeks or onions, tomatoes, and herbs. The fish are rapidly boiled in an aromatic broth and are removed to a platter; the broth is served in a tureen. Each guest helps himself to both and eats them together in a big soup plate. If you wish to serve wine, choose a *rosé*, or a light, strong, young red such as a Côtes de Provence or Beaujolais, or a strong, dry, white wine from the Côtes de Provence, or a Riesling.

Ideally you should pick six or more varieties of fresh fish, which is why a bouillabaisse is at its best when made for at least six people. Some of the fish should be firm-fleshed and gelatinous like halibut, eel, and winter flounder, and some tender and flaky like hake, baby cod, small pollock, and lemon sole. Shellfish are neither necessary nor particularly typical, but they always add glamor and color if you wish to include them.

The fish, except for live lobsters and crabs, may be cleaned, sliced, and refrigerated several hours before the final cooking. The soup base may be boiled and strained. The actual cooking of the fish in the soup will take only about 20 minutes, and then the dish should be served immediately.

For 6 to 8 people

Ingredients for the preceding *soupe de poisson,* minus the *pasta.* Use fish heads, bones, and trimmings, and if you have not enough of them, strengthen the soup base with bottled clam juice

Boil the soup ingredients for 30 to 40 minutes as described in the fish soup recipe, page 50. Strain, pressing juices out of ingredients. Taste carefully for seasoning and strength. It should be delicious at this point, so it will need no further fussing with later. You should have about 2½ quarts in a high, rather narrow kettle.

6 to 8 pounds assorted lean fish, and shellfish if you wish, selected and prepared from the suggestions on page 50

Bring the soup to a rapid boil 20 minutes before serving. Add lobsters, crabs, and firm-fleshed fish. Bring quickly back to the boil and boil rapidly for 5 minutes. Add the tender-fleshed fish, the clams, mussels, and scallops. Bring rapidly to the boil again and boil 5 minutes more or until the fish are just tender when pierced with a fork. Do not overcook.

A hot platter
A soup tureen
Rounds of hard-toasted French bread, page 44
⅓ cup roughly chopped fresh parsley
Optional: A bowl of *rouille* (page 51)

Immediately lift out the fish and arrange on the platter. Correct seasoning, and pour the soup into the tureen over rounds of French bread. Spoon a ladleful of soup over the fish, and sprinkle parsley over both fish and soup. Serve immediately accompanied by the optional *rouille.*

CHAPTER TWO

SAUCES

Sauces

Sauces are the splendor and glory of French cooking, yet there is nothing secret or mysterious about making them. While their roster is stupendous to look at, it is not mind-boggling when you begin to realize that their multitude divides itself into a half-dozen very definite groups, and that each sauce in a particular group is made in the same general way. For instance, every sauce in the white sauce group of béchamels and *veloutés* calls for an identical technique, but any change in ingredients or trimmings gives the sauce a new name: béchamel with grated cheese is a *mornay,* with minced herbs, a *chivry;* while a white-wine fish *velouté* with dollops of cream, egg yolk, and butter becomes an elegant *sauce parisienne.* The same is true of the egg yolk and butter group. When flavored with tarragon, pepper, and vinegar it's a *béarnaise,* but lemon makes it a hollandaise—yet hollandaise with a folding-in of whipped cream becomes a *mousseline.* Thus as soon as you have put into practice the basic formulas for the few mother sauces, you are equipped to command the whole towering edifice. Here are the mother groups in the sauce family:

The White Sauces These stem from those two cousins, béchamel and *velouté.* Both use a flour and butter *roux* as a thickening agent but béchamel is a milk-based sauce while the *velouté* has a fish, meat, or poultry base. These are fundamental to the great tradition of French cooking, as well as being indispensable to the home cook. Their most useful function, these easy white sauces, is to make an appetizing and interesting dish out of such simple ingredients as hard-boiled eggs and diced mushrooms—*gratiner* them with a *sauce mornay.* Or flake left-over poached fish, mix it with cooked onions, and fold it with a cream sauce before browning it with buttered bread crumbs in the oven. A boiled hen becomes a *poule à l'ivoire* when napped with a creamy chicken *velouté* and accompanied with little braised onions and steamed rice. It would be hard for the everyday cook to get along without these good simple sauces.

The Brown Sauces Long simmered *daubes* and pot roasts, stews and ragouts, these need brown sauces, as do sautés, brown fricassees, and roasts. More complicated to make than the white sauces, they have gone through some changes since the *grande cuisine* of Escoffier, as you will see in their discussion on page 66–7.

Tomato Sauce, Egg Yolk and Butter Sauces (Hollandaise family), and The Oil and Vinegar (French dressing) Group These need no introduction.

Flavored Butters Butters creamed with various herbs, seasonings, or purées are included in the sauce roster. But the most important here is the hot butter sauce *beurre blanc,* a signature of the *nouvelle cuisine* which emerged in the early 1970s. Originally it was a specialty sauce reserved usually for boiled fish and vegetables, but, easy to make (once you know how!), it has become the ubiquitous restaurant sauce for all manner of fish, meat, and fowl.

Rich sauces, especially the butter sauces and white sauces with cream and butter, should be used sparingly, never more than one to a meal. A sauce should not be considered a disguise or a mask; its role is to point up, to prolong, or to complement the taste of the food it accompanies, or to contrast with it, or to give variety to its mode of presentation.

WHITE SAUCES
Sauces Blanches

White sauces are rapidly made with a white *roux* (butter and flour cooked together) plus milk, or white stock. They go with eggs, fish, chicken, veal, and vegetables. They are also the base for cream soups, soufflés, and many of the hot hors d'oeuvres.

Sauce béchamel in the time of Louis XIV was a more elaborate sauce than it is today. Then it was a simmering of milk, veal, and seasonings with an enrichment of cream. In modern French cooking, a béchamel is a quickly made milk-based foundation requiring only the addition of butter, cream, herbs, or other flavorings to turn it into a proper sauce.

Sauce velouté is made in exactly the same way, but its *roux* is moistened with chicken, veal, or fish stock, often with a wine flavoring. Milk or cream are included if you wish.

The roux

In French cooking, the flour and butter, which act as a thickening agent for the sauce, are always cooked slowly together for several minutes before any liquid is added. This is called a *roux*. The cooking eliminates that raw, pasty taste uncooked flour will give to a sauce, and also prepares the flour particles to absorb the liquid. The thickness of a sauce is in direct relation to the proportion of flour you use per cup of liquid. The following table is based on American all-purpose hard-wheat flour. All flour measurements are for level tablespoons or fractions.

THIN SAUCE OR SOUP	1 Tb flour per cup of liquid
MEDIUM, GENERAL-PURPOSE SAUCE	1½ Tb flour per cup of liquid
THICK SAUCE	2 Tb flour per cup of liquid
SOUFFLÉ BASE	3 Tb flour per cup of liquid

Cooking time

Many of the old cookbooks recommend that a white sauce, especially a *velouté,* be simmered for several hours, the object being to rid the sauce of its floury taste, and to concentrate flavor. However, if the flour and butter *roux* is properly cooked to begin with, and a concentrated, well-flavored stock is used, both of these problems have been solved at the start. After a long simmering, a perfectly executed *velouté* will acquire a certain added finesse; and if you have the time to simmer, by all means do so. But for the practical purposes of this book, we shall seldom consider it necessary.

Saucepan note

White sauces should always be made in a heavy-bottomed enameled, stainless steel, pyrex, porcelain, or tin-lined copper saucepan. If a thin-bottomed pan is used, it is a poor heat conductor and the sauce may scorch in the bottom of the pan. Aluminum tends to discolor a white sauce, particularly one containing wine or egg yolks.

A NOTE ON STOCKS FOR VELOUTÉ SAUCES

The recipe for homemade white stock is on page 109; for white chicken stock on page 237; for fish stock on page 114; and for clam-juice fish stock on page 115. Canned chicken broth may be substituted for homemade white stock if you give it the following preliminary treatment:

Canned chicken broth

2 cups canned chicken broth or strained clear chicken and vegetable soup 3 Tb each: sliced onions, carrots, and celery ½ cup dry white wine or ⅓ cup dry white vermouth 2 parsley sprigs, ⅓ bay leaf, and a pinch of thyme	Simmer the chicken broth or soup with the vegetables, wine, and herbs for 30 minutes. Season to taste, strain, and it is ready to use.

✳ *SAUCE BÉCHAMEL*
SAUCE VELOUTÉ

[White Sauce]

This basic sauce takes about 5 minutes to make, and is then ready for the addition of flavors or enrichments. Suggestions for these are at the end of the master recipe.

For 2 cups (*medium thickness*)

A heavy-bottomed, 6-cup enameled, stainless steel, lined copper, porcelain, or pyrex saucepan 2 Tb butter 3 Tb flour A wooden spatula or spoon	In the saucepan melt the butter over low heat. Blend in the flour, and cook slowly, stirring, until the butter and flour froth together for 2 minutes without coloring. This is now a white *roux*.
2 cups of milk and ¼ tsp salt heated to the boil in a small saucepan OR 2 cups boiling white stock (see notes in preceding paragraph) A wire whip	Remove *roux* from heat. As soon as *roux* has stopped bubbling, pour in all the hot liquid at once. Immediately beat vigorously with a wire whip to blend liquid and *roux*, gathering in all bits of *roux* from the inside edges of the pan. Set saucepan over moderately high heat and stir with the wire whip until the sauce comes to the boil. Boil for 1 minute, stirring.

Salt and white pepper	Remove from heat, and beat in salt and pepper to taste. Sauce is now ready for final flavorings or additions.
	(*) If not used immediately, clean sauce off inside edges of pan with a rubber scraper. To prevent a skin from forming on its surface, float a thin film of milk, stock, or melted butter on top. Set aside uncovered, keep it hot over simmering water, refrigerate, or freeze it.

Remarks

If you follow the preceding directions, you will always obtain a smooth sauce of the correct consistency. But here are some remedial measures in case you need them:

If sauce is lumpy	If your *roux* is hot, and your liquid near the boil, you should never have a lumpy sauce. But if there are lumps, force the sauce through a very fine sieve or whirl it in an electric blender. Then simmer it for 5 minutes.
If sauce is too thick	Bring the sauce to the simmer. Thin it out with milk, cream, or stock, beaten in a tablespoon at a time.
If sauce is too thin	*Either* boil it down over moderately high heat, stirring continually with a wooden spoon, until it has reduced to the correct consistency;
	Or blend half a tablespoon of butter into a paste with half a tablespoon of flour (*beurre manié*). Off heat, beat the paste into the sauce with a wire whip. Boil for 1 minute, stirring.

ENRICHMENTS FOR WHITE SAUCES

The three following enrichments complete the whole master system of white-sauce making. While a plain, well-seasoned béchamel or *velouté* may be served just as it is, the addition of butter, cream, or egg yolks transforms it into something infinitely more delicious.

Butter Enrichment

Fresh butter stirred into a sauce just before serving is the simplest of the enrichments. It smooths out the sauce, gives it a slight liaison, and imparts that certain French taste which seems to be present in no other type of cooking.

For a cup of simple sauce, ½ to 1 tablespoon of butter is sufficient; as much as ½ cup may be beaten into a fine fish sauce. But if more than a tablespoon of butter is beaten into a cup of sauce, the sauce should then be served immediately. If it is reheated, or is kept hot, or if it is used for a *gratinéed* dish, the butter either liquefies and the sauce thins out just as though it had been diluted with milk, or the butter releases itself from suspension and floats on top of the sauce. However, if you slip up and heat a heavily buttered sauce, it will quickly reconstitute itself if you treat it like turned hollandaise, page 81.

To enrich 2 cups of béchamel or velouté, page 57

2 to 8 Tb butter (1 to 2 Tb is the usual amount) **A wire whip**	Just before serving the sauce, and after all the final flavorings have been added, remove it from heat. Stir in the butter, a half-tablespoon at a time, beating until each piece of butter has been absorbed into the sauce before adding the next. Spoon the sauce over the hot food, or pour the sauce into a warmed bowl, and serve immediately.

Cream Enrichment – Cream Sauce

[*Sauce Crème – Sauce Suprême*]

With the addition of cream, a béchamel becomes a *sauce crème;* and a *velouté,* a *sauce suprême.* As the cream thins out the sauce, the basic béchamel or *velouté* must be thick enough initially so the finished sauce will be of the correct consistency.

Cream sauces are used for vegetables, eggs, fish, poultry, hot hors d'oeuvres, and for dishes which are to be *gratinéed.*

For 2 cups

1½ cups of thick béchamel or *velouté*, page 57 (3 Tb flour, 2½ Tb butter, and 1½ cups liquid) **½ cup whipping cream** **Salt and white pepper** **Lemon juice**	Bring the sauce to the simmer. Beat in the cream by spoonfuls, simmering, until the sauce is the consistency you wish it to be. Season to taste with salt, pepper, and drops of lemon juice.
Optional: 1 to 2 Tb softened butter (no butter if sauce is to be used for a *gratinéed* dish)	Off heat, and just before serving, beat in the optional butter by half-tablespoons.

Egg Yolk and Cream Enrichment

[*Sauce Parisienne* – formerly *Sauce Allemande*]

Sauces enriched with egg yolks and cream are among the richest and most velvety in all the French repertoire. *Sauce parisienne*, or *sauce allemande*, is the generic term, but it invariably goes by another name according to its special flavorings or to the dish it accompanies. The simplest, *sauce poulette*, has a base of *velouté* flavored with meat or fish, onions and mushrooms. The famous *sauce normande* is a *velouté* based on white-wine fish stock and the cooking liquors of mussels, oysters, shrimps, *écrevisses*, and mushrooms. The shellfish sauces such as *cardinal, Nantua,* and *Joinville* are shellfish *veloutés* with special trimmings and a shellfish butter enrichment beaten in at the end. As all of these sauces are a basic *velouté* with a final enrichment of egg yolks, cream, and usually butter, if you can make one, you can make all.

Success in making the egg yolk liaison is but a realization that egg yolks will curdle and turn granular unless they are beaten with a bit of cold liquid first, before a hot liquid is gradually incorporated into them so that they are slowly heated. Once this preliminary step has been completed, the sauce may be brought to the boil; and because the egg yolks are supported by a flour-based sauce they may boil without danger of curdling.

The *sauce parisienne* described in the following recipe is used with eggs, fish, poultry, hot hors d'oeuvres, and dishes which are to be *gratinéed*. A heavily buttered *sauce parisienne* is used principally for fish poached in white wine, as described beginning on page 214 in the Fish chapter.

For about 2 cups

1½ cups thick béchamel or *velouté,* page 57 (3 Tb flour, 2½ Tb butter, and 1½ cups liquid)

A heavy-bottomed, 8-cup enameled saucepan

Bring the sauce to the simmer in its saucepan.

---

2 egg yolks
½ cup whipping cream
An 8-cup mixing bowl
A wire whip

Blend the egg yolks and cream in the mixing bowl with a wire whip. A few drops at a time, beat in ½ cup of hot sauce. Slowly beat in the rest of the sauce in a thin stream. Pour the mixture back into the saucepan.

A wooden spatula or spoon	Set over moderately high heat and stir constantly with a wooden spoon, reaching all over the bottom of the pan until the sauce comes to the boil. Boil and stir for 1 minute.
Salt and white pepper **Lemon juice** **More cream if necessary**	Strain the sauce through a fine sieve to remove coagulated bits of egg white which always cling to the yolk. Rinse out the saucepan and return the sauce to it. Simmer over low heat to check seasoning, adding salt, pepper, and drops of lemon juice to taste. If sauce is too thick, beat in more cream by spoonfuls. (*) If not used immediately, clean off sides of pan, and float a film of cream or stock over the surface. Sauce will thicken and look custardy as it cools, which is normal. It will smooth out when it is reheated. (Sauce may be frozen.)
Optional: 1 to 2 Tb softened butter (occasionally more is called for; use no butter if sauce is for a *gratinéed* dish)	Off heat, and just before serving, stir in the optional butter by bits.

SAUCES DERIVED FROM BÉCHAMEL AND VELOUTÉ

Here are some of the principal sauces derived from *sauce béchamel* and *sauce velouté,* the recipes for which are on page 57.

Sauce Mornay

[Cheese Sauce]

For: eggs, fish, poultry, veal, vegetables, *pastas,* and hot hors d'oeuvres

Note: If the sauce covers foods which are to be baked or *gratinéed,* use the minumum amount of cheese suggested, and omit the butter enrichment at the end of the recipe. Too much cheese can make the sauce stringy, and a butter enrichment will exude from the top of the sauce.

2 cups of medium béchamel or *velouté,* page 57

¼ to ½ cup of coarsely grated Swiss cheese, or a combination of coarsely grated Swiss and finely grated Parmesan

Bring the sauce to the boil. Remove from heat, and beat in the cheese until it has melted and blended with the sauce.

Salt and pepper
Pinch of nutmeg
Optional: pinch of cayenne pepper and 1 to 2 Tb softened butter

Season to taste with salt, pepper, nutmeg, and optional cayenne. Off heat and just before serving, stir in the optional butter a bit at a time.

Sauce Aurore

[Béchamel or *Velouté* with Tomato Flavoring]

For: eggs, fish, chicken, vegetables

2 cups béchamel or *velouté,* page 57, or the cream sauce, page 59

2 to 6 Tb cooked, fresh tomato purée, page 78, or tomato paste

Bring the sauce to the simmer. Stir in the tomato, a spoonful at a time, until you have achieved the color and flavor you wish. Correct seasoning.

1 to 2 Tb softened butter
Optional: 1 to 2 Tb minced fresh parsley, chervil, basil, or tarragon

Off heat and just before serving, stir in the butter, and the optional herbs.

Sauce Chivry
Sauce à L'Estragon

[Herbal White Wine Sauce and Tarragon Sauce]

For: eggs, fish, vegetables, or poached chicken

A small enameled saucepan
1 cup dry white wine or ⅔ cup dry white vermouth

Place all ingredients in the saucepan and boil slowly for 10 minutes, allowing the wine to reduce to about 3 tablespoons. This is now an herb essence.

4 Tb minced fresh chervil,
   tarragon, and parsley, or
   tarragon only; OR 2 Tb
   dried herbs
2 Tb minced shallots or
   green onions

2 cups béchamel or *velouté*, page 57, or the cream sauce, page 59	Strain the essence into the sauce, pressing the juice out of the herbs. Simmer for 2 to 3 minutes.
3 to 4 Tb minced fresh green herbs, or parsley, or tarragon 1 to 2 Tb softened butter	Off heat, and just before serving, stir in the fresh herbs and the enrichment butter.

Sauce au Cari

[Light Curry Sauce]

For: fish, veal, lamb, chicken, turkey, eggs, and vegetables
Here the béchamel or *velouté* sauce is made simultaneously with the curry flavorings.

For 2½ cups

½ cup finely minced white or yellow onions 4 Tb butter An 8-cup enameled saucepan	Cook the onions and butter over low heat for 10 minutes without allowing the onions to color.
2 to 3 Tb curry powder	Stir in the curry powder and cook slowly for 2 minutes.
4 Tb flour	Add the flour and stir over low heat for 3 minutes more.
2 cups boiling milk, white stock, or fish stock	Off heat, blend in the boiling liquid. Return sauce to heat and simmer slowly for 10 to 15 minutes, stirring occasionally.
4 to 6 Tb whipping cream Salt and pepper Lemon juice	Then stir in the cream by tablespoons, until sauce has thinned to consistency you wish. Check seasoning, and add lemon juice to taste.

1 to 2 Tb softened butter Optional: 2 to 3 Tb minced parsley	Off heat, and just before serving, stir in the butter by bits, then the optional parsley.

Sauce Soubise

[Onion Sauce]

For: eggs, veal, chicken, turkey, lamb, vegetables, and foods which are to be *gratinéed*

Another version of this excellent sauce is in the Veal section, page 355.

For about 2½ cups

1 lb. or 4 cups of sliced yel- low onions ¼ tsp salt 6 Tb butter A 2½-quart, heavy-bot- tomed, enameled sauce- pan	Cook the onions slowly with salt and butter in a covered saucepan for 20 to 30 minutes, or until the onions are very tender but not browned.
4 Tb flour	Add the flour and stir over low heat for 3 minutes.
2 cups boiling milk, white stock, or fish stock	Off heat, blend in the boiling liquid. Then simmer the sauce slowly for 15 minutes, stirring occasionally. Force the sauce through a sieve or food mill, or purée it in the electric blender.
6 to 8 Tb whipping cream Salt and pepper Pinch of nutmeg	Bring again to the simmer, and thin out to desired consistency with spoonfuls of cream. Add salt, pepper, and nutmeg to taste.
1 to 2 Tb softened butter (no butter if sauce is to be used for a *gratinéed* dish)	Off heat and just before serving, stir in the enrichment butter.

∗ SAUCE BÂTARDE
SAUCE AU BEURRE

[Mock Hollandaise]

For: boiled fish, boiled chicken, boiled lamb, boiled potatoes, asparagus, cauliflower, celery, broccoli

This quickly made and useful sauce does not belong to the béchamel and *velouté* family because it is made with an uncooked *roux,* or *beurre manié.* A golden color is given it by the addition of an egg yolk, and when flavored with enough butter it suggests a hollandaise.

For 2 cups (*medium thickness*)

2 Tb melted or softened butter 3 Tb flour An 8-cup, heavy-bottomed, enameled saucepan A rubber scraper	Place the butter and flour in the saucepan and blend them into a smooth paste with a rubber scraper.
2 cups boiling white stock, or vegetable cooking water, or water and ¼ tsp salt A wire whip	Pour on all the boiling liquid at once and blend vigorously with a wire whip.
1 egg yolk 2 Tb whipping cream An 8-cup mixing bowl Salt and white pepper 1 to 2 Tb lemon juice	Blend the egg yolk and cream with a wire whip, then, a few drops at a time, beat in ½ cup of sauce. Beat in the rest in a thin stream. Pour the mixture back into the saucepan. Bring to the boil over moderately high heat, beating, and boil 5 seconds. Remove from heat and season to taste with salt, pepper, and lemon juice. (*) If not used immediately, film surface with a half-tablespoon of melted butter.
4 to 8 Tb softened butter	Off heat, and just before serving, beat in the butter, a tablespoon at a time.

VARIATIONS

Sauce aux Câpres

[Caper Sauce]

For: boiled fish or boiled leg of lamb

2 cups *sauce bâtarde* 2 to 3 Tb capers	Just before stirring in the enrichment butter, beat in the capers. Then, off heat, beat in the enrichment butter.

Sauce à la Moutarde

[Mustard Sauce]

For: broiled mackerel, herring, tuna, or swordfish

2 cups *sauce bâtarde* omitting final butter enrichment 2 Tb strong Dijon-type prepared mustard 4 to 8 Tb softened butter	Blend the mustard and butter together with a rubber scraper. Off heat, and just before serving, beat the mustard/butter by tablespoons into the hot sauce.

Sauce aux Anchois

[Anchovy Sauce]

For: boiled fish or boiled potatoes

2 Tb canned anchovies mashed into a purée or 1 Tb anchovy paste 2 cups *sauce bâtarde*	Just before buttering the sauce, beat in the anchovy mixture to taste. Then off heat, and before serving, beat in the enrichment butter.

BROWN SAUCES
Sauces Brunes

The classical French brown sauce starts out with a long-simmered brown meat stock that goes into the making of an equally long-simmered, lightly thickened sauce base called an *espagnole*. The *espagnole* is simmered and skimmed for several hours more with additional stock and flavorings until it finally develops into the traditional mother of the brown sauces, *demi-glace*. This may take several days to accomplish, and the result is splendid. But as we are concerned with less formal cooking, we shall discuss it no further.

A good brown sauce may have as its thickening agent a brown *roux* of flour and butter, or cornstarch, potato starch, rice starch, or arrowroot. A flour-thickened brown sauce must be simmered and skimmed for two hours at least if it is to develop its full flavor. Starch and arrowroot thickenings take but a few minutes; and when properly made they are very good indeed. Because they are far more useful in home cooking than the long simmered and more conventional sauce, we have used them in most of the main-course recipes throughout this book.

Following are three interchangeable methods for making a basic brown sauce. Any of them may rapidly be converted into one of the composed sauces starting on page 71.

A NOTE ON MEAT STOCKS FOR BROWN SAUCES

Recipes for making brown stocks are on pages 107 to 110. Canned beef bouillon may be substituted, as is, for stocks in the first two recipes for brown sauce. If it is to be used in the last recipe, for starch-thickened sauce, its canned flavor should first be disguised and enriched as follows (canned consommé tends to be sweet and is not recommended):

Canned beef bouillon

2 cups canned beef bouillon

3 Tb each: finely minced onions and carrots

1 Tb finely minced celery

½ cup red wine, dry white wine, or dry white vermouth

2 parsley sprigs

⅓ bay leaf

⅛ tsp thyme

Optional: 1 Tb tomato paste

Simmer the canned bouillon with the rest of the ingredients listed for 20 to 30 minutes. Strain through a fine sieve, and the bouillon is ready to be turned into a sauce.

BROWN SAUCE (1)

SAUCE BRUNE

[Flour-based Brown Sauce]

This is the best of the group and the one most nearly approaching the traditional *demi-glace*. Its preliminaires are somewhat exacting, and it requires at least two hours of simmering; the longer it cooks the better it will be. It may be refrigerated for several days and freezes perfectly for several weeks.

A NOTE ON BROWN ROUX

Brown *roux,* which is the thickening for this type of sauce, is flour and fat cooked together until the flour has turned an even, nut-brown color. For an ordinary sauce, the flour is cooked in rendered fresh pork fat, or in cooking oil. But if the sauce is to accompany a delicate dish, such as *foie gras,* eggs, or *vol-au-vent,* the flour should be cooked in clarified butter—meaning the butter is melted and decanted, leaving its milky particles behind, as these burn and taste bitter.

It is important that the *roux* be cooked slowly and evenly. If the flour is burned, it will not thicken the sauce as it should, and it will also impart an unpleasant taste.

For about 1 quart of brown sauce

A heavy-bottomed, 2-quart saucepan ⅓ cup each: finely diced carrots, onions, and celery 3 Tb diced boiled ham (or diced lean bacon simmered for 10 minutes in water, rinsed, and drained) 6 Tb clarified butter, page 15, rendered fresh pork fat, or cooking oil	Cook the vegetables and ham or bacon slowly in the butter, fat, or oil for 10 minutes.
4 Tb flour A wooden spatula or spoon	Blend the flour into the vegetables and stir continually over moderately low heat for 8 to 10 minutes, until the flour slowly turns a golden, nut brown.
A wire whip 6 cups boiling brown stock or canned beef bouillon 2 Tb tomato paste A medium herb bouquet: 3 parsley sprigs, ½ bay leaf, and ¼ tsp thyme tied in cheesecloth	Remove from heat. With a wire whip, immediately blend in all the boiling liquid at once. Beat in the tomato paste. Add the herb bouquet.
	Simmer slowly, partially covered, for 2 hours or more, skimming off fat and scum as necessary. Add more

liquid if sauce thickens too much. You should end up with about 4 cups of sauce, thick enough to coat a spoon lightly.

Salt and pepper	Correct seasoning. Strain, pressing juice out of vegetables. Degrease thoroughly, and the sauce is ready to use.

(*) If not used immediately, clean off sides of pan, and float a film of stock over the top of the sauce to prevent a skin from forming. When cold, cover and refrigerate or freeze.

BROWN SAUCE (2)

✳ SAUCE RAGOÛT

[Flour-based Brown Sauce with Giblets]

Sauce ragoût is essentially like the preceding brown sauce, but has more character, as it includes bones, trimmings, or giblets gathered from the game, beef, lamb, veal, goose, duck, or turkey the sauce is to be served with.

For 4 cups

A heavy-bottomed, 3- to 4-quart saucepan 1 to 4 cups of giblets, bones, and meat trimmings, raw or cooked ½ cup chopped carrots ½ cup chopped onions 6 Tb clarified butter (page 15), rendered fresh pork fat, or cooking oil; more if needed	Brown the giblets, bones, meat trimmings and vegetables in hot clarified butter, fat, or oil. Remove them to a side dish.
4 Tb flour	Slowly brown the flour in the fat remaining in the saucepan, adding more fat if necessary.
5 to 6 cups boiling brown stock or canned beef bouillon Optional: 1 cup dry white wine, red wine, or ⅔ cup dry white vermouth	Off heat, beat in the boiling liquid, optional wine, and optional tomato paste. Add the herb bouquet and return the browned ingredients. Simmer, skimming as necessary, for 2 to 4 hours. Strain, degrease, correct seasoning, and the sauce is ready to use.

Optional: 3 Tb tomato paste
A medium herb bouquet: 3
  parsley sprigs, ½ bay leaf,
  ¼ tsp thyme tied in
  cheesecloth

VARIATIONS

Sauce Poivrade

[Brown Game Sauce]

This is the same as *sauce ragoût*. If the game has been marinated, a cup or two of the marinade is used instead of the optional wine. The final sauce is highly seasoned with pepper.

Sauce Venaison

[Brown Sauce for Venison]

This is *sauce poivrade* with ½ cup red currant jelly and ½ cup whipping cream beaten into it just before serving.

BROWN SAUCE (3)

* *JUS LIÉ*

[Starch-thickened Brown Sauce]

Jus lié is a most useful alternative to the preceding long-simmered brown sauces, and takes about 5 minutes to prepare. But it has no culinary interest whatsoever if it is not made with an excellent base, as it is only stock thickened with cornstarch or arrowroot. The sauce is usually made with the liquids obtained from the simmering or stewing of meats, and therefore acquires a good, strong flavor. If it is made from canned bouillon, the bouillon should first be simmered with wine and seasonings as described under meat stocks on page 67. Cornstarch is the thickening for ordinary brown sauces of this type. Arrowroot is used when the sauce is to be very clear and limpid, such as that for the ham braised in Madeira on page 393, or the duck with orange, page 276. (Potato starch and rice starch are French equivalents of cornstarch.)

For 2 cups

2 Tb cornstarch or arrow-
root
2 cups of excellent brown
stock, or canned beef
bouillon simmered with
wine and seasonings, page
67
A 4-cup saucepan
A wire whip

Blend the cornstarch or arrowroot with 2 tablespoons
of cold stock, then beat in the rest of the stock. Simmer for 5 minutes, or until sauce has cleared and is
lightly thickened. Correct seasoning.

Optional: ¼ cup Madeira,
port, or cognac

Add optional wine or cognac, and simmer for 2 to 3
minutes, tasting, until the alcohol has evaporated.
(*) Sauce may be set aside, and reheated when
needed.

SAUCES DERIVED FROM BROWN SAUCE

Following are some of the principal composed sauces which are made with
any of the three preceding brown sauces. They are almost always combined
with the cooking juices of the dishes they accompany, and thereby pick up
additional flavor.

Sauce Diable

[Peppery Brown Sauce]

For: broiled chicken, roast or braised pork, pork chops, hot meat leftovers

A 4-cup saucepan or your
meat-cooking pan with its
degreased juices
1 to 2 Tb minced shallots or
green onions
1 Tb butter or cooking fat
1 cup dry white wine or ⅔
cup dry white vermouth

Cook the shallots or green onions slowly with the
butter or cooking fat for 2 minutes without browning. Then add the wine and boil it down rapidly until
it has reduced to 3 or 4 tablespoons.

2 cups brown sauce (pages
67 to 71)
Black pepper
Cayenne pepper

Pour in the sauce and simmer for 2 minutes. Season
with enough pepper to give it a spicy taste.

1 to 3 Tb softened butter 2 to 3 Tb fresh minced parsley or mixed green herbs	Off heat, and just before serving, swirl butter into the sauce a bit at a time. Stir in the parsley or herbs.

Sauce Piquante

[Brown Sauce with Pickles and Capers]

For: roast or braised pork, pork chops, boiled or braised tongue, boiled beef, and hot meat leftovers

The preceding sauce diable *plus:*

2 Tb finely chopped pickles 2 Tb capers	Just before removing the sauce from heat, stir in the pickles and capers. Simmer a moment, then, off heat, beat in the butter and herbs.

Sauce Robert

[Brown Mustard Sauce]

For: roast or braised pork, pork chops, boiled beef, broiled chicken, or turkey, hot meat leftovers, hamburgers

A heavy-bottomed, 6-cup saucepan or your meat-cooking pan with its de-greased juices ¼ cup finely minced yellow onions 1 Tb butter 1 tsp oil or cooking fat	Cook the onions slowly with the butter and oil or fat, for 10 to 15 minutes until they are tender and lightly browned.
1 cup dry white wine or ⅔ cup dry vermouth	Add the wine and boil it down rapidly until it has reduced to 3 or 4 tablespoons.
2 cups brown sauce, pages 67 to 71	Add the brown sauce and simmer 10 minutes. Correct seasoning.
3 to 4 Tb Dijon-type prepared mustard creamed with 2 or 3 Tb softened butter and ⅛ tsp sugar 2 to 3 Tb fresh minced parsley	Off heat and just before serving, beat the mustard mixture into the sauce, tasting. Beat in the parsley, and serve.

Sauce Brune aux Fines Herbes
Sauce Brune à l'Estragon

[Brown Herb or Tarragon Sauce]

For: sautéed chicken, veal, rabbit, braised vegetables, hot meat leftovers, and poached or baked eggs

A 2- to 3-cup enameled saucepan 1 cup dry white wine or ⅔ cup dry white vermouth 2 Tb minced shallots or green onions 4 Tb fresh herbs or 2 Tb dried herbs as follows: parsley, basil, chervil, rosemary, oregano, and tarragon only	Place all the ingredients in the saucepan and boil slowly for 10 minutes, reducing the wine to 2 or 3 tablespoons. This is now an herb essence.
2 cups of brown sauce, pages 67 to 71 A 6- to 8-cup saucepan	Strain the herb essence into the brown sauce, pressing the juices out of the herbs. Simmer for 1 minute.
1 to 3 Tb softened butter 2 to 3 Tb fresh minced parsley, mixed green herbs, or tarragon	Off heat, and just before serving, beat the butter into the sauce by bits, then beat in the herbs.

Sauce Brune au Cari

[Brown Curry Sauce]

For: lamb, chicken, beef, rice, and egg dishes

A heavy-bottomed, 8-cup saucepan 1½ cups finely minced yellow onions 2 Tb butter 1 tsp oil	Cook the onions slowly in the butter and oil for about 15 minutes, until they are tender and lightly browned.

3 to 4 Tb curry powder	Blend in the curry powder and cook slowly for 1 minute.
Optional: 2 cloves mashed garlic	Stir in the optional garlic and cook slowly for half a minute.
2 cups brown sauce, pages 67 to 71	Add the brown sauce and simmer for 10 minutes.
2 to 3 tsp lemon juice	Correct seasoning and add lemon juice to taste.
1 to 3 Tb softened butter 2 to 3 Tb fresh minced parsley	Off heat, and just before serving, beat in the butter by bits. Stir in the parsley.

Sauce Duxelles

[Brown Mushroom Sauce]

For: broiled or sautéed chicken, veal, rabbit, or for egg dishes, hot meat leftovers, or *pastas*

A heavy-bottomed, 8-cup saucepan ¼ lb. (1 cup) finely minced fresh mushrooms or mushroom stems only 2 Tb shallots or green onions 1 Tb butter ½ Tb oil	Sauté the mushrooms with the shallots or onions in hot butter and oil for 4 to 5 minutes.
½ cup dry white wine or ⅓ cup dry white vermouth	Add the wine and boil it down rapidly until it has reduced almost completely.
1½ cups brown sauce, pages 67 to 71 1½ Tb tomato paste	Stir in the brown sauce and tomato paste and simmer for 5 minutes. Correct seasoning.
1 to 3 Tb softened butter 3 to 4 Tb mixed green herbs or parsley	Off heat and just before serving, stir in the butter by bits, then the herbs or parsley.

Sauce Chasseur

[Brown Mushroom Sauce with Fresh Tomatoes, Garlic, and Herbs]

For: same as preceding *sauce duxelles*

Sauce chasseur is almost the same as *sauce duxelles,* but a bit more hearty in flavor. The recipe for it is described in the Veal section under *escalopes de veau chasseur* on page 368.

Sauce Madère
[Brown Madeira Sauce]

Sauce au Porto
[Brown Port-wine Sauce]

For: *filet* of beef, or for ham, veal, chicken livers, and egg dishes, or to sauce a garniture for *vol-au-vents*

½ cup Madeira or port A 6-cup saucepan	Boil the wine in the saucepan until it has reduced to about 3 tablespoons.
2 cups excellent brown sauce, pages 67 to 71 Optional: 1 to 2 tsp meat glaze, page 110 3 to 4 Tb Madeira or port, if necessary	Add the brown sauce and simmer for a minute or two. Taste carefully for seasoning and strength, adding meat glaze if you have it and feel it necessary. If more wine is needed, add it by tablespoons, simmering briefly to evaporate the alcohol.
2 to 3 Tb softened butter	Off heat and just before serving, beat in the butter by bits.

Sauce Périgueux

[Brown Madeira Sauce with Truffles]

For: *filet* of beef, fresh *foie gras,* ham, veal, egg dishes, and timbales

The preceding sauce Madère 2 to 4 diced canned truffles and their juice	Prepare the Madeira sauce as in the preceding recipe, but add the truffle juice to reduce with the Madeira at the beginning. After flavoring the sauce, stir in the truffles and simmer for a minute. Off heat, beat the butter into the sauce just before serving.

OTHER BROWN SAUCES

The following brown sauces are incorporated into recipes in other parts of the book.

Brown deglazing sauce

This sauce is made by dissolving the coagulated cooking juices in a roasting or sautéing pan with wine or stock after the meat has been removed. The liquid is boiled down until it is syrupy. Off heat a lump of butter is swirled in to give the sauce a slight liaison. It is one of the most delicious, useful, and simple of all the brown sauces, and is described in countless recipes. A good illustration is the deglazing sauce for roast chicken, page 240.

Sauce à l'Italienne, a brown sauce with ham, mushrooms, and herbs, as described under braised sweetbreads, page 411. The sauce may also be used for brains, sautéed liver, egg dishes, and *pastas.*

Sauce Bordelaise, a red wine sauce with beef marrow, described in the Kidney section under *rognons de veau à la bordelaise,* page 419. The sauce is also good with steaks, hamburgers, and egg dishes.

Sauce à l'Orange, a brown sauce with orange flavoring and orange peel, as described in the Duck section for *canard à l'orange,* page 276. The same sauce could also be used with baked ham or roast pork.

Sauce Bourguignonne, a red wine sauce always accompanied by a garniture of bacon, mushrooms, and braised onions, as described under poached eggs *à la bourguignonne* on page 121. It also goes with sweetbreads or brains, sautéed beef, and chicken. *Boeuf bourguignon* and *coq au vin* are examples, pages 315 and 263.

TOMATO SAUCES
Sauces Tomate

SAUCE TOMATE

[Tomato Sauce]

This good basic tomato sauce is served just as it is, or may be flavored with herbs or combined with other sauces whenever you wish a tomato flavoring. It is at its best with fresh tomatoes, but canned tomatoes or canned tomato purée will also produce a good sauce. You will notice, during its simmering, that it really should cook for about an hour and a half to develop its full flavor.

For about 2½ cups

A heavy-bottomed, 2½-quart saucepan

¼ cup each: finely diced carrots, onions, and celery

2 Tb minced boiled ham; OR 2 Tb minced lean bacon, simmered for 10 minutes in water, rinsed, and drained

3 Tb butter

1 Tb oil

Cook the vegetables and the ham or bacon slowly in the butter and oil for 10 minutes without letting them brown.

1½ Tb flour

Blend the flour into the ham and vegetables, and cook slowly for 3 minutes, stirring.

1½ cups boiling stock or canned beef bouillon

Off heat, beat in the stock or bouillon.

2 lbs. (4 cups) chopped, ripe, red tomatoes which need not be peeled; OR 3 cups canned tomatoes; OR 1½ cups canned tomato purée and 1½ cups water

¼ tsp salt

⅛ tsp sugar

2 unpeeled cloves garlic

4 parsley sprigs

½ bay leaf

¼ tsp thyme

Stir in the tomatoes, salt, and sugar. Add the garlic and herbs. Simmer for 1½ to 2 hours, skimming occasionally, and adding water if sauce reduces and thickens too much. You should end up with about 2½ cups of rich, fairly thick sauce.

1 to 2 Tb tomato paste, if necessary

Strain, pressing juice out of ingredients. Correct seasoning. Stir in 1 to 2 tablespoons of tomato paste if you feel the sauce lacks color, and simmer again for 5 minutes.

(*) If not used immediately, film surface with stock or a few drops of oil. May be refrigerated or frozen.

COULIS DE TOMATES À LA PROVENCALE

[Fresh Tomato Purée with Garlic and Herbs]

For: broiled or boiled chicken, boiled beef, meat patties, hot meat left-overs, eggs, *pastas,* and pizzas

Here is a thick, concentrated tomato sauce with real Mediterranean flavor.

For about 2 cups

A heavy-bottomed, 3-quart saucepan
⅓ cup finely minced yellow onions
2 Tb olive oil

Cook the onions and olive oil slowly together for about 10 minutes, until the onions are tender but not browned.

---

2 tsp flour

Stir in the flour and cook slowly for 3 minutes without browning.

---

3 lbs. ripe red tomatoes, peeled, seeded, juiced, and chopped, page 505 (about 4½ cups)
⅛ tsp sugar
2 cloves mashed garlic
A medium herb bouquet: 4 parsley sprigs, ½ bay leaf, and ¼ tsp thyme tied in cheesecloth
⅛ tsp fennel
⅛ tsp basil
Small pinch of saffron
Small pinch of coriander
A 1-inch piece (¼ tsp) dried orange peel
½ tsp salt

1 to 2 Tb tomato paste, if necessary
Salt and pepper

Stir in the tomatoes, sugar, garlic, herbs, and season-ings. Cover pan and cook slowly for 10 minutes, so the tomatoes will render more of their juice. Then uncover and simmer for about half an hour, adding spoonfuls of tomato juice or water if the sauce be-comes so thick it risks scorching. The purée is done when it tastes thoroughly cooked and is thick enough to form a mass in the spoon. Remove herb bouquet. If necessary, stir in 1 or 2 tablespoons of tomato paste for color, and simmer 2 minutes. Correct seasoning. Strain the sauce if you wish.

(*) May be refrigerated or frozen.

THE HOLLANDAISE FAMILY

SAUCE HOLLANDAISE

[Hollandaise Sauce: Egg Yolk and Butter Sauce flavored with Lemon Juice]

Hollandaise sauce is made of warmed egg yolks flavored with lemon juice, into which butter is gradually incorporated to make a thick, yellow, creamy sauce. It is probably the most famous of all sauces, and is often the most dreaded, as the egg yolks can curdle and the sauce can turn. It is extremely easy and almost foolproof to make in the electric blender, and we give the recipe on page 81. But we feel it is of great importance that you learn how to make hollandaise by hand, for part of every good cook's general knowledge is a thorough familiarity with the vagaries of egg yolks under all conditions. The following recipe takes about 5 minutes, and is almost as fast as blender hollandaise. It is only one of numerous methods for hollandaise, all of which accomplish the same result, that of forcing egg yolks to absorb butter and hold it in creamy suspension.

TWO POINTS TO REMEMBER when making hollandaise by hand

The heating and thickening of the egg yolks

So that the egg yolks will thicken into a smooth cream, they must be heated slowly and gradually. Too sudden heat will make them granular. Over-cooking scrambles them. You may beat them over hot water or over low heat; it makes no difference as long as the process is slow and gentle.

The butter

Egg yolks will readily absorb a certain quantity of butter when it is fed to them gradually, giving them time to incorporate each addition before another is presented. When too much is added at a time, particularly at first, the sauce will not thicken. And if the total amount of butter is more than the yolks can absorb, the sauce will curdle. About 3 ounces of butter is the usual maximum amount per yolk. But if you have never made hollandaise before, it is safer not to go over 2 ounces or ¼ cup.

For 1 to 1½ cups hollandaise—serving 4 to 6 people

6 to 8 ounces of butter (¾ to 1 cup or 1½ to 2 sticks) A small saucepan	Cut the butter into pieces and melt it in the saucepan over moderate heat. Then set it aside.

A 4- to 6-cup, medium-weight, enameled or stainless steel saucepan A wire whip 3 egg yolks	Beat the egg yolks for about 1 minute in the saucepan, or until they become thick and sticky.
1 Tb cold water 1 Tb lemon juice Big pinch of salt	Add the water, lemon juice, and salt, and beat for half a minute more.
1 Tb cold butter A pan of cold water (to cool off the bottom of the saucepan if necessary)	Add the tablespoon of cold butter, but do not beat it in. Then place the saucepan over very low heat or barely simmering water and stir the egg yolks with a wire whip until they slowly thicken into a smooth cream. This will take 1 to 2 minutes. If they seem to be thickening too quickly, or even suggest a lumpy quality, immediately plunge the bottom of the pan in cold water, beating the yolks to cool them. Then continue beating over heat. The egg yolks have thickened enough when you can begin to see the bottom of the pan between strokes, and the mixture forms a light cream on the wires of the whip.
1 Tb cold butter	Immediately remove from heat and beat in the cold butter, which will cool the egg yolks and stop their cooking.
The melted butter	Then beating the egg yolks with a wire whip, pour on the melted butter by droplets or quarter-teaspoonfuls until the sauce begins to thicken into a very heavy cream. Then pour the butter a little more rapidly. Omit the milky residue at the bottom of the butter pan.
Salt and white pepper Drops of lemon juice	Season the sauce to taste with salt, pepper, and lemon juice.

Keeping the sauce warm

Hollandaise is served warm, not hot. If it is kept too warm, it will thin out or curdle. It can be held perfectly for an hour or more near the very faint heat of a gas pilot light on the stove, or in a pan of lukewarm water. As hollandaise made with the maximum amount of butter is difficult to hold, use the minimum suggested in the recipe, then beat softened or tepid butter into the sauce just before serving.

A restaurant technique

A tablespoon or two of béchamel or *velouté* sauce, page 57, beaten into the hollandaise, or a teaspoon of cornstarch beaten into the egg yolks at the beginning, will help to hold a sauce that is to be kept warm for a long period of time.

If the sauce is too thick

Beat in 1 to 2 tablespoons of hot water, vegetable cooking liquid, stock, milk, or cream.

If the sauce refuses to thicken

If you have beaten in your butter too quickly, and the sauce refuses to thicken, it is easily remedied. Rinse out a mixing bowl with hot water. Put in a teaspoon of lemon juice and a tablespoon of the sauce. Beat with a wire whip for a moment until the sauce creams and thickens. Then beat in the rest of the sauce half a tablespoon at a time, beating until each addition has thickened in the sauce before adding the next. This always works.

If the sauce curdles or separates—"turned sauce"

If a finished sauce starts to separate, a tablespoon of cold water beaten into it will often bring it back. If not, use the preceding technique.

Leftover hollandaise

Leftover hollandaise may be refrigerated for a day or two, or may be frozen. It is fine as an enrichment for *veloutés* and béchamels; beat it into the hot white sauce off heat and a tablespoon at a time just before serving.

If the leftover sauce is to be used again as a hollandaise, beat 2 tablespoons of it in a saucepan over very low heat or hot water. Gradually beat in the rest of the sauce by spoonfuls.

Hollandaise Sauce Made in the Electric Blender

This very quick method for making hollandaise cannot fail when you add your butter in a small stream of droplets. If the sauce refuses to thicken, pour it out, then pour it back into the whizzing machine in a thin stream of droplets. As the butter cools, it begins to cream and forms itself into a thick sauce. If you are used to handmade hollandaise, you may find the blender variety lacks something in quality; this is perhaps due to complete homogenization. But as the technique is well within the capabilities of an 8-year-old child, it has much to recommend it.

For about ¾ cup

3 egg yolks	Place egg yolks, seasonings, and 1 tablespoon lemon
¼ tsp salt	juice in the blender jar. You can beat in more when
Pinch of pepper	sauce is done and will know what proportions you
1 to 2 Tb lemon juice	like for the next time.

4 ounces or 1 stick of butter	Cut the butter into pieces and heat it to foaming hot in a small saucepan.
A towel, if you do not have a splatterproof blender jar	Cover the jar and blend the egg yolk mixture at top speed for 2 seconds. Uncover, and still blending at top speed, immediately start pouring on the hot butter in a thin stream of droplets. (You may need to protect yourself with a towel during this operation.) By the time two thirds of the butter has gone in, the sauce will be a thick cream. Omit the milky residue at the bottom of the butter pan. Taste the sauce, and blend in more seasonings if necessary. (*) If not used immediately, set the jar in tepid, but not warm, water.

For More Sauce

The amount of butter you can use in a blender is only half the amount the egg yolks could absorb if you were making the sauce by hand, when 3 egg yolks can take 8 to 9 ounces of butter rather than the 4 ounces in the preceding recipe. However, if you added more butter to the blender than the 4 ounces specified, the sauce would become so thick that it would clog the machine. To double your amount of sauce, then, pour it out of the blender jar into a saucepan or bowl and beat into it an additional ½ cup of melted butter, added in a stream of droplets.

OTHER MEMBERS OF THE HOLLANDAISE FAMILY

Except for the *mousseline sabayon* mentioned at the end of this section, all the other members of the family are made in exactly the same way as hollandaise sauce. The basic flavorings may be vinegar and herbs instead of lemon juice, or concentrated white-wine fish stock, but the technique does not vary.

Stirred-in Trimmings

A plain hollandaise may have a number of trimmings such as the following stirred into it:

HERBS

For poached eggs or boiled fish, stir in a mixture of minced parsley, chives, and tarragon.

PURÉES AND MINCES

From 2 to 3 tablespoons of puréed artichoke hearts, asparagus tips, or cooked shellfish stirred into a hollandaise make it a good sauce for egg dishes. Or use finely minced sautéed mushrooms—see the recipe for mushroom *duxelles* on page 515.

Hollandaise avec Blancs d'Oeufs

[Hollandaise with Beaten Egg Whites]

For: fish, soufflés, asparagus, egg dishes
Stiffly beaten egg whites folded into hollandaise swell and lighten the sauce so that it may serve more people.

2 or 3 stiffly beaten egg whites, page 159 1½ cups *sauce hollandaise,* page 79	Just before serving, fold the egg whites into the hollandaise.

Sauce Mousseline
Sauce Chantilly

[Hollandaise with Whipped Cream]

For: fish, soufflés, asparagus

½ cup chilled whipping cream	Beat the chilled cream in a chilled bowl with a chilled beater as described on page 580.
1½ cups *sauce hollandaise,* page 79	Fold it into the hollandaise just before serving.

Sauce Maltaise

[Orange-flavored Hollandaise]

For: asparagus or broccoli

This sauce is made like an ordinary hollandaise except for the orange flavoring. Proceed as follows:

3 egg yolks 1 Tb lemon juice 1 Tb orange juice Pinch of salt 2 Tb cold butter ⅓ to ⅔ cup melted butter	Beat the egg yolks until thickened, then beat in the liquids and salt. Add 1 tablespoon of cold butter, and thicken the mixture over low heat. Beat in the other tablespoon of cold butter, then the melted butter.
2 to 4 Tb orange juice The grated peel of an orange	Finish the sauce by beating in the orange juice by spoonfuls, then the orange peel.

HOLLANDAISE SAUCES FOR FISH

When a hollandaise type of sauce is to accompany *filets* of fish poached in white wine, or a fish soufflé, the fish-poaching liquid is boiled down to a concentrated essence, or *fumet,* and is used in place of lemon juice as a flavoring for the sauce.

Sauce Vin Blanc

[Hollandaise with White-wine Fish *Fumet*]

1 cup white-wine fish stock	Boil down the fish stock until it has reduced to 3 tablespoons. This is now a *fumet de poisson.* Allow it to cool.
Ingredients for the *sauce hollandaise,* page 79, omitting lemon juice and water	Proceed with the hollandaise as usual, substituting the fish *fumet* for the lemon juice and water.

Sauce Mousseline Sabayon

[Hollandaise with Cream and White-wine Fish *Fumet*]

The recipe for this extremely good sauce, in which the egg yolks are thickened with cream and fish *fumet,* is on page 169 under *soufflé de poisson.*

✳ Sauce Béarnaise

[*Béarnaise* Sauce]

For: steaks, boiled or fried fish, broiled chicken, egg dishes, timbales
Béarnaise sauce differs from hollandaise only in taste and strength; in-

stead of lemon juice, its basic flavoring is a reduction of wine, vinegar, shallots, pepper, and tarragon. The techniques for making the two sauces are similar.

For 1½ cups

¼ cup wine vinegar ¼ cup dry white wine or dry white vermouth 1 Tb minced shallots or green onions 1 Tb minced fresh tarragon or ½ Tb dried tarragon ⅛ tsp pepper Pinch of salt A small saucepan	Boil the vinegar, wine, shallots or onions, herbs, and seasonings over moderate heat until the liquid has reduced to 2 tablespoons. Let it cool.
3 egg yolks 2 Tb cold butter ½ to ⅔ cup melted butter 2 Tb fresh minced tarragon or parsley	Then proceed as though making a hollandaise, page 79. Beat the egg yolks until thick. Strain in the vinegar mixture and beat. Add 1 tablespoon of cold butter and thicken the egg yolks over low heat. Beat in the other tablespoon of cold butter, then the melted butter by droplets. Correct seasoning, and beat in the tarragon or parsley.

VARIATIONS

The two following sauces are also for steaks, fish, chicken, and eggs.

Sauce Choron

[Tomato-flavored *Béarnaise*]

2 to 4 Tb tomato paste or purée 1½ cups *sauce béarnaise*	Beat the tomato by tablespoons into the *sauce béarnaise* and correct seasoning.

Sauce Colbert

[*Béarnaise* with Meat Glaze]

1 to 1½ Tb meat glaze, page 110, melted in 1 Tb white wine 1½ cups *sauce béarnaise*	Stir the melted meat glaze into the *sauce béarnaise*.

THE MAYONNAISE FAMILY

MAYONNAISE

[Mayonnaise: Egg Yolk and Oil Sauce]

Mayonnaise like hollandaise is a process of forcing egg yolks to absorb a fatty substance, oil in this case, and to hold it in thick and creamy suspension. But as the egg yolks do not have to be warmed, the sauce is that much simpler to make than hollandaise. You can make it by machine in a blender, although the processor produces a larger and better sauce. Either way it is almost automatic, and takes no skill whatsoever. Mayonnaise done by hand or with an electric beater requires familiarity with egg yolks. And again, as with hollandaise, you should be able to make it by hand as part of your general mastery of the egg yolk. It is certainly far from difficult once you understand the process, and after you have done it a few times, you should easily and confidently be able to whip together a quart of sauce in less than 10 minutes.

POINTS TO REMEMBER when making mayonnaise by hand

Temperature
Mayonnaise is easiest to make when all ingredients are at normal room temperature. Warm the mixing bowl in hot water to take the chill off the egg yolks. Heat the oil to tepid if it is cold.

Egg Yolks
Always beat the egg yolks for a minute or two before adding anything to them. As soon as they are thick and sticky, they are ready to absorb the oil.

Adding the Oil
The oil must be added very slowly at first, in droplets, until the emulsion process begins and the sauce thickens into a heavy cream. After this, the oil may be incorporated more rapidly.

Proportions
The maximum amount of oil one U.S. Large egg yolk will absorb is 6 ounces or ¾ cup. When this maximum is exceeded, the binding properties of the egg yolks break down, and the sauce thins out or curdles. If you have never made mayonnaise before, it is safest not to exceed ½ cup of oil per egg yolk. Here is a table giving proportions for varying amounts of sauce:

Number of Egg Yolks	Cups of Oil	Vinegar and/or Lemon Juice	Amount of Finished Sauce
2	1 to 1½ cups	2 to 3 Tb	1¼ to 1¾ cups
3	1½ to 2¼ cups	3 to 5 Tb	2 to 2¾ cups
4	2 to 3 cups	4 to 6 Tb	2½ to 3⅔ cups
6	3 to 4½ cups	6 to 10 Tb	3¾ to 5½ cups

For 2 to 2¾ Cups of Hand-beaten Mayonnaise

NOTE: The following directions are for a hand-beaten sauce. Exactly the same system is followed for an electric beater. Use the large bowl, and the moderately fast speed for whipping cream. Continually push the sauce into the beater blades with a rubber scraper.

A round-bottomed, 2½- to 3-quart glazed pottery, glass, or stainless-steel mixing bowl. Set it in a heavy casserole or sauce-pan to keep it from slipping.
3 egg yolks
A large wire whip

Warm the bowl in hot water. Dry it. Add the egg yolks and beat for 1 to 2 minutes until they are thick and sticky.

---

1 Tb wine vinegar or lemon juice
½ tsp salt
¼ tsp dry or prepared mustard

Add the vinegar or lemon juice, salt, and mustard. Beat for 30 seconds more.

1½ to 2¼ cups of olive oil, salad oil, or a mixture of each. If the oil is cold, heat it to tepid; and if you are a novice, use the minimum amount.

The egg yolks are now ready to receive the oil, and while it goes in, drop by drop, you must not stop beating until the sauce has thickened. A speed of 2 strokes per second is fast enough. You can switch hands or switch directions, it makes no difference as long as you beat constantly. Add the drops of oil with a teaspoon, or rest the lip of the bottle on the edge of the bowl. Keep your eye on the oil rather than on the sauce. Stop pouring and continue beating every 10 seconds or so, to be sure the egg yolks are absorbing the oil. After ⅓ to ½ cup of oil has been incorporated, the sauce will thicken into a very heavy cream and the crisis is over. The beating arm may rest a moment.

Then beat in the remaining oil by 1 to 2 tablespoon dollops, blending it thoroughly after each addition.

Drops of wine vinegar or lemon juice as needed

When the sauce becomes too thick and stiff, beat in drops of vinegar or lemon juice to thin it out. Then continue with the oil.

2 Tb boiling water
Vinegar, lemon juice, salt, pepper, and mustard

Beat the boiling water into the sauce. This is an anti-curdling insurance. Season to taste.

If the sauce is not used immediately, scrape it into a small bowl and cover it closely so a skin will not form on its surface.

REMEDY FOR TURNED MAYONNAISE

You will never have trouble with freshly made mayonnaise if you have beaten the egg yolks thoroughly in a warmed bowl before adding the oil, if the oil has been added in droplets until the sauce has commenced to thicken, and if you have not exceeded the maximum proportions of ¾ cup of oil per egg yolk. A mayonnaise has turned when it refuses to thicken, or, in a finished mayonnaise, when the oil releases itself from suspension and the sauce curdles. In either case, the remedy is simple.

Warm a mixing bowl in hot water. Dry it. Add 1 teaspoon of prepared mustard and 1 tablespoon of sauce. Beat with a wire whip for several seconds until they cream and thicken together. Beat in the rest of the sauce by teaspoons, thickening each addition before adding the next. This always works. Just be sure you add the turned sauce a little bit at a time, particularly at first.

REFRIGERATION

After several days under refrigeration, mayonnaise has a tendency to thin out, especially if it is stirred before it comes to room temperature. If it does turn, bring it back using the preceding system.

Mayonnaise Made in the Electric Blender or Food Processor

Mayonnaise in the blender takes a whole egg whirled with a pinch of mustard and salt for 30 seconds, then a tablespoon of lemon juice whirled another 10 seconds, and finally, with the machine at full speed, in goes a thin stream of oil, about a cupful. Add more, and the machine clogs. You scrape it out, your rubber spatula impaling itself on the sharp-pointed blade, and you get less than the 1¼ cups of mayonnaise you should have because part of it remains plastered in the machine. It's mayonnaise, all right, but the processor makes more sauce of a better quality. Here's how:

For about 2 cups of mayonnaise in the food processor (with steel blade)

1 egg and 2 yolks	Process the egg and the yolks for 1 minute.
¼ tsp dry mustard ½ tsp salt Fresh lemon juice and/or wine vinegar	With the machine running, add the mustard, salt, and 1 teaspoon of lemon juice or vinegar.
2 cups best quality oil—olive oil and/or salad oil More salt, pepper, and lemon juice or vinegar as needed	With the machine still running, start adding the oil in a stream of droplets, continuing until you have used half the oil and the sauce is very thick—do not stop processing until sauce has thickened. Thin out with lemon juice or vinegar, then continue with the oil. Season carefully with more salt, pepper, and lemon juice or vinegar.

MAYONNAISE VARIATIONS

Mayonnaise aux Fines Herbes
[Mayonnaise with Green Herbs]

For: hors d'oeuvres, eggs, fish, meats

3 to 4 Tb of fresh, minced green herbs, such as tarragon, basil, chervil, chives, parsley, oregano 1½ cups mayonnaise, page 86 or 88	If the sauce is to be kept for several days, blanch the herbs for 1 minute in boiling water. Drain, run cold water over them, and pat dry with a towel. The herbs will look greener, and will not turn sour in the sauce. Stir them into the mayonnaise.

Mayonnaise Verte
[Green Herbal Mayonnaise]

For: hors d'oeuvres, eggs, fish, meats

Ingredients for about 4 Tb of herb purée:	Bring 1 cup of water to the boil in a small saucepan. Add the spinach and shallots or onions and boil 2

8 to 10 spinach leaves

2 Tb chopped shallots or green onions

¼ cup water-cress leaves

¼ cup parsley leaves

1 Tb fresh tarragon or ½ Tb dried tarragon

Optional: 2 Tb fresh chervil

minutes. Then add the rest of the ingredients and boil 1 minute more. Strain, run cold water over the herbs, and pat dry with a towel.

Ingredients for 1½ cups of mayonnaise, page 86 or 88

If you are making the mayonnaise in an electric blender, add the herbs to the blender with the egg, then proceed as usual. For a handmade mayonnaise, either purée the herbs in a blender, or chop them into a purée and force them through a sieve, then stir the herbs into the finished sauce.

Sauce Riviera

Beurre Montpellier

[Green Mayonnaise with Butter or Cream Cheese, Pickles, Capers, and Anchovies]

For: hors d'oeuvres, sandwich spreads, eggs, fish, and as a spread for cold sliced veal, beef, or pork

For about 2¼ cups

2 Tb each: sour pickles, capers, and canned anchovies or anchovy paste

½ cup softened butter or cream cheese

The preceding *mayonnaise verte*

Chop the pickles, capers, and anchovies into a very fine mince, then cream them with the butter or cheese. Beat the mixture, a tablespoon at a time, into the green mayonnaise.

Sauce Tartare

[Hard Yolk Mayonnaise]

The yolks of hard-boiled eggs will also absorb oil and turn into a mayonnaise, but with its own characteristic taste and consistency. When sieved egg whites are beaten into it, the sauce acquires a nice lightness and body which makes it useful for spooning over cold foods. This sauce cannot be made in an electric blender; it becomes so stiff the machine clogs.

For 1½ to 2 cups

3 hard-boiled egg yolks 1 Tb prepared mustard ¼ tsp salt	Pound and mash the egg yolks in a mixing bowl with the mustard and salt until you have a very smooth paste. Unless the yolks are smooth and free from lumps, they will not absorb the oil.
1 cup oil Wine vinegar or lemon juice as needed	Proceed as for regular mayonnaise, page 86, beating in the oil by droplets at first until the sauce has thickened, and thinning out with vinegar or lemon juice as necessary.
3 to 4 Tb minced sour pickles 3 to 4 Tb minced capers 2 to 4 Tb minced fresh green herbs such as parsley, chives, tarragon Optional: 2 or 3 sieved hard-boiled egg whites	Twist the minced pickles and capers into a ball in the corner of a towel to extract their juice. Beat them gradually into the sauce. Then beat in the herbs, and finally the optional egg whites. Correct seasoning.

Sauce Rémoulade

[Mayonnaise with Anchovies, Pickles, Capers, and Herbs]

With the addition of half a teaspoon or so of anchovy paste, *sauce rémoulade* has the same flavorings as *sauce tartare,* but it is a regular mayonnaise rather than one made with hard yolks.

Mayonnaise Collée

[Gelatin Mayonnaise – for Decorating Cold Dishes]

When gelatin is dissolved and congealed in mayonnaise, the sauce will hold its shape and can be used for coating cold eggs, fish, and vegetables, or may be squeezed out of a pastry bag to make fancy decorations.

For about 1¾ cups

(This is the correct consistency for coating cold foods with a spoon. If the mayonnaise is to be forced through a pastry bag, it must be stiffer; you would use 2 tablespoons of gelatin dissolved in ½ cup of liquid then beaten into 2 cups of mayonnaise.)

⅓ cup of liquid as follows:

2 Tb white wine or white vermouth

1 Tb wine vinegar

2½ Tb chicken-, beef-, or fish-stock

1 Tb (1 envelope) gelatin

Pour the liquid into a small saucepan. Sprinkle the gelatin on it and let it dissolve for several minutes. Then stir the mixture over low heat until the gelatin is completely free of granules. Let it cool to tepid.

1½ cups mayonnaise, page 86 or 88

Beat the gelatin mixture gradually into the mayonnaise. Correct seasoning. The sauce will thin out, then gradually thicken as the gelatin sets.

Use it just before it sets. If it becomes too stiff, stir it briefly over gentle heat.

Sauce Aïoli

[Provençal Garlic Mayonnaise]

For: boiled fish, especially cod, *bourride* (Provençal fish soup), snails, boiled potatoes, green beans, and hard-boiled eggs

This rich, thick mayonnaise with its fine garlic flavor must be made in a fairly traditional way if it is to have its correct taste and consistency. The garlic should be pounded in a mortar until it is mashed into a very smooth paste. You cannot make it successfully in an electric blender because for some unfortunate reason the garlic acquires a raw and bitter taste, and the egg white required for blender-made sauce does not produce the fine, heavy texture that is characteristic of a proper Mediterranean *aïoli*.

For about 2 cups

1 slice—⅜ inch thick—of stale, white homemade-type bread

3 Tb milk or wine vinegar

Remove crusts and break the bread into a small bowl. Stir in the milk or vinegar and let the bread soak for 5 to 10 minutes into a soft pulp. Twist the bread into a ball in the corner of a towel to extract the liquid.

A heavy bowl or mortar

A wooden pestle

4 to 8 cloves mashed garlic

Place the bread and garlic in the bowl and pound with the pestle for at least 5 minutes to mash the garlic and bread into a very, very smooth paste.

1 egg yolk

¼ tsp salt

Pound in the egg yolk and salt until the mixture is thick and sticky.

1½ cups good olive oil
A wire whip
3 to 4 Tb boiling water or
    fish stock
2 to 3 Tb lemon juice

Then, drop by drop, pound and blend in the olive oil. When the sauce has thickened into a heavy cream, you may switch from a pestle to a wire whip and add the oil a little bit faster. Thin out the sauce as necessary with drops of water or stock, and lemon juice. Sauce should remain quite heavy, so it holds its shape in a spoon. Correct seasoning.

NOTE: If the sauce turns or curdles, you can reconstitute it by following the directions for turned mayonnaise on page 88.

Fish Soup Note

If the *aïoli* is to be stirred into a fish soup, more egg yolks are used, usually one per person.

Sauce Alsacienne
Sauce de Sorges

[Herbal Mayonnaise Made with Soft-boiled Eggs]

For: hot boiled beef, chicken, or fish
For about 2 cups

2 eggs

Boil the eggs for 3 minutes (3½ if they are chilled). Place the yolks in a mixing bowl and put the whites—which should be just set—aside.

1 Tb prepared mustard
½ tsp salt
1 Tb wine vinegar or lemon
    juice
1 cup oil

Proceed as for making mayonnaise, page 86, beating the yolks until they are thick and sticky, then beating in the mustard, salt, and vinegar or lemon juice. Finally beat in the oil, drop by drop at first.

¼ cup whipping cream, sour
    cream, or beef, chicken, or
    fish stock
1½ Tb finely minced shallot
    or green onions
1½ Tb capers
3 to 4 Tb minced parsley,

Gradually beat the additional liquid into the sauce. Beat in the rest of the ingredients. Season to taste.

tarragon, basil, etc.; or
dill only
The soft-boiled egg whites,
chopped or seived

OIL AND VINEGAR SAUCES
Vinaigrettes

✳ *SAUCE VINAIGRETTE*

[French Dressing]

For: salads and simple marinades

The basic French dressing of France is a mixture of good wine vinegar, good oil, salt, pepper, fresh green herbs in season, and mustard if you like it. Garlic is employed usually only in southern France. Worcestershire, curry, cheese, and tomato flavorings are not French additions, and sugar is heresy.

The usual proportion of vinegar to oil is one to three, but you should establish your own relationship. Lemon juice or a mixture of lemon and vinegar may be used, and the oil may be a tasteless salad oil, or olive oil. For salads, make the dressing in the empty bowl or a jar, so that all ingredients are well blended and flavored before the salad is mixed with the dressing. And be sure the salad greens are perfectly dry so the dressing will adhere to the leaves. Salad dressings are always best when freshly made; if they stand around for several days they tend to acquire a rancid taste.

For about ½ cup

½ to 2 Tb good wine vinegar or a mixture of vinegar and lemon juice
⅛ tsp salt
Optional: ¼ tsp dry mustard
6 Tb salad oil or olive oil
Big pinch of pepper

Either beat the vinegar or lemon juice in a bowl with the salt and optional mustard until the salt is dissolved, then beat in the oil by droplets, and season with pepper, *or* place all ingredients in a screw-top jar and shake vigorously for 30 seconds to blend thoroughly.

Optional: 1 to 2 Tb minced green herbs, such as parsley, chives, tarragon, basil; or pinch of dried herbs.

Stir in the optional herbs and correct seasoning just before dressing the salad.

VARIATIONS

Sauce Ravigote

[Vinaigrette with Herbs, Capers, and Onion]

For: cold or hot boiled beef, boiled chicken, boiled fish, pig's feet, calf's head, and vegetables

1 cup vinaigrette, page 94	Stir all the ingredients into the vinaigrette and taste for seasoning.
1 tsp chopped capers	
1 tsp very finely minced shallot or green onions	
2 Tb minced fresh green herbs, parsley, chives, tarragon, chervil, or parsley only	

Vinaigrette à la Crème

[Sour Cream Dressing—Dill Sauce]

For: cold eggs, vegetables, and cold or hot fish

1 egg yolk	Beat the egg yolk and cream in a bowl until thoroughly blended. Then beat in the vinaigrette in a stream of droplets as though making a mayonnaise. Season to taste with lemon juice, and stir in the herbs.
4 Tb whipping cream or sour cream	
½ cup vinaigrette, page 94	
Lemon juice to taste	
2 Tb minced fresh green herbs, parsley, chives, tarragon, chervil, burnet, or just dill	

Sauce Moutarde

[Cold Mustard Sauce with Herbs]

For: cold beef, pork, and vegetables

2 Tb prepared mustard, preferably the strong Dijon type 3 Tb boiling water	Rinse a small mixing bowl in hot water. Add the mustard and beat with a wire whip, adding the water by droplets.
⅓ to ½ cup olive oil or salad oil	Again by droplets, beat in the olive oil to make a thick, creamy sauce.
Salt and pepper Lemon juice 1 to 2 Tb parsley or minced fresh green herbs	Beat in salt, pepper, and lemon juice to taste. Then beat in the herbs.

HOT BUTTER SAUCES
Sauces au Beurre

✳ BEURRE BLANC–BEURRE NANTAIS
[White Butter Sauce]

For: boiled fish originally, but now for all kinds of fish and shellfish, and vegetables such as asparagus, broccoli, cauliflower, as well as for sautés of veal, chicken, kidneys, livers, and so forth.

This famous sauce originated in Nantes, on the Loire River, and is traditionally served with pike, *brochet au beurre blanc*. Warm, thick, creamy, and butter-colored, the original sauce is only butter creamed with shallots, wine vinegar, lemon, and seasonings. The idea was taken up by *nouvelle cuisine* chefs in the early seventies because it is a far easier sauce system than the long-simmered classics, and it is delicious with so many dishes. Rather than a lemon and vinegar base, you use a strong reduction of fish or meat juices—the residue, for instance, of sautéed chicken livers or *foie gras* deglazed with wine and shallots and, perhaps, a dash of wine vinegar all reduced almost to a syrup; this is then enriched by the beating in of a large quantity of butter. It is, in fact, the usual buttered deglazing sauce, but rather than beating in 2 or 3 tablespoons of butter for 4 to 6 servings, you might add as much as half a pound. With butter at 100 calories per tablespoon, an otherwise simple sauté can be marvelously yet astronomically (even lethally) fattening; but, as we imply in most of our recipes, "the amount of butter is up to you."

The trick in making a *beurre blanc* is to prevent the butter from turning oily like melted butter; it must retain its warm, thick, creamy consistency. A chemical process takes place once the base is boiled down and the acids are well concentrated so that the milk solids remain in suspension rather than sinking to the bottom of the pan. We give two methods here, first the classic way where the butter is slowly creamed in, and second the newer fast-boil system. In either case you may beat in more butter than the amount given, but if you beat in less you may have too acid-tasting a sauce.

For about 1 cup

The flavor base

A 6-cup medium-weight, stainless saucepan
2½ Tb white-wine vinegar
2½ Tb dry white wine, vermouth, or lemon juice
1 Tb very finely minced shallots or green onions
½ tsp salt
⅛ tsp white pepper
2 Tb butter

Boil the liquid, shallots or onions, and seasonings with the butter until reduced to a syrupy consistency —about 1½ tablespoons should remain.

The butter—Added the classic way

A wire whip
8 ounces (2 sticks) best quality unsalted butter, well chilled, and cut into 16 pieces
Salt, pepper, and lemon juice as needed

Remove saucepan from heat and immediately beat in 2 pieces of chilled butter. As the butter softens and creams in the liquid, beat in another piece. Then set the saucepan over very low heat and, beating constantly, continue adding successive pieces of butter as each previous piece has almost creamed into the sauce. The sauce will be thick and ivory-colored, the consistency of a light hollandaise. Immediately remove from heat as soon as all the butter has been used. Beat in additional seasonings to taste.

OR—Adding butter—The fast-boil way

Make the same flavor base described above, and cut the same amount of butter into pieces; however, the butter need not be chilled. Bring the reduced flavor base to the fast boil and start beating in butter piece by piece—it will at once produce thick creamy bubbles. When all the butter has been added, boil for 2 seconds only and pour the sauce into a bowl or another saucepan to stop the cooking. (If you continue boiling you will reduce the sauce base liquid to nothing and the butter will quickly clarify itself—no more creamy sauce.)

Holding the sauce. It will thin out and turn oily almost at once if you reheat it or if you keep it too warm. Hold it over barely tepid water, or place it near the faint heat of a gas pilot light, or on the slightly warm shelf over a cooktop. If it does thin out, cream it by beating a spoonful of sauce in a cold mixing bowl, gradually beat in the rest by very small spoonfuls; reheat it by beating in dribbles (2 to 3 tablespoons in all) of hot liquid such as wine, concentrated meat juices, or heavy cream.

VARIATION

Beurre au Citron

[Lemon Butter Sauce]

For: broiled or boiled fish, asparagus, broccoli, cauliflower
A minor variation of *beurre blanc,* and very nice with fish or vegetables.
For about ½ cup

A 2- to 4-cup, medium-weight, enameled saucepan ¼ cup lemon juice ⅛ tsp salt Pinch of white pepper	Boil down the lemon juice with the salt and pepper until it has reduced to 1 tablespoon.
A wire whip 4 ounces (1 stick) chilled butter cut into 8 pieces	Remove from heat and immediately beat in 2 pieces of chilled butter. Set over very low heat and beat in the rest of the butter, a piece at a time, to make a thick, creamy sauce. Immediately remove from heat.
2 to 3 Tb hot fish or vegetable stock or hot water	Just before serving, beat in the hot liquid by driblets to warm the sauce. Correct seasoning and serve in a barely warmed sauceboat.

BEURRE NOIR–BEURRE NOISETTE

[Brown Butter Sauce]

For: shirred eggs, calf's brains, boiled or sautéed fish, chicken breasts, vegetables

A properly made brown butter sauce has a deliciously nutty smell and taste, but is never black despite the poesy of the title. When you heat butter to the boil, its milk solids begin to darken from golden nutty, *noisette,* to golden brown, *noir,* but you never let it darken to black, burned, and bitter. It is a quick sauce, and you can make it right in the pan when you are serving it over browned foods like liver or sautéed chicken breasts. For pale foods like poached eggs or poached calf's brains, make it separately and pour the browned butter off the dark sediment in the pan.

For about ¾ cup, serving 6 to 8

6 ounces (1½ sticks) butter
Salt and pepper
3 to 4 Tb fresh minced
   parsley
3 to 4 Tb wine vinegar or
   lemon juice, or 1 to 2 Tb
   capers

Making the sauce in the sauté pan—just before serving

Cut the butter into pieces, and add to pan after food has been sautéed and removed. Salt and pepper food if necessary, and sprinkle the parsley over it. Holding sauté pan by handle, swirl over moderate heat as butter foams up; it will begin to color as foam subsides. At the moment the butter is a nutty brown—a matter of seconds—pour it over the food. Then add the vinegar, lemon juice or capers to the pan, rapidly boil down to reduce excess acidity, pour over the brown butter, and serve at once.

Making the sauce separately—may be done in advance

Cut the butter into pieces and add to a small saucepan. Swirl pan by its handle over moderate heat as butter melts and foams up. Continue cooking for a few seconds as foam subsides and butter starts to color. As soon as it is a nutty brown, remove from heat and let sediment settle for a moment. Either pour clear brown butter over hot food that you have seasoned and sprinkled with parsley, or pour the butter off its sediment and into a bowl or another pan. Rinse out butter pan, add vinegar, lemon juice or capers, and boil down rapidly to reduce excess acidity. Either pour over the food and serve; or pour the browned butter back in, set aside, and reheat before serving.

COLD FLAVORED BUTTERS
Beurres Composés

Butter can be put to a variety of appetizing uses when it has been creamed with herbs, wine, mustard, egg yolks, shellfish meat, or other flavorings.

On Hot Dishes: Place a piece of cold flavored butter on top of grilled fish or meat just as it is sent to the table.

For Basting: Baste meat, fish, or mushrooms with flavored butter as it cooks in oven.

Sauce and Soup Enrichment: Stir flavored butter into a sauce or soup just before serving.

Egg Filling or Sandwich Spread: Cream butter, egg yolks, and herbs together and use as a filling for hard-boiled eggs, or as a sandwich spread.

Decorations: Fill a pastry bag with chilled but still malleable flavored butter and squeeze it out in fancy designs to decorate appetizers or cold dishes.

Cutout Designs: Spread flavored butter on a plate and chill it. Then dip a knife or cutter in hot water and form fancy shapes for canapés or cold dishes.

HOW TO CREAM BUTTER

[*Beurre en Pommade*]

The butter must always be creamed or beaten before the flavoring is added to it. You can blend the butter to a cream in an electric beater, pound it in a bowl with a pestle, or mash it, a bit at a time, with the back of a wooden spoon, then beat it vigorously until it is light and creamy. Then the flavorings and the butter are creamed together, and the mixture is put in a cool place to firm up. If it is refrigerated, it will become as hard as an ordinary piece of chilled butter.

Beurre de Moutarde

[Mustard Butter]

For: kidneys, liver, steaks, broiled fish, and sauce enrichments

---

½ cup butter
1 to 2 Tb prepared mustard, the strong Dijon type
Salt and pepper to taste
Optional: 2 Tb fresh minced parsley or mixed green herbs

Cream the butter well. A half-teaspoon at a time, beat in the mustard. Beat in seasonings and optional parsley or mixed herbs to taste.

Beurre d'Anchois
[Anchovy Butter]

For: broiled fish, egg fillings, sandwiches, sauce enrichments

½ cup butter
2 Tb mashed canned ancho-
  vies or 1 Tb anchovy paste
Pepper
Lemon juice to taste
Optional: 1 to 2 Tb minced
  parsley or mixed green
  herbs

Cream the butter well. A half-teaspoon at a time, beat in the anchovies or anchovy paste. Season to taste with pepper, drops of lemon juice, and optional herbs.

Beurre d'Ail
[Garlic Butter]

For: broiled or boiled fish, steaks, hamburgers, lamb chops, boiled potatoes, canapés, sauce and soup enrichments

The smoothest and best-tasting result will be obtained if the garlic is pounded to a paste with a pestle and the butter is gradually pounded into it. A garlic press may be used if you have not the time or patience to pound, but the result will not be as good either in flavor or in texture.

2 to 8 cloves garlic
1 quart boiling water

Set the unpeeled cloves of garlic in the boiling water, bring to the boil for 5 seconds. Drain, peel, and rinse under cold water. Bring to the boil again for 30 seconds, drain, and rinse. Pound to a smooth paste in a mortar (or put through a garlic press).

½ cup butter
Salt and pepper
Optional: 1 to 2 Tb minced
  parsley or mixed green
  herbs

Pound or cream the butter and garlic together. Season to taste with the salt, pepper, and optional herbs.

Beurre à l'Oeuf
[Egg Yolk Butter]

For: sandwiches, canapés, hard-boiled eggs, and general decoration

| ½ cup butter | Cream the butter well. |
| 4 sieved hard-boiled egg yolks
Salt and pepper
Optional: 1 to 2 Tb minced chives or mixed green herbs. | Beat the sieved egg yolks into the butter and season to taste with salt, pepper, and optional herbs. |

Beurre Maître d'Hôtel

[Parsley Butter]

Beurre de Fines Herbes

[Mixed Herb Butter]

Beurre d'Estragon

[Tarragon Butter]

For: broiled meats and fish, and for sauce and soup enrichments

| ½ cup butter
1 Tb lemon juice
2 to 3 Tb fresh minced parsley, or mixed green herbs, or tarragon (or dried tarragon and fresh parsley)
Salt and pepper | Cream the butter. Drop by drop, beat in the lemon juice. Then beat in the herbs, and season to taste with salt and pepper. |

Beurre Colbert

[Tarragon Butter with Meat Flavoring]

For: broiled meats and fish

| Ingredients for the preceding butter using tarragon
1 Tb melted meat glaze (meat stock reduced to a syrup), page 110 | Drop by drop, beat the meat glaze into the tarragon butter. |

Beurre pour Escargots

[Snail Butter]

For: snails, broiled meats and fish; for basting baked or broiled fish or mushrooms; for broiled mussels, clams, or oysters

½ cup butter
2 Tb minced shallots or green onions
1 to 3 cloves mashed garlic, depending on your taste for garlic
2 Tb minced parsley
Salt and pepper

Cream the butter well. Twist the shallots or onions into a ball in the corner of a towel to extract their juice. Beat them into the butter with the garlic and parsley. Season to taste with salt and pepper.

Beurre Marchand de Vins

[Shallot Butter with Red Wine]

For: steaks, hamburgers, liver, and enrichment of brown sauces

¼ cup red wine
1 Tb minced shallot or green onions
1 Tb meat glaze or ½ cup brown stock or canned beef bouillon
Big pinch of pepper

Boil the wine with the shallots or onions, meat flavoring, and pepper until the liquid has reduced to about 1½ tablespoons. Let it cool.

½ cup butter
1 to 2 Tb minced parsley
Salt and pepper

Cream the butter well, then beat it, a tablespoon at a time, into the wine flavoring. Beat in the parsley, and season to taste.

Beurre Bercy

[Shallot Butter with White Wine]

For: steaks, hamburgers, liver, and enrichment of brown sauces

Ingredients for the preceding shallot butter, but substitute dry white wine or vermouth for the red wine

Follow the preceding recipe, then proceed to the optional next step.

Optional: 3 to 4 Tb diced   Stir in the optional beef marrow along with the final
beef marrow softened for   seasonings.
3 or 4 minutes in hot
salted water, page 19

Beurre de Crustacés

[Shellfish Butter]

For: sandwich spreads, canapés, hard-boiled eggs, decoration of cold
dishes; for enrichment of shellfish sauces and bisques, and canned and frozen
shellfish soups

Shellfish butters are made with the cooked debris, such as legs, chests,
eggs, and green matter of lobster, crab, crayfish, or shrimps. The red shells
color the butter a creamy rose, and both shell and bits of flesh give a lovely
flavor to the mixture. You can also make shellfish butter with the meat alone,
and color the butter with a bit of tomato paste.

Traditionally, the shells and meat are placed in a large marble mortar,
and are pounded into a purée with a heavy wooden pestle. Then they are
pounded with the butter so every bit is thoroughly mixed together. Finally
the whole mass is forced through a fine-meshed drum sieve to remove all
minute pieces of shell. This long and arduous process needs no further explanation. You just pound; the result is exquisite. An excellent butter may be
made in an electric blender in a fraction of the time:

For about 2/3 cup

---

1 cup cooked shellfish debris   Chop the debris or meat into 1/4-inch pieces, or put it
OR 1/2 cup cooked, whole,   through a meat grinder.
unpeeled shrimp
Or 1/2 cup cooked shellfish
meat and 1 1/2 Tb tomato
paste

1/4 lb (1/2 cup) hot melted   Fill the electric blender jar with hot water to heat it
butter   thoroughly. Empty and dry quickly. Then add the
                               shellfish. Immediately pour in the hot melted butter,
                               cover, and blend at top speed. The butter will cream
                               into a stiff paste in a few seconds. Pour the mixture
                               into a saucepan, heat until the butter has warmed and
                               melted. Blend again. Repeat, if you feel it necessary.

A fine-meshed sieve set over a bowl **A pestle or wooden spoon** **Salt and white pepper**	Rub through a very fine sieve, extracting as much butter and shellfish meat as possible. As the butter cools and partially congeals, beat it with a wooden spoon. Season to taste with salt and pepper. (*) May be frozen.

Second pressing

To extract the remaining butter and flavor from the debris left in the sieve, steep the debris in an equal amount of almost simmering water for 5 minutes in a saucepan over very low heat. Strain, and chill. The congealed butter on top of the liquid may be used for sauce enrichments. The liquid itself may serve as the basis for a fish stock.

OTHER SAUCES

Following is a list of regional or special sauces described in recipes elsewhere in this book.

Sauce Speciale à l'Ail pour Gigot, a special garlic sauce for roast lamb, page 334

Sauce Moutarde à la Normande, a cream and mustard sauce for pork, page 382

Sauce Nénette, cream, mustard, and tomato sauce for pork or boiled beef, page 387

Sauce Fondue de Fromage, a creamy, wine-flavored cheese sauce with a whiff of garlic, in the Poached Egg section, page 118. This is also good for vegetables, fish, chicken, or *pastas* which are to be *gratinéed* under a broiler, or as a spread for hot hors d'oeuvres that are to be browned quickly in the oven or under the broiler.

Sauce Chaud-froid, Blanche-neige, a reduction of heavy cream, meat, poultry, or fish stock, and tarragon, plus gelatin. For coating cold chicken, fish, or cold molded mousses. This is an excellent cold sauce, and in our opinion far more delicate than the traditional *sauce chaud-froid* made from a flour-thickened *velouté*. See the recipes for cold breast of chicken on page 551, for crab on page 553, and for fish mousse on page 562.

STOCKS AND ASPICS
Fonds de Cuisine – Gelée

The wonderful flavor of good French food is the result, more often than not, of the stock used for its cooking, its flavoring, or its sauce. The French term *fonds de cuisine* means literally the foundation and working capital of the kitchen. A stock is the liquid obtained from the simmering together of meat, bones—or fish trimmings—with vegetables, seasonings, and water. This liquid, strained, and boiled down to concentrate its flavor if necessary, is the basis for soups, the moistening element for stews, braised meats, or vegetables, and the liquid used in making all the sauces that have a meat or fish flavoring. Stocks are extremely easy to make, and can simmer quietly by themselves with little or no attention from the cook. They may be frozen and stored for weeks, or they may be boiled down until all their water content has evaporated, and they become a *glace de viande,* or flavor concentrate.

SUBSTITUTES FOR HOMEMADE STOCK

If you do not have a homemade stock in the larder, you can always use canned beef bouillon, canned chicken broth, canned mushroom broth, or bottled clam juice. Such economical substitutes for stock are not usually available to French cooks, and when simmered with meats, or with wine and aromatic vegetables, these canned alternatives are entirely satisfactory. A recipe for improving canned beef bouillon is on page 67; for canned chicken broth, on page 57; and for bottled clam juice, on page 115. Bouillon cubes are less successful, but they should certainly be used in an emergency. Canned consommé tends to be sweet and we do not recommend it.

INGREDIENTS FOR MAKING STOCKS

The most luxurious stocks are made from fresh soup bones, fresh meat, and vegetables. But unless you intend to make a stock for an absolutely remarkable consommé, use what you have on hand and add any fresh ingredients you wish to buy. It is a good idea to make a collection in the freezer of beef, veal, and poultry bones, and meat scraps. Then when a sufficient amount has accumulated, you can boil up a stock. Both meat and bones give flavor, and the bones, in addition, contain a certain amount of gelatin which gives body to the stock. Raw veal bones, especially the knuckle, and calf's feet, if you can find them, contain the most gelatin. If you want a stock that will jell naturally, include these in the proportions listed on page 112.

Lamb, Ham, and Pork

A few pork bones may be added to the stock kettle, but too much pork tends to give the stock a sweet flavor. Lamb or ham bones should not be used; their flavor is too strong for a general-purpose stock. But lamb or ham stocks are made in the same way as simple stock.

Vegetables

Carrots, onions, celery, and leeks are the usual soup vegetables. A parsnip or two may be included if you wish. Starchy vegetables will cloud the stock. Turnips, cauliflower, and the cabbage family in general have too strong a flavor for a general-purpose stock.

THE PRESSURE COOKER

One would expect a pressure cooker to be the ideal stock-making instrument; but our experiments have shown otherwise. After about 45 minutes of cooking under 15 pounds of pressure, a meat stock acquires its maximum pressure-cooked flavor. To reach its optimum flavor, it must then be simmered quietly in an open pot an hour or two more. Poultry stock, in our experience, acquires an unpleasant flavor if cooked for more than 20 minutes under 15 pounds of pressure. After this lapse of time the pressure should be released and the stock allowed to simmer, uncovered, for an hour or so longer.

---

* FONDS DE CUISINE SIMPLE

[Simple Meat Stock]

This is the general formula for a simple stock made from a miscellaneous collection of bones and meat scraps. It may be employed for meat sauces, the braising of meats and vegetables, the flavoring of soups, and for deglazing a roasting pan. The stock may be made from bones alone, but will have more character if some meat is included; ideal proportions are about half and half. The more elaborate stocks follow exactly the same cooking procedure.

For 2 to 3 quarts

3 quarts of meat and bones chopped into 2- to 3-inch pieces (raw or cooked veal or beef bones and meat, and/or poultry carcasses, scraps, and giblets)
An 8- to 10-quart kettle
Cold water

Place the meat and bones in the kettle and add cold water to cover them by 2 inches. Set over moderate heat. As the liquid comes slowly to the simmer, scum will start to rise. Remove it with a spoon or ladle for 5 minutes or so, until it almost ceases to accumulate.

2 tsp salt
2 medium-sized scraped carrots
2 medium-sized peeled onions
2 medium-sized celery stalks
The following tied in washed cheesecloth:
    ¼ tsp thyme
    1 bay leaf
    6 parsley sprigs
    2 unpeeled garlic cloves
    2 whole cloves
Optional: 2 washed leeks

Add all the ingredients at the left, and more water if the liquid does not cover the ingredients by a full inch. When liquid is simmering again, skim as necessary. Partially cover the kettle, leaving a space of about 1 inch for steam to escape. Maintain liquid at a very quiet simmer—just a bubble or two of motion at the surface—for 4 to 5 hours or more. Accumulated fat and scum may be skimmed off occasionally. Boiling water should be added if the liquid evaporates below the level of the ingredients.

Never allow the liquid to boil; fat and scum incorporate themselves into the stock and will make it cloudy.

Cooking may be stopped at any time, and continued later.

Never cover the kettle airtight unless its contents have cooled completely, or the stock will sour.

When your taste convinces you that you have simmered the most out of your ingredients, strain the stock out of the kettle into a bowl.

TO DEGREASE

Either let the stock settle for 5 minutes, remove the fat from its surface with a spoon or ladle, then draw scraps of paper toweling over the top of the stock to blot up the last globules of fat;

Or set the stock, uncovered, in the refrigerator until the fat has hardened on the surface and can be scraped off.

FINAL FLAVORING

Taste the degreased stock for strength. If its flavor is weak, boil it down to evaporate some of its water content and to concentrate its strength. Correct seasoning, and it is ready to use.

When the stock is cold, cover and refrigerate it, or bottle and freeze it. Stock kept in the refrigerator must be brought to the boil every 3 or 4 days to keep it from spoiling.

VARIATIONS

The following are traditional recipes for classical stocks made with fresh ingredients. You can, of course, vary the proportions according to your pocketbook and store of leftover bones and meat scraps. These are all simmered in exactly the same way as the simple stock in the preceding master recipe.

Fonds Blanc

[White Stock – Veal Stock]

White stock is used when you want to make a particularly fine white *velouté* sauce or soup. Raw veal releases a tremendous amount of gray and granular scum that can cloud your stock if it is not completely removed. The easiest way to deal with this problem is to blanch the veal as described here.

For 2 to 3 quarts

3 lbs. lean, raw veal shank meat 4 lbs. cracked, raw veal bones	Place the meat and bones in a kettle. Cover with cold water, bring to the boil and boil slowly for 5 minutes. Drain, and rinse the bones and meat under cold water to remove all scum. Rinse the kettle clean.
Same vegetables, herbs, and seasonings as for the master recipe, page 107	Place the bones and meat again in the kettle, cover with cold water, bring to the simmer, and skim as necessary. Then add the vegetables, herbs, and seasonings. Simmer the stock for 4 to 5 hours or more as described in the master recipe.

Fonds Blanc de Volaille

[White Poultry Stock]

This stock is used for soups and sauces. Employ the same method and ingredients as for the preceding white veal stock, but add a whole or parts of a stewing hen to the kettle along with the vegetables. The chicken may be removed when tender, and the stock simmered several hours longer.

Fonds Brun

[Brown Stock]

Brown stock is used for brown sauces, consommés, and for the braising of vegetables and red meats. To give the stock a good color, the meat, bones, and vegetables are browned before they go into the kettle, otherwise the cooking procedure is the same as for a simple stock, which may also be turned into a brown stock if you brown the ingredients.

For 3 to 4 quarts

A shallow roasting pan **3 lbs. beef shank meat** **3 to 4 lbs. cracked beef and** ** veal bones** **2 scrubbed, quartered carrots** **2 halved, peeled onions**	Heat oven to 450 degrees. Arrange the meat, bones, and vegetables in the roasting pan and place in the middle portion of the oven. Turn the ingredients occasionally so they will brown evenly, in 30 to 40 minutes.
An 8- to 10-quart kettle	Remove from oven and drain fat out of roasting pan. Transfer the browned ingredients to a soup kettle. Pour a cup or two of water into the pan, set over heat, and scrape up all coagulated browning juices. Pour them into the kettle.
2 tsp salt **2 celery stalks** **Herbs and flavorings listed** ** in the master recipe, page** ** 107, tied in cheesecloth**	Then, following the procedure in the master recipe on page 107, cover the ingredients in the kettle with cold water, bring to the simmer, skim. Add the ingredients at the left and proceed with the recipe. Simmer the stock 4 to 5 hours or more.

Fonds Brun de Volaille

[Brown Poultry Stock]

The recipe for a simple brown poultry stock is on page 236 in the Poultry chapter. You will note that poultry bones and scraps should be browned in a skillet, as they tend to burn and to acquire an unpleasant flavor if browned in the oven.

Glace de Viande

[Meat Glaze]

Meat glaze is any one of the preceding stocks boiled down until it has reduced to a syrup that becomes a hard jelly when it is cold. Three quarts of stock will reduce to 1½ cups or less of glaze, so it is easily stored. Half a tea-spoon stirred into a sauce or a soup will often give it just that particular boost of flavor which it lacks. Meat glaze dissolved in hot water may always be used in place of stock. It is thus a most useful commodity to have on hand and al-most invariably has a better flavor than commercial meat extracts and bouillon cubes.

2 to 3 quarts of any home-made stock	Strain the stock and degrease it thoroughly. Bring it to the boil in an uncovered saucepan and boil it slowly until it has reduced to about 1 quart. Strain it through a very fine sieve into a smaller saucepan and continue to boil it down until it has reduced to a syrup which coats the spoon lightly. Watch it during the last stages to be sure it does not burn. Strain it into a jar. When it is cold and has turned to a jelly, cover and refrigerate, or freeze it.

Meat glaze will keep for weeks under refrigeration. If it develops a few spots of mold, no harm is done. Pry it out of its jar, wash it under warm water. Then simmer it in a saucepan over low heat with a spoonful of water until it has again reduced to a thick syrup.

CLARIFICATION OF STOCK
Clarification du Bouillon

If you wish to serve a rich homemade consommé, jellied soup, or aspic, you should clarify your stock so it is beautifully clear and sparkling. This is accomplished by beating egg whites into cold stock, then heating it to just be-low the simmer for 15 minutes. The egg-white globules dispersed into the stock act as a magnet for all its minute cloudy particles. These gradually rise to the surface, leaving a crystal-clear liquid below them.

Clarification is a simple process if you remember that the stock must be perfectly degreased, that all equipment must be absolutely free of grease, and that you must handle the stock gently so the egg whites are not unduly dis-turbed.

For about 1 quart

5 cups cold stock **Salt and pepper**	Degrease the stock thoroughly; any fat particles will hinder the clarification process. Taste carefully for

A very clean 2½-quart
saucepan

seasoning and oversalt slightly if stock is to be served
cold; salt loses savor in a cold dish.

A very clean 2-quart mixing
  bowl
A wire whip
2 egg whites
Optional: ¼ cup or 2 ounces
  of absolutely lean, scraped,
  or minced beef
  ¼ cup minced green leek
    tops or green onion tops
  2 Tb minced parsley
  ½ Tb tarragon or chervil

Beat 1 cup of stock in the mixing bowl with the egg
whites and add optional ingredients for richer flavor.
Bring the rest of the stock to the boil in the saucepan.
Then, beating the egg-white mixture, gradually pour
on the hot stock in a very thin stream. Pour the mixture back into the saucepan and set over moderate
heat. Until the stock reaches the simmer, agitate it
slowly and continually with a wire whip so that the
egg whites, which will begin to turn white, are being
constantly circulated throughout the liquid. Immediately the simmer is reached, stop stirring. The egg
whites now will have mounted to the surface. Gently
move the saucepan to the side of the heat so that one
edge of the liquid is barely bubbling. In 5 minutes,
rotate the saucepan a quarter turn. Turn it again in 5
minutes, and once more for a final 5 minutes.

---

5 layers of well-washed,
  damp cheesecloth
A very clean colander
A very clean 3-quart bowl
A very clean ladle
⅓ cup Madeira, port, or
  cognac

Line the colander with the cheesecloth and place it
over the bowl. The colander should be of a size so
that its bottom will remain above the surface of the
liquid which is to be poured into the bowl. Very
gently ladle the stock and egg whites into the cheesecloth, disturbing the egg whites as little as possible.
The clarified stock will drain through the cheesecloth, leaving the egg-white particles behind. Allow
the egg whites to drain undisturbed for 5 minutes,
then remove the colander, and stir the wine or cognac into the clarified stock.

JELLIED STOCKS—ASPICS
Gelée

Homemade Jellied Stock

Calf's feet and veal knuckles contain enough natural gelatin to make
a stock jell by itself; pork rind helps the process. They are added to simmer
with any of the stocks on pages 107 to 110 and will provide about 3 quarts of
jelly. Prepare them as follows:

Either 2 calf's feet	These can usually be ordered from your butcher, and come skinned and cleaned. Scrub them under cold water. Soak them for 8 hours in several changes of cold water. Then cover them with cold water, boil for 5 minutes, and wash under cold water. They are now ready to use, and are added to the stock along with the vegetables.
Or 1 lb. cracked veal knuck-les	Cover the knuckles with cold water, boil for 5 minutes, then wash under cold water. Add the knuckles to the stock along with the vegetables.
And ¼ lb. fresh or salt pork rind	Scrub the pork rind in cold water. Cover with cold water and simmer for 10 minutes. Rinse under cold water. Add the rind to the stock along with the vegetables, calf's feet, or knuckles.

USING COMMERCIAL GELATIN

Plain stock, clarified stock, canned bouillon, and canned consommé are turned into aspic (or meat jelly) by adding unflavored gelatin in the following proportions:

(1 envelope of powdered American gelatin equals ¼ ounce, 8 grams, or a scant tablespoon. 1 sheet of French gelatin equals 2 grams; 4 sheets are the equivalent of 1 envelope of powdered gelatin.)

For jellied soup: 1 envelope of gelatin for each 3 cups of liquid

For aspics or for the decoration of cold dishes: 1 envelope of gelatin for each 2 cups of liquid

For lining a mold: 1 envelope of gelatin for each 1½ cups of liquid

How to Use Powdered Gelatin

Sprinkle 1 envelope of gelatin into ¼ to ½ cup of cold stock and let it soften for 3 to 4 minutes. Then blend it into the rest of the stock and stir over moderate heat for several minutes until the gelatin has completely dissolved and the liquid is absolutely free of granules.

How to Use Sheet Gelatin

If you are living in France, you will usually buy gelatin in sheets. Soak the sheets in cold water for about 10 minutes, until they are soft. Drain them, then stir them in the stock over gentle heat until the gelatin has completely dissolved.

Wine Flavoring

The wine used for flavoring a jelly is almost always port, Madeira, or cognac. From 1 to 2 tablespoons per cup is usually sufficient. Stir the wine or cognac into the hot stock after the gelatin has been dissolved. As most of the alcohol will evaporate, this small additional amount of liquid will not disturb the proportions of gelatin.

TESTING JELLIES

Always test out a jelly before using it; the few minutes you spend can save you from disaster. Pour ½ inch of jelly into a chilled saucer and refrigerate it for about 10 minutes until it has set. Then break it up with a fork and let it sit at room temperature for 10 minutes. For jellied soups it should hold its shape softly. For aspics its broken lumps should stand alone, but not be rubbery. A jelly that is to line a mold should be stiffer, so it can support the ingredients it is to enclose. If the jelly is too hard, add unjellied stock and test again. If the jelly is too soft, add more gelatin and test again.

FISH STOCKS
Fumets de Poisson

Fumet de Poisson au Vin Blanc
[White-wine Fish Stock]

The following proportions are for the production of a fine, well-flavored fish stock to be used as the basis of a fish *velouté* sauce. A smaller quantity of fish would produce a lighter stock suitable for fish-poaching, or fish soups.
For about 2 cups

A 6- to 8-quart enameled or stainless steel saucepan or kettle	Place all the ingredients in the saucepan or kettle. Bring to the simmer, skim, then simmer uncovered for 30 minutes. Strain through a fine sieve, and correct
2 pounds (about 2 quarts)	seasoning. Fish stock may be refrigerated or frozen.

lean, fresh fish, fish heads, and/or bones and trimmings (halibut, whiting, or flounder are recommended, or use frozen fish of good quality. Fresh or cooked shellfish leftovers may be included.)

1 thinly sliced onion

6 to 8 parsley stems—not the leaves, which will darken the stock

1 tsp lemon juice

¼ tsp salt

1 cup dry white wine or ⅔ cup dry white vermouth

Cold water to cover ingredients

Optional: ¼ cup fresh mushroom stems

If refrigerated, boil it up every 2 days to keep it from spoiling.

Emergency Fish Stock – Clam Juice

A good substitute for fresh fish stock may be made with bottled clam juice; but remember that clam juice is very salty and becomes even saltier if it is reduced.

For about 2 cups

A 6-cup enameled or stainless steel saucepan

1½ cups bottled clam juice

1 cup water

1 cup dry white wine or ⅔ cup dry white vermouth

1 thinly sliced onion

6 parsley stems

Optional: ¼ cup fresh mushroom stems

Place all ingredients in the saucepan and simmer for 30 minutes, allowing the liquid to reduce to about 2 cups. Strain, and correct seasoning. If very salty, use in diluted form.

CHAPTER THREE

EGGS

Oeufs

O<small>NCE AN EGG</small> is taken out of the breakfast category and put to use as a hot entrée, a luncheon, or a supper dish, it offers a great variety of presentations and you can draw on practically your whole cooking experience for its saucing and garnishing. In the following selection of recipes, we have concentrated on poaching, shirring, baking, scrambling, and omelette making, with a fundamental recipe for each, and a group of variations.

Wine and eggs have no great sympathy for each other, but as one usually likes to serve wine with an entrée, the best choice would be a fairly dry white wine with some body—such as Graves, Chablis, or Pouilly-Fuissé—or a *rosé*.

---

* *POACHED EGGS*

[Oeufs Pochés]

A poached egg is one that has been dropped without its shell into a pan of barely simmering liquid and cooked for about 4 minutes until the white is set but the yolk remains liquid. A perfect specimen is neat and oval in shape, and the white completely masks the yolk. The most important requirement for poaching is that the eggs be very fresh; the yolk stands high, the white clings to it in a cohesive mass, and only a small amount of watery liquid falls away from the main body of the white. A stale egg with a relaxed and watery white is unpoachable because the white trails off in wisps in the water leaving the yolk exposed. If the eggs are not quite as fresh as you could wish, simmer them in their shells for 8 to 10 seconds before poaching. This will often firm up the white just enough so it will hold its shape around the yolk when the egg is broken into the water. And a fine solution is the oval metal perforated egg poacher, carried in most gourmet-type cookware shops. Simmer the eggs 10 seconds in their shells, as suggested; place the poachers in the simmering water, adding vinegar if you think your eggs need help, and break an egg into each poacher, time as usual, and you get a beautiful egg. A final solution is the 6-minute boiled egg, *l'oeuf mollet;* when you peel it, you can substitute it for poached eggs in any recipe.

How to poach eggs

To transfer the egg from the shell to the water you may either break it directly into the water as described below, or break it into a saucer, tilt the saucer directly over the water, and slip the egg in.

A saucepan or a skillet 8 to 10 inches in diameter and 2½ to 3 inches deep **Vinegar (which helps the eggs to hold their shape)**	Pour 2 inches of water into the pan or skillet and add 1 tablespoon of vinegar per quart of water. Bring to the simmer.
4 very fresh eggs **A wooden spoon or spatula** **A skimmer or slotted spoon**	Break one of the eggs, and, holding it as closely over the water as possible, let it fall in. Immediately and gently push the white over the yolk with a wooden spoon for 2 to 3 seconds. Maintain the water at the barest simmer and proceed with the other eggs in the same manner.
A bowl of cold water	After 4 minutes, remove the first egg with the skimmer and test with your finger. The white should be set, the yolk still soft to the touch. Place the egg in the cold water; this washes off the vinegar and stops the cooking. Remove the rest of the eggs as they are done, and poach others in the same water if you are doing more. (*) The eggs may remain for several hours in cold water, or may be drained and refrigerated.
A bowl of hot water containing 1½ tsp salt per quart **A clean towel**	To reheat the eggs, trim off any trailing bits of white with a knife. Place them in hot salted water for about half a minute to heat them through. Remove one at a time with a slotted spoon. Holding a folded towel under the spoon, roll the egg back and forth for a second to drain it, and it is ready to serve.

A SUBSTITUTE FOR POACHED EGGS

Oeufs Mollets

[Six-minute Boiled Eggs]

This is a boiled egg with a set white and a soft yolk which can be peeled and substituted for poached eggs.

2 quarts boiling water	Lower the eggs into the boiling water and boil slowly
6 eggs with uncracked shells	according to the following table, adding 1 minute if the eggs are chilled.

U.S. Large Eggs	6 minutes
Extra Large	6½ minutes
Jumbo	7 minutes

As soon as the time is up, drain off the boiling water and run cold water into the pan for a minute to set the white, and to cool the eggs enough to remove the shells. Tap gently on a hard surface to break the shells, peel carefully under a stream of water.

If to be served cold, refrigerate. If to be served hot, warm for a minute in a bowl of hot water.

OEUFS SUR CANAPÉS
OEUFS EN CROUSTADES

[Poached Eggs on Canapés, Artichoke
Bottoms, Mushroom Caps, or in
Pastry Shells]

A practically limitless series of elegant little hot first courses or luncheon dishes may be concocted with poached eggs, sauces, minces, and imagination. Here are some ideas:

Oeufs à la Fondue de Fromage

[Poached Eggs on Canapés with
Cheese Fondue Sauce]

This is a particularly good sauce for eggs; it is creamy, wine-flavored, cheesy, and has just a whiff of garlic. *Sauce mornay* (béchamel with cheese), page 61 may always be substituted.

For 6 servings (1½ cups)

A 4-cup saucepan
1 Tb minced shallot or green onions
1 Tb butter
A small clove mashed garlic

Cook the shallots or onions for 1 to 2 minutes in the butter without browning. Add garlic and cook 30 seconds more.

1½ cups dry white wine or ¾ cup dry white vermouth
¼ cup stock or canned beef bouillon

Then add the wine and stock and boil rapidly until liquid has reduced to 3 or 4 tablespoons.

1½ Tb cornstarch
1¼ cups whipping cream
A small mixing bowl

Blend the cornstarch with 2 tablespoons of the cream, then stir in half of the remaining cream. Pour it into the wine and shallots and simmer, stirring, for 2 minutes. Add more cream by spoonfuls to thin the sauce—it should coat a spoon fairly heavily.

½ to ⅔ cup grated Swiss cheese
Salt and pepper
Pinch of nutmeg

Stir in the cheese and simmer, stirring, until the cheese has melted and the sauce is smooth and creamy. Add more spoonfuls of cream if necessary. Correct seasoning, set aside, and reheat when needed.

6 poached eggs or 6-minute boiled eggs
6 canapés (oval slices of white bread sautéed in clarified butter), page 199

Prepare the eggs and canapés.

3 Tb grated Swiss cheese
1 Tb melted butter
A broiling pan or fireproof serving platter

Shortly before serving, preheat broiler to very hot. Place a cold drained egg on each canapé, spoon the sauce over, sprinkle with cheese and butter. Run for about a minute under the hot broiler to reheat the eggs but not to overcook them, and to brown the top of the sauce lightly. Serve on a platter or on serving plates.

Other Ideas

Mix a spoonful or two of cooked, chopped spinach, or minced sautéed ham with a bit of the sauce and spread over each canapé to act as a bed for the egg. Use pastry shells, broiled mushroom caps, or cooked artichoke bottoms instead of canapés.

Oeufs en Croustades à la Béarnaise

[Poached Eggs and Mushrooms,
Béarnaise Sauce]

For 8 servings

---

1 lb. finely minced fresh mushrooms
3 Tb butter
3 Tb minced shallots or green onions
An enameled skillet

A handful at a time, twist the mushrooms into a ball in the corner of a towel to extract their juice. Sauté the mushrooms in hot butter with the shallots or onions for 7 to 8 minutes, until the pieces begin to separate from each other.

1½ Tb flour

Sprinkle on the flour and stir over moderate heat for 3 minutes.

¼ cup Madeira or port
½ cup whipping cream
½ tsp salt
Pinch of pepper

Stir in the wine and boil for a minute. Then stir in two thirds of the cream. Add the seasonings. Simmer for 2 to 3 minutes, adding more cream by spoonfuls if the mushroom mixture becomes too thick. Correct seasoning and set aside.

---

8 cooked pastry shells 2 to 2½ inches in diameter and 1½ inches high, page 200
8 poached eggs or 6-minute boiled eggs
2 to 2½ cups *sauce béarnaise,* or *sauce choron* (béarnaise with tomato), pages 84–5

Just before serving, reheat the mushrooms, pastry shells, and eggs. Put 2 or 3 tablespoons of the mushroom mixture into each shell, lay an egg over it, and coat with the sauce. Serve immediately on a platter or individual serving plates.

Other Ideas

Instead of mushrooms, use creamed shellfish; follow the recipe for *fondue de crustacés* on page 202, and top with hollandaise. Broiled mushroom caps, broiled tomatoes, or cooked artichoke bottoms may replace pastry shells.

Oeufs à la Bourguignonne

[Eggs Poached in Red Wine]

This is a good dish for a light supper or a winter luncheon, and can be made more important if it is garnished with sautéed chicken livers or braised onions, and sautéed or broiled mushrooms. Accompany it with a light red Burgundy or Beaujolais. Traditionally the eggs are poached in the wine, but they may be done in water in the usual way, if you wish.

For 8 servings

2 cups of brown stock or canned beef bouillon
2 cups good, young red wine
An 8-inch saucepan
8 very fresh eggs

Bring the stock and wine to the simmer and poach the eggs in it. Remove the eggs to a fireproof dish, add $\frac{1}{16}$ inch of poaching liquid, and set aside. About 5 minutes before serving, set the dish uncovered over simmering water to reheat the eggs.

½ bay leaf tied with 2 or 3 parsley sprigs
¼ tsp thyme
1 clove mashed garlic
1 Tb minced shallot or green onion
Pinch of cayenne pepper
Pinch of pepper

After poaching the eggs, add the herbs, garlic, shallot or onion, and seasonings to the wine and boil it down rapidly until it has reduced to 2 cups. Remove parsley and bay leaf.

1½ Tb softened butter
2 Tb flour
Optional: 1 Tb red currant jelly

Blend the butter and flour to a smooth paste—*beurre manié*. Off heat, beat it into the wine mixture with a wire whip. Boil for 30 seconds. Beat in the optional currant jelly for color and flavor, and correct seasoning.
(*) If not to be used immediately, set aside uncovered, top dotted with part of the enrichment butter.

1 to 2 Tb softened butter

Just before serving, reheat the sauce to the simmer. Off heat, beat in the butter.

8 canapés (ovals of white bread sautéed in clarified butter, page 199. They may be rubbed with a cut

Place a hot egg on each canapé and arrange on a platter or serving plates. Surround with whatever garniture you may have chosen, and spoon the hot sauce over. Decorate with parsley, and serve.

clove of garlic if you
  wish.)
2 to 3 Tb fresh minced parsley

Oeufs en Gelée

[Poached Eggs in Aspic]

This recipe is in the chapter on cold buffets, page 547.

✳ *SHIRRED EGGS*

[Oeufs sur le Plat – Oeufs Miroir]

A shirred egg is one that is broken into a small, flat, buttered dish and cooked quickly under the broiler. The white is softly set and tender, and the yolk is liquid, but covered by a shimmering, translucent film. Shirred eggs should never be attempted in the oven, as it toughens them.

For each serving

Preheat broiler to very hot.

A shallow, fireproof dish about 4 inches in diameter
½ Tb butter
1 or 2 eggs

Place the dish over moderate heat and add the butter. As soon as it has melted, break the egg or eggs into the dish and cook for about 30 seconds until a thin layer of white has set in the bottom of the dish. Remove from heat, tilt dish, and baste the egg with the butter. Set aside.

Salt and pepper

A minute or so before serving, place the dish an inch under the hot broiler. Slide it in and out every few seconds and baste the egg with the butter. In about a minute the white will be set, and the yolk filmed and glistening. Remove, season, and serve immediately.

VARIATIONS

Using the technique of the preceding recipe, shirred eggs may be dressed up in the following ways:

Au Beurre Noir

[With Black Butter Sauce]

Substitute *beurre noir,* page 98, for plain butter.

Aux Fines Herbes

[With Herb Butter]

Substitute herb or tarragon butter, page 102, for plain butter.

À la Crème

[With Cream]

Use half the amount of butter. After bottom of egg has been lightly cooked on top of the stove, pour 2 tablespoons of whipping cream over the egg, then set it under the broiler. Basting is not necessary.

Gratinés

[Browned with Cheese]

This is the same as *à la crème,* but sprinkle a teaspoon of grated cheese over the cream, and dot with butter.

Pipérade

[With Tomatoes, Onions, and Peppers]

Prepare the *pipérade* mixture of cooked onions, green peppers, and tomatoes described on page 137. Then proceed as for the main recipe, spooning the *pipérade* around the egg before it goes under the broiler.

Other Suggestions

Just before serving, surround the egg with sautéed mushrooms, kidneys, chicken livers, sausages, asparagus tips, broiled tomatoes, tomato sauce, or whatever else strikes your fancy.

✳ EGGS BAKED IN RAMEKINS

[Oeufs en Cocotte]

These are individual servings of 1 or 2 eggs baked in porcelain, pyrex, or earthenware ramekins. The ramekins must be set in a pan of boiling water, otherwise the intense heat of the oven toughens the outside layer of egg before the inside has cooked.

For each serving

Preheat oven to 375 degrees.

½ tsp butter
1 ramekin 2½ to 3 inches in diameter and about 1½ inches high
2 Tb whipping cream
A pan containing ¾ inch of simmering water
1 or 2 eggs

Butter the ramekin, saving a dot for later. Add 1 tablespoon of cream and set the ramekin in the simmering water over moderate heat. When the cream is hot, break into it one or two eggs. Pour the remaining spoonful of cream over the egg and top with a dot of butter.

Place in middle level of the hot oven and bake for 7 to 10 minutes. The eggs are done when they are just set but still tremble slightly in the ramekins. They will set a little more when the ramekins are removed, so they should not be overcooked.

Salt and pepper

Season with salt and pepper, and serve.
(*) The ramekins may remain in the pan of hot water, out of the oven, for 10 to 15 minutes before serving. To prevent overcooking, remove eggs from oven when slightly underdone.

VARIATIONS

Aux Fines Herbes

[With Herbs]

Add half a teaspoon of mixed fresh parsley, chives, and chervil, or tarragon to the cream in the preceding recipe.

Sauces

Instead of cream, use one of the brown sauces on pages 71 to 75, especially those with herbs, mushrooms, or tomatoes. Or substitute one of the white sauces, pages 61 to 64 of which *sauce soubise* with onions, or *sauce au cari* (curry sauce) are especially good. The tomato sauces on pages 76 to 78 are other alternatives.

Other Suggestions

A spoonful or two of any of the following cooked ingredients may be put in the bottom of the ramekins along with either cream or sauce:

Minced mushrooms, asparagus, spinach, artichoke hearts
Diced lobster, shrimp, crab
Diced truffles, and/or a slice of *foie gras*

✳ SCRAMBLED EGGS

[Oeufs Brouillés]

Scrambled eggs in French are creamy soft curds that just hold their shape from fork to mouth. Their preparation is entirely a matter of stirring the eggs over gentle heat until they slowly thicken as a mass into a custard. Salt plus half a teaspoon of liquid per egg helps blend yolks and white, but no more liquid or liquid-producing ingredients or the eggs will turn watery.

For 4 or 5 servings

A fork or a wire whip 8 eggs, or 7 eggs and 2 yolks A mixing bowl Salt and pepper 4 tsp water or milk	Beat the eggs in the bowl with the seasonings and liquid for 20 to 30 seconds, just to blend yolks and whites.
2 Tb softened butter A heavy-weight saucepan or skillet 7 to 8 inches bottom diameter (no-stick suggested). Depth of eggs in pan should be ⅔ to 1 inch A rubber spatula or wooden spoon	Smear the bottom and sides of the pan with the butter. Pour in the eggs and set over moderately low heat. Stir slowly and continually, reaching all over the bottom of the pan. Nothing will seem to happen for 2 to 3 minutes as the eggs gradually heat. Suddenly they will begin to thicken into a custard. Stir rapidly, moving pan on and off heat, until the eggs have almost thickened to the consistency you wish. Then remove from heat, as they will continue to thicken slightly.
1½ to 2 Tb softened butter or whipping cream A warm buttered platter Parsley sprigs	Just as soon as they are of the right consistency, stir in the enrichment butter or cream, which will stop the cooking. Season to taste, turn out onto the platter, decorate with parsley, and serve. (✳) The eggs may be kept for a while in their saucepan over tepid water, but the sooner they are served the better.

VARIATIONS

Aux Fines Herbes

[With Herbs]

Beat a tablespoon of minced fresh herbs such as parsley, chervil, chives, and tarragon into the eggs at the start. Sprinkle more herbs over the eggs just before serving.

Au Fromage

[With Cheese]

Stir 4 to 6 spoonfuls of grated Swiss cheese into the eggs along with the enrichment butter at the end.

Aux Truffes

[With Truffles]

Stir 1 or 2 diced truffles into the eggs before scrambling them. Sprinkle a bit of chopped truffle over the eggs before serving.

Garnishings

Aside from ham, bacon, or sausages, the platter may be garnished with such things as: broiled or sautéed mushrooms, kidneys, or chicken livers; sautéed eggplant or zucchini; broiled tomatoes, tomato sauce, or the *pipérade* mixture on page 137; diced sautéed potatoes; buttered peas, asparagus tips, or artichoke hearts.

OMELETTES

A good French omelette is a smooth, gently swelling, golden oval that is tender and creamy inside. And as it takes less than half a minute to make, it is ideal for a quick meal. There is a trick to omelettes, and certainly the easiest way to learn is to ask an expert to give you a lesson. Nevertheless we hope one of the two techniques we describe will enable you, if you have never made an omelette before, to produce a good one. The difficulty with all written recipes for omelettes is that before you even start to make one you must read, remember, and visualize the directions from beginning to end, and practice the movements. For everything must go so quickly once the eggs are in the pan that there is no time at all to stop in the middle and pore over your book in order to see what comes next. Learning to make a good omelette is entirely a matter of practice. Do one after another for groups of people every chance you get for several days, and even be willing to throw some away. You should soon develop the art, as well as your own personal omelette style.

The two methods set forth here are rapid, professional techniques. The first is the simplest. The second takes more .manual skill.

OMELETTE PANS

An omelette cannot be made in a sticky pan; the eggs must be able to slide around freely, and if they cannot, you simply cannot make an omelette at all. Since the first edition of this book, professionally shaped omelette pans of heavy aluminum with no-stick.interiors are everywhere available, and that's what we use—gratefully. However, the great omelette maker Dione Lucas insisted on her specially made cast-aluminum pan half an inch thick, while that other famous omelette queen Mme Romaine de Lyon and many another French cook swear only by the plain iron pan ⅛ inch thick like the one in our illustrations. Whatever you buy, you should have the long handle and the straight-sloping sides 2 inches deep; the bottom diameter should be about 7 inches, since this is the perfect size for the perfect 2- to 3-egg omelette.

If you prefer the French iron pan illustrated, you must first scrub it with steel wool and scouring powder, rinse and dry it, then heat it for a minute or two just until its bottom is too hot for your hand. Rub it with paper towels and cooking oil and let it stand overnight. Before making your first omelette, sprinkle a teaspoon of table salt in the pan, heat it again, and rub vigorously for a moment with paper towels; rub the pan clean, and it is ready for an omelette. If the pan is used only for omelettes (a wise decision), it needs no washing afterwards; merely rub it clean with paper towels. If the pan *is* washed, dry, warm, and oil it lightly before putting it away. If it becomes sticky again, rub again with salt. Never allow any pan, particularly an iron one, to sit empty over heat—this does something to its internal structure so that foods stick to it forevermore.

EGGS AND HOW TO BEAT THEM

An omelette can contain up to 8 eggs, but the individual 2- to 3-egg omelette is usually the tenderest, and by far the best size to practice making. At under 30 seconds an omelette, a number of people can be served in a very short time. In fact, unless you are extremely expert and have a restaurant-size heat source, we do not recommend larger omelettes at all. But if you do want to attempt them, be sure to have the correct size of pan. The depth of the egg mass in the pan should not be over ¼ inch, as the eggs must cook quickly. A pan with a 7-inch bottom is right for the 2- to 3-egg omelette; a 10- to 11-inch pan is required for 8 eggs.

Just before heating the butter in the pan, break the eggs into a mixing bowl and add salt and pepper. With a large table fork, beat the eggs only enough to blend the whites and yolks thoroughly. From 30 to 40 vigorous strokes should be sufficient.

If you are making several 2- to 3-egg omelettes, beat the necessary number of eggs and seasonings together in a large mixing bowl, and provide yourself with a ladle or measure. Two U.S. large eggs measure about 6 tablespoons; 3 eggs, about 9 tablespoons. Measure out the required quantity for each omelette as you are ready to make it, giving the eggs 4 or 5 vigorous beats before dipping them out with your measure.

TRANSFERRING THE OMELETTE FROM PAN TO PLATE

In each of the methods described, the finished omelette ends up in the far lip of the pan. This is the way to transfer it from the pan to the plate.

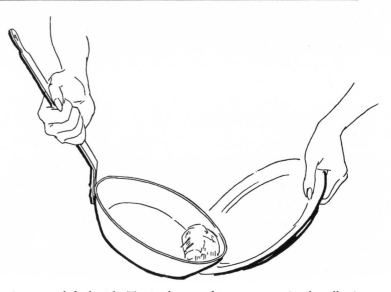

Hold the plate in your left hand. Turn the omelette pan so its handle is to your right. Grasp the handle with your right hand, thumb on top. Rest the lip of the pan slightly off the center of the plate so the omelette will land in the middle of the plate. Then tilt plate and pan against each other at a 45-degree angle.

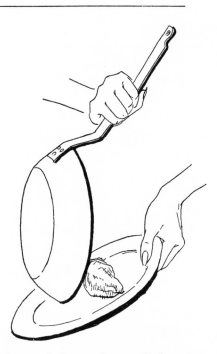

Quickly turn the pan upside down over the plate and the omelette will drop into position.

If it has not formed neatly, push it into shape with the back of a fork. Rub the top of the omelette with softened butter and serve as soon as possible, for omelettes toughen if they are kept warm.

I · L'OMELETTE BROUILLÉE

[Scrambled Omelette]

This is best in a French omelette pan, but a skillet can be used.

For 1 omelette, 1 to 2 servings. Time: Less than 30 seconds of cooking

2 or 3 eggs **Big pinch of salt** **Pinch of pepper** **A mixing bowl** **A table fork**	Beat the eggs and seasonings in the mixing bowl for 20 to 30 seconds until the whites and yolks are just blended.

1 Tb butter
An omelette pan 7 inches in
    diameter at the bottom
A table fork

Place the butter in the pan and set over very high heat. If you have an electric heat element, it should be red hot. As the butter melts, tilt the pan in all directions to film the sides. When you see that the foam has almost subsided in the pan and the butter is on the point of coloring, it is an indication that it is hot enough to pour in the eggs.

Hold the panhandle with your left hand, thumb on top, and immediately start sliding the pan back and forth rapidly over the heat. At the same time, fork in right hand, its flat side against the bottom of the pan, stir the eggs quickly to spread them continuously all over the bottom of the pan as they thicken. In 3 or 4 seconds they will become a light, broken custard. (*A filling would go in at this point.*)

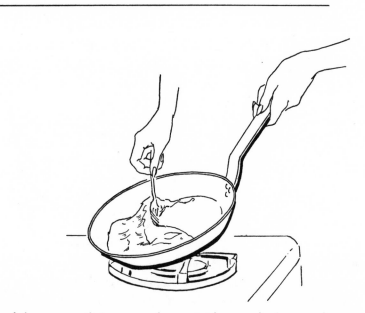

Then lift the handle of the pan to tilt it at a 45-degree angle over the heat, and rapidly gather the eggs at the far lip of the pan with the back of your fork. Still holding the pan tilted over the heat, run your fork around the lip of the pan under the far edge of the omelette to be sure it has not adhered to the pan.

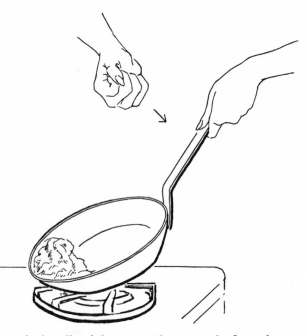

Give 4 or 5 short, sharp blows on the handle of the pan with your right fist to loosen the omelette and make the far edge curl over onto itself.

Hold the pan tilted over heat for 1 or 2 seconds to brown the bottom of the omelette very lightly, but not too long or the eggs will overcook. The center of the omelette should remain soft and creamy.

A warm plate
Softened butter

Turn the omelette onto the plate as illustrated on page 128, rub the top with a bit of butter, and serve as soon as possible.

II · L'OMELETTE ROULÉE

[Rolled Omelette]

This omelette should be made in a French omelette pan and a high gas flame is usually more successful than an electric heat element. The rolled omelette is the most fun of any method, but requires more practice. Here the pan is jerked over high heat at an angle so that the egg mass is continually hurled against the far lip of the pan until the eggs thicken. Finally, as the pan is tilted further while it is being jerked, the eggs roll over at the far lip of the pan, forming an omelette shape. A simple-minded but perfect way to master the movement is to practice outdoors with half a cupful of dried beans. As soon as you are able to make them flip over themselves in a group, you have the right feeling; but the actual omelette-making gesture is sharper and rougher.

For 1 omelette, 1 to 2 servings. Time: Less than 30 seconds of cooking

---

2 or 3 eggs **Big pinch of salt** **Pinch of pepper** **A mixing bowl** **A table fork**	Beat the eggs and seasonings in the mixing bowl for 20 to 30 seconds until the whites and yolks are just blended.

---

1 Tb butter **An omelette pan 7 inches in diameter at the bottom** **A table fork**	Place the butter in the pan and set over very high heat. As the butter melts, tilt the pan in all directions to film the sides. When you see that the foam has almost subsided in the pan and the butter is on the point of coloring (indicating it is hot enough), pour in the eggs. It is of utmost importance in this method that the butter be of the correct temperature.

Let the eggs settle in the pan for 2 or 3 seconds to form a film of coagulated egg in the bottom of the pan.

Grasp the handle of the pan with both hands, thumbs on top, and immediately begin jerking the pan vigorously and roughly toward you at an even, 20-degree angle over the heat, one jerk per second.

It is the sharp pull of the pan toward you which throws the eggs against the far lip of the pan, then back over its bottom surface. You must have the courage to be rough or the eggs will not loosen themselves from the bottom of the pan. After several jerks, the eggs will begin to thicken. (*A filling would go in at this point.*)

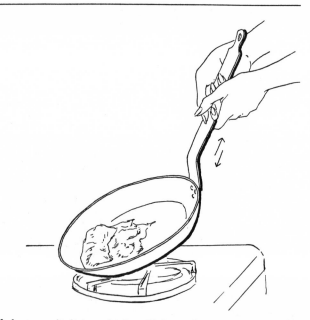

Then increase the angle of the pan slightly, which will force the egg mass to roll over on itself with each jerk at the far lip of the pan.

As soon as the omelette has shaped up, hold it in the angle of the pan to brown the bottom a pale golden color, but only a second or two, for the eggs must not overcook. The center of the omelette should remain soft and creamy. If the omelette has not formed neatly, push it with the back of your fork.

Turn the omelette onto the plate as illustrated on page 128, rub the top with a bit of butter, and serve as soon as possible.

GARNISHINGS AND FILLINGS FOR OMELETTES

Aux Fines Herbes

[With Herbs]

Beat into the eggs at the beginning 1 tablespoon of minced fresh herbs such as chervil, parsley, chives, and tarragon. Sprinkle more of the same over the finished omelette.

Au Fromage

[With Cheese]

After the eggs have set for 2 or 3 seconds in the pan at the point indicated in either of the two omelette recipes, sprinkle in 1 or 2 tablespoons of grated

Swiss or Parmesan cheese and finish the omelette. If you wish, sprinkle more cheese over the completed omelette, dot with butter, and run quickly under a very hot broiler to melt and brown the cheese.

Aux Épinards

[With Spinach]

Beat 2 or 3 tablespoons of cooked purée of spinach, page 469, into the eggs at the beginning, then proceed with the omelette as usual.

Other Suggestions

Sprinkle ¼ cup of any of the following cooked ingredients over the eggs after they have set for 2 or 3 seconds in the pan at the point indicated in either of the two omelette recipes, then proceed with the omelette as usual:

Diced sautéed potatoes and minced herbs
Diced truffles
Diced sautéed ham, chicken livers, or mushrooms
Diced cooked asparagus tips or artichoke hearts
Diced cooked shrimp, crab, or lobster
Cubes of stale white bread sautéed in butter

Omelettes Gratinées à la Tomate

[Tomato-filled Omelettes *Gratinéed* With Cream and Cheese]

Here is a delicious supper or luncheon dish that can be prepared ahead and *gratinéed* just before serving.

For 4 to 6 people

---

4 two-egg omelettes or 2 three-egg omelettes A buttered plate A shallow, buttered, fireproof serving platter	Cook the omelettes according to one of the master recipes, but leave them slightly underdone. Slip each as it is made onto a buttered plate, then slide it onto the buttered platter, arranging the omelettes side by side.

---

1 cup fresh tomato purée, page 78	Cut a slit along the length of each omelette to within ½ inch of the 2 ends. Fill the slits with the tomato purée.

(*) If not to be used immediately, rub tops of omelettes with softened butter and cover with waxed paper.

Preheat broiler to very hot.

½ to ⅔ cup whipping cream or *crème fraîche*, page 16

⅓ cup grated Swiss cheese

½ Tb melted butter

Just before serving, pour the cream over the omelettes, and sprinkle with cheese and melted butter. Set platter 3 inches from hot broiler for 1 or 2 minutes to reheat the omelettes and to brown the cheese lightly, but do not let the omelettes overcook. Serve immediately.

Pipérade

[Open-faced Omelette Garnished with Onions, Peppers, Tomatoes, and Ham]

This is a Basque specialty, and quick to make if the *pipérade* mixture has been prepared in advance. As the omelette is not folded, and is served in its cooking vessel, it is not a disaster if it sticks a little on the bottom. You may therefore cook the eggs in a low, glazed pottery dish, or a fancy skillet.

For 4 to 6 servings

---

8 to 12 strips of ham ¼ inch thick and about 2 by 3 inches across

2 Tb olive oil or butter

An 8- to 9-inch enameled skillet

Brown the ham slices lightly on both sides in hot oil or butter. Set them aside, and reheat just before using them at the end of the recipe.

½ cup thinly sliced yellow onions

½ cup thinly sliced green or red bell peppers

Salt and pepper to taste

In the same oil or butter in which you browned the ham, cook the onions and peppers slowly, covering the skillet, until they are tender but not browned. Season to taste with salt and pepper.

½ clove mashed garlic

Speck of cayenne pepper

2 or 3 firm, ripe, red toma-

Stir in the garlic and pepper. Lay the tomatoes over the onions and sprinkle with salt. Cover and cook slowly for 5 minutes. Uncover, raise heat, and boil for

toes peeled, seeded, juiced, and sliced, page 505
Salt and pepper

a few minutes, shaking the pan occasionally until the juice from the tomatoes has almost entirely evaporated. Season to taste, and reheat just before using.
(*) Recipe may be prepared ahead to this point.

1½ Tb olive oil or butter
An 11- to 12-inch serving skillet or shallow, fireproof serving dish
8 to 10 eggs beaten lightly with ¼ tsp salt and a pinch of pepper
A large table fork
2 to 3 Tb minced parsley or mixed fresh green herbs

Heat the oil or butter in the skillet or dish. When very hot, pour in the eggs. Stir rapidly with a fork until the eggs have just set into a creamy mass. Remove from heat and spread over them the hot *pipérade,* mixing a bit of it delicately into the eggs. Lay the warm ham strips over the *pipérade.* Sprinkle with the herbs and serve immediately.

CHAPTER FOUR

ENTRÉES AND LUNCHEON DISHES

PIE DOUGH—PASTRY CRUSTS
Pâte Brisée

PÂTE BRISÉE

[Short Paste, Pastry Dough, Pie Crust]

A good French pastry crust is tender, crunchy, and buttery. The best one, *pâte brisée fine,* is made in the proportions, according to weight, of 5 parts flour to 4 parts butter. American all-purpose, hard-wheat flour produces a slightly brittle crust if only butter is used. However, a mixture of 3 parts butter and 1 part vegetable shortening will give a tender crust with a good buttery flavor. Unlike standard American methods, the French system calls for a *fraisage* at the end of the operation, which is a short pushing out of the dough with the heel of the hand to insure an even blending of fat and flour.

Proportions per cup of flour

(Directions for measuring flour and tables of equivalents are on pages 17–
   18.)
1 cup all-purpose flour (5 ounces)
3 ounces (¾ stick) butter and 1 ounce (2 Tb) vegetable shortening
3 to 4½ Tb iced water
½ tsp salt
⅛ tsp sugar (optional, for color)

Directions for making short paste by hand and in the food processor

Hand mixing. You must train yourself to work rapidly, particularly if your kitchen is warm, so that the butter will soften as little as possible. Use very quick, light finger movements, and do not linger on the dough at all with the warm palms of your hands. A pastry blender may be used if you wish, but a necessary part of learning how to cook is to get the feel of the dough in your fingers. *Il faut mettre la main à la pâte!*

---

2 cups all-purpose flour (scooped and leveled, see page 17)
1 tsp salt
¼ tsp sugar
6 ounces (1½ sticks) chilled butter cut into ½-inch bits
4 Tb chilled shortening

Place flour, salt, sugar, butter, and vegetable shortening in a big mixing bowl. Rub the flour and fat together rapidly between the tips of your fingers until the fat is broken into pieces the size of oatmeal flakes. Do not overdo this step as the fat will be blended more thoroughly later.

A scant half cup of iced water, plus droplets more as needed

Add the water and blend quickly with one hand, fingers held together and slightly cupped, as you rapidly gather the dough into a mass. Sprinkle up to 1 tablespoon more water by droplets over any unmassed remains and add them to the main body of the dough. Then press the dough firmly into a roughly shaped ball. It should just hold together and be pliable, but not sticky. Proceed to the *fraisage,* page 141.

Short paste in the food processor. The preceding proportions are right for machines with a 2-quart capacity; a large container would take double the amount. Measure the dry ingredients into the bowl (equipped with the steel blade). Quarter the chilled sticks of butter lengthwise and cut crosswise into ⅜-inch pieces; add to the flour along with the chilled shortening. Flick the machine on and off 4 or 5 times, then measure out a scant half cup of iced water. Turn the machine on and pour it all in at once; immediately flick the machine on and off several times, and the dough should begin to mass on the blade. If not, dribble in a little more water and repeat, repeating again if necessary. Dough is done when it has begun to mass; do not overmix it. Scrape the dough out onto your work surface, and proceed to the *fraisage.*

The fraisage—or final blending (for hand-made and machine dough)

Place the dough on a lightly floured pastry board. With the heel of one hand, not the palm which is too warm, rapidly press the pastry by two-spoonful bits down on the board and away from you in a firm, quick smear of about 6 inches. This constitutes the final blending of fat and flour, or *fraisage*.

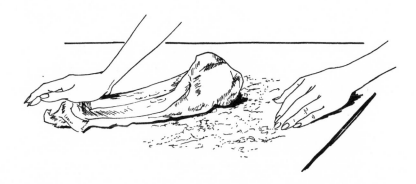

With a scraper or spatula, gather the dough again into a mass; knead it briefly into a fairly smooth round ball. Sprinkle it lightly with flour and wrap it in waxed paper. Either place the dough in the freezing compartment of the refrigerator for about 1 hour until it is firm but not congealed, or refrigerate for 2 hours or overnight.

Uncooked pastry dough will keep for 2 to 3 days under refrigeration, or may be frozen for several weeks. Always wrap it airtight in waxed paper and a plastic bag.

Rolling out the dough

Because of its high butter content, roll out the dough as quickly as possible, so that it will not soften and become difficult to handle.

Place the dough on a lightly floured board or marble. If the dough is hard, beat it with the rolling pin to soften it. Then knead it briefly into a fairly flat circle. It should be just malleable enough to roll out without cracking.

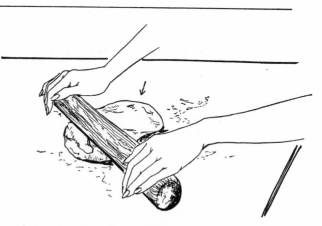

Lightly flour the top of the dough. Place rolling pin across center and roll the pin back and forth with firm but gentle pressure to start the dough moving. Then, with a firm, even stroke, and always rolling away from you, start just below the center of the dough and roll to within an inch of the far edge.

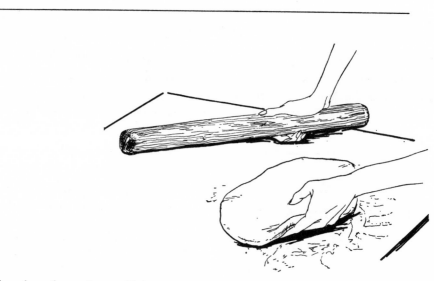

Lift dough and turn it at a slight angle.

Give it another roll. Continue lifting, turning, and rolling, and, as necessary, sprinkle board and top of dough lightly with flour to prevent sticking. Roll it into a circle ⅛ inch thick and about 2 inches larger all around than your pie pan or *flan* ring. If your circle is uneven, cut off a too-large portion, moisten the

edge of the too-small portion with water, press the two pieces of pastry together, and smooth them with your rolling pin.

The dough should be used as soon as it has been rolled out, so that it will
not soften.

Making a pastry shell

Flan *ring, false-*
bottomed cake pan

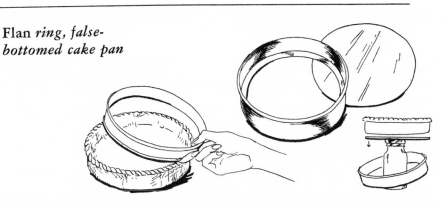

A French tart, *quiche,* or pie is straight sided and open faced, and stands
supported only by its pastry shell. In France the shell is molded in a bottomless
metal *flan* ring that has been set on a baking sheet. When the tart is done, the
ring is removed and the tart is slid from the baking sheet to a rack or the serving dish. You can achieve the same effect by molding your pastry in a false-
bottomed, straight-sided, cake pan 1 to 1½ inches deep. When the shell is ready
for unmolding, the pan is set over a jar and the false bottom frees the shell
from the sides of the pan. It is then, with the aid of a long-bladed spatula, slid
off its false bottom and onto a rack or the serving dish. You can also make
pastry shells using two matching pie pans; once in a while the weight of the
filling will force the outward-slanting sides of the shell to collapse, so we are
not recommending it.

Quiches

Partially baked pastry shells are used for *quiches* and for tarts whose filling cooks in the shell. Fully baked shells are for tarts filled with cooked ingredients that need only a brief reheating, or for fresh fruit tarts that are served cold.

Butter the inside of the mold. If you are using a *flan* mold, butter the baking sheet also.

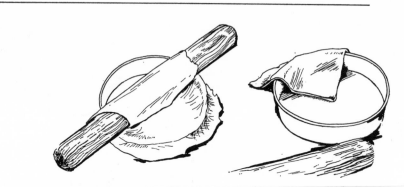

Either reverse the dough onto the rolling pin, and unroll it over the mold; *or* fold the dough in half, in half again, then lay it in the mold and unfold it.

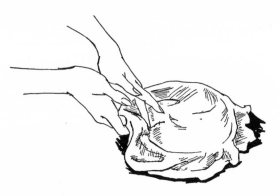

Press the dough lightly into the bottom of the cake pan, or onto the baking sheet if you are using a *flan* ring. Then lift the edges of the dough and work it gently down the inside edges of mold with your fingers, taking in about ⅜ inch of dough all around the circumference. This will make the sides of the pastry shell a little thicker and sturdier. Trim off excess dough by rolling the pin over the top of the mold.

Then with your thumbs, push the dough ⅛ inch above the edge of the mold, to make an even, rounded rim of dough all around the inside circumference of the mold.

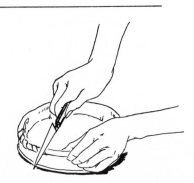

Press a decorative edge around the rim of the pastry with the dull edge of a knife.

Prick bottom of pastry with a fork at ½-inch intervals.

To keep the sides of the pastry shell from collapsing and the bottom from puffing up, *either* butter the bottom of another mold, weight it with a handful of dry beans, and place it inside the pastry; *or* line the pastry with buttered, lightweight foil, or buttered brown paper. Press it well against the sides of the pastry, and fill it with dried beans. The weight of the beans will hold the pastry against the mold during the baking.

Refrigerate if not baked immediately.

For a partially cooked shell: Bake at the middle level of a preheated 400-degree oven for 8 to 9 minutes until pastry is set. Remove mold or foil and beans. Prick bottom of pastry with a fork to keep it from rising. Return to oven for 2 to 3 minutes more. When the shell is starting to color and just beginning to shrink from sides of mold, remove it from the oven. If it seems to you that the sides of the shell are fragile, or are liable to crack or leak with the weight of the filling to come, do not unmold until your tart or *quiche* is filled and finally baked.

For a fully cooked shell: Bake 7 to 10 minutes more, or until the shell is very lightly browned.

Unmolding: When the shell is done, unmold it and slip it onto a rack. Circulation of air around it while it cools will prevent it from getting soggy.

OPEN-FACED TARTS
Quiches

Quiche Lorraine, although it seems to be the most well known, is only one of a series of generally simple-to-make and appetizing entrées. A *quiche* is a mixture of cream and bacon, such as the *quiche Lorraine,* or cheese and milk, or tomatoes and onions, or crab, or anything else which is combined with eggs, poured into a pastry shell, and baked in the oven until it puffs and browns. It is practically foolproof, and you can invent your own combinations. Serve it with a salad, hot French bread, and a cold white wine; follow it with fruit, and you have a perfect lunch or supper menu. Or let it be the first course of your dinner. You can also make tiny *quiches* for hot hors d'oeuvres.

The following recipes are all designed for pastry shells 8 inches in diameter. The *quiche* ingredients should fill the shell by no more than three fourths, to allow room for puffing. An 8-inch shell will hold about 2½ cups of filling and serves 4 to 6 people. A 10-inch shell, serving 6 to 8, will hold one and a half times this amount of filling or slightly more.

The partially cooked shell may be baked hours ahead of time, and the filling prepared and refrigerated in its mixing bowl. Half an hour before serving, the filling is poured into the shell and the *quiche* is set in a 375-degree oven. In 25 to 30 minutes it will have puffed and the top browned. A knife plunged into the center should come out clean, and the *quiche* is ready to serve. It will stay puffed for about 10 minutes in the turned-off hot oven with the door ajar. As it cools, it sinks down. It may be reheated, but will not puff again. A cold *quiche* makes a good snack and is easy to take along on a picnic.

✳ *QUICHE LORRAINE*

[Cream and Bacon *Quiche*]

The classic *quiche Lorraine* contains heavy cream, eggs, and bacon, no cheese. The bacon is usually blanched in simmering water to remove its smoky, salty taste, but this step is optional. Diced, cooked ham, sautéed briefly in butter, may replace the bacon.

For 4 to 6 servings

Preheat oven to 375 degrees.

3 to 4 ounces lean bacon (6 to 8 slices, medium thickness)

1 quart water

An 8-inch partially cooked pastry shell placed on a baking sheet, page 146

Cut bacon into pieces about an inch long and ¼ inch wide. Simmer for 5 minutes in the water. Rinse in cold water. Dry on paper towels. Brown lightly in a skillet. Press bacon pieces into bottom of pastry shell.

3 eggs or 2 eggs and 2 yolks

1½ to 2 cups whipping cream or half cream and half milk

½ tsp salt

Pinch of pepper

Pinch of nutmeg

1 to 2 Tb butter cut into pea-sized dots

Beat the eggs, cream or cream and milk, and seasonings in a mixing bowl until blended. Check seasonings. Pour into pastry shell and distribute the butter pieces on top.

Set in upper third of preheated oven and bake for 25 to 30 minutes, or until *quiche* has puffed and browned. Slide *quiche* onto a hot platter and serve.

Quiche au Fromage de Gruyère

[Swiss Cheese *Quiche*]

Follow the preceding recipe, but stir 2 to 4 ounces (½ to 1 cup) grated Swiss cheese into the egg and cream mixture. The bacon is usually omitted, and you may use all milk instead of cream.

✱ *QUICHE AU ROQUEFORT*
[Roquefort Cheese *Quiche*]

For 4 to 6 servings

Preheat oven to 375 degrees.

3 ounces (6 Tb) Roquefort
   or blue cheese
6 ounces (2 small packages)
   cream cheese or cottage
   cheese
2 Tb softened butter
3 Tb whipping cream
2 eggs
Salt and white pepper
Cayenne pepper to taste
½ Tb minced fresh chives
   or ½ tsp minced green
   onion tops
An 8-inch partially cooked
   pastry shell placed on a
   baking sheet, page 146

Blend the cheese, butter, and cream with a fork, then beat in the eggs. Force the mixture through a sieve, to get rid of the lumps. Season to taste and stir in the chives or green onion tops. Pour into the pastry shell and set in upper third of preheated oven. Bake for 25 to 30 minutes, or until *quiche* has puffed and top has browned.

Quiche au Camembert
[Camembert Cheese *Quiche*]

Instead of Roquefort cheese, use the same amount of Camembert, Brie, or Liederkranz, but remove the outside crust of the cheese. Or use a mixture of all or some of these, including Roquefort cheese, if you have leftovers.

QUICHE À LA TOMATE, NIÇOISE
[Fresh Tomato *Quiche* with Anchovies and Olives]

For 4 to 6 servings

Preheat oven to 375 degrees.

An 8- to 9-inch enameled or stainless steel skillet
¼ cup minced onions
2 Tb olive oil

Cook the onions slowly in the olive oil for 5 minutes or so, until tender but not browned.

1¾ to 2 lbs. firm, ripe, red tomatoes
1 large clove mashed garlic
½ tsp oregano, basil, or thyme
½ tsp salt
⅛ tsp pepper

Peel, seed, and juice the tomatoes, page 505, and chop the pulp roughly. Stir the tomatoes into the skillet and add the garlic, herbs, and seasonings. Cover skillet and cook for 5 minutes over low heat. Uncover, raise heat and cook for 5 minutes or so more, shaking pan occasionally, to evaporate the juice almost entirely. Allow to cool slightly.

1 egg and 3 egg yolks
8 chopped anchovy *filets*
3 Tb olive oil (including oil from anchovy can)
3 Tb tomato paste
3 Tb chopped parsley
1 tsp paprika
Pinch of cayenne pepper

Beat the egg, egg yolks, anchovies, oil, tomato paste, parsley and seasonings in a mixing bowl until blended. Gradually fold in the cooked tomatoes. Check seasoning.

An 8-inch partially cooked pastry shell on a baking sheet, page 146
12 pitted black olives (the dry Mediterranean type)
¼ cup grated Parmesan or Swiss cheese
1 Tb olive oil

Spread tomato mixture in pastry shell. Place olives over the top in a decorative design. Spread on the cheese and dribble the oil over it. Bake in upper third of preheated oven for 25 to 30 minutes, or until *quiche* has puffed and browned on top.

QUICHE AUX FRUITS DE MER

[Shrimp, Crab, or Lobster *Quiche*]

For 4 to 6 servings

Preheat oven to 375 degrees.

2 Tb minced shallots or green onions
3 Tb butter

Cook the shallots or onions in the butter for 1 to 2 minutes over moderate heat until tender, but not browned. Add shellfish meat and stir gently for 2

¼ lb. (1 cup) cooked fresh or canned crab, or diced cooked fresh or canned shrimp or lobster
¼ tsp salt
Pinch of pepper
2 Tb Madeira or dry white vermouth

minutes. Sprinkle on salt and pepper. Add wine, raise heat, and boil for a moment. Allow to cool slightly.

---

3 eggs
1 cup whipping cream
1 Tb tomato paste
¼ tsp salt
Pinch of pepper

Beat the eggs in a mixing bowl with the cream, tomato paste, and seasonings. Gradually blend in the shellfish and taste for seasoning.

An 8-inch partially cooked pastry shell on a baking sheet, page 146
¼ cup grated Swiss cheese

Pour mixture into pastry shell and sprinkle the cheese over it. Bake in upper third of preheated oven for 25 to 30 minutes, until *quiche* has puffed and browned.

QUICHE AUX OIGNONS

[Onion *Quiche*]

For 4 to 6 servings

---

2 lbs. minced onions (about 7 cups)
3 Tb butter
1 Tb oil

Cook the onions in a heavy skillet with the oil and butter over very low heat, stirring occasionally until they are extremely tender and a golden yellow. This will take about an hour.

1½ Tb flour

Sprinkle with the flour, mix well, and cook slowly for 2 or 3 minutes. Allow to cool slightly.

Preheat oven to 375 degrees.

---

2 eggs or 3 yolks
⅔ cup whipping cream
1 tsp salt
⅛ tsp pepper
Pinch of nutmeg

Beat the eggs or egg yolks in a mixing bowl with the cream and seasonings until blended. Gradually mix in the onions and half of the cheese. Check seasoning. Pour into tart shell. Spread on the rest of the cheese and distribute the butter over it. Bake in

2 ounces (½ cup) grated
Swiss cheese
An 8-inch partially cooked
pastry shell on a baking
sheet, page 146
1 Tb butter cut into pea-
sized dots

upper third of preheated oven for 25 to 30 minutes,
until *quiche* has puffed and browned.

PISSALADIÈRE NIÇOISE

[Onion Tart with Anchovies and Black Olives]

This is not a *quiche,* properly speaking, because it contains no eggs. In
Nice it is made either in a pastry shell or on a flat round of bread dough like
the Italian pizza.

For 4 to 6 servings

2 lbs. minced onions
4 Tb olive oil
1 medium herb bouquet: 4
parsley sprigs, ¼ tsp
thyme, and ½ bay leaf
tied in washed cheesecloth
2 cloves unpeeled garlic
½ tsp salt
1 pinch of powdered cloves
⅛ tsp pepper

Cook the onions very slowly in the olive oil with the
herb bouquet, garlic, and salt for about 1 hour, or
until very tender. Discard herb bouquet and garlic.
Stir in cloves and pepper, and taste carefully for
seasoning.

Preheat oven to 400 degrees.

An 8-inch partially cooked
pastry shell on a baking
sheet, page 146
8 canned anchovy *filets*
16 pitted black olives (the
dry Mediterranean type)
1 Tb olive oil

Spread the onions in the pastry shell. Arrange anchovy
filets over it in a fan-shaped design. Place the olives at
decorative intervals. Drizzle on the oil. Bake in upper
third of the preheated oven for 10 to 15 minutes, or
until bubbling hot.

---

* FLAMICHE – QUICHE AUX POIREAUX

[Leek *Quiche*]

For 4 to 6 servings

Preheat oven to 375 degrees.

1 lb. sliced white of leek (about 3½ cups)
½ cup water
1 tsp salt
3 Tb butter

Boil the leeks over moderately high heat in a heavy-bottomed, covered saucepan with the water, salt, and butter until liquid has almost evaporated. Lower heat and stew gently for 20 to 30 minutes until leeks are very tender.

3 eggs
1½ cups whipping cream
Pinch of nutmeg
⅛ tsp pepper
An 8-inch partially cooked pastry shell on a baking sheet, page 146
¼ cup grated Swiss cheese
1 Tb butter cut into pea-sized dots

Beat the eggs, cream, and seasonings in a mixing bowl to blend. Gradually stir in the leeks. Check seasoning. Pour into pastry shell. Spread on the cheese and distribute the butter over it. Bake in upper third of preheated oven for 25 to 30 minutes, or until puffed and browned.

Quiche aux Endives
[Endive *Quiche*]

Follow the preceding recipe, using sliced endive rather than leeks; add a teaspoon of lemon juice to their cooking water.

Quiche aux Champignons
[Mushroom *Quiche*]

Use the same proportions of cream, eggs, grated cheese, and dots of butter as for the preceding leek *quiche* and an 8-inch partially cooked pastry shell. Prepare the mushrooms as follows:

2 Tb minced shallots or green onions
3 Tb butter
1 lb. sliced fresh mushrooms
1 tsp salt
1 tsp lemon juice
Optional: 2 Tb Madeira or port

Cook the shallots or onions in a heavy-bottomed saucepan with the butter for a moment. Stir in the mushrooms, salt, lemon juice and optional wine. Cover pan and cook over moderately low heat for 8 minutes. Uncover. Raise heat and boil for several minutes until liquid is completely evaporated and mushrooms are beginning to sauté in their butter.

Gradually stir the mushrooms into the eggs and cream. Pour into pastry shell, sprinkle with cheese, dot with butter, and bake for 25 to 30 minutes in a preheated 375-degree oven.

Quiche aux Épinards
[Spinach *Quiche*]

Use the same proportions of cream, eggs, cheese, and butter as for the leek *quiche,* page 151, and an 8-inch partially cooked pastry shell. Prepare the spinach as follows:

An enameled saucepan
2 Tb finely minced shallots or green onion
2 Tb butter
1¼ cups chopped blanched spinach, page 468, or frozen spinach, page 475
½ tsp salt
⅛ tsp pepper
Pinch of nutmeg

Cook the shallots or onions for a moment in the butter. Add the spinach and stir over moderate heat for several minutes to evaporate all its water. Stir in salt, pepper, and nutmeg and taste carefully for seasoning. Gradually stir the spinach into the eggs and cream. Pour into pastry shell, sprinkle with cheese, dot with butter, and bake for 25 to 30 minutes in a preheated 375-degree oven.

GRATINÉED DISHES
Gratins

Any of the *quiche* mixtures in the preceding section may be baked in a shallow fireproof dish or pyrex pie plate rather than a pastry shell. They then officially become *gratins.* Most of the following, although they look more grand in a shell, are so substantial that they are perhaps better in a dish.

RÂPÉE MORVANDELLE
[*Gratin* of Shredded Potatoes with Ham and Eggs and Onions]
For 4 people

Preheat oven to 375 degrees.

½ cup finely minced onions
2 Tb olive oil
2 Tb butter

Cook the onions slowly in the oil and butter for 5 minutes or so, until tender but not browned.

½ cup (3 ounces) finely diced cooked ham

Raise heat slightly, stir in ham, and cook a moment more.

4 eggs
½ clove crushed garlic
2 Tb minced parsley and/or chives and chervil
⅔ cup (3 ounces) grated Swiss cheese
4 Tb whipping cream, light cream, or milk
Pinch of pepper
¼ tsp salt

Beat the eggs in a mixing bowl with the garlic, herbs, cheese, cream or milk, and seasonings. Then blend in the ham and onions.

3 medium-sized potatoes (about 10 ounces)

Peel the potatoes and grate them, using large holes of grater. A handful at a time, squeeze out their water. Stir potatoes into egg mixture. Check seasoning. (*) May be prepared ahead to this point.

2 Tb butter
An 11- to 12-inch baking dish or skillet about 2 inches deep or individual baking dishes about 6 inches in diameter
½ Tb butter cut into pea-sized dots

Heat the butter in the dish. When foaming, pour in the potato and egg mixture. Dot with butter. Set in upper third of preheated oven and bake for 30 to 40 minutes, or until top is nicely browned. Serve directly from the dish or skillet.

---

* *GRATIN DE POMMES DE TERRE AUX ANCHOIS*

[*Gratin* of Potatoes, Onions, and Anchovies]

For 4 people

Preheat oven to 375 degrees.

⅔ cup minced onions
2 Tb butter

Cook the onions slowly in butter for 5 minutes or so, until tender but not browned.

½ lb. diced raw potatoes (about 2 cups)	Drop potatoes in boiling salted water and cook for 6 to 8 minutes, or until barely done. Drain thoroughly.
A 3- to 4-cup baking dish, 1½ to 2 inches deep, such as an 8-inch pyrex pie plate 8 to 10 anchovy *filets* packed in olive oil	Butter the baking dish. Spread half the potatoes in the bottom, then half the cooked onions. Over them lay the anchovy *filets,* then the rest of the onions, and finally the remaining potatoes.
3 eggs beaten with 1½ cups whipping cream, ½ tsp salt, and ⅛ tsp pepper; OR 2 cups well-seasoned béchamel sauce, page 57	Pour the eggs and cream, or the béchamel sauce, over the potatoes and shake dish to send liquid to bottom.
¼ cup grated Swiss cheese 1 Tb oil from anchovy can or butter	Spread on the cheese. Dribble on the oil, or dot with the butter. (*) May be prepared ahead to this point.
	Bake for 30 to 40 minutes in upper third of oven until top is nicely browned.

VARIATIONS

Gratin de Pommes de Terre et Saucisson

[*Gratin* of Potatoes, Onions, and Sausages]

Follow the preceding master recipe, but cut the potatoes in slices rather than dice, and substitute sliced uncooked Polish sausage for the anchovies, interspersing the sausage between the potato slices.

Gratin de Poireaux

[*Gratin* of Leeks with Ham]

Use the same amount of eggs and cream or of béchamel sauce, as in the preceding potato and anchovy *gratin,* or substitute a *sauce mornay* (béchamel with cheese), page 61, and prepare the leeks as follows:

12 leeks, ¾ inch thick	Use the white of the leeks only. Cut each into crosswise sections about 2 inches long.

A heavy-bottomed saucepan ½ tsp salt 2 Tb butter 1 cup water	Boil the leeks in a covered saucepan over moderately high heat with salt, butter, and water until liquid has almost completely evaporated. Lower heat and stew gently for 20 to 30 minutes until the leeks are very tender.
6 to 8 thin slices of cooked ham	Wrap each piece of leek in a piece of ham, arrange in buttered dish, cover with eggs and cream, or sauce, and bake as in the preceding master recipe.

Gratin d'Endives

[*Gratin* of Endive with Ham]

Use whole endives braised in butter, page 493, wrap in ham, cover with eggs and cream, or béchamel sauce, and bake as in the preceding master recipe.

* GRATIN AUX FRUITS DE MER

[*Gratin* of Creamed Salmon or Other Fish]

A quick and delicious main-course dish can be made by combining a good cream sauce with canned salmon, tuna, or clams, or leftover cooked fish or shellfish. If you are using a baking dish, all may be prepared ahead, then set in the oven shortly before serving, but a pastry shell should not be filled until just before it goes into the oven. The following recipe is for salmon, but other fish may be substituted:

For 4 to 6 people

	Preheat oven to 425 degrees.
¼ cup finely minced onions 3 Tb butter A heavy-bottomed, 2-quart saucepan	Cook the onions in butter in the saucepan over low heat for 5 minutes or so, until onions are tender but not browned.
3 Tb flour	Stir in the flour, and cook slowly for 2 minutes without coloring.
1 cup boiling milk ¼ cup dry white wine or dry white vermouth	Off heat, beat in the boiling milk, then the wine, salmon juice, and the seasonings. Now bring this sauce to boil over moderately high heat, stirring. Boil sev-

Juice from salmon can, if any
¼ tsp salt
Pinch of pepper
¼ tsp oregano
4 to 6 Tb whipping cream

1½ cups cooked or canned salmon
Optional: sautéed mushrooms; sliced hard-boiled eggs
An 8-inch, shallow, baking dish 1½ to 2 inches deep, or a cooked pastry shell, page 146
¼ cup grated Swiss cheese
1 Tb butter

eral minutes to evaporate the alcohol in the wine, and allow the sauce to thicken considerably. Then thin it out to a medium consistency with tablespoons of cream. Taste carefully for seasoning.

Fold the salmon and optional ingredients into the sauce, and check seasoning again. Spread in baking dish or pastry shell. Sprinkle on the cheese, and distribute the butter in pea-sized dots. Bake in upper third of preheated oven for about 15 minutes, or until top is nicely browned.

VARIATIONS

Gratin de Volaille
Gratin de Cervelles
Gratin de Ris de Veau

[*Gratin* of Chicken, Turkey, Brains, or Sweetbreads with Mushrooms]

Exactly the same system as that for the preceding master recipe for fish *gratin* may be followed, using diced cooked chicken, turkey, brains, or sweetbreads. Combine with sautéed mushrooms, and warm the mixture briefly in butter with shallots or green onions. If you are short on meat, or wish to make the dish more filling, include cooked rice or noodles. Concentrated chicken stock or mushroom juice, or leftover chicken sauce may substitute for part of the milk in the béchamel sauce. If your sauce is carefully flavored, this is an attractive way to use leftovers.

SOUFFLÉS

A soufflé, quickly described, is a sauce containing a flavoring or purée into which stiffly beaten egg whites are incorporated. It is turned into a mold and baked in the oven until it puffs up and the top browns.

EGG WHITES

The glory and lightness of French soufflés are largely a matter of how voluminously stiff the egg whites have been beaten and how nicely they have been incorporated into the soufflé base. Both beating and folding are perfectly simple operations when you know the reasons behind the directions.

A fluffy mass of beaten egg whites is actually hundreds of minute air bubbles all connected and enclosed by a film of egg white; the bubbles of air expand as the soufflé cooks in the oven, and that is what pushes it into its magnificent puff. Whether you beat them by hand in a copper bowl in the time-honored way of the old chefs of France, or whether you use electricity, your egg whites should mount 7 or 8 times their original volume. They should be perfectly smooth and have a velvety sheen, and they should be firm enough to stand in peaks as in the illustration on the opposite page.

Warnings

Egg whites will not mount properly if they contain particles of egg yolk, or if either bowl or beater is oily or greasy. Any of these elements interfere with the action of the egg whites in forming and sustaining those all-important air bubbles. Before you begin, therefore, wash your equipment with an efficient detergent, and dry it well. Room-temperature egg whites mount more voluminously than chilled egg whites, and chilled egg whites will often form coagulated specks when beaten. Thus either set chilled whole eggs in a bowl of tepid water for 10 minutes before separating them, or let the whites sit 15 to 20 minutes at room temperature before beating.

Whips and bowls

One of the unexplained mysteries of *la cuisine* is that the unlined copper bowl used by old French chefs produces splendidly smooth, velvety, and high-rising egg whites that remain stable for a surprisingly long time. Stable means that they do not lose their sheen or get watery a few minutes after you beat them. Fortunately a stainless steel bowl or a plastic bowl used only for egg whites (oil might get into the pores of plastic if you use it for mayonnaise, for instance), plus a pinch of cream of tartar, works very well also. The cream of tartar acts as a stabilizer. Glass and porcelain bowls are not recommended because their slippery sides don't hold up the whites. You may use a large balloon-shaped wire whip 5 to 6 inches across at its widest diameter, or an electric beater. Here are directions for each.

How to beat egg whites by hand – for 2 to 8 egg whites

Provide yourself with a clean, dry balloon whip and a clean, dry round-bottomed bowl of unlined copper, stainless steel, or pristine plastic. The bowl should be 9 to 10 inches in diameter and 5 to 6 inches deep, and the whip 5 to 6 inches in diameter. To keep the bowl from jumping about, either place it on a wet pot holder or set it in a heavy pot or casserole.

Place the egg whites in the bowl, letting them sit for 15 to 20 minutes at room temperature if they have just come from the refrigerator. Start beating at a speed of 2 strokes per second with a vertical, circular motion for 20 to 30 seconds, until the egg whites have begun to foam. Then, for 4 egg whites, add a pinch of salt—salt gives a slight flavor to the egg whites and is added even for sweet soufflés. If you are not using unlined copper, add also a scant ¼ teaspoon of cream of tartar for the 4 egg whites.

Using your lower-arm and wrist muscles for beating—shoulder muscles tire quickly—gradually increase the beating speed to 4 strokes per second, beating as much air as possible into the mixture, and circulating the bowl so all the egg whites are entering into the action.

Start testing as soon as the whites seem to be stiff by gathering a dollop in the wires of the whip and holding it upright. If peaks are formed like those in the illustration, you have achieved "stiffly beaten egg whites." If not, beat a few seconds more and test again. When you arrive at the right consistency, the egg whites should be folded almost immediately into the soufflé mixture.

How to beat egg whites by machine—for 2 or more egg whites

For the successful beating of egg whites by machine, you must have the kind of equipment that will keep all of the egg whites in motion all of the time. This is best accomplished by the kind of whip mechanism that rotates about itself as well as circulating about the bowl, and that bowl must be of a rather narrow and rounded shape. In other words, you want a machine of the type illustrated on page 10. If you have the old-fashioned mixer with a wide flat-bottomed bowl, substitute a narrower rounded bowl and you will be more successful. Otherwise use a rounded bowl and a hand-held electric beater that you circulate all around the bowl, pretending you are a heavy-duty mixer.

Always start at slow speed for a minute or more, until the egg whites are broken up and begin to foam; gradually increase your speed and when the whites are softly foaming—in about another minute—beat in ¼ teaspoon of cream of tartar and a big pinch of salt (for 4 egg whites). Gradually increase your speed to fast, taking another minute or so. Stand right over your egg whites all the time because it is easy to overbeat them. Stop and check them when the beater begins to leave traces on the surface, and beat to stiff shining peaks as in the previous illustration.

Egg whites with sugar added

When the egg whites are to be folded into a cake or sweet soufflé batter, you are usually directed to sprinkle in sugar after the whites have formed soft peaks, and you continue to the stiff shining-peak stage. Sugar stabilizes the egg whites and also makes for a stiffer texture.

Overbeaten egg whites

You can easily overbeat egg whites in an efficient machine—they lose their velvety shine, turn dull, look grainy and slightly lumpy, and, worse, lose their puffing abilities. You can usually bring them back into shape by beating in another egg white, which will not disturb your recipe proportions.

Freezing egg whites

Raw egg whites freeze, thaw, and whip up perfectly. Two egg whites make ¼ cup, which you can freeze in custard cups, unmold, and pack in plastic containers for later defrosting.

Folding in the egg whites

After the main ingredients of the soufflé have been blended together and seasoned, the beaten egg whites are incorporated gently and delicately so that they will retain as much of their volume as possible. This process is known as folding, and is accomplished as follows:

The technique of folding

First stir a big spoonful of egg whites into the soufflé mixture to lighten it. Then with a rubber scraper, scoop the rest of the egg whites on top. Finally, still using your rubber scraper, cut down from the top center of the mixture to the bottom of the saucepan, then draw the scraper quickly toward you against the edge of the pan, and up to the left and out, as illustrated. You are thus bringing a bit of the soufflé mixture at the bottom of the pan up over the egg whites. Continue the movement while slowly rotating the saucepan, and rapidly cutting down, toward you, and out to the left, until the egg whites have been folded into the body of the soufflé. The whole process should not take more than a minute, and do not attempt to be too thorough. It is better to leave a few unblended patches than to deflate the egg whites.

AHEAD-OF-TIME NOTES

After your soufflé mold has been filled and is ready for the oven, you may set it aside in a warm place free from drafts. Cover it with a big empty pot or soup kettle. As long as it is protected, it will not begin to collapse for an hour.

SOUFFLÉ MOLDS

Although a soufflé can be cooked in a fairly shallow porcelain or pyrex dish—the usual type sold in America for this purpose—a more practical one is the cylindrical, metal mold known in France as a *charlotte*. *Charlotte* molds come in the following sizes, are inexpensive, and can be ordered from one of the French import shops if you cannot find them elsewhere.

CHARLOTTE MOLDS

HEIGHT	BOTTOM DIAMETER	APPROXIMATE CAPACITY
3⅜ inches	4⅜ inches	3 cups
3½ inches	5½ inches	6 cups
4 inches	6 inches	8 to 9 cups

If you do not have one of these, use a porcelain or pyrex mold holding whatever capacity your recipe specifies. American recipes for soufflés often direct that you use the regular American type of mold and give it added height by tying a double strip of buttered foil or brown paper around the dish and removing it when the soufflé is done. We have found this a nuisance, but if you like this method, calculate the capacity of the mold-plus-paper-collar according to the height and diameter measurements in the preceding table.

Soufflé Molds

Preparing the mold for the soufflé

So that the soufflé may slide easily up during its rise, butter the sides and bottom of the mold heavily. Then roll grated cheese or bread crumbs around in it, paying particular attention to the inner circumference, which must be lightly but evenly coated. Turn the mold upside down and knock it on the table to dislodge excess cheese or bread crumbs.

PLACEMENT IN THE OVEN

A soufflé will always perform as it should if it is placed on a rack in the middle level of a preheated 400-degree oven and the temperature is immediately reduced to 375 degrees.

GENERAL PROPORTIONS

Whether your soufflé is made with cheese, fish, spinach, or anything else, the proportions with few exceptions remain the same.

Ingredients	**Amounts** for a 6-cup mold	**Amounts** for an 8-cup mold
Thick béchamel or *velouté* sauce	2½ Tb butter 3 Tb flour 1 cup liquid	3½ Tb butter 4½ Tb flour 1½ cups liquid
Egg yolks, beaten into sauce	4	6
Flavoring added: cheese, fish, meat, vegetables	¾ cup	1¼ cups
Stiffly beaten egg whites folded in	5	7 or 8

WHEN IS IT DONE?

After 25 to 30 minutes of baking in a 375-degree oven, the soufflé will have risen 2 or 3 inches over the rim of the mold and will have browned on top. If you like the center creamy, it may be served at this point, but it is fragile and will sink rapidly. It will collapse less readily if you allow it to cook 4 to 5 minutes more, until a trussing needle or thin knife plunged into the center through the side of the puff comes out clean. A well-cooked soufflé will stay puffed for about 5 minutes in the turned-off hot oven. As it cools, it begins to sink. Therefore, there should be no lingering when a soufflé is to be eaten.

HOW TO SERVE A SOUFFLÉ

Puncture the top of the soufflé lightly with a serving spoon and fork—held vertically—and spread it apart for each serving.

✳ *SOUFFLÉ AU FROMAGE*

[Cheese Soufflé]

This recipe is intended as a detailed guide to those that follow. All main-course soufflés follow this general pattern:

For 4 people

The soufflé sauce base

A 6-cup soufflé mold, page   Preheat oven to 400 degrees.
162

1 tsp butter
1 Tb grated Swiss or Parmesan cheese

Measure out all your ingredients. Butter inside of soufflé mold and sprinkle with cheese.

3 Tb butter
A 2½-quart saucepan
3 Tb flour
A wooden spatula or spoon
1 cup boiling milk
A wire whip
½ tsp salt
⅛ tsp pepper
A pinch of cayenne pepper
Pinch of nutmeg

Melt the butter in the saucepan. Stir in the flour with a wooden spatula or spoon and cook over moderate heat until butter and flour foam together for 2 minutes without browning. Remove from heat; when mixture has stopped bubbling, pour in all the boiling milk at once. Beat vigorously with a wire whip until blended. Beat in the seasonings. Return over moderately high heat and boil, stirring with the wire whip, for 1 minute. Sauce will be very thick.

4 egg yolks

Remove from heat. Immediately start to separate the eggs. Drop the white into the egg white bowl, and the yolk into the center of the hot sauce. Beat the yolk into the sauce with the wire whip. Continue in the same manner with the rest of the eggs. Correct seasoning.

(*) May be prepared ahead to this point. Dot top of sauce with butter. Heat to tepid before continuing.

The egg whites and cheese

5 egg whites
A pinch of salt
Coarsely grated Swiss, or Swiss and Parmesan cheese—¾ to 1 cup (3 to 4 ounces) depending on its strength

Add an extra egg white to the ones in the bowl and beat with the salt until stiff, as described and illustrated, page 159. Stir a big spoonful (about one quarter of the egg whites) into the sauce. Stir in all but a tablespoon of the cheese. Delicately fold in the rest of the egg whites. Be careful not to overfold (see page 161).

Baking

Turn the soufflé mixture into the prepared mold, which should be almost three quarters full. Tap bottom of mold lightly on the table, and smooth the surface of the soufflé with the flat of a knife. Sprinkle the remaining cheese on top.

Set on a rack in middle level of preheated 400-degree oven and immediately turn heat down to 375. (Do not open oven door for 20 minutes.) In 25 to 30 minutes the soufflé will have puffed about 2 inches over the rim of the mold, and the top will be nicely browned. Bake 4 to 5 minutes more to firm it up, then serve at once.

VARIATION

Soufflé Vendôme

[Soufflé with Poached Eggs]

Prepare the soufflé mixture as in the preceding master recipe. Turn half of it into the prepared mold. Arrange 4 to 6 cold poached eggs (page 116) over the soufflé, and cover with the rest of the soufflé mixture. Sprinkle with cheese and bake for 25 to 30 minutes in a 375-degree oven. Dig carefully into the soufflé so as to lift out an unbroken egg with each serving. Poached eggs also may be baked in the following spinach soufflé:

* SOUFFLÉ AUX ÉPINARDS

[Spinach Soufflé]

For 4 people

A 6-cup soufflé mold, page 162	Butter the mold and sprinkle with cheese. Preheat oven to 400 degrees. Measure out your ingredients.
An enameled saucepan 1 Tb minced shallots or green onion 1 Tb butter ¾ cup blanched chopped spinach (or chopped frozen spinach—which will take several minutes more cooking) ¼ tsp salt	Cook the shallots or onions for a moment in the butter. Add spinach and salt, and stir over moderately high heat for several minutes to evaporate as much moisture as possible from the spinach. Remove from heat.
The soufflé sauce base, page 163	Prepare the soufflé sauce base. After the egg yolks have been beaten in, stir in the spinach. Correct seasoning.
5 egg whites A pinch of salt ⅓ to ½ cup (1½ to 2 ounces) grated Swiss cheese	Beat the egg whites and salt until stiff, page 159. Stir one fourth of them into the sauce. Stir in all but a tablespoon of the cheese. Fold in the rest of the egg whites and turn mixture into prepared mold. Sprinkle with remaining cheese and set on a rack in the middle level of preheated oven. Turn heat down to 375 degrees and bake for 25 to 30 minutes.

VARIATIONS to be added to the preceding spinach soufflé:

Ham

⅓ cup finely minced boiled ham	Cook the ham with the butter and shallots for a moment before adding the spinach.

Mushrooms

¼ lb. finely minced mushrooms 1 Tb butter Salt and pepper	A handful at a time, twist the mushrooms in the corner of a towel to extract their juice. Sauté in the butter for 5 minutes or so until the mushroom pieces begin to separate from one another. Season to taste. Stir them into the soufflé mixture with the spinach.

Other vegetable soufflés

These are all done in exactly the same manner as the spinach soufflé. Use ¾ cup of cooked vegetables, finely diced or puréed, such as mushrooms, broccoli, artichoke hearts, or asparagus tips.

---

* SOUFFLÉ DE SAUMON

[Salmon Soufflé]

For 4 people

A 6-cup soufflé mold, page 162 1 tsp butter 1 Tb grated Swiss or Parmesan cheese	Butter the mold and sprinkle with cheese. Preheat oven to 400 degrees. Measure out all your ingredients.

2 Tb minced shallots or green onions 3 Tb butter A 2½-quart saucepan 3 Tb flour 1 cup boiling liquid (juice from canned salmon, if any, and milk) ½ tsp salt ⅛ tsp pepper	Cook the shallots or onions in the butter for a moment in the saucepan. Add the flour and cook 2 minutes. Off heat, beat in the boiling liquid, then the seasonings, tomato paste, and herbs. Bring to boil, stirring, for 1 minute.

1 Tb tomato paste (for color)

½ tsp oregano or marjoram

---

4 egg yolks
¾ cup shredded cooked or canned salmon
½ cup (2 ounces) grated Swiss cheese

Off heat, beat in the egg yolks one by one. Then beat in the salmon and all but a tablespoon of cheese.

---

5 egg whites
A pinch of salt

Beat the egg whites and salt until stiff, see page 159. Stir one fourth of them into the soufflé mixture. Fold in the rest. Turn into prepared mold and sprinkle with the remaining cheese. Set in middle level of pre-heated oven. Turn heat down to 375 degrees and bake for about 30 minutes.

VARIATIONS

With the same method and proportions, you can make a soufflé using ¾ cup of any of the following:

Flaked canned tuna or any cooked fish

Finely diced or ground cooked lobster, shrimp, or crab

Ground cooked chicken or turkey

Puréed cooked sweetbreads or brains

If you wish to use raw fish or chicken, grind it, add it to the sauce base with the boiling milk, and boil for 2 minutes. Then beat in the egg yolks and proceed with the recipe.

FISH SOUFFLÉS FROM THE HAUTE CUISINE

These are only more complicated than the preceding soufflés in that each requires fish *filets* poached in white wine, and each is accompanied by a delicious type of hollandaise called *sauce mousseline sabayon*. The fish may be poached ahead of time, and the soufflé sauce base as well as the hollandaise may also be prepared in advance. Remember that if the hollandaise is to wait, it must be kept barely warm or it will thin out. If it is set aside to cool, reheat it very gently and not too much.

⁎ SOUFFLÉ DE POISSON

[Fish Soufflé]

For 4 to 6 people

A 6-cup soufflé mold, page 162
1 tsp butter
1 Tb grated Swiss or Parmesan cheese

Butter the mold and sprinkle with cheese. Measure out ingredients. Preheat oven to 400 degrees.

Preparing the fish

¾ lb. skinless flounder filets
¼ tsp salt
Pinch of pepper
1 Tb minced shallots or green onions
½ cup dry white wine or dry white vermouth

Grind half the fish; you will have ⅔ to ¾ cup of purée. Set it aside. Following directions for fish *filets* in white wine on page 208, season the rest of the *filets,* arrange them in a buttered baking dish with the shallots, wine, and enough water barely to cover them. Bring to the simmer, cover with buttered paper, and bake in bottom third of oven for 8 to 10 minutes or until a fork just pierces them easily. Strain out all the cooking liquor, boil it down in an enameled saucepan until it has reduced to ¼ cup, and set it aside until later for your *sauce mousseline sabayon.*

The soufflé mixture

2½ Tb flour
3 Tb butter
A 2½-quart saucepan
1 cup boiling milk
½ tsp salt
⅛ tsp pepper
The ground fish

Cook the flour and butter together slowly in the saucepan for 2 minutes without coloring. Off heat, beat in the boiling milk, salt, pepper, and ground fish. Boil, stirring, for 2 minutes.

4 egg yolks

Remove from heat and immediately beat in the egg yolks one by one. Taste for seasoning.

5 egg whites
A pinch of salt
⅓ cup (1½ ounces) grated Swiss cheese

Beat the egg whites and salt until stiff, page 159. Stir one fourth of them into the soufflé mixture. Stir in the cheese. Delicately fold in the rest of the egg whites.

Filling the mold

Turn a third of the soufflé mixture into the prepared mold. Cut the poached fish *filets* into 2-inch strips about ½ inch wide, and arrange half of them over the soufflé. Cover them with half the remaining soufflé mixture, and arrange the rest of the *filets* over it. Cover them with the last of the soufflé mixture.

Baking the soufflé

1 Tb grated Swiss cheese

Sprinkle the cheese on top, and set the mold in the middle level of the preheated, 400-degree oven. Immediately reduce heat to 375 degrees, and bake for about 30 minutes, or until the soufflé has puffed and browned and a needle or knife plunged into the side of the puff comes out clean. While the soufflé is cooking, prepare the following sauce as an accompaniment. Serve the soufflé as soon as it is done.

Sauce Mousseline Sabayon (1½ cups)

3 egg yolks
½ cup whipping cream
The ¼ cup concentrated fish liquor
A 4-cup enameled saucepan and a wire whip

Beat the egg yolks, cream, and fish liquor over low heat until they gradually thicken into a light cream that coats the wires of the whip (165 degrees). Do not overheat or the egg yolks will scramble.

---

6 ounces (1½ sticks) softened butter divided into 10 pieces

Off heat, beat in the butter a piece at a time, beating until each is almost absorbed before adding another. The sauce will thicken like a hollandaise.

Salt and pepper
Lemon juice if necessary

Taste carefully for seasoning, and add drops of lemon juice if you feel they are needed. Keep sauce over tepid—not hot—water, and when the soufflé is done, pour the sauce into a warm sauceboat to accompany the soufflé.

VARIATIONS

Soufflé de Homard

Soufflé de Crabe

Soufflé aux Crevettes

[Lobster, Crab or Shrimp
Soufflé]

Use the same soufflé mixture as in the preceding recipe, with about
¾ cup of ground flounder *filets*. Instead of poached fish *filets* in the center of
the soufflé, use:

⅔ cup cooked diced lobster, crab, or shrimp	Cook the diced shellfish gently in the butter and seasonings for 3 minutes. Then add the wine, cover the pan, and simmer for 1 minute. Raise heat and let liquid boil off quickly.
2 Tb butter	
¼ tsp salt	
Pinch of pepper	
3 Tb Madeira, sherry, or dry white vermouth	

Filets de Poisson en Soufflé

[Fish Soufflé Baked on a Platter]

A soufflé will also rise impressively when baked on a platter. This recipe
is lighter than the preceding fish soufflé as it has no ground fish in its sauce
base and only one egg yolk.

For 6 people

Preheat oven to 350 degrees.

½ lb. skinless flounder filets	Measure out ingredients. Poach the fish *filets* for 8 to 10 minutes in wine, seasonings, and shallots as described in *filets* poached in white wine, page 208. Drain out all the cooking liquor and boil it down in an enameled saucepan until it has reduced to ¼ cup. Set it aside for your *sauce mousseline sabayon*. Turn oven up to 425 degrees.
½ cup dry white wine or dry white vermouth	
½ tsp salt	
Pinch of pepper	
1 Tb minced shallots or green onions	
2½ Tb butter	Cook the butter and flour slowly in the saucepan for 2 minutes without coloring. Off heat, beat in the boil-
3 Tb flour	

A 2½-quart saucepan
1 cup boiling milk
½ tsp salt
Pinch of pepper
Pinch of nutmeg
1 egg yolk

ing milk and seasonings. Boil, stirring, for 1 minute. Off heat, beat in the egg yolk. Check seasoning.

4 or 5 egg whites
Pinch of salt
½ cup (2 ounces) coarsely grated Swiss cheese

Beat the egg whites and salt until stiff, page 159. Stir one fourth of them into the soufflé base. Stir in all but two tablespoons of the cheese. Delicately fold in the rest of the egg whites.

A buttered oval fireproof platter about 16 inches long

Spread a ¼-inch layer of soufflé in the bottom of the platter. Flake the poached fish *filets* and divide into 6 portions on the platter. Heap the rest of the soufflé mixture over the fish, making 6 mounds. Sprinkle with the remaining cheese and set on a rack in upper third of preheated 425-degree oven. Bake for 15 to 18 minutes, or until soufflé has puffed and browned on top.

Ingredients for 1½ cups *sauce mousseline sabayon,* page 169

Meanwhile, prepare the sauce as directed in the master fish soufflé recipe. Pass it separately in a warm sauceboat.

SOUFFLÉ DÉMOULÉ, MOUSSELINE

[Unmolded Soufflé]

Most unmolded soufflés are heavy, puddinglike affairs, but this one is light and delicious. You bake it slowly in a pan of water for over an hour, and then unmold it. Although it does not rise as high as its molded relatives, it sinks only a little bit, and may be kept warm for a good 30 minutes before it is served. You may adapt any of the soufflé combinations in the preceding recipes for unmolding if you use the same number of egg yolks and egg whites, and the same cooking method specified in the following recipe. Unmolded cheese soufflé makes a handsome first course, and a fine main course surrounded by or accompanied with chicken livers, sausages, mushrooms, green peas, or asparagus tips.

For 6 people as a first course; 4, as a main course

Preheat oven to 350 degrees.

1½ cups tomato sauce or fresh tomato purée, page 76 or 78

Set the tomato sauce to simmering.

½ Tb butter
An 8-cup soufflé mold, preferably one 4 inches deep
2 Tb finely grated Swiss or Parmesan cheese

Butter your mold heavily, especially on the bottom so the soufflé will unmold easily. Roll cheese around in it to cover the bottom and sides.

2½ Tb butter
3 Tb flour
A 2½-quart saucepan
A wooden spoon
¾ cup boiling milk
A wire whip
½ tsp salt
Big pinch of pepper
Pinch of nutmeg

Stir the butter and flour over moderate heat in the saucepan until they foam and froth together for 2 minutes without coloring. Off heat, vigorously beat in the boiling milk, then the seasonings. Boil over moderate heat, stirring, for 1 minute. Remove from heat.

---

3 egg yolks
A wire whip

One by one, beat the egg yolks into the hot sauce. Correct seasoning.

---

6 egg whites
A pinch of salt
1 cup (4 ounces) coarsely grated Swiss cheese, or a combination of Swiss and Parmesan

In a separate bowl, beat the egg whites and salt until stiff peaks are formed, page 159. Stir one fourth of the egg whites into the sauce base; then stir in the cheese. Delicately fold in the rest of the egg whites.

Turn the mixture into the prepared mold, which the soufflé will fill by about two thirds. Set in a pan and pour boiling water around the mold to come up to the level of the soufflé mixture. Place in middle level of preheated oven and bake for about 1¼ hours. Regulate heat so water in pan never quite simmers—this is important; soufflé must cook slowly. The soufflé is done when it has risen about half an inch over the top of the mold, is brown and crusty, and has just begun to show a faint line of shrinkage from the sides of the mold.

Turn a warm serving plate over the soufflé; reverse them. Then, clamping mold and plate together, give a sharp downward jerk or two, and the soufflé will dislodge itself. If the mold was properly buttered, and the soufflé sufficiently cooked, it will unmold perfectly, and present a golden brown exterior. Surround the soufflé with the tomato sauce, and serve. In the case of blemishes, pour the sauce over the soufflé and decorate with parsley.

(*) For a wait of 30 minutes or so, leave the soufflé unmolded in its pan of hot water, and return to hot, turned-off oven with door ajar.

SOUFFLÉ AUX BLANCS D'OEUFS

[Cheese Soufflé with Egg Whites Only]

The following light soufflé with its strong cheese flavor is one way of using leftover egg whites. Remember that egg whites take well to freezing, so you can make a collection and do the soufflé when you have the right amount. One egg white equals 2 tablespoons.

If you wish to make this type of soufflé with other flavorings, substitute ⅔ cup of ground fish, chicken, sweetbreads, ham, or vegetables for two thirds of the diced cheese.

For 4 people

Preheat oven to 400 degrees.

A 6-cup soufflé mold

Butter the soufflé mold and sprinkle with grated cheese, page 162. Measure out your ingredients.

2½ Tb butter
3 Tb flour
A 2½-quart saucepan
¾ cup simmering light cream
½ tsp salt
⅛ tsp pepper
Big pinch of nutmeg

Cook the butter and flour slowly together in the saucepan for 2 minutes without coloring. Off heat, beat in the simmering cream and seasonings. Boil, stirring, for 1 minute. Remove from heat.

6 or 7 egg whites (¾ to ⅞ cup)
Big pinch of salt
¾ cup (3 ounces) coarsely grated Swiss cheese
¾ cup (3 ounces) Swiss cheese cut into ¼-inch dice

Beat the egg whites and salt until stiff, page 159. Stir one fourth of them into the soufflé mixture. Stir in all but a tablespoon of the grated cheese, then the diced cheese. Fold in the rest of the egg whites.

Turn mixture into the prepared mold, sprinkle with the remaining cheese, and set in middle level of preheated, 400-degree oven. Immediately reduce heat to 375 degrees and bake for 25 to 30 minutes, until soufflé has puffed and browned. Serve immediately.

---

* TIMBALES DE FOIES DE VOLAILLE

[Unmolded Chicken Liver Custards]

These delicate little entrées (also called *mousses, pains,* and *soufflés*) are usually baked in individual ramekins and served hot with a *béarnaise* sauce. Or you can bake the ingredients in one large ring mold and fill the center with the sauce. It can be prepared very quickly in an electric blender, but if you do not have one, put the livers through a meat grinder, push them through a sieve, then beat in the rest of the ingredients.

For 4 cups serving 8 people

Preheat oven to 350 degrees.

1½ Tb butter
2 Tb flour
1 cup boiling milk
¼ tsp salt
Pinch of pepper

Make a thick béchamel sauce in a small saucepan by cooking the butter and flour together until they foam for 2 minutes without coloring. Off heat, beat in the boiling milk and seasonings. Boil, stirring, for 1 minute. Allow to cool while preparing other ingredients, beating occasionally.

1 lb. or about 2 cups of chicken livers
2 eggs
2 egg yolks
¼ tsp salt
⅛ tsp pepper

Place the livers, eggs, egg yolks, and seasonings in the blender, cover, and blend at top speed for 1 minute.

6 Tb whipping cream
2 Tb port, Madeira, or cognac

Add the cool béchamel sauce, cream, and wine to the liver and blend for 15 seconds. Strain through a sieve into a bowl.

Optional: 1 chopped, canned truffle

Stir in the optional truffle and correct seasoning.
(*) If not used immediately, cover and refrigerate.

1 Tb butter
8 ramekins of ½-cup capacity, or a 4-cup ring mold

Butter the interior of the ramekins or mold heavily. Pour in the liver mixture filling each ramekin or the mold to within about ⅛ inch of the top.

A pan containing 1 to 1½ inches of boiling water	Set in pan of boiling water, then place on a rack in middle level of preheated oven for 25 to 30 minutes, until a needle or knife plunged into the center comes out clean, and the timbales have just begun to show a line of shrinkage from the ramekins. (*) If not served immediately, leave in hot turned-off oven, with door ajar, for 15 to 20 minutes.
2 cups *sauce béarnaise,* page 84	Run a knife around the edge of each timbale and reverse onto a serving platter or serving plates. Top each with a spoonful of sauce, and pass the rest of the sauce separately.

VARIATIONS

Using the same proportions and method, substitute for the chicken livers any of the following cooked ingredients: ham, chicken, turkey, sweetbreads, salmon, lobster, crab, scallops, mushrooms, asparagus tips, or spinach.

Other Sauces

Sauce Aurore, béchamel or *velouté* with cream and a flavoring of tomato paste, page 62

Sauce Madère, brown sauce with Madeira wine, page 75

Sauce Périgueux, brown sauce with truffles, page 75

Sauce Estragon, brown sauce with tarragon, page 73

PUFFS, GNOCCHI, AND QUENELLES

✳ *PÂTE À CHOUX*

[Cream Puff Paste]

Pâte à choux is one of those quick, easy, and useful preparations like béchamel sauce which every cook should know how to make. Probably the only reason for the packaged mix, which in addition to its purchase price requires fresh eggs and hot water, is that most people do not realize cream puff paste is only a very, very thick white sauce or *panade* of flour, water, seasonings, and buttter, into which eggs are beaten. The eggs make the paste swell as it cooks. For half the price of a packaged mix, and in less than ten minutes, you can make your own cream puff paste with the good taste of fresh butter.

Baked just as it is in the following recipe or mixed with cheese, *pâte à choux* becomes puffs for hors d'oeuvres. Sweetened with sugar, it is ready to be cream puffs. When mashed potatoes or cooked semolina is beaten in, it turns into *gnocchi*. And with ground fish, veal, or chicken, it is quenelle paste, or can become a mousse.

For about 2 cups

A 1½-quart, heavy-bottomed saucepan 1 cup water 3 ounces (6 Tb or ¾ stick) butter cut into pieces 1 tsp salt ⅛ tsp pepper Pinch of nutmeg	Bring water to boil with the butter and seasonings and boil slowly until the butter has melted. Meanwhile measure out the flour.
¾ cup all-purpose flour (scooped and leveled, see page 17)	Remove from heat and immediately pour in all the flour at once. Beat vigorously with a wooden spatula or spoon for several seconds to blend thoroughly. Then beat over moderately high heat for 1 to 2 minutes until mixture leaves the sides of the pan and the spoon, forms a mass, and begins to film the bottom of the pan.
4 eggs (U.S. graded "large")	Remove saucepan from heat and make a well in the center of the paste with your spoon. Immediately break an egg into the center of the well. Beat it into the paste for several seconds until it has absorbed. Continue with the rest of the eggs, beating them in one by one. The third and fourth eggs will be absorbed more slowly. Beat for a moment more to be sure all is well blended and smooth.

Pâte à choux for Dessert Puffs

For dessert puffs, only a suggestion of sugar—1 teaspoon—is added to boil with the water and butter in the preceding recipe, and the salt is reduced from 1 teaspoon to a pinch. Otherwise there is no difference in ingredients or method.

Leftover pâte à choux

Pâte à choux is usually employed as soon as it is made, and while it is still warm. If it is not used immediately, rub the surface with butter and cover with waxed paper to prevent a skin from forming over it. If your recipe then specifies warm *pâte à choux,* beat it vigorously in a heavy-bottomed saucepan over low heat for a moment until it is smooth and free from lumps and is barely warm to your finger. Be very careful not to warm it to more than tepid or the paste will lose its puffing ability. *Pâte à choux* may be kept under refrigeration for several days, or it may be frozen. Reheated gently as just described, it will produce a good small puff; large puffs may not always rise as high as those made with fresh paste.

If you wish to make hot hors d'oeuvres in a hurry, leftover *pâte à choux* can help you. Beat 3 or 4 tablespoons of heavy cream into ½ cup of warmed *pâte à choux,* then several tablespoons of grated cheese, minced ham, or minced clams. Spread the mixture on crackers, toast, or triangles of bread, pop them into a hot oven, and in 15 minutes you will have lovely puffed canapés.

PUFF SHELLS

Choux

You cannot fail with puff shells—as mounds of *pâte à choux* puff and brown automatically in a hot oven—if you take the proper final measures to insure the shells remain crisp. A perfect puff is firm to the touch, tender and dry to the taste. Hot puffs will seem perfectly cooked when taken from the oven, but, if left as they are, they will become soggy as they cool because there is always an uncooked center portion that gradually spreads its dampness through to the outside crust. To prevent this sad effect, small puffs are punctured to release steam; large puffs are slit, and often their uncooked centers are removed. This is actually the only secret to puff making.

When you have done puff shells once or twice you will find that it takes less than 30 minutes from start to finish to make them ready for the oven, and that they are a wonderfully useful invention. Hot, bite-sized, filled puffs make delicious appetizers. Large ones may contain creamed fish, meat, or mushrooms and be a hot first course. And sweet puffs with ice cream or custard filling and chocolate or caramel topping are always an attractive dessert.

The Pastry Bag

A pastry bag makes the neatest puffs. If you do not have one, drop the paste on the baking sheet with a spoon.

Small Puffs

For 36 to 40 puffs 1¼ to 1½ inches in diameter

Preheat oven to 425 degrees.

Ingredients for 2 cups warm *pâte à choux* from the preceding recipe

A pastry bag with ½-inch, round tube opening

Make the *pâte à choux*.

Fold the top 3 inches of the pastry bag over your left hand as illustrated. Using a rubber spatula, fill the bag with the warm *choux* paste.

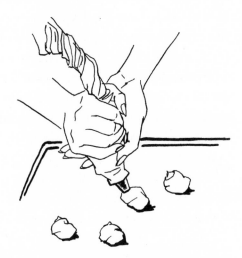

2 buttered baking sheets

Squeeze the paste onto the baking sheets, making circular mounds about 1 inch in diameter and ½ inch high. Space the mounds 2 inches apart.

1 egg beaten with ½ tsp water in a small bowl
A pastry brush

Then dip your pastry brush into the beaten egg and flatten each puff very slightly with the side of the brush. Avoid dripping egg down the puff and onto the baking sheet, as this will prevent the puff from rising.

Set the sheets in the upper and lower thirds of your preheated, 425-degree oven, and bake for about 20 minutes. The puffs are done when they have doubled in size, are a golden brown, and firm and crusty to the touch. Remove them from the oven and pierce the side of each puff with a sharp knife. Then set in the turned-off oven and leave the door ajar for 10 minutes. Cool the puffs on a rack.

Large Puffs

For 10 to 12 puffs about 3 inches in diameter

Use the same ingredients as in the preceding recipe, but provide your pastry bag with a ¾-inch, round tube opening. Squeeze the *choux* paste onto the baking sheets in mounds 2 to 2¼ inches in diameter and 1 inch at the highest point. Space the mounds 2 inches apart. Flatten each mound slightly with the flat of your pastry brush dipped into the beaten egg. Place the baking sheets in the upper and lower thirds of a preheated, 425-degree oven and bake for 20 minutes, or until the puffs have doubled in size and are lightly browned. Then reduce heat to 375 degrees and bake for 10 to 15 minutes more, or until the puffs are golden brown, and firm and crusty to the touch. Remove from oven, and make a 1-inch slit in the side of each puff. Return the puffs to the hot, turned-off oven, and leave its door ajar for 10 minutes. Then open one puff as a test. If its center is damp, *either* reach into the other puffs through their slits with the handle of a teaspoon and remove their damp centers, *or* cut all the puffs in two horizontally, and scrape out the uncooked portions with a fork. Allow the halves to cool and crisp, then re-form the puffs.

Freezing Puff Shells

Puff shells freeze perfectly. Just before using frozen puffs, set them in a 425-degree oven for 3 to 4 minutes to thaw and crisp them.

Filling Puff Shells

For appetizer or entrée puffs, use any of the cream fillings on pages 201 to 203. *Either* place the filling in a pastry bag, slit the sides of the puffs, and squeeze in the filling, *or* remove the tops of the puffs and insert the filling

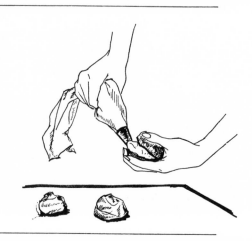

with a spoon. Reheat for 2 to 3 minutes in a 425-degree oven. For dessert puffs, use ice cream, or the custard filling, *crème pâtissière* on page 590, plain or with beaten egg whites.

Petits Choux au Fromage

[Cheese Puffs]

As cocktail appetizers, these may be served hot or cold, and need no filling. Because of the large amount of cheese, they do not rise as high as plain puffs.

For about 40 puffs, 1½ inches in diameter when baked

Preheat oven to 425 degrees.

1 **cup (4 ounces) grated Swiss, or Swiss and Parmesan, cheese**	Beat the cheese into the warm *pâte à choux*. Correct seasoning. Squeeze into circular mounds on a baking sheet, paint with beaten egg, and bake as in the preceding recipe for small puffs. After painting with egg, you may, if you wish, sprinkle each puff with a pinch of grated cheese.
2 **cups warm** *pâte à choux,* **page 175**	

GNOCCHI

Gnocchi and quenelles are types of dumplings made of *pâte à choux* into which a purée is beaten. They are shaped into ovals or cylinders and are poached for 15 to 20 minutes in salted water or bouillon until they swell almost double in size. After they have drained, they may be covered with a hot sauce, or they may be *gratinéed* with cheese and butter, or with a sauce.

Both *gnocchi* and quenelles are relatively simple to make, and as they may be poached ahead of time and either refrigerated or frozen, they are a useful addition to one's cooking repertoire.

* *GNOCCHI DE POMMES DE TERRE*

[Potato *Gnocchi*]

These make a good luncheon dish, or may be used as a starchy vegetable to accompany a roast.

For about 12 gnocchi, 3 by 1½ inches when cooked

3 **to 4 medium-sized baking potatoes (1 pound)**	Peel and quarter the potatoes. Boil in salted water until tender. Drain and put through a ricer. You should have 2 cups.

Dry out the potatoes by stirring them in a heavy-bottomed saucepan over moderate heat for a minute or two until they film the bottom of the pan. Remove from heat.

1 cup warm *pâte à choux*, page 175
⅓ cup (1½ ounces) grated Swiss, or Swiss and Parmesan, cheese

Beat the *pâte à choux* and the cheese into the potatoes. Correct seasoning.

Take the mixture by dessert-spoonfuls and roll it with the palms of your hands on a lightly floured board to form cylinders about 2½ inches long and 1 inch in diameter.

A 12-inch skillet of simmering salted water

Slip the *gnocchi* into the simmering water and poach, uncovered, for 15 to 20 minutes. Water should remain almost but not quite at the simmer throughout the cooking. If it boils, the *gnocchi* may disintegrate. When they have swelled almost double, and roll over easily in the water, they are done. Drain on a rack or a towel. Serve as in the following suggestions:

TO SERVE

Gnocchi Gratinés au Fromage
[*Gnocchi* Baked with Cheese]

The preceding *gnocchi*
½ cup grated Swiss or Parmesan cheese
2 Tb butter cut into pea-sized dots

Arrange the drained *gnocchi* in a shallow, buttered, baking dish. Spread the cheese over them and dot with the butter. Set aside uncovered.

Ten minutes before serving time, reheat and brown them slowly under a moderately hot broiler.

Gnocchi Mornay
[*Gnocchi* Baked with Cheese Sauce]

For about 3 cups of sauce

4 Tb butter	Cook the butter and flour together slowly in the
4½ Tb flour	saucepan for 2 minutes without coloring. Off heat,
A 2-quart saucepan	beat in the boiling milk and seasonings. Boil, stirring,
3 cups boiling milk	for 1 minute.
¾ tsp salt	
⅛ tsp pepper	
Big pinch of nutmeg	
¾ cup (3 ounces) coarsely grated Swiss cheese	Remove from heat and beat for a moment to cool slightly. Then beat in the cheese and correct seasoning.
The potato *gnocchi*, page 181	Arrange the *gnocchi* in a buttered baking dish about 2 inches deep. Spoon the cheese sauce over them,
3 Tb finely grated Swiss cheese	sprinkle with cheese, and dot with the butter. Set aside uncovered.
1 Tb butter cut into pea-sized dots	
	About 10 minutes before serving time, reheat and brown slowly under a moderately hot broiler.

ADDITIONS TO THE POTATO GNOCCHI PASTE on page 181.

Any of the following may be mixed into the *gnocchi* paste along with the cheese, and are especially good if your *gnocchi* are to be served as a main course.

3 to 4 TB minced fresh green herbs, such as chives and parsley
¼ to ½ cup minced cooked ham or bacon
¼ to ½ cup sautéed diced mushrooms or chicken livers

GNOCCHI DE SEMOULE AVEC PÂTE À CHOUX – PATALINA

[Semolina *Gnocchi*]

Italian *gnocchi* are made of semolina with butter and seasonings. This French version with *pâte à choux* gives the semolina a puff and a lighter texture. Semolina is farina, which in turn is the residue of middle-sized particles left over from the sifting of durum wheat, the type of wheat used for making macaroni. Untreated semolina takes 20 to 30 minutes to cook. Quick-cooking farina breakfast cereal, which is semolina, cooks in 3 or 4 minutes.

For about 12 pieces, 3 by 1½ inches when cooked

1½ cups water 1 Tb butter ½ tsp salt ⅛ tsp pepper Pinch of nutmeg	Bring the water to a boil in a saucepan with the butter and seasonings.
¼ cup (2 ounces) quick-cooking farina breakfast cereal	Stirring the boiling water with a wooden spoon, gradually sprinkle in the farina. Boil, stirring, for 3 to 4 minutes until the cereal is thick enough to form a mass on the back of the spoon. (You will have about 1¼ cups of cereal.)
½ cup (2 ounces) grated Swiss or Parmesan cheese 2 cups warm *pâte à choux,* page 175	Beat the cereal, then the cheese, into the *pâte à choux.* Correct seasoning.
	Roll the *gnocchi* paste into cylinders on a floured board, poach in salted water, drain, and brown under the broiler with grated cheese or cheese sauce as for the potato *gnocchi* in the preceding recipes.

QUENELLES

A quenelle, for those who are not familiar with this delicate triumph of French cooking, is a mixture of *pâte à choux,* cream, and purée of raw fish, veal, or chicken that is formed into ovals or cylinders and poached in a seasoned liquid. Served hot in a fine sauce, quenelles make a distinguished first course or luncheon dish—they are individual small independent mousses really, almost as light as a soufflé, with just enough body to hold themselves in shape for poaching. If the mixture is too solid, the quenelle will have a dry and heavy texture. You therefore want to choose the kind of fish—if it's fish quenelles you're making—that has the firm gelatinous flesh that will absorb the maximum amount of cream. It's the cream that makes for lightness and delicacy of texture.

Manufacturing note
In the 1950s, when we were working on our book in France, any kind of

a mousse mixture like this was an arduous process because it was the era BFP—Before Food Processor. Quenelles were the province of the *haute cuisine,* or at least of the great restaurants with plenty of young apprentice cooks to do the dog work. First the fish had to be pounded with a large wooden pestle in a vast marble mortar. When reduced to a purée, it was beaten into a *pâte à choux* and turned out onto a large drum-shaped sieve. Then began the hateful process of rubbing it through that sieve with a wooden masher—you had to eliminate gristly bits, bones, and so forth. After you rubbed it through, you removed the sticky mass off the bottom of the sieve with an oval-shaped palm-sized scraper made of horn—actual animal horn. (That was also the era BP, Before Plastics.) Then you beat the mixture over ice to chill it so that you could beat in as much cream as it would take and still hold its shape. It took, literally, hours to do, and was perfectly delicious—but not the least of it was the washing of that drum sieve when you were through, scrubbing bone bits out of tiny mesh crevices. Not an everyday affair, for the home cook at least.

We thought we were clever indeed, in our first edition, to have eliminated the mortar and pestle. The electric blender, which did exist at that time, was not at all satisfactory, but we found that two times through the fine blade of the meat grinder, a chilling, and a beating up with the electric mixer made a more than satisfactory quenelle. We eliminated that self-torture, the sieve, and eliminate it still; some cooks, however, do use it, and sieving does undeniably produce a more velvety texture. Sieving is optional, in this book.

Now, of course, with the food processor, all of the preceding is ancient lore. Quenelles and mousses take literally minutes and have stepped out of the never-never land of ultra fancy food into the everyday life of the average home cook.

✳ *QUENELLES DE POISSON*
[Fish Quenelles]

Fish quenelles in France are usually labeled *quenelles de brochet,* and are presumably made from pike, a fish of excellent flavor but so webbed with little shadlike bones that a quenelle is the most convenient way of eating it. If you do use pike, then, you will have to pound it in a mortar and then sieve it or you'll never rid it of bones. However, boneless fish *filets* may be puréed as is.

Choice of fish
Choose fish with lean, close-grained flesh of a slightly gelatinous quality. Flimsy, light-textured fish, like most flounder, will absorb little cream and

will therefore produce a rather dull and dry quenelle. Halibut and monkfish do nicely, as does gray sole or winter flounder. Very fresh petrale sole is also excellent. Less available choices are silver hake (*merlan*), green or ocean cod (*colin*), conger or sea eel (*congre*).

For about 16 quenelles
The pâte à choux—for 2 cups

1 cup water

A 1½-quart heavy-bottomed saucepan

1 tsp salt

4 Tb butter

¾ cup flour (scooped and leveled, see page 17)

2 "large" eggs

2 egg whites (¼ cup)

A 4-quart mixing bowl with a tray of ice cubes and water to cover them

Following the general directions for *pâte à choux* on page 175, bring the water to the boil in the saucepan with the salt and butter. As soon as the butter has melted, remove the saucepan from heat and beat in all the flour at once with a wooden spatula or spoon. Then beat over moderately high heat for several minutes until the mixture forms a mass. Off heat and one by one, beat in the eggs, then the egg whites. Set saucepan in the bowl of ice and stir for several minutes to cool; leave in the ice while you prepare the fish, and be sure the *pâte à choux* is well chilled before you combine the two.

The quenelle mixture

1¼ lbs. (2½ packed cups) well-chilled skinless and boneless lean fish *filets* from the preceding suggestions

A food processor (steel blade)

½ tsp salt

¼ tsp white pepper

4 to 6 to 8 or more Tb chilled heavy whipping cream

A rubber spatula

Cut the chilled fish *filets* into 1-inch strips, then into 1-inch pieces, and place in the bowl of the processor, along with the chilled *pâte à choux* from the previous step, salt, pepper, and 4 tablespoons of chilled cream. Process 30 seconds or so, stopping if necessary to scrape down sides of bowl with rubber spatula. If the mixture seems stiff, blend in more cream by the tablespoon—you want to add as much as it will take, but the mixture must hold its shape well in a mass on the spoon.

A saucepan of almost simmering salted water

2 Tb chopped truffle
OR, a big pinch of nutmeg

Scoop out a dollop as a test, drop it into the almost simmering water, and let it poach several minutes. Taste it: process in more cream if you think it can be absorbed—but better too little than too much! Add more seasonings, too, if you think them necessary. Then blend in the truffle or nutmeg. (If you are not proceeding at once to the next step, refrigerate the mixture.)

Shaping quenelles and poaching them

(The spoon method described here makes the most delicate quenelles. A neater-looking but less light-textured alternative is to roll them into cylinders on a floured board as for the *gnocchi* on page 181.)

2 dessert spoons in a cup of cold water

A 12-inch skillet containing 3 to 4 inches of barely simmering fish stock or salted water

With a wet spoon, dip out a rounded mass of the cold quenelle paste. Transfer the spoon to your left hand. Smooth the top of the paste with the inverted bowl of the second wet spoon. Then slip the bowl of the second spoon under the quenelle to loosen it and drop it into the barely simmering liquid. Rapidly form quenelles with the rest of the paste in the same manner. Poach them uncovered for 15 to 20 minutes, never allowing the water to come beyond the barest suggestion of a simmer. The quenelles are done when they have about doubled in size and roll over easily. Remove with a slotted spoon, and drain on a rack or a towel.

(*) If the quenelles are not to be served immediately, arrange them in a lightly buttered dish, brush them with melted butter, cover with waxed paper, and refrigerate. They will keep perfectly for one to two days.

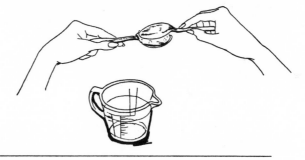

Fish Mousse
In Case of Disaster

If by any chance your quenelle paste turns out to be too soft to poach as quenelles, it will taste every bit as good if you declare it to be a mousse. Pack it into a buttered soufflé mold, a ring mold, or individual serving molds. Set in a pan of boiling water and bake in a preheated 350-degree oven until the mousse has risen and shows a faint line of shrinkage from the sides of the mold. Unmold and serve with any of the fish sauces suggested on pages 214 to 216, or with the delicious *sauce mousseline sabayon* in the fish soufflé recipe on page 169.

Sauces for Quenelles

Quenelles may be served as in the following recipe, in which they may be sauced ahead of time and *gratinéed* just before serving; or hot quenelles may be coated with a hot sauce. If you choose the latter system and the quenelles have been prepared in advance, cover them and heat them through in a buttered dish for 10 to 15 minutes in a 350-degree oven. Then sauce them. Fish quenelles may be substituted for poached fish *filets* in any of the recipes for fish on pages 214 to 216, which include the fine, rich, buttery sauces such as *Nantua* and *normande*.

Gratin de Quenelles de Poisson

[Quenelles *Gratinéed* in White Wine Sauce]

Sauce suprème de poisson (4 cups) enough for 16 poached quenelles, page 185

5 Tb butter
7 Tb flour
A 2-quart enameled saucepan
1½ cups boiling milk
1½ cups boiling, concentrated, white-wine fish stock, page 114
½ tsp salt
⅛ tsp white pepper

Cook the butter and flour slowly together in the saucepan for 2 minutes without coloring. Off heat, beat in the boiling milk, fish stock, and seasonings. Boil, stirring, for 1 minute. Sauce will be very thick.

¾ to 1 cup whipping cream
Salt and pepper
Lemon juice

Slowly simmering the sauce, thin it out with the cream, stirred in by tablespoons. Sauce should be thick enough to coat the spoon fairly heavily. Taste carefully for seasoning, adding salt, pepper and drops of lemon juice as you feel it necessary.

A lightly buttered baking dish 2 inches deep
3 Tb grated Swiss cheese
1 Tb butter cut into pea-sized dots

Pour ¼ inch of sauce in the baking dish. Arrange the drained quenelles on top and spoon the rest of the sauce over them. Sprinkle with cheese and dot with the butter. Set aside uncovered.

About 10 to 15 minutes before serving time, reheat and brown slowly under a moderate broiler.

Quenelles aux Huîtres

[Fish Quenelles with Oysters]

½ Tb minced shallots or green onions 1 Tb butter 12 large oysters, shelled ½ cup dry white wine or ⅓ cup dry white vermouth ¼ tsp salt Pinch of pepper	Sauté the shallots in butter for a moment in a small saucepan. Add the oysters, wine, and seasonings. Poach at just below the simmer for 3 to 4 minutes, until the oysters swell. Drain the oysters. Boil the poaching liquid over high heat until it is reduced by half, and reserve it for your sauce.
Ingredients for the fish quenelle paste, page 185	Roll one oyster into each cylinder of the fish quenelle paste. Poach and sauce the quenelles in the same manner as the fish quenelles in the preceding recipes.

Quenelles de Saumon

[Salmon Quenelles]

Use exactly the same proportions and method as given in the master recipe for the fish quenelles, page 185, substituting 2 cups of raw salmon, or well-drained canned salmon, for the white-fleshed fish. You may wish to include a tablespoon of tomato paste for added color. Serve with the fish *velouté* sauce, or with any of the other sauces suggested for fish quenelles.

Quenelles de Crustacés

[Shrimp, Lobster, or Crab Quenelles]

Using exactly the same proportions and method as given in the master recipe for the fish quenelles on page 185, substitute 2 cups of raw, cooked, or canned shrimps, lobster, or crab for the fish. The same sauces also apply.

Quenelles de Veau–Quenelles de Volaille

[Veal, Chicken, or Turkey Quenelles]

These can be delicious as a light luncheon or supper dish, and follow the same procedure as for the fish quenelles in the master recipe.

Ingredients for quenelles, page 185, but substitute the following for the 2	Have both meat and *pâte à choux* well chilled before puréeing in the processor, and cut the meat into 1-inch cubes. You can probably add more cream for meat

cups of fish: 2 cups raw veal, chicken, or turkey, minus all skin, bones, and gristle

A 12-inch buttered skillet

Boiling well-seasoned chicken or veal stock, or salted water

than fish, because meat has more body. Test in almost simmering stock or lightly salted water before forming, and make sure of the seasoning. Then form into quenelles and arrange in the skillet. Cover by 2 inches with boiling stock or water. Poach for 15 to 20 minutes. Drain, and serve in one of the following ways:

TO SERVE

Quenelles au Gratin. Use the same proportions and method as for the *velouté* with cream in the *gratin* recipe, page 188, substituting the veal or chicken stock in which you poached the quenelles for the fish stock and all or part of the milk.

Or use the cheese sauce in the *gnocchi* recipe on page 182.

Quenelles, Sauce Madère. Pour over the hot quenelles a brown sauce flavored with Madeira: *sauce madère*, page 75, or *sauce périgueux* (with truffles), page 75.

FRENCH PANCAKES
Crêpes

Every French household makes use of *crêpes*, not only as a festive dessert for Mardi Gras and Candlemas Day, but as an attractive way to turn leftovers or simple ingredients into a nourishing main-course dish. *Crêpes* may be rolled around a filling of fish, meat, or vegetables, spread with sauce, and browned under the broiler. More spectacular is a *gâteau de crêpes* in which the pancakes are piled upon each other in a stack of 24, each spread with a filling. This is then heated in the oven and *gratinéed* with a good sauce. Or the *crêpes* may be piled in a soufflé mold with alternating layers of filling, heated in the oven, unmolded, and coated with sauce. Whatever system you decide upon, including rolled *crêpes*, your dish may be prepared in advance and heated up when you are ready to serve.

Dessert *crêpes*, called *crêpes sucrées*, and entrée *crêpes*, *crêpes salées*, have slightly different proportions, but their batters are blended and cooked in the same way. The following recipe is made with an electric blender, because it is so quick. If you do not have one, gradually blend the eggs into the flour, beat in the liquid by spoonfuls, then the butter, and strain the batter to get rid of any possible lumps. *Crêpe* batter should be made at least 2 hours before it is to be used; this allows the flour particles to expand in the liquid and insures a tender, light, thin *crêpe*.

PÂTE À CRÊPES

[*Crêpe* Batter]

For about 25 to 30 crêpes, 6 to 6½ inches in diameter

---

1 cup cold water
1 cup cold milk
4 eggs
½ tsp salt
1½ cups flour (scooped and leveled, see page 17)
4 Tb melted butter
A rubber scraper

Put the liquids, eggs, and salt into the blender jar. Add the flour, then the butter. Cover and blend at top speed for 1 minute. If bits of flour adhere to sides of jar, dislodge with a rubber scraper and blend for 2 to 3 seconds more. Cover and refrigerate for at least 2 hours.

The batter should be a very light cream, just thick enough to coat a wooden spoon. If, after making your first *crêpe,* it seems too heavy, beat in a bit of water, a spoonful at a time. Your cooked *crêpe* should be about ¹⁄₁₆ inch thick.

Method for Making Crêpes

The first *crêpe* is a trial one to test out the consistency of your batter, the exact amount you need for the pan, and the heat.

An iron skillet or a *crêpe* pan with a 6½- to 7-inch bottom diameter
A piece of fat bacon or pork-rind; OR 2 to 3 Tb cooking oil and a pastry brush

Rub the skillet with the rind or brush it lightly with oil. Set over moderately high heat until the pan is just beginning to smoke.

Iron Crêpe Pans

Top—French Crêpe Pan

Left—American Skillet

Right—Omelette Pan

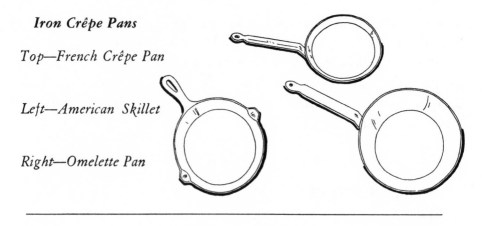

A ladle or measure to hold 3 to 4 Tb or ¼ cup

Immediately remove from heat and, holding handle of pan in your right hand, pour with your left hand a scant ¼ cup of batter into the middle of the pan. Quickly tilt the pan in all directions to run the batter all over the bottom of the pan in a thin film. (Pour any batter that does not adhere to the pan back into your bowl; judge the amount for your next *crêpe* accordingly.) This whole operation takes but 2 or 3 seconds.

Return the pan to heat for 60 to 80 seconds. Then jerk and toss pan sharply back and forth and up and down to loosen the *crêpe*. Lift its edges with a spatula and if the under side is a nice light brown, the *crêpe* is ready for turning.

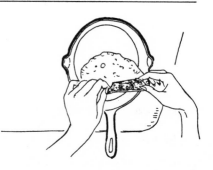

Turn the *crêpe* by using 2 spatulas; *or* grasp the edges nearest you in your fingers and sweep it up toward you and over again into the pan in a reverse circle; *or* toss it over by a flip of the pan.

Brown lightly for about ½ minute on the other side. This second side is rarely more than a spotty brown, and is always kept as the underneath or nonpublic aspect of the *crêpe*. As they are done, slide the *crêpes* onto a rack and let cool several minutes before stacking on a plate. Grease the skillet again, heat to just smoking, and proceed with the rest of the *crêpes*. *Crêpes* may be kept warm by covering them with a dish and setting them over simmering water or in a slow oven. Or they may be made several hours in advance and reheated when needed. (*Crêpes* freeze perfectly.)

As soon as you are used to the procedure, you can keep 2 pans going at once, and make 24 *crêpes* in less than half an hour.

---

* *Gâteau de Crêpes à la Florentine*

[Mound of French Pancakes Filled with Cream Cheese, Spinach, and Mushrooms]

An amusing entrée or main-course dish can be made by piling *crêpes,* a filling between each, in a shallow baking dish. (It looks like a many-layered cake or cylindrical mound.) Then the whole mound is covered with a good sauce and heated in the oven. Instead of the spinach, cheese, and mushrooms suggested, use any type of filling you wish, even three or four different kinds rather than one or two. Like the cream fillings on page 201, they are all a combination of well-flavored sauce and a mince or purée of cooked fish, shellfish, veal, ham, chicken or chicken livers, to which are added cooked vegetables such as asparagus tips, eggplant, tomatoes, spinach, or mushrooms if you wish. Other sauce suggestions, depending on your filling, are tomato sauce, page 76, brown Madeira sauce, page 75, *sauce soubise* (béchamel with puréed onions), page 64. You may use one or more types of sauce for the fillings, and still another to top the mound of *crêpes.*

This type of dish may be made ready for the oven in the morning, and heated up at dinnertime.

For 4 to 6 people

Batter for 24 *crêpes* 6½ inches in diameter, page 191	Make the *crêpes* and set them aside.

Sauce Mornay (béchamel with cheese), 3 cups

5 Tb flour **4 Tb butter** **A 1½-quart saucepan**	Cook the flour and butter slowly together in the saucepan for 2 minutes without coloring.

2¾ cups boiling milk **½ tsp salt** **⅛ tsp pepper** **Big pinch of nutmeg**	Off heat, beat in the boiling milk and seasonings. Boil, stirring, for 1 minute.

¼ cup whipping cream
I cup coarsely grated Swiss cheese

Reduce to the simmer and stir in the cream by table-spoons. Sauce should be thick enough to coat the spoon fairly heavily. Remove from heat and correct seasoning. Stir in all but two tablespoons of the cheese. Film top of sauce with milk to prevent a skin from forming.

The spinach filling

I Tb minced shallots or green onions
2 Tb butter
1½ cups blanched chopped spinach, page 468
¼ tsp salt

Cook the shallots or onions in butter for a moment in an enameled saucepan. Add spinach and salt, and stir over moderately high heat for 2 to 3 minutes to evaporate moisture. Stir in ½ to ⅔ cup of the cheese sauce. Cover and simmer slowly for 8 to 10 minutes, stirring occasionally. Correct seasoning and set aside.

The cheese and mushroom filling

I cup cottage cheese or 8 ounces cream cheese
Salt and pepper
I egg

Mash the cheese in a mixing bowl with the seasonings. Beat in ⅓ to ½ cup of the cheese sauce, and the egg.

¼ lb. (I cup) minced mush-rooms
I Tb minced shallots or green onions
I Tb butter
½ Tb oil

Sauté the mushrooms and shallots in butter and oil for 5 to 6 minutes in a skillet. Stir them into the cheese mixture, and correct seasoning.

Forming the mound

A round baking dish about 9 inches in diameter and 1½ inches deep
3 Tb grated cheese
½ Tb butter

Butter the baking dish, and center a *crêpe* in the bottom. Spread it with a layer of cheese and mushroom filling. Press a *crêpe* on top and spread it with a layer of spinach filling. Continue with alternating layers of *crêpes* and filling, ending with a *crêpe*. Pour the remaining cheese sauce over the top and sides of the mound. Sprinkle with the 3 tablespoons of cheese and dot with 3 or 4 pea-sized bits of butter. Set aside.

Baking

About 25 to 30 minutes before serving time, place in upper third of a preheated 350-degree oven to heat through thoroughly and brown the top lightly. To serve, cut in pie-shaped wedges.

VARIATIONS

Timbale de Crêpes

[Molded French Pancakes with Various Fillings]

For 6 people

A 1½-quart cylindrical mold, preferably a charlotte, about 3½ inches high and 6¼ inches in diameter

10 cooked *crêpes* 6½ to 7 inches in diameter and 12 *crêpes* 6 inches in diameter

3 to 4 cups of cream fillings, pages 201 to 203, one or several varieties

Butter the mold. Cut the 10 large *crêpes* in half. Line the mold with them—their best sides against the mold, their pointed ends meeting at the bottom center of the mold, and the other ends folded down the outside of the mold. Fill the mold with alternating layers of stuffing and *crêpes*. Fold the dangling ends of the halved *crêpes* over the last layer of stuffing and top with a final *crêpe*.

2½ cups of sauce, such as tomato, cheese, or whatever will go with your fillings

Set mold in a pan of boiling water and bake in lower third of a preheated 350-degree oven for 30 to 40 minutes, or until thoroughly heated. Unmold on a buttered serving dish and cover with whatever sauce you have chosen.

Crêpes Farcies et Roulées

[Stuffed and Rolled French Pancakes]

Place a big spoonful of filling on the lower third of each *crêpe* and roll the *crêpes* into cylinders.

Either sauté in butter, remove to a hot serving dish and sprinkle with parsley;

Or arrange in a shallow baking dish, cover with sauce, sprinkle with cheese and brown slowly under a moderate broiler.

The shellfish or chicken fillings on page 202 are especially good for this if you wish to be fairly elaborate. Both call for a good *sauce velouté;* in making it, use half the sauce to mix with an equal amount of shellfish or chicken for your filling. Thin out the rest with a bit of heavy cream, and use that for coating the *crêpes*.

COCKTAIL APPETIZERS
Hors d'Oeuvres

For those who enjoy making pastries, here are a few good hot hors d'oeuvres and one cold one. The series of canapés and tartlets starting on page 199, and the *chaussons* on page 204, can be made larger, and served as a first course or luncheon dish.

AMUSE-GUEULE AU ROQUEFORT

[Roquefort Cheese Balls – Cold]

For about 24

½ lb. Roquefort or blue cheese
4 to 6 Tb softened butter
1½ Tb chives or minced green onion tops
1 Tb finely minced celery
Pinch of cayenne pepper
Salt if needed
⅛ tsp pepper
1 tsp cognac or a few drops of Worcestershire sauce

Crush the cheese in a bowl with 4 tablespoons of the butter and work it into a smooth paste. Beat in the chives or onion tops, celery, seasonings, and cognac or Worcestershire. If mixture is very stiff, beat in more butter by fractions. Check seasoning carefully. Roll into balls about ½ inch in diameter.

½ cup fine, stale, white breadcrumbs
2 Tb very finely minced parsley

Toss bread crumbs and parsley in a plate. Roll the cheese balls in the mixture so they are well covered. Chill.

Serve as they are or pierced with a toothpick.

CHEESE BISCUITS
Bouchées, Galettes, Baguettes

Any of the following are more attractive when hot, but are quite good served cold. They may be baked, then frozen, and reheated for 5 minutes or so in a hot oven.

* GALETTES AU FROMAGE

[Cheese Wafers]

These featherweight wafers are often made of Swiss cheese, but you can use other cheese or a mixture of cheeses if you wish, and thus employ leftovers. The dough contains just enough flour to hold the *galettes* together while they bake, and ¾ cup of flour is usually right for Swiss cheese. You will probably need more if you are using soft cheeses, and should always bake one as a test.

For about 30 wafers

Preheat oven to 425 degrees.

½ lb. (about 2 pressed-down cups) grated Swiss cheese or a mixture of cheeses
½ lb. softened butter
½ cup all-purpose flour, more if needed
¼ tsp pepper
Pinch of cayenne pepper
Salt to taste

Knead all ingredients together in a bowl or on a board. The mixture will be sticky. Roll a 1-tablespoon bit into a ball in the palms of your hands, then flatten it into a cake ¼ inch thick. Bake 10 to 15 minutes in hot oven to observe how it holds together; it should spread slightly, puff lightly, and brown. If it spreads out more than you wish, or is too fragile, knead in ¼ cup more flour and make another test.

Lightly buttered baking sheets
1 egg beaten with ½ tsp water in a small bowl
A pastry brush
½ cup grated Swiss cheese
A cooling rack

When you are satisfied, form the rest of the dough into cakes and place on baking sheets. Paint the tops with beaten egg and top each with a pinch of grated cheese. Bake for 10 to 15 minutes until the *galettes* have puffed, and browned lightly. Cool them on a rack.

Galettes au Roquefort

[Roquefort Cheese Biscuits]

The dough for these *galettes* may also serve as a pastry dough for tarts and turnovers.

For about 30 biscuits

¼ lb. Roquefort or blue cheese

Mash the cheese in the bowl with a mixing fork. Beat in the butter, cream, and egg yolk. Then knead in

A 2-quart mixing bowl
¼ lb. softened butter
2 Tb whipping cream
1 egg yolk
¾ cup flour (scooped and
  leveled, see page 17)

the flour. Form into a ball, wrap in waxed paper, and chill until firm. Roll out ¼ inch thick, cut into 1½-inch rounds, brush with egg, and bake as in the preceding recipe.

Galettes au Camembert

[Camembert Biscuits]

This dough may substitute for the usual pastry dough for tarts and turnovers.

For about 50 biscuits

---

6 to 8 ounces ripe Camembert, Brie, or Liederkranz cheese
A 2-quart mixing bowl
3 ounces (¾ stick) softened butter
2 eggs
½ tsp salt
⅛ tsp pepper
Pinch of cayenne pepper
2 cups sifted all-purpose flour

Scrape off the crusts and mash the cheese in the bowl with a mixing fork. Blend in the butter, then beat in the eggs and seasoning. Work in the flour and knead everything together for a moment to make a smooth and fairly supple dough. Knead in a tablespoon or so more flour if dough seems too soft. Wrap in waxed paper and chill until firm. Roll out ¼ inch thick, cut into 1½-inch rounds, and brush with egg as in the preceding master recipe for cheese biscuits. Bake in upper third of a preheated 350-degree oven for about 15 minutes, or until lightly browned.

BOUCHÉES PARMENTIER AU FROMAGE

[Potato Cheese Sticks]

Mashed potato gives these little cheese mouthfuls a nice, tender quality.

For about 60 pieces

½ lb. baking potatoes (2 medium potatoes)

Peel and quarter the potatoes. Boil in salted water until tender. Drain, and put through a ricer. You should have 1 cup.

Stir the potatoes over moderate heat in a heavy-bottomed saucepan for 2 to 3 minutes until they form a light film on the bottom of the pan, indicating most of their moisture has been evaporated.

⅔ cup flour (scooped and leveled, see page 17)

4 ounces (1 stick) softened butter

1 egg

4 ounces (1 cup) grated Swiss cheese

⅛ tsp white pepper

Pinch of nutmeg

Pinch of cayenne pepper

Salt as needed

Beat the flour into the potatoes, then the butter by fractions, then the egg, cheese, and seasonings. Taste for seasoning. Preheat oven to 425 degrees.

2 lightly buttered baking sheets

With a fluted pastry tube ¼ inch in diameter, squeeze the mixture into 2½-inch lengths spaced ½ inch apart onto the baking sheets.

Bake both sheets at a time in preheated oven for about 15 minutes, or until sticks are lightly browned.

CANAPÉS, BREAD CASES, AND TARTLET SHELLS

Although Melba toast and crackers make good foundations for hot appetizers, the following are more elegant. They may be used interchangeably, all of them may be prepared ahead, and they may also be filled and browned, then reheated. When bread is specified, use only a homemade type of white bread with body, not the soft squashy type. French recipes call for *pain de mie*.

Canapés – Croûtons

[Plain or Sautéed Bread Rounds]

Plain, sliced, white bread works perfectly well for canapés when cut into triangles or rounds, spread with a filling, then set in a preheated 425-degree oven until the bread is toasted on the bottom and the filling has puffed and browned on top. But if you wish to be more elaborate, proceed as follows:

Slice the bread ¼ inch thick, and cut it into rounds 1½ to 2 inches in diameter with a fluted cutter. Heat ⅛ inch of clarified butter (page 15) in a skillet and sauté the rounds on each side until very lightly browned, adding more butter as necessary. (These are called *croûtons* when they are triangular and garnish an entrée.)

Heap the filling (recipes are on following pages) upon each canapé in a ½-inch dome. Top with a pinch of grated cheese, and a drop of melted butter. Arrange on a baking sheet and slip for a moment under a hot broiler to brown the tops lightly. If prepared in advance, reheat in a 350-degree oven for several minutes.

Croûtes

[Toasted Bread Cases]

Slice off the crust. Cut the bread into 1-inch slices, and the slices either into 1-inch cubes or, with a cutter, into rounds. Cut out a well in the center of each. Tamp down the bread on the sides and bottom of the well with your finger to make an open-topped case about ¼ inch thick. Paint the tops and sides with melted butter. Place on a baking sheet and brown lightly for 5 minutes in the upper third of a preheated 450-degree oven.

Place filling (following pages) in the hollow centers. Top with a pinch of grated cheese and a drop of melted butter. Brown top of filling delicately under a hot broiler for a moment. Reheat, if they have been prepared in advance, in a 350-degree oven for several minutes.

Tartelettes

[Little Pastry Shells]

Following the general procedure for pastry dough, and for pastry shells, pages 139 to 146, roll the dough a bit less than ⅛ inch thick. Line buttered pastry molds ½ inch deep and 2 to 2½ inches in diameter, or shallow muffin tins, with the dough. Flute the rims with the back of a knife. Prick the bottom of the dough with a fork. Fill each mold or cup with a round of buttered brown paper and a small handful of dried beans; or set another mold on the pastry. Either will keep the bottom from puffing up and the sides from collapsing. Bake in a preheated 400-degree oven for 7 to 8 minutes, or until pastry will hold its shape. Remove paper and beans or empty molds. Prick bottom of shells again and return to oven for 2 to 3 minutes more, or until shells are just beginning to color and to shrink from sides of molds. Remove shells and cool on a rack.

Place a filling (following) in center. Top with a pinch of cheese and a drop of melted butter. Arrange on a baking sheet and set in a 450-degree oven for 5 minutes or so, until filling has browned on top. If done ahead, reheat in a 350-degree oven for several minutes.

SPREADS AND FILLINGS

Farces

Use these multipurpose cream fillings for the sautéed bread rounds, bread cases or *tartelettes*. They may also garnish the cream puffs on page 177, the pastry turnovers on page 204, the croquettes on page 203, and the *crêpes* on pages 190 to 195.

✳ *FONDUE AU GRUYÈRE*

[Cream Filling with Swiss Cheese]

For about 2 cups

2½ Tb butter
3 Tb flour
A 2-quart saucepan
A wire whip
1½ cups boiling milk or boiling light cream
½ tsp salt
⅛ tsp pepper
Pinch of nutmeg
Pinch of cayenne pepper

Cook the butter and flour slowly together in the saucepan for 2 minutes without coloring. Off heat, beat in the boiling milk or cream, then the seasonings. Boil, stirring, for 1 minute. Sauce should be very thick. Taste for seasoning.

1 egg yolk
4 ounces (1 cup) coarsely grated Swiss, or Swiss and Parmesan, cheese
2 Tb butter

Remove sauce from heat. Place egg yolk in center of sauce and immediately beat it vigorously in with the wire whip. Beat for a moment to cool slightly, then beat in the cheese, and finally the butter. Taste carefully for seasoning. If not used immediately, dot top of sauce with butter to prevent a skin from forming.

VARIATIONS

Garlic and Wine Flavoring

½ Tb butter
1½ Tb minced shallots or
    green onions
1 small clove mashed garlic
½ cup dry white vermouth

Using a small enameled saucepan, cook the shallots
or onions, and garlic slowly in butter for a moment.
Add wine, raise heat, and boil down rapidly until
wine is reduced to ¼ cup. Substitute this for ¼ cup
of milk in the master recipe.

Ham

½ cup minced ham or Cana-
    dian bacon
½ Tb butter

Sauté the ham for a moment in butter. Substitute it
for half of the cheese in the master recipe.

Mushrooms or Chicken Livers

¼ lb. diced mushrooms or
    chicken livers
1 Tb butter
Salt and pepper

Sauté the mushrooms or chicken livers in the butter.
Season to taste, and substitute for half of the cheese
in the master recipe.

* FONDUE DE CRUSTACÉS

[Cream Filling with Shellfish or Clams]

For about 2 cups

1½ Tb minced shallots or
    green onions
2 Tb butter
1¼ cups diced or flaked,
    cooked or canned shell-
    fish; or canned minced
    clams
⅓ cup dry white wine or
    dry white vermouth; or

Using a 2-quart saucepan or a small enameled skillet,
cook the shallots or onions in the butter for a moment
over low heat. Stir in the shellfish or clams and cook
slowly for 2 minutes over low heat. Add the wine.
Cover and simmer for 1 minute. Uncover, raise heat,
and boil rapidly until liquid has almost evaporated.
Season to taste and stir in optional herbs.

3 to 4 **Tb Madeira or sherry**
Salt and pepper to taste
Optional: 1 Tb minced fresh herbs such as tarragon or chervil; or ½ tsp dried tarragon or oregano

2 **Tb butter**
2½ **Tb flour**
1 **cup boiling liquid** (milk, plus—if you have it—concentrated fish stock or mushroom juice, or clam juice)
⅛ **tsp pepper**
Salt to taste

In a separate 2-quart saucepan, cook the butter and flour slowly together for 2 minutes without coloring. Off heat, beat in the boiling liquid, pepper, and salt to taste. Boil, stirring, for 1 minute.

1 **egg yolk**
¼ **cup whipping cream**

Beat egg yolk and cream in a bowl. Remove sauce from heat and beat it into the bowl by tablespoons. Return to saucepan and boil, stirring, for 1 minute. Sauce should be very thick. Correct seasoning.

¼ **cup grated Swiss cheese**

Fold the previously prepared shellfish, then the cheese into the sauce, and check seasoning again. If not used immediately, dot top of sauce with butter to prevent a skin from forming.

VARIATION

Fondue de Volaille

[Cream Filling with Chicken or Turkey]

Using exactly the same method and proportions as for the preceding *fondue de crustacés,* substitute 1 cup of diced, cooked chicken, turkey, duck, or game for the shellfish or clams.

CROQUETTES

Crèmes Frites, Fondues, Cromesquis

Any of the preceding fondues, starting on page 201, may be chilled, cut into squares or balls, rolled in egg and bread crumbs, then browned in deep fat. But as you need a far thicker sauce, here is a different method.

For 24 pieces 1½ inches square and ½ inch thick

½ cup flour (measure by scooping into cup; level off with knife)

1½ cups milk

2 egg yolks

Salt, pepper, and nutmeg

2 Tb butter

1 cup any of the preceding flavorings

1 Tb melted butter

Place flour in a heavy saucepan, gradually blend in milk with a wire whip. Stir over moderate heat until mixture begins to lump. Remove from heat and vigorously blend in egg yolks. When smooth, beat over heat 2 minutes to thicken sauce. Remove from heat; beat in seasonings and butter. When sauce is slightly cool, add flavoring. Spread ½ inch thick in a lightly buttered platter. Film surface with melted butter; cover and chill several hours.

---

1 cup flour

3 pie plates

1 egg and 2 egg whites beaten with 1 Tb oil, 1 tsp water, salt and pepper

2 cups fine, dry, white bread crumbs

Frying oil and deep-fat frying equipment

Turn the flour in one plate, beaten egg in second, and crumbs in third. Scoop up 1½ tablespoons chilled mixture with a spatula; drop into flour. Dredge lightly and shape into a square with fingers. Drop into egg and spoon it over entire surface. Drain on a fork and drop into crumbs. Pat crumbs evenly over entire surface. (*) Croquettes may be crumbed a day in advance; cover and refrigerate.

Brown 4 to 5 croquettes at a time for 2 to 3 minutes in frying oil at 375 degrees. Drain on crumpled paper towels. Reheat if necessary for 2 to 3 minutes only in a preheated 450-degree oven.

TURNOVERS

Chaussons

PETITS CHAUSSONS AU ROQUEFORT

[Pastry Turnovers with Roquefort Cheese]

These nice little mouthfuls are made of pastry dough rolled out and cut into squares, ovals, or circles. In the center a small lump of filling is placed.

The edges of the pastry are moistened with beaten egg, then either another piece of pastry is placed on top, or the original pastry is folded over upon itself to enclose the filling. They are then baked in a hot oven until they puff and brown. In making them, avoid putting in so much filling that the pastry cannot be sealed, and be sure to seal carefully so the turnovers do not burst while baking. A ravioli stamp—a heavy metal ring about 2 inches in diameter with serrated teeth—will seal 2 rounds of pastry most efficiently together.

Turnovers may enclose a variety of stuffings other than Roquefort, such as the cream fillings on pages 201 to 203, or any of the liver, sausage, or veal mixtures in the *pâté* section, pages 565 to 569, or the ground meat mixtures in the Beef, Lamb, or Veal sections. You can also use little pork sausages or store-bought sausage meat. *Chaussons* may be made in any size or shape, from about 2½ inches for appetizers to 12 inches for an entrée.

For about 40 pieces

½ lb. Roquefort or blue cheese

A 3-quart mixing bowl

¼ lb. (1 stick) softened butter

2 egg yolks

1 to 2 Tb kirsch or cognac

1¼ tsp pepper

2 Tb minced chives or minced green onion tops

Mash the cheese in the bowl with a mixing fork. Beat in the butter, then the egg yolks, kirsch or cognac, pepper, and chives or onion tops.

2 to 6 Tb whipping cream

Beat in the cream by tablespoons but do not let the mixture thin out too much. It should remain a fairly thick paste. Correct seasoning.

Chilled pastry dough made from 4 cups of flour, page 139

Roll out the dough into a rectangle ⅛ inch thick. With a ravioli wheel or a knife, cut the dough into 2½-inch squares.

Preheat oven to 425 degrees.

1 egg beaten in a bowl with ½ tsp water

A pastry brush

Lightly buttered baking sheets

Place 1 teaspoon of filling in the center of each square. One by one, paint a ¼-inch border of beaten egg around the edges of the pastry. Fold the pastry over on itself into a triangle. Press the edges together firmly with your fingers. Press them again making a design with the tines of a fork. Place on a buttered baking sheet and continue with the rest of the turnovers. Paint the tops with beaten egg. Make shallow crosshatch lines with the point of a knife, and poke a ⅛-inch hole through the center of each pastry top so cooking steam can escape.

Bake in upper third of preheated oven for about 15 minutes, or until puffed and lightly browned.

Turnovers may be baked, then reheated. Baked turnovers may also be frozen, then set in a 425-degree oven for 5 minutes or so to thaw and heat through.

CHAPTER FIVE

FISH

Poisson

THE FRENCH are magnificent with fish. Not only is fresh fish abundant all year round, but the art of its cooking and saucing is accomplished with great taste and skill.

This chapter includes two fine recipes for scallops, one for tuna or swordfish, three for lobster, and a group for mussels. But the main emphasis is on the important and typically French method of poaching *filets* of fish in white wine and serving them in a wine sauce, starting with the simplest type of sauce and ending with several of the most famous of *la grande cuisine*. These last, as you will observe, are fish *veloutés* (flour and butter *roux* simmered with the fish cooking liquid), which are then enriched with cream and egg yolks. They are all the same basic sauce described in detail on page 60 in the Sauce chapter. Under numerous disguises and with various flavorings, this sauce appears throughout almost every phase of French cookery.

A NOTE ON BUYING FISH

Fish must be fresh smelling and fresh tasting. If it is whole, its eyes are bright and full, not filmed, opaque, and flat. Its gills are bright red, its flesh firm to the touch, its skin fresh and glistening.

Frozen fish should be bought from a dealer who has the proper facilities to ship and store it at a constant temperature of zero degrees. It should be solidly frozen. A block of frozen juices at the bottom of the package is proof that it has been thawed and refrozen. Before cooking, defrost it in the refrigerator, or under cold running water.

A beautifully sauced fish can well be considered as a separate course and needs nothing but French bread and a good wine to go with it. If it is a main course, include *risotto* or steamed rice for shellfish, boiled potatoes for other fish. A salad or vegetable should come afterward, so as not to disturb the harmony of the fish, the sauce, and the wine.

FISH FILETS IN WHITE WINE SAUCE

THE FISH FILETS

Most of the famous French dishes involving *filet* of sole center around fish poached in white wine and coated with a lovely, creamy sauce made from the poaching liquid. Although many types of American flat fish and fish *filets* are called sole, they are usually flounder because the true sole is not a native American fish. European sole is flown over to America, and can be bought, but it is rarely seen in the usual American market. The sole's ease of skinning and filleting, and its close-grained yet delicate flesh make it ideal for poaching. The best substitutes for European sole are winter flounder or gray sole, Pacific petrale sole or brill. Each of these is a common sole *filet* in America, depending on where you live. Other worthy substitutes of a different nature are whiting or silver hake, dab, tilefish, fresh-water trout, and (if the *filets* are too thick, slice these horizontally to make them about ⅜ inch thick) halibut, cod, pollack, striped bass, monkfish. Any of the lean white fish, in other words, may be used in these recipes in place of sole; if they flake during poaching, plan to sauce and serve them in their baking dish.

✳ *FILETS DE POISSON POCHÉS AU VIN BLANC*

[Fish *Filets* Poached in White Wine]

For 6 people

Preheat oven to 350 degrees.

A buttered, 10- to 12-inch, fireproof baking and serving dish, 1½ to 2 inches deep

2 Tb finely minced shallots or green onions

2½ lbs. skinless and boneless sole or flounder filets cut into serving pieces

Salt and pepper

1½ Tb butter cut into bits

1¼ to 1½ cups cold, white-wine fish stock made from heads, bones, and trimmings, page 114

OR ¾ cup dry white wine or ⅔ cup dry white vermouth plus ¼ cup bottled clam juice, and water

OR 1½ cups wine and water mixed

Sprinkle half the shallots or onions in the bottom of the dish. Season the *filets* lightly with salt and pepper and arrange them in one slightly overlapping layer in the dish. If *filets* are thin, they may be folded in half so they make triangles. Sprinkle the *filets* with the remaining shallots or onions, and dot with butter. Pour in the cold liquid and enough water so fish is barely covered.

Buttered brown paper or waxed paper (do not use aluminum foil—it will discolor the wine)

Bring almost to the simmer on top of the stove. Lay the buttered paper over the fish. Then place dish in bottom third of preheated oven. Maintain liquid almost at the simmer for 8 to 12 minutes depending on the thickness of the *filets*. The fish is done when a fork pierces the flesh easily. Do not overcook; the fish should not be dry and flaky.

An enameled saucepan

Place a cover over the dish and drain out all the cooking liquid into an enameled saucepan.

(*) The fish is now poached and ready for saucing. It may be covered and kept warm for a few minutes over hot, but not simmering, water. Or set it aside, covered with its piece of paper, and reheat later for a few minutes over simmering water. Be very sure the fish does not overcook as it reheats. Before saucing the fish, drain off any liquid which may have accumulated in the dish.

✳   *Filets de Poisson Bercy aux Champignons*

[Fish *Filets* Poached in White Wine with Mushrooms]

Bercy is the simplest of the white-wine fish sauces. The poaching liquid
is thickened with *beurre manié*—a flour and butter paste—then enriched with
cream. This combination of fish, mushrooms, and cream sauce is an informal
version of *sole bonne femme*. Serve with it a white Burgundy, Graves, or
Traminer.

> *For 6 people*

¾ lb. or 3½ cups sliced fresh mushrooms 2 Tb butter An enameled skillet ⅛ tsp salt Pinch of pepper	Toss the mushrooms in hot butter over moderately high heat for a minute or two without browning. Season with salt and pepper, and set aside.
2½ lbs. *filets* of sole or flounder and the ingredients for poaching them in white wine (see preceding recipe) A 2-quart enameled or stainless steel saucepan	Arrange the seasoned *filets* in a buttered baking dish as described in the master recipe. Spread the mushrooms over them. Pour in the liquids, and poach the fish. Then drain the poaching liquid into the saucepan. Preheat broiler.
	Rapidly boil down the poaching liquid until it has reduced to 1 cup.
2½ Tb flour blended to a paste with 3 Tb softened butter ¾ to 1 cup whipping cream Salt and pepper Lemon juice	Off heat, beat the flour and butter paste into the hot liquid, then ½ cup of the cream. Bring to the boil. Thin out the sauce with additional tablespoons of cream until it coats the spoon nicely. Season to taste with salt, pepper, and drops of lemon juice.
¼ cup grated Swiss cheese 1 Tb butter cut into bits	Spoon the sauce over the fish. Sprinkle on the cheese, and dot with butter. Place dish 6 to 7 inches from a hot broiler for 2 to 3 minutes to reheat fish and brown top of sauce lightly. Serve as soon as possible. (✳) Dish may be prepared ahead and reheated as follows: After sprinkling on the cheese and butter, set

aside. Before serving, reheat just to the simmer on top
of the stove, then run for a minute or two under a hot
broiler to brown the top of the sauce.

VARIATION

Filets de Poisson à la Bretonne

[Fish *Filets* Poached in White Wine and a Julienne of Vegetables]

This is the same recipe, but with a julienne of carrots, onions, celery,
and mushrooms cooked in butter, then spread over the fish. It makes a pretty
dish with a delicious flavor.

Ingredients for the preceding recipe, but use only ¼ lb. of mushrooms, and the following vegetables: 1 carrot 2 leeks, white part only; or 2 yellow onions 2 tender celery stalks	Cut the vegetables into julienne matchsticks 1½ inches long and ⅛ inch across. Keep the mushrooms separate. Cook the other vegetables slowly in butter for about 20 minutes in a covered saucepan, until they are tender but not browned. Then add the mushrooms and cook for 2 minutes. Season with salt and pepper.
	Spread the vegetables over the seasoned fish *filets,* cover with the liquids, and poach the fish. Make the sauce as in the preceding recipe.

---

* Filets de Poisson Gratinés, à la Parisienne

[Fish *Filets* Poached in White Wine; Cream and Egg Yolk Sauce]

In the following recipe, the fish poaching liquid is cooked with a flour
and butter *roux* to make a fish *velouté.* The *velouté* is then combined with
cream and egg yolks to produce a delicious, velvety sauce called a *parisienne.*
Although it uses almost the same elements as the *sauce Bercy,* because of its
cooked *roux* and its egg yolks, *sauce parisienne* is far more subtle in taste and
texture. It is the basis for all the great fish sauces described later. When the
sauce is to be used for a *gratin,* as in this recipe, the whole dish may be prepared
ahead of time, and reheated later. Before the fish is sauced, it may be surrounded
with various cooked shellfish as suggested at the end of the recipe. Serve with
this a chilled white Burgundy, or an excellent white Graves.

For 6 people

2½ lbs. sole or flounder filets poached in white
wine, page 208

Poach the fish in white wine as described in the master recipe. Drain the poaching liquid into an enameled saucepan and rapidly boil it down until it has reduced to 1 cup.

Sauce Parisienne (2½ cups)

A 2-quart, heavy-bottomed,
enameled or stainless steel
saucepan
3 Tb butter
4 Tb flour
A wooden spatula or spoon
The boiling fish-poaching
liquid
¾ cup milk
A wire whip

Melt the butter, blend in the flour, and cook slowly, stirring, until they foam and froth together for 2 minutes without coloring. Off heat, beat in the boiling liquid, then the milk. Boil, stirring, for 1 minute. Sauce will be very thick.

Preheat broiler.

2 egg yolks
½ cup whipping cream
A 2-quart mixing bowl
A wire whip
A wooden spoon
More cream as needed
Salt and white pepper
Lemon juice

Blend the yolks and cream in the mixing bowl. Beat in driblets of hot sauce until a cup has been added. Beat in the rest of the hot sauce in a thin stream. Return the sauce to the pan. Set over moderately high heat and stir with wooden spoon, reaching all over the bottom of the pan, until the sauce comes to the boil. Boil and stir for 1 minute. Thin out with additional spoonfuls of cream until the sauce coats the spoon nicely. Season carefully to taste with salt, pepper, and drops of lemon juice. Strain.

2 Tb grated Swiss cheese, to
help brown top of sauce
1 Tb butter cut into bits

Spoon the sauce over the fish. Sprinkle with cheese, and dot with butter.
(*) If not to be served immediately, set aside.

Just before serving, reheat slowly almost to simmer on top of the stove. Run under hot broiler to brown the top of the sauce.

SHELLFISH GARNITURES

Before saucing the fish in the preceding or following recipes, you may surround it with one or various types of cooked shellfish meat. Their cooking juices are added to reduce with the liquid in which your fish *filets* were poached, giving it even more character.

The following brief directions include the cooking of the raw shellfish, and then the warming of the meat in butter and seasonings to give it additional flavor. If you are using previously cooked or canned meat, it will need only the final warming in butter.

Lobster

Steam the lobster in wine and aromatic flavorings as described at the beginning of the lobster Thermidor recipe on page 221. When the lobster is cool, remove the meat and dice or slice it. Sauté the meat for 2 to 3 minutes in 2 tablespoons of hot butter, 1 tablespoon of minced shallots or green onions, and salt and pepper. Stir in 3 tablespoons of dry white wine or dry white vermouth and boil for 1 minute until the liquid has almost completely evaporated. The lobster is now ready to be used.

Shrimp

Follow the preceding directions for lobster, but simmer the whole, unpeeled shrimp for 5 minutes only. Allow them to cool in the cooking liquid. Then peel them, and warm them in butter, seasonings, and wine.

Écrevisses

These fresh-water shellfish are also called crayfish or crawfish, depending on what part of the country you come from. They look exactly like baby lobsters but are only 4 to 5 inches long. Prepare them like the shrimps in the preceding directions. Only the tail meat is used as a garnish. The chests and the rest of the shells may be ground up to make a shellfish butter, page 104.

Shelled Fresh Oysters

Poach the oysters at just below the simmer for 3 or 4 minutes in their natural juices until they swell. Drain them, and they are ready to use.

Mussels

Scrub and soak 1 quart of fresh mussels as directed on page 226. Then place them in a covered enameled or stainless steel saucepan with ½ cup of dry white wine or ⅓ cup of dry white vermouth, 3 tablespoons of minced shallot or green onion, 3 parsley sprigs, and a pinch of pepper. Boil rapidly for about

5 minutes, tossing several times, until the shells swing open. Remove the mussels from their shells, and they are ready to use.

SOME CLASSIC COMBINATIONS

The same cream and egg-yolk fish sauce described in the recipe for *filets de poisson gratinés à la parisienne* on page 211 becomes even more rich and velvety if a fairly large quantity of butter is beaten into it just before serving. The more you beat in, the more delicious the sauce becomes. But as in all heavily buttered sauces, it cannot be kept warm once buttered or the butter will liquefy and either thin out the sauce, or rise up and float on top. Here in outline are some traditional combinations of poached fish *filets* and various shellfish garnitures to give you an idea of what you can do. You can, of course, make up your own selection. In each case, in the following recipes, the sauce takes on the name of the dish. Serve your finest white Burgundy with any of these, and they should be considered a separate course, accompanied only by hot French bread.

---

* *SOLE À LA DIEPPOISE*

[Fish *Filets* with Mussels and Shrimp]

This recipe is the model for the variations to follow.
For 6 people

Poaching the fish

2½ lbs. sole or flounder filets poached in white
wine, page 208
1 quart fresh mussels
steamed in white wine,
page 213
½ lb. shelled shrimp
warmed in butter and
seasonings, page 213

Arrange the poached fish *filets* on a lightly buttered serving platter and surround them with the mussels and shrimp. Just before serving, cover the platter and reheat the fish for a few minutes over simmering water. Drain off any accumulated liquid before napping the fish with the following sauce:

For 2½ cups of sauce

A 2½-quart enameled saucepan
3 Tb butter

Following the technique for *sauce parisienne* on page 212, cook the flour and butter slowly together until they foam and froth for 2 minutes. Off heat, beat in

4 Tb flour

The fish-poaching and mussel-steaming liquids combined and boiled down to 1 cup

¾ cup milk

2 egg yolks and ½ cup whipping cream blended in a 2-quart mixing bowl

Salt and pepper

Drops of lemon juice

the hot fish cooking liquid, then the milk. Boil 1 minute. Beat the hot sauce by droplets into the yolks and cream. Return mixture to saucepan and boil, stirring, for 1 minute. Thin out with more cream if necessary, and correct seasoning. Strain. Film top of sauce with a tablespoon of melted butter if not to be served immediately.

4 to 16 Tb softened butter (6 to 8 Tb is usual)

Just before serving the fish, bring the sauce to the simmer. Then remove it from heat and beat in the butter 1 tablespoon at a time.

Final assembly

6 whole cooked shrimp in their shells

6 to 12 thin slices of canned truffles

Immediately spoon the sauce over the hot fish and shellfish. Decorate with the shrimp and truffles and serve.

VARIATIONS

The following are all constructed in exactly the same manner as the preceding *sole à la dieppoise*. Directions for poaching the fish are on page 208; for the shellfish garnitures, on page 212.

Sole à la Normande

[Fish *Filets* with Shellfish and Mushrooms]

Follow the preceding recipe, but to the garniture add oysters, mushrooms, and *écrevisses,* if available. Decorate the sauced fish with whole shrimps or *écrevisses,* truffle slices, and *croûtons* (triangles of white bread sautéed in butter), page 199.

Sole Walewska

[Fish *Filets* with Shellfish and Truffles]

Same as the *sole à la dieppoise,* but the *filets* are garnished with *écrevisses* or shrimp, and lobster meat, and instead of beating plain butter into the sauce, use the shellfish butter on page 104. Decorate the sauced fish with truffle slices, and cooked lobster claws or whole shrimp.

Sole à la Nantua

[Fish *Filets* with *Écrevisses*]

Same as the *sole à la dieppoise,* but the fish is garnished with *écrevisses,* and shellfish butter, page 104, rather than plain butter is beaten into the sauce.

Sole Bonne Femme

[Fish *Filets* with Mushrooms]

Poach the fish *filets* in white wine and sliced mushrooms as for the *sole Bercy* on page 210. Make the sauce following the recipe for the *sole à la dieppoise.* Garnish the sauced fish with 6 fluted mushroom caps, page 510, which have been stewed in butter and lemon juice, page 511.

Filets de Sole Farcis

[Stuffed Fish *Filets*]

Make 1 cup of the fish quenelle mixture on page 185. Mix into it ¼ cup of finely diced mushroom *duxelles,* page 515, and 2 to 3 tablespoons additional whipping cream. Place a spoonful in the center of each seasoned, raw *filet,* and fold or roll the *filet* to enclose the filling. Tie with white string. Poach, garnish, and sauce the *filets* following any of the preceding suggestions.

COQUILLES ST. JACQUES À LA PARISIENNE

[Scallops and Mushrooms in White Wine Sauce]

Exactly the same *sauce parisienne* as that for the poached fish *filets* in the preceding recipes is delicious with scallops *gratinéed* in their shells. This dish may be prepared ahead, and *gratinéed* just before serving. A fine, chilled white Burgundy or a very good white Graves would go well with it. Scallops are usually served as a first course, or as a light luncheon dish.

For 6 scallop shells

Cooking the scallops

1 cup dry white wine or ¾ cup dry white vermouth
½ tsp salt
Pinch of pepper
½ bay leaf
2 Tb minced shallots or green onions
A 2-quart enameled or stainless steel saucepan

Simmer the wine and flavorings for 5 minutes.

1 lb. washed scallops
½ lb. sliced fresh mushrooms

Add the scallops and mushrooms to the wine, and pour in enough water barely to cover ingredients. Bring to the simmer. Cover, and simmer slowly for 5 minutes. Remove scallops and mushrooms with a slotted spoon, and set aside in a bowl.

The sauce

Rapidly boil down the cooking liquid until it has reduced to 1 cup.

A 2-quart enameled or stainless steel saucepan
3 Tb butter
4 Tb flour
¾ cup milk
2 egg yolks
½ cup whipping cream, more if needed
Salt and pepper
Drops of lemon juice

Following the directions in *sauce parisienne,* page 212, cook the butter and flour slowly together for 2 minutes. Off heat, blend in the boiling cooking liquid, then the milk. Boil 1 minute. Blend the egg yolks and cream in a bowl, then beat the hot sauce into them by driblets. Return the sauce to the pan and boil, stirring, for 1 minute. Thin out with more cream if necessary. Season to taste with salt, pepper, and lemon juice. Strain.

Final assembly

6 scallop shells or pyrex or porcelain shells of ⅓ cup capacity

Cut the scallops into crosswise pieces about ⅛ inch thick.

½ Tb butter
6 Tb grated Swiss cheese

Blend two thirds of the sauce with the scallops and mushrooms. Butter the shells. Spoon the scallops and mushrooms into them, and cover with the rest of the

1½ Tb butter cut into 6 pieces

sauce. Sprinkle with cheese and dot with butter. Arrange the shells on a broiling pan.

(*) Set aside or refrigerate until ready to *gratiné*.

Fifteen minutes before serving, set the scallops 8 to 9 inches under a moderately hot broiler to heat through gradually, and to brown the top of the sauce. Serve as soon as possible.

TWO RECIPES FROM PROVENCE

COQUILLES ST. JACQUES À LA PROVENÇALE

[Scallops *Gratinéed* with Wine, Garlic, and Herbs]

This good recipe may be prepared in advance and *gratinéed* just before serving. The following proportions are sufficient for a first course. Double them for a main course. Serve a chilled *rosé,* or a dry white wine such as *côtes de Provence.*

For 6 scallop shells

⅓ cup minced yellow onions
1 Tb butter
1½ Tb minced shallot or green onions
1 clove minced garlic

Cook the onions slowly in butter in a small saucepan for 5 minutes or so, until tender and translucent but not browned. Stir in the shallots or onions, and garlic, and cook slowly for 1 minute more. Set aside.

1½ lbs. washed scallops
Salt and pepper
1 cup sifted flour in a dish

Dry the scallops and cut into slices ¼ inch thick. Just before cooking, sprinkle with salt and pepper, roll in flour, and shake off excess flour.

2 Tb butter
1 Tb olive oil
A 10-inch enameled skillet

Sauté the scallops quickly in very hot butter and oil for 2 minutes to brown them lightly.

⅔ cup dry white wine, or ½ cup dry white vermouth and 3 Tb water
½ bay leaf
⅛ tsp thyme

Pour the wine, or the vermouth and water, into the skillet with the scallops. Add the herbs and the cooked onion mixture. Cover the skillet and simmer for 5 minutes. Then uncover, and if necessary boil down the sauce rapidly for a minute until it is lightly thickened. Correct seasoning, and discard bay leaf.

6 buttered scallop shells, or porcelain or pyrex shells, of ⅓ cup capacity ¼ cup grated Swiss cheese 2 Tb butter cut into 6 pieces	Spoon the scallops and sauce into the shells. Sprinkle with cheese and dot with butter. (*) Set aside or refrigerate until ready to *gratiné*.
	Just before serving, run under a moderately hot broiler for 3 to 4 minutes to heat through, and to brown the cheese lightly.

THON À LA PROVENÇALE

[Tuna or Swordfish Steaks with Wine, Tomatoes, and Herbs]

Tomatoes, wine, herbs, and garlic are a good contrast to tuna or swordfish, and this dish can be served either hot or cold. Boiled potatoes and green beans would go well, and a chilled *rosé* wine, or a dry white such as *côtes de Provence,* or Riesling.

For 6 to 8 people

3 lbs. fresh tuna or swordfish cut into steaks ¾ inch thick (if fish is frozen, thaw it) A 9- by 14- inch pyrex baking dish about 2½ inches deep 1 tsp salt 2 Tb lemon juice 6 Tb olive oil ⅛ tsp pepper	Remove skin, and cut fish steaks into serving pieces. Blend salt and lemon juice in baking dish, then beat in the oil and pepper. Arrange the fish in the dish, and baste with the marinade. Cover with waxed paper and marinate 1½ to 2 hours, turning and basting the fish with the marinade several times. Drain the fish and dry it thoroughly on paper towels. Discard the marinade, which will be strong and fishy.
3 to 4 Tb olive oil, more if needed A skillet	Sauté the fish rapidly in very hot olive oil for a minute or two on each side to brown lightly. Rearrange the fish in the baking dish.
	Preheat oven to 350 degrees.
1 cup minced yellow onions 3 lbs. fresh, ripe, red toma-	Cook the onions slowly in the skillet for 5 minutes or so until tender but not browned. Stir in the tomato

toes peeled, seeded, juiced, and chopped, page 505
2 cloves mashed garlic
½ tsp oregano
¼ tsp thyme
¼ tsp salt
⅛ tsp pepper

pulp, garlic, seasonings, and herbs. Cover skillet and cook slowly for 5 minutes. Correct seasoning, and spread the tomato mixture over the fish.

---

1 cup dry white wine or ⅔ cup dry white vermouth

Place a cover or aluminum foil over the baking dish and bring to the simmer on top of the stove. Then set in lower third of preheated oven and bake for 15 minutes. Pour in the wine and bake for 30 minutes more, turning oven down to 325 degrees as soon as fish is simmering.

A serving platter

Remove fish to a serving platter, scraping the sauce off the fish and back into the baking dish. Keep fish warm for about 5 minutes while finishing the sauce.

---

1 to 2 Tb tomato paste for added flavor and color
Optional: 1 Tb meat glaze, page 110, for depth of flavor

Boil down the sauce over high heat until it has reduced to about 2 cups. Stir in the tomato paste and optional meat glaze. Simmer for a moment, and correct seasoning.

---

1 Tb flour blended to a paste with 1 Tb softened butter
2 to 3 Tb chopped parsley

Off heat, beat in the flour and butter paste, and bring again to the simmer for 1 minute. Stir in the chopped parsley, spoon the sauce over the fish, and serve. (*) Fish may be set aside, then covered and reheated in the oven, but be careful not to overcook it.

Other Fish—Green cod or coalfish, ocean pollack, and halibut may be cooked in the same way. They need no marinating and require only 20 to 30 minutes of baking.

TWO FAMOUS LOBSTER DISHES

A NOTE ON DEALING WITH LIVE LOBSTERS

If you object to steaming or splitting a live lobster, it may be killed almost instantly just before cooking if you plunge the point of a knife into the head between the eyes, or sever the spinal cord by making a small incision in the back of the shell at the juncture of the chest and the tail.

HOMARD THERMIDOR

[Lobster Thermidor – *Gratinéed* in its Shell]

So many steps are involved in the preparation of a really splendid lobster Thermidor, no wonder it costs a fortune in any restaurant! But it is not a particularly difficult dish to execute, and everything may be prepared in advance and heated up just before serving. This is an especially attractive recipe for lobster Thermidor because the meat is stirred in hot butter before it is sauced, and turns a rosy red. Buy lobsters weighing a good 2 pounds each, so the shells will be large enough to hold the filling.

For 6 people

Steaming the lobsters

A covered, enameled or stainless steel kettle with tight-fitting cover

3 cups dry white wine (or 2 cups dry white vermouth) and 2 cups water

A large onion, a medium carrot, and a celery stalk, all thinly sliced

6 parsley sprigs

1 bay leaf

¼ tsp thyme

6 peppercorns

1 Tb fresh or dried tarragon

3 live lobsters, 2 lbs. each

Simmer wine, water, vegetables, herbs, and seasonings in the kettle for 15 minutes. Then bring to a rolling boil and add the live lobsters. Cover and boil for about 20 minutes. The lobsters are done when they are bright red and the long head-feelers can be pulled from the sockets fairly easily.

½ lb. sliced fresh mushrooms

1 Tb butter

1 tsp lemon juice

¼ tsp salt

A covered enameled or stainless steel saucepan

While the lobsters are steaming, stew the mushrooms slowly in the covered saucepan with the butter, lemon juice, and salt for 10 minutes.

The sauce

When the lobsters are done, remove them from the kettle. Pour the mushroom cooking juices into the lobster steaming juices in the kettle and boil down rapidly until liquid has reduced to about 2¼ cups.

A 4-cup enameled or stainless steel saucepan	Strain into the saucepan and bring to the simmer.
5 Tb butter **6 Tb flour** **A 1½-quart, heavy-bottomed, enameled or stainless steel saucepan** **A wooden spoon** **A wire whip** **1 Tb cream**	Cook the butter and flour slowly together in the second saucepan for 2 minutes without browning. Off heat, beat in the simmering lobster-cooking liquid. Boil, stirring, for 1 minute. Set aside. Film top of sauce with the cream.
A 3-quart mixing bowl **1 Tb dry mustard** **2 egg yolks** **½ cup whipping cream** **Pinch of cayenne pepper**	Split the lobsters in half lengthwise, keeping the shell halves intact. Discard sand sacks in the heads, and the intestinal tubes. Rub lobster coral and green matter through a fine sieve into the mixing bowl, and blend into it the mustard, egg yolks, cream, and pepper. Beat the sauce into this mixture by driblets.
4 to 6 Tb more whipping cream	Return the sauce to the pan and, stirring with a wooden spoon, bring it to the boil and boil slowly for 2 minutes. Thin out with tablespoons of cream. Sauce should be thick enough to coat a spoon fairly heavily. Taste carefully for seasoning. Set aside, top filmed with a spoonful of cream.

Sautéing the lobster meat

Remove the meat from the lobster tails and claws, and cut it into ⅜-inch cubes.

A 12-inch enameled or stainless steel skillet **4 Tb butter** **⅓ cup cognac**	Set the skillet with the butter over moderate heat. When the butter foam begins to subside, stir in the lobster meat and sauté, stirring slowly, for about 5 minutes until the meat has turned a rosy color. Pour in the cognac and boil for a minute or two, shaking the skillet, until the liquid has reduced by half.

Final assembly

Preheat oven to 425 degrees.

Fold the cooked mushrooms and two thirds of the sauce into the skillet with the lobster meat.

A shallow roasting pan or fireproof serving platter	Arrange the split lobster shells in the roasting pan. Heap the lobster mixture into the shells; cover with the remaining sauce. Sprinkle with cheese and dot with butter.
½ cup grated Parmesan or Swiss cheese	
2 Tb butter cut into bits	(*) May be prepared ahead up to this point and refrigerated.

Place in upper third of 425-degree oven for 10 to 15 minutes, until lobster is bubbling and the top of the sauce is nicely browned. Serve immediately on a platter or serving plates.

VARIATION

Homard aux Aromates

[Lobster Steamed in Wine with Herb Sauce]

This is not a variation of lobster Thermidor at all, but it fits well into this niche.

Ingredients for steaming 3 lobsters in wine, herbs, and aromatic vegetables as in the preceding Thermidor recipe	Steam the lobsters for about 20 minutes as described in the preceding recipe. Remove them. Rapidly boil down their cooking liquid until it has reduced to 2 cups. The sliced carrots and onions need not be removed.
1½ Tb flour blended to a paste with 1½ Tb softened butter	Off heat, beat in the flour and butter paste. Then bring to the boil for 15 seconds. Reduce to the simmer and stir in the cream by tablespoons until the sauce is the consistency of a light cream soup. Correct seasoning and stir in the herbs.
About 1 cup of whipping cream	
3 to 4 Tb fresh minced green herbs: parsley, chervil, and tarragon, or parsley only	Split the lobsters in two, lengthwise. Remove stomach sacks in heads and intestinal tubes. Arrange the lobsters in a serving dish, pour the sauce over them, and serve.

HOMARD À L'AMÉRICAINE

[Lobster Simmered with Wine, Tomatoes, Garlic, and Herbs]

Homard à l'américaine is live lobster chopped into serving pieces, sautéed in oil until the shells turn red, then flamed in cognac, and simmered with wine, aromatic vegetables, herbs, and tomatoes. In France, unless you are at a formal dinner, the meat is left in the shells and guests dig in, flanked by finger bowl and napkin. We have noticed that many Americans prefer that the meat be removed from the shells before the dish is served, which is too bad, as it makes more work for the cook.

The origin of *homard à l'américaine* is a subject for discussion. Some authorities call it *à l'armoricaine,* after the ancient province of Armorique in Brittany where lobsters grow. Others say *armoricaine* is nonsense because the tomato flavoring is quite untypical of Brittany and that the recipe is far more likely the product of a Paris chef with Provençal inclinations who titled his dish after an American client, or after the exotic origins of the tomato. In any case it is a splendid creation for fresh lobster, and though we are not partial to frozen lobster tails, it is one of the best ways we know to cook them.

Risotto simmered in fish stock, or steamed rice, and a dry white wine with body such as Burgundy, Côtes du Rhône, or Graves would make fine accompaniments.

For 6 people

Three 1½-lb. live lobsters (or 6 frozen lobster tails partially defrosted and cut in half lengthwise)	Split the lobsters in two lengthwise. Remove stomach sacks (in the head) and intestinal tubes. Reserve coral and green matter. Remove claws and joints and crack them. Separate tails from chests.
3 Tb olive oil **A heavy 12-inch enameled skillet or casserole**	Heat the oil in the skillet until it is very hot but not smoking. Add the lobster pieces, meat-side down, and sauté for several minutes, turning them, until the shells are bright red. Remove lobster to a side dish.
1 medium carrot, finely diced **1 medium onion, finely diced**	Stir in the diced carrot and onion, and cook slowly for 5 minutes or until almost tender.
	Preheat oven to 350 degrees.
Salt and pepper **3 Tb minced shallots or green onions** **1 clove mashed garlic**	Season the lobster, return it to the skillet, and add the shallots or green onions, and the garlic. With the skillet over moderate heat, pour in the cognac. Avert your face and ignite the cognac with a lighted match and

⅓ cup cognac

1 lb. fresh, ripe, tomatoes, peeled, seeded, juiced, and chopped, page 505

2 Tb tomato paste

1 cup fish stock, page 114, or ⅓ cup bottled clam juice

1½ cups dry white wine or 1 cup dry white vermouth

Optional: ½ Tb meat glaze, page 110

2 Tb chopped parsley

1 Tb fresh tarragon or 1 tsp dried tarragon

shake the skillet slowly until the flames have subsided. Stir in all the ingredients to the left. Bring to the simmer on top of the stove. Cover and place in middle level of preheated oven. Regulate heat so lobster simmers quietly for 20 minutes.

---

6 Tb softened butter

The lobster coral and green matter

A 3-quart mixing bowl

While the lobster is simmering, force the lobster coral and green matter with the butter through a fine sieve into the mixing bowl and set aside.

When the lobster is done, remove it to a side dish. Take the meat out of the shells if you wish. Set skillet with its cooking liquids over high heat and boil down rapidly until sauce has reduced and thickened slightly. It will acquire more body later when the butter and coral mixture is added. Taste very carefully for seasoning.

(*) Recipe may be completed to this point, and finished later.

Return the lobster to the sauce and bring to the simmer to reheat the lobster. Beat a cupful of hot sauce by driblets into the coral and butter mixture, then pour the mixture into the skillet with the lobster. Shake and swirl the skillet over low heat for 2 to 3 minutes to poach the coral and green matter, but do not bring the sauce near the simmer again.

A ring of *risotto* or steamed rice

2 to 3 Tb minced parsley, or parsley and fresh tarragon

Arrange the lobster and sauce in the rice ring, decorate with herbs, and serve immediately.

MUSSELS

Moules

Mussels, with their long, oval, blue-black shells and delicious pink-orange flesh are often called the poor man's oyster. Clinging to rocks and piers along the seacoasts everywhere, they can be had for the picking at low tide. If you are gathering mussels yourself, take them only from places washed by clear, clean, sea water.

SCRUBBING AND SOAKING MUSSELS

Before they can be cooked, mussels must have a rather long and careful cleaning process to remove all possible sand from their interiors, and to rid the shells of any slime and dirt which might spoil the excellent juices they render as they steam open. Discard any mussels that are not firmly closed, or which feel lighter in weight than the rest. Discard also any too-heavy mussels, as they may be nothing but sand enclosed between two mussel shells. Scrub each mussel very clean with a rough brush under running water. Then with a small knife, scrape off the tuft of hairs, or beard, which protrudes from between one side of the closed shell halves. Set the mussels in a basin or bucket of fresh water for an hour or two so they will disgorge their sand and also lose a bit of their saltiness. Lift the mussels out of the water into a colander, wash and drain them again, and they are ready to cook.

Note: Some cooks add flour to the soaking water on the theory that while the mussels eat the flour and become fatter and more succulent, they are at the same time disgorging their sand more thoroughly. Use ⅓ cup of flour for each 2 quarts of water, beating the flour and a bit of water with a whip first, to mix it thoroughly. Then, after soaking the mussels, lift them into a colander, and rinse them in cold water.

CANNED MUSSELS

Beware of sand if you are using canned mussels. If there is any sand at all in the juices at the bottom of the can, soak the mussels in several changes of cold water. Eat one, and if it is sandy, continue washing the mussels. Good quality canned mussels may be substituted for fresh mussels in all but the first two of the following recipes; the canned juices may be used as stock for your sauce. Simmer the juices with a bit of white wine or vermouth, and fill out the quantity of stock called for in your recipe with boiling milk.

MOULES À LA MARINIÈRE · I

[Fresh Mussels Steamed Open in Wine and Flavorings]

Here is the simplest version of this most typical of French methods for cooking mussels. They are steamed open in a big pot with wine and flavorings, and it takes only about 5 minutes. Then the mussels, shells and all, are dipped out into soup plates, and the cooking liquor is poured over them. Each guest removes the mussels one by one from their shells with fingers or a fork and discards the shells into a side dish. In addition to shell dish and fork, provide your guests with a soupspoon for drinking up the mussel juices, a big napkin, and a finger bowl. Along with the mussels serve French bread, butter, and a chilled, light, dry white wine such as Muscadet, dry Graves, or one of the Pouillys.

For 6 to 8 people

2 cups of light, dry white wine or 1 cup dry white vermouth

An 8- to 10-quart enameled kettle with cover

½ cup minced shallots, or green onions, or very finely minced onions

8 parsley sprigs

½ bay leaf

¼ tsp thyme

⅛ tsp pepper

6 Tb butter

Bring the wine to the boil in the kettle with the rest of the ingredients listed. Boil for 2 to 3 minutes to evaporate its alcohol and to reduce its volume slightly.

6 quarts scrubbed, soaked mussels, page 226

Add the mussels to the kettle. Cover tightly and boil quickly over high heat. Frequently grasp the kettle with both hands, your thumbs clamped to the cover, and toss the mussels in the kettle with an up and down slightly jerky motion so the mussels will change levels and cook evenly. In about 5 minutes the shells will swing open and the mussels are done.

½ cup roughly chopped parsley

With a big skimmer, dip the mussels into wide soup plates. Allow the cooking liquid to settle for a moment so any sand will sink to the bottom. Then ladle the liquid over the mussels, sprinkle with parsley and serve immediately.

MOULES À LA MARINIÈRE · II
[Mussels Steamed with Wine, Flavorings, and Bread Crumbs]

In this quite different method, bread crumbs cook with the mussels and give a liaison to the sauce. Here you must be sure that the mussels are most carefully washed and soaked so there will be no sand to mix itself with the crumbs.

For 6 to 8 people

3 cups finely minced onions
¼ lb. (8 Tb) butter
An 8- to 10-quart enameled kettle with cover

Cook the onions slowly in the butter for about 10 minutes, until they are tender and translucent but not browned.

2 cups light, dry white wine or 1 cup dry white vermouth
1½ cups fine, dry, white bread crumbs from home-made type of bread
½ cup chopped parsley
⅛ tsp pepper
1 bay leaf
¼ tsp thyme

Stir in all the ingredients at the left, cover the kettle, and simmer very slowly for 10 minutes, stirring occasionally, and making sure the mixture does not scorch. Remove bay leaf.

6 quarts scrubbed, soaked mussels, page 226
⅓ cup chopped parsley

Add the mussels. Cover and toss them in the kettle. Set over high heat, tossing frequently until the mussel shells swing open. Ladle the mussels and sauce into soup plates, sprinkle with parsley, and serve.

MOULES AU BEURRE D'ESCARGOT
MOULES À LA PROVENÇALE
[Mussels on the Half Shell, *Gratinéed*]

These are delicious as a first course. Serve them with French bread and a rather strong, dry, white wine such as Mâcon, *côtes de Provence,* white Chianti, or a domestic equivalent.

For 4 to 6 people

48 extra large, scrubbed and soaked mussels, page 226

For this recipe you may steam the mussels open as for *moules à la marinière I,* preceding, or you may open the raw mussels with a knife. We prefer the latter method. When the mussels are open, discard the empty shell halves. Arrange the remaining half shells holding the mussels in a shallow baking and serving dish, or individual fireproof dishes.

6 ounces or 1½ sticks of softened butter
A 2-quart mixing bowl
A wooden spoon
3 Tb finely minced shallots or green onions
1 to 3 cloves mashed garlic, depending on your love of garlic
¼ cup minced parsley
½ cup fine, white, dry bread crumbs
Salt and pepper to taste

Beat the butter in the mixing bowl until it is light and creamy. Beat in the rest of the ingredients and taste for seasoning. Spread a bit of the mixture over each mussel.
(*) May be prepared ahead of time to this point. Cover the mussels with waxed paper and refrigerate.

About 2 or 3 minutes before serving, run the mussels under a very hot broiler until the butter is bubbling in the shells and the crumbs have browned lightly. Serve immediately.

SALADE DE MOULES

[Mussels Marinated in Oil and Herbs]

2 cups of cooked, fresh mussels (or canned or frozen mussels)

Steam fresh mussels open as directed in *moules à la marinière I,* page 227. Discard shells.

4 Tb light olive oil or salad oil
1 Tb dry white vermouth and 1 Tb lemon juice
2 Tb finely minced shallots or green onions
3 Tb minced parsley or a mixture of fresh green herbs
Pinch of pepper

Toss the mussels in a bowl with the ingredients at the left and allow them to marinate half an hour before serving. They may be served just as they are, or you may drain them and fold into them half a cup of mayonnaise, page 87. Place them in a bowl or individual shells.

∗   *MOULES EN SAUCE*
    MOUCLADES
    MOULES À LA POULETTE
    MOULES À LA BÉARNAISE

[Sauced Mussels Served in Scallop Shells]

This is a more formal recipe for mussels. They are steamed open with wine and flavorings, then a rich, creamy, buttery sauce is made with their cooking liquid. This is the same heavily buttered *sauce parisienne* found on page 214, but with a quite different flavor. If the mussels are served on the half shell, as they often are in Brittany, they are called *mouclades*. We have suggested in the following recipe that they be shelled, sauced, and served in scallop shells; done this way they may be prepared ahead of time. There are naturally many versions and flavorings for mussels served in a sauce. For instance, if you omitted the curry, garlic, and fennel in the recipe, and substituted ½ cup of mushroom stems, your mussel dish would be *à la poulette*. Also, if you omitted the special flavorings, and the cream, egg yolks, and butter enrichment, then stirred a cup of *béarnaise* sauce into your *velouté* just before serving, you would have *moules à la béarnaise*.

For 6 people

5 to 6 quarts scrubbed, soaked mussels, page 226. (A 2-hour soaking is advisable here to rid the mussels of as much salt as possible)

The wine and flavoring for *moules à la marinière I*, page 227, plus:
¼ tsp curry powder
A pinch of fennel
1 clove mashed garlic

Steam the mussels open in wine and flavorings, following the method for *moules à la marinière I*, page 227. Shell the mussels and place them in a bowl. Strain the mussel cooking liquor into an enameled saucepan and rapidly boil it down over high heat to concentrate its flavor. Taste it frequently as it boils; you may find that if you reduce it too much, the salt content will be overpowering. Measure out 1½ cups of the concentrated liquor to be used in the following sauce:

3 Tb butter
4 Tb flour
A 2-quart, heavy-bottomed enameled saucepan
A wooden spoon

Stir the butter and flour over low heat in the saucepan until they foam and froth together for 2 minutes without coloring. Remove *roux* from heat.

A wire whip	Strain the hot mussel cooking liquor into the flour and butter *roux,* being sure not to add any sand that may have collected at the bottom of the mussel kettle. Beat *roux* and liquid with a wire whip to blend thoroughly. Bring to the boil, stirring, for 1 minute. Sauce will be very thick.
2 egg yolks ½ cup whipping cream A mixing bowl A wire whip A wooden spoon Salt and pepper Drops of lemon juice	Blend the egg yolks and cream in the mixing bowl. Gradually beat in the hot sauce, in a thin stream of droplets. Pour the sauce back into the pan. Set over moderately high heat and stir with a wooden spoon, reaching all over the bottom of the pan, until the sauce comes to the boil. Boil 1 minute, stirring. Remove from heat and taste carefully for seasoning, stirring in salt, pepper, and drops of lemon juice if necessary. Fold the mussels into the sauce. (*) If not to be served immediately, clean sauce off sides of pan and film top of sauce with milk. Set aside uncovered, and reheat to simmer when ready to use.
4 to 8 Tb softened butter 6 buttered scallop shells or porcelain or pyrex shells of ½ cup capacity Parsley sprigs	Just before serving, and off heat, fold the butter into the hot sauce and mussels 1 tablespoon at a time. Fold until each bit is absorbed before adding the next. Heap the mixture into the shells, decorate with parsley, and serve immediately.

VARIATIONS

Pilaf de Moules

[Sauced Mussels in a Rice Ring]

Prepare and sauce the mussels exactly as in the preceding recipe, but serve them in a ring of *risotto,* page 532.

Soupe aux Moules

[Mussel Soup]

The very same recipe may also be turned into a mussel soup. After enriching the sauce with cream and egg yolks, thin it out to a cream soup consistency with several cups of boiling milk. Then add the mussels, and bring just to the simmer. Off heat, and just before serving, fold in 2 tablespoons of butter, one by one. Decorate with minced parsley or chervil.

OTHER RECIPES–OTHER SAUCES

Fish Recipes Appearing in Other Chapters

FISH SOUFFLÉS
Salmon Soufflé, page 166
Flounder Soufflé with *sauce mousseline sabayon,* page 168
Shellfish Soufflé, page 170
Fish Soufflé Baked on a Platter, page 170
Unmolded Soufflés, page 171

Fish Timbales, pages 174–5
Fish Quenelles, page 185
Creamed Shellfish, page 202
Shellfish *Quiche,* open-faced tart, page 149
Gratin of Canned Salmon or Tuna, or of Fish Leftovers, page 156
Bouillabaisse, page 52
Crab or Lobster in Aspic, pages 549, 553
Salmon Mousse, page 562
Fish and Shellfish Mousse, pages 562, 564

Sauces for Boiled or Baked Fish

Hollandaise and Variations, pages 79 to 85
Mock Hollandaise and Variations, page 64
White Butter Sauce and Lemon Butter Sauce, pages 96 and 98
Brown Butter Sauce, page 98
Sauce Chivry, white-wine herb sauce, page 62
Aïoli, garlic mayonnaise, page 92
Sauce Alsacienne, herbal mayonnaise with soft-boiled eggs, page 93
Sauce Ravigote, vinaigrette with herbs, capers and onions, page 95
Sour Cream Dressing, page 95

Sauces for Sautéed or Broiled Fish

Mustard Sauce, page 66
Brown Butter Sauce, page 98
Many of the Flavored Butters, pages 100 to 105

Sauces for Cold Fish

Mayonnaise and Variations, pages 86 to 94
Sauce Ravigote, vinaigrette with herbs, capers, and onions, page 95
Sour Cream Dressing, page 95

CHAPTER SIX

POULTRY

Volaille

CHICKEN

Poulet – Poularde

Some of the most glorious dishes of the French *cuisine* have been created for chicken, and almost all the fundamentals of French cookery and sauce making are to be found somewhere in the chicken realm. The most important aspect of chicken cooking is that you procure a good and flavorsome bird. Modern poultry raising has done wonders in making it possible to grow a fine-looking chicken in record time and to sell it at a most reasonable price, but rarely does anyone in the country discuss flavor. If you are interested in price alone, you will often end up with something that tastes like the stuffing inside a teddy bear and needs strong dousings of herbs, wines, and spices to make it at all palatable. A chicken should taste like chicken and be so good in itself that it is an absolute delight to eat as a perfectly plain, buttery roast, sauté, or grill. So when you buy chicken, make every attempt to find a market which takes special pride in the quality and flavor of its poultry.

CHICKEN TYPES

Chickens fall into several categories, all of which relate to age. Age dictates the cooking method. A broiler, for instance, may be broiled, or roasted, but its very tender flesh becomes dry and stringy if it is fricasseed. The full-flavored stewing hen, on the other hand, must be fricasseed or stewed, as its flesh is too firm to be cooked in any other way.

AMERICAN CHICKEN	NEAREST FRENCH EQUIVALENT	USUAL U.S. WEIGHT READY TO COOK	COOKING METHOD
SQUAB CHICKEN or Baby Broiler	*Poussin* *Coquelet*	¾ to 1 lb.	Broil, Grill, Roast
BROILER (2 to 3 months old)	*Poulet Nouveau*	1½ to 2½ lbs.	Broil, Grill, Roast
FRYER	*Poulet de Grain* (small) *Poulet Reine* (larger)	2½ to 3½ lbs.	Fry, Sauté, Roast, Casserole Roast, Fricassee, Poach
ROASTER	*Poulet Gras* *Poularde*	Usually 4 to 6½ lbs.	Roast, Casserole Roast, Poach, Fricassee
CAPON and CAPONETTE	*Chapon*	Usually 4 to 7 lbs.	Roast, Casserole Roast, Poach, Fricassee
STEWING CHICKEN or FOWL (8 to 12 months old)	*Poule de l'Année*	Usually over 4 lbs.	Stew, Fricassee
OLD HEN, COCK, or ROOSTER (over 12 months old)	*Vielle Poule* *Coq*	Usually over 4 lbs.	*If still tender:* Stew, Fricassee *If tough:* Soup Stock, Forcemeat, *Pâté;* Pressure cook

DEFROSTING FROZEN CHICKEN

The best method for defrosting frozen chicken, according to those in the business, is the slowest: leave it in its transparent wrapper and let it thaw in the refrigerator. It will lose much less of its juice and flavor. The best alternative is to unwrap it and thaw it in a basin of cold, running water, removing the package of giblets from the cavity as soon as it can be pried loose, and pulling the legs and wings away from the body as soon as they will move.

Sometimes frozen roasters, fryers, and broilers can be quite tough and stringy. According to the Poultry and Egg National Board, this is usually the result of their having been frozen while they were too fresh. If the frozen chicken is flavorless, it may have thawed and been refrozen several times, so the juices escaped; or it may be too young a bird to have a developed flavor.

WASHING AND DRYING

Because commercially raised chickens, on the whole, are packed in a communal tub of ice during at least part of their processing, it is probably wise to give them a thorough washing and drying before storing or cooking—just to be on the safe side.

SINGEING

Usually American chickens have been plucked absolutely clean. If not, pluck and squeeze out feather follicles, then turn the chicken rapidly over a gas or alcohol flame to burn off any hairs or feather bits.

* CHICKEN STOCK

A little concentrated chicken stock is easy to make with the giblets and neck of a chicken and will always give more character to your sauce, however simple it may be.

Brown Chicken Stock

For about 1 cup

A heavy-bottomed, 2-quart saucepan
The chicken neck, gizzard, heart, and miscellaneous scraps
1 sliced onion
1 sliced carrot
1½ Tb rendered fresh pork fat or cooking oil

Chop the chicken into pieces of 1½ inches or less. Brown them with the vegetables in hot fat or oil.

2 cups white or brown stock, or canned beef bouillon, or chicken broth

Pour out the browning fat. Add the liquid, the herbs, and enough water to cover the chicken by ½ inch. Simmer partially covered for 1½ hours or more,

2 parsley sprigs
⅓ bay leaf
⅛ tsp thyme

skimming as necessary. Strain, degrease, and the stock is ready to use.

White Chicken Stock

Same as brown chicken stock, but do not brown the ingredients, and use white stock or canned chicken broth.

STUFFING WARNING

Stuffings may be prepared in advance, but a chicken should never be stuffed until just before it is cooked, as the mixture may sour inside the chicken and spoil the meat.

HOW TO TRUSS A CHICKEN

A whole chicken should be trussed so the legs, wings, and neck skin are held in place during its cooking, and the bird will make a neat and attractive appearance on the table. The following French method calls for a trussing or mattress needle and white string. There are two ties, one at the tail end to secure the drumsticks, and one at the breast end to fasten the wings and neck skin.

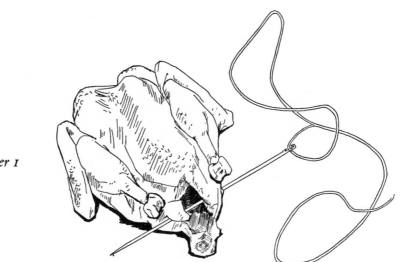

Tie Number 1

Thrust the needle through the lower part of the carcass.

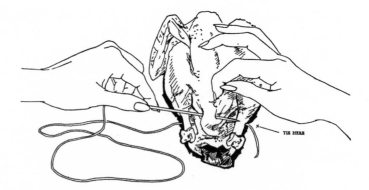

Come back over one drumstick, through the tip of the breastbone, and over the second drumstick. Tie.

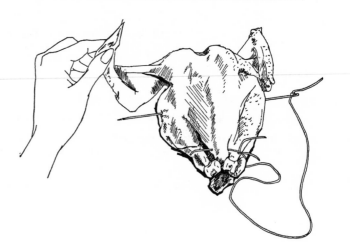

Tie Number 2

Push the needle through the carcass where the second joint and drumstick join, coming out at the corresponding point on the other side.

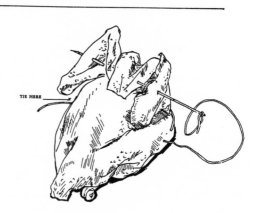

Turn the chicken on its breast. Fold the wings akimbo. Go through one wing, catch the neck skin against either side of the backbone, and come out the other wing. Draw the string tightly and tie.

The chicken is now ready for oven roasting, spit roasting, or poaching.

HOW TO TELL WHEN A CHICKEN IS DONE

A stewing chicken is done when its meat is tender if pierced with a fork. Roasters, fryers, and broilers are tender to begin with and are done when the flesh is cooked through so that the juices, when the meat is pricked deeply with a fork, run clear yellow with no trace of rosy color. For a whole chicken, the last drops of juice drained from the vent will run clear yellow with no rosy traces. While an underdone chicken is not fit to eat, it is a shame to over-cook chicken, allowing the meat to dry out and lose its juice and flavor. How-ever, we have noticed that the French criterion of doneness seems like under-doneness to some American palates. We consider a chicken to be cooked at a meat-thermometer reading of 175 to 180 degrees, and have based our recipes on these figures. The figure on American thermometers is 190 degrees.

TIMETABLE FOR WHOLE CHICKENS: Oven Roasting, Casserole Roasting, Spit Roasting, and Poaching

This table is based on unchilled, unstuffed chicken. Oven temperature for open-pan roasting is 350 degrees, for covered roasting, 325 degrees. Meat-thermometer reading is 175 to 180 degrees. Add 5 to 10 minutes more to the total roasting time if you wish a reading of 190 degrees. You will note that larger chickens require less cooking time per pound than smaller chickens. A 4-pound chicken takes an hour and 10 to 20 minutes, while a 7-pound bird re-quires only 20 to 30 minutes more. Stuffed chicken will take 10 to 30 minutes additional roasting than the total time indicated.

ROASTING TIMETABLE – OVEN TEMPERATURE: 350 DEGREES

READY-TO-COOK WEIGHT	UNDRAWN WEIGHT (DRESSED WEIGHT)	NUMBER OF PEOPLE SERVED	APPROXIMATE TOTAL COOKING TIME
¾ lb.	1 lb.	1 or 2	30 to 40 minutes
1 ¼ lbs.	2 lbs.	2	40 to 50 minutes
2 lbs.	3 lbs.	2 or 3	50 to 60 minutes
3 lbs.	4 lbs.	4	1 hour and 10 to 20 minutes
4 lbs.	5 lbs.	4 or 5	1 hour and 15 to 30 minutes
4½ lbs.	6 lbs.	5 or 6	1 hour and 25 to 40 minutes
5¼ lbs.	7 lbs.	6 or 8	1 hour and 30 to 45 minutes

ROAST CHICKEN

* *POULET RÔTI*

[Roast Chicken]

You can always judge the quality of a cook or a restaurant by roast chicken. While it does not require years of training to produce a juicy, brown, buttery, crisp-skinned, heavenly bird, it does entail such a greed for perfection that one is under compulsion to hover over the bird, listen to it, above all see that it is continually basted, and that it is done just to the proper turn. Spit roasting, where the chicken is wrapped in fat and continually rotated, is far less exacting than oven roasting where you must constantly turn and baste.

Small French chickens are frequently roasted without a stuffing. The cavity is seasoned with salt and butter, and the skin rubbed with butter. For oven roasting, it is browned lightly for 10 to 15 minutes at a temperature of 425 degrees, then the temperature is reduced to 350, and the chicken is turned and basted until it is done. A simple, short deglazing sauce is made with stock and the juices in the pan, giving just a scant spoonful for each serving.

VEGETABLE SUGGESTIONS

Broiled tomatoes, buttered green beans or peas, and sautéed, roasted, souffléed, or fried potatoes, or potato *crêpes*

One of the potato casseroles on page 523, and green peas or beans
Stuffed mushrooms, glazed carrots, and glazed onions
Ratatouille (eggplant casserole), page 503, and sautéed potatoes

WINE SUGGESTIONS

A light red wine, such as a Bordeaux-Médoc, or a *rosé*

For 4 people

Estimated roasting time for a 3-pound chicken: 1 hour and 10 to 20 minutes

Preheat oven to 425 degrees.

A 3-lb., ready-to-cook roasting or frying chicken
¼ tsp salt
2 Tb softened butter

Sprinkle the inside of the chicken with the salt, and smear in half the butter. Truss the chicken, page 237. Dry it thoroughly, and rub the skin with the rest of the butter.

A shallow roasting pan just large enough to hold the chicken easily
To flavor the sauce: a small sliced carrot and onion
For basting: a small saucepan containing 2 Tb melted butter, 1 Tb good cooking oil; a basting brush

Place the chicken breast up in the roasting pan. Strew the vegetables around it, and set it on a rack in the middle of the preheated oven. Allow the chicken to brown lightly for 15 minutes, turning it on the left side after 5 minutes, on the right side for the last 5 minutes, and basting it with the butter and oil after each turn. Baste rapidly, so oven does not cool off.
Reduce oven to 350 degrees. Leave the chicken on its side, and baste every 8 to 10 minutes, using the fat in the roasting pan when the butter and oil are exhausted. Regulate oven heat so chicken is making cooking noises, but fat is not burning.

¼ tsp salt

Halfway through estimated roasting time, salt the chicken and turn it on its other side. Continue basting.

¼ tsp salt

Fifteen minutes before end of estimated roasting time, salt again and turn the chicken breast up. Continue basting.

Indications that the chicken is almost done are: a sudden rain of splutters in the oven, a swelling of the breast and slight puff of the skin, the drumstick is tender when pressed and can be moved in its socket. To check further, prick the thickest part of the drumstick with a fork. Its juices should run clear yellow. As a final check, lift the chicken and drain the juices from its vent. If the last drops are clear yellow, the chicken is definitely done. If not, roast another 5 minutes, and test again.

When done, discard trussing strings and set the chicken on a hot platter. It should sit at room temperature for 5 to 10 minutes before being carved, so its juices will retreat back into the tissues.

½ Tb minced shallot or green onion
1 cup brown chicken stock, canned chicken broth, or beef bouillon
Salt and pepper
1 to 2 Tb softened butter

Remove all but two tablespoons of fat from the pan. Stir in the minced shallot or onion and cook slowly for 1 minute. Add the stock and boil rapidly over high heat, scraping up coagulated roasting juices with a wooden spoon and letting liquid reduce to about ½ cup. Season with salt and pepper. Off heat and just before serving, swirl in the enrichment butter by bits until it has been absorbed. Pour a spoonful of the sauce over the chicken, and send the rest to the table in a sauceboat.

(*) AHEAD-OF-TIME NOTE

Roast chicken can wait for 20 to 30 minutes in the turned-off hot oven, its door ajar. It cannot be reheated or it loses its fresh and juicy quality.

Poulet à la Broche

[Spit-roasted Chicken]

Estimated roasting time: same as for oven-roasted chicken, see chart on page 240.

3 to 4 strips of blanched bacon, page 15 (never use regular bacon; it will flavor the whole chicken)

Season and truss the chicken as described in the preceding master recipe. Push the spit through it starting at the breast end. Dry it thoroughly, rub with butter and sprinkle with salt. Secure the strips of blanched bacon over the breast and thighs with white string. Because of the bacon, no basting is necessary until the very end.

If you have a rotisserie, use the moderate heat and roast with the door closed. Remove bacon 15 minutes before the end, and baste with the pan drippings until the chicken is browned and done.

If you have a spit attachment in the oven, use a moderate broiler temperature, leave oven door ajar, and place a pan under the chicken to catch the fat and juices. Fifteen minutes before the end, remove the bacon, increase broiler temperature, and continue roasting, basting frequently until the chicken is browned and done.

Use the same tests as for oven roasting in determining when the chicken is done, and the same method for making the sauce.

Poulet Rôti à la Normande

[Roast Chicken Basted with Cream, Herb and Giblet Stuffing]

In this lush combination, the chicken is roasted as usual, but is basted for the last minutes with heavy cream, which rolls off the buttery, brown chicken skin and combines with the pan and stuffing juices.

VEGETABLE SUGGESTIONS

Serve sautéed mushrooms and sautéed potatoes, or green peas and braised onions.

WINE SUGGESTIONS

A chilled white Burgundy or white Graves, or a red Bordeaux-Médoc would be appropriate.

For 4 or 5 people

Herb and giblet stuffing

The chicken gizzard, peeled and minced	Sauté the gizzard in hot butter and oil for 2 minutes. Then stir in the heart, liver, and shallots or onions.
1 Tb butter	Sauté for 2 minutes more, or until the liver has stiff-

⅛ tsp oil
A small skillet
The chicken heart, chopped
1 to 4 chopped chicken livers
1 Tb minced shallots or
green onions

ened but is still rosy inside. Scrape into a mixing bowl.

⅔ cup coarse crumbs from
fresh homemade type of
bread
4 Tb cream cheese
2 Tb softened butter
3 Tb minced parsley
⅛ tsp tarragon or thyme
⅛ tsp salt
Pinch of pepper

Blend in the rest of the ingredients and taste carefully for seasoning. Let the stuffing cool.

A 3-lb. ready-to-cook roasting or frying chicken
¼ tsp salt
1 Tb butter

Sprinkle salt inside the chicken, and loosely fill with the stuffing. Sew or skewer the vent. Truss and dry the chicken, and rub its skin with butter.

Roasting the chicken

1 cup whipping cream

Roast it either in the oven, page 240, or on a spit, page 242. About 10 minutes before the end of the estimated roasting time, remove all but 1 spoonful of fat from the roasting pan. Start basting with 2 or 3 tablespoons of cream every 3 to 4 minutes until the chicken is done. The cream will probably look curdled in the pan, but this will be corrected later.

¼ tsp salt

Remove the chicken to a hot platter and sprinkle with salt.

The sauce

3 Tb strong brown chicken
stock or canned beef
bouillon

Add the stock or bouillon to the cream in the roasting pan and boil rapidly for 2 to 3 minutes, scraping up coagulated chicken roasting juices.

3 to 4 Tb whipping cream
Salt and pepper
Drops of lemon juice

Just before serving, remove from heat and stir in additional cream by spoonfuls to smooth out the sauce. Correct seasoning, and add drops of lemon juice to taste.

Spoon a bit of sauce over the chicken and send the rest to the table in a warmed sauceboat.

Poulet au Porto

[Roast Chicken Steeped with Port Wine, Cream, and Mushrooms]

Chicken, cream, and mushrooms occur again and again, as it is one of the great combinations. This perfectly delicious recipe is not difficult, but it cannot be prepared ahead of time or the chicken will lose its fresh and juicy quality. The chicken is roasted, then carved, flamed in cognac, and allowed to steep for several minutes with cream, mushrooms, and port wine. It is the kind of dish to do when you are entertaining a few good, food-loving friends whom you can receive in your kitchen.

VEGETABLE SUGGESTIONS

Nothing should interfere with these special flavors. It would be best to serve only potatoes sautéed in butter, page 526, or a perfectly seasoned *risotto*, page 532. Peas, or asparagus tips, or braised onions, page 481, could be added if you feel the necessity for more vegetables.

WINE SUGGESTIONS

Serve very good, chilled, white Burgundy such as a Meursault or Montrachet, or an excellent, château-bottled white Graves.

For 4 people

A 3-lb., ready-to-cook, roasting or frying chicken	Roast the chicken as described in the master recipe on page 240. Be sure not to overcook it.
1 lb. fresh mushrooms	Meanwhile, trim and wash the mushrooms. Quarter them if large, leave them whole if small.
A 2½-quart enameled or stainless steel saucepan ¼ cup water ½ Tb butter ½ tsp lemon juice ¼ tsp salt	Bring the water to boil in the saucepan with the butter, lemon, and salt. Toss in the mushrooms, cover, and boil slowly for 8 minutes. Pour out the cooking liquid and reserve.
1 cup whipping cream ½ Tb cornstarch blended with 1 Tb of the cream Salt and pepper	Pour the cream and the cornstarch mixture into the mushrooms. Simmer for 2 minutes. Correct seasoning, and set aside.

When the chicken is done, remove it to a carving board and let it rest at room temperature while completing the sauce.

½ Tb minced shallots or green onions
⅓ cup medium-dry port
The mushroom cooking liquid
The mushrooms in cream
Salt and pepper
Drops of lemon juice

Remove all but 2 tablespoons of fat from the roasting pan. Stir in the shallots or onions and cook slowly for 1 minute. Add the port and the mushroom juice, and boil down rapidly, scraping up coagulated roasting juices, until liquid has reduced to about ¼ cup. Add the mushrooms and cream and simmer for 2 to 3 minutes, allowing the liquid to thicken slightly. Correct seasoning and add lemon juice to taste.

A fireproof casserole or a chafing dish
1 Tb butter
⅛ tsp salt

Smear the inside of the casserole or chafing dish with butter. Rapidly carve the chicken into serving pieces. Sprinkle lightly with salt, and arrange in the casserole or chafing dish.

¼ cup cognac

Set over moderate heat or an alcohol flame until you hear the chicken begin to sizzle. Then pour the cognac over it. Avert your face, and ignite the cognac with a lighted match. Shake the casserole slowly until the flames have subsided. Then pour in the mushroom mixture, tilting the casserole and basting the chicken. Cover and steep for 5 minutes without allowing the sauce to boil. Serve.
(*) Chicken may remain in its casserole over barely simmering water or in the turned-off hot oven with its door ajar, for 10 to 15 minutes, but the sooner it is served, the better it will be.

Coquelets sur Canapés

[Roast Squab Chickens with Chicken Liver Canapés and Mushrooms]

Also for: squab pigeons, game hens, partridge, quail, dove

This is one of the classic French recipes for serving small roast birds. The livers are chopped, seasoned, and spread over sautéed bread rectangles; just before serving, these are run under the broiler. Then the roast birds are placed on them, and the dish is garnished with a wine-flavored deglazing sauce and sautéed mushrooms.

VEGETABLE SUGGESTIONS

Only sautéed, shoestring, or souffléed potatoes, or homemade potato chips are suggested.

WINE SUGGESTIONS

Serve a red Bordeaux-Médoc for chicken, game hens, or pigeon; red Bordeaux–St. Émilion or red Burgundy for game.

For 6 people, 1 bird apiece

A Note on the Order of Battle: Although the mushrooms and canapés may be prepared while the birds are roasting, it seems best to do them ahead and relieve pressure, for the roast birds should be served almost as soon as they are done.

The mushrooms

1½ lbs. fresh mushrooms 2 Tb butter 1 Tb oil A 10- to 12-inch enameled skillet	Trim and wash the mushrooms. Leave whole if small, quarter if large. Dry in a towel. Sauté for 5 to 6 minutes in hot butter and oil until they are very lightly browned.
1 Tb minced shallots or green onions ½ clove mashed garlic	Stir in the shallots or onions, and garlic, and cook over moderate heat for 2 minutes. Set aside.

The canapés

Homemade-type of white bread	Cut 6 slices of bread ¼ inch thick. Remove crusts, and cut slices into rectangles 2 by 3½ inches.
½ cup clarified butter, page 15 A skillet	Sauté the bread lightly on each side in hot clarified butter.
6 poultry or game livers from the birds 3 Tb fresh, raw pork fat; OR fat bacon simmered in water for 10 minutes, rinsed, and dried	Trim the livers, cutting off any black or green spots. Chop very fine, almost into a purée, with the pork fat or bacon. Then blend the liver in a bowl with the seasonings, wine, and optional *foie gras*. Spread the mixture on one side of each rectangle of sautéed bread. Arrange on a broiling pan and set aside. (Pre-

¼ tsp salt

Big pinch of pepper

1 Tb Madeira, port, or cognac

Optional: 2 to 3 Tb *foie gras*

Roasting the birds

heat broiler in time to cook the canapés just before serving.)

Preheat oven to 400 degrees.

Six 10- to 12-ounce, ready-to-cook squab chickens, game hens, squab pigeons, or game birds

½ Tb salt

2 Tb finely minced shallots or green onions

½ tsp dried tarragon

4 Tb butter

6 strips of bacon simmered in water for 10 minutes, rinsed, and dried

Season the cavities of the birds with a sprinkling of salt, shallots or onion, and tarragon, and 1 teaspoon of butter. Truss the birds, dry them, and rub with butter. Cut the blanched bacon in half, crosswise, and tie 2 strips over the breast and thighs of each bird.

A shallow roasting pan just large enough to hold the birds easily on their sides

3 Tb butter melted with 1 Tb good cooking oil

A basting brush

Place the birds in the roasting pan, and set on a rack in the middle of the preheated oven. Baste and turn the birds every 5 to 7 minutes until they are done:

CHICKENS will take from 30 to 40 minutes; they are done when the last drops of juice from their vents run clear yellow with no trace of rose.

GAME HENS, as their flesh is usually firmer than chicken, take about 45 minutes; they are done when the flesh of their drumsticks is soft.

PARTRIDGE and QUAIL, if young and tender, may be judged like chicken; if older, like game hens.

PIGEON and DOVE may be served slightly underdone if you wish, when their juices run a very pale rose rather than a clear yellow.

½ Tb salt

When done, remove trussing strings, sprinkle the birds with salt, and place them on a warm platter. Set in turned-off oven, its door ajar.

The sauce

1 Tb minced shallots or green onions

Remove all but 2 tablespoons of fat from the roasting pan. Stir in the shallots or onions and cook slowly for

1½ cups brown chicken stock, brown stock, or canned beef bouillon
¼ cup Madeira or port
1 to 2 Tb softened butter

1 minute. Add the stock or bouillon and wine and boil rapidly, scraping up coagulated cooking juices until liquid has reduced to about ½ cup. Correct seasoning. Off heat and just before serving, swirl the butter into the sauce.

Final assembly

Just before serving, run the liver canapés under a hot broiler for a minute, until they are sizzling.

---

1 Tb butter
¼ tsp salt
Pinch of pepper

Toss the mushrooms over moderately high heat with the butter, salt, and pepper.

A handful of water-cress leaves or parsley sprigs

Place a canapé under each bird. Surround with the mushrooms, and decorate with water cress or parsley. Spoon the sauce over the birds, and serve.

CASSEROLE-ROASTED CHICKEN

✻ *POULET POÊLÉ À L'ESTRAGON*

[Casserole-roasted Chicken with Tarragon]

For: roasters, large fryers, and capons

When a chicken is cooked this way, it is trussed, browned in butter and oil, then set to roast in a covered casserole with herbs and seasonings. It is a lovely method, as the buttery, aromatic steam in the casserole gives the chicken great tenderness and flavor. While oven cooking is more even, the top of the stove may be used if your casserole is heavy; then the chicken must be turned and basted frequently, and the cooking will be a little longer than for oven cooking.

VEGETABLE AND WINE SUGGESTIONS

They are the same as for a roast chicken, page 240.

For 4 people

Estimated roasting time: 1 hour and 10 to 20 minutes for a 3-lb. bird. See chart on page 240 for other sizes.

Preheat oven to 325 degrees.

A 3-lb., ready-to-cook roasting chicken
¼ tsp salt
Pinch of pepper
2 Tb butter
3 or 4 sprigs of fresh tarragon or ½ tsp of dried tarragon

Season the cavity of the chicken with salt, pepper, and
1 tablespoon of the butter. Insert the tarragon leaves,
or sprinkle in dried tarragon. Truss the chicken, page
237. Dry it thoroughly and rub the skin with the rest
of the butter.

A heavy fireproof casse-
role just large enough to
hold the chicken on its
back and on its side
2 Tb butter
1 Tb oil, more if needed

Set the casserole over moderately high heat with the
butter and oil. When the butter foam has begun to
subside, lay in the chicken, breast down. Brown for 2
to 3 minutes, regulating heat so butter is always very
hot but not burning. Turn the chicken on another
side, using 2 wooden spoons or a towel. Be sure not
to break the chicken skin. Continue browning and
turning the chicken until it is a nice golden color almost all over, particularly on the breast and legs. This
will take 10 to 15 minutes. Add more oil if necessary
to keep the bottom of the casserole filmed.

3 Tb butter, if necessary

Remove the chicken. Pour out the browning fat if it
has burned, and add fresh butter.

½ cup sliced onions
¼ cup sliced carrots
¼ tsp salt
3 or 4 sprigs of fresh tarragon or ½ tsp dried tarra-
gon

Cook the carrots and onions slowly in the casserole
for 5 minutes without browning. Add the salt and
tarragon.

¼ tsp salt
A bulb baster
Aluminum foil
A tight-fitting cover for the
casserole

Salt the chicken. Set it breast up over the vegetables
and baste it with the butter in the casserole. Lay a
piece of aluminum foil over the chicken, cover the
casserole, and reheat it on top of the stove until you
hear the chicken sizzling. Then place the casserole on
a rack in the middle level of the preheated oven.

Roast for 1 hour and 10 to 20 minutes, regulating heat
so chicken is always making quiet cooking noises.
Baste once or twice with the butter and juices in the

casserole. The chicken is done when its drumsticks move in their sockets, and when the last drops drained from its vent run clear yellow.

Remove the chicken to a serving platter and discard trussing strings.

Brown tarragon sauce

2 cups brown chicken stock, or 1 cup canned beef bouillon and 1 cup canned chicken broth

1 Tb cornstarch blended with 2 Tb Madeira or port

2 Tb fresh minced tarragon or parsley

1 Tb softened butter

Add the stock or bouillon and broth to the casserole and simmer for 2 minutes, scraping up coagulated roasting juices. Then skim off all but a tablespoon of fat. Blend in the cornstarch mixture, simmer a minute, then raise heat and boil rapidly until sauce is lightly thickened. Taste carefully for seasoning, adding more tarragon if you feel it necessary. Strain into a warmed sauceboat. Stir in the herbs and the enrichment butter.

To serve

Optional but attractive: 10 to 12 fresh tarragon leaves blanched for 30 seconds in boiling water then rinsed in cold water, and dried on paper towels

Pour a spoonful of sauce over the chicken, and decorate the breast and legs with optional tarragon leaves. Platter may be garnished with sprigs of fresh parsley or—if you are serving them—sautéed potatoes and broiled tomatoes.

(*) AHEAD-OF-TIME NOTE

If the chicken is not to be served for about half an hour, make the sauce except for its butter enrichment, and strain it into a saucepan. Return the chicken to the casserole. Place aluminum foil over it and set the cover askew. Keep the casserole warm over almost simmering water, or in the turned-off hot oven, its door ajar. Reheat and butter the sauce just before serving.

OPTIONAL:

Farce Duxelles

[Mushroom Stuffing]

A chicken will need 10 to 15 minutes more cooking if you fill it with this stuffing.

For a 3-lb. chicken

¾ lb. finely minced fresh mushrooms
1 Tb butter
1 Tb oil
1½ Tb minced shallots or green onions
A 10-inch skillet

A handful at a time, twist the mushrooms into a ball in the corner of a towel to extract their juice. Sauté them in hot butter and oil with the shallots or onions for 5 to 8 minutes, until the pieces begin to separate from each other. Place them in a mixing bowl.

The chicken gizzard, peeled and minced
The chopped chicken liver
1 Tb butter
A small skillet

Sauté the gizzard for 2 minutes in hot butter. Add the liver and sauté 2 minutes more. Add to the mixing bowl.

¼ cup Madeira or port

Pour the wine into the mushroom cooking skillet and boil it down rapidly until it has reduced to a spoonful. Scrape into the mixing bowl.

¼ cup dry, white crumbs from homemade-type of bread
3 Tb cream cheese
1 Tb softened butter
½ tsp minced fresh or dried tarragon
2 Tb minced parsley
¼ tsp salt
Big pinch of pepper

Blend the rest of the ingredients into the mixing bowl and season carefully to taste. Let the stuffing cool. Pack it loosely into the chicken. Sew or skewer the vent and truss the chicken. Then brown and roast it as described in the preceding master recipe.

VARIATION

Poulet en Cocotte Bonne Femme

[Casserole-roasted Chicken with Bacon, Onions, and Potatoes]

This is an all-in-one dish where bacon and vegetables are cooked with the chicken and each item takes on a bit of flavor from its neighbors. No other vegetables are needed to make up a main course, but you may wish to serve broiled tomatoes along with it for color.

For 4 people

A ½-lb. chunk of bacon
A fireproof casserole for cooking the chicken
1 Tb butter

Remove the rind and cut the bacon into *lardons* (rectangular strips ½ inch wide and 1½ inches long). Simmer for 10 minutes in 2 quarts of water. Rinse in cold water, and dry. In the casserole, sauté the bacon for 2 to 3 minutes in butter until very lightly browned. Remove to a side dish, leaving the fat in the casserole.

A 3-lb., ready-to-cook roasting chicken, trussed and buttered

Brown the chicken in the hot fat, as described in the master recipe on page 249. Remove it to a side dish and pour the fat out of the casserole.

Preheat oven to 325 degrees.

15 to 25 peeled white onions about 1 inch in diameter

Drop the onions in boiling, salted water and boil slowly for 5 minutes. Drain and set aside.

1 to 1½ lbs. "boiling" potatoes or small new potatoes

Peel the potatoes and trim them into uniform ovals about 2 inches long and 1 inch in diameter. Cover with cold water, and bring to the boil. Drain immediately.

3 Tb butter
¼ tsp salt
A medium herb bouquet: 4 parsley sprigs, ½ bay leaf, and ¼ tsp thyme tied in washed cheesecloth
A bulb baster
Aluminum foil
A tight-fitting cover for the casserole

Heat the butter in the casserole until it is foaming. Add the drained potatoes and roll them around over moderate heat for 2 minutes to evaporate their moisture; this will prevent their sticking to the casserole. Spread them aside, salt the chicken, and place it breast up in the casserole. Place the bacon and onions over the potatoes, and the herb bouquet. Baste all ingredients with the butter in the casserole, lay the aluminum foil over the chicken, and cover the casserole.

Heat the casserole on top of the stove until the contents are sizzling, then place in the middle level of the preheated oven and roast for 1 hour and 10 to 20 minutes or until the chicken is done, page 239. Baste once or twice with the butter and juices in the pan. No sauce is necessary.

SAUTÉED CHICKEN

✳ *POULET SAUTÉ*

[Sautéed Chicken]

For: frying chickens

In a true sauté the cut-up chicken is cooked entirely in butter, or butter and oil, with seasonings. No liquid comes in contact with it until the very end. It is a quick and delicious way to cook chicken, but should be served as soon as possible after it is done or it loses the fresh and juicy characteristics of a sauté. The fricassees, however, as they cook in a sauce, take well to reheating.

A NOTE ON DISJOINTING THE CHICKEN

French chicken is disjointed so that each wing includes a strip from the lower part of the breast. The breast minus ribs is cut in two, crosswise. The drumsticks are separated from the second joints. This makes 8 good serving pieces, plus the back cut in two, crosswise, if you wish to include it.

American chicken is usually disjointed into 2 drumsticks, 2 second joints, the 2 halves of the breast, and the 2 wings with no breast meat attached. So that the breasts will cook evenly, slip a knife under the ribs and remove them. Each breast half may be chopped in two, crosswise, if you wish.

WINE AND VEGETABLE SUGGESTIONS

These are the same as for roast chicken, page 240.

For 4 to 6 people.

Total cooking time: 30 to 35 minutes

Browning the chicken (8 to 10 minutes)

2½ to 3 lbs. of cut-up frying chicken	Dry each piece of chicken thoroughly. It will not brown if it is damp.
A heavy, 10-inch casserole, skillet, or electric skillet 2 Tb butter and 1 Tb oil, more if necessary to keep bottom of pan filmed with fat	Place the casserole or skillet over moderately high heat with the butter and oil (360 degrees for an electric skillet). When you see that the butter foam has almost subsided, add as many chicken pieces, skin-side down, as will fit easily in one layer. In 2 to 3 minutes, when the chicken has browned to a nice golden color on one

Tongs for turning the chicken

side, turn it to brown on another side. Regulate heat so fat is always very hot but not burning. Remove browned pieces as they are done and add fresh ones until all pieces have browned.

Finishing the cooking (20 to 25 minutes)

Salt and pepper
Optional: 1 to 2 tsp fresh green herbs: thyme, basil, and tarragon, or tarragon only; or 1 tsp dried herbs
2 or 3 Tb butter, if necessary

Season the dark meat with salt, pepper, and optional herbs. (The wings and breasts are done later, as they cook faster.) If the browning fat has burned, pour it out of the casserole and add the fresh butter. Place over moderate heat (300 degrees for an electric skillet). Add the dark meats, cover the casserole, and cook slowly for 8 to 9 minutes.

Salt and pepper
A bulb baster

Season the white meat, add it to the dark meat, and baste the chicken with the butter in the casserole. Cover and continue cooking for about 15 minutes, turning and basting the chicken 2 or 3 times.

The meat is done when the fattest part of the drumsticks is tender if pinched and the chicken juices run clear yellow when the meat is pricked deeply with a fork.

Remove the chicken to a hot serving platter. Cover and keep warm for 2 to 3 minutes while finishing the sauce.

Brown deglazing sauce

1 Tb minced shallot or green onions
Optional: ½ cup dry white wine or ⅓ cup dry white vermouth
¾ to 1 cup brown chicken stock, canned beef bouillon, or canned chicken broth
1 to 2 Tb softened butter
Optional: 1 to 2 Tb minced parsley or fresh green herbs

Remove all but 2 or 3 tablespoons of fat from the casserole. Add the shallots or onions and cook slowly for 1 minute. Pour in the optional wine, and the stock. Raise heat and boil rapidly, scraping up coagulated sauté juices and reducing liquid to about ⅓ cup. Correct seasoning. Off heat and just before serving, swirl in the enrichment butter and optional herbs.

Arrange around the platter whatever vegetables you have chosen. Pour the sauce over the chicken and serve.

(*) FOR A WAIT UP TO HALF AN HOUR

Finish the sauce except for its final buttering. Arrange the cooked chicken in an enameled, glazed, pyrex, or stainless steel casserole and baste it with the sauce. Cover loosely and set over barely simmering water. Just before serving, and off heat, tip casserole, add enrichment butter, and baste the chicken with the sauce.

(*) PARTIAL COOKING IN ADVANCE

The chicken may be browned, the dark meat cooked for 8 to 9 minutes, and the white meat added and cooked for 5 minutes more. Then set the casserole aside, uncovered. About 10 to 15 minutes before serving time, cover and finish the cooking on top of the stove; or heat the casserole and set it in a preheated 350-degree oven for 15 to 20 minutes.

OTHER SAUCES

Poulet Sauté à la Crème

[Deglazing Sauce with Cream]

1 Tb minced shallots or green onions ½ cup dry white wine or ⅓ cup dry white vermouth 1 cup whipping cream	Sauté the chicken as described in the preceding recipe and place it on a hot platter. Remove all but 1 tablespoon of fat from the casserole. Stir in the shallots or onions and cook slowly for 1 minute. Then add the wine and boil it rapidly down to about 3 tablespoons, scraping up coagulated cooking juices. Add the cream and boil it down until it has thickened slightly.
1 to 2 Tb softened butter Optional: 1 to 2 Tb minced parsley or mixed green herbs	Correct seasoning. Off heat and just before serving, swirl in the butter and optional herbs.
	Pour the sauce over the chicken.

Poulet Sauté Chasseur

[Tomato and Mushroom Sauce]

Use the same technique as for the veal scallops on page 368, *escalopes de veau chasseur*

VARIATION

Poulet Sauté aux Herbes de Provence

[Chicken Sautéed with Herbs and Garlic, Egg Yolk and Butter Sauce]

Basil, thyme or savory, a pinch of fennel, and a bit of garlic give this sauté a fine Provençal flavor that is even more pronounced if your herbs are fresh. The sauce is a type of hollandaise, as the herbal, buttery pan juices are beaten into egg yolks to make a thick and creamy liaison. Serve this dish with potatoes sautéed in butter or potato *crêpes,* pages 521 or 526, broiled tomatoes and a chilled *rosé* wine.

For 4 to 6 people

A heavy- 10-inch fireproof casserole, skillet, or electric skillet set at 300 degrees
¼ lb. (1 stick) butter
2½ to 3 lbs. of cut-up frying chicken dried in a towel
1 tsp thyme or savory
1 tsp basil
¼ tsp ground fennel
Salt and pepper
3 cloves unpeeled garlic

Heat the butter until it is foaming, then turn the chicken pieces in it for 7 to 8 minutes, not letting them color more than a deep yellow. Remove the white meat. Season the dark meat with herbs, salt, and pepper, and add the garlic to the casserole. Cover and cook slowly for 8 to 9 minutes. Season the white meat and add it to the casserole, basting the chicken with the butter. Cook for about 15 minutes, turning and basting 2 or 3 times, until the chicken is tender and its juices run pale yellow when the meat is pricked with a fork.

When the chicken is done, remove it to a hot platter, cover, and keep warm.

⅔ cup dry white wine or ½ cup dry white vermouth

Mash the garlic cloves in the casserole with a spoon, then remove the garlic peel. Add the wine and boil it down over high heat, scraping up coagulated sauté juices until the wine has been reduced by half.

2 egg yolks
1 Tb lemon juice
1 Tb dry white wine or white vermouth
A small enameled saucepan
A wire whip

Beat the egg yolks in the saucepan until they are thick and sticky. Beat in the lemon juice and wine. Then beat in the casserole liquid, a half-teaspoon at a time to make a thick creamy sauce like a hollandaise.

Optional: 2 or 3 Tb softened butter

Beat the sauce over very low heat for 4 to 5 seconds to warm and thicken it. Remove from heat and beat in

2 **Tb fresh minced basil,**   more butter by tablespoons if you wish. Beat in the
   fresh fennel tops, or pars-   herbs, and correct seasoning. Spoon the sauce over the
   ley   chicken, and serve.

CHICKEN FRICASSEE

For: fryers, roasters, and young stewing chicken

One frequently runs into chicken recipes labeled sautés which are actually fricassees, and others labeled fricassees which are actually stews. The fricassee is halfway between the two. No liquid is included in the cooking of a sauté. For a stew, the chicken is simmered in liquid from the start of its cooking. When chicken is fricasseed, the meat is always cooked first in butter—or butter and oil—until its flesh has swelled and stiffened, then the liquid is added. There is a subtle but definite difference in taste between the three methods. Fricassees can be white, like the following recipe, or brown, like the *coq au vin* on page 263. It is an ideal technique for ahead-of-time dishes, as the chicken loses none of its essential qualities if it is allowed to cool in its sauce and is then reheated.

TYPE OF CHICKEN TO USE

The following recipes are all based on frying chicken. Younger chickens, such as broilers, should never be used; their flesh is so soft and tender that it dries out and becomes stringy. Older chickens need longer cooking than the 25 to 30 minutes of simmering required for a fryer.

Roasting chicken—35 to 45 minutes of simmering

Young stewing chicken—1½ hours or more of simmering, or until the flesh is tender when pricked with a fork.

---

* *FRICASSÉE DE POULET À L'ANCIENNE*

[Old-fashioned Chicken Fricassee with Wine-flavored Cream Sauce, Onions, and Mushrooms]

For this traditional Sunday dinner dish, which is not difficult to execute, the chicken pieces are turned in hot butter, sprinkled with flour and seasonings, then simmered in wine and white stock. The sauce is a reduction of the cooking liquid, enriched with cream and egg yolks. Braised onions and mushrooms accompany the chicken. Include also steamed rice or *risotto,* pages 529 or 532, or buttered noodles. If you want other vegetables, buttered peas or asparagus tips may serve as a garnish.

WINE SUGGESTIONS

Serve a chilled, fairly full-bodied white Burgundy, Côtes du Rhône, or Bordeaux-Graves.

For 4 to 6 people

Preliminary cooking in butter

2½ to 3 lbs. of cut-up frying chicken

Dry the chicken thoroughly in a towel.

A heavy, 10-inch, fireproof
casserole or electric skillet
1 thinly sliced onion, carrot,
and celery stalk
4 Tb butter

Cook the vegetables slowly in the butter for about 5 minutes, or until they are almost tender but not browned (260 degrees for an electric skillet). Push them to one side. Raise heat slightly (290 degrees), and add the chicken. Turn it every minute for 3 or 4 minutes until the meat has stiffened slightly, without coloring to more than a light golden yellow.

Lower heat (260 for an electric skillet), cover, and cook very slowly for 10 minutes, turning the chicken once. It should swell slightly, stiffen more, but not deepen in color.

Adding the flour

½ tsp salt
⅛ tsp white pepper
3 Tb flour

Sprinkle salt, pepper, and flour on all sides of the chicken, turning and rolling each piece to coat the flour with the cooking butter. Cover and continue cooking slowly for 4 minutes, turning it once.

Simmering in stock and wine

3 cups boiling white chicken
stock, white stock, or
canned chicken bouillon
1 cup dry white wine or ⅔
cup dry white vermouth
A small herb bouquet: 2
parsley sprigs, ⅓ bay leaf
and ⅛ tsp thyme tied in
washed cheesecloth

Remove from heat and pour in the boiling liquid, shaking casserole to blend the liquid and flour. Add the wine, the herb bouquet, and more stock, or water, so the liquid just covers the chicken. Bring to the simmer. Taste for seasoning, and salt lightly if necessary.

Cover and maintain at a slow simmer for 25 to 30 minutes (180 to 190 degrees for an electric skillet). The chicken is done when the drumsticks are tender if pinched and the chicken juices run clear yellow when the meat is pricked with a fork. When done, remove the chicken to a side dish.

Onion and mushroom garniture

16 to 20 white-braised on-ions, page 481
½ lb. fresh mushrooms stewed in butter, lemon juice, and water, page 511

While the chicken is cooking, prepare the onions and mushrooms. Add their cooking juices to the chicken cooking sauce in the next step.

The sauce

Simmer the cooking liquid in the casserole for 2 to 3 minutes, skimming off fat. Then raise heat and boil rapidly, stirring frequently, until the sauce reduces and thickens enough to coat a spoon nicely. Correct seasoning. You should have 2 to 2½ cups.

2 egg yolks
½ cup whipping cream
A 2-quart mixing bowl
A wire whip

Blend the egg yolks and cream in the mixing bowl with a wire whip. Continue beating, and add the hot sauce by small tablespoonfuls until about a cupful has gone in. Beat in the rest of the sauce in a thin stream.

A wooden spoon

Pour the sauce back into the casserole, or into an enameled or stainless steel saucepan (do not use aluminum). Set over moderately high heat and, stirring constantly, reach all over the bottom and sides of the casserole, until the sauce comes to a boil. Boil for 1 minute, stirring.

Salt and white pepper
Drops of lemon juice
Pinch of nutmeg

Correct seasoning, adding drops of lemon juice to taste, and a pinch of nutmeg. Strain the sauce through a fine sieve.

Final assembly

A clean casserole

Arrange the chicken, and the onion and mushroom garniture, in the casserole. Pour the sauce over it.
(*) Except for reheating, and the final buttering of

the sauce, the dish is now ready and can wait indefinitely. To prevent a skin from forming over the sauce,
spoon over it a film of cream, stock, or milk. Set it
aside uncovered.

Reheating and serving

Set casserole over moderate heat and bring to the simmer. Cover and simmer very slowly for 5 minutes, or
until the chicken is hot through, basting it frequently
with the sauce.

---

1 to 2 Tb softened butter

Off heat and just before serving, tilt casserole, add enrichment butter, and baste the chicken with the sauce
until the butter has absorbed into it.

Sprigs of fresh parsley

Serve the chicken from the casserole; or arrange it
with the onions and mushrooms on a hot platter, surrounded with rice or noodles, and covered with the
sauce. Decorate with sprigs of fresh parsley.

VARIATIONS: SAUCES

Using the preceding recipe, you may vary the sauce in a number of ways.
The egg yolk liaison at the end may be omitted and a cream sauce substituted;
just reduce the cooking liquid until it is quite thick, then simmer it slowly
while thinning it out with spoonfuls of heavy cream until it is the consistency
you wish it to be. Here are some other ideas:

VARIATIONS

Fricassée de Poulet à l'Indienne

[Curry Sauce]

**1 to 2 Tb fragrant curry
powder**

After the chicken has had its preliminary turning of 5
minutes in butter, blend in the curry powder. Cover,
and proceed with the 10-minute cooking period. Then
continue with the recipe.

Fricassée de Poulet au Paprika

[Paprika Sauce]

1½ Tb fresh-smelling and fragrant paprika	After the chicken has had its preliminary turning of 5 minutes in butter, blend in the paprika. Cover, and proceed with the 10-minute cooking period. Then continue with the recipe.
½ Tb more paprika, if necessary	After completing the sauce, stir in more paprika if the sauce needs color. It should be a creamy pink.

Fricassée de Poulet à l'Estragon

[Tarragon Sauce]

4 or 5 sprigs fresh tarragon or 2 tsp dried tarragon	Add the tarragon to the wine and stock for the simmering of the chicken.
2 Tb fresh minced tarragon or parsley	Stir fresh tarragon or parsley into the finished sauce.

FONDUE DE POULET À LA CRÈME

[Chicken Simmered with Cream and Onions]

In this rich and delectable dish, the chicken is cooked in butter and onions, then simmered with wine and heavy cream. Serve it with steamed rice or *risotto,* page 532, buttered green peas or baked cucumbers, page 499, and a fairly full-bodied white Burgundy or white Bordeaux-Graves.

For 4 to 6 people

2½ to 3 lbs. of cut-up frying chicken 3 Tb butter A heavy, 10-inch, fireproof casserole	Dry the chicken thoroughly. Turn it in hot butter for 4 to 5 minutes, until the meat has stiffened slightly but has not browned. Remove it to a side dish.
1½ cups thinly sliced yellow onions	Stir the onions into the butter in the pan. Cover and cook very slowly for 5 minutes, or until the onions are fairly tender but not browned.

Return the chicken to the casserole, cover and cook slowly for 10 minutes until it swells slightly and stiffens, but does not brown. Turn it once during this period.

½ tsp salt
⅛ tsp white pepper
¼ tsp curry powder
⅓ cup cognac, Calvados, Madeira, or port; or ¾ cup dry white wine, or ½ cup dry white vermouth

Season the chicken with salt, pepper, and curry powder. Pour in the spirits or wine, raise heat, and boil rapidly until the liquid has almost entirely evaporated.

3 cups whipping cream brought to the boil in a small saucepan

Pour on the hot cream, bring to the simmer, baste the chicken, and cover the casserole. Maintain at the barest simmer for 30 to 35 minutes, or until the chicken is tender and its juices run a clear yellow when the meat is pricked with a fork. The cream may look slightly curdled, but will be smoothed out later.

Remove the chicken to a hot platter, cover, and keep warm for 5 minutes while finishing the sauce.

Salt and white pepper
Drops of lemon juice
3 to 4 Tb whipping cream

Skim fat off the sauce, then boil it rapidly, stirring, until it reduces enough to coat the spoon lightly. Correct seasoning, adding lemon juice to taste. Off heat, beat in additional cream by spoonfuls to smooth out the sauce.

Sprigs of fresh parsley

Pour the sauce over the chicken, decorate with parsley, and serve.

COQ AU VIN

[Chicken in Red Wine with Onions, Mushrooms, and Bacon]

This popular dish may be called *coq au Chambertin, coq au riesling,* or *coq au* whatever wine you use for its cooking. It is made with either white or red wine, but the red is more characteristic. In France it is usually accompanied only by parsley potatoes; buttered green peas could be included if you wish a green vegetable. Serve with it a young, full-bodied red Burgundy, Beaujolais, or Côtes du Rhône.

For 4 to 6 people

A 3- to 4-ounce chunk of lean bacon	Remove the rind and cut the bacon into *lardons* (rectangles ¼ inch across and 1 inch long). Simmer for 10 minutes in 2 quarts of water. Rinse in cold water. Dry.
A heavy, 10-inch, fireproof casserole or an electric skillet 2 Tb butter	Sauté the bacon slowly in hot butter until it is very lightly browned (temperature of 260 degrees for an electric skillet). Remove to a side dish.
2½ to 3 lbs. cut-up frying chicken	Dry the chicken thoroughly. Brown it in the hot fat in the casserole (360 degrees for the electric skillet).
½ tsp salt ⅛ tsp pepper	Season the chicken. Return the bacon to the casserole with the chicken. Cover and cook slowly (300 degrees) for 10 minutes, turning the chicken once.
¼ cup cognac	Uncover, and pour in the cognac. Averting your face, ignite the cognac with a lighted match. Shake the casserole back and forth for several seconds until the flames subside.
3 cups young, full-bodied red wine such as Burgundy, Beaujolais, Côtes du Rhône, or Chianti 1 to 2 cups brown chicken stock, brown stock, or canned beef bouillon ½ Tb tomato paste 2 cloves mashed garlic ¼ tsp thyme 1 bay leaf	Pour the wine into the casserole. Add just enough stock or bouillon to cover the chicken. Stir in the tomato paste, garlic, and herbs. Bring to the simmer. Cover and simmer slowly for 25 to 30 minutes, or until the chicken is tender and its juices run a clear yellow when the meat is pricked with a fork. Remove the chicken to a side dish.
12 to 24 brown-braised onions, page 483 ½ lb. sautéed mushrooms, page 513	While the chicken is cooking, prepare the onions and mushrooms.

Salt and pepper	Simmer the chicken cooking liquid in the casserole for a minute or two, skimming off fat. Then raise heat and boil rapidly, reducing the liquid to about 2¼ cups. Correct seasoning. Remove from heat, and discard bay leaf.
3 Tb flour **2 Tb softened butter** **A saucer** **A rubber spatula** **A wire whip**	Blend the butter and flour together into a smooth paste (*beurre manié*). Beat the paste into the hot liquid with a wire whip. Bring to the simmer, stirring, and simmer for a minute or two. The sauce should be thick enough to coat a spoon lightly.
	Arrange the chicken in the casserole, place the mushrooms and onions around it, and baste with the sauce. (*) If the dish is not to be served immediately, film the top of the sauce with stock or dot with small pieces of butter. Set aside uncovered. It can now wait indefinitely.
	Shortly before serving, bring to the simmer, basting the chicken with the sauce. Cover and simmer slowly for 4 to 5 minutes, until the chicken is hot through.
Sprigs of fresh parsley	Serve from the casserole, or arrange on a hot platter. Decorate with sprigs of parsley.

BROILED CHICKEN

POULETS GRILLÉS À LA DIABLE

[Chicken Broiled with Mustard, Herbs, and Bread Crumbs]

Here is a fine method for broiled chicken which is good either hot or cold. The chicken is partially cooked under the broiler, then smeared with mustard and herbs, rolled in fresh bread crumbs, and returned to the broiler to brown and finish cooking. A practical attribute is that it can be almost entirely cooked ahead of time, set aside or refrigerated, and then finished off in the oven. With the mustard dip, a sauce is not a necessity. But if you want one, serve melted butter mixed with lemon juice and minced herbs, or *sauce diable* (herbal brown sauce with shallots and wine), page 71. Baked, whole tomatoes and green beans would go well with it, and a chilled *rosé* wine.

For 4 to 8 people

Preheat oven broiler to moderately hot.

Two ready-to-cook, 2½-lb. broilers, halved or quartered
A saucepan containing 6 Tb melted butter and 2 Tb oil
A pastry brush
A broiling pan minus rack
Salt

Dry the chicken thoroughly, paint it with butter and oil, and arrange it skin-side down in the bottom of the broiling pan. Place it so that the surface of the chicken is 5 to 6 inches from the hot broiling element and broil 10 minutes on each side, basting every 5 minutes. The chicken should be very lightly browned. Salt it lightly.

6 Tb prepared mustard of the strong Dijon type
3 Tb finely minced shallots or green onions
½ tsp thyme, basil, or tarragon
⅛ tsp pepper
Pinch of cayenne pepper

Blend the mustard with the shallots or onions, herbs, and seasonings in a bowl. Drop by drop, beat in half the basting fat to make a mayonnaiselike cream. Reserve the rest of the basting fat for later. Paint the chicken pieces with the mustard mixture.

4 cups fresh, white crumbs from homemade-type of bread (make the crumbs in an electric blender, 3 or 4 slices of bread at a time)

Pour the crumbs into a big plate, then roll the chicken in the crumbs, patting them on so they will adhere.

A broiling pan with rack
The rest of the basting fat

Arrange the chicken pieces skin-side down on the rack in the broiling pan and dribble half the remaining basting fat over them. Brown slowly for 10 minutes under a moderately hot broiler. Turn, baste with the last of the fat, and brown 10 minutes more on the other side. The chicken is done when the thickest part of the drumstick is tender, and, when the meat is pricked with a fork, the juices run clear yellow.

Transfer to a hot platter and serve.

(*) AHEAD-OF-TIME NOTES

If you wish to do most of the cooking in advance, brown the crumbed chicken under the broiler for 5 minutes only on each side. It then may be finished off several hours later, placed in a preheated 350-degree oven for 20 to 30 minutes. Do not allow it to overcook.

CHICKEN BREASTS
Suprêmes de Volaille

Breast of chicken when it is removed raw from one side of the bird in a skinless, boneless piece is called a *suprême*. Each chicken possesses two of them. If the upper part of the wing is left on, the *suprême* becomes a *côtelette*. The breast of a cooked chicken is not a *suprême,* but a *blanc de poulet,* or white meat of chicken. A *suprême* may be poached in butter in a covered casserole *à blanc,* or sautéed or broiled with butter *à brun*. It is never, in good French cooking, simmered in a liquid. The *suprême* is an easy morsel to cook, but attention must be exercised to be sure it is not overdone, as even a minute too much can toughen the meat and make it dry. The flesh of a perfectly cooked *suprême* is white with the faintest pinky blush, its juices run clear yellow, and it is definitely juicy. Its point of doneness is easily determined as it cooks. Press the top of it with your finger; if it is still soft and yields slightly to the touch, it is not yet done. As soon as the flesh springs back with gentle resilience, it is ready. If there is no springiness, it is overcooked. As a *suprême* cooks in only 6 to 8 minutes and may be served very simply, it can make an exquisite quick meal.

PREPARING THE SUPRÊMES FOR COOKING

Choose whole or half breasts from a 2½- to 3-lb. fryer. Slip your fingers between skin and flesh, and pull off the skin. Then cut against the ridge of the breastbone to loosen the flesh from the bone. Disjoint the wing where it joins the carcass and continue down along the rib cage, pulling flesh from bone as you cut until the meat from one side of the breast separates from the bone in one piece. Remove the wing. Cut and pull out the white tendon that runs about two thirds of the way down the under side of the meat. Trim off any jagged edges and flatten the *suprêmes* lightly with the side of a heavy knife. They are now ready for cooking. If they are not to be used immediately, wrap in waxed paper and refrigerate.

✷ *SUPRÊMES DE VOLAILLE À BLANC*

[Breast of Chicken with Cream]

Serve these with buttered asparagus tips, green peas, artichoke hearts, or creamed spinach, a good *risotto* cooked in chicken stock, and a bottle of chilled white Burgundy or Traminer.

For 4 people

Preheat oven to 400 degrees.

4 *suprêmes* (boned breasts from two fryers; see directions in paragraph preceding recipe)
½ tsp lemon juice
¼ tsp salt
Big pinch white pepper
A heavy, covered, fireproof casserole about 10 inches in diameter
A round of waxed paper 10 inches in diameter and buttered on one side
4 Tb butter

Rub the *suprêmes* with drops of lemon juice and sprinkle lightly with salt and pepper. Heat the butter in the casserole until it is foaming. Quickly roll the *suprêmes* in the butter, lay the buttered paper over them, cover casserole and place in hot oven. After 6 minutes, press top of *suprêmes* with your finger. If still soft, return to oven for a moment or two. When the meat is springy to the touch it is done. Remove the *suprêmes* to a warm platter and cover while making the sauce (2 to 3 minutes).

For the sauce:

¼ cup white or brown stock or canned beef bouillon
¼ cup port, Madeira, or dry white vermouth
1 cup whipping cream
Salt and pepper
Lemon juice as needed
2 Tb fresh minced parsley

Pour the stock or bouillon and wine into the casserole with the cooking butter and boil down quickly over high heat until liquid is syrupy. Stir in the cream and boil down again over high heat until cream has thickened slightly. Off heat, taste carefully for seasoning, and add drops of lemon juice to taste. Pour the sauce over the *suprêmes,* sprinkle with parsley, and serve at once.

VARIATIONS

Suprêmes de Volaille Archiduc

[Chicken Breasts with Paprika, Onions, and Cream]

This is a delicious combination, the onions giving the chicken and the sauce a subtle flavor, while the paprika lends fragrance and rosiness to the finished dish.

⅔ cup finely minced white onions 5 Tb butter 1 Tb fragrant red paprika ⅛ tsp salt	Drop the minced onions into boiling water for 1 minute. Drain, run cold water over them, and drain again. Cook the onions with the salt, paprika, and butter in the covered casserole for about 10 minutes over very low heat until the onions are tender and translucent, but not browned.
4 *suprêmes* and the sauce ingredients in the preceding master recipe	Following the master recipe, cook the *suprêmes* in the onions, paprika, and butter. Remove when done, leaving the onions in the casserole. Complete the sauce, also as described in the master recipe.

Suprêmes de Volaille à l'Écossaise

[Chicken Breasts with Diced Aromatic Vegetables and Cream]

The following vegetables cut into neat ¹⁄₁₆-inch cubes, making ⅔ to ¾ cup in all: 1 medium carrot 1 to 2 tender celery stalks 1 medium white onion	Cook the diced vegetables slowly with the salt and butter for about 10 minutes in the covered casserole until tender, but not browned.
⅛ tsp salt 5 Tb butter 4 *suprêmes* and the sauce ingredients in the master recipe	Following the master recipe, cook the *suprêmes* in the vegetables and butter. Remove them when done, leaving the vegetables in the casserole. Complete the sauce, as described in the master recipe.

Suprêmes de Volaille aux Champignons

[Chicken Breasts with Mushrooms and Cream]

5 Tb butter 1 Tb minced shallot or green onion ¼ lb. diced or sliced fresh mushrooms ⅛ tsp salt	Heat the butter in the casserole over moderate heat until foaming. Stir in the minced shallots or green onion and sauté a moment without browning. Then stir in the mushrooms and sauté lightly for a minute or two without browning. Sprinkle with salt.

4 *suprêmes* and the sauce ingredients in the master recipe	Following the master recipe, cook the *suprêmes* in the mushrooms and butter. Remove when done, leaving the mushrooms in the casserole. Complete the sauce, as described in the master recipe.

---

* *SUPRÊMES DE VOLAILLE À BRUN*

[Chicken Breasts Sautéed in Butter]

Here the chicken breasts are lightly dusted with flour and are sautéed in clarified butter. (Ordinary butter will burn and form black specks on the *suprêmes*. Clarified butter may be heated to a higher temperature before burning.) A good accompaniment for this dish would be grilled or stuffed tomatoes, buttered green peas or beans, and potato balls sautéed in butter. Serve with it a red Bordeaux-Médoc.

For 4 people

4 *suprêmes* (boned breasts from 2 fryers), page 267 ¼ tsp salt Big pinch of pepper 1 cup flour spread on an 8-inch plate	Just before sautéing, sprinkle the *suprêmes* with salt and pepper, roll them in the flour, and shake off excess flour.

An 8- to 9-inch skillet 6 to 8 Tb clarified butter, page 15 (note that you will need ¼ cup more for your sauce) A hot platter	Pour clarified butter into skillet to a depth of about ¹⁄₁₆ inch. Set over moderately high heat. When the butter begins to deepen in color very slightly, put in the *suprêmes*. Regulate heat so butter is always hot but does not turn more than a deep yellow. After 3 minutes, turn the *suprêmes* and sauté on the other side. In two minutes, press tops of *suprêmes* with your finger. As soon as they are springy to the touch, they are done. Remove to a hot platter, leaving the butter in the skillet.

Brown Butter Sauce (Beurre Noisette)

4 Tb clarified butter 3 Tb minced parsley 1 Tb lemon juice	Add additional clarified butter to skillet and set over moderately high heat until the butter has turned a very light golden brown (a minute or two). Immediately remove from heat, sir in parsley and lemon juice, and taste for seasoning. Pour over the *suprêmes* and serve.

VARIATIONS

Brown Deglazing Sauce with Wine

1 Tb minced shallot or green onion
1/4 cup port or Madeira
2/3 cup brown stock or canned beef bouillon
2 Tb minced parsley

After removing the sautéed *suprêmes,* stir minced shallot or onion into skillet and sauté a moment. Then pour in the wine and stock or bouillon and boil down rapidly over high heat until liquid is lightly syrupy. Pour over the *suprêmes,* sprinkle with parsley, and serve.

Deglazing Sauce with Truffles

1 minced canned truffle and the juice from its can
Ingredients for the preceding brown deglazing sauce minus the parsley

After sautéing the shallots or onions, as in the preceding master recipe, add the wine, stock or bouillon, and the truffle and its juice. Boil down liquid until syrupy, and pour over the *suprêmes.*

Suprêmes de Volaille à la Milanaise

[Chicken Breasts Rolled in Parmesan and Fresh Bread Crumbs]

4 *suprêmes* (boned breasts from two fryers), page 267
1/4 tsp salt
Big pinch of pepper
1 cup flour spread on an 8-inch plate
1 egg, 1/8 tsp salt, and 1/2 tsp olive oil beaten together in an 8-inch soup plate
1/2 cup freshly grated Parmesan cheese and 1/2 cup fine, white, fresh bread crumbs mixed together in an 8-inch dish

Season the *suprêmes* with salt and pepper. One at a time, roll them in the flour and shake off excess. Dip in beaten egg. Then roll in the cheese and bread crumbs, patting them in place with the flat of a knife. Lay the *suprêmes* on waxed paper and allow cheese and bread crumbs to set for 10 to 15 minutes or several hours.

Ingredients for brown butter sauce, master recipe

Sauté on both sides in clarified butter until resilient to the pressure of your finger. Serve with brown butter sauce as described in the master recipe.

DUCK

Canard – Caneton

Only the genuine duckling or *caneton*—a bird under 6 months old—is good for roasting. Fortunately that is the only kind of duck you are liable to find in any American market. It generally weighs 4½ to 5½ pounds ready to cook, has been beautifully plucked and cleaned, and is usually frozen, a state to which it takes much better than chicken. It needs only to be thawed out in the refrigerator or in a basin of cold, running water, and it is ready for cooking.

A NOTE ON FRENCH DUCKS

While American commercially raised birds are usually of one variety— the White Pekin—French ducks are of various breeds. These are: the *nantais,* which rarely weighs over 3 pounds and is the most common table duckling; the *rouennais,* famous as pressed duck; and the *canard de barbarie,* often older and always larger, which is used for braising.

PREPARING A DUCK FOR ROASTING

Pull out all loose fat from the cavity and from around the neck. To make the carving of the breast meat easier, cut out the wishbone. The lower part of the wing is mostly bone; chop it off at the elbow and add it to the stock pot. Be sure the fat glands on the back at the base of the tail have been removed; dig out any yellow residue that may remain, and rub the area with salt and lemon juice. To help the layer of subcutaneous duck fat to escape during cook- ing, prick the skin at ½-inch intervals along the thighs, the back, and the lower part of the breast. After seasoning the cavity, or stuffing it, sew or skewer the legs, wings, and neck skin to the body so the bird will make a neat appearance on the table; see the illustrated directions for trussing a chicken on page 237, which may be adapted for duck.

DUCK STOCK

The neck, heart, gizzard, and lower wings may be used for the making of a duck stock. Follow the same method as for chicken stock, page 236.

CARVING NOTE

Duck has far more carcass and far less meat than a chicken of the same weight; a 4½-pound duck will serve only 4 or 5 people. The French method of carving is to make as many thin slices of breast meat as possible, 4 to 6 per side, as follows: After the second joints and drumsticks have been removed, the duck is turned on its side, its tail facing the carver. Thin slices of meat are cut diagonally starting from the lower part of the breast nearest the tail and running toward the breastbone. The same system is used for the other side, cutting in the opposite direction.

ROASTING TIMETABLE

French taste is for ducks roasted to a medium rare—the juices run slightly rosy when the meat is pricked. If the duck is to be served well done, its juices should run clear yellow. Overcooked duck meat is brown, dry, and disappointing.

The following table is for unstuffed, unchilled duck. Add 20 to 30 minutes to the times listed if the duck is stuffed.

READY-TO-COOK WEIGHT	NUMBER OF PEOPLE SERVED	MEDIUM RARE	WELL DONE
		Oven at 350 degrees	
3½ lbs.	3 or 4	65 to 70 minutes	1 hour and 15 to 25 minutes
4½ lbs.	4	1 hour and 15 to 20 minutes	1 hour and 25 to 35 minutes
5½ lbs.	5 or 6	1 hour and 25 to 30 minutes	1 hour and 35 to 40 minutes

VEGETABLE SUGGESTIONS

Caneton aux petits pois, duckling with green peas, is one of the favorite French combinations, especially in the spring. Other vegetable suggestions are broccoli or Brussels sprouts, or braised lettuce, celery, celeriac, onions, or turnips. Among starchy vegetables, if you wish to serve one, are braised or puréed chestnuts, potatoes mashed with celery root or turnips, or a purée of lentils or navy beans.

WINE SUGGESTIONS

Serve full red wine, such as Burgundy, Côtes du Rhône, Châteauneuf-du-Pape, or Bordeaux–St. Émilion. Or a chilled Alsatian Traminer.

* *CANETON RÔTI*

[Roast Duckling]

For 5 to 6 people

Estimated roasting time: 1 hour and 20 to 40 minutes

Preheat oven to 425 degrees.

A   5½-lb.   ready-to-cook
duckling
½ tsp salt
⅛ tsp pepper
A pinch of thyme or sage
A small sliced onion

Season the inside of the duck with salt, pepper, herbs, and the sliced onion. Secure the legs, wings, and neck skin to the body. Prick the skin around the thighs, back, and lower breast. Dry the duck thoroughly.

A shallow roasting pan just
large enough to hold the
duck easily
1 medium sliced carrot
1 medium sliced onion

Place the duck breast up in the roasting pan, strew the vegetables around it, and set it in the middle level of the oven for 15 minutes to brown lightly.

A bulb baster

Reduce oven to 350 degrees, and turn the duck on its side. Regulate heat so duck is always making cooking noises but fat is not burning. Remove accumulated fat occasionally (a bulb baster will suck it up easily). Basting is not necessary.

About 30 minutes later, or about halfway through, turn the duck on its other side.

½ tsp salt

Fifteen minutes before the end of the estimated roasting time, salt the duck and turn it breast up.

The duck is done to a medium rare if the juices from the fattest part of the thigh or drumstick run faintly rosy when the meat is pricked, and when the duck is lifted and drained, the last drops of juice from the vent are a pale rose. The duck is well done when the juices run pale yellow.

When done, discard trussing strings, and place the duck on a serving platter. Set in turned-off oven and leave the door open while preparing the sauce, which will take 3 to 4 minutes.

1½ to 2 cups brown duck stock, beef stock, or canned beef bouillon Optional: 3 or 4 Tb port	Tilt the roasting pan and spoon out all but 1 table-spoon of fat. Add the stock or bouillon and boil rapidly, scraping up coagulated roasting juices, and crushing the vegetables, until liquid is reduced at least by half. Correct seasoning. Add optional wine and simmer a minute to evaporate its alcohol.
1 to 2 Tb softened butter	Off heat and just before serving, swirl the butter into the sauce and strain it into a sauceboat. Pour a bit of sauce over the duck, and serve.

(*) AHEAD-OF-TIME NOTE

Roast duck may wait in the turned-off hot oven, its door ajar, for about 30 minutes before serving.

SPIT ROASTING

Duck does very well indeed on a rotary spit. Follow the directions for spit-roasted chicken on page 242, but omit the bacon wrapping. No basting is necessary. Roasting time is the same as for oven roasting on the chart, page 273.

VARIATIONS

Caneton Rôti à l'Alsacienne

[Roast Duck with Sausage and Apple Stuffing]

Apples and duck are a fine combination, and sausages make it an even better one. The platter may be garnished with more apples and sausages if you wish, braised onions, and sautéed potatoes or potato *crêpes*. A chilled Alsatian Traminer would go well with it, or hard cider.

For 5 or 6 people

Estimated roasting time: 1 hour and 45 to 60 minutes

Sausage and apple stuffing

½ lb. pork link sausages	Sauté the sausages in a skillet until they are lightly browned. Drain them. Mash them roughly with a fork in a mixing bowl.
4 or 5 crisp eating apples	Peel, quarter, and core the apples. Cut the quarters into 2 or 3 lengthwise segments. Sauté them, a few at

a time, in the hot sausage fat in the skillet. They should be very lightly browned, and almost tender, but still retain their shape.

1 Tb sugar ¼ tsp cinnamon ¼ tsp salt ¼ tsp sage 2 Tb cognac	Place them on a platter and sprinkle with the seasonings and cognac.

¼ cup port ¼ cup stock or canned beef bouillon	Pour the fat out of the skillet. Add the wine and stock or bouillon and boil rapidly until liquid has reduced to 2 or 3 tablespoons. Pour it over the cooked sausages.

When both apples and sausages have cooled, mix them delicately together. Stuff loosely into the duck. Sew or skewer the vent, truss the duck, and roast it according to the preceding master recipe.

---

* *Caneton à l'Orange*

[Roast Duck with Orange Sauce]

One of the most well known of all the duck dishes, *caneton à l'orange,* is roast duck decorated with fresh orange segments and accompanied by an orange-flavored brown sauce. Its most important element is its sauce—a rich, strong, meaty, duck essence darkened with caramel, flavored with wine and orange peel, and given a light liaison of arrowroot. You can and should prepare the sauce well ahead of time so that when the duck is roasted, the dish is within 2 to 3 minutes of being done.

VEGETABLE AND WINE SUGGESTIONS

Nothing should interfere with the flavors of the duck, the sauce, and the oranges. Sautéed or shoestring potatoes, or homemade potato chips are your best choice. Serve a good red Bordeaux-Médoc, or a chilled white Burgundy—Meursault, Montrachet, or Corton-Charlemagne.

For 5 or 6 people

Note: Under the ingredients needed for the sauce are 2 cups of excellent duck stock. This should be prepared ahead of time, as it must simmer about 2 hours.

Blanching the orange peel

4 brightly colored navel oranges	Remove the orange part of the skin in strips with a vegetable peeler. Cut into julienne (small strips $\frac{1}{16}$ inch wide and $1\frac{1}{2}$ inches long). Simmer for 15 minutes in a quart of water. Drain. Pat dry in paper towels.

Roasting the duck

A 5½-lb. ready-to-cook duckling ½ tsp salt Pinch of pepper	Season the duck cavity with salt and pepper, add a third of the prepared orange peel, and truss the duck. Roast it according to the master recipe, page 274.

The sauce base

A 4-cup saucepan 3 Tb granulated sugar ¼ cup red wine vinegar 2 cups strong, brown duck stock (follow directions for brown chicken stock, page 236, using duck giblets instead of chicken giblets) 2 Tb arrowroot blended with 3 Tb port or Madeira The rest of the blanched orange peel	While the duck is roasting, make a sweet-and-sour caramel coloring as follows: Boil the sugar and vinegar over moderately high heat for several minutes until the mixture has turned into a mahogany-brown syrup. Immediately remove from heat and pour in ½ cup of the duck stock. Simmer for a minute, stirring, to dissolve the caramel. Then add the rest of the stock, beat in the arrowroot mixture, and stir in the orange peel. Simmer for 3 to 4 minutes or until the sauce is clear, limpid, and lightly thickened. Correct seasoning, and set aside.

The orange segments

The 4 oranges, skinned	Cut the 4 oranges into neat, skinless segments and place in a covered dish.

Final assembly

	When the duck is done, discard trussing strings, and set it on a platter. Place it in the turned-off hot oven, leaving the door ajar.
½ cup port or Madeira	Remove as much fat as you can from the roasting pan. Add the wine and boil it down rapidly, scraping up coagulated roasting juices and reducing the liquid to 2 or 3 tablespoons.
The prepared sauce base 2 or 3 Tb good orange liqueur	Strain the wine reduction into the sauce base and bring to the simmer. Stir in the orange liqueur by spoonfuls, tasting. The sauce should have a pleasant

Drops of orange bitters or lemon juice

orange flavor but not be too sweet. Add drops of orange bitters or lemon juice as a corrective.

2 Tb softened butter

Just before serving, and off heat, swirl in the butter enrichment, and pour the sauce into a warmed sauce-boat.

Place a line of orange segments over the length of the duck and heap the rest at the two ends of the platter. Spoon a bit of sauce with peel over the duck, and serve.

VARIATIONS

Caneton aux Cerises

Caneton Montmorency

[Roast Duck with Cherries]

Cherries or peaches are also good as a garnish for roast duck. Roast the bird as directed in the master recipe, page 274. Make the caramel-colored and arrowroot-thickened sauce described for the preceding *caneton à l'orange,* omitting the orange peel and orange liqueur. The fruit is heated in the sauce as follows:

36 to 48 red or black pitted cherries (if frozen, thaw and drain)
A 4-cup enameled saucepan
1 Tb lemon juice
3 Tb port or cognac
2 to 3 Tb granulated sugar

Toss the cherries in the saucepan with the lemon juice, port or cognac, and sugar. Let them soak for at least 20 to 30 minutes.

After the duck has roasted, and the pan juices have been deglazed with wine and added to the sauce, pour the sauce into the cherries. Heat to below the simmer for 3 to 4 minutes to poach the cherries (if liquid simmers, the fruit may shrivel). Remove the cherries with a slotted spoon and distribute them over and around the duck.

2 Tb softened butter

Boil the sauce rapidly to reduce and thicken it slightly. Correct seasoning. Off heat, swirl in the enrichment butter. Pour the sauce into a warmed bowl, spoon a bit over the duck, and serve.

Caneton aux Pêches

[Roast Duck with Peaches]

3 large or 6 small, firm, ripe, freestone peaches (or drained canned peaches, minus the sugar below) 2 Tb lemon juice 2 to 3 Tb port or cognac 2 to 3 Tb granulated sugar	If using fresh peaches, peel and halve them not more than 30 minutes before serving so they will not discolor. Arrange the peaches in a fireproof dish and baste them with the liquids and sugar. Baste several times more before using.
	After the duck has roasted and the pan juices have been deglazed with wine and added to the sauce, pour the sauce over the peaches. Proceed as for the preceding duck with cherries recipe.

* CANETON POÊLÉ AUX NAVETS

[Casserole-roasted Duck with Turnips]

In casserole roasting, the duck is browned on all sides, then set to roast in a covered casserole. Cooked in its own steam, the duck's flesh becomes wonderfully tender, and the layer of subcutaneous fat is even more effectively dissolved than by roasting. The turnips, which finish their cooking with the duck absorbing cooking juices, are particularly succulent. No other vegetable is necessary, but you could serve green peas or broccoli. A red Bordeaux, Beaujolais, or Côtes du Rhône would be the choice of wines.

For 5 to 6 people.

Estimated roasting time: 1 hour and 20 to 40 minutes

Preheat oven to 325 degrees.

A 5½-lb. ready-to-cook duckling ½ tsp salt ⅛ tsp pepper A heavy, oval casserole just large enough to hold the duck easily 3 Tb rendered fresh pork fat or cooking oil	Season the inside of the duck with salt and pepper, truss it, prick the skin around the thighs, back, and lower part of the breast. Dry it thoroughly. Brown it slowly on all sides in hot fat in the casserole—as for browning a chicken, page 249.

½ tsp salt

A medium herb bouquet: 4 parsley sprigs, ½ bay leaf, and ¼ tsp thyme tied in washed cheesecloth

Pour out the browning fat. Salt the duck and place it breast up in the casserole. Add the herb bouquet, cover the hot casserole, and place it in the middle level of the preheated oven. Roast for 50 to 60 minutes, regulating heat so the duck is always making quiet cooking noises. Basting is not necessary.

2 lbs. firm, crisp, white or yellow turnips

While the duck is cooking, prepare the turnips: Peel them and cut into large olive shapes about 1¾ inches long, or into ¾-inch dice. Drop into boiling, salted water, and boil slowly for 5 minutes. Drain.

A bulb baster

After the duck has roasted for 50 to 60 minutes, or 30 to 40 minutes before the end of its estimated cooking time, degrease casserole with bulb baster. Arrange the turnips around the duck, cover the casserole, and return it to the oven. Baste turnips occasionally with the juices in the casserole.

The duck is done when its juices run a pale rose for medium rare, or a clear yellow for well done.

2 to 3 Tb minced parsley

Drain the duck, discard trussing strings, and place it on a hot platter. Remove the turnips with a slotted spoon, arrange them around the duck, and decorate with parsley. Degrease the cooking juices, correct seasoning, pour into a warmed sauceboat, and serve.

(*) AHEAD-OF-TIME NOTE

The duck, turnips, and degreased cooking juices can be returned to the hot casserole. Set the cover askew, and keep it warm for 30 minutes in the turned-off hot oven, or over barely simmering water.

VARIATIONS

Canard Braisé avec Choucroute – à la Badoise

[Duck Braised in Sauerkraut]

Canard Braisé aux Choux Rouges

[Duck Braised in Red Cabbage]

These two classic combinations are both done in the same way: after the sauerkraut or cabbage is about two thirds braised, the browned duck is added to cook in the casserole, and all ingredients benefit from their mutual exchange of flavors. Parsley potatoes or braised chestnuts and a chilled Alsatian Traminer go well with this.

For 5 or 6 people

Ingredients for 2 lbs. of braised sauerkraut, page 498, or braised red cabbage, page 496	Follow the recipe for braised sauerkraut or braised red cabbage, and cook for 3½ hours.
A casserole large enough to include the duck as well	
A 5½-lb. ready-to-cook duckling	Season, truss, prick, and dry the duck. Brown it in hot fat as described in the preceding recipe. Salt it and bury it in the casserole with the sauerkraut or cabbage. Cover, and braise for about 1½ hours more, or until the duck is done.
Parsley sprigs	When done, remove the duck to a hot platter and discard trussing strings. Lift out the sauerkraut or cabbage, draining its juices back into the casserole, and arrange it about the duck. Decorate with parsley.
	Degrease the cooking juices. Set casserole over high heat and boil rapidly until the liquid has reduced and its flavor is concentrated. Strain into a sauceboat, pour a spoonful over the duck, and serve.

CANETON BRAISÉ AUX MARRONS

[Braised Duck with Chestnut and Sausage Stuffing]

Follow the recipe for braised goose with chestnut and sausage stuffing, page 285. Use the timetable for roast duck on page 273, adding 30 minutes more because of the stuffing.

CANARD EN CROÛTE

[Boned, Stuffed Duck Baked in a Crust]

This recipe is on page 571.

GOOSE

Oie

Goose, like duck, can only be considered gastronomically interesting when it is under 6 months old, and that is probably the only kind you will find in American markets. It usually comes frozen, and should be defrosted either in the refrigerator or in a pan with cold, running water. It is prepared for cooking like duck, page 272.

GOOSE FAT

Goose fat is extremely good as a sauté or basting medium, or as a flavoring for braised cabbage or sauerkraut. Once rendered, it will keep for weeks in the refrigerator. To render the fat, pull out all the loose fat from inside the goose. Chop it up into ½-inch pieces. Simmer it in a covered saucepan with 1 cup of water for 20 minutes to draw the fat out of the tissues. Then uncover the pan and boil the liquid slowly to evaporate the water. As the moisture evaporates, the fat will make spluttering noises. As soon as these have stopped, the fat is rendered, the liquid will be a pale yellow, and the fat particles will have browned very lightly. Strain the liquid into a jar.

Frittons

Grattons

[Goose Cracklings]

The browned fat particles may be turned into a spread for *croûtons,* toast, or crackers. Pound them in a mortar or put them through the meat grinder. Warm them briefly in a skillet and stir in salt, pepper, and allspice to taste. Pack them into a jar. When cold, pour a ⅛-inch layer of hot goose fat over them to seal them. They will keep for several weeks in the refrigerator.

GOOSE STOCK

A good goose stock is easy to make with the gizzard, neck, heart, and wing tips of the goose. The liver may be included, unless you wish to treat it like chicken liver, or add it to your stuffing. Follow the general procedure for chicken stock, page 236. It should simmer for 2 hours or so.

STUFFINGS FOR GOOSE

Goose may be cooked with or without a stuffing. Besides the prune and *foie gras,* and the chestnut stuffing, both of which are described in the pages following, another good one for goose is the apple and sausage mixture in the Duck section, page 275. Count on ¾ to 1 cup of stuffing for each ready-to-cook pound of goose. An 8-lb. bird, for instance, will take 6 to 8 cups of stuffing. Although you may prepare a stuffing ahead of time, never stuff the goose until just before cooking, or both goose and stuffing may spoil.

TIMETABLE FOR ROAST OR BRAISED GOOSE

The following table is based on unstuffed, unchilled goose cooked to the well-done stage—when its juices run pale yellow. Be sure not to overcook your goose, or the breast meat especially will be dry and disappointing. You will see in the table that the larger the goose, the less time per pound it takes to cook. A 9-lb. goose requires about 2 hours, and a 12½-lb. bird, only about 30 minutes longer. The best sizes to buy are from 9 to 11 lbs.; larger geese may be a bit older and tougher. Oven temperature for roasting is 350 degrees; for braising, 325 degrees. A meat thermometer should register 180 degrees.

READY-TO-COOK WEIGHT	NUMBER OF PEOPLE SERVED	APPROXIMATE TOTAL COOKING TIME (UNSTUFFED GOOSE) *
8 lbs.	6	1 hour and 50 to 55 minutes
9 lbs.	6 to 8	About 2 hours
9½ lbs.	8 to 9	2 hours and 10 to 15 minutes
10½ lbs.	9 to 10	2 hours and 15 to 20 minutes
11½ lbs.	10 to 12	2 hours and 20 to 30 minutes
12½ lbs.	12 to 14	2 hours and 30 to 40 minutes

* For a stuffed goose, add from 20 to 40 minutes to the times given.

OIE RÔTIE AUX PRUNEAUX

[Roast Goose with Prune and *Foie Gras* Stuffing]

Goose is roasted exactly like duck, the only exception being that the goose is basted every 15 to 20 minutes with boiling water to help in the dissolution of its subcutaneous fat, which is more copious for goose than for duck. Prunes and goose are an exceptionally fine combination. With the goose you can serve braised onions and chestnuts, and a full red wine such as a Burgundy or Châteauneuf-du-Pape.

For 6 to 8 people.

Estimated roasting time: About 2½ hours

Note: A good brown goose stock will give you an excellent sauce, but it must be prepared in advance; see preceding remarks.

Prune and foie gras stuffing

40–50 "tenderized" prunes	Soak the prunes in hot water for 5 minutes. Pit them as neatly as possible.
1 cup white wine or ⅔ cup dry white vermouth 2 cups brown goose stock, brown stock, or canned beef bouillon	Simmer them slowly in a covered saucepan with the wine and stock or bouillon for about 10 minutes, or until they are just tender. Drain them and reserve the cooking liquid.
The goose liver, minced 2 Tb finely minced shallots or green onions 1 Tb butter	Sauté the goose liver and shallots or onions in butter, using a small skillet, for 2 minutes. Scrape into a mixing bowl.
⅓ cup port	Boil the wine in the same skillet until it is reduced to 2 tablespoons. Scrape it into the mixing bowl with the liver.
½ cup or 4 ounces of *foie gras* (goose liver), or very good liver paste Pinch: allspice and thyme 2 to 3 Tb bread crumbs Salt and pepper	Blend the *foie gras* or liver paste and flavorings into the mixing bowl with the sautéed liver. If mixture seems too soft for easy stuffing, beat in bread crumbs. Taste carefully for seasoning. Fill each prune with a teaspoon of the stuffing.

Preheat oven to 425 degrees.

A 9-lb. ready-to-cook young roasting goose 1 tsp salt	Salt the cavity of the goose. Stuff it loosely with the prunes. Sew or skewer the vent. Secure the legs, wings, and neck skin to the body. Prick the skin over the

A shallow roasting pan

thighs, back, and lower breast. Dry thoroughly, and set it breast up in the roasting pan.

Boiling water
A bulb baster

Following directions for roast duck, page 274, brown the goose for 15 minutes in the hot oven. Turn goose on its side, lower heat to 350 degrees, and continue roasting. Baste every 15 to 20 minutes with 2 or 3 tablespoons of boiling water, and remove excess accumulated fat. A bulb baster is useful for this; tilt the pan and suck the fat out. Turn goose on its other side at the halfway mark, and on its back 15 minutes before the end. The goose should be done in 2 hours and 20 to 30 minutes, when the drumsticks move slightly in their sockets, and, when the fleshiest part of one is pricked, the juices run a pale yellow. Do not allow the goose to overcook or the meat will dry out.

When done, discard trussing strings and set the goose on a platter.

The prune cooking juices
Optional: ⅓ to ½ cup port
Salt and pepper
2 Tb softened butter

Tilt the pan and spoon out the fat, but leave the brown roasting juices. Pour in the prune cooking juices and optional port. Boil down rapidly, scraping up coagulated roasting juices, until liquid has reduced and is full of flavor. Correct seasoning. Off heat and just before serving, swirl in the enrichment butter by bits. Pour into a warmed sauceboat, spoon a bit of sauce over the goose, and serve.

(*) AHEAD-OF-TIME NOTE

Roast goose may wait for 30 to 40 minutes in the turned-off hot oven with its door ajar.

OIE BRAISÉE AUX MARRONS

[Braised Goose with Chestnut and Sausage Stuffing]

There are many who prefer braised goose to roast goose because the meat is more tender and more flavorful, and the closed, moist cooking of a braise renders out more fat than open-pan roasting. A good combination to go with this would be more chestnuts, either braised or puréed, and braised lettuce, onions or leeks. Brussels sprouts, or braised green or red cabbage are other choices. Serve a red Burgundy, Côtes du Rhône, Châteauneuf-du-Pape, or chilled Alsatian Traminer.

For a 9-lb. bird, serving 8 to 10 people—because of the meat stuffing the goose will go further.

Estimated roasting time: 2½ hours

Sausage and chestnut stuffing (8 cups)

1½ pounds of fresh chest-nuts, or 4 cups of drained, canned, and unsweetened chestnuts	If using fresh chestnuts, peel them, and simmer them in stock and seasonings as described on page 518. Drain, and allow them to cool.
4 cups of the fresh ground veal and pork stuffing de-scribed on page 565 The goose liver, chopped, and sautéed in butter	Prepare the stuffing and beat the sautéed liver into it. Sauté a spoonful to check seasoning.
	Preheat oven to 450 degrees.
A 9-lb. ready-to-cook young roasting goose ½ tsp salt A shallow roasting pan	Season the cavity of the goose with salt. Starting with the meat stuffing, loosely pack alternate layers of stuffing and of chestnuts into the goose, leaving a good inch of unfilled space at the vent. Sew or skewer the vent, truss the goose, and prick its skin. Dry it thoroughly, and set it breast up in the roasting pan.
	Brown the goose lightly in the hot oven for 15 to 20 minutes, turning it several times so it will color evenly.
1 tsp salt A covered roaster just large enough to hold the goose easily	Salt the goose and place it breast up in the roaster. Turn oven down to 325 degrees.
The goose neck, wing tips, gizzard, and heart 1½ cup sliced onions ½ cup sliced carrots 4 Tb rendered goose fat, rendered fresh pork fat, or cooking oil A skillet	Brown the goose bits and vegetables in hot fat in the skillet.

6 Tb flour	Stir the flour into the skillet and brown slowly for several minutes.
4 cups boiling brown stock or canned beef bouillon **3 cups dry white wine or 2 cups dry white vermouth**	Off heat, blend in the boiling stock or bouillon, and then the wine. Simmer for a moment. Then pour the contents of the skillet into the roaster around the goose. Add additional stock if necessary, so liquid reaches about one third the way up the goose.
	Bring to the simmer on top of the stove. Cover, and set in the middle level of the preheated 325-degree oven.
A bulb baster	Braise for about 2 hours and 20 to 30 minutes, regulating oven heat so liquid simmers very quietly. Basting is not necessary. Accumulated fat may be removed occasionally with the bulb baster. The goose is done when its drumsticks move slightly in their sockets, and, when their fleshiest part is pricked, the juices run pale yellow.
	Remove the goose to a serving platter and discard trussing strings.
Salt and pepper to taste **⅓ to ½ cup port**	Skim the fat out of the roaster (degreasing directions are on page 12), boil the cooking liquid down rapidly until it has thickened enough to coat a spoon lightly. Correct seasoning. Stir in the port and simmer a minute or two to evaporate its alcohol. Strain the sauce into a bowl or a saucepan, pressing juice out of the ingredients. You should have about 5 to 6 cups of sauce. Pour a spoonful over the goose, and serve.

(*) AHEAD-OF-TIME NOTE

For a 30- to 40-minute wait, return the goose to the roaster, and set the cover askew. Place in turned-off hot oven with its door ajar, or over barely simmering water.

CHAPTER SEVEN

MEAT

Viandes

Faced with the awesome problem of what to choose from among the wonderful store of French recipes for beef, lamb, pork, ham, sweetbreads, kidneys, liver, and brains, we have picked those which seemed to us especially French, or of particular interest to American cooks. We have not gone into roast beef or broiled chops as they are practically the same everywhere. Besides numerous traditional dishes, we have included a number of French regional recipes for *ragoûts,* stews, and *daubes;* their comparative economy and ease of execution, in addition to their robust flavors, make them most appealing.

For those who have collections of original French recipes, or who are living in France, we have in most instances given translations, approximations, or explanations of French meat cuts. Cross-cultural comparisons are a maze of complication as the systems of the two countries are entirely different: the French cut meat following muscle separations, while American butchers usually cut across the grain. Identification is made more confusing as different regions in each country use different names for the same cuts. We have used the Chicago terminology for American cuts, and the Paris terminology for French cuts.

BEEF
Boeuf

Any cook or housewife is well advised to learn as much as possible about grades and cuts of beef, as a vague beef-buyer is open to countless unnecessary disappointments and expenses. Both the grade of beef and the cut determine the cooking method. Beef carcasses are divided into five grades which are rated according to the form and shape of the carcass, the amount and distribution of fat, and the color and quality of the flesh, fat, and bone. Some packers use their own wording. Federal meat inspectors use Prime, Choice, Good, Commercial, and Utility in descending order, and stamp the grade on the beef so it is visible for each retail cut. Grade is an indication of flavor and tenderness especially for roasting and broiling cuts. A Choice or Prime sirloin steak or roast will be more tender and juicy than one graded Good because the flesh of the latter is less marbled with fat. Chuck or rump from a Good carcass will be quite tough when roasted, while the same cut from a Choice carcass should be reasonably tender. However, both cuts are suitable for braising, so there is no reason to buy Prime beef when Good will do. At most retail markets, the higher grades used for roasting and broiling are aged from three to six weeks to improve their flavor and tenderness.

The best way to learn beef cuts is step by step, or cut by cut. You could begin by peering closely at sirloin steaks every time you go into a market. Is the flesh cherry red and marbled with little veins of fat, and is the surrounding fat creamy white and firm? If so, it is a Choice or Prime steak. Is it a double-bone or round-bone sirloin—the two best cuts, or is it from the wedge-bone or pinbone end? When you feel you have mastered the sirloin, you might move to the leg, familiarizing yourself with top round, bottom round, and sirloin tip. Then proceed to other cuts. Ask questions. Your butcher will be much more interested in serving you well if you show interest in learning about his meat.

STEAKS

Biftecks

French and American methods for cutting up a beef carcass are so dissimilar that it is rarely possible to find in America the same steak cut you could find in France. But this is a point of small significance as the various steak recipes differ from one another only in their sauces, butters, or garnitures.

In France the tenderloin or *filet,* which runs from the thirteenth rib to the rump, is usually removed in one piece. Then the loin strip, under which the *filet* was cut, is boned and used for steaks or roasts. Thus there is neither short loin nor sirloin left intact, and consequently no T-bone, porterhouse, or sirloin steak. The best part of the rib-roast section is usually boned and cut into rib steaks called *entrecôtes*.

Since you often find French steak names on a menu, here is a list explaining them.

Entrecôte. Rib steak, or rib eye steak, from the rib-roast section, ribs 9 to 11. Delmonico or club steak, cut from the rib end of the short loin, is a near equivalent.

Romsteck, or Rumsteck. Rump steak, cut from the end of a rump which faces the sirloin. Rump steaks must be from a well aged Prime or Choice carcass to be tender.

Faux Filet, or Contre Filet. Loin strip steak, or strip steak, corresponds to the loin part of a porterhouse or T-bone steak rather than to the tenderloin part. Top-quality strip steaks are rarely available in American retail markets because of the heavy call for porterhouse and T-bone steaks. Delmonico or club steak is practically equivalent.

Bifteck. Tenderloin butt, or New York butt, cut from the larger and less tender end of the *filet,* which also makes up the best part of a sirloin steak. In France the term *bifteck* can also include any lean, boneless steak such as a trimmed Delmonico, club, strip, or rump steak, or a tender steak from the round or chuck. We shall also include T-bone, porterhouse, and sirloin as *biftecks*.

FILET OF BEEF

If the *filet* is taken from a large Choice or Prime carcass, the meat should be 3½ to 4 inches in diameter at the heart, and the slices delicately marbled with fat. Because most butchers reserve their best beef carcasses for T-bone and

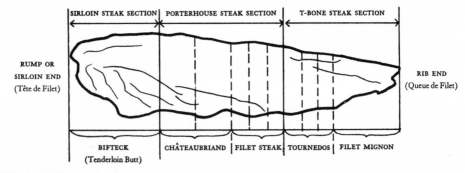

Whole Filet of Beef

porterhouse steaks, it is not always possible to find a *filet* of this size and quality.

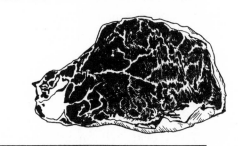

Untrimmed Center Cut of Filet, the Château-briand Section

Bifteck, or tenderloin butt, is considered to be the less tender part of the *filet* and is classified in the preceding list of steaks.

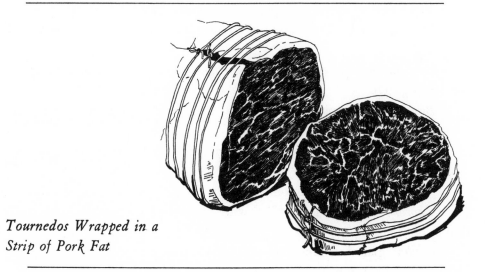

Tournedos Wrapped in a Strip of Pork Fat

Châteaubriand (which can also be spelled with a final "t" rather than "d") corresponds to the tenderloin portion of a Choice or Prime porterhouse steak. It is cut 2 inches thick, should weigh a pound or more before trimming, and is always broiled or grilled. A thinner steak cut from this portion of the tenderloin is called a *filet.*

Tournedos and *filet mignons,* which become progressively smaller near the tail of the *filet,* correspond to the tenderloin of T-bone steaks.

WINE SUGGESTIONS

With all but the *filet* steaks, which are discussed separately, serve a good, rather young red wine with a certain amount of body, such as a Côtes du Rhône, Bordeaux–St. Émilion, or Beaujolais.

VEGETABLE SUGGESTIONS

Bifteck et pommes frites are just as popular in France as steak and baked potatoes are in America. A good change from the old rhythm would be the garlic mashed potatoes on page 520, or one of the scalloped potato casseroles on pages 523 to 526, or potatoes sautéed in butter, page 526. Vegetables which would go well include the following:

Buttered green peas, page 462, or beans, page 444, or Brussels sprouts, pages 449 to 455

Baked or stuffed tomatoes, pages 506 to 508

Broiled or stuffed mushrooms, pages 512 and 516

Ratatouille, egg plant casserole, page 503

Turnips, including the excellent casserole on page 488

Braised celery, leeks, or lettuce, pages 489 to 496

Here are some of the classical French vegetable garnitures for a steak platter:

Beauharnais, stuffed mushrooms, page 516, artichoke hearts cooked in butter, page 431

Brabançonne, Brussels sprouts with cheese sauce, page 453, potato balls sautéed in butter, page 528

Catalane, stuffed tomatoes, page 507, artichoke hearts cooked in butter, page 431

Chartres, stuffed mushrooms, page 516, braised lettuce, page 489

Choron, artichoke hearts filled with buttered peas, page 431, potato balls sautéed in butter, page 528

Maillot, glazed turnips, page 488, carrots, page 479, and onions, page 483, with braised lettuce, page 489, and buttered green peas and beans

Sévigné, braised lettuce, page 489, broiled mushrooms, page 512, potatoes sautéed in butter, page 526

---

* *BIFTECK SAUTÉ AU BEURRE*

[Pan-broiled Steak]

Pan-broiled steak is very French and also a very nice method for cooking small steaks. None of the juice essences are lost, and it is easy to tell when the steak is done.

A 1-inch steak takes 8 to 10 minutes to cook, and the sauce, or pan gravy,

1 to 2 minutes to prepare after the steak is on its platter. The sauce, you will observe, is a deglazing of the pan with stock, wine, or water, and a swish of butter at the end. It is purely an extension of the pan juices, and amounts to only 1 or 2 tablespoons of buttery, concentrated essence per serving.

KIND OF STEAK TO BUY

In France you would select an *entrecôte, romsteck, faux-filet,* or *bifteck.* In America buy any tender, well-aged ¾- to 1-inch steak or steaks which will fit easily into a skillet such as:

Club or Delmonico	Small Sirloin	Tenderloin Butt
T-Bone	Loin Strip Steak	Rump Steak
Porterhouse	Rib Steak	Chuck Steak

AMOUNT TO BUY

One pound of boneless steak will serve 2 people, 3 if the rest of the menu is copious. For large sirloins, T-bones, and porterhouse steaks, count on about ¾ pound per person.

PREPARATION FOR COOKING

Trim off excess fat. Cut small incisions around the circumference of the steak wherever there is a layer of gristle, usually between the fat and the meat. This will prevent the steak from curling as it cooks. Dry the steak thoroughly on paper towels. It will not brown if it is moist.

For 4 to 6 people, depending on your menu

One or two heavy skillets just large enough to hold the meat easily in one layer

1½ Tb butter and 1½ Tb oil, or rendered fresh beef suet, more if needed

2 to 2½ lbs. steak ¾ to 1 inch thick

Put the butter and oil, or beef suet, in the skillet and place over moderately high heat until you see the butter foam begin to subside, or the beef fat almost smoking; this indicates the fat is hot enough to sear the meat. Sauté the steak on one side for 3 to 4 minutes, and regulate the heat so the fat is always very hot but is not burning. Turn the steak and sauté the other side for 3 to 4 minutes. The steak is done to a medium rare (*à point*) the moment you observe a little pearling of red juice beginning to ooze at the surface of the steak. Another test is to press the steak with your finger; it is medium rare when it just begins to take on a suggestion of resistance and spring in contrast to its soft raw state. If you have any doubts at all, cut a small incision in the steak.

A hot platter	Remove the steak to a hot platter and season it
Salt and pepper	quickly with salt and pepper. Keep warm for a moment while completing the sauce.

½ cup stock, canned beef bouillon, red wine, dry white wine, dry white vermouth, or water	Pour the fat out of the skillet. Add the liquid, and set the skillet over high heat. Scrape up coagulated juices with a wooden spoon while rapidly boiling down the liquid until it is reduced almost to a syrup.
2 to 3 Tb softened butter	Off heat, swirl the butter into the liquid until it is absorbed; the butter will thicken the liquid into a light sauce. Pour the sauce over the steak and serve.

VARIATIONS: FLAVORED BUTTERS

Any of the following are delicious when beaten into your sauce in place of plain butter. They are simply butters creamed with flavorings. If you are serving a broiled steak, spread one of the butters over it just before taking it to the table.

Parsley Butter, page 102
Herb Butter, page 102
Mustard Butter, page 100
Shallot Butter, page 103
Garlic Butter, page 101
Snail Butter (with shallot, garlic, and herbs), page 103

VARIATIONS

Bifteck Sauté Bercy

[Pan-broiled Steak, with Shallot and White Wine Sauce]

For broiled steak, use a *beurre Bercy,* page 103, and spread it over the steak just before serving.

For 4 to 6 people, depending on your menu

2 to 2½ lbs. steak	Sauté the steak as described in the master recipe and
1 Tb butter	remove it to a hot platter. Pour the fat out of the
3 Tb minced shallots or green onions	skillet. Add the butter. Stir in the shallots or onions and cook slowly for a minute.

½ cup dry white wine or dry white vermouth	Pour the wine into the skillet and boil it down rapidly, scraping up the coagulated juices from the bottom of the pan until the liquid has reduced almost to a syrup.

4 to 6 Tb softened butter Salt and pepper to taste 2 to 3 Tb minced parsley Optional: 2 to 3 Tb diced, poached beef marrow, page 19	Off heat, beat in the butter a spoonful at a time until it is absorbed and has thickened the sauce. Beat in salt and pepper to taste, then the parsley. Fold in the optional beef marrow. Spread sauce over the steak and serve.

Bifteck Sauté Marchand de Vins

Bifteck Sauté à la Bordelaise

[Pan-broiled Steak with Red Wine Sauce]

Use the same procedure described for the preceding *Bercy* sauce, but substitute red wine for white. If you add the optional beef marrow, the sauce becomes a *bordelaise*.

Bifteck Sauté Béarnaise

[Pan-broiled Steak with *Béarnaise* Sauce]

For 4 to 6 people, depending on your menu

2 to 2½ lbs. steak ½ cup brown stock, canned beef bouillon, dry white wine, or dry white vermouth. ¾ cup *sauce béarnaise*, page 84	Sauté the steak as described in the master recipe, preceding. Deglaze skillet with stock, bouillon, or wine, boiling it down rapidly to reduce it to 1½ spoonfuls. Beat the liquid by droplets into the *sauce béarnaise*.

Sautéed or fried potatoes Fresh water cress A warmed sauceboat	Decorate the steak platter with sautéed or fried potatoes and fresh water cress. Serve the sauce in a warmed sauceboat.

Steak au Poivre

[Pepper Steak with Brandy Sauce]

Steak au poivre can be very good when it is not so buried in pepper and doused with flaming brandy that the flavor of the meat is utterly disguised. In fact, we do not care at all for flaming brandy with this dish; it is too reminiscent of restaurant show-off cooking for tourists. And the alcohol taste, as it is not boiled off completely, remains in the brandy, spoiling the taste of the meat.

For 4 to 6 people, depending on your menu

2 Tb of a mixture of several kinds of peppercorns, or white peppercorns	Place the peppercorns in a big mixing bowl and crush them roughly with a pestle or the bottom of a bottle.
2 to 2½ lbs. steak ¾ to 1 inch thick	Dry the steaks on paper towels. Rub and press the crushed peppercorns into both sides of the meat with your fingers and the palms of your hands. Cover with waxed paper. Let stand for at least half an hour; two or 3 hours are even better, so the flavor of the pepper will penetrate the meat.
A hot platter Salt	Sauté the steak in hot oil and butter as described in the preceding master recipe. Remove to a hot platter, season with salt, and keep warm for a moment while completing the sauce.
1 Tb butter 2 Tb minced shallots or green onions ½ cup stock or canned beef bouillon ⅓ cup cognac 3 to 4 Tb softened butter Sautéed or fried potatoes Fresh water cress	Pour the fat out of the skillet. Add the butter and shallots or green onions and cook slowly for a minute. Pour in the stock or bouillon and boil down rapidly over high heat while scraping up the coagulated cooking juices. Then add the cognac and boil rapidly for a minute or two more to evaporate its alcohol. Off heat, swirl in the butter a half-tablespoon at a time. Decorate the platter with the potatoes and water cress. Pour the sauce over the steak, and serve.

FILET STEAKS–TENDERLOIN STEAKS
Filets, Tournedos, Filet Mignons

Filets, tournedos, and *filet mignons* are steaks 1 inch thick cut from the *filet* of beef as illustrated on page 290. The *filet,* the largest, should be 3 to 3½ inches in diameter, the *tournedos* about 2½ inches, and the *filet mignon* can be as small as 1½ inches. Since they are all cooked and served in the same way, we shall refer to all three as *tournedos* in French, and as *filet* steaks in English. *Filet* steaks are trimmed of all fat and surrounding filament. The circumference is usually wrapped in a strip of fresh pork fat or blanched bacon, and tied with string so the steaks will keep their neat circular shape while they are being cooked. The string is removed before serving and also, if you wish, the strip of fat or bacon. Although *filet* steaks may be broiled, they are usually sautéed quickly in hot butter to a nice brown on the outside and a juicy red inside.

Filet steaks may be sauced and served exactly like the beefsteaks in the preceding recipes, but because of their expense they are usually surrounded with fine wines and truffles or other elaborations. They cook in 8 to 10 minutes, and the sauce takes about 2 minutes, so you can afford to spend a bit of time on the vegetables and garniture you wish to serve with them. Here are three classical combinations. See also the vegetable suggestions for steak on page 292.

* *TOURNEDOS SAUTÉS AUX CHAMPIGNONS*
TOURNEDOS SAUTÉS CHASSEUR

[*Filet* Steaks with Mushroom and Madeira Sauce]

A handsome presentation for these steaks would be a platter decorated with whole baked tomatoes, artichoke hearts cooked in butter, and potato balls sautéed in butter. Serve with them a good red Bordeaux from the Médoc district.

For 6 steaks

6 crustless rounds of white bread, 2½ inches in diameter and ³⁄₁₆ inch thick 3 to 4 Tb clarified butter, page 15	Sauté bread rounds in hot clarified butter to brown very lightly on each side. Reheat them for a minute in a 350-degree oven just before serving.
½ lb. fresh mushrooms, whole if very small, quartered if large	Sauté mushrooms in hot butter and oil for 5 minutes to brown them lightly. Stir in the shallots or onions

2 Tb butter

1 Tb oil

2 Tb minced shallots or green onions

¼ tsp salt

Pinch of pepper

and cook slowly for a minute or 2 more. Season, and set aside.

---

6 *filet* steaks 1 inch thick and 2½ inches in diameter, each wrapped in a strip of fat as illustrated on page 291

2 Tb butter, more if needed

1 Tb oil

1 or 2 heavy skillets just large enough to hold the steaks easily

Dry the steaks on paper towels. Place the butter and oil in the skillet and set over moderately high heat. When you see the butter foam begin to subside, indicating it is hot enough to sear and brown the steaks, sauté them for 3 to 4 minutes on each side. They are medium rare if, when pressed with your finger, they offer a suggestion of resistance in contrast to their soft, raw state.

Salt and pepper

A warm serving platter

Immediately remove from heat. Discard the strings and, if you wish, the strip of fat. Season quickly with salt and pepper. Place each steak on a canapé, and keep warm for several minutes while preparing the sauce.

½ cup stock or canned beef bouillon

1 Tb tomato paste

Pour the fat out of the skillet; stir in the stock or bouillon and tomato paste. Boil rapidly, scraping up the coagulated cooking juices, until liquid is reduced to 2 or 3 tablespoons.

¼ cup Madeira mixed with ½ Tb of arrowroot or cornstarch

2 Tb minced parsley, tarragon and chervil, or parsley only

Pour in the starch and wine mixture; boil rapidly for a minute to evaporate the alcohol and to thicken the sauce lightly. Then add the sautéed mushrooms and simmer a minute more to blend flavors. Correct seasoning. Spread the sauce and mushrooms over the steaks, sprinkle with herbs, and serve.

VARIATIONS

Tournedos Henri IV

[*Filet* Steaks with Artichoke Bottoms and *Béarnaise* Sauce]

For 6 steaks

6 *filet* steaks sautéed in oil
and butter

6 canapés (rounds of white
bread sautéed in clarified
butter, page 199)

¼ cup Madeira, dry white
wine, or dry white ver-
mouth

¼ cup beef stock or canned
beef bouillon

6 fresh artichoke bottoms
cooked in butter, page 431

¾ to 1 cup *sauce béarnaise,*
page 84

Potato balls sautéed in butter, page 528, and rolled in
2 Tb minced parsley

Asparagus tips cooked in
butter, page 438

Sauté the steaks as described in the master recipe. Season and place on canapés on a hot platter. Keep warm
for a few minutes. Pour sauté fat out of skillet, add
wine and stock or bouillon, and boil down rapidly reducing liquid to 3 tablespoons while scraping coagulated sauté juices into it. Spoon liquid over steaks.
Top each steak with a hot artichoke bottom filled with
béarnaise. Decorate platter with the hot potatoes and
asparagus. Serve immediately.

Tournedos Rossini

[*Filet* Steaks with *Foie Gras,* Truffles, and Madeira Sauce]

A platter of *tournedos Rossini* takes the *filet* steak about as far as it can
go. Were you living in France during the midwinter, your *foie gras* and
truffles would, of course, be fresh. Most recipes use *canapés* (rounds of white
bread sautéed in butter) as a bed for the steaks; we have chosen artichoke
bottoms as a further improvement to an already elegant presentation.

Fitting accompaniments would be potato balls sautéed in butter, buttered peas, asparagus tips, or braised lettuce, and an excellent, château-bottled
red Bordeaux from the Médoc district.

For 6 steaks

3 large, fresh artichoke
bottoms cooked in a
blanc, page 430

Salt and pepper

3 Tb melted butter

Slice each cooked artichoke bottom in two, horizontally. Season with salt, pepper, and melted butter.
Place in a covered dish. Fifteen minutes before serving, heat them in a 350-degree oven.

6 slices canned "block" *foie gras,* ¼ inch thick and about 1½ inches in diameter

2 Tb Madeira

3 Tb rich stock, mushroom essence, page 512, or canned beef bouillon

Place the *foie gras* slices in a covered dish and baste with the Madeira and stock, essence, or bouillon. Ten minutes before serving, set over barely simmering water to heat through gently.

18 to 24 slices of canned truffle, 1/16 inch thick

2 Tb Madeira

Pinch of pepper

1 Tb butter

Place the truffle slices and their juices in a small saucepan with the Madeira, pepper, and butter. Five minutes before serving, warm over gentle heat.

6 *filet* steaks 1 inch thick and 2½ inches in diameter

Salt and pepper

Sauté the steaks as directed in the master recipe on page 297. Season with salt and pepper.

A warm serving platter

Arrange the hot artichoke bottoms on the serving platter and place a steak on each. Over each steak lay a warm slice of *foie gras,* and top with slices of truffle. Decorate the platter with whatever vegetables you have chosen, and keep warm for 2 to 3 minutes while finishing the sauce.

½ cup stock or canned bouillon

Juice from the *foie gras* and truffles

1 tsp arrowroot or cornstarch blended with 2 Tb Madeira

Salt and pepper

3 to 4 Tb softened butter

Pour the fat out of the steak skillet. Pour in the stock or bouillon, and the juices from the *foie gras* and truffles. Boil down rapidly, scraping up all coagulated juices, until liquid has reduced by half. Pour in the starch and wine mixture and simmer for a minute. Correct seasoning. Off heat, swirl in the butter. Pour the sauce over the steaks and serve.

GROUND BEEF–HAMBURGERS

Bifteck Haché

Shock is the reaction of some Americans we have encountered who learn that real French people living in France eat hamburgers. They do eat them, and when sauced with any of the suggestions in the following recipes, the French hamburger is an excellent and relatively economical main course for an informal party. Serve with them the same types of red wines and vegetables listed for steaks on page 291–2.

The best hamburgers are made from the leanest beef. Actually some of the least expensive cuts, chuck and neck, are the most flavorful. Top sirloin, rump, and round are really second choice for hamburgers although they are more expensive. Be fussy in choosing your meat; have all the fat and sinews removed, and have it ground before your eyes or better, grind it yourself. The fat content of hamburger should be only 8 to 10 per cent, or 1¼ to 1½ ounces per pound. This may be in the form of butter, ground beef suet, beef marrow, or ground fresh pork fat.

---

* *BIFTECK HACHÉ À LA LYONNAISE*

[Ground Beef with Onions and Herbs]

For 6 hamburgers

¾ cup finely minced yellow onions 2 Tb butter	Cook the onions slowly in the butter for about 10 minutes until very tender but not browned. Place in a mixing bowl.
1½ lbs. lean, ground beef 2 Tb softened butter, ground beef suet, beef marrow, or fresh pork fat 1½ tsp salt ⅛ tsp pepper ⅛ tsp thyme 1 egg	Add the beef, butter or fat, seasonings, and egg to the onions in the mixing bowl and beat vigorously with a wooden spoon to blend thoroughly. Correct seasoning. Form into patties ¾ inch thick. Cover with waxed paper and refrigerate until ready to use.
½ cup flour spread on a plate	Just before sautéing, roll the patties lightly in the flour. Shake off excess flour.
1 Tb butter and 1 Tb oil, or sufficient to film the bottom of the skillet 1 or 2 heavy skillets just large enough to hold the patties easily in one layer	Place the butter and oil in the skillet and set over moderately high heat. When you see the butter foam begin to subside, indicating it is hot enough to sear the meat, sauté the patties for 2 to 3 minutes or more on each side, depending on whether you like your hamburgers rare, medium, or well done.

A warm serving platter	Arrange the hamburgers on the serving platter and keep warm for a moment while finishing the sauce.
½ cup beef stock, canned beef bouillon, dry white wine, dry white vermouth, red wine, or ¼ cup water 2 to 3 Tb softened butter	Pour the fat out of the skillet. Add the liquid and boil it down rapidly, scraping up the coagulated pan juices, until it has reduced almost to a syrup. Off heat, swirl the butter by half-tablespoons into the sauce until it is absorbed. Pour the sauce over the hamburgers and serve.

VARIATION

Bitokes à la Russe

[Hamburgers with Cream Sauce]

Ingredients for 6 plain beef hamburgers or the preceding flavored hamburgers	Sauté the hamburgers in oil and butter as described in the preceding master recipe. Remove them to a hot serving platter.
¼ cup stock or canned beef bouillon ⅔ cup whipping cream Salt and pepper Pinch of nutmeg Drops of lemon juice	Pour the fat out of the skillet. Add the stock or bouillon and boil it down rapidly, scraping up coagulated cooking juices, until reduced almost to a syrup. Pour in the cream and boil it down rapidly for a minute or two until it has reduced, and thickened slightly. Season to taste with salt, pepper, nutmeg, and drops of lemon juice.
2 to 3 Tb softened butter 2 Tb minced green herbs such as parsley, chives, tarragon, chervil, or parsley only	Off heat, swirl in the butter by half-tablespoons until it is absorbed. Stir in the herbs, spoon the sauce over the hamburgers, and serve.

VARIATION: FLAVORED BUTTERS

Any of the butters listed here may be swirled into the skillet after it has been deglazed with stock, wine, or water.

Parsley Butter, page 102   Shallot Butter, page 103
Herb Butter, page 102   Garlic Butter, page 101
Mustard Butter, page 100   Snail Butter (shallots, garlic, and
                                       herbs), page 103

VARIATION: OTHER SAUCES

Any of the following sauces are made separately. After the hamburgers have been sautéed and removed from the skillet, the sauce is poured in and boiled for a moment while the coagulated sauté juices are scraped into it. The sauce is then poured over the hamburgers.

Sauce Tomate, or *Coulis de Tomates,* tomato sauce, pages 76 to 78

Sauce Poivrade, brown sauce with strong pepper flavoring, page 70

Sauce Robert, brown sauce with mustard, page 72

Sauce Brune aux Fines Herbes, brown sauce with herbs or tarragon, page 73

Sauce Madère, brown sauce with Madeira wine, page 75

Sauce au Cari, brown sauce with curry and onions, page 73

See also the red wine and the white wine sauce for steaks on page 294, and the mushroom sauce for *filet* steak on page 297.

FILET OF BEEF

Filet de Boeuf

* FILET DE BOEUF BRAISÉ PRINCE ALBERT

[Braised *Filet* of Beef Stuffed with *Foie Gras* and Truffles]

Here is a magnificent recipe for an important dinner, and it is not a difficult one in spite of the luxury of its details. We have chosen braised *filet* because it is more unusual than roast *filet.* Everything except the actual cooking of the meat may be done in advance as indicated by the asterisk in the recipe.

Braised lettuce and potato balls sautéed in butter would go beautifully with this, and you should accompany it with a fine château-bottled red Bordeaux from the Médoc district. See also the other vegetables suggested for steaks on page 292.

For 8 people

4 to 6 canned truffles about 1 inch in diameter 3 Tb Madeira	Cut the truffles in quarters. Place in a small bowl with juice from the can and the Madeira. Cover and marinate while preparing the rest of the ingredients.
The braising vegetables (matignon)	
¾ cup each: finely diced carrots and onions	Cook the vegetables, ham, seasonings, herbs, and butter slowly together in a small covered saucepan for

½ cup finely diced celery
3 Tb diced boiled ham
¼ tsp salt
Pinch of pepper
A small herb bouquet: 2 parsley sprigs, ⅓ bay leaf, ⅛ tsp thyme tied in cheesecloth
3 Tb butter
⅓ cup Madeira

10 to 15 minutes, until the vegetables are tender but not browned. Then pour in the wine and boil it down rapidly until it has almost entirely evaporated. Set aside.

The foie gras stuffing

2 Tb very finely minced shallots or green onions
1 Tb butter
4 ounces or ½ cup *mousse de foie d'oie* (or "block" *foie gras,* which is much more expensive but also much better)
1 Tb Madeira
1 Tb cognac
Pinch of allspice
Pinch of thyme
⅛ tsp pepper

Cook the shallots or onions slowly in butter for 3 minutes in a small saucepan without browning them. Scrape into a mixing bowl. Beat in the *foie gras* and other ingredients. Correct seasoning.

A 3-lb. trimmed *filet* of beef, at least 3 inches in diameter
Salt and pepper

Cut a deep slit down the length of the least presentable side of the *filet,* going to within ¼ inch of the two ends and to within ¼ inch of the other side, or top. Season the interior of the slit lightly with salt and pepper, and spread it with the *foie gras* mixture. Insert the truffles in a line down the center of the filled slit—reserve their marinade for later. Do not stuff the *filet* so full that the slit cannot be closed.

A 2½-inch strip of fresh pork fat as long as the *filet* (or strips of blanched bacon, page 15)
White string

Lay the pork fat or bacon strips the length of the closed slit. Tie securely but not too tightly with loops of white string at 1-inch intervals.

Braising the filet

Preheat oven to 350 degrees.

A heavy, oval, fireproof casserole just large enough to hold the *filet*
2 Tb butter
1 Tb oil
Salt and pepper
A meat thermometer

Brown the *filet* lightly on all sides in the casserole in hot butter and oil. Discard the browning fat. Season the meat lightly with salt and pepper. (Insert meat thermometer, unless you are using the "instant" kind.) Spread the cooked vegetables over the *filet*.
(*) May be prepared in advance to this point.

2 to 3 cups good brown stock or canned beef bouillon (or a very good brown sauce, page 66, in which case the starch liaison at the end of the recipe is omitted)
An oval of aluminum foil
A bulb baster

Pour in enough stock, bouillon, or sauce to come half way up the sides of the *filet*. Bring to a simmer on top of the stove. Lay foil over the meat. Cover the casserole and set in lower third of pre-heated oven for 45 to 55 minutes. Regulate heat so liquid remains at a very slow boil. Baste the meat with the braising stock 3 or 4 times during its cooking. The *filet* is done at a meat-thermometer reading of 125 degrees for rare beef, or 135 for medium rare, and if, when you press the *filet* with your finger, it offers a slight resistance in contrast to its soft, raw state.

A hot serving platter

Place the *filet* slit-side down on a hot serving platter after removing the trussing strings and pork fat or bacon. The meat should cool for 10 minutes or more before carving, so that its juices will retreat back into the tissues.

Sauce and serving

Wine marinade from the truffles

Skim the fat off the braising juices. Pour the truffle marinade into them, and rapidly boil down this liquid until it has reduced to about 2 cups and its flavor is rich and concentrated.

1 Tb arrowroot or cornstarch mixed with 2 Tb Madeira
Optional: 2 or 3 Tb diced truffles

Beat in the starch mixture (unless you have used the brown sauce) and the optional truffles. Simmer for 2 to 3 minutes, then correct seasoning. The diced *matignon* vegetables remain in the sauce.

Decorate the platter with whatever vegetables you have chosen. Pour a spoonful or two of the sauce and diced vegetables over the meat, and pass the rest of the sauce in a bowl. The *filet* is carved into crosswise slices about ⅜ inch thick.

VARIATION

If you do not wish to stuff the *filet,* cook it exactly the same way but without slitting and filling it. When you have placed it on a serving platter, you may garnish the top with broiled mushroom caps alternating with sliced truffles.

VARIATION

Marinade, for Filet of Beef

The following marinade is particularly good if you do not have top-quality *filet.*

½ cup dry white wine or dry white vermouth
¼ cup Madeira
2 Tb cognac
1 tsp salt
6 peppercorns
¼ tsp thyme
¼ tsp basil
3 parsley sprigs
3 Tb minced shallots or green onions
2 or more canned truffles and their juice

Place the raw, trimmed *filet* in an enameled or pyrex dish or casserole. Pour on the wines and mix in the seasonings, herbs, shallots or onions, and truffles. Cover and marinate for 6 hours or overnight, turning the meat and basting it several times. Drain and dry the meat thoroughly before browning it. Include the marinade, but not the truffles, with your braising liquid. Reserve the truffles for your sauce.

BOILED BEEF

Pot-au-feu

* *POTÉE NORMANDE*

POT-AU-FEU

[Boiled Beef with Pork, Chicken, Sausage, and Vegetables]

Here is a sumptuous family-style boiled dinner which will serve 12 or more, and always makes a great hit with guests. It is brought to the table in its kettle or a reasonable facsimile, looking for all the world like a plain *pot-au-*

feu. The host starts the proceedings as usual by spearing out the beef and placing it on a platter. Then he finds a sausage, and after that a big piece of pork. Finally, to wild acclaim, he brings out a chicken. Two or three sauces may be served, such as a cream sauce with mustard and tomato, an herbal mayonnaise, and a big bowl of the cooking stock. The *potée,* like all boiled dinners, is easy on the cook because it can simmer quietly by itself for 4 to 5 hours and if it is done before serving time, it can remain in its kettle where it will keep warm for a good hour.

VEGETABLE AND WINE SUGGESTIONS

Carrots, turnips, onions, and leeks cook along with the meats. Boiled potatoes, *risotto,* or buttered noodles are prepared and served separately. A nice, simple red wine goes well: Beaujolais, Bordeaux, or Chianti, or a chilled *rosé.*

BEEF CUTS FOR BOILING—POT-AU-FEU

First Choice: Rump Pot Roast—*Pointe de Culotte* or *Aiguillette de Rumsteck*

> Other Choices: Sirloin Tip, Knuckle—*Tranche Grasse*
> Bottom Round—*Gîte à la Noix*
> Chuck Pot Roast—*Paleron* or *Macreuse à Pot-au-feu*
> Brisket—*Milieu de Poitrine*

For 12 to 16 people

A kettle large enough to hold all the ingredients listed

Beef (cooking time 2½ to 3 hours): a 4-lb. boneless piece of rump pot roast, sirloin tip, bottom round, chuck pot roast, or brisket

Pork (cooking time about 3 hours): a 4-lb. piece from the butt, picnic, rolled shoulder, or fresh ham

Chicken (cooking time 2½ to 3 hours): a 4-lb. ready-to-cook stewing hen of good quality

Sausage (cooking time 30

All the meats and vegetables listed at the left are simmered together in the kettle, but are added at various times, depending on how long they take to cook. Start the cooking 5 hours before you expect to serve, to be sure the meats will be done. Trim excess fat off the beef and pork. Tie each piece so it will hold its shape during cooking. Truss the chicken. To each piece of meat and to the chicken, tie a string long enough to fasten to the handle of the kettle, so that the meats may be removed easily for testing.

NOTE: You could do with this chicken only, and it would be called a *poule au pot.*

minutes): 2 lbs. lightly
smoked country or Polish
sausage

Vegetable Garnish (cooking
time 1½ hours): carrots,
onions, turnips, and, if
available, leeks; 1 to 2 of
each vegetable per person

Prepare the vegetable garnish: Peel the carrots and
turnips and quarter them lengthwise; peel the onions;
trim and wash the leeks. Tie the vegetables in one or
several bundles of washed cheesecloth so they may be
removed easily from the kettle.

Soup Vegetables and Herbs:
  3 scraped carrots
  3 peeled onions, each stuck
    with a whole clove
  2 scraped parsnips
  2 celery stalks
  2 leeks, if available
  A large herb bouquet as
    follows: 6 parsley sprigs,
    1 bay leaf, ½ tsp thyme,
    4 garlic cloves, 8 pepper-
    corns tied in cheese-
    cloth
Cooking Stock: sufficient
meat stock to cover in-
gredients by 6 inches; OR
3 cans of beef bouillon, 3
cans of chicken broth, and
water
Optional: raw or cooked
beef or veal bones, meat
scraps, poultry carcasses,
necks, gizzards

Place the beef in the kettle with the soup vegetables,
herb bouquet, and optional bones and scraps. Cover
with cooking stock by 6 inches. More liquid may be
added later if necessary. Set kettle over moderate heat,
bring to the simmer, skim. Partially cover the kettle
and simmer slowly for 1 hour, skimming occasionally.

Add the pork and chicken. Bring kettle quickly back
to the simmer. Skim. Simmer 1½ hours more and
skim from time to time.

Then add the vegetable garnish and bring kettle
quickly back to the simmer. Taste cooking stock for
seasoning and salt lightly if necessary. Simmer 1½ to
2 hours more, adding the sausage ½ hour before the
end. The meats and chicken are done when they are
tender if pierced with a sharp-pronged fork or skewer.
If any piece is tender before the others are done, re-

move to a bowl and keep moist with several ladlefuls of cooking stock. Return to kettle to reheat before serving.

(*) If the *potée* is ready before you are, it will stay warm for at least 45 minutes in the kettle, or may be reheated.

While the kettle is simmering, prepare one or two of the sauces suggested at the end of the recipe, using some of the liquid from the kettle if you need stock.

Serving

Drain the meats and the vegetable garnish. Discard trussing strings. Arrange vegetables on a large, hot platter and moisten them with a ladleful of cooking stock. Decorate with parsley. Either place the meats in a large casserole for presentation and carving at the table, or carve in the kitchen and arrange on a platter. Strain, degrease, and season enough cooking stock to fill a large serving bowl, and pass it along with whatever sauce or sauces you have chosen from the following suggestions.

Sauce suggestions

Make 6 to 8 cups if only one sauce is to be served; 4 cups each if two sauces are served.

Sauce Alsacienne, hard-boiled egg mayonnaise with herbs, capers, and cooking stock, page 93

Sauce Nénette, heavy cream simmered until it has reduced and thickened, then flavored with mustard and tomato, page 387

Sauce Tomate or *Coulis de Tomates,* a good tomato sauce, page 76–8

Sauce Suprême, a *velouté* sauce made with the cooking stock, and enriched with cream, page 59

BRAISED BEEF–POT ROAST
Pièce de Boeuf Braisée

* *BOEUF À LA MODE*

[Beef Braised in Red Wine]

Braised beef is a wonderful party dish; it is not only delicious to smell, look at, and eat, but you have no worries about overdone meat, and you can cook it ahead of time if you need to. The following recipe calls for a 6- to 24-hour marination of the beef in red wine and aromatic vegetables before cooking. If you prefer to omit this step, pour the marinade ingredients into the casserole after browning the meat.

VEGETABLE AND WINE SUGGESTIONS

Boeuf à la mode is traditionally garnished with braised carrots and onions, and is usually accompanied by buttered noodles, parsley potatoes, or steamed rice. Other vegetables could be braised lettuce, celery, or leeks, or buttered green peas. Serve with it a good, characterful red wine, such as a Burgundy, Hermitage, Côte Rôtie, or Châteauneuf-du-Pape.

BEEF CUTS FOR BRAISING

Although it is not essential, beef for braising is usually larded. That is, strips of fresh pork fat are inserted into it, going in the direction of the grain. They baste the interior of the meat as it cooks, and make an attractive design when the meat is sliced. Most butchers will lard the meat for you.

Choose a piece of beef of at least 3 pounds, and, however long it is, its width should be at least 4 inches. It shrinks quite a bit during cooking. Count on 1 pound of boneless beef for 2 or 3 people.

First Choice: Rump Pot Roast—*Pointe de Culotte,* or *Aiguillette de Rumsteck*

Other Choices: Sirloin Tip, Knuckle—*Tranche Grasse*
                Chuck Pot Roast—*Paleron* or *Macreuse à Pot-au-feu*
                Top Round—*Tende de Tranche*
                Bottom Round—*Gîte à la Noix*
                Eye of Round—*Rond de Gîte à la Noix*

For 10 to 12 people

Red wine marinade

An enameled, pyrex, or porcelain bowl just large enough to hold all the ingredients listed	Place half the vegetables, herbs, and spices in the bottom of the bowl. Rub the meat with salt and pepper and place it over the vegetables. Spread the rest of the vegetables and herbs over the meat. Pour on the wine, brandy, and olive oil. Cover and marinate for at least 6 hours (12 to 24 hours if the meat is refrigerated). Turn and baste the meat every hour or so.
1 cup each: thinly sliced carrots, onions, and celery stalks	
2 halved cloves unpeeled garlic	
1 Tb thyme	
2 bay leaves	

¼ cup minced parsley

2 whole cloves or 4 allspice
berries

A 5-lb. piece of braising beef
trimmed and tied for
cooking

1 Tb salt

¼ tsp pepper

5 cups young red wine with
body—Burgundy, Côtes
du Rhône, Mâcon, or
Chianti

⅓ cup brandy

½ cup olive oil

Half an hour before cooking, drain the meat on a
rack. Just before browning, dry it thoroughly with
paper towels. It will not brown if it is damp.

Browning and braising the beef

Preheat oven to 350 degrees.

A fireproof casserole or
heavy roaster just large
enough to hold the meat
and braising ingredients

4 to 6 Tb rendered pork fat
or cooking oil

Add the fat to the casserole and place over moderately
high heat. When fat is on the point of smoking,
brown the meat on all sides. This takes about 15 minutes. Pour out the browning fat.

(*) Recipe may be prepared in advance up to this
point.

One or all of these to give
body to the sauce:

1 or 2 cracked veal knuckles

1 or 2 split calf's feet

4 to 8 ounces fresh pork
rind, bacon rind, or
ham rind simmered 10
minutes in a quart of
water, rinsed, and
drained

4 to 6 cups beef stock, or
canned beef bouillon

Pour in the wine marinade and boil it down rapidly
until it has reduced by half. Then add the veal knuckles, calf's feet, and rind, and pour in enough stock or
bouillon to come two thirds of the way up the beef.
Bring to a simmer on top of the stove, skim, cover
tightly, and set in lower third of preheated oven.
Regulate heat so liquid remains at a gentle simmer for
2½ to 3 hours, and turn the meat several times during
its braising. The beef is done when a sharp-pronged
fork will pierce it easily.

2 lbs. quartered carrots braised in butter, page 477
24 to 36 small white onions, brown-braised in stock, page 483

While the beef is being braised, cook the carrots and onions. Set them aside until needed.

A hot serving platter

When the meat is tender, remove it to the platter. Discard trussing strings. Trim off any loose fat, and keep the meat warm while finishing the sauce (5 to 10 minutes).

1 Tb arrowroot or corn-starch mixed with 2 Tb Madeira or port, if needed

Skim the fat off the braising juices, and strain them through a sieve into a saucepan, pressing the liquid out of the vegetables. Simmer for a minute or two, skimming, then boil rapidly until liquid is reduced to about 3½ cups and is full of flavor. Taste carefully for seasoning. Sauce should be lightly thickened. If too thin, beat in the starch and wine mixture and simmer for 3 minutes. Then add the cooked carrots and onions and simmer for 2 minutes to blend flavors.

A slotted spoon
Parsley sprigs
A warmed sauceboat

Remove vegetables with a slotted spoon and arrange them around the meat. Decorate with parsley. Pour a bit of sauce over the meat and send the rest to the table in a warmed sauceboat. (Or carve the meat and arrange on the platter with the vegetables and parsley, and spoon some of the sauce over the meat.)

(*) AHEAD-OF-TIME NOTES

For a wait of up to one hour, return meat, vegetables and sauce to casserole, cover loosely, and set over barely simmering water.

For a longer wait, slice the meat and arrange it on a fireproof platter. Place the vegetables around the meat. Baste with the sauce. Half an hour before serving, cover and reheat in a 350-degree oven. Leftover braised beef will be just as good the next day, heated up the same way.

VARIATIONS

Cold Braised Beef

This recipe for beef braised in red wine may easily be turned into an aspic by following the directions for *boeuf à la mode en gelée,* page 556. Cold braised beef may also be served as a salad, by following the directions for *salade de boeuf à la parisienne,* page 543.

Pièce de Boeuf à la Cuillère
[Minced Braised Beef Served in a Beef Shell]

From *la vieille cuisine française* comes an unusual way to serve braised beef for a dinner party. First the beef is braised; then meat is cut out from its top and center to leave a shell of beef which is crumbed and browned in the oven. The removed beef is chopped, combined with sautéed mushrooms, minced ham, and sauce, and is returned to the shell for serving. A nice thing about this recipe is that all may be readied in advance for a 5- to 10-minute heating just before serving.

For 10 to 12 people

Braising the beef

Braise the beef and make the sauce following the master recipe, but simmer the meat only until it is almost tender, about 3 hours for a 5-pound piece. It should still be firm enough to hold its shape when the shell is made. Choose a solid, lean piece of top round with no muscle separations. It should weigh at least 5 pounds and be cut into an even rectangular block about 5 inches wide and 5 inches deep.

Making the shell

When the meat is done, remove it from the sauce. Place it under a board and a 2-pound weight to preserve its shape for about an hour while it cools to tepid. Then trim it, if necessary, into a neat rectangle. Hollow out the center, leaving an open-topped rectangular trough or shell of meat with sides and bottom half an inch thick. Chop the removed meat, including any trimmed-off bits, into ⅛-inch pieces. Place them in a large, heavy-bottomed, enameled saucepan, skillet, or casserole.

Preparing the filling

½ lb. fresh mushrooms, quartered and sautéed in oil and butter with 1 Tb minced shallots or green onions, page 513

¾ cup (4 ounces) lean, minced, boiled ham

1½ cups sauce from the braised beef

Stir the mushrooms and ham into the chopped beef, and blend in the sauce. Simmer slowly, covered, for 15 to 20 minutes, stirring frequently. Add a little more sauce if the mixture becomes too thick. It should hold its shape fairly solidly in a spoon. Carefully correct seasoning. Film top of mixture with a spoonful of stock or a bit of melted butter and set aside, uncovered, or refrigerate, until needed.

Finishing the shell

A pastry brush

2 eggs beaten in a small bowl with 1 tsp water and a pinch of salt

2 cups fine, dry, white bread crumbs tossed with ½ cup grated Parmesan cheese

½ cup melted butter

A rack set on a roasting pan

Using a pastry brush, paint the whole beef shell with beaten egg. Pat on a layer of cheese and bread crumbs. Sprinkle with butter and set the shell on the rack. Refrigerate until needed.

(*) Recipe may be completed even a day ahead up to this point.

Final assembly

Preheat oven to 450 degrees.

A vegetable garnish such as braised onions and carrots, and sautéed potatoes, OR baked tomatoes, and green beans or braised lettuce

The rest of the sauce from the braised beef poured into a gravy bowl

A hot serving platter

¼ cup minced parsley

About 5 to 10 minutes before serving, set the beef shell in the oven to brown the crumb and cheese covering lightly. Reheat the filling to the simmer. Heat the vegetable garniture and the sauce. Then place the browned shell on the platter, heap with meat mixture, and sprinkle parsley over it. Arrange the vegetables about the platter. Pass the sauce separately. Each guest cuts down the crusty, tender shell with a serving spoon to help himself to part of it and its filling.

BEEF STEWS

Ragoûts de Boeuf

Of the several types of beef stew in which the meat is browned, then simmered in an aromatic liquid, *boeuf bourguignon* is the most famous. The *daubes, estouffades,* and *terrines* usually require no browning, and are much simpler to do. To be technically correct, any recipe describing meat which is browned before it is simmered should be labeled a fricassee; we shall not always make the distinction here because stew has become current usage.

CUTS FOR STEWING

The better the meat, the better the stew. While cheaper and coarser cuts may be used, the following are most recommended. Count on 1 pound of boneless meat, trimmed of fat, for 2 people; 3 if the rest of the menu is large.

First Choice: Rump Pot Roast—*Pointe de Culotte,* or *Aiguillette de Rumsteck*

Other Choices: Chuck Pot Roast—*Paleron,* or *Macreuse à Pot-au-feu*
Sirloin Tip—*Tranche Grasse*
Top Round—*Tende de Tranche*
Bottom Round—*Gîte à la Noix*

COOKING TIME

Beef stews take 2 to 3 hours of simmering depending on the quality and tenderness of the meat. If it has been marinated before cooking, it may take less time. Stews may be cooked either in the oven or on top of the stove; the oven is preferable because its heat is more uniform.

BOEUF BOURGUIGNON
BOEUF À LA BOURGUIGNONNE

[Beef Stew in Red Wine, with Bacon, Onions, and Mushrooms]

As is the case with most famous dishes, there are more ways than one to arrive at a good *boeuf bourguignon.* Carefully done, and perfectly flavored, it is certainly one of the most delicious beef dishes concocted by man, and can well be the main course for a buffet dinner. Fortunately you can prepare it completely ahead, even a day in advance, and it only gains in flavor when reheated.

VEGETABLE AND WINE SUGGESTIONS

Boiled potatoes are traditionally served with this dish. Buttered noodles or steamed rice may be substituted. If you also wish a green vegetable, buttered peas would be your best choice. Serve with the beef a fairly full-bodied, young red wine, such as Beaujolais, Côtes du Rhône, Bordeaux–St. Émilion, or Burgundy.

For 6 people

A 6-ounce chunk of bacon	Remove rind, and cut bacon into *lardons* (sticks, ¼ inch thick and 1½ inches long). Simmer rind and bacon for 10 minutes in 1½ quarts of water. Drain and dry.

Preheat oven to 450 degrees.

A 9- to 10-inch fireproof casserole 3 inches deep
1 Tb olive oil or cooking oil
A slotted spoon

Sauté the bacon in the oil over moderate heat for 2 to 3 minutes to brown lightly. Remove to a side dish with a slotted spoon. Set casserole aside. Reheat until fat is almost smoking before you sauté the beef.

3 lbs. lean stewing beef cut into 2-inch cubes (see preceding list of cuts)

Dry the beef in paper towels; it will not brown if it is damp. Sauté it, a few pieces at a time, in the hot oil and bacon fat until nicely browned on all sides. Add it to the bacon.

1 sliced carrot
1 sliced onion

In the same fat, brown the sliced vegetables. Pour out the sautéing fat.

1 tsp salt
¼ tsp pepper
2 Tb flour

Return the beef and bacon to the casserole and toss with the salt and pepper. Then sprinkle on the flour and toss again to coat the beef lightly with the flour. Set casserole uncovered in middle position of preheated oven for 4 minutes. Toss the meat and return to oven for 4 minutes more. (This browns the flour and covers the meat with a light crust.) Remove casserole, and turn oven down to 325 degrees.

3 cups of a full-bodied, young red wine such as one of those suggested for serving, or a Chianti
2 to 3 cups brown beef stock or canned beef bouillon
1 Tb tomato paste
2 cloves mashed garlic
½ tsp thyme
A crumbled bay leaf
The blanched bacon rind

Stir in the wine, and enough stock or bouillon so that the meat is barely covered. Add the tomato paste, garlic, herbs, and bacon rind. Bring to simmer on top of the stove. Then cover the casserole and set in lower third of preheated oven. Regulate heat so liquid simmers very slowly for 2½ to 3 hours. The meat is done when a fork pierces it easily.

18 to 24 small white onions, brown-braised in stock, page 483
1 lb. quartered fresh mushrooms sautéed in butter, page 513

While the beef is cooking, prepare the onions and mushrooms. Set them aside until needed.

When the meat is tender, pour the contents of the casserole into a sieve set over a saucepan. Wash out the casserole and return the beef and bacon to it. Distribute the cooked onions and mushrooms over the meat.

Skim fat off the sauce. Simmer sauce for a minute or two, skimming off additional fat as it rises. You should have about 2½ cups of sauce thick enough to coat a spoon lightly. If too thin, boil it down rapidly. If too thick, mix in a few tablespoons of stock or canned bouillon. Taste carefully for seasoning. Pour the sauce over the meat and vegetables.

(*) Recipe may be completed in advance to this point.

Parsley sprigs

FOR IMMEDIATE SERVING: Cover the casserole and simmer for 2 to 3 minutes, basting the meat and vegetables with the sauce several times. Serve in its casserole, or arrange the stew on a platter surrounded with potatoes, noodles, or rice, and decorated with parsley.

FOR LATER SERVING: When cold, cover and refrigerate. About 15 to 20 minutes before serving, bring to the simmer, cover, and simmer very slowly for 10 minutes, occasionally basting the meat and vegetables with the sauce.

CARBONNADES À LA FLAMANDE

[Beef and Onions Braised in Beer]

Beer is typical for the Belgian braise, and gives a quite different character to beef than the red wine of the *bourguignon*. A bit of brown sugar masks the beer's slightly bitter quality, and a little vinegar at the end gives character. Serve this with parsley potatoes or buttered noodles, a green salad, and beer.

For 6 people

A 3-lb. piece of lean beef from the chuck roast or rump

2 to 3 Tb rendered fresh pork fat or good cooking oil

A heavy skillet

Preheat oven to 325 degrees. Cut the beef into slices about 2 by 4 inches across and ½ inch thick. Dry on paper towels. Put a 1/16-inch layer of fat or oil in the skillet and heat until almost smoking. Brown the beef slices quickly, a few at a time, and set them aside.

1½ lbs. or 6 cups of sliced onions

Salt and pepper

4 cloves mashed garlic

Reduce heat to moderate. Stir the onions into the fat in the skillet, adding more fat if necessary, and brown the onions lightly for about 10 minutes, stirring frequently. Remove from heat, season with salt and pepper, and stir in the garlic.

A 9- to 10-inch fireproof casserole about 3½ inches
   deep
Salt and pepper

Arrange half the browned beef in the casserole and
season lightly with salt and pepper. Spread half the
onions over the beef. Repeat with the rest of the beef
and onions.

1 cup strong beef stock or
   canned beef bouillon
2 to 3 cups light beer, Pilsner
   type
2 Tb light brown sugar
1 large herb bouquet: 6
   parsley sprigs, 1 bay leaf,
   and ½ tsp thyme tied in
   cheesecloth

Heat the stock or bouillon in the browning skillet,
scraping up coagulated cooking juices. Pour it over
the meat. Add enough beer so the meat is barely
covered. Stir in the brown sugar. Bury the herb
bouquet among the meat slices. Bring casserole to the
simmer on top of the stove. Then cover the casserole
and place in lower third of preheated oven. Regulate
heat so liquid remains at a very slow simmer for 2½
hours at the end of which time the meat should be
fork-tender.

1½ Tb arrowroot or corn-
   starch blended with 2 Tb
   wine vinegar

Remove herb bouquet. Drain the cooking liquid out
of the casserole into a saucepan, and skim off fat.
Beat the starch and wine vinegar mixture into the
cooking liquid and simmer for 3 to 4 minutes. Carefully correct seasoning. You should have about 2 cups
of sauce. Pour the sauce back over the meat.
(*) May be prepared in advance to this point.

Parsley potatoes or buttered
   noodles
Parsley sprigs

When ready to serve, cover the casserole and simmer
slowly for 4 to 5 minutes until the meat is thoroughly
heated through. Either bring the casserole to the table,
or arrange the meat on a hot serving platter, spoon the
sauce over it, surround with potatoes or noodles, and
decorate with parsley.

✳ *PAUPIETTES DE BOEUF*
ROULADES DE BOEUF
PETITES BALLOTINES DE BOEUF
[Braised Stuffed Beef Rolls]

Paupiettes are thin slices of beef wrapped around a filling, and braised in
wine and stock with herbs and aromatic vegetables. Although they follow the
same general pattern as other fricassees of beef, their pork and veal stuffing
gives them a special character. *Paupiettes* can be cooked in advance, and any
leftovers may be reheated or may be served cold. Accompany hot *paupiettes*

with rice, *risotto,* or noodles, and a garniture of sautéed mushrooms, braised onions, and carrots, or with buttered green peas or green beans, broiled tomatoes, and French bread. Serve a good simple red wine such as Beaujolais, Côtes du Rhône, Chianti, or a *rosé.*

For about 18 paupiettes serving 6 people

½ cup finely minced onions 1 Tb butter A 3-quart mixing bowl	Cook the onions slowly in butter for 7 to 8 minutes until they are tender but not browned. Scrape them into the mixing bowl.
6 ounces lean pork ground with 6 ounces lean veal and 3 ounces fresh pork fat, making about 1½ cups ground meat A wooden spoon 1 clove mashed garlic ⅛ tsp thyme Pinch of allspice Big pinch of pepper ¼ tsp salt ¼ cup chopped parsley 1 egg	Add all ingredients at the left to the mixing bowl and beat vigorously with a wooden spoon until thoroughly blended.
2½ lbs. lean beef (top round or chuck) cut into 18 cross-grain slices ¼ inch thick and about 3 inches in diameter Salt and pepper White string	Flatten each slice of beef to a thickness of ⅛ inch by pounding it between 2 sheets of waxed paper with a wooden mallet or rolling pin. Lay the meat flat on a board and sprinkle lightly with salt and pepper. Divide the stuffing into 18 portions and place one on the lower third of each slice. Roll the meat around the stuffing to form cylinders about 4 inches long and 1½ inches thick. Secure each with 2 ties of string. Dry in paper towels.
	Preheat oven to 325 degrees.
2 to 3 Tb rendered pork fat or good cooking oil A heavy fireproof casserole about 10 inches in diameter and 2½ to 3 inches deep	Heat the fat or oil in the casserole until almost smoking. Brown the *paupiettes* lightly, a few at a time, and remove to a side dish. Lower heat to moderate and brown the vegetables slowly for 4 to 5 minutes, stirring. Then add the flour and brown it slowly for 2 to 3 minutes. Remove casserole from heat and im-

½ cup sliced carrots
½ cup sliced onions
3 Tb flour
1 cup dry white wine or dry white vermouth
1½ cups brown stock or canned beef bouillon

mediately beat in the wine, then the stock or bouillon.

A 4-inch square of fresh pork rind, bacon rind or salt-pork rind, simmered 10 minutes in a quart of water, then drained
1 large herb bouquet plus 2 cloves of garlic: 6 parsley sprigs, 1 bay leaf, ½ tsp thyme, and the garlic tied together in cheesecloth

Lay rind in the bottom of the casserole. Place the *paupiettes* over it, and add more stock or bouillon, or water, if necessary, to the liquid in the casserole so *paupiettes* are barely covered. Add the herb bouquet.

Bulb baster

Bring to the simmer on top of the stove. Cover the casserole and set in lower third of preheated oven. Regulate heat so the *paupiettes* simmer very slowly for 1½ hours. Baste them two or three times with the liquid in the casserole.

Remove the *paupiettes* to a side dish and cut off trussing strings. Strain the cooking liquid into a saucepan and degrease thoroughly. Boil down the sauce if necessary, to concentrate its flavor. You should have 1½ to 2 cups thick enough to coat a spoon lightly. Correct seasoning.

---

1 Tb prepared mustard of the strong Dijon type blended with ⅓ cup whipping cream
A wire whip

Off heat, beat the mustard and cream into the sauce. Simmer for 1 minute. Rearrange the *paupiettes* in the casserole or a fireproof serving dish, and pour the sauce over them.
(*) Recipe may be prepared in advance to this point. Film top of sauce with a spoonful of stock or melted butter. When cold, cover and refrigerate.

Parsley sprigs

About 10 minutes before serving, reheat barely to the simmer on top of the stove. Cover and simmer slowly for 5 minutes or so, basting the *paupiettes* frequently with the sauce. Serve from the casserole, or arrange the *paupiettes* on a platter, spoon the sauce over them,

and surround with rice or noodles. Decorate with
parsley.

VARIATIONS

Prepare, brown, and braise the *paupiettes* as in the preceding recipe but
use the sauce ingredients and techniques outlined either for the *boeuf bourguignon* on page 315, or for the *carbonnades à la flamande* on page 317.

BOEUF À LA CATALANE

[Beef Stew with Rice, Onions, and Tomatoes]

Here is a hearty dish from the Spanish-Mediterranean corner of France.
Serve it with a green salad, French bread, and a strong, young red wine.

For 6 people

Preheat oven to 325 degrees.

A ¼-lb. chunk of bacon
2 Tb olive oil
A heavy, 10-inch skillet
A slotted spoon
A 3-quart fireproof casserole
about 3 inches deep

Remove rind and cut bacon into *lardons* (1½-inch
strips, ⅜ of an inch thick.) Simmer in 1 quart of
water for 10 minutes. Drain, dry, and brown lightly
in oil in the skillet. Remove with a slotted spoon to
the casserole.

3 lbs. lean stewing beef cut
into squares 2½ inches
across and 1 inch thick
(see cuts listed on page
315)

Dry the meat on paper towels. Heat fat in skillet until
almost smoking then brown the meat a few pieces at a
time. Place it when browned in the casserole.

1½ cups sliced onions

Lower heat to moderate, and brown the onions lightly.
Remove them with a slotted spoon and add to the
casserole.

1 cup clean, unwashed, raw
white rice

Still in the same fat, stir the rice over moderate heat
for 2 to 3 minutes until it turns a milky color. Scrape
into a bowl and set aside until later.

1 cup dry white wine or dry
white vermouth

Pour any remaining fat out of the skillet, add the
wine and stir for a moment over heat to dissolve
coagulated cooking juices. Pour into the casserole.

2 to 3 cups beef stock or canned beef bouillon
Salt to taste
¼ tsp pepper
2 cloves mashed garlic
½ tsp thyme
Pinch of saffron
1 crumbled bay leaf

Add stock or bouillon almost to the height of the meat. Salt lightly. Stir in the pepper, garlic, and herbs. Bring to simmer on top of the stove, cover tightly, and set in lower position of preheated oven to simmer slowly for 1 hour.

1 lb. ripe, red tomatoes, peeled, seeded, juiced, and chopped, page 505 (this will make about 1½ cups tomato pulp)

Remove casserole from oven. Stir in the tomatoes, bring to simmer on top of the stove, cover, and return to the oven for an additional hour or so of very slow simmering. When the meat is almost fork-tender, remove casserole from oven. Raise oven heat to 375 degrees.

Sautéed rice from above
Stock or canned bouillon if necessary

Tilt casserole and skim off fat. You should have 2 to 2½ cups of liquid; add more stock or bouillon, or water, if necessary. Stir in the rice. Bring to simmer on top of stove, cover, and set again in lower third of oven. Regulate heat to keep liquid at a full simmer for 20 minutes so the rice will cook. Do not stir the rice. At the end of this time it should be tender and have absorbed almost all the liquid. Remove from oven and correct seasoning.

(*) May be prepared in advance to this point. Set aside, cover askew. To reheat, cover casserole and place in a pan of boiling water for about half an hour.

1 cup (4 ounces) grated Swiss or Parmesan cheese

Just before serving, delicately fold the cheese with a fork into the hot beef and rice. Serve from the casserole or on a hot platter.

✳ *DAUBE DE BOEUF*
ESTOUFFADE DE BOEUF
TERRINE DE BOEUF

[Casserole of Beef with Wine and Vegetables – Hot or Cold]

Daube comes from *daubière*, a covered casserole. *Estouffade* is a stifling or smothering, in a covered casserole. Almost every region of France has its own *daubes, estouffades,* and *terrines.* Some of them are for a whole piece of braised beef; others are like a *boeuf bourguignon*. In many the meat is larded, and in most it is marinated in wine with vegetables before the cooking begins. Here is a savory, country-style *daube,* an informal main dish to serve with boiled potatoes, *risotto,* or noodles, a green salad, and a simple red wine or a chilled *rosé*.

Note: We have not directed that the meat be larded, but you may do so if you wish, by inserting two ¼-inch strips of larding pork or blanched bacon through each piece of meat. You may also omit the marination of the meat, and add all the marinade ingredients to the casserole with the beef.

For 6 people

3 lbs. lean stewing beef cut into 2½-inch squares, 1 inch thick (beef cuts are listed on page 315)

A large glazed earthenware bowl

1½ cups dry white wine, dry white vermouth, or red wine

Optional: ¼ cup brandy, *eau de vie,* or gin

2 Tb olive oil

2 tsp salt

¼ tsp pepper

½ tsp thyme or sage

1 crumbled bay leaf

2 cloves mashed garlic

2 cups thinly sliced onions

2 cups thinly sliced carrots

Place the beef in the bowl and mix with the wine, optional spirits, olive oil, seasonings, herbs, and vegetables. Cover and marinate at least 3 hours (6 if refrigerated), stirring up frequently.

½ lb. lean bacon cut into 1-inch slices ¼ inch thick and 2 inches long approximately

1½ cups (6 ounces) sliced fresh mushrooms

1½ lbs. ripe, red tomatoes, peeled, seeded, juiced, and chopped, page 505 (this will make about 2¼ cups tomato pulp)

Simmer the bacon for 10 minutes in 2 quarts of water. Drain and dry. Prepare the mushrooms and tomatoes.

Remove the beef from the marinade and drain in a sieve.

Preheat oven to 325 degrees.

A 5- to 6-quart fireproof casserole 3½ inches deep
1 cup sifted flour on a plate

Line the bottom of the casserole with 3 or 4 strips of bacon. Strew a handful of the marinade vegetables, mushrooms, and tomatoes over them. Piece by piece, roll the beef in the flour and shake off excess. Place closely together in a layer over the vegetables. Cover with a few strips of bacon, and continue with layers of vegetables, beef, and bacon. End with a layer of vegetables and 2 or 3 strips of bacon.

1 to 2 cups beef stock or canned beef bouillon

Pour in the wine from the marinade and enough stock or bouillon almost to cover the contents of the casserole. Bring to simmer on top of the stove, cover closely, and set in lower third of preheated oven. Regulate heat so liquid simmers slowly for 2½ to 3 hours. The meat is done when a fork pierces it easily.

Tip casserole and skim out fat. Correct seasoning.
(*) May be prepared ahead and reheated, and is good either hot or cold.

VARIATION

Daube de Boeuf à la Provençale

[Casserole of Beef with Garlic and Anchovy Sauce]

This is the same *daube* given a Provençal flavoring at the end. Any cold leftovers are delicious, served with a green salad and French bread. Follow the master recipe with these additions:

10 flat anchovy *filets* packed in olive oil
2 Tb capers
A table fork
3 Tb wine vinegar

Using a fork, mash the anchovies and capers to a paste in a bowl. Beat in the other ingredients. After the *daube* has cooked for 2½ hours remove it from the oven and skim off the fat. Pour on the anchovy mixture and baste the beef with the cooking juices in

3 Tb olive oil from the anchovy can and/or plain olive oil

2 cloves mashed garlic

¼ cup minced parsley

Bulb baster

the casserole. Cover and return to oven until the meat is tender.

BEEF SAUTÉS

Sauté de Boeuf

* *SAUTÉ DE BOEUF À LA PARISIENNE*

[Beef Sauté with Cream and Mushroom Sauce]

This sauté of beef is good to know about if you have to entertain important guests in a hurry. It consists of small pieces of *filet* sautéed quickly to a nice brown outside and a rosy center, and served in a sauce. The following recipe can easily be prepared in 30 minutes, or in less than half the time if the meat has been sliced and the mushrooms sautéed ahead. In the variations at the end of the recipe, all the sauce ingredients may be prepared in advance. If the whole dish is cooked ahead of time, be very careful indeed in its reheating that the beef does not overcook. The cream and mushroom sauce here is a French version of beef Stroganoff, but less tricky as it uses fresh rather than sour cream, so you will not run into the problem of curdled sauce.

Serve the beef in a casserole, or on a platter surrounded with steamed rice, *risotto,* or potato balls sautéed in butter. Buttered green peas or beans could accompany it, and a good red Bordeaux wine.

For 6 people

½ lb. sliced fresh mushrooms

A heavy, 9- to 10-inch enameled skillet

2 Tb butter and 1 Tb good cooking oil

3 Tb minced shallots or green onions

¼ tsp salt and a pinch of pepper

Following directions on page 513, sauté the mushrooms in the skillet in hot butter and oil for 4 to 5 minutes to brown them lightly. Stir in the shallots or onions, and cook for a minute longer. Season the mushrooms, and scrape them into a side dish.

2½ lbs. *filet* of beef; the tenderloin butt and the tail of the *filet* are usually used (see illustrations, page 290)

Remove all surrounding fat and filament, and cut the *filet* into 2-ounce pieces, about 2 inches across and ½ inch thick. Dry thoroughly on paper towels.

2 Tb butter and 1 Tb cooking oil, more if needed

Place the butter and oil in the skillet and set over moderately high heat. When the butter foam begins to subside, sauté the beef, a few pieces at a time, for 2 to 3 minutes on each side to brown the exterior but keep the interior rosy red. Set the beef on a side dish, and discard sautéing fat.

¼ cup Madeira (best choice), or dry white vermouth
¾ cup good brown stock or canned beef bouillon
1 cup whipping cream
2 tsp cornstarch blended with 1 tablespoon of the cream

Pour the wine and stock or bouillon into the skillet and boil it down rapidly, scraping up coagulated cooking juices, until liquid is reduced to about ⅓ cup. Beat in the cream, then the cornstarch mixture. Simmer a minute. Add the sautéed mushrooms and simmer a minute more. The sauce should have a slight liaison (be lightly thickened). Taste carefully for seasoning.

Salt and pepper

Season the beef lightly with salt and pepper and return it to the skillet along with any juices which may have escaped. Baste the beef with the sauce and mushrooms; or transfer everything to a serving casserole.

2 Tb softened butter
Parsley sprigs

When you are ready to serve, cover the skillet or casserole and heat to below the simmer for 3 to 4 minutes, being very careful not to overdo it or the pieces of *filet* will be well done rather than rare. Off heat and just before serving, tilt casserole, add butter to sauce a bit at a time while basting the meat until the butter has absorbed. Decorate with parsley, and serve at once.

VARIATIONS

Sauté de Boeuf à la Bourguignonne

[Beef Sauté with Red Wine, Mushrooms, Bacon, and Onions]

For 6 people

2½ lbs. filet of beef pre-pared and sautéed as in preceding master recipe

A 3-ounce chunk blanched bacon, page 15

1½ cups red wine

1½ cups brown stock or canned beef bouillon

1 clove mashed garlic

1 Tb tomato paste

¼ tsp thyme

Sauté the beef and set it aside. Cut the blanched bacon into 1-inch strips ¼ of an inch thick. Brown lightly in the sauté skillet and pour out fat. Add rest of ingredients at left and slowly boil down by half.

1 Tb flour mashed to a paste with 1 Tb butter—*beurre manié*

A wire whip

Remove from heat and beat in the flour-butter paste. Simmer for 1 minute, beating with wire whip.

18 small braised onions, page 481

½ lb. sliced mushrooms sautéed in butter, page 513

Salt and pepper

A fireproof serving casserole

Add onions and mushrooms and simmer 2 minutes. Correct seasoning. Season the sautéed beef, and arrange it and the sauce, bacon, and vegetables in the serving casserole.

(*) Recipe may be prepared ahead to this point. Set casserole aside uncovered.

2 Tb softened butter

Parsley sprigs

When ready to serve, cover and reheat at below simmer for 3 to 4 minutes. Off heat, add the butter by bits, basting the meat and vegetables with the sauce until the butter has absorbed. Decorate with parsley and serve immediately.

Sauté de Boeuf à la Provençale

[Beef Sauté with Fresh Tomato Sauce, Olives, and Herbs]

For 6 people

2½ lbs. filet of beef

Cut and sauté the beef as described in the preceding master recipe. Remove to a side dish.

⅓ cup dry white wine or dry white vermouth

Pour the fat out of the sauté skillet and pour in the wine. Boil it down rapidly until reduced to 2 table-

2 cups fresh tomato purée
  with garlic and herbs,
  page 78
⅓ cup pitted black olives,
  preferably the dryish
  Mediterranean type
2 Tb mixed fresh green
  herbs, or parsley

spoons, scraping up coagulated sauté juices. Add the tomato purée and simmer a moment. Then add the sautéed beef and reheat without simmering. Decorate with olives and herbs or parsley, and serve immediately.

LAMB AND MUTTON

Agneau et Mouton

American scientific methods have achieved the miracle of our growing some of the world's finest wines, and this same approach has worked tremendous improvements in chicken raising, as well as in the cross-breeding, feeding, and raising of lamb. We can now buy large young lamb, 5 to 7 months old, all through the year. From mid-February through April we get lamb grown in the Imperial Valley of California, from May through July it comes from Nevada and Idaho, mountain lamb from Colorado comes to us in the fall, and winter lamb is raised in Ohio and Iowa. Furthermore, over 90 percent of the lamb we see in our big supermarkets has the purple USDA inspection stamps that guarantee a healthy animal, as well as the official grading stamp CHOICE. A whole leg averages 8 to 9 pounds—2 or more pounds over the old average—and makes wonderful eating.

The old labels of spring lamb, milk-fed lamb, and mutton do not apply at all anymore to commercially raised American lamb, but because this is a book of classic French cooking, it is good to know the traditional terminology, and you may still find that these labels apply among private meat purveyors and individual raisers. (Imported lamb from Australia and New Zealand is raised from a smaller breed of animal, and always comes to us frozen.)

TRADITIONAL TERMS FOR LAMB AND MUTTON

Hothouse Lamb, Milk-fed Lamb—*Agneau de Lait, Agneau de Pauillac.* Very young lamb raised, like veal, on milk, and considered a prime delicacy. Roast it whole with one of the stuffings on pages 336 to 338, or cut it up and brown with a mustard coating, like that on the broiled chicken, page 265. You may find this in ethnic Greek or Italian markets around Easter time.

Genuine Spring Lamb, Milk-finished Lamb—*Agneau Pascal.* Lamb that is 3 to 4 months old with delicate, pale red flesh. You'd have to order this from a private breeder or purveyor. Roast, broil, or grill it, stew it *en blanquette* like veal, page 362, or poach it, page 342.

Lamb—*Agneau.* Young lamb, ideally from 5 to 7 months old, the kind we buy today in our large markets. The best French lamb, by the way, has always been considered to be from those fed on the salty grasses of the northern coastal areas, *les près salés.*

Mutton—*Mouton.* No longer lamb, from between 12 months and 2 years old, it is mutton. Full-flavored and in need of proper aging, mutton is roasted like lamb, or the chops are broiled, and the rest makes mutton stew. Unfortunately it is rare to find mutton anywhere today, even in France.

LEG OR SHOULDER OF LAMB

Gigot ou Épaule de Pré-salé

PREPARING A LEG OF LAMB FOR COOKING

Trim off all but a thin layer of fat, and remove any loose fat. Shave off the purple inspection stamps.

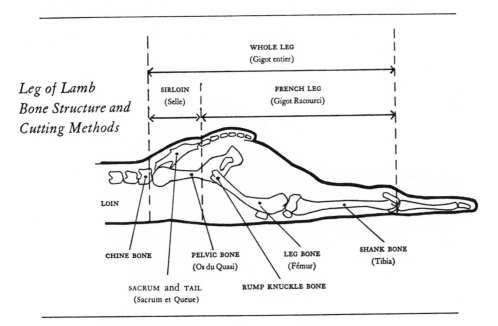

Leg of Lamb Bone Structure and Cutting Methods

WHOLE LEG
(Gigot entier)

SIRLOIN
(Selle)

FRENCH LEG
(Gigot Racourci)

LOIN

CHINE BONE

PELVIC BONE
(Os du Quasi)

LEG BONE
(Fémur)

SHANK BONE
(Tibia)

SACRUM and TAIL
(Sacrum et Queue)

RUMP KNUCKLE BONE

In the following recipes, a 6-pound leg of lamb means the French leg, without the sirloin, since the whole 9-pound leg is more than the average oven wants; however, the whole leg roasts in almost the same amount of time.

Although some meat fanciers object to any tampering at all with a leg of lamb, carving is much easier if some of the bones are removed. The tail and the pelvic bone may be cut out, and the meat sewn or skewered together to cover the rump knucklebone. Or if you wish only the shank to remain after the pelvic bone has been removed, the leg bone may be taken from inside the meat without making an outside incision; the meat is then sewn or skewered at the large end. If the leg is boned entirely, then rolled and tied, it makes a compact roast which may be cooked on a spit. Most butchers will perform any of these operations for you, but they are not too difficult to manage by yourself. The bones and trimmings may be turned into a good sauce for your roast, see *sauce ragoût,* page 69.

FLAVORINGS AND STUFFINGS

For a mild garlic flavor, insert 3 or 4 slivers of garlic in the meat at the shank end. For a more pronounced flavor, make several incisions in the meat and insert more garlic slivers. See also the garlic and herb stuffing and other suggestions for boned lamb beginning on page 336, and the herbal-mustard coating on page 335.

SHOULDER OF LAMB

Shoulder of lamb in America is one half the forequarter of lamb, minus the lower part of the ribs and the shank. It thus forms a square shape, and consists of the upper leg, all or part of the shoulder blade, 3 to 5 shoulder chops, and 2 or 3 vertebrae in the neck. Whole, it weighs 4 to 6 pounds; boned, a third less, or 2½ to 4 pounds. In France the shank is considered to be part of the shoulder, but not the chops. So if you are living there and want to stuff a shoulder of lamb, ask that some of the shoulder chops, *côtes découvertes,* be included. Otherwise there will be little room for your stuffing. When the shoulder is boned, the fell or top filament, is left intact to form a covering for the roast. After boning, the shoulder may be rolled, tied, and roasted as is. Or it may be stuffed and either rolled and tied into a fat cylindrical shape, or formed into a square cushion roast. Boned shoulder may be substituted for leg of lamb in any of the recipes in this section.

TIMING FOR ROAST LAMB AND MUTTON

Lamb and mutton cooked in the French manner are seared for 15 minutes in a 450-degree oven, then the roasting is continued in a 350-degree oven until the meat is frankly rare, rosy, and juicy. If you prefer lamb well done, do not go over a meat-thermometer reading of 160 degrees or the meat will lose much of its juice and flavor. Medium, from bright to pale pink, would be 140 to 150. A boned leg or shoulder will weigh approximately 30 per cent less than a bone-in piece, but its cooking time per pound usually more than doubles, depending on the thickness of the meat. The estimates in the following list are based on unchilled meat, and the recipes refer to unboned meat unless otherwise specified.

A 6-pound leg or shoulder, bone in

Rare—1 to 1¼ hours (10 to 12 minutes per pound)
Meat Thermometer Reading—125 to 130 degrees

Medium to Well Done—1¼ to 1½ hours (13 to 15 minutes per pound)
Meat Thermometer Reading—145 to 160 degrees

A 4-pound piece of boned and rolled leg or shoulder

Rare—1¾ to 2 hours (25 to 30 minutes per pound)
Meat Thermometer Reading—125 to 130 degrees

Medium to Well Done—2 to 2¼ hours (30 to 35 minutes per pound)
Meat Thermometer Reading—145 to 160 degrees

VEGETABLE SUGGESTIONS FOR ROAST LAMB

Beans

Gigot, haricots—lamb and beans—are a favorite combination. The beans may be plain buttered green beans, page 444, or green beans and fresh shell beans (otherwise known as white or cranberry beans), or the dried beans on page 400. A mixture of the two is called *haricots panachés*. Another suggestion is green beans with tomatoes, page 447. Additional bean recipes are in the Bean section, pages 442 to 447.

Potatoes

With plain buttered green vegetables you could serve one of the potato casseroles, pages 523 to 526, or the garlic mashed potatoes on page 520. Potatoes sautéed in butter, page 526, go with either plain or sauced vegetables.

Other vegetables

Rice with mushrooms, page 531, could be accompanied by one of the recipes for peas, pages 461 to 467, and baked tomatoes, page 506.

Tomatoes stuffed with herbs or mushrooms, page 507, green beans, and sautéed potatoes are always good with roast lamb.

Eggplant and lamb are an excellent flavor combination. See the eggplant casserole, *ratatouille*, page 503, and the eggplant stuffed with mushrooms on page 501.

Brussels sprouts or broccoli, pages 449 to 456, or cauliflower, pages 456 to 461, are other ideas. If the vegetables are served plain, you could accompany them with one of the potato casseroles on pages 523 to 526.

TRADITIONAL GARNITURES

Here are some of the traditional French vegetable combinations for garnishing a roast of lamb.

Bruxelloise, braised endive, page 493, Brussels sprouts braised in butter, page 451, potatoes sautéed in butter, page 526.

Châtelaine, quartered artichoke hearts braised in butter, page 431, whole baked tomatoes, page 506, braised celery, page 491, potatoes sautéed in butter, page 526.

Clamart, cooked artichoke hearts, page 431, filled with buttered peas, page 462, potatoes sautéed in butter, page 526

Florian, braised lettuce, page 489, brown-braised onions, page 483, carrots braised in butter, page 477, potatoes sautéed in butter, page 526

Judic, tomatoes stuffed with herbs or mushrooms, page 507, braised lettuce, page 489, potatoes sautéed in butter, page 526

Provençale, whole baked tomatoes, page 506, baked stuffed mushrooms, page 516

Viroflay, spinach braised with stock or cream, page 470, quartered artichoke hearts braised in butter, page 431, potatoes sautéed in butter, page 526

WINE SUGGESTIONS

Red wine goes with lamb and mutton. A light red, such as Bordeaux-Médoc, is best with the delicate flavor of young spring lamb. Serve a stronger red, such as Bordeaux–St. Émilion, with more mature lamb. Mutton, or lamb roasted with a strong, herbal stuffing or mustard coating, calls for a sturdier wine, Côtes du Rhône or Burgundy.

✳ *GIGOT DE PRÉ-SALÉ RÔTI*

[Roast Leg of Lamb]

For 8 to 10 people

Preheat oven to 450 degrees.

A 6-lb. leg of lamb

Prepare the lamb for cooking as described in the preceding paragraphs, and wipe it dry with paper towels.

4 Tb rendered fresh pork or beef fat, or a mixture of melted butter and cooking oil

A roasting pan 1½ inches deep and just large enough to hold the meat

A rack to fit the pan

A bulb baster or long-handled spoon

Brush the lamb with melted fat or butter and oil. Place it on the rack in the roasting pan and set in the upper third of the preheated oven. Turn and baste it every 4 to 5 minutes for 15 to 20 minutes, or until it has browned lightly on all sides. This sears the outside of the meat and prevents its juices from bursting out.

A meat thermometer

1 large carrot, roughly sliced

1 large onion, roughly sliced

Optional: 3 to 6 cloves unpeeled garlic, added to pan ½ hour before end of cooking

Reset oven for 350 degrees. Insert a meat thermometer into the fleshiest part of the lamb. Strew the vegetables in the bottom of the pan. Set lamb in middle level of oven and roast until done. Basting is not necessary.

Total Cooking Time

Rare, 1 to 1¼ hours, 125 to 130 degrees. Meat is slightly resistant when pressed, and if the meat is pricked deeply with a fork, the juices run rosy red.

Medium, 1¼ to 1½ hours, 145 to 150 degrees. Meat is firmer when pressed, juices run a pale rose when meat is pricked.

1 tsp salt

¼ tsp pepper

A hot platter

Discard any trussing strings or skewers. Season the lamb, and place it on a platter. It should rest at room temperature for 20 to 30 minutes before being carved, to let its juices retreat back into the tissues.

1 cup stock, brown lamb stock, or canned beef bouillon

A hot sauceboat

Remove the rack, and spoon the cooking fat out of the pan. Pour in the stock or bouillon and boil rapidly, scraping up coagulated roasting juices and mashing the vegetables into the stock. Taste for seasoning. Just before serving, strain into a hot sauceboat, pressing the juices out of the vegetables. Stir in any juices which may have escaped from the roast.

Water cress or parsley

Hot plates

Decorate the roast with water cress or parsley, and be sure to serve the lamb on hot plates as lamb fat congeals when cold.

VARIATION: OTHER SAUCES

The preceding directions are for a deglazing sauce which furnishes about a spoonful per serving. If you wish more sauce, prepare in advance 2 to 3 cups of *sauce ragoût* with the lamb bones and trimmings, page 69. Omit the stock in the master recipe and stir the sauce into the degreased roasting juices; simmer a moment, and pour into a sauceboat.

Sauce Spéciale à l'Ail pour Gigot

[Garlic Sauce for Roast Lamb]

This very good sauce uses a whole head of garlic which, after two blanchings and a long simmering, becomes tamed and develops a delicious flavor.
For 1½ to 2 cups of sauce

1 large head of garlic A saucepan containing 1 quart of cold water	Separate the garlic cloves. Bring them to the boil in the saucepan and boil 30 seconds. Drain and peel. Set again in cold water, bring to the boil, and drain.
A 1-quart heavy-bottomed saucepan ¾ cup milk, more if needed ⅛ tsp salt ¼ tsp rosemary or thyme 1½ Tb raw white rice	In the saucepan bring the milk, salt, herbs, and rice to the simmer. Add the garlic, and simmer very slowly for 45 minutes, putting in more milk by spoonfuls if the rice is in danger of scorching.
1 cup brown lamb stock, beef stock, or canned beef bouillon A sieve, a bowl, and a wooden spoon, or an electric blender Salt and pepper	Pour in the stock or bouillon and simmer 1 minute. Then force through a sieve, or purée in the electric blender. Correct seasoning. Set sauce aside and reheat when needed.
A hot gravy boat	After the lamb has been roasted as described in the master recipe and the roasting pan degreased, deglaze the pan with 2 to 3 tablespoons of stock or water, scraping up coagulated juices. Strain into the hot garlic sauce. Pass the sauce in a hot gravy boat.

VARIATION

Gigot à la Moutarde

[Herbal Mustard Coating for Roast Lamb]

When lamb is brushed with this mixture, garlic slivers and herbal stuffings are not necessary, and the lamb becomes a beautiful brown as it roasts.

For a 6-lb. leg of lamb

½ cup Dijon-type prepared mustard 2 Tb soy sauce 1 clove mashed garlic 1 tsp ground rosemary or thyme ¼ tsp powdered ginger 2 Tb olive oil	Blend the mustard, soy sauce, garlic, herbs, and ginger together in a bowl. Beat in the olive oil by droplets to make a mayonnaise-like cream.
A rubber spatula or brush	Paint the lamb with the mixture and set it on the rack of the roasting pan. The meat will pick up more flavor if it is coated several hours before roasting.
	Roast in a 350-degree oven, 1 to 1¼ hours, for medium rare; or 1¼ to 1½ hours for well done. The searing step at the beginning of the master recipe is omitted.

❋ GIGOT OU ÉPAULE DE PRÉ-SALÉ, FARCI

[Stuffed Leg or Shoulder of Lamb]

Boned leg and shoulder of lamb lend themselves nicely to any of the following stuffings, and cold leftovers are particularly good. Lay the boned meat skin side down on a flat surface. Season lightly with salt and pepper. Spread the stuffing over the meat and into the pockets left by the bones. Then roll the meat into a cylindrical shape to enclose the stuffing completely. Sew or skewer if necessary, then tie loops of string around its circumference at 1-inch intervals so the meat will hold its shape. Roast either in the oven or on a spit, or braise it as described in the recipe on page 338. The following are for 3 to 4 pounds of boned meat.

Farce aux Herbes

[Garlic and Herb Stuffing]

½ cup chopped parsley
½ tsp ground rosemary or thyme
2 Tb minced shallots or green onions
½ to 1 clove mashed garlic
¼ tsp powdered ginger
1 tsp salt
¼ tsp pepper

Mix all the ingredients together in a bowl. Spread the mixture on the lamb. Roll and tie as described in the preceding instructions.

Farce de Porc

[Pork and Herb Stuffing]

¾ cup finely minced onions
2 Tb butter
A 3-quart mixing bowl

Cook the onions and butter slowly together in a small saucepan until tender but not browned. Scrape into a mixing bowl.

1 cup fresh white bread crumbs (French or home-made-type bread)
½ cup lukewarm stock or canned beef bouillon

Soak the bread crumbs in stock or bouillon for 5 minutes. Drain in a sieve and press out as much liquid as you can. Save the liquid for your sauce, and place the bread crumbs in the mixing bowl.

½ lb. (1 cup) lean, fresh pork ground with 4 ounces (½ cup) fresh pork fat
1 clove mashed garlic
¼ tsp ground rosemary, sage, or thyme
¼ cup minced parsley
Pinch of allspice
½ tsp salt
¼ tsp pepper
1 egg
A wooden spatula or spoon

Add the rest of the ingredients to the mixing bowl and beat vigorously with a wooden spoon until well mixed. Sauté a teaspoonful until cooked through, and taste for seasoning. Add more seasonings to the stuffing if you feel it necessary.

Spread the stuffing on the lamb. Roll and tie as described at the beginning of this section.

Farce aux Rognons

[Rice and Kidney Stuffing]

¼ cup finely minced onions
1 Tb butter
⅓ cup raw white rice
⅔ cup white stock or canned chicken bouillon

In a small, heavy-bottomed saucepan, cook the onions in butter for 4 to 5 minutes until tender but not browned. Add the rice and stir over low heat for 2 to 3 minutes until it turns a milky color. Pour in the stock or chicken bouillon, bring to a boil, cover, and simmer not too slowly for 15 minutes without stirring, at which point the liquid should be absorbed and the rice almost tender. It will finish cooking in the lamb.

½ tsp ground rosemary, sage, or thyme
Pinch of allspice
¼ tsp pepper
½ clove mashed garlic
Salt to taste

Fluff in the herbs, spice, pepper, and garlic with a fork. Add salt to taste.

4 lamb kidneys, or a mixture of lamb kidneys, heart, and liver making about 1 cup in all
1 Tb butter and 1 Tb oil
Salt and pepper

Dry the meat in paper towels, and leave the pieces whole. Sauté quickly in hot butter and oil to brown very lightly, leaving the interior of the meat rosy. Cut into ⅛-inch slices. Season lightly with salt and pepper, and fold into the rice.

When the stuffing is cool, spread it on the lamb. Roll and tie the meat as described at the beginning of this section.

VARIATIONS: Other Stuffings Following the General Procedures Outlined

Farce Duxelles

[Ham and Mushroom Stuffing]

½ cup minced onions, cooked in butter
¼ lb. minced fresh mushrooms, cooked in butter
¾ cup minced, lean boiled ham
¼ cup finely minced fresh pork fat (or ham fat)
Salt, pepper, herbs

Farce aux Olives

[Olive and Ground Lamb Stuffing]

½ cup ground lean lamb
½ cup minced onions, cooked in butter
1 cup stale white bread crumbs soaked in stock or bouillon and squeezed dry
12 pitted black Greek olives, simmered 10 minutes in 1 quart of water, drained, and chopped
1 egg
Salt, pepper, herbs, allspice, and garlic

Farce Mentonnaise

[Salmon and Anchovy Stuffing]

An unlikely combination, but a good one

½ cup drained, canned salmon
6 drained, mashed anchovies (packed in olive oil)
½ cup ground lean lamb
¾ cup minced onions, sautéed in butter
Salt, pepper, herbs, garlic

GIGOT OU ÉPAULE DE PRÉ-SALÉ BRAISÉ (aux Haricots)

[Braised Leg or Shoulder of Lamb—with Beans]

Braising is a succulent way to do almost mature lamb or young mutton, particularly if it has been stuffed with any of the preceding suggestions. Beans may finish their cooking with the lamb, and will absorb a fine flavor from the braising liquid. If you do not wish to include them, serve with the lamb a purée of lentils or chestnuts, mashed potatoes, rice, or *risotto*. Other vegetables to serve with braised lamb are green beans, peas, Brussels sprouts, baked tomatoes, or a garniture of glazed carrots, turnips, onions, and sautéed mushrooms. A fairly full red wine goes well—Beaujolais, Bordeaux–St. Émilion, Côtes du Rhône, or Burgundy.

A NOTE ON TIMING

Almost mature lamb or young mutton is usually braised 40 to 50 minutes per pound, long enough for the meat, its stuffing, and the braising liquid to exchange flavors. This makes 3½ to 4 hours for a leg, and around 2½ hours for a shoulder. Boned and stuffed lamb will usually take an hour longer. The meat is done when a fork pierces it easily. You may, if you wish, cut the time in half, and cook the meat only until the thermometer indicates 150 degrees for medium rare, or 160 to 165 degrees for well done; in this case, there will be little exchange of flavor between the various elements.

Beans. If you are to use dry white beans, their soaking and precooking will take a good two hours. This is done while the lamb is braising.

For 8 to 10 people

Preheat oven to 350 degrees.

A 6- to 7-lb. leg or 4- to 5-lb. shoulder of lamb, boned, and stuffed, if you wish, with one of the preceding fillings

The lamb bones, sawed or chopped

3 to 4 Tb rendered fresh pork fat or cooking oil

A heavy fireproof casserole or covered roaster just large enough to hold all ingredients

2 large sliced carrots

2 large sliced onions

2 cups of dry white wine, or red wine, or 1½ cups dry white vermouth

½ tsp salt

¼ tsp pepper

3 to 4 cups beef stock or canned beef bouillon

4 parsley sprigs

1 bay leaf

1 tsp rosemary, thyme, or sage

3 unpeeled cloves garlic

Optional: 3 Tb tomato paste

Aluminum foil

Brown the lamb on all sides, and then the bones in hot fat or oil in the casserole or roaster. This will take 15 to 20 minutes. Remove to a side platter. Then brown the vegetables for 2 to 3 minutes. Remove them with a slotted spoon to the platter. Pour out the browning fat. Add the wine or vermouth and boil it down rapidly, scraping up coagulated browning juices, until reduced by half. Season the lamb and place it, its fattiest side up, in the casserole or roaster. Surround it with the browned bones and vegetables. Pour in enough stock or bouillon to come two thirds of the way up the meat. Stir in the herbs, garlic, and optional tomato paste. Bring to the simmer on top of the stove. Lay aluminum foil over the top of the casserole, then the casserole cover. Place in lower third of preheated oven and regulate so liquid is maintained at a slow simmer. Turn and baste the meat every half hour.

Remove the lamb from the casserole when it is to within half an hour of being done. (See A Note on Timing, at beginning of recipe.) Strain and degrease the cooking stock, and correct its seasoning. Return meat and stock to the casserole and surround with the beans which have been precooked as follows:

2½ cups dry white Great
    Northern beans
6½ cups boiling water
A 4-quart kettle
1½ Tb salt

Drop the beans into the boiling water. Bring quickly to the boil again and boil exactly 2 minutes. Set aside for 1 hour. Immediately the soaking time is up, add the salt to the kettle, bring to the simmer, and simmer 1 hour. Set aside. The beans will finish their cooking later with the lamb. After the lamb stock has been degreased as described in the preceding paragraph, drain the beans and add them to the casserole with the lamb.

(*) May be prepared ahead to this point. See note at end of recipe.

Bring the casserole again to the simmer on top of the stove. Cover, and return to the oven until the meat is tender when pierced with a fork, about 30 minutes.

A hot platter
Parsley sprigs
A hot sauceboat

Drain the lamb, remove trussing strings, and place it on a hot platter. Strain the beans and place them around the meat. Decorate with parsley sprigs. Degrease the cooking stock, correct seasoning, and pour it into a hot sauceboat.

(*) AHEAD-OF-TIME NOTES

If you wish to cook the meat in advance, braise it until tender. Then strain and degrease the cooking stock and place meat and stock in the casserole. An hour before serving, reheat on top of the stove, then cover and place in a 350-degree oven. In 20 minutes, add the beans and continue cooking for about 30 minutes more. The meat should reach an internal temperature of about 130 degrees.

Or follow the recipe but carve the meat when it is done. Arrange it in a fireproof serving dish or casserole with the beans, and spoon part of the sauce over it. Cover and reheat slowly for 10 minutes before serving.

GIGOT EN CHEVREUIL

[Leg of Lamb or Mutton Marinated in Red Wine]

A large well-aged leg of lamb or a leg of young mutton marinated for several days in wine will taste very much like a marinated leg of venison. It is roasted and served, like venison, with a *sauce poivrade* or *chevreuil*. Braised red cabbage with chestnuts, and a purée of celery root and potatoes go well with it, plus a good red Burgundy wine. Any cold sliced leftovers will be delicious.

Since the meat is marinated for a relatively long period of time, it takes on a definitely gamy taste—which is the whole reason for the recipe. The first marinade vegetables are cooked, therefore, so they will not turn sour.

Marinade Cuite

[Cooked Wine Marinade]

1 cup thinly sliced onions
1 cup thinly sliced carrots
⅓ cup thinly sliced celery
2 halved cloves garlic
½ cup olive oil
A 3-quart enameled saucepan with cover

Cook the vegetables slowly in the olive oil in the covered saucepan for 5 minutes without allowing them to brown.

6 cups full-bodied, young red wine: Mâcon, Côtes du Rhône, Beaujolais, Burgundy, Chianti
1½ cups red wine vinegar
1 Tb salt
1 tsp peppercorns
2 cloves
5 parsley sprigs
2 bay leaves
1 Tb rosemary
½ tsp juniper berries, if available, or ¼ cup gin

Add the wine, the vinegar, and all the rest of the ingredients. Simmer, partially covered, for 20 minutes. Allow the marinade to cool completely before using it.

Marinade au Laurier

[Uncooked Wine Marinade with Bay Leaves]

6 cups red wine
1½ cups wine vinegar
½ cup olive oil
35 bay leaves
1 Tb salt
½ tsp peppercorns

This alternative marinade needs no cooking, and is just poured over the lamb.

Marinating and Roasting the Lamb

A 7- to 8-pound leg of well aged lamb or young mutton

Prepare the lamb for cooking as described on page 329. It may be boned if you wish.

Place it in an enameled, pyrex, porcelain, or stainless steel bowl, roaster, or tub just large enough to hold it. Pour the marinade over it. Turn and baste the lamb 3 or 4 times a day for 4 to 5 days at room temperature, for 6 to 8 days if it is refrigerated.

Drain the lamb for half an hour or more on a rack. Just before roasting, dry it thoroughly with paper towels. Following directions in the master recipe for roast lamb on page 332, baste it with fat and sear it for 15 to 20 minutes in a 450-degree oven, then roast it at 350 degrees to a medium rare, 147 to 150 degrees on the meat thermometer.

If you are serving with it a *sauce poivrade*, page 70, or *sauce venaison*, page 70, include ½ cup of the marinade liquid as part of the ingredients.

GIGOT À L'ANGLAISE

[Boiled Leg of Lamb with Onion, Caper, or Tomato Sauce]

The English, according to the French, boil everything, thus anything boiled (or poached) and served simply is *à l'anglaise* in French cuisine. This method is truly a delicious and utterly simple way to cook a leg of lamb; simmer it in salted water until it is done, and it can stay quietly in that hot water for an hour or more before serving. But you do need a young tender "genuine spring leg of lamb" for this because the fat of older lamb penetrates the meat, giving it a strong taste. (See lamb discussion, pages 328–9.)

VEGETABLE AND WINE SUGGESTIONS

For a family-style vegetable garnish, carrots, turnips, onions, leeks, and potatoes may be cooked for an hour with the lamb; tie them in cheesecloth bundles for easy removal. For a more formal array, here are some other suggestions to be cooked separately and combined as you wish:

Purée of turnips and potatoes, page 487

Garlic mashed potatoes, page 520

Soubise (rice and onions), page 485

Brussels sprouts, pages 449 to 455

String beans, pages 442 to 447

Ratatouille (eggplant casserole), page 503

If you choose onion sauce for the lamb, serve a red Bordeaux from the Médoc district. With caper or tomato sauce, serve a chilled *rosé*.

For 6 to 8 people

A 4- to 5-lb. whole leg of genuine spring lamb

Prepare the lamb for cooking as described on page 329; if a whole leg, remove pelvic bone.

A meat thermometer

A kettle of rapidly boiling water, large enough to hold the lamb completely submerged

1½ tsp salt per quart of water

Insert a meat thermometer into the fleshiest part of the lamb. Plunge the lamb into the boiling, salted water. When the water comes back to the simmer, begin timing 10 to 12 minutes per pound, or about 1 hour (125 to 130 degrees on the thermometer for rare; 140 to 150 for medium). The water must remain at a very slow simmer throughout the cooking. (*) After the lamb has been removed from the kettle, it should cool at room temperature for about 20 minutes before it is carved. But if it is to be served later than that, pour cold water into the kettle to cool it to just below 120 degrees, so the lamb will not continue to cook. (Add 1½ tsp salt per quart of water poured into the kettle.) The lamb may rest thus for an hour or more, and the kettle may be gently reheated if necessary.

3 cups of one of the follow-
  ing sauces:
  Sauce aux Câpres (mock
    hollandaise with egg
    yolks, cream, capers,
    and butter), page 65
  Sauce Soubise (béchamel
    with onion purée), page
    64
  Coulis de Tomates (fresh
    tomato sauce with
    herbs), page 78

While the lamb is simmering, prepare the sauce: 5
minutes or less for caper sauce, about 30 for onion
sauce, 1½ hours of simmering for tomato sauce.

3 Tb melted butter
¼ cup minced parsley
A hot platter
A warmed sauceboat

Drain the lamb when you are ready to serve, and
place it on a hot platter. Baste it with the melted butter and sprinkle it with parsley. Pass the sauce in a
warmed sauceboat.

LAMB STEW

Ragoûts, Navarins, et Haricots de Mouton

In France, mutton rather than lamb is preferred for stews because the
flesh of the more mature animal has more character. But, except for the tender-
fleshed stewing cuts of "genuine spring lamb" which are best in a *blanquette*,
lamb or mutton may be used interchangeably. *Ragoût, navarin,* and *haricot* all
mean stew. *Haricot* according to most linguists is a corruption of *halicoter*, to
cut up. It does not therefore mean a lamb stew with beans. Stew meat is very
inexpensive; one can only wonder why, but be grateful when a dish like a
navarin is so delicious. Other lamb stews may be made like beef stew, and suggestions are listed at the end of the *navarin* recipe.

CUTS FOR STEWING

All of the lamb for a stew may be from the same cut, but a more interesting texture and sauce will be obtained if you use a mixture from the following
suggestions. Chop and leg meat are not recommended as they become dry and
stringy. Count on 1 pound of boneless meat for 2 people if your menu is small;
for 3, if large.

Shoulder—*Épaule* and *Basses Côtes*. Lean and meaty, a bit dry
Breast—*Poitrine*. Provides fat and texture

Short Ribs—*Haut de Côtelettes.* Provide fat and texture, and the bones give flavor

Neck—*Collet.* Has a gelatinous quality which gives body to the sauce.

PREPARATION FOR COOKING

Have excess fat and the fell or covering filament removed, and the meat cut into 2-inch cubes weighing 2 to 2½ ounces. Any bones left in the meat will give added flavor to the sauce. Most of them may be removed before serving.

TIMING

Allow about 2 hours for the cooking. Stews may be simmered on top of the stove but the more uniform and surrounding heat of the oven is preferable.

✻ *NAVARIN PRINTANIER*

[Lamb Stew with Spring Vegetables]

Navarin printanier, a most delectable lamb stew with its carrots, onions, turnips, potatoes, peas, and green beans, is presumably done in the spring when all the vegetables are young and tender. But as it can be made any time of the year, it is not a seasonal dish any more thanks to deep freezing. Frozen peas and beans are discussed on pages 449 and 466. The written recipe is long as each detail is important if the *navarin* is to taste like a French masterpiece. But none of the steps is difficult and everything except the addition of the green vegetables at the very end may be made ready in the morning. The stew can then be finished in 10 to 15 minutes just before dinner time.

With the stew serve hot French bread, and a red Beaujolais or Bordeaux wine, a chilled *rosé,* or a fairly full-bodied, dry, chilled white wine such as a Mâcon, Hermitage, or one of the lesser Burgundies.

For 6 people

Preheat oven to 450 degrees.

---

3 lbs. lamb stew meat (see list preceding recipe)

2 to 4 Tb rendered fresh pork fat or cooking oil

A 10- to 12-inch skillet

A fireproof covered casse-

Cut the lamb into 2-inch cubes and dry with paper towels. The meat will not brown if it is damp. Brown a few pieces at a time in hot fat or oil in the skillet. As they are browned, place them in the casserole.

role large enough to hold
the meat, and all the vegetables to come

1 Tb granulated sugar

Sprinkle the lamb in the casserole with sugar and toss
over moderately high heat for 3 to 4 minutes until the
sugar has caramelized. This will give a fine amber
color to the sauce.

1 tsp salt
1/4 tsp pepper
3 Tb flour

Toss the meat with the salt and pepper, then with the
flour. Set casserole uncovered in middle level of preheated oven for 4 to 5 minutes. Toss the meat and
return it to the oven for 4 to 5 minutes more. This
browns the flour evenly and coats the lamb with a
light crust. Remove casserole and turn oven down to
350 degrees.

2 to 3 cups brown lamb- or
beef-stock or canned beef
bouillon
3/4 lb. ripe, red tomatoes,
peeled, seeded, juiced, and
chopped (1 cup of pulp),
page 505; or 3 Tb tomato
paste
2 cloves mashed garlic
1/4 tsp thyme or rosemary
1 bay leaf

Pour out the fat; add 2 cups of stock or bouillon to
the sauté skillet. Bring to the boil and scrape up coagulated sauté juices. Then pour the liquid into the casserole. Bring to the simmer for a few seconds shaking
and stirring to mix liquid and flour. Add the tomatoes
or tomato paste and the other ingredients. Bring to
the simmer for 1 minute, then add more stock if
necessary; meat should be almost covered by liquid.

Put the lid on the casserole and set in lower third of
preheated oven; regulate heat so casserole simmers
slowly and regularly for 1 hour. Then pour the contents of the casserole into a sieve set over a bowl.
Rinse out the casserole. Remove any loose bones and
return the lamb to the casserole. Skim the fat off the
sauce in the bowl, correct seasoning, and pour sauce
back into casserole. Then add the vegetables which
have been prepared as follows:

6 to 12 peeled "boiling"
potatoes
6 peeled carrots
6 peeled turnips
12 to 18 peeled white onions
about 1 inch in diameter

While the lamb is simmering, trim the potatoes into
ovals 1 1/2 inches long, and cover with cold water until
ready to use. Quarter the carrots and turnips, cut them
into 1 1/2 inch lengths, and, if you have the patience,
trim the edges to round them slightly. Pierce a cross
in the root ends of the onions so they will cook evenly.

Press the vegetables into the casserole around and between the pieces of lamb. Baste with the sauce. Bring to the simmer on top of the stove, cover and return to the oven. Regulate heat so liquid simmers slowly and steadily for about an hour longer or until the meat and vegetables are tender when pierced with a fork. Remove from oven, tilt casserole, and skim off fat. Taste sauce again, and correct seasoning.

1 cup shelled green peas
¼ lb. or about 1 cup green beans cut into ½-inch pieces
3 quarts boiling water
1½ Tb salt

While the casserole is in the oven, drop the peas and beans into the boiling salted water and boil rapidly, uncovered, for 5 minutes or until the vegetables are almost tender. Immediately drain in a colander. Run cold water over them for 2 to 3 minutes to stop the cooking and to set the color. Put aside until ready to use.

(*) May be prepared ahead to this point. Set casserole aside, cover askew. Bring to the simmer on top of the stove before proceeding with recipe.

Shortly before serving, place the peas and beans in the casserole on top of the other ingredients and baste with the bubbling sauce. Cover and simmer about 5 minutes or until the green vegetables are tender.

Serve the *navarin* from its casserole or arrange it on a very hot platter.

VARIATIONS

The preceding *navarin* is a model for other stews. You may, for instance, omit the green beans, peas, and potatoes, and add navy beans or lentils simmered in salted water until almost tender, or canned kidney beans, then finish them off for half an hour with the lamb. The following are prepared exactly like beef stews.

Civet de Mouton

[Lamb or Mutton Stew with Red Wine, Onions, Mushrooms, and Bacon]

Follow the recipe for *boeuf bourguignon,* page 315, braising the lamb 2 hours rather than the 3½ to 4 hours required for beef.

Pilaf de Mouton à la Catalane

[Lamb or Mutton Stew with Rice, Onions, and Tomatoes]

Follow the recipe for *boeuf à la catalane,* page 321, using boned shoulder or shank. Time the cooking for about 2 hours rather than the 3 or 4 required for beef.

Daube de Mouton

[Casserole of Lamb or Mutton with Wine, Mushrooms, Carrots, Onions, and Herbs]

Follow the recipe for *daube de boeuf,* page 322, using boned shoulder or shank. Cook the lamb for 2 hours rather than the 3 or 4 in the recipe.

Blanquette d'Agneau

[Spring Lamb Stew with Onions and Mushrooms]

This is a delicious stew for "genuine spring lamb," and is cooked exactly like the *blanquette de veau* on page 362 in the Veal section.

Lamb Shanks

Lamb shanks, *jarrets de devant,* are considered part of the shoulder in France, so no special recipes are given for them. They may be boned or left whole, and you should allow one shank per person. Use any of the preceding lamb stew recipes. (Braised lamb shanks means that the meat is browned, then simmered in a liquid, and is just another name for stew or fricassee.)

LAMB PATTIES

Fricadelles d'Agneau

Delicious "lamburgers" may be made using freshly ground neck or other lean meat and mixing it with any of the stuffing suggestions for boned lamb on page 336–8.

Except for the garlic and herb stuffing, which is a flavoring only, use 1 part of stuffing for 3 to 4 parts of ground lamb. Sauté and sauce them according to directions in the hamburger recipes which begin on page 301.

MOUSSAKA

MOUSSAKA

[Lamb and Eggplant Mold]

Lamb can hardly be considered a leftover when it receives this elaborate treatment. A mold is lined with the skins of cooked eggplant, and filled with a carefully seasoned mixture of cooked lamb, eggplant, and mushrooms. It presents itself after baking and unmolding as a shiny, dark purple cylinder surrounded with a deep red tomato sauce. It is delicious either hot or cold.

Serve the *moussaka* with steamed rice or *risotto,* and buttered green beans or a green salad. A fairly full-bodied, dry, chilled white wine such as a Mâcon or Hermitage goes well with it. *Moussaka* also makes a handsome cold dish served with tomato salad and French bread.

For 8 people

Preheat oven to 400 degrees, in time to bake the eggplant.

Ingredients for 3 cups of tomato sauce, page 76

Set tomato sauce to simmer.

5 lbs. of eggplant (five 1-lb. eggplants if possible, each 7 to 8 inches long)
1 Tb salt
2 Tb olive oil
A shallow roasting pan

Remove green caps and slice eggplants in half lengthwise. Cut deep gashes in the flesh of each half, but do not pierce the skin. Sprinkle flesh with salt and let stand for 30 minutes. Wash under cold water, squeeze out juice, and dry on paper towels. Rub with olive oil and set eggplants skin side down in a roasting pan. Pour in ½ inch of water. Bake in upper third of preheated oven for about half an hour, or until just tender.

A 9- to 10-inch skillet
⅔ cup (3 ounces) finely minced onions
1 Tb olive oil
A 3-quart mixing bowl

While eggplants are baking, cook the onions slowly in olive oil for 10 to 15 minutes, until tender but not browned. Scrape into mixing bowl.

½ lb. finely minced mushrooms
2 Tb minced shallots or green onions

A handful at a time, twist mushrooms into a ball in the corner of a towel to extract their juice. Add the juice to the tomato sauce. Sauté the mushrooms and shallots or onions in olive oil for 5 minutes or so,

1½ Tb olive oil

until pieces separate from each other. Add to mixing bowl.

---

3 Tb olive oil

When eggplants are tender, carefully scoop out the flesh with a spoon, leaving the skin intact. Chop half the flesh and place in the mixing bowl. Dice or slice the rest and toss it briefly in very hot olive oil to brown lightly. Set aside until later.

½ tsp olive oil
A 2-quart cylindrical mold
  (preferably a *charlotte*)
  4 inches high and 7 inches
  in diameter

Oil the mold. Line it with the eggplant skins, their purple sides against the mold; place each lengthwise, a pointed end at the center of the bottom of the mold, the other end falling down outside the mold.

2¼ cups ground cooked
  lamb
1 tsp salt
½ tsp thyme
½ tsp pepper
½ tsp rosemary
1 medium clove crushed
  garlic
⅔ cup thick brown sauce,
  pages 66 to 71 (prefer-
  ably Numbers I or II; but
  the quick sauce, Number
  III, can be used)
3 Tb tomato paste
3 eggs
Aluminum foil

Reset oven to 375 degrees. Add all ingredients at the left to the mixing bowl containing the onions, mushrooms, and chopped eggplant. Beat vigorously with a wooden spoon to blend thoroughly. Taste carefully for seasoning. Spread an inch of the mixture in the bottom of the mold. Arrange over that a layer of the previously sautéed eggplant. Continue thus, ending with a layer of the lamb mixture. Fold the dangling ends of eggplant skin up over the surface. Cover the mold with foil and a lid or plate.
(*) May be prepared ahead to this point.

A pan of boiling water
A hot serving platter
The tomato sauce
A sauceboat

Set mold in a pan of boiling water. Bake in bottom third of oven for 1½ hours. Remove and let cool for 10 minutes. Reverse on a hot serving platter and surround with ½ cup of the tomato sauce. Pass the rest of the sauce separately.

VEAL
Veau

Veal is an interesting and delicious meat when it is cooked well, and like chicken it lends itself to a variety of flavorings and sauces. The best quality of veal is milk-fed and is between 5 and 12 weeks old. The flesh is firm, smooth, fine-grained, and of a very pale pink color. The fat, which is white and satiny, is concentrated almost entirely inside the carcass around the kidneys. The bones are soft and reddish and can easily be sawed without splintering. After 12 weeks veal becomes calf and is of no further culinary interest until it develops into beef. At whatever age the veal animal leaves its milk diet and starts in on grain or grass, its flesh becomes increasingly rosy until, when it is almost of calf age, it is frankly reddish. A considerable amount of the veal found in American markets is partially grass or grain fed, and its flesh color ranges from dark pink to light red. It can make reasonably good eating, but never has the delicacy, flavor, and tenderness of milk-fed veal. Train yourself when shopping for veal to look carefully at its color. Once you are aware of what good quality should look like, you can avoid the reddish pieces. You will be more likely to find the better qualities of veal in markets catering to a European clientele.

CASSEROLE-ROASTED VEAL
Veau Poêlé

With no natural fat covering and no marblings of fat inside the meat, a roast of veal will always be juicier and have more flavor if it is cooked in a covered casserole with aromatic vegetables. This is a particularly good method for the rather dark pink veal most frequently found in American markets.

CUTS FOR ROASTING

Count on 1 pound of boneless meat for 2 or 3 people.

Round Roast—*Cuisseau Raccourci*. An American duplication of French cuts of the hind leg of veal is not possible as the two cutting methods are entirely different. Because the French animal is larger and older, between 5 and 12 weeks rather than the usual 3 to 6 of American veal, the French round is separated into lengthwise muscles like beef. These are top round or *noix,* bottom round or *sous noix,* and sirloin tip or *noix pâtissière;* they make compact, boneless, cylindrical roasts which carve into neat slices. Top round and sirloin tip are the choice morsels, and top round is also used for scallops. The American round is formed into roasts, steaks, or scallops by cutting directly across the grain, so one piece contains the top and bottom rounds and the sirloin tip.

Rump—*Culotte*. This should be boned and rolled.

Sirloin—*Quasi*. This should be boned and rolled.

Loin or Saddle—*Longe,* or, *Selle,* or if the kidneys are included, *Rognon-nade.* This is the loin-chop section. When used for roasts, it is usually boned and rolled, and is an expensive cut.

Shoulder—*Épaule.* This is boned and rolled, and is less expensive than the previously listed roasts. It is not always available as some markets do not buy the forequarters of veal.

PREPARATION FOR COOKING

Select a boneless roast from any of the veal cuts in the list. It should weigh at least 3 pounds. Have it tied to make, if possible, a compact cylindrical shape 4 to 5½ inches in diameter. As it is usually not the custom of American butchers to place thin strips of fresh pork fat along the top, bottom, and sides of a roast, we have suggested strips of blanched bacon in the recipes to follow; the bacon bastes the veal as it cooks.

TIMING AND TEMPERATURES

Veal is always cooked to well done; that is, until its juices run a clear yellow with no trace of rosy color—about 175 degrees on a meat thermometer. If the meat is at room temperature when it goes into the oven, estimate 30 to 40 minutes per pound depending on the thickness of the meat.

VEGETABLE SUGGESTIONS

Starchy vegetables

Risotto, page 532, or *soubise* (rice and onions), page 485
Potatoes scalloped in cream, page 524, or sautéed in butter, page 526
Buttered noodles

Other vegetables

Braised lettuce, page 489, endive, page 493, or celery, page 491, or baked cucumbers, page 499
Spinach braised in cream or in stock, page 470
Brussels sprouts with cream, page 452, or with cheese sauce, page 453
Creamed, stuffed, or sautéed mushrooms, pages 513 to 516
Buttered peas, page 462, and tomatoes stuffed with herbs, page 507
A garniture of glazed carrots, page 479, onions, page 481, turnips, page 488 and sautéed mushrooms, page 513

WINE SUGGESTION

A good, red Bordeaux from the Médoc district is usually the best choice.

* *VEAU POÊLÉ*

[Casserole-roasted Veal]

This is a very simple and savory recipe for veal. The meat renders a certain amount of juice as it roasts, so no special sauce is necessary if you are content with the French system of a spoonful per serving to moisten the meat. For more sauce, see the suggestion at the end of the recipe.

For 6 people

Preheat oven to 325 degrees.

A 3-lb. roast of veal, boned and tied

Dry the veal on paper towels.

A heavy fireproof casserole just large enough to hold the veal easily
2 Tb butter
2 Tb oil

Place the casserole over moderately high heat with the butter and oil. When you see the butter foam begin to subside, brown the veal lightly on all sides; this takes 10 to 15 minutes. Remove the veal.

3 Tb butter, if needed
2 sliced carrots
2 sliced onions
A medium herb bouquet: 4 parsley sprigs, ½ bay leaf, and ¼ tsp thyme tied in cheesecloth

If the browning fat has burned, pour it out and add butter. Stir in the vegetables and herb bouquet, cover, and cook over low heat for 5 minutes without browning.

½ tsp salt
¼ tsp pepper
A meat thermometer
2 strips of fat bacon, simmered for 10 minutes in 1 quart of water, rinsed, drained, and dried
Aluminum foil
Bulb baster

Sprinkle salt and pepper over the veal. Return it to the casserole and baste with the butter in the casserole. Insert meat thermometer. Lay the blanched bacon over the meat, then the foil. Cover the casserole and set in lower third of preheated oven. Regulate heat so meat cooks slowly and steadily for about 1½ hours. Baste it 2 or 3 times with the juices in the casserole. The roast is done at a thermometer reading of 175 degrees, or as soon as its juices run clear yellow when the meat is pricked deeply with a fork.

A hot platter
Salt and pepper
A hot gravy boat

Place the veal on a hot platter and discard trussing strings. The veal and vegetables will have produced a cup or more of juice in the casserole. Remove all but

2 tablespoons of fat from them. Set casserole over moderate heat while scraping up any coagulated cooking juices from the bottom and sides with a wooden spoon, and mashing the vegetables into the liquid. Boil down rapidly if necessary; you should have ¾ to 1 cup. Correct seasoning, and strain into a hot gravy boat. Garnish the meat platter with whatever vegetables you have chosen, and serve.

(*) If you are not serving immediately, return the veal and sauce to the casserole, cover partially, and set in turned-off hot oven where it will stay warm for half an hour at least.

VARIATION

Veau Poêlé à la Matignon

[Casserole-roasted Veal with Diced Vegetables]

⅓ cup Madeira

Follow the master recipe for roast veal, but instead of slicing the carrots and onions, cut them into ⅛-inch dice. After browning the veal, remove it and cook the vegetables slowly in butter for 10 minutes. Then add the Madeira and boil it down rapidly until it has almost completely evaporated. Return the meat to the casserole and spread half the vegetables over it, leaving the rest in the bottom of the casserole. Proceed with the recipe.

---

1 cup good brown stock or canned beef bouillon
1 Tb arrowroot or cornstarch blended with 2 Tb Madeira
Optional: 1 diced canned truffle and juice from the can

When the veal is done and has been removed from the casserole, add the stock or bouillon and simmer for 5 minutes. Then remove the herb bouquet and bacon, and degrease the sauce. Pour in the starch mixture and optional truffles and truffle juice. Simmer for 5 minutes. Correct seasoning. Sauce should be lightly thickened.

---

2 Tb softened butter
A warmed sauceboat

Off heat, and just before serving, add the butter by bits, swirling the sauce in the casserole until each addition has been absorbed. Ladle a spoonful of sauce and vegetables over the meat. Pour the rest into the warmed sauceboat.

VEAU PRINCE ORLOFF

[Veal *Gratinéed* with Onions and Mushrooms]

This delicious creation is fine for a party as it may be prepared in the morning and reheated in the evening. The veal is cooked and sliced, re-formed with a spreading of onions and mushrooms between each slice, and covered with a light cheese sauce. It is reheated and browned before serving. Braised lettuce or endive go particularly well with this roast, and either a red Bordeaux wine from the Médoc district or a chilled white Burgundy.

For 10 to 12 people

Roasting the veal

A 5-lb. boned and tied roast of veal

Brown the veal, and roast it for about 2½ hours (to 175 degrees on a meat thermometer) in a covered casserole as described in the master recipe, page 353. Then allow the meat to rest for 30 minutes at room temperature; it will be carved when the preparations which follow are ready.

A 1-quart saucepan

Strain the roasting juices into the saucepan and skim off fat. Boil juices down rapidly to reduce to 1 cup. They will go into your *velouté* sauce later.

While the veal is roasting, prepare the onions and mushrooms as follows:

Soubise (rice and onions)

¼ cup raw white rice
2 quarts boiling water
1 Tb salt

Drop the rice into boiling salted water. Boil 5 minutes. Drain.

3 Tb butter
A 6- to 8-cup, heavy, fire-proof casserole with cover
1 lb. (3½ cups) sliced yellow onions
½ tsp salt

Melt the butter in the casserole, stir in the onions and salt, and coat well with butter; stir in the rice. (No liquid is added; the onions provide enough for the rice.) Cover and cook over very low heat or in the oven next to the veal for 45 minutes to 1 hour, until the rice and onions are very tender but not browned.

Mushroom duxelles

½ lb. finely minced fresh mushrooms (makes 2 cups)

A handful at a time, squeeze the mushrooms in the corner of a towel to extract their juice. Then sauté them with the shallots or onions in hot butter and oil

3 **Tb minced shallots or**
green onions
2 **Tb butter**
1 **Tb oil**
An 8-inch enameled skillet
or heavy-bottomed enam-
eled saucepan
Salt and pepper

for 5 to 6 minutes, or until the pieces begin to separate from each other. Season to taste and set aside.

When the roast is done, prepare the following sauce and the filling:

Thick velouté sauce

6 **Tb butter**
A 2-quart, heavy-bottomed
enameled saucepan
8 **Tb flour**
A wooden spoon
3 **cups boiling liquid: the**
veal-roasting juices plus
milk
A wire whip
Pinch of nutmeg
¼ **tsp salt**
⅛ **tsp pepper**

Melt the butter in the saucepan. Stir in the flour and cook slowly together, stirring, until they foam for 2 minutes without coloring. Remove from heat, pour in all the boiling liquid at once and beat vigorously with wire whip. Beat in the seasonings. Bring to the boil, stirring, and boil for 1 minute. Correct seasoning. Sauce will be very thick.

½ **cup whipping cream**

Pour 1 cup of sauce into the cooked rice and onions. Beat the cream into the rest of the sauce and set it in a pan of simmering water to continue cooking slowly.

Rice, onion, and mushroom filling

The cooked rice and onions
The mushroom *duxelles*
¼ **cup whipping cream,**
more if needed
Salt and pepper

Purée the rice and onions through a sieve or in an electric blender. Add the purée to the mushrooms, pour in ¼ cup cream, and simmer for 5 minutes, stirring. The filling should be thick enough to hold its shape quite solidly in a spoon. Boil down if not thick enough; thin out with spoonfuls of cream if too thick. Correct seasoning.

Final assembly

A lightly buttered, fireproof
serving platter 1½ inches
deep and about 14 inches
long

Carve the veal into neat serving slices about ³⁄₁₆ of an inch thick, piling them to one side in the order in which you sliced them. The roast is now to be re-turned in slices to the serving platter: Place the last

Salt and pepper
The filling

slice you carved in the platter, sprinkle lightly with salt and pepper, then spread with a spoonful of the filling. Overlap the next slice of veal on the first, sprinkle with salt and pepper, spread with filling, and continue thus down the length of the platter. Spread any extra filling around and over the meat.

The remaining velouté sauce

2 to 3 Tb cream, if needed
⅓ cup grated Swiss cheese

Bring the sauce to the simmer and correct seasoning. It should be thick enough to coat a spoon fairly heavily; thin out with more spoonfuls of cream, if necessary. Off heat, beat in the cheese.

---

3 Tb grated Swiss cheese
3 Tb melted butter

Spoon the sauce over the roast. Sprinkle the cheese over it, and dribble on the melted butter.
(*) May be prepared ahead to this point. Set aside uncovered until ready to reheat.

About 30 to 40 minutes before serving, set in the upper position of a preheated, 375-degree oven until the sauce is bubbling and the top has browned lightly. Do not overcook, or the meat will dry out and lose character.

Once ready, the dish will stay warm for 20 to 30 minutes in the turned-off hot oven, its door ajar.

VEAU SYLVIE

[Veal Roasted with Ham and Cheese]

In this recipe, deep slits are cut in the roast of veal from one end to the other, and the meat is marinated in brandy, Madeira, and aromatic vegetables, then stuffed with slices of ham and cheese. It is roasted in a covered casserole and, when sliced, the ham and cheese appear to have melted into the veal. Serve with the roast any of the wine and vegetable suggestions on page 352. *Veau Sylvie* also makes a good cold roast just as it is or glazed with aspic.

The French cut for this would be a *noix* or top round of veal, as it is a long, cylindrical piece with no muscle separations. Rump, round, and sirloin are more difficult to handle but can be managed perfectly well; a boned section from the rib roast would be the best alternative, though more expensive.

For 10 to 12 people

A 5-lb. boneless roast of veal, as solid as possible and in a loaf shape

So that the roast may be stuffed, deep slits are cut from one end to the other to make it open like the leaves of a book: make a series of deep, parallel cuts 1 to 1½ inches apart starting at the top and going with the grain the length of the meat from one end of the roast to the other, and to within ½ inch of the bottom of the roast. You will thus have 3 or 4 thick pieces of meat which are free at the top and sides, but which are all attached together at the bottom of the roast. If your meat contains many muscle separations it will look very messy and uneven at this point, but the roast is tied into shape later.

½ cup cognac
½ cup Madeira
2 Tb olive oil
¾ cup sliced carrots
¾ cup sliced onions
1 Tb salt
A large herb bouquet with peppercorns: 6 parsley sprigs, 1 bay leaf, ½ tsp thyme, and 6 peppercorns tied in cheesecloth
6 or more large slices of boiled ham 1⁄16 inch thick
12 or more large slices of Swiss cheese 1⁄16 inch thick
White string

Choose a glazed bowl large enough to hold the meat easily. Mix the marinade ingredients at the left in the bowl. Add the meat and baste it with the marinade. Turn and baste the meat every hour or so, and marinate for 6 hours or overnight. Then scrape off the marinade ingredients and dry the meat in paper towels. Reserve the marinade. Lay the roast so its bottom rests on your cutting board. Completely cover each leaf of meat with a layer of ham between two layers of cheese. The exterior of the two outside leaves is not covered. Then close the leaves of meat together to re-form the roast. Tie loops of white string around the circumference of the meat to hold it in shape. If the roast is not neat looking, no matter; it will firm up during its cooking. Dry the roast again with paper towels so it will brown nicely.

Preheat oven to 450 degrees.

4 Tb butter
2 Tb oil
A covered fireproof casserole large enough to hold the meat
A bulb baster

Strain the marinade, reserving the liquid. Cook the marinade vegetables slowly in the butter and oil in the casserole for 5 minutes. Push them to the sides of the casserole. Raise heat to moderately high, put the veal in, uncut side down, and let the bottom brown for 5 minutes. Then baste with the butter and oil in the casserole. Place the casserole uncovered in the upper third of the oven to brown the top and sides of the meat for about 15 minutes. Baste every 4 to 5 minutes with the butter in the casserole.

½ tsp salt
⅛ tsp pepper
2 strips of fat bacon simmered for 10 minutes in 1 quart of water, rinsed, drained, and dried
A meat thermometer
Aluminum foil

Turn oven down to 325 degrees. Remove the casserole, pour in the marinade liquid and boil it down rapidly on top of the stove until it is reduced to one third of its volume. Season the meat with salt and pepper. Place the bacon over it. Insert a meat thermometer, lay the foil over the meat, cover the casserole and place it in the lower third of the oven. Regulate heat so meat cooks slowly and steadily for about 2½ hours, or to a thermometer reading of 175 degrees. Baste 3 or 4 times with the juices in the casserole during this period.

Serve the veal and prepare the sauce as described in the master recipe, *veau poêlé,* on page 353.

The meat should rest at room temperature for about 20 minutes before being carved, and it is carved in crosswise slices so each piece has lardings of cheese and ham.

VEAL STEW

Sauté de Veau – Blanquette de Veau

In France the favorite cut of veal for stews is *tendron,* the part of the breast which contains the cartilaginous false ribs. Its combination of meat and gelatin gives the sauce a fine body, and the cooked *tendron* has a special and slightly crunchy eating-quality all its own. However, this particular morsel does not charm all American palates. Time and again we have noticed a guest push it off to the side of his plate, obviously indicating he has no intention of eating that inferior bit of budget meat. Therefore, unless you know or can train your American audience, it is probably wiser to choose other parts of the veal. A combination of cuts is the best alternative, some with bones, some with cartilage, and some lean meat. Rump, sirloin, and round tend to be dry, but there are those who prefer them anyway. If you are using boneless meat, include a cupful or so of cracked veal bones with the stew so your sauce will develop more flavor and body.

RECOMMENDED STEWING CUTS

Allow 1 pound of boneless meat for 2 or 3 people, depending on the rest of your menu; about ¾ pound per person for bone-in meat such as breast and ribs.

Breast—*Poitrine, Tendron*
Short Ribs—*Haut de Côtes*
Shoulder and Shoulder Chops—*Épaule* and *Côtes Découvertes*
Neck—*Collet*
Heel of Round or Shank—*Nerveux Gîte à la Noix or Jarret*

(Rump, Round, and Sirloin are less recommended but may be used if you wish)

STEWING TIME

Allow 1½ to 1¾ hours.

SAUTÉ DE VEAU MARENGO

[Brown Veal Stew with Tomatoes and Mushrooms]

The flavors of Provence go into this uncomplicated and hearty dish. Steamed rice or noodles go well with it, and green peas or beans. Serve a chilled *rosé* wine, or a strong, young, white wine. As with all stews, this one may be cooked in advance and reheated just before serving.

For 6 people

Preheat oven to 325 degrees.

3 lbs. veal stew meat from the preceding list, cut into 2-ounce, 2-inch pieces
2 to 3 Tb olive oil, more if needed
A 10- to 12-inch skillet
A 4-quart fireproof casserole

Dry the veal on paper towels. Heat the oil in the skillet until almost smoking. Then brown the meat, a few pieces at a time, and arrange the browned pieces in the casserole.

1 cup minced yellow onions

Lower heat to moderate. Pour all but a tablespoon of oil out of the skillet, and brown the onions lightly for 5 to 6 minutes.

1 tsp salt
¼ tsp pepper
2 Tb flour

While the onions are browning, toss the meat in the casserole with salt and pepper, then with the flour. Toss and stir over moderate heat for 3 to 4 minutes to brown the flour lightly. Remove from heat.

2 cups dry white wine or dry white vermouth

Add the wine to the skillet with the browned onions. Boil for 1 minute, scraping up coagulated sauté juices. Pour the wine and onions into the casserole and bring to the simmer, shaking and stirring to mix the liquid and flour.

1 lb. firm, ripe, red tomatoes peeled, seeded, juiced, and roughly chopped (1½ cups), page 505
OR, 1 cup drained and strained canned tomatoes or tomato purée
½ tsp basil or tarragon
½ tsp thyme
A 3-inch strip of orange peel ½ inch wide or ½ tsp bottled ground orange peel
2 cloves mashed garlic
Salt and pepper to taste

Stir the tomatoes into the casserole. Add the herbs, orange peel, and garlic. Bring again to the simmer and season lightly to taste. Cover and set in lower third of oven to simmer slowly for 1¼ to 1½ hours or until the meat is almost tender when pierced with a fork.

½ lb. fresh button mushrooms or quartered larger mushrooms

Add the mushrooms to the casserole and baste them with the sauce. Bring again to the simmer on top of the stove. Then cover and return the casserole to the oven for 15 minutes more.

½ Tb cornstarch mixed with 1 Tb water, if needed

Remove casserole from oven. Pour contents into a sieve placed over a saucepan. Remove the strip of orange peel and return the meat and vegetables to the casserole. Skim the fat off the sauce in the saucepan and boil the sauce down rapidly until it has reduced to about 2½ cups. It should be lightly thickened, and a rich reddish brown. If too thin, blend in the starch and water and simmer for 2 minutes. Correct seasoning, and pour the sauce back into the casserole over the veal.

(*) May be done ahead to this point. Set aside, cover askew.

2 to 3 Tb minced fresh tarra-gon, basil, or parsley	Shortly before serving, cover and bring to the simmer for 5 to 10 minutes. Present the stew in its casserole, or on a platter surrounded by rice or noodles. Decorate with fresh herbs.

BLANQUETTE DE VEAU À L'ANCIENNE

[Veal Stew with Onions and Mushrooms]

Blanquette de veau, a much-loved stew in France, is veal simmered in a lightly seasoned white stock. It is served in a *sauce velouté* made from the veal cooking stock and enriched with cream and egg yolks. A *blanquette* is certainly not difficult to make, and except for the cream and egg yolk liaison at the end, which takes less than 10 minutes, all of it may be cooked in advance. However, as it is supposed to be a lovely and delicate dish, it should really not be attempted unless you can find veal of good quality and of the palest pink color.

Serve it with noodles or rice, or boiled or mashed potatoes. No other vegetables are needed with the mushrooms and onions, but you could include green peas, artichoke hearts, or baked cucumbers. A red Bordeaux-Médoc or chilled *rosé* wine would go well.

TECHNICAL NOTE ON SCUM REMOVAL

As veal comes to the simmer it releases a tremendous amount of gray-brown scum which must be removed by one means or another. American veal, probably because it is younger than most French veal, seems particularly scum-productive. You can skim continually while the veal simmers for the first 30 to 40 minutes. You can let it simmer for 10 minutes, then remove the veal and wash it rapidly in cold water, wash out the casserole, strain the stock through several thicknesses of damp cheesecloth, and continue with the recipe. Or you can adopt the following blanching process, which is the simplest. As long as all the scum is removed, it makes no difference which method you use; pick the one which best suits your predilections and prejudices.

For 6 people

Cooking the veal

3 lbs. veal stew meat cut into 2-ounce, 2-inch pieces	Place the veal in the casserole and cover with cold water by 2 inches. Bring to the simmer and simmer 2

(cuts are listed on page 360)

A 3- to 4-quart, fireproof, enameled casserole

minutes. Drain the veal and wash it rapidly under cold water to remove all traces of scum. Wash out the casserole. Return the meat to the casserole.

---

5 to 6 cups cold white stock or good canned chicken broth

1 large onion studded with 1 clove

1 large carrot, peeled and quartered

A medium herb bouquet and 2 celery stalks: 8 parsley stems (not the leaves), ½ bay leaf, ½ tsp thyme, and 2 medium celery stalks tied in cheesecloth

Salt

Pour on stock or broth to cover the veal by ½ inch. Bring slowly to the simmer, and skim as necessary for several minutes. Add the vegetables and herb bouquet. Taste for seasoning and salt lightly if necessary. Cover partially and simmer very slowly for 1¼ to 1½ hours, or until the veal is tender when pierced with a fork. It should not be overcooked.

The onions

18 to 24 peeled white onions about 1 inch in diameter

½ cup of stock dipped from the simmering veal casserole

¼ tsp salt

1 Tb butter

While the *blanquette* is simmering, prepare the onions: Following directions for white-braised onions on page 481, pierce a cross in the root ends and simmer for 30 to 40 minutes in a small, covered saucepan with the veal stock, salt, and butter. Set them aside.

When the veal is tender, pour the contents of the casserole into a colander set over a bowl. Rinse out the casserole and return the meat to the casserole, removing any loose bones. Arrange the cooked onions over the meat.

Sauce velouté (3½ cups), and mushrooms

An 8-cup, heavy-bottomed, enameled saucepan

4 Tb butter

5 Tb flour

A wooden spoon

3¼ cups of veal cooking stock

In the saucepan, melt the butter, add the flour, and stir over low heat until they foam together for 2 minutes. Off heat, pour in the veal stock, beating vigorously with a wire whip. Bring the sauce to the boil, stirring. Simmer for 10 minutes, frequently skimming off the film which rises to the surface. Fold in the mushroom caps and simmer 10 minutes more,

A wire whip

18 to 24 fresh mushroom
caps about 1 inch in di-
ameter, tossed with 1 Tb
lemon juice

Salt and white pepper

1 to 2 Tb lemon juice

skimming. Taste the sauce very carefully for seasoning, adding salt, pepper, and lemon juice to taste.

---

2 Tb cream or stock

Pour the sauce and mushrooms over the veal. Film
the top of the sauce with 2 spoonfuls of cream or
stock to prevent a skin from forming. Set aside,
partially covered.

(*) May be done ahead to this point.

Cream and egg yolk enrichment

About 10 to 15 minutes before serving, reheat slowly
to the simmer, basting the veal with the sauce. Cover
and simmer for 5 minutes. Remove from heat.

---

3 egg yolks

½ cup whipping cream

A 6-cup mixing bowl

A wire whip

Blend the egg yolks and cream in the bowl with wire
whip. Beat in by spoonfuls 1 cup of the hot sauce.
Then pour the mixture into the casserole, tilting it and
basting the veal and vegetables to blend the rest of the
sauce with the egg yolk mixture.

Set over moderate heat, gently shaking the casserole
until sauce has thickened lightly, but do not let it
come to the simmer. (If not served at once, film the
top of the sauce with a spoonful or two of stock,
partially cover the casserole, and keep warm over hot
but not simmering water for 10 to 15 minutes.)

---

2 Tb minced parsley

Serve from the casserole or on a platter surrounded
with rice, noodles, or potatoes. Decorate with parsley.

VEAL SCALLOPS

Escalopes de Veau

French veal scallops are boneless slices of meat cut ⅜ inch thick which
are flattened to a thickness of ¼ inch. So that each scallop will constitute a
neat, flat serving piece, it is cut across the grain from a solid piece of veal which
contains no muscle separations. Scallops take from 8 to 10 minutes to cook,

may be elegantly or simply sauced, and are always an expensive delicacy. They may be breaded or floured but are best, in our opinion, when sautéed *au naturel*.

AMOUNT TO BUY

Allow 2 or 3 scallops per person, depending on the size of the pieces of meat.

QUALITY

Because it is cooked so quickly, the veal should be of good quality, tender, and of the palest pink you can find. Dark pink and reddish veal tends to be tough when cooked this way.

SCALLOPS CUT FROM THE ROUND ROAST

In France, because of the French method of cutting the leg into lengthwise muscles, scallops are usually taken from the top round or *noix*. This cut gives solid slices of meat, with no muscle separations, which cook without curling. You may obtain the same effect if you buy slices of round roast ⅜ inch thick, and then separate them into their natural muscle divisions. The largest piece is the top round, which may be cut in half. The bottom round with its eye insert will furnish one or two more scallops. Usually one more of reasonable size can be found among the muscle divisions which make up the sirloin tip at the side of the meat nearest the bone. Smaller pieces may be saved for second helpings or reserved for stew or for ground meat.

SCALLOPS CUT FROM RIB CHOPS

Rib chops are more expensive but easier to use and furnish scallops all of the same size. Have your butcher bone a length of the rib section (rack) and cut the meat into ⅜-inch slices across the grain. Bones and trimming may be saved for veal stock.

PREPARATION FOR COOKING

Remove the transparent filaments, or the skin and any fat surrounding the scallops. If left on, the meat will curl up as it cooks. Place each scallop between sheets of waxed paper and pound briefly and not too roughly; use a mallet, the flat of a cleaver, or a rolling pin to reduce the scallop to a thickness of ¼ inch. If they are not to be cooked immediately, wrap the scallops in waxed paper and refrigerate them.

✳ *ESCALOPES DE VEAU À LA CRÈME*

[Sautéed Veal Scallops with Mushrooms and Cream]

This recipe for veal scallops makes a perfect main course for a chic little luncheon. If you are reasonably quick you can complete it in 30 minutes or less, and you may prepare it in advance; it only needs a 5-minute heating before it is ready to eat. Serve with it buttered rice or *risotto,* green beans, peas, or braised endive, and a chilled white Burgundy wine.

For 6 people

12 veal scallops prepared according to the preceding directions	Dry the scallops thoroughly on paper towels. The meat will not brown if it is damp.
2 Tb butter and 1 Tb oil, more as necessary A 10- to 12-inch enameled skillet	Place the butter and oil in the skillet over moderately high heat. When you see that the butter foam has almost subsided, arrange 3 or 4 pieces of veal in the skillet. Do not crowd them together. Sauté on one side for a minute or so regulating heat so fat is very hot but is not burning. Turn, and sauté the meat on its other side. (Each scallop should be lightly browned and cooked to the point where the juices have turned from rose to yellow. It is done when it has just become springy rather than squashy to the pressure of your finger.) Remove the scallops to a dish, and continue with the rest in the same manner, adding more butter and oil as needed.
3 Tb minced shallots or green onions 2 Tb butter if needed	Pour all but 2 tablespoons of fat out of the skillet. If fat has burned, discard it and add 2 Tb butter. Stir in the shallots or onions and cook slowly for 1 minute.
½ cup dry white wine or ⅓ cup dry white vermouth or Madeira ⅔ cup brown stock or canned beef bouillon A wooden spoon	Pour the wine and stock or bouillon into the skillet and scrape up all the coagulated cooking juices with wooden spoon. Boil rapidly until liquid has reduced to about ¼ cup.
1½ cups whipping cream ½ Tb arrowroot or corn-	Pour the cream and the starch mixture into the skillet and boil for several minutes until cream has reduced

starch blended with 1 Tb
water
Salt and pepper to taste

and thickened slightly. Remove from heat and season
with salt and pepper.

½ lb. sliced fresh mush-
rooms
2 Tb butter
1 Tb oil
Salt and pepper

In a separate skillet, sauté the mushrooms in very hot
butter and oil for 4 to 5 minutes to brown them
lightly. Season to taste with salt and pepper, and
scrape them into the cream sauce. Simmer for 1
minute. Remove from heat and correct seasoning.

Salt and pepper

Sprinkle salt and pepper over the sautéed scallops and
arrange in the skillet, basting with the cream and
mushrooms.
(*) May be done ahead to this point. Set skillet aside,
partially covered.

Several minutes before serving, cover the skillet and
bring almost to the simmer for 4 to 5 minutes, to
warm the veal thoroughly but not to overcook it.

A hot platter
Parsley sprigs

Arrange the scallops on a hot platter. Spoon the cream
and mushrooms over them and surround, if you wish,
with the rice or *risotto*. Decorate with parsley, and
serve.

VARIATIONS

Escalopes de Veau à l'Estragon

[Sautéed Veal Scallops with Brown Tarragon Sauce]

Rice, noodles, or sautéed potatoes go well with this, and green peas or
beans. Accompany with a red Bordeaux wine.

For 6 people

---

12 veal scallops

Prepare and sauté the veal as described in the preceding master recipe. Place on a plate while completing
the following sauce.

---

3 Tb minced shallots or
green onions
½ cup dry white wine or

Cook the shallots or onions for a minute in the sauté
skillet, then deglaze the skillet with the wine and
tarragon, reducing the liquid to 2 or 3 spoonfuls. Add

⅓ cup dry white vermouth
1 Tb fragrant tarragon, fresh or dried
1 cup brown sauce, page 66, or 1 cup brown stock or canned beef bouillon plus 1 Tb arrowroot or cornstarch blended with 1 Tb water

the brown sauce, or the stock and starch mixture, and boil for 2 to 3 minutes until the sauce has reduced and thickened lightly. Correct seasoning.

Salt and pepper
A hot platter
2 Tb softened butter
1 Tb fresh minced tarragon or minced parsley

Season the veal with salt and pepper. Return it to the skillet, and baste with the sauce. Cover the skillet and heat for 4 to 5 minutes without boiling. Arrange the meat on a hot platter. Off heat, swirl the butter into the sauce by small spoonfuls. Swirl in the herbs. Spoon the sauce over the veal and serve.

Escalopes de Veau Chasseur

[Sautéed Veal Scallops with Mushrooms and Tomatoes]

Serve rice, noodles, or sautéed potatoes with this, green peas or beans, or sautéed eggplant, and a Beaujolais or chilled *rosé* wine.

For 6 people

12 veal scallops

Prepare and sauté the veal as described in the preceding master recipe. Place the meat on a plate while completing the following sauce.

¼ cup minced shallots or green onions
¾ lb. firm, ripe, red tomatoes, peeled, seeded, juiced, and chopped, page 505 (makes 1 cup of pulp)
½ clove mashed garlic
¼ tsp salt
Pinch of pepper
½ tsp basil or tarragon
½ cup white wine or ⅓ cup dry white vermouth
½ cup brown sauce, page 66, or ½ cup brown stock

Cook the shallots or onions for 1 minute in the skillet. Stir in the tomatoes, garlic, seasonings, and herbs. Cover the skillet and simmer for 5 minutes. Pour in the wine, and the brown sauce or the stock and starch. Boil rapidly for 4 to 5 minutes until the sauce has reduced and thickened. Correct seasoning and remove from heat.

or canned beef bouillon
plus 1 Tb arrowroot or
cornstarch blended with 1
Tb water

½ lb. sliced fresh mushrooms 2 Tb butter 1 Tb oil Salt and pepper	In a separate skillet, sauté the mushrooms in very hot butter and oil to brown lightly. Season to taste and scrape them into the tomato sauce. Simmer for 1 minute and correct seasoning again.
A hot platter 2 Tb fresh minced tarragon, basil, or parsley	Sprinkle the veal scallops with salt and pepper and return them to the skillet. Baste with the sauce. Cover and heat for 4 to 5 minutes without boiling. Serve on a hot platter and decorate with the herbs.

VEAL CHOPS OR CUTLETS

Côtes de Veau

The best treatment for veal chops, in our opinion, is the simple one of browning them, then cooking them slowly in a covered skillet or casserole for 15 to 20 minutes until their juices have turned from rose to yellow. They are particularly good if aromatic herbs and vegetables are braised with them as veal usually needs other flavors to make it more interesting.

PREPARATION FOR COOKING

Buy loin, rib, or shoulder chops 1 to 1¼ inches thick. Have the corner of the backbone at the top of the chop cut off so the meat will lie as flat as possible on either side.

* CÔTES DE VEAU AUX HERBES

[Veal Chops Braised with Herbs]

This is an excellent basic recipe for all veal chops, whether they are served with a plain deglazing sauce made from the pan juices, or with any of the suggestions listed at the end of the recipe. Sautéed potatoes, broiled tomatoes, string beans, and a chilled *rosé* wine would go well with chops prepared in the following manner.

Cooking Note: For 2 or 3 chops, the final cooking may be done on top of the stove in a covered skillet. For 6 chops, it is easier to finish cooking them in the oven.

For 6 people

Preheat oven to 325 degrees.

6 large veal chops cut 1 inch thick

A 10- to 12-inch skillet

2 Tb butter and 1 Tb oil, more if needed

Salt and pepper

A heavy, 10- to 12-inch fire-proof casserole with cover

Dry the chops on paper towels. Heat the butter and oil in the skillet until you see that the butter foam has almost subsided, then brown the chops, two or three at a time, for 3 to 4 minutes on each side. As they are done, season with salt and pepper and arrange in the casserole, overlapping them slightly.

3 Tb butter, if needed

3 Tb minced shallots or green onions

Optional: 1 clove mashed garlic

½ cup dry white wine or dry white vermouth

1 tsp mixed basil and thyme, or tarragon

Pour all but 3 tablespoons of fat out of the skillet. If fat has burned, pour it all out and add butter. Stir in the shallots or onions and optional garlic, and cook slowly for 1 minute. Then pour in the wine, add the herbs, and simmer for a few minutes, scraping up the coagulated sautéing juices. Scrape the mixture into the casserole over the chops.

Heat the casserole on top of the stove until the liquid is simmering. Cover and set in lower third of pre-heated oven for 15 to 20 minutes. Turn the chops and baste them with the liquid in the casserole 2 or 3 times during this period. The chops are done as soon as their juices run yellow when the meat is pierced with a fork.

A hot platter

¼ cup stock, canned bouillon, or cream

Salt and pepper

1 to 2 Tb softened butter

Remove the chops to a hot platter. Add the stock, bouillon, or cream to the casserole and boil rapidly for a few minutes until the liquid has reduced and thickened slightly. Correct seasoning. Off heat, swirl in the butter by bits. Pour the sauce over the chops and serve.

(*) AHEAD-OF-TIME NOTE

Veal chops may be browned well in advance of their final cooking. Once cooked, they may be kept in the hot, turned-off oven, casserole cover askew, for about 20 minutes. But do not allow them to overcook or overheat for they will dry out.

VARIATIONS: SAUCES

In addition to the following sauces, you may use the mushrooms and cream, mushrooms and tomato, or brown tarragon sauces described in the recipes for veal scallops, pages 366 to 368.

Sauce Tomate or *Coulis de Tomates,* tomato sauce, pages 76 to 78

Sauce Madère, brown sauce with Madeira wine, page 75

Sauce Robert, brown sauce with mustard and onions, page 72

Sauce Duxelles, brown sauce with diced mushrooms and herbs, page 74

Before cooking the chops, prepare 2 cups of one of the sauces listed at the left. When the chops are done, pour the sauce into the casserole, basting the chops. If not to be served immediately, set aside. Shortly before serving, cover the casserole and reheat for 4 to 5 minutes without simmering. Arrange the chops on a platter. Off heat, swish 1 or 2 tablespoons of butter into the casserole, then pour the sauce over the chops.

OTHER VARIATIONS

The recipe for sautéed chicken *aux herbes de Provence,* page 257, has an herb-and-garlic type of hollandaise sauce which can be adapted for veal chops. Another idea is to add almost cooked small potatoes and onions, and browned *lardons* of blanched bacon, all of which will finish cooking with the chops; follow the directions for them in *poulet en cocotte,* pages 252-3, but boil the vegetables long enough so they are almost tender before arranging them in the casserole to bake with the chops. Following the same system with other vegetables, you could use a combination of butter-braised carrots and artichoke hearts with sautéed mushrooms.

VEAL STEAKS

Veal steaks 1 to 1¼ inches thick cut from the round roast or the sirloin may be cooked exactly the same way as veal chops.

GROUND VEAL PATTIES

Fricadelles de Veau

Here is a fine recipe for ground veal patties. Arranged on a bed of braised spinach, surrounded with baked or stuffed tomatoes, and served with a chilled *rosé* wine, they make a most attractive informal main course. Other vegetables are suggested in the list under roast veal on page 352. Neck, shoulder, shank, or breast meat may be used for grinding; be sure the meat has first been pared of gristle, tendons, filaments and other miscellaneous matter. Always include a proportion of ham fat, pork fat, or sausage meat; otherwise the patties will be too dry.

✷ *FRICADELLES DE VEAU À LA NIÇOISE*

[Veal Patties with Tomatoes, Onions, and Herbs]

Onions, garlic, and tomatoes are particularly good mixed with ground veal. If you happened to have the remains of a *ratatouille* (eggplant and tomato casserole, page 503), half a cup of it could replace the tomatoes and onions in the following recipe.

For 6 people

½ cup finely minced onions
2 Tb butter

Cook the onions slowly with the butter in a small skillet for 8 to 10 minutes, until they are tender but not browned.

2 medium tomatoes, peeled, seeded, juiced, and chopped, page 505
1 clove mashed garlic
¼ tsp salt
½ tsp basil or thyme
A 3-quart mixing bowl

Add the tomatoes, and other ingredients. Cover and cook slowly for 5 minutes. Uncover, raise heat, and boil rapidly until the tomato juices have almost entirely evaporated. Scrape into the mixing bowl.

1 cup stale white bread crumbs and ½ cup milk
OR, grind ½ cup of cooked rice with the veal

While the tomatoes are cooking, soak the bread crumbs in the milk for 5 minutes. Pour into a strainer and press out as much of the milk as you can. Add bread crumbs to mixing bowl.

1 lb. or 2 cups lean raw veal, ground with 2 ounces (½

Add the meat, seasonings, parsley, and egg to the mixing bowl and beat vigorously with wooden spoon

cup) of boiled ham and 2
ounces (½ cup) of ham
fat or fresh pork fat

1 tsp salt

¼ tsp pepper

3 Tb minced parsley

1 egg

A wooden spoon

to blend thoroughly. Taste carefully for seasoning, adding more if you feel it necessary. Form the mixture into 6 or 12 balls. Flatten them into patties ½ inch thick with the palm of your hand. If not to be cooked immediately, cover with waxed paper and refrigerate.

½ cup sifted flour spread on
a dish

Just before sautéing, dredge the patties in the flour and shake off excess flour.

---

1 to 2 skillets each containing 2 Tb butter and 1 Tb oil

Set the skillet or skillets over moderately high heat. When you see that the butter foam has almost subsided, brown the patties for 2 to 3 minutes on each side. Pour out excess fat, cover and cook very slowly for 15 minutes, turning the patties once.

A hot platter

Arrange the meat on a hot platter with whatever vegetables you have chosen, and keep warm for a moment while finishing the sauce.

⅔ cup brown stock or
canned beef bouillon

1 to 2 Tb softened butter

Pour the fat out of the skillet. Add the stock or bouillon and boil rapidly, scraping up coagulated cooking juices and reducing liquid to 3 or 4 spoonfuls. Off heat, swirl in the butter by small spoonfuls. Pour the sauce over the patties, and serve.

(*) AHEAD-OF-TIME NOTE

After the patties have been browned, arrange them in a casserole. Deglaze the skillet with stock and set aside. About 20 to 30 minutes before serving, heat the casserole until the meat is sizzling, cover and finish cooking in a 325-degree oven. Reheat and butter the sauce just before pouring it over the patties.

VARIATION

Fricadelles de Veau à la Crème

[Veal Patties with Cream and Herb Sauce]

½ Tb tarragon or basil

½ cup dry white wine, dry
white vermouth, or stock

Cook the patties and remove them to a hot platter as directed in the master recipe. Add the tarragon or basil and wine or stock to the degreased skillet. Boil

½ to ¾ cup whipping cream

2 Tb softened butter

½ Tb fresh minced tarragon, basil, or parsley

down liquid to 3 tablespoons, scraping up coagulated cooking juices. Then pour in the cream and boil it down rapidly to reduce and thicken it lightly. Off heat, swirl in the butter by bits, then swirl in the herbs. Pour over the patties.

VARIATIONS: SAUCES

Coulis de Tomates à la Provençale, fresh tomato sauce with herbs, page 78

Sauce Brune aux Fines Herbes or *à l'Estragon,* brown sauce with mixed green herbs or tarragon, page 73

Sauce Madère, brown sauce with Madeira wine, page 75

Sauce Robert, brown sauce with mustard and onions, page 72

Sauce Duxelles, brown sauce with diced mushrooms and herbs, page 74

After cooking the patties, deglaze the skillet with half a cup of white wine or white vermouth, then add 1½ to 2 cups of any of the sauces listed at the left. Simmer for a minute or two. Off heat, swirl in 1 to 2 tablespoons of softened butter and pour the sauce over the meat.

VARIATIONS

Use the same mixture of ground veal, onions, and tomatoes as described in the master recipe on page 372.

Fricadelles de Veau Duxelles

[Veal Patties with Mushrooms]

¼ lb. finely minced fresh mushrooms

Squeeze the mushrooms, a handful at a time, in the corner of a towel to extract their juice. When the minced onions in the master recipe are tender, add the mushrooms. Raise heat and sauté for 4 to 5 minutes. Then add the tomatoes and proceed with the recipe.

Fricadelles de Veau Mentonnaise

[Veal Patties with Tuna and Anchovies]

This Italian and Mediterranean combination is especially good accompanied by braised spinach and grilled or baked tomatoes, or fried or sautéed potatoes and a salad of fresh tomatoes.

½ cup drained and mashed canned tuna fish	Prepare the ground veal mixture as described in the master recipe and beat into it the tuna and anchovies.
6 canned anchovy *filets* drained and mashed, or 1 Tb anchovy paste	Then proceed with the recipe.

Patties Using Cooked Ground Veal

Follow any of the preceding combinations, substituting cooked veal for raw veal. To prevent the meat from being too dry, add to the mixture ½ cup of sausage meat or an additional ¼ cup of ground ham fat or pork fat.

Pain de Veau

[Veal Loaf]

Use any of the preceding ground veal combinations and pack the meat in a loaf pan or a soufflé mold. Over the top of the meat lay 2 or 3 strips of blanched bacon, page 15. Bake in a 350-degree oven for 1 to 1½ hours.

The loaf is done when the meat has shrunk slightly from the sides of the mold and the surrounding juices are clear yellow with no trace of rosy color, or at a meat-thermometer reading of 175 to 180 degrees. Unmold the loaf and serve it with a tomato sauce, page 76. If the loaf is to be served cold, place a weight on top of it after cooking to compress the meat as it cools.

PORK

Porc

MARINADES

Fresh pork, whether it is a large piece for roasting, or a thin piece for sautéing, will be tenderer and have a more interesting flavor if it receives a marination before cooking. This is not an essential step, but you will find it most effective, and cold leftovers will be even better than usual. You may use a simple dry mixture of salt, herbs, and spices, or a liquid marinade of either lemon juice or wine and vinegar with herbs and aromatic vegetables.

Always marinate the meat in a noncorroding container: porcelain, pyrex, enamelware, or stainless steel.

TIME REQUIRED

(If the meat is refrigerated, increase the minimum marination time by at least one third.)

Chops and steaks—a minimum of 2 hours; 6 to 12 are even better.

Loin roasts—a minimum of 6 hours, but 24 are recommended.

Fresh hams and picnic shoulders—a minimum of 2 days, but 4 to 5 are more effective.

MARINADE SÈCHE

[Salt Marinade with Herbs and Spices]

Fine for all types of fresh pork. This is our favorite, as it tenderizes the pork and accentuates its natural flavor.

Per pound of pork

1 tsp salt
⅛ tsp freshly ground pepper
¼ tsp ground thyme or sage
⅛ tsp ground bay leaf
Pinch of allspice
Optional: ½ clove mashed garlic

Mix all the ingredients together and rub them into the surface of the pork. Place in a covered bowl. Turn the meat 2 or 3 times if the marinade is a short one; several times a day if it is of long duration.

Before cooking, scrape off the marinade, and dry the meat thoroughly with paper towels.

MARINADE SIMPLE

[Lemon Juice and Herb Marinade]

For chops, steaks, and small, boned roasts. This is also an effective marinade giving the pork a slightly different flavor than the dry one.

Per pound of pork

1 tsp salt
⅛ tsp pepper
3 Tb lemon juice
3 Tb olive oil
3 parsley sprigs
¼ tsp thyme or sage
1 bay leaf
1 clove mashed garlic

Rub salt and pepper into the meat. Mix the other ingredients in a bowl, add the pork and baste it. Place a lid over the bowl. Turn and baste the meat 3 or 4 times during its marination period.

Before cooking, scrape off the marinade, and dry the meat thoroughly with paper towels.

MARINADE AU VIN

[Wine Marinade]

May be used for chops, steaks, and small roasts, but is usually reserved for fresh hams and picnic shoulders. This is a special 2- to 4-day marinade which gives pork a taste akin to that of wild boar, *marcassin*.

[NOTE: If the pork is to be marinated for more than 3 days, cook the carrots, onions, and garlic very slowly in the olive oil before proceeding with the recipe.]

Per each 3 pounds of pork

1 Tb salt
1 cup dry white wine or ⅔ cup dry white vermouth
½ cup wine vinegar
4 Tb olive oil
3 halved cloves garlic
½ cup thinly sliced carrots
½ cup thinly sliced onions
½ tsp peppercorns
2 bay leaves
1 tsp thyme
Optional: ¼ tsp each of basil, tarragon, sage, and mint; 5 coriander seeds; 5 juniper berries

Rub salt into the pork. Mix the other ingredients in a bowl, add the meat and baste it. Place a lid over the bowl. Turn and baste the meat 3 or 4 times a day. Before cooking, scrape off the marinade and drain the meat for half an hour or so. Then dry it thoroughly with paper towels.

ROAST PORK
Rôti de Porc

Pork may be roasted slowly in an open pan in a 325-degree oven, and basted occasionally with a spoonful or two of wine, stock, or water to aid in the dissolution of its fat. But we think pork is more tender and juicy if it is browned in hot fat, then roasted like veal in a covered casserole. This slow, steamy cooking tenderizes the meat and renders out the fat very effectively.

PREPARATION OF ROASTS FOR COOKING

The flavors of a marinade will penetrate pork more thoroughly if the meat is boned; it is rolled and tied after marination. All but a ⅛-inch layer of outside fat should be cut off, as well as any loose interior fat or heavy layers of fat. If you are using a fresh ham or shoulder, remove the rind; it may be frozen and used whenever you are cooking braised meat to give body to the sauce.

CUTS FOR ROASTING OR BRAISING

One pound of boneless pork will serve 2 or 3 people. For bone-in roasts, particularly the loin, allow ¾ pound per person.

Loin of Pork—*Longe*. The loin is divided into the following cuts:

Center Cut—*Milieu de Filet*. This is lean meat, and corresponds to the porterhouse and T-bone steak section of beef with both loin and tenderloin. If it is not boned and rolled, have the backbone part removed for easier carving.

Rib Cut—*Carré*. This is lean meat, and corresponds to the rib section of beef with loin but no tenderloin. If it is not boned and rolled, have the backbone section removed.

Loin End—*Pointe de Filet*. This corresponds to the rump of beef and should be boned. It makes a juicy roast with a combination of fat and lean.

Shoulder or Blade End—*Échine*. This combination of fat and lean is a favorite roasting cut in France; it is the shoulder-chop end of the loin and should be boned.

Shoulder Butt or Boston Butt—*Palette*. The shoulder butt is a combination of fat and lean and should be boned.

Picnic Shoulder or Shoulder Arm—No French equivalent: part of it is *palette;* part is *jambonneau.* This is lean meat, and should be boned.

Fresh Ham—*Jambon Frais.* Fresh ham is lean meat. It may be bought whole, or in part, and may be boned or not, as you wish.

TEMPERATURE AND TIMING FOR ROAST PORK

Pork, in our opinion, develops its best flavor and texture when it is cooked to an interior temperature of 180 to 185 degrees on a meat thermometer. At this point all its juices have turned clear yellow with no trace of rosy color, and the meat is somewhat gray with only a suggestion of pink overtone. It was authoritatively established as far back as the year 1919 that trichinae are killed at a meat temperature of 131 degrees (137 degrees for official purposes) or when the pork is still rare. In view of this fact there is no reason whatsoever for overcooking pork until it is dry and lifeless.

From 30 to 45 minutes per pound are required to roast a 3- to 8-pound piece of unchilled fresh pork to an internal temperature of 180 to 185 degrees. A long, thin, pork loin takes less time to roast than a thick fresh ham or shoulder of the same weight. Boned roasts usually require 5 to 10 minutes per pound more than bone-in roasts. As it takes a good hour for a large roast to cool off when it is out of the oven, you can afford to allow yourself plenty of time. Here are some examples for covered roasting in a 325-degree oven:

A 3-pound loin
Bone In—1½ to 1¾ hours
Boned and Rolled—1¾ to 2 hours
A 5-pound loin
Bone In—2½ to 3 hours
Boned and Rolled—3 to 3½ hours
A 5-pound fresh ham or picnic
Bone In—About 3½ hours
Boned and Rolled—About 4 hours

VEGETABLE SUGGESTIONS

Potatoes
Roast potatoes, which may cook with the pork
Sautéed potatoes, which may be done in pork fat rather than butter, page 526
Boiled potatoes, plain, mashed potatoes, or the garlic mashed potatoes on page 520

Scalloped potatoes with stock and cheese, page 524, or with tomatoes and onions, page 525

Other vegetables

Braised white cabbage, page 383, red cabbage, page 384, or sauerkraut, page 385, which may cook with the pork

Brussels sprouts braised in butter, or with cheese, page 451 or 453

Braised leeks, page 495, or braised celery root, page 492

Stuffed tomatoes, page 507; *ratatouille* (eggplant and tomato casserole), page 503

Glazed onions, page 481, or turnips, page 488, which may cook with the pork

See also the fruit suggestions (apples, peaches, and cherries) in the Duck section, pages 275 to 279; and the prunes in the Goose section, page 283

WINE SUGGESTIONS

Serve a dry white wine, Riesling, Traminer, white Côtes du Rhône, or a *rosé*.

---

* RÔTI DE PORC POÊLÉ

[Casserole-roasted Pork]

As most French recipes call for a boneless roast, we shall so specify in this recipe and its variations. The loin is the most expensive cut and also the most attractive looking. But any other cut among those listed on page 378 may be substituted, and may be boned or not.

For 6 people

A 3-lb. boneless roast of pork, previously marinated, if you wish, according to one of the suggestions on page 376

4 Tb rendered pork fat, lard, or cooking oil

A heavy fireproof casserole just large enough to hold the meat

Preheat oven to 325 degrees. Dry the meat thoroughly on paper towels. Place the fat in the casserole and set over moderately high heat. When fat is almost smoking, brown the pork on all sides. This will take about 10 minutes. Remove pork to a side dish.

2 Tb butter, if needed
1 sliced yellow onion
1 sliced carrot
Optional: 2 cloves unpeeled garlic
A medium herb bouquet: 4 parsley sprigs, ½ bay leaf, and ¼ tsp thyme tied in cheesecloth

Pour all but 2 spoonfuls of fat out of the casserole. If fat has burned, throw it all out and add more butter. Stir in the vegetables, optional garlic, and herb bouquet. Cover and cook slowly for 5 minutes.

A bulb baster

Place the meat in the casserole, its fattiest side up. (If pork was not marinated, season it with salt and pepper, and half a teaspoon of sage or thyme.) Cover the casserole and heat it until the meat is sizzling, then place in lower third of preheated oven for about 2 hours or to a meat-thermometer reading of 180 to 185 degrees. Baste the roast 2 or 3 times during this period with the juices in the casserole, and regulate oven heat so the pork is cooking slowly and evenly. The pork and vegetables will render about 1 cup of juices as they roast.

A hot platter

When it is done, place the pork on a hot serving platter and discard trussing strings.

½ cup dry white wine, stock, canned bouillon, or water
A hot gravy boat

Pour the liquid into the casserole and simmer slowly for 2 to 3 minutes. Then tilt the casserole and skim out all but a tablespoon or two of fat. Mash the vegetables into the juices; boil rapidly until you have about 1 cup. Strain into a hot gravy boat. Surround the pork roast with whatever vegetable garnish you have chosen, and serve.

(*) AHEAD-OF-TIME NOTE

If you are not serving immediately, return pork and sauce to casserole. Cover loosely and set in turned-off hot oven with door ajar. The meat will stay warm for a good half hour.

VARIATIONS: SAUCES

Any of the following sauces may be prepared while the pork is roasting, then simmered for a moment to blend with the degreased juices in the casserole.

Sauce Diable, peppery brown sauce, page 71

Sauce Piquante, spicy brown sauce with pickles and capers, page 72

Sauce Robert, brown mustard sauce, page 72

Sauce Poivrade, peppery brown sauce with vinegar and wine for use especially if the pork has been marinated in wine, page 70

Sauce Tomate, a good tomato sauce, page 76

Sauce Moutarde à la Normande

[Mustard Sauce with Cream]

For about 2 cups

	After the pork has been cooked and placed on a platter, keep it warm for 10 to 15 minutes while preparing the sauce.
	Strain the meat juices into a bowl and degrease them.
⅓ cup cider vinegar 10 crushed peppercorns	Pour the vinegar and peppercorns into the casserole and boil until the vinegar has reduced to about a tablespoon. Pour in the meat juices and boil them down rapidly until they have reduced to about ⅔ cup.
1½ cups whipping cream Salt 2 tsp dry mustard mixed with 2 tsp water	Add the cream and simmer for 5 minutes, stirring in salt to taste. Beat in the mustard mixture and simmer 2 or 3 minutes more. Sauce should be thick enough to coat a spoon lightly. Correct seasoning.
1 to 2 Tb softened butter A warm gravy boat	Off heat and just before serving, swirl in the butter by bits, then pour the sauce into a warm gravy boat.

VARIATIONS

Rôti de Porc Grand' Mère

[Casserole-roasted Pork with Potatoes and Onions]

Onions and potatoes absorb a distinctive flavor when they cook with pork in this manner.

For 6 people

A 3-lb. boneless roast of pork previously marinated	Roast the pork in a covered casserole with seasonings as described in the master recipe, page 380, but omit

in salt for several hours, if you wish, page 376

12 to 18 peeled white onions 1 to 1½ inches in diameter

the vegetables. After 1 hour, add potatoes and onions which have been prepared as follows:

Pierce a cross in the root end of the onions, and boil them for 5 minutes in salted water. Drain.

12 to 18 small new potatoes or "boiling" potatoes, peeled and cut into 1½ inch ovals
A skillet
2 Tb rendered pork fat or cooking oil
Salt and pepper

Drop the potatoes into a pan of boiling salted water. Bring to the boil and boil ½ minute. Drain. Just before adding the potatoes to the casserole, roll them for 1 to 2 minutes in hot fat in skillet to brown very lightly. Season with salt and pepper.

After the pork has cooked for an hour, arrange the potatoes and onions around it and baste them with the juices in the casserole. Cover the casserole and return it to the oven until the meat is done, basting the vegetables once or twice.

A hot platter
1 to 2 Tb chopped parsley

Remove the pork to a hot platter and arrange the vegetables around it. Decorate with chopped parsley. Degrease the meat juices and either pour them over the vegetables, or into a hot gravy boat.

Rôti de Porc aux Navets

[Casserole-roasted Pork with Turnips]

Turnips are wonderful when cooked in pork juices. Use the same general system described for the onions and potatoes in the preceding recipe. Peel and quarter the turnips; allow 4 to 6 pieces per person. Drop them in boiling water and boil 2 minutes. Drain. Add them to the casserole for the last hour of cooking.

Rôti de Porc aux Choux

[Casserole-roasted Pork with Cabbage]

This is a great dish for lovers of cabbage. Serve it with boiled potatoes and a dry Alsatian wine, or beer.

For 6 people

A 3-lb. boneless roast of pork previously marinated for several hours in salt, if you wish, page 376

Roast the pork in a covered casserole with carrots, onions, and seasonings as described in the master recipe, page 380. After an hour, add the cabbage which has been prepared as follows:

1 lb. (about 6 cups) green or white cabbage cut into ½-inch slices

A kettle containing 7 to 8 quarts of rapidly boiling water with 1½ tsp salt per quart of water

Drop the cabbage into the boiling water. Bring rapidly to the boil and boil uncovered for 2 minutes. Immediately drain in a colander, and run cold water over the cabbage for a minute or two. Drain thoroughly and set aside.

½ tsp salt
⅛ tsp pepper
Optional: ½ tsp caraway seeds

After the pork has cooked for an hour, arrange the cabbage around it. Fluff salt, pepper, and the optional caraway seeds into the cabbage, and baste it with the juices in the casserole. Cover the casserole, bring to the simmer, and return it to the oven until the pork is done. Baste the cabbage several times with the meat juices during this period.

A hot platter
Salt and pepper
Parsley sprigs

Then remove the pork to a hot platter. Lift the cabbage out of the casserole with a fork and spoon so it will drain, and arrange it around the meat. Season it with salt and pepper if necessary. Degrease the juices in the casserole and pour them over the cabbage. Decorate with sprigs of fresh parsley.

✳ PORC BRAISÉ AUX CHOUX ROUGES

[Pork Braised with Red Cabbage]

A good dish of red cabbage is even better when a roast of pork is cooked with it. The casserole of cabbage cooks for 3 hours before the pork goes into it, and needs 2 hours more in the oven until the pork is done.

For 6 people

Ingredients for the braised red cabbage on page 496 (omit the chestnuts if you wish, but they are a good accompaniment)

Braise the cabbage for 3 hours in a 325-degree oven, following the directions in the recipe.

A 3-lb. boneless roast of pork, previously marinated for several hours in salt, if possible, page 376	Brown the pork in hot fat in a skillet. After the cabbage has cooked for 3 hours, place the pork in the casserole with the cabbage. Cover the casserole and return it to the oven to braise for two hours more or until the pork is done.
A hot platter Salt and pepper	Then place the pork on a platter, drain the cabbage and arrange it around the pork. Correct seasoning. Degrease and season the cooking juices, and pour them over the cabbage.

VARIATION

Porc Braisé avec Choucroute

[Pork Braised with Sauerkraut]

Use exactly the same method as for red cabbage but substitute sauerkraut, page 498. After the sauerkraut has braised for 3 hours, brown the pork, add it to the casserole, and cook for another 2 hours or until the pork is done.

PORC SYLVIE

[Pork Stuffed with Cheese]

A loin of pork is cut lengthwise from the top almost to the bottom to make 3 or 4 long leaves or slices so the roast may be opened up like a book. It is marinated for several hours, then stuffed with slices of Swiss cheese and cooked in a covered casserole. Follow the recipe for *veau Sylvie*, page 357, but use one of the pork marinades on page 376, and omit the slices of ham.

PORK CHOPS AND STEAKS
Côtes de Porc

Pork chops and steaks are best, we think, when they are cut thick, browned on each side, then cooked in a covered casserole or skillet like the preceding casserole roasts of pork.

Have the chops or steak cut between 1 to 1¼ inches thick, and ask that the backbone corners of chops be leveled or removed so the meat will lie perfectly flat on either side. All but a thin layer of fat should be trimmed off. The best chops are from the center loin or the rib loin. Second choices are the loin end or rump, shoulder loin chops, and blade and round-bone chops from the shoulder. Steaks are usually cut from the picnic shoulder or shoulder arm, or from the fresh ham.

Usually 1 thick chop per person is sufficient. For steaks, count on 1 pound for 2 or 3 people. As steaks or chops are interchangeable in these recipes, we will call everything chops.

VEGETABLE AND WINE SUGGESTIONS

These are the same as the suggestions for roast pork on pages 379–80.

✳ *CÔTES DE PORC POÊLÉES*

[Casserole-sautéed Pork Chops]

Three or four chops or one or two steaks may be cooked in a covered skillet on top of the stove. For a larger quantity oven-cooking in a covered casserole is easier.

For 6 people

Preheat oven to 325 degrees.

6 pork chops cut 1 inch thick and previously marinated for several hours, if you wish, in salt, lemon juice, or wine, page 376–7
3 to 4 Tb rendered pork fat, lard, or cooking oil
A heavy, 10- to 12-inch fire-proof casserole

Dry the pork chops on paper towels. Heat the fat or oil in the casserole until it is moderately hot, then brown the chops, 2 or 3 at a time, on each side for 3 to 4 minutes. As they are browned, transfer them to a side dish.

If the chops have not been marinated, season them with salt, pepper, and ¼ teaspoon of thyme or sage.

2 Tb butter
Optional: 2 halved cloves garlic

Pour the fat out of the casserole and add the butter and optional garlic. Return the chops, overlapping them slightly. Baste them with the butter. Cover and heat the casserole until the meat is sizzling, then set in lower third of preheated oven for 25 to 30 minutes.

Turn and baste the chops once or twice. They are done when the meat juices run a clear yellow with no trace of rose. Make a deep cut next to the bone if you have any doubts.

A hot platter ½ cup dry white wine, dry white vermouth, brown stock, canned beef bouillon, or marinade liquid	Arrange the chops on a hot platter with whatever vegetable garnish you have chosen. The chops will have rendered about ½ cup of juices during their cooking; remove all but 2 tablespoons of fat from them. Pour in the ½ cup of liquid and boil rapidly, scraping up all coagulated cooking juices, until you have about ½ cup of concentrated sauce. Taste for seasoning, and pour it over the chops.

(*) AHEAD-OF-TIME-NOTE

If the chops are not to be served immediately, return them to the casserole, baste them with the sauce, cover loosely, and keep warm in turned-off oven for 20 minutes or so.

VARIATIONS: SAUCES

Any of the sauces suggested for roast pork on page 382 may also be used for pork chops. Here is another suggestion:

Côtes de Porc Sauce Nénette

[Pork Chops with Mustard, Cream, and Tomato Sauce]

	While the pork chops are cooking according to directions in the master recipe, prepare the following:
1½ cups whipping cream ¼ tsp salt Pinch of pepper	Simmer the cream, salt, and pepper in a small saucepan for 8 to 10 minutes, or until it has reduced to 1 cup.
1 Tb dry English mustard 2 Tb tomato paste	Beat the mustard and tomato paste together in a small bowl, then beat in the hot cream. Set aside.
2 Tb fresh chopped basil, chervil, or parsley	After removing the chops from the casserole and degreasing the meat juices, pour in the cream mixture and simmer for 3 or 4 minutes. Correct seasoning, stir in the herbs, and pour the sauce over the chops.

VARIATIONS

Côtes de Porc Robert
Côtes de Porc Charcutière

[Pork Chops Braised in Fresh Tomato Sauce]

Include sautéed potatoes and a chilled *rosé* wine on the menu with this good dish of pork chops. If you stir chopped pickles and capers into the sauce just before serving the chops, they become *côtes de porc charcutière*.

For 6 people

6 pork chops cut 1 inch thick and previously marinated for several hours, if you wish, according to one of the formulas on page 376	Preheat oven to 325 degrees. Brown the chops in hot fat in the casserole as described in the master recipe, page 386, and set them aside.
A heavy, 10- to 12-inch fire-proof casserole	
2 Tb butter	Pour out the browning fat, add the butter and onions, cover and cook slowly for 10 minutes. Mix in the flour and stir over low heat for 2 minutes more. Stir in the tomatoes and other flavorings. Cover and cook slowly for 5 minutes.
1 cup minced yellow onions	
1 Tb flour	
1 lb. ripe tomatoes peeled, seeded, and chopped (1½ cups), page 505	
½ tsp salt	
⅛ tsp pepper	
¼ tsp sage or thyme	
1 large clove mashed garlic	
1 cup dry white wine or ⅔ cup dry vermouth (include marinade liquid, if any)	Stir in the wine and stock or bouillon and simmer for 10 minutes. Correct seasoning and stir in enough tomato paste to deepen the flavor and color of the sauce.
½ cup brown stock or canned beef bouillon	
1 to 2 Tb tomato paste	

If the chops have not been marinated, season them with salt and pepper. Arrange them, slightly overlapping, in the casserole and baste them with the tomato sauce.

(*) May be done in advance to this point.

Cover the casserole and bring to the simmer on top of the stove, then set it in the lower third of the preheated oven. Regulate oven temperature so casserole simmers slowly and regularly for 25 to 30 minutes or until the chops are done.

A hot platter
1 to 2 Tb fresh chopped basil or parsley

Arrange the chops on a serving platter. Degrease the sauce and if necessary boil it down rapidly until it is lightly thickened. Correct seasoning and pour it over the chops. Sprinkle with herbs and serve.

VARIATIONS: VEGETABLE SUGGESTIONS

Browned pork chops may also finish their cooking for half an hour or so in a casserole of braised red cabbage, page 496, or braised sauerkraut, page 498. Or you can add blanched onions, carrots, new potatoes, or turnips to the casserole with the browned chops so the meat and vegetables finish their cooking in the oven together.

PORK STEWS

Ragoûts de Porc

The following recipes for beef stew are also very good with pork rather than beef. Use boneless pork cuts which contain a mixture of fat and lean, such as shoulder loin chops, loin-end chops, or shoulder (Boston) butt. Cooking time is 2 to 2½ hours rather than the 3½ hours required for beef.

Boeuf à la Catalane, stew with rice, onions, and tomatoes, page 321

Daube de Boeuf, casserole with wine and vegetables, page 322

Daube de Boeuf à la Provençale, casserole with wine, vegetables, anchovies, and garlic, page 324

HAM

Jambon

Ham is a fine dish for large parties, but a parade of plain boiled or baked hams can become woefully monotonous especially around Christmas and

Easter. Here are a handful of French recipes which will lift any ham into *la grande classe*.

VEGETABLE SUGGESTIONS

Classic accompaniment

Spinach braised with cream or with stock, page 470–1

Other vegetables

Braised celery, page 491, celeriac, page 492, or lettuce, page 489
Braised chestnuts, page 519, puréed chestnuts, page 518
Braised onions, page 481, or leeks, page 495
Mashed potatoes

Fruits

The French do not go in much for fruits and ham, but if you like them, see the prunes in wine in the Goose section, page 283, and the fruits suggested for duck on pages 278 to 279.

WINE SUGGESTIONS

The best choice is a not-too-heavy red wine such as Bordeaux-Médoc, or a Beaujolais, Mâcon, or Chinon.

TYPE OF HAM TO BUY

All of the recipes in this section call for cooked, mild-cured ham. In the recipes for whole braised ham, we have specified 8 to 10 pounds; a pound or two more will make little difference except in the braising time. You may buy whole ham, which always looks more festive, or half a ham, or a picnic or boned shoulder butt. We have allowed about 1 pound of bone-in ham for 2 people. If the ham has been boned, 1 pound should serve 3 and possibly 4 people. When you buy ham, have the skin or rind removed, and cut off all but a ⅛-inch layer of covering fat. Hams labeled "fully cooked" usually require reheating to an internal temperature of between 130 and 140 degrees. But you should test the meat anyway, to see if a fork will pierce it fairly easily; if not, continue cooking until the ham is tender.

* *JAMBON BRAISÉ MORVANDELLE*

[Ham Braised in Wine—Cream and Mushroom Sauce]

Ham heated in a covered roaster with aromatic vegetables, herbs, stock, and wine absorbs these different flavors, and the braising liquid is easily transformed into a good sauce.

For 16 to 20 people

¼ lb. (about 1 cup) sliced carrots

¼ lb. (about 1 cup) sliced onions

2 Tb butter and 1 Tb oil, or 3 Tb rendered ham fat

A heavy covered roaster or fireproof casserole just large enough to hold the ham

Preheat oven to 325 degrees. Sauté the vegetables in butter and oil or ham fat for about 10 minutes in the roaster or casserole until they are tender and very lightly browned.

An 8- to 10-lb. cooked ham or picnic shoulder, skinned, and trimmed of excess fat

6 parsley sprigs

1 bay leaf

6 peppercorns

½ tsp thyme

3 whole cloves

4 cups white Burgundy wine (Chablis or Pouilly-Fuissé) or 3 cups dry white vermouth

4 to 6 cups white or brown stock or canned beef bouillon

Place the ham over the vegetables, its fattiest side up, and add the rest of the ingredients at the left. Bring to the simmer on top of the stove, cover, and place the roaster or casserole in the middle level of the preheated oven. Regulate heat so liquid barely simmers for about 2 hours. Baste every 20 minutes. The ham is done when a trussing needle or sharp-pronged fork will pierce the thickest part of it fairly easily.

Optional glazing

Powdered sugar in a shaker

A shallow roasting pan containing a rack

When the ham is done, drain it. If you wish to glaze it, dust the top and sides with powdered sugar, and place it on the rack in the roasting pan. Heat oven to

450 degrees. Place the ham in the upper third of the oven and let it brown lightly for 10 to 15 minutes. Basting is not necessary.

Let the ham sit at room temperature for 20 to 30 minutes before carving. If it is to wait longer, put it in the turned-off hot oven with door ajar where it can stay for an hour. The braising liquid is turned into a sauce as follows:

Cream and Mushroom Sauce

Version I

2 lbs. sliced fresh mush-rooms
3 Tb butter
1 Tb oil
3 Tb minced shallots or green onions
A large enameled skillet
Salt and pepper

Dry the mushrooms in a towel. Sauté them for 5 to 6 minutes in hot butter and oil until they are very lightly browned. Stir in the shallots or onions and sauté for a minute more. Season to taste and set aside.

The ham braising liquid
¼ cup Marc de Bourgogne, Madeira, or port
A 2½-quart enameled sauce-pan
4 Tb flour mixed to a paste with 4 Tb softened butter
2 to 3 cups whipping cream

Degrease the braising liquid in the roaster. Set roaster over high heat and boil rapidly until liquid has reduced to about 3 cups and is full of flavor. Add the *marc* or wine and simmer for a minute or two to evaporate the alcohol. Strain into a saucepan and beat in the flour and butter paste. Beat in 2 cups of cream, then stir in the sautéed mushrooms. Simmer for 5 minutes. The sauce should be just thick enough to coat a spoon very lightly. Stir in more cream if sauce seems too thick. Taste carefully for seasoning.
(*) If not to be served immediately, set aside uncovered, top of sauce filmed with a spoonful of cream to keep a skin from forming. Reheat when ready to serve.

Version II, with egg yolks

2 lbs. fresh sliced mush-rooms
3 Tb butter

Following Version I of the sauce, sauté the mushrooms in butter and oil, adding the shallots or onions at the end. Degrease the ham braising liquid, reduce

1 Tb oil
3 Tb minced shallots or green onions
The ham braising liquid
¼ cup Marc de Bourgogne, Madeira, or port
A 2½-quart enameled saucepan

it to about 3 cups, add the *marc* or wine and simmer for a moment. Strain into the saucepan, add the sautéed mushrooms and simmer for 5 minutes.

---

5 egg yolks
1 tsp cornstarch (anticurdling insurance)
A 2-quart mixing bowl
A wire whip
2 cups whipping cream

Blend the egg yolks and cornstarch in the mixing bowl with wire whip. Beat in the cream. Then gradually beat in about 1½ cups of the ham braising liquid from the saucepan. Pour the mixture back into the saucepan with the rest of the braising liquid and mushrooms.

(*) May be done in advance to this point.

A wooden spoon
½ to 1 cup whipping cream
A warmed sauce bowl

Shortly before serving, set saucepan over moderate heat and stir with a wooden spoon until the sauce thickens lightly, but do not let it come near the simmer (maximum temperature, 165 degrees) or the egg yolks will curdle. Stir in more cream by spoonfuls if the sauce seems too thick. It should coat a spoon lightly. Taste carefully for seasoning, pour into a warmed sauce bowl, and serve.

VARIATION

Jambon Braisé au Madère

[Ham Braised in Madeira Wine]

The combined flavors of Madeira and ham have always been a favorite in France. Spinach braised in stock, broiled or stuffed mushrooms, and a red Bordeaux-Médoc wine are good accompaniments for this dish.

For 16 to 20 people

1 cup sliced onions
1 cup sliced carrots
2 Tb butter
1 Tb oil
A covered roaster
An 8- to 10-lb. cooked ham or picnic shoulder,

Following the general directions in the preceding master recipe, preheat oven to 325 degrees. Cook the vegetables in butter and oil in the roaster until lightly browned. Place the ham in the roaster, pour in the wine, the stock or bouillon, and add the herbs. Bring to the simmer on top of the stove, cover, and bake very slowly for 2 to 2½ hours, basting every 20 min-

skinned and trimmed of
excess fat

2 cups Madeira

3 cups stock or canned beef
bouillon

6 parsley sprigs

1 bay leaf

½ tsp thyme

Powdered sugar in a shaker

utes. When the ham is tender, glaze it with powdered
sugar as described in the master recipe.

Degrease the braising liquid and boil it down rapidly
to 3 cups. Strain it into a saucepan.

---

3 Tb arrowroot (preferable
to cornstarch as it does not
cloud the sauce)

2 Tb cold stock, wine, or
truffle juice

2 or 3 chopped, canned
truffles and their juice
OR, ½ cup mushroom
duxelles (finely diced,
sautéed mushrooms), page
515

Blend the arrowroot with the cold liquid and beat it
into the hot braising liquid. Stir in the truffles or
mushrooms. Simmer for 5 minutes. Correct seasoning. Sauce will have a very light thickening; the butter enrichment will give it more body and character.

---

3 Tb softened butter

A warmed sauceboat

Reheat when ready to serve. Off heat, beat in the butter by bits, and pour the sauce into a warmed sauceboat.

✳ *JAMBON FARCI ET BRAISÉ*

[Braised Ham with Mushroom Stuffing]

A fine dish for an important dinner is ham sliced into serving pieces, re-
constructed with a stuffing between each slice, then braised in Madeira.

For 12 to 14 people

2 lbs. fresh mushrooms

3 Tb butter

1 Tb oil

½ cup minced shallots or
green onions

Trim, wash, and mince the mushrooms. A handful at
a time, twist them into a ball in the corner of a towel
to extract their juice. Sauté in the butter and oil with
the shallots or onions for 8 to 10 minutes until the
mushroom pieces begin to separate from each other.

¼ cup Madeira or port

Add the wine to the mushrooms and boil rapidly until the liquid has almost completely evaporated.

Salt and pepper
6 to 7 ounces or ¾ cup *mousse de foie gras,* or *mousse de foie d'oie* (the latter is puréed liver from a plain goose and is much less expensive)
½ tsp sage or thyme
Pinch of allspice
Optional: 1 or 2 diced, canned truffles (reserve their juice for your sauce)

Scrape the mushrooms into a mixing bowl and season with salt and pepper. Blend in the rest of the ingredients. Taste carefully for seasoning, but do not salt too heavily because the ham is salted.

A 10-lb. cooked ham, skinned, and trimmed of excess fat
A large square of well washed cheesecloth, if needed

Cut the upper two thirds of the ham into neat, thin, horizontal serving slices, piling them to one side in the order in which you slice them. Leave the lower third of the ham intact to act as a cradle to hold the slices when you put them back. Spread a spoonful of the mushroom stuffing in the center of each slice and pile the slices back onto the ham, reconstructing it into approximately its original shape. If the slices have been arranged neatly and solidly on the ham, no tying is necessary to keep them in place while the ham braises. But if you are doubtful, wrap the ham in cheesecloth.

Then braise the ham for about 2½ hours with cooked vegetables, herbs, stock, and Madeira as described in the braising recipe, page 393. Serve it with the same Madeira sauce, and braised spinach, page 470.

VARIATION

Jambon Farci en Croûte

[Stuffed Ham Baked in a Pastry Crust]

A splendid way to serve the preceding sliced and stuffed ham is to bake it in a pastry crust. To do so, after stuffing and braising it, allow it to cool for about an hour. Then, following the directions for duck in a crust, page 571, surround it with a decorated pastry dough and bake it in a 375-degree oven for 30 to 40 minutes until the crust is cooked and nicely browned.

HAM SLICES

Tranches de Jambon

Sliced ham responds to a number of interesting preparations which are relatively quick and simple to do.

TRANCHES DE JAMBON EN PIPÉRADE

[Ham Slices Baked with Tomatoes, Onions, and Peppers]

This savory recipe for thick slices of smoked ham may be prepared for baking several hours before it is set in the oven. Sautéed potatoes, green beans, and a light red wine or a *rosé* go well with it.

For 6 people

2½ to 3 lbs. of cooked ham, sliced ½ inch thick, and cut into serving pieces if you wish
3 Tb rendered ham fat or olive oil
A large skillet
A shallow baking dish large enough to hold ham in one layer

Trim off excess fat, and dry the ham slice or slices on paper towels. Heat the fat or olive oil in the skillet until it is almost smoking, then brown the ham lightly for a minute or two on each side. Remove skillet from heat and place the ham in the baking dish.

1 cup sliced yellow onions
1 cup sliced green bell peppers

Lower heat, and stir the onions into the fat in the skillet. Cover and cook slowly for 5 minutes. Stir in the peppers and cook 5 minutes more or until the vegetables are tender but not browned.

2 lbs. firm, ripe, red tomatoes, peeled, seeded, juiced, and sliced, page 505 (makes 3 cups of pulp)

Spread the tomato pulp over the onions and peppers, add the garlic and seasonings. Cover and cook slowly for 5 minutes so the tomatoes will render their remaining juice. Then uncover and boil for several

2 cloves mashed garlic
⅛ tsp pepper
Pinch of cayenne pepper
¼ tsp sage or thyme

minutes, shaking the skillet, until the tomato juice has almost entirely evaporated.

Cover the browned ham with the vegetables.
(*) May be done in advance to this point.

---

2 to 3 Tb minced parsley

Preheat oven to 350 degrees. About 20 to 30 minutes before serving time, cover the baking dish and place it in the middle level of the oven and bake until the ham is heated through and tender when pierced with a fork. Baste with the juices in the dish and correct seasoning, adding salt if necessary. Decorate with parsley and serve.

TRANCHES DE JAMBON MORVANDELLE

[Sautéed Ham Slices—Cream and Madeira Sauce]

Placed on a bed of spinach braised in stock, surrounded with broiled mushrooms or sautéed potatoes, this is a delectable ham dish. Serve with it a light red wine, or a Chablis or Pouilly-Fuissé.

For 6 people

2½ to 3 lbs. of cooked ham, sliced ¼ inch thick

Trim off excess fat, and cut the ham into serving pieces. Dry on paper towels.

2 Tb butter
1 Tb oil
An enameled skillet

A few pieces at a time, brown the ham lightly for a minute on each side in hot butter and oil. Set the ham aside.

3 Tb flour
2 Tb minced shallots or green onions
A wooden spoon

Pour all but 2½ tablespoons of fat out of the skillet. Stir in the flour with a wooden spoon, then the shallots or onions, and cook slowly for 2 or 3 minutes without browning. Remove from heat.

1 cup very good ham stock, white or brown stock, or canned beef bouillon
½ cup Madeira or port
A wire whip
1 Tb tomato paste
Big pinch of pepper

Bring the stock or bouillon and wine to the simmer in a small saucepan. Blend it into the flour in the skillet with a wire whip. Beat in the tomato paste and pepper.

1½ cups whipping cream
3 Tb cognac

Bring the sauce to the simmer, stirring, then beat in the cream. Simmer for 4 or 5 minutes, allowing the sauce to reduce until it coats the spoon lightly. Taste carefully for seasoning but do not oversalt. Stir in the cognac. Then add the ham slices and spoon the sauce over them.

(*) May be done in advance to this point. Film surface with a spoonful of cream and set aside.

A hot platter on which, if you wish, is a mound of spinach braised in stock, page 470

Shortly before serving, bring to the simmer, cover, and simmer slowly for a minute or two until the ham is tender when pierced with a fork. Taste again for seasoning. Transfer the ham to a platter, or place it over a bed of braised spinach. Spoon the sauce over the ham and serve.

VARIATION

Mix sliced, sautéed mushrooms into the sauce to simmer with the ham.

TRANCHES DE JAMBON À LA CRÈME

[Sautéed Ham Slices—Fresh Cream Sauce]

This famous recipe is the same idea as the preceding one, but is made with a richer and more delicate sauce.

For 6 people

2½ to 3 lbs. cooked ham, sliced ¼ inch thick
2 Tb butter
1 Tb oil
A 9- to 10-inch skillet
2 Tb shallots or green onions
⅔ cup Madeira or port and 3 Tb cognac
A wooden spoon

Trim off excess fat, cut the ham into serving pieces, and dry on paper towels. Brown the slices lightly on each side in hot butter and oil and set them aside. Pour all but a tablespoon of sautéing fat out of the skillet, stir in the shallots or onions, and cook slowly for 2 minutes. Pour in the wine and cognac and, scraping up the coagulated sauté juices with a wooden spoon, boil rapidly until the liquid has reduced to 3 or 4 tablespoons.

2 cups whipping cream
2 Tb Dijon-type prepared

Add the cream to the skillet, beat in the mustard mixture, and the pepper. Simmer slowly for 10 to 15

mustard mixed with 1 Tb tomato paste and 2 Tb whipping cream
Big pinch of pepper

minutes, until the cream has reduced to about 1½ cups and has thickened lightly. Correct seasoning, but do not oversalt.

Return the ham slices to the skillet and baste them with the sauce.
(*) May be done ahead to this point.

A hot platter on which, if you wish, is a mound of spinach braised in stock, page 470

Shortly before serving, bring to the simmer, cover and simmer for several minutes until the ham is reheated and tender. Arrange the ham on a hot platter or on the bed of spinach. Spoon the sauce over the ham and serve.

FRENCH BAKED BEANS
Cassoulet

Cassoulet is a rich combination of beans baked with meats, as much a part of southwestern France as Boston baked beans are of New England. The composition of a *cassoulet* is, in typical French fashion, the subject of infinite dispute, so much so that if you have read or heard about *cassoulet* and never tasted it, you come to expect a kind of rare ambrosia rather than the nourishing country fare it actually is. As *cassoulet* is native to a relatively large region of France, each part of which has its own specialties, arguments about what should go into this famous dish seem based on local traditions. *Toulousains* insist that it must include among its meats preserved goose, *confit d'oie,* or it is not a real·*cassoulet*. After all, something must be done with all the geese which housed the *foie gras,* and *cassoulet* is a natural solution in the Toulouse area. Then there are those who declare the *cassoulet* was born in Castelnaudary, and originally contained only beans, pork, and sausages. A heretical few suggest the *cassoulet* was not a French invention at all, but an adaption from the Arab *fava* bean and mutton stew. And so on, with variations and dogmatisms rampant. Fortunately all the talk can be regarded as so much historical background, for an extremely good *cassoulet* can be made anywhere out of beans and whatever of its traditional meats are available: goose, game, pork, sausages, lamb, mutton. The important item is flavor, which comes largely from the liquid the beans and meats are cooked in. And truth to tell, despite all the to-do about preserved goose, once it is cooked with the beans you may find difficulty in distinguishing goose from pork.

The following recipe makes no attempt to cut corners, for the concoction of a good *cassoulet* is a fairly long process. You can prepare it in one day, but two or even three days of leisurely on-and-off cooking are much easier. It calls for a roast loin of pork, shoulder of lamb braised in wine, homemade sausage cakes, and beans cooked with pork rind, fresh bacon or salt pork, and aromatic vegetables. The meats are cut into serving pieces and arranged in a casserole with the beans and various cooking juices. Then the dish is baked in the oven for an hour to blend flavors. Time could be saved if the lamb were roasted whole or if leftover roast were used, but flavor would be lost, and there would be no splendid braising liquid to give character to the *cassoulet*. Polish sausage could cook with the beans, replacing the homemade sausage cakes. But after you have made the dish once or twice, you will see that you can pretty well invent your own formula as long as you supply excellent flavor through one means or another. Suggestions for other meats are at the end of the recipe.

MENU SUGGESTIONS

Any *cassoulet* worthy of the name is not a light dish, and is probably best served as a noontime dinner. The rest of the menu should consist of a simple first course if any—a clear soup, jellied soup, or oysters—then a green salad and fruits. For wine, choose a strong, dry *rosé* or white, or a young, full-bodied red.

THE BEANS

Most French recipes specify simply "dry white beans." A few call for white beans from certain localities in France such as Cayence, Pamiers, Mazères, Lavelanet. We have found American Great Northern beans to be entirely satisfactory, but they should not be old and stale. If you wish to pressure-cook them instead of using the open-pot method, soak them as directed in the recipe, then add all the ingredients listed and, following the directions for your cooker, bring them quickly to 15 pounds pressure. Cook for exactly 3 minutes, then allow the pressure to go down slowly by itself, 15 to 20 minutes. Let the beans stand uncovered in the cooking liquid for at least 30 minutes so they will absorb its flavor.

A NOTE ON THE ORDER OF BATTLE

All of the various steps leading up to the final assembly in the recipe below may be carried on at various times or almost simultaneously. Once the *cas-*

soulet is made ready for the oven, it may be refrigerated and baked a day or two later.

✳ *CASSOULET DE PORC ET DE MOUTON*

[Beans Baked with Pork Loin, Shoulder of Mutton or Lamb, and Sausage]

For 10 to 12 people

The pork loin

2½ lbs. of boned pork loin, excess fat removed (It will taste even better if marinated overnight in salt and spices, page 376.)

Following directions on page 380, roast the pork to an internal temperature of 175 to 180 degrees. Set it aside to cool. Reserve cooking juices.

The beans

2 lbs. or 5 cups dry white beans (Great Northern, preferably)

An 8-quart kettle containing 5 quarts of rapidly boiling water

Drop the beans into the boiling water. Bring rapidly back to the boil and boil for 2 minutes. Remove from heat and let the beans soak in the water for 1 hour; they will cook in the soaking water, and the cooking should proceed as soon as possible after the soaking process is completed.

½ lb. fresh pork rind or salt pork rind

A heavy saucepan

Heavy shears

While the beans are soaking, place the rind in the saucepan and cover with 1 quart of cold water. Bring to the boil and boil 1 minute. Drain, rinse in cold water, and repeat the process. Then, with shears, cut the rind into strips ¼ inch wide; cut the strips into small triangles. Cover the rind again with a quart of cold water, bring to the simmer, and simmer very slowly for 30 minutes. Set saucepan aside. This process freshens the rind, and softens it so it will lose itself as it cooks with the beans.

A 1-lb. chunk of fresh, unsalted, unsmoked lean bacon (or very good quality lean salt pork simmered for 10 minutes in 2 quarts of water and drained)

Place all the ingredients at the left in the kettle with the soaked beans. Bring to the simmer. Skim off any skum which may rise. Simmer slowly, uncovered, for about 1½ hours or until the beans are just tender. Add boiling water if necessary during cooking, to keep beans covered with liquid. Season to taste near end of cooking. Leave beans in their cooking liquid

1 cup (4 ounces) sliced onions

The pork rind and its cooking liquid

A large herb bouquet, with garlic and cloves: 6 to 8 parsley sprigs, 4 unpeeled cloves garlic, 2 cloves, ½ tsp thyme, and 2 bay leaves tied in cheesecloth

No salt until later if you have used salt pork; otherwise 1 Tb salt

until ready to use, then drain. Reserve cooking liquid. Remove the bacon or salt pork and set aside. Discard the herb packet.

The lamb or mutton

2 to 2½ lbs. boned shoulder or breast of mutton or almost mature lamb, fell (skin covering meat) and excess fat removed

4 to 6 Tb rendered fresh pork fat, pork-roast drippings, goose fat, or cooking oil; more if needed

A heavy, 8-quart fireproof casserole

About 1 lb. cracked mutton or lamb bones; some pork bones may be included

2 cups (½ lb.) minced onions

Cut the lamb or mutton into chunks roughly 2 inches square. Dry each piece in paper towels. Pour a $\frac{1}{16}$-inch layer of fat into the casserole and heat until the fat is almost smoking. Brown the meat, a few pieces at a time, on all sides. Set the meat on a side dish. Brown the bones and add them to the meat. If fat has burned, discard it and add 3 tablespoons of fresh fat. Lower heat, and brown the onions lightly for about 5 minutes.

4 cloves mashed garlic

6 Tb fresh tomato purée, tomato paste, or 4 large tomatoes peeled, seeded, and juiced, page 505

½ tsp thyme

2 bay leaves

3 cups dry white wine or 2 cups dry white vermouth

1 quart brown stock or 3

Return the bones and lamb or mutton to the casserole and stir in all ingredients on the left. Bring to the simmer on top of the stove, season lightly with salt. Cover and simmer slowly on top of the stove or in a 325-degree oven for 1½ hours. Then remove the meat to a dish; discard the bones and bay leaves. Remove all but 2 tablespoons fat and carefully correct seasoning of cooking liquid.

cups canned beef bouillon
and 1 cup water
Salt and pepper

Final flavoring of beans

Pour the cooked and drained beans into the lamb cooking juices. Stir in any juices you may have from the roast pork. Add bean cooking liquid, if necessary, so beans are covered. Bring to the simmer and simmer 5 minutes, then let the beans stand in the liquid for 10 minutes to absorb flavor. Drain the beans when you are ready for the final assembly farther on.

Homemade sausage cakes—a substitute for Saucisse de Toulouse

1 lb. (2 cups) lean fresh pork
⅓ lb. (⅔ cup) fresh pork fat
A meat grinder
A 3-quart mixing bowl
A wooden spoon
2 tsp salt
⅛ tsp pepper
Big pinch allspice
⅛ tsp crumbled bay leaf
¼ cup armagnac or cognac
A small clove mashed garlic
Optional: 1 chopped truffle and the juice from the can

Put the pork and fat through the medium blade of the meat grinder. Place in bowl and beat in the rest of the ingredients on the left. Sauté a small spoonful and taste for seasoning, adding more to the mixture if you feel it necessary. Form into cakes 2 inches in diameter and ½ inch thick. Brown lightly over moderate heat in a skillet. Drain on paper towels.

Final assembly

An 8-quart fireproof casserole 5 to 6 inches high: brown earthenware glazed inside is typical, but other types of glazed pottery or enameled iron will do nicely
2 cups dry white bread crumbs mixed with ½ cup chopped parsley
3 to 4 Tb pork roasting fat or goose fat

Cut the roast pork into 1½ to 2 inch serving chunks. Slice the bacon or salt pork into serving pieces ¼ inch thick. Arrange a layer of beans in the bottom of the casserole, then continue with layers of lamb or mutton, roast pork, bacon slices, sausage cakes, and beans, ending with a layer of beans and sausage cakes. Pour on the meat cooking juices, and enough bean cooking juice so liquid comes just to the top layer of beans. Spread on the crumbs and parsley, and dribble the fat on top.

(*) Set aside or refrigerate until you are ready to take up the final cooking of about an hour. The *cassoulet* should be served soon after its baking, so it will not dry out or overcook.

_____

Baking

Preheat oven to 375 degrees. Bring the casserole to the simmer on top of the stove. Then set it in the upper third of the preheated oven. When the top has crusted lightly, in about 20 minutes, turn the oven down to 350 degrees. Break the crust into the beans with the back of a spoon, and baste with the liquid in the casserole. Repeat several times, as the crust forms again, but leave a final crust intact for serving. If the liquid in the casserole becomes too thick during the baking period, add a spoonful or two of bean cooking liquid. The *cassoulet* should bake for about an hour; serve it from its casserole.

_____

VARIATIONS

Here are some additions or substitutions for the meats in the preceding recipe.

Preserved Goose, Confit d'Oie. This is goose, usually from the *foie gras* regions of France, which has been cut into wing, leg, and breast sections, poached in goose fat, and preserved in goose fat. It can usually be bought in cans from one of the food-importing stores. Use it instead of, or even in addition to, the roast pork in the recipe. Scrape the fat off the pieces of goose, and cut the goose into serving portions. Brown them lightly in some of the fat from the can. Arrange the goose in the casserole with the beans and meats for the final baking.

Fresh Goose, Duck, Turkey, or Partridge. Roast or braise any of these, and carve into serving pieces. Use along with or instead of the roast pork in the recipe, arranging the pieces with the beans and meats in the casserole for the final baking.

Ham Hock or Veal Shank. Simmer either of these with the beans. Cut into serving pieces before arranging in the casserole for the final baking.

Polish Sausage. This sausage can usually be bought in any American market, and is a good substitute for such French sausages as *de campagne, de ménage, à cuire, à l'ail,* or *de Morteau.* First simmer the whole sausage for ½ hour with the beans. Then cut it into ½-inch slices and arrange in the casserole with the beans and the other meats for the final baking. Polish sausage may be used instead of or in addition to the sausage cakes in the recipe.

SAUTÉED CALF'S LIVER
Foie de Veau Sauté

It is most important that calf's liver be sautéed in very hot butter and oil, so a crust will form on the outside which will keep the juices in. Do not crowd the skillet, use two skillets if necessary, and do not use a skillet too large for your source of heat. Sautéed liver should be pink inside, its juices will run a very pale rose when the meat is pricked with a fork. Have the liver cut into even slices ⅜ inch thick, and ask that the surrounding filament be peeled off each slice; if this is left on, the liver will curl as it cooks.

WINE AND VEGETABLE SUGGESTIONS

Broiled tomatoes, braised spinach, or *ratatouille* (eggplant and tomato casserole, page 503), and sautéed potatoes go well with liver. Wine choices would be chilled *rosé,* or a light red such as Bordeaux or Beaujolais.

---

* *FOIE DE VEAU SAUTÉ*

[Sautéed Calf's Liver]

For 6 people

6 to 12 slices of calf's liver ⅜ inch thick, with surrounding filament removed
Salt and pepper
½ cup of sifted flour on a large plate

Just before sautéing, season the slices with salt and pepper, roll in flour, and shake off excess flour.

1 or 2 heavy skillets
2 Tb butter and 1 Tb oil for each skillet
A hot platter
A vegetable garniture, water cress, or parsley

Place the butter and oil in the skillet or skillets and set over high heat until you see that the butter foam has almost subsided, indicating it is hot enough. Then arrange the liver in the skillet, leaving a ¼-inch space between each slice. Sauté for 2 to 3 minutes, regulating heat so butter is always very hot but not burning. Turn the liver with a spatula and sauté for a minute or so on the other side. The liver is done when its juices run a very pale pink if a slice is pricked with a fork. Remove the liver to a hot platter and serve, surrounded by whatever garniture you have chosen, or decorated with water cress or sprigs of parsley.

SAUCES TO SERVE WITH SAUTÉED LIVER

Sauce Crème à la Moutarde

[Cream and Mustard Sauce]

For about 1 cup

½ cup brown stock or canned beef bouillon ¾ cup whipping cream	As soon as the liver has been removed to a platter, pour the stock or bouillon into the skillet and boil down rapidly until it has reduced by half. Then add the cream and boil for a moment to reduce and thicken it slightly.
1 Tb prepared mustard, mashed with 2 Tb softened butter Parsley sprigs	Off heat, swirl the mustard-butter into the skillet. Pour the sauce around the liver, decorate with parsley, and serve.

Other Sauces

The sauces in the following list can be prepared in advance; either serve them separately, or pour them around the sautéed liver. About 1½ cups should be sufficient.

Coulis de Tomates, fresh tomato purée with herbs, page 78

Sauce Robert, brown sauce with mustard and onions, page 72

Sauce Brune aux Fines Herbes, brown herb sauce, page 73

Sauce à l'Italienne, tomato-flavored brown sauce with diced mushrooms, diced ham, and herbs, page 411

Beurres Composés, flavored butters, pages 100 to 103. These include butter creamed with mustard, with herbs, with garlic, and with wine and herbs. Spread a spoonful over each slice of sautéed liver, or cut chilled, flavored butter into pieces and pass separately.

FOIE DE VEAU À LA MOUTARDE

[Liver with Mustard, Herbs, and Bread Crumbs]

This is an appealing way to prepare liver. It is sautéed very briefly to brown lightly, then painted with mustard and herbs, rolled in fresh bread crumbs, basted with melted butter, and set under a hot broiler to brown the crumbs. The preliminary sautéing and crumbing may be done several hours in advance of the final cooking, which takes about 5 minutes. For this recipe, the liver is sliced thicker, so it will not cook too quickly.

For 6 servings

6 slices of calf's liver cut ½ inch thick, outside filament removed
Salt and pepper
½ cup sifted flour on a large plate
2 Tb butter
1 Tb oil
A heavy skillet

Season the liver with salt and pepper, dredge in flour, and sauté for 1 minute on each side in very hot butter and oil. The slices should be very lightly browned and slightly stiffened, but not cooked through. Remove to a dish.

3 Tb prepared mustard of the strong, Dijon type
1 Tb finely minced shallots or green onions
3 Tb minced parsley
½ clove mashed garlic
Pinch of pepper
3 cups fine, white, fresh bread crumbs spread on a large plate
A greased broiling pan

Beat the mustard in a small bowl with the shallots or onions and seasonings. Drop by drop, beat in the liver sautéing fat to make a mayonnaiselike cream. Paint the liver slices with the mixture. One by one, lay the slices in the bread crumbs and heap bread crumbs on top, gently shake off excess, and pat the adhering crumbs in place with the flat of a knife. Arrange the liver on the broiling pan.
(*) If not to be broiled immediately, cover with waxed paper and refrigerate.

Shortly before serving, heat broiler to very hot.

6 Tb melted butter
A hot platter

Baste the liver with half the melted butter. Place so its surface is about 2 inches from the broiler heat to brown for a minute or two. Turn, baste with the remaining butter, and brown the other side quickly. Arrange on a hot platter and serve.

SWEETBREADS AND BRAINS

Ris de Veau et Cervelles

Sweetbreads and brains have much the same texture and flavor, but brains are more delicate. They both receive almost the same treatments. Both must be soaked for several hours in cold water before they are cooked, to soften the filament which covers them so that it may be removed, to dissolve their bloody patches, and to whiten them. Some authorities direct that they always be blanched before cooking—that is, poached in salted and acidulated water or a court bouillon; others do not agree. If the sweetbreads or brains are to be braised, blanching is a useless and flavor-losing step. If they are to be sliced and sautéed, blanching firms them up so they are easier to cut, but removes some of their delicacy and tenderness. Both brains and sweetbreads are perishable, and if they are not to be cooked within 24 hours, they should be soaked and blanched which will help to preserve them.

SOAKING SWEETBREADS AND BRAINS

Wash in cold water, then place in a bowl and soak in several changes of cold water or under a dripping tap for 1½ to 2 hours. Delicately pull off as much as you easily can of the filament which encloses them, without tearing the flesh. This is a rather slow process. Soak them again for 1½ to 2 hours, this time in several changes of cold water containing 1 tablespoon of vinegar per quart. Peel off as much more filament as you can, and they are ready for trimming and cooking.

TRIMMING

A whole sweetbread, which is the thymus gland of a calf and usually weighs about 1 pound, consists of 2 lobes connected by a soft, white tube, the *cornet*. The smoother, rounder, and more solid of the two lobes is the kernel, heart, or *noix,* and choicest piece. The second lobe, called throat sweetbread or *gorge,* is more uneven in shape, broken by veins, and is often slit. Separate the two lobes from the tube with a knife. The tube may be added to the stock pot.

For brains, cut off white, opaque bits at the base.

BLANCHING SWEETBREADS

Sweetbreads, trimmed and soaked as in preceding directions
An enameled saucepan just large enough to hold them
Cold water
Per quart of water: 1 tsp salt and 1 Tb lemon juice

Place sweetbreads in saucepan and cover by 2 inches with cold water; add salt and lemon juice. Bring to simmer and cook, uncovered, at barest simmer for 15 minutes. Drain and plunge into cold water for 5 minutes. Drain. The sweetbreads are now ready for sautéing.

BLANCHING BRAINS

Brains, trimmed and soaked as in preceding directions
An enameled saucepan just large enough to hold them
Boiling water
Per quart of water: 1 tsp salt and 1 Tb lemon juice

Place brains in saucepan and cover by 2 inches with boiling water; add salt and lemon juice or vinegar. Heat to just below simmer and maintain water at a not-quite-simmering temperature, timing as follows:

Lamb brains, 15 minutes

Calf or pork brains, 20 minutes

Beef brains, 30 minutes

Then set saucepan aside and let the brains cool for 20 minutes in the cooking liquid; if they are not to be used until later, set saucepan in refrigerator. Drain the brains, and they are ready for sautéing, page 413.

PRESSING BLANCHED BRAINS OR SWEETBREADS UNDER A WEIGHT

Some cooks like to weight blanched sweetbreads or brains for 2 to 3 hours under a heavy dinnerplate. This forces the water out of them, and flattens them so they are easy to cut into narrow slices. Follow this system or not, as you wish.

SWEETBREADS

* *RIS DE VEAU BRAISÉS*

[Braised Sweetbreads]

Braising is a preliminary cooking for sweetbreads, and you will note that no blanching is required. The soaked and peeled sweetbreads are first cooked slowly in butter to firm them a little and to render some of their juices; they are then baked with wine and other flavorings. After this cooking, or braising, which may take place as long as the day before you are to use them, the sweet-breads are ready for saucing and serving. Sauced sweetbreads may be arranged in a ring of rice or *risotto,* in a *vol-au-vent* or pastry shell, on a platter, or they may be gratinéed. Drained, braised sweetbreads are also good cold, in a salad.

VEGETABLE AND WINE SUGGESTIONS

Rice or *risotto,* and buttered peas or creamed or braised spinach go well with sweetbreads. Serve a light red wine such a Bordeaux-Médoc, or a *rosé* with sweetbreads in brown sauce; a white Burgundy or a white Graves with sweetbreads in cream sauce.

For 6 people

¼ cup each: finely diced carrots, onions, celery, and diced ham
4 Tb butter
A medium herb bouquet: 4 parsley sprigs, ¼ tsp thyme, and ½ bay leaf tied in cheesecloth
⅛ tsp salt
Pinch of pepper
A 10-inch enameled skillet

Cook the diced vegetables and ham slowly in the butter with the herb bouquet and seasonings for 10 to 15 minutes, until tender but not browned.

½ tsp salt
Big pinch of pepper
1½ to 2 lbs. sweetbreads previously soaked, peeled, and trimmed as directed on page 408

Season the sweetbreads. Arrange them in the skillet and baste them with the butter and vegetables. Cover and cook slowly for 5 minutes. Turn, baste, and cook 5 minutes more. They will render quite a bit of juice.

A buttered fireproof casserole or baking dish about 7 inches in diameter, or just large enough to hold the sweetbreads in one layer

Transfer the sweetbreads to the casserole.

Preheat oven to 325 degrees.

¾ cup dry white wine or ½ cup dry white vermouth

1 cup brown stock or canned beef bouillon if you are serving a brown sauce; 1 cup white stock or canned chicken broth if you are serving a white sauce

Pour the wine into the skillet with the sweetbread juices and vegetables, and boil down rapidly until the liquids have reduced to ½ cup. Then pour the liquids, vegetables, and herb bouquet over the sweetbreads; add sufficient stock, bouillon, or broth barely to cover them.

Bring to the simmer on top of the stove. Cover the casserole and place in lower third of oven. Regulate heat so the sweetbreads cook at the barest simmer for 45 minutes.

(*) Let the sweetbreads cool in their cooking stock until you are ready to use them.

VARIATIONS

Ris de Veau Braisés à l'Italienne

[Braised Sweetbreads with Brown Mushroom Sauce]

For 6 people

The braised sweetbreads in the preceding recipe

Remove the sweetbreads from the braising casserole. Drain, cut into ½-inch slices, and set aside.

1 Tb cornstarch blended with 1 Tb dry white wine or vermouth
1 Tb tomato paste
½ lb. finely diced fresh mushrooms sautéed in butter, page 513
¼ cup diced, boiled ham
Salt and pepper

Rapidly boil down the cooking stock in the casserole to 1½ cups. Remove from heat and discard herb bouquet. (The braising vegetables and ham remain, and become a part of the sauce.) Beat in the starch mixture and the tomato paste. Stir in the mushrooms and additional ham; simmer for 3 minutes, stirring. Correct seasoning and fold in the sliced sweetbreads.

(*) If not to be served immediately, film sauce with a spoonful of stock.

2 Tb minced green herbs such as parsley, chervil, and tarragon, or parsley only

Reheat for 2 to 3 minutes at below the simmer just before serving. Arrange on a serving dish, or in a patty shell or ring of rice. Sprinkle with herbs, and serve.

Ris de Veau à la Crème
Ris de Veau à la Maréchale

[Creamed Sweetbreads]

1½ to 2 lbs. braised sweetbreads, master recipe	Cut the braised sweetbreads into slices ½ inch thick and set aside. Rapidly boil down their cooking stock until it has reduced to 1¼ cups.
A 6-cup enameled saucepan 2½ Tb butter 3 Tb flour	In a separate pan, cook the butter and flour slowly together until they foam for 2 minutes without browning. Off heat, strain in the hot cooking stock and beat vigorously to blend. Bring to the simmer, stirring, for 1 minute. Sauce will be very thick.
⅔ to 1 cup whipping cream Salt and pepper Drops of lemon juice	Beat in ½ cup of cream, simmering, then beat in more by spoonfuls until the sauce thins out and coats the spoon nicely. Correct seasoning, adding drops of lemon juice if you feel it necessary.
	Replace the sweetbreads in their original casserole, or in a fireproof serving dish, and pour the sauce over them. (*) If not to be served immediately, film top with a spoonful of cream.
2 Tb minced, mixed green herbs or parsley	Reheat for 3 to 4 minutes at below the simmer before serving, then decorate with the herbs.

Ris de Veau à la Crème et aux Champignons

[Creamed Sweetbreads with Mushrooms]

Ingredients for the preceding creamed sweetbreads ½ lb. sliced fresh mushrooms	After making the sauce, stir in the mushrooms and simmer for 10 minutes, allowing the sauce to reduce slightly as the mushrooms will thin it out. Then proceed with the recipe.

Ris de Veau au Gratin

[Sweetbreads au Gratin]

Ingredients for the braised sweetbreads on page 409 and any of the preceding sauces

¼ cup grated Swiss cheese

1 Tb butter, cut into bits

Arrange the sliced sweetbreads in a buttered baking dish or individual shells or dishes. Pour sauce over them. Sprinkle on the cheese, and dot with the butter. Set aside until ready to serve.

About 10 minutes before serving, place 7 to 8 inches under a moderately hot broiler to heat the sweetbreads through and to brown the top of the sauce lightly.

ESCALOPES DE RIS DE VEAU SAUTÉS

[Sweetbreads Sautéed in Butter]

These are done exactly like brains sautéed in butter, and are accompanied by any of the sauces suggested at the end of that recipe, page 415.

BRAINS

Although calf's brains are those most universally known in America, lamb brains are equally good. Mutton, pork, and beef brains are less delicate in texture than calf brains and are best when braised, but you may sauté them if you wish. Soaking and peeling directions for brains are at the beginning of this section on page 408. We shall call everything in the following recipes calf's brains with the understanding that calf, lamb, mutton, pork, and beef brains are interchangeable though their cooking times differ slightly as indicated in the blanching directions on page 409.

* CERVELLES AU BEURRE NOIR

[Calf's Brains in Brown Butter Sauce]

Brown butter sauce and calf's brains are almost synonyms, they go so well together. To be at its best, the sauce should always be made separately, not in the pan in which you sautéed the brains. It is thus clear and unspeckled, and also much more digestible. In addition, as the brains can be sautéed only at the last minute, the dish will then be ready to serve almost at once.

Of the several methods for *cervelles au beurre noir,* we have chosen that of pre-cooking the brains, slicing them, marinating them in a vinaigrette, then sautéing and saucing them. As alternatives, you may simply pour a brown butter sauce over hot, blanched brains, or you may omit the pre-cooking and marination altogether. In this case, slice raw, soaked, and trimmed brains, season, dredge in flour, and sauté them; then pour the sauce over them.

VEGETABLE AND WINE SUGGESTIONS

This dish often constitutes a separate course, but if you wish to serve the brains as a main course, accompany them with mashed or parsley potatoes and either buttered green peas or the spinach braised in stock on page 470. Wine choices would be a light red, such as Bordeaux-Medoc, or a *rosé;* good but less usual would be a white Burgundy.

For 6 people as a main course

1½ lbs. calf's brains, previously soaked, trimmed, and blanched according to directions on page 409

Cut the blanched brains into slices ½ inch thick.

---

3 Tb lemon juice
⅛ tsp salt
A 2½ quart mixing bowl
Pinch of pepper
1 Tb olive oil
2 Tb minced parsley

Beat the lemon juice and salt in the bowl until the salt has dissolved. Then beat in the pepper, oil, and parsley. Fold the sliced brains into the sauce. Marinate for 30 minutes, or until you are ready to sauté them.

---

1 cup brown butter sauce, page 98, with or without capers

While the brains are marinating, prepare the sauce and keep hot over simmering water.

---

1 cup flour sifted into a dish

Just before sautéing, drain the brains. Roll in the flour and shake off excess flour.

---

1 or 2 heavy skillets
2 Tb butter and 1 Tb oil for each skillet

Set the skillet or skillets over moderately high heat with the butter and oil. As soon as you see that the butter foam has almost subsided, brown the brains lightly for 3 to 4 minutes on each side.

A hot platter	Arrange on a hot platter, pour the hot butter sauce over them, and serve.

VARIATIONS: SAUCES

Sauce à l'Italienne, tomato-flavored brown sauce with diced mushrooms, diced ham, and herbs, page 411

Coulis de Tomates, fresh tomato sauce with herbs, page 78

CERVELLES BRAISÉES

[Braised Calf's Brains]

The brains are cooked in butter with aromatic vegetables, herbs, wine, and stock. Follow the recipe for braised sweetbreads, page 409, and use the same sauces, but the oven-simmering times are:

20 minutes for lamb brains

30 minutes for calf and pork brains

45 minutes for beef brains

CERVELLES EN MATELOTE

[Calf's Brains in Red Wine with Mushrooms and Onions]

This dish makes a complete course in itself. Serve a light red Burgundy or Mâcon wine.

For 6 people

2 cups good, young, red wine (Mâcon or Burgundy)	Bring the wine and stock or bouillon to the simmer in the saucepan with the herbs and garlic. Add the brains, bring to the simmer, and cook uncovered at just below the simmer for 20 minutes. Allow the brains to cool in the cooking liquid for 20 minutes, so they will absorb flavor, and firm up. Then drain
1 cup brown stock or canned beef bouillon	
An enameled saucepan just	

large enough to hold the
brains in one layer
¼ tsp thyme
4 sprigs of parsley
½ bay leaf
1 clove mashed garlic
1½ lbs. calf's brains, previously soaked and peeled,
page 408
A buttered, fireproof serving
dish

them, slice into ½-inch pieces, and arrange in the
buttered serving dish.

½ Tb tomato paste
2 Tb flour mashed to a paste
with 2 Tb softened butter
Salt and pepper

Beat the tomato paste into the cooking stock, and
boil down rapidly until the liquid has reduced to 1½
cups. Off heat, beat in the flour-butter paste. Boil,
stirring, for 1 minute. Correct seasoning.

---

24 small, brown-braised onions, page 483
½ lb. fresh mushrooms sautéed in butter, page 513

Arrange the onions and mushrooms around the
brains, and strain the sauce over the brains and vegetables.
(*) If not to be served immediately, film the sauce
with a spoonful of stock or melted butter.

---

1 to 2 Tb softened butter

Just before serving, set over low heat to warm
through for 3 to 4 minutes without simmering. Off
heat, tip dish, add butter, a half-tablespoon at a time,
and baste brains and vegetables with the sauce until
the butter has absorbed.

---

12 heart-shaped *croûtons*
(white bread sautéed in
clarified butter), page 199
2 to 3 Tb minced parsley

Decorate with *croûtons* and parsley, and serve.

VEAL AND LAMB KIDNEYS
Rognons de Veau et de Mouton

Cooked kidneys should be tender and slightly pink near the center. The
bursting-out of juices is always a problem when they are sautéed in slices. Unless your source of heat is a very strong one, within a few seconds after the
slices hit the pan their juices pour out and the kidneys boil and toughen rather

than sauté. An excellent solution—and, in fact, the best method for kidneys in our experience—is to cook the whole kidney in butter, then slice it, and warm the slices briefly in a sauce. However, if you prefer to sauté raw sliced kidneys, do so in very hot butter and oil for only 2 to 3 minutes. They do not brown; they just cook through, turning a uniform gray outside but remaining somewhat pink inside. Then remove the kidneys to a hot dish, make one of the sauces described in the following recipes, and return the kidneys to warm in the sauce without boiling.

Any of the following recipes may be done at the table in a chafing dish.

LAMB KIDNEYS

All of the following recipes are for veal kidneys, but are equally applicable to lamb kidneys. Allow 2 or 3 lamb kidneys per person. Cook them whole in butter as described in the master recipe, but only for 4 to 5 minutes rather than the 10 for veal kidneys. Then proceed with the recipe.

PREPARATION FOR COOKING

Both lamb and veal kidneys are encased in a layer of fat which has usually been peeled off, presumably without breaking the kidneys, before you buy them. Under this is a thin filament surrounding the kidney; it should also be peeled off. Cut out most of the button of fat on the underside of lamb kidneys, and most of the knob of fat under a veal kidney. A trimmed veal kidney will weigh 6 to 8 ounces; a lamb kidney, 1½ to 2 ounces. Kidneys should have a good, fresh odor and only the faintest suggestion, if any, of an ammonia smell. Veal and lamb kidneys should never be washed or soaked in water, as they absorb too much of it.

✳ *ROGNONS DE VEAU EN CASSEROLE*

[Kidneys Cooked in Butter—Mustard and Parsley Sauce]

If you want to serve this as a main course rather than as a hot hors d'oeuvre, potatoes sautéed in butter and braised onions make good accompaniments. Red Burgundy goes especially well with kidneys.

For 4 to 6 people

---

4 Tb butter	Heat the butter in the casserole or chafing dish until
A fireproof casserole or	you see the foam begin to subside. Roll the kidneys

chafing dish which will just hold the kidneys easily side by side

3 veal kidneys, peeled and trimmed of fat

A hot plate and cover

in the butter, then cook them uncovered for about 10 minutes; turn them every minute or two. Regulate heat so butter is always very hot but is not discoloring. A little juice from the kidneys will exude and coagulate in the bottom of the casserole. The kidneys should stiffen but not become hard, brown very lightly, and be pink at the center when sliced. Remove them to a hot plate and cover to keep warm for a few minutes.

---

1 Tb minced shallots or green onions

½ cup dry white wine or dry vermouth

1 Tb lemon juice

Stir the shallots or onions into the butter in the casserole and cook for 1 minute. Then add the wine or vermouth and lemon juice. Boil, scraping up coagulated cooking juices, until the liquids have reduced to about 4 tablespoons.

1½ Tb prepared mustard of the strong Dijon type, mashed with 3 Tb softened butter

Salt and pepper

Off heat, swirl the mustard-butter by spoonfuls into the casserole, and a sprinkling of salt and pepper.

Salt and pepper

3 Tb minced parsley

Rapidly cut the kidneys into crosswise slices ⅛ inch thick. Sprinkle with salt and pepper and put them and their juices into the casserole. Sprinkle on the parsley. Shake and toss them over low heat for a minute or two to warm them through without allowing the sauce to come near the simmer.

Hot plates

Serve immediately on very hot plates.

VARIATIONS

Rognons de Veau Flambés

[Veal Kidneys Flamed in Brandy—Cream and Mushroom Sauce]

This extremely good combination is one which is often prepared beside your table in a good restaurant. If you are making it at home in a chafing dish, have all the sauce ingredients, including the sautéed mushrooms, at hand in separate containers. Kidneys cooked this way are best as a separate course, served with hot French bread, and a full, red Burgundy wine.

For 4 to 6 people

3 veal kidneys, peeled and trimmed of fat 4 Tb butter A fireproof casserole or chafing dish	Cook the kidneys for about 10 minutes in hot butter as described in the master recipe.
⅓ cup cognac A hot plate and cover	Pour the cognac over the kidneys. Avert your face and ignite the cognac with a lighted match. Shake the casserole or chafing dish and baste the kidneys for a few seconds until the flames have subsided. Remove the kidneys to a hot plate, and cover them.
½ cup brown sauce, page 66, or ½ cup canned beef bouillon mixed with 1 tsp cornstarch ⅓ cup Madeira	Pour the brown sauce or bouillon and starch, and the wine into the casserole. Boil for a few minutes until reduced and thickened.
1 cup whipping cream ½ lb. sliced fresh mushrooms sautéed in butter with 1 Tb minced shallots or green onions, page 513 Salt and pepper	Stir in the cream and mushrooms and boil a few minutes more. Sauce should be thick enough to coat the spoon lightly. Season to taste with salt and pepper.
½ Tb prepared mustard of the strong Dijon type, blended with 2 Tb softened butter and ½ tsp Worcestershire	Off heat, swirl in the mustard-butter.
Salt and pepper Hot plates	Rapidly cut the kidneys into crosswise slices ⅛ inch thick. Season with salt and pepper, and put them and their juices into the sauce. Shake and toss the kidneys over low heat for a moment to reheat them without bringing the sauce near the simmer. Serve immediately on hot plates.

Rognons de Veau à la Bordelaise

[Veal Kidneys in Red Wine Sauce with Marrow]

Sauce à la bordelaise is a reduction of red wine, brown sauce, shallots, and herbs into which poached marrow is folded just before serving. It goes very well with kidneys. With sautéed potatoes and braised onions or buttered peas, this would make a fine main course served with a red Burgundy wine.

For 4 to 6 people

3 veal kidneys, peeled and trimmed of fat
4 Tb butter
A fireproof casserole or chafing dish
A hot plate and cover

Cook the kidneys for about 10 minutes in hot butter in a casserole or chafing dish as described in the master recipe, page 417. Remove them to a hot plate and cover them.

2 Tb minced shallots or green onions
½ cup good, young, red wine such as a Burgundy or Mâcon
Big pinch each of thyme, pepper, and powdered bay leaf

Stir the shallots or onions into the casserole and cook for 1 minute. Pour in the wine, add seasonings, and boil until reduced by half.

1 cup brown sauce or 1 cup canned beef bouillon, mixed with 1 Tb arrowroot or cornstarch
Salt and pepper

Then pour in the brown sauce or bouillon and starch. Simmer for 3 to 4 minutes until lightly thickened. Correct seasoning.

Salt and pepper
⅓ cup diced beef marrow softened for 2 to 3 minutes in hot water, page 19
2 to 3 Tb fresh parsley
Hot plates

Rapidly cut the kidneys into crosswise slices ⅛ inch thick, and season with salt and pepper. Mix them and their juices in with the sauce. Fold in the marrow. Shake and toss for a moment over low heat to reheat the kidneys without bringing the sauce near the simmer. Sprinkle with parsley and serve on very hot plates.

CHAPTER EIGHT

VEGETABLES

Légumes

Anyone who has been fortunate enough to eat fresh, home-cooked vegetables in France remembers them with pleasure. Returning voyagers speak of them with trembling nostalgia: "Those delicious little green beans! They even serve them as a separate course. Why I'll never forget the meal I had . . . ," and so forth. Some people are even convinced that it is only in France that you can enjoy such experiences because French vegetables are somehow different. Fortunately this is not the case. Any fine, fresh vegetable in season will taste just as good in America or anywhere else if the French vegetable-cooking techniques are used.

The French are interested in vegetables as food rather than as purely nutrient objects valuable for their vitamins and minerals. And it is in the realm of the green vegetable that French methods differ most radically from American. The French objective is to produce a cooked green vegetable so green, fresh-tasting, and full of flavor that it really can be served as a separate course. They do not hesitate to peel, boil, squeeze, drain, or refresh a vegetable, which is often upsetting to those very Americans who weep in delighted remembrance of vegetables in France. For many Americans have been taught that by performing any of these acts one is wickedly "throwing away the best part."

BLANCHING

You will note that before anything else in the way of cooking or flavoring takes place, all the green vegetables in this chapter are blanched—dropped into a very large kettle of rapidly boiling salted water. This is the great secret of French green-vegetable cookery, and also happens to be the same process used in America to prepare green vegetables for the freezer. Success is entirely dependent on having a great quantity of boiling water: 7 to 8 quarts for 2 to 3 pounds of vegetables. The more water you use in proportion to your vegetables, the quicker the water will return to the boil after the vegetables have gone in, and the greener, fresher, and more full of flavor they will be. Baking soda is never necessary when you cook green vegetables this way.

REFRESHING

A second important French technique is that of refreshing. As soon as green vegetables have been blanched, and if they are not to be served immediately or are to be served cold, they are plunged for several minutes into a large quantity of cold water. This stops the cooking immediately, sets the color, and preserves the texture and flavor. If the vegetables are not refreshed in this manner and sit steaming in a saucepan or colander, their collective warmth softens and discolors them, and they lose their fresh taste. Following the refreshing technique, then, you can cook all your green vegetables well in advance of a party, and have only the final touches left to do at the last minute.

OVERCOOKING

A cardinal point in the French technique is: *Do not overcook*. An equally important admonition is: *Do not attempt to keep a cooked green vegetable warm for more than a very few moments*. If you cannot serve it at once, it is better to set it aside and then to reheat it. Overcooking and keeping hot ruin the color, texture, and taste of green vegetables—as well as most of the nutritive qualities.

SCOPE OF VEGETABLE CHAPTER

This chapter does not pretend to offer a complete treatise on vegetables. The French repertoire is so large that we have felt it best to go into more detail on a selection than to give tidbits on all. Most of our emphasis is on green vegetables. There is a modest but out-of-the-ordinary section on potatoes. Other vegetables rate only one or two recipes—but good ones—and some we have not mentioned at all.

GREEN VEGETABLES
ARTICHOKES
Artichauts

French or globe artichokes are in season from October to June. April and May are the peak months when their prices are most attractive. A fresh, de-

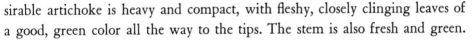

Cooked Artichoke Filled with Hollandaise Sauce

sirable artichoke is heavy and compact, with fleshy, closely clinging leaves of a good, green color all the way to the tips. The stem is also fresh and green.

As baby artichokes are not generally available in this country, all the following recipes are based on the large, 10- to 12-ounce artichoke which is about 4½ inches high and 4 to 4½ inches at its largest diameter.

SERVING SUGGESTIONS

Hot or cold boiled artichokes are served as a separate course, either at the beginning of the meal or in place of a salad. Most wine authorities agree that water should be served with them rather than wine, for wine changes its character when drunk with this vegetable. But, if you insist, serve a strong, dry, chilled white wine such as a Mâcon, or a chilled and characterful *rosé* such as a Tavel.

PREPARATION FOR COOKING

One at a time, prepare the artichokes as follows:

Remove the stem by bending it at the base of the artichoke until it snaps off, thus detaching with the stem any tough filaments which may have pushed up into the heart.

*Sectional View of
Artichoke*

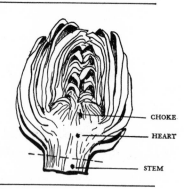

CHOKE

HEART

STEM

Break off the small leaves at the base of the artichoke. Trim the base with a knife so the artichoke will stand solidly upright.

Lay the artichoke on its side and slice three quarters of an inch off the top of the center cone of leaves. Trim off the points of the rest of the leaves with scissors. Wash under cold running water.

*Trim off ends of leaves
with scissors*

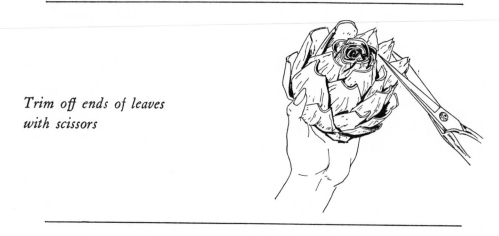

Rub the cut portions of the artichoke with lemon juice. Drop it into a basin of cold water containing 1 tablespoon of vinegar per quart of water. The acid prevents the artichoke from discoloring.

* *ARTICHAUTS AU NATUREL*

[Whole Boiled Artichokes—Hot or Cold]

Artichokes should be boiled in a large kettle so that they have plenty of room. It is not necessary to tie the leaves in place. Because they must cook a comparatively long time, artichokes turn an olive green. Any Frenchman would look with disfavor on a bright green boiled artichoke, knowing that baking soda had been added to the water.

---

6 artichokes prepared for cooking as in the preceding directions
A large kettle containing 7 to 8 quarts of rapidly boiling water
1½ tsp salt per quart of water
Washed cheesecloth

Drop the prepared artichokes in the boiling salted water. To help prevent discoloration, lay over the artichokes a double thickness of cheesecloth; this will keep their exposed tops moist. Bring the water back to the boil as rapidly as possible and boil slowly, uncovered, for 35 to 45 minutes. The artichokes are done when the leaves pull out easily and the bottoms are tender when pierced with a knife.

A skimmer or slotted spoon
A colander

Immediately remove them from the kettle with skimmer or spoon and drain them upside down in a colander.

Boiled artichokes may be served hot, warm, or cold.

HOW TO EAT AN ARTICHOKE

If you have never eaten an artichoke before, here is how you go about it. Pull off a leaf and hold its tip in your fingers. Dip the bottom of the leaf in melted butter or one of the sauces suggested farther on. Then scrape off its tender flesh between your teeth. When you have gone through all the leaves, you will come to the heart, which you eat with a knife and fork after you have scraped off and discarded the choke or hairy center growth.

TO REMOVE THE CHOKE BEFORE SERVING

It is not necessary to remove the choke, but it makes a nicer presentation if you wish to take the time. To do so, gently spread the leaves apart enough so you can reach into the interior of the artichoke. Pull out the tender center cone of leaves in one piece. Down in the center of the artichoke, at the point where you removed the cone of leaves, is the choke or hairy growth which covers the top of the heart. Scrape off and remove the choke with a spoon to expose the tender flesh of the artichoke heart. Sprinkle salt and pepper over the heart. Turn the cone of leaves upside down and set it in the hollow formed by the top of the artichoke.

Sauces for Hot or Warm Artichokes

Beurre Fondu, melted butter

Beurre au Citron, lemon butter sauce, page 98

Sauce Hollandaise, page 79. If you have removed the choke, you may wish to spread the leaves apart enough to expose the heart, then heap 3 or 4 spoonfuls of the hollandaise into it, and top with a sprig of parsley.

Sauces for Cold Artichokes

Vinaigrette, French dressing, page 94

Sauce Ravigote, vinaigrette with herbs, capers, and onions, page 95

Sauce Moutarde, mustard sauce with olive oil, lemon juice, and herbs, page 95

Sauce Alsacienne, soft-boiled egg mayonnaise with herbs, page 93

Mayonnaise, page 86

✳ *ARTICHAUTS BRAISÉS À LA PROVENÇALE*

[Artichokes Braised with Wine, Garlic, and Herbs]

Most of the many recipes for braised artichokes follow the general lines of this one. You may, if you wish, add to the casserole a cup of diced tomato pulp, or ½ cup of diced ham, and, 10 minutes before the end of the cooking, ½ pound of sautéed mushrooms. Another suggestion with different vegetables follows this recipe. Braised artichokes go well with roast or braised meats, or they can constitute a first course. As they are rather messy to eat with the fingers, guests should be furnished with a spoon as well as a knife and fork, so the flesh may be scraped off the artichoke leaves.

For 6 to 8 people

6 large artichokes

A large kettle containing 7 to 8 quarts of rapidly boiling water

1½ tsp salt per quart of water

Prepare the artichokes for cooking as directed at the beginning of this section, but cut off the leaves so that the artichokes are only about 1½ inches long. Then slice the artichokes into lengthwise quarters and cut out the chokes. Drop the quarters in boiling water and boil for 10 minutes only. Drain.

Preheat oven to 325 degrees.

1 cup (4 ounces) diced onions
6 Tb olive oil
A 10- to 11-inch covered
fireproof casserole large
enough to hold the arti-
chokes in one layer
2 large cloves minced garlic
Salt and pepper

Cook the onions slowly in olive oil in the casserole for 5 minutes without letting the onions color. Stir in the garlic. Arrange the artichoke quarters in the casserole. Baste with the olive oil and onions. Sprinkle on salt and pepper. Cover casserole and cook slowly over low heat for 10 minutes, not allowing artichokes to brown.

¼ cup wine vinegar
½ cup dry white wine or
dry white vermouth
1½ cups stock, canned beef
bouillon, or water
An herb bouquet: 4 parsley
sprigs, ½ bay leaf, and ¼
tsp thyme tied in cheese-
cloth
A round of waxed paper

Pour in the vinegar and wine. Raise heat and boil un-til liquid is reduced by half. Then pour in the stock, bouillon, or water. Add the herb bouquet. Bring to the simmer, then lay the waxed paper over the artichokes. Cover casserole and place it in the middle level of the preheated oven. Casserole should simmer slowly for 1¼ to 1½ hours, or until liquid has almost entirely evaporated.

(*) If not to be served immediately, set casserole aside, its cover askew. Reheat when needed.

2 to 3 Tb minced parsley

Discard herb bouquet. Serve from casserole or on a warm serving dish. (The artichokes may be sur-rounded with baked tomatoes and sautéed potatoes.) Sprinkle with parsley before bringing to the table.

VARIATION

Artichauts Printaniers

[Artichokes Braised with Carrots, Onions, Turnips, and Mushrooms]

Except for the addition of other vegetables, this recipe is the same as the master recipe. You may wish to use butter instead of olive oil, cut down on the garlic, and omit all or part of the vinegar, increasing the wine accordingly.

Ingredients for the preceding braised artichokes, including diced onions, oil
(or butter), wine, stock,
and seasonings

Following the preceding recipe, quarter and blanch the artichokes, and cook the diced onions in the olive oil (or butter). Then add the artichokes and place the whole onions and the other vegetables around the edge of the casserole. Baste with the diced onions and

12 small white onions, about
1 inch in diameter, peeled

3 or 4 carrots, peeled, quartered and cut into 1½-inch
lengths

3 or 4 white turnips, peeled
and quartered

oil (or butter), and season with salt and pepper. Proceed with the recipe.

---

12 to 18 mushroom caps
lightly sautéed in olive oil
or butter

About 10 minutes before the end of the cooking, add
the mushroom caps. Finish the sauce and serve the
casserole as in the preceding recipe.

ARTICHOKE HEARTS OR BOTTOMS

Fonds d'Artichauts

Although there is a tendency to lump artichoke hearts and bottoms
together, they are technically different. The heart is the tender central part of
baby artichokes; it includes the inner cone of leaves, the choke, and the bottom.
The bottom is just the meaty bottom part, usually of larger artichokes, minus
leaves and choke. Unless you live near a market catering to the baby artichoke
desires of a foreign clientele, you will probably only see artichoke hearts in a
can, a jar, or a frozen package. Bottoms, however, you can prepare yourself,
and they are even more of a delicacy in this country, owing to the price of
artichokes, than they are in France. Sliced, and braised in butter, they make a
delicious vegetable garnish; quartered and served in a vinaigrette sauce, they
are a delightful first course. Or you may top the whole bottom with poached
eggs and a sauce for an elegant hot first course, or fill it with shellfish mayonnaise for a cold luncheon dish. Whatever your plans for them, you must first
trim the leaves off your artichokes to expose the bottoms, and then poach them
in a *blanc* to preserve their whiteness.

HOW TO PREPARE ARTICHOKE BOTTOMS

Choose the largest artichokes you can find. Ideally they should be 4½
inches in diameter, which will do for one serving. Otherwise, allow two per
person. Prepare them as illustrated on the opposite page.

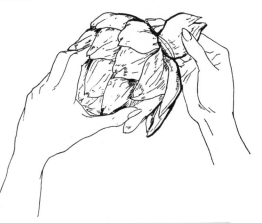

Break the stem off close to the base of the artichoke. Holding the artichoke bottom up, bend a lower leaf back on itself until it snaps. Then pull it off. Continue all around the artichoke until you have gone beyond the curve of the artichoke bottom, where the cone of leaves folds inward.

Cut off remaining cone of leaves close above top of artichoke bottom. Immediately rub cut parts with lemon juice to prevent discoloration.

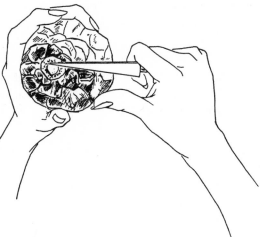

Trim bottom part, rotating it slowly with your left hand against the blade of a knife held firmly in your right hand. Remove all bits of green to expose the whitish tender surface. Frequently rub cut portions with lemon juice. Drop each as it is finished into a bowl of acidulated water (2 Tb lemon juice per quart of water).

Trimmed bottom ready to
cook; choke is removed
after cooking

FONDS D'ARTICHAUTS À BLANC

[Cooked Artichoke Bottoms—Preliminary Cooking]

A *blanc* is a solution of salted water with lemon juice and flour. It is used for the preliminary cooking of any food which discolors easily, such as artichoke bottoms, salsify, calf's head. Flour and lemon juice blanch the food and keep its whiteness.

Never cook artichoke bottoms in anything but enamel, pyrex, stainless steel, or earthenware. Aluminum or iron pans will give them a grayish color.

For 6 to 8 large artichoke bottoms

¼ cup flour	Put the flour in the saucepan and beat in a bit of cold
An enameled saucepan	water to make a smooth paste. Then beat in the rest
A wire whip	of the water, the lemon juice, and the salt. Bring to
1 quart cold water	the boil and simmer 5 minutes.
2 Tb lemon juice	
1½ tsp salt	

Add the artichokes. Bring liquid again to the boil, then simmer 30 to 40 minutes or so until tender when pierced with a knife. Be sure they are completely covered with liquid at all times. Add more water if necessary.

Allow them to cool in their liquid. If they are to be refrigerated for a day or two, film the top of the liquid with oil. Just before using, remove from the liquid and wash under cold water. Delicately scoop out the choke with a spoon, and trim off the remaining leaf ends.

Cooked Artichoke Bottom,
Choke Removed

* FONDS D'ARTICHAUTS AU BEURRE

[Buttered Artichoke Bottoms, Whole]

This is the method for heating cooked artichoke bottoms which are to be filled with hot vegetables, poached eggs, *béarnaise* sauce, truffles, or whatever is called for.

Preheat oven to 325 degrees.

6 cooked artichoke bottoms (see preceding recipe)
Salt and white pepper
4 Tb butter
A covered fireproof casserole (enameled, pyrex, or stainless steel) just large enough to hold the artichokes in one layer
A round of buttered waxed paper

Season the artichokes with salt and pepper. Heat the butter in the casserole until it is bubbling. Remove from heat. Baste each artichoke bottom with butter as you place it upside down (to keep center moist) in the casserole. Lay the buttered paper over them. Reheat the casserole, then place it in the middle level of the preheated oven for about 20 minutes, or until they are well heated through. Do not overcook.

The artichokes are now ready to receive any filling your recipe directs.

VARIATIONS

Quartiers de Fonds d'Artichauts au Beurre

[Buttered Artichoke Bottoms, Quartered]

This is basically the same as the preceding recipe, except that the artichoke bottoms are cut into quarters, and shallots or onions are included with the butter. Use quartered artichokes as a vegetable garnish or combine them with other vegetables such as braised carrots and onions, or sautéed mushrooms. They go well with veal, chicken, and egg dishes.

6 cooked artichoke bottoms, page 430

Cut the artichoke bottoms in quarters, and preheat oven to 325 degrees.

4 Tb butter
A 6-cup, enameled casserole
2 Tb minced shallots or green onions
Salt and pepper
A round of waxed paper, buttered
2 Tb minced parsley

Melt the butter in the casserole. Stir in the shallots or onions, then fold in the artichokes. Season with salt and pepper, and lay over them the round of buttered paper. Cover the casserole and bake in middle level of preheated oven for about 20 minutes, or until the vegetables are well steeped in the butter. Do not overcook. Sprinkle with parsley before serving.
(*) May be cooked in advance.

Fonds d'Artichauts Mirepoix

[Buttered Artichoke Bottoms with Diced Vegetables]

This is particularly good if the artichoke bottoms are to be served as a separate vegetable.

3 Tb each: finely diced carrots, onions, and celery
2 Tb finely diced, lean, boiled ham
Ingredients for the preceding buttered artichoke bottoms

Cook the carrots, onions, celery, and ham for 8 to 10 minutes in the butter called for in the preceding recipe. When the vegetables are tender but not browned, add the rest of the ingredients listed, and proceed with the recipe.

Fonds d'Artichauts à la Crème

[Creamed Artichoke Bottoms]

Serve creamed artichoke bottoms with roast veal or chicken, or sautéed brains or sweetbreads. They also go with omelettes.

Ingredients for 6 quartered artichoke bottoms cooked as in either of the two preceding variations
1½ cups whipping cream
Salt and pepper
1 tsp lemon juice, more if needed
A hot vegetable dish
2 Tb minced parsley

While the artichoke bottoms are cooking as directed in either of the two preceding recipes, boil the cream in a small saucepan until it has reduced by half. Season to taste with salt, pepper, and lemon juice. When the artichokes are done, fold the hot cream into them. Simmer for a moment on top of the stove to blend flavors. Turn into a hot vegetable dish and sprinkle with parsley.

Fonds d'Artichauts Mornay

[Artichoke Bottoms *Gratinéed* with Cheese Sauce]

Serve *gratinéed* artichoke bottoms with roast chicken or veal, sautéed chicken, veal scallops, or liver. Or you could use them as a hot first course or luncheon dish; in this case, you might fold into the artichoke bottoms before saucing them 1 cup of sautéed mushrooms, diced boiled ham, or diced cooked chicken.

Ingredients for 6 buttered artichoke bottoms, quartered, page 431

1½ cups *sauce mornay* (béchamel with cheese), page 61

A lightly buttered baking dish about 8 inches in diameter and 2 inches deep

3 Tb grated Swiss cheese

1 Tb butter

While the artichoke bottoms are cooking, make the *sauce mornay*. When they are done, spread one third of the sauce in the dish and arrange the artichokes over it. Pour on the rest of the sauce, sprinkle on the cheese, and dot with butter.

About 30 minutes before serving, place in upper third of a preheated, 375-degree oven to heat through thoroughly and brown the top of the sauce lightly. Serve as soon as possible.

FONDS D'ARTICHAUTS AU GRATIN

[Stuffed Artichoke Bottoms *au Gratin*]

Stuffed artichoke bottoms make an attractive hot first course or luncheon dish.

For 6 people

6 large artichoke bottoms cooked in a *blanc,* page 430

A buttered baking dish

1 to 1½ cups of one of the creamed fillings on pages 201 to 203, such as ham,

Arrange the cooked artichoke bottoms in the baking dish. Place several spoonsful of the filling in each, heaping it into a slight dome. Sprinkle with cheese and dot with butter. About 20 minutes before serving, bake in upper third of a preheated 375-degree oven until thoroughly warmed through and the cheese has browned lightly.

chicken, mushrooms or
shellfish
⅓ cup grated Swiss cheese
1½ Tb butter

FROZEN ARTICHOKE HEARTS

These usually come in 10-ounce packages and are baby, halved hearts
with the tender center leaves still attached. We find it to be more satisfactory
if you allow the vegetables to thaw enough so they can be detached from each
other. They will then cook more evenly.

For 6 servings

1 cup chicken stock, canned
chicken broth, half mush-
room broth and half wa-
ter, or water only
2 Tb minced shallots or
green onions (or 2 Tb
each: finely diced onions,
celery, carrots, and ham,
previously cooked until
tender in the butter)
2 Tb butter
¼ tsp salt
An 8-inch enameled sauce-
pan or skillet
2 packages frozen artichoke
hearts, partially thawed
(10 ounces each)

Bring the liquid, shallots or onions, butter, and salt
to the boil in an enameled saucepan. Add the partially
thawed artichoke hearts. Cover saucepan and bring
to the boil. Boil slowly for 7 to 10 minutes, or until
artichoke hearts are tender. Uncover, raise heat, and
boil off any remaining liquid.

Serve them sprinkled with parsley, or in the cream
sauce or cheese sauce described in the previous recipes. Or you may combine them with other cooked
vegetables such as sautéed mushrooms or glazed carrots and onions.

ASPARAGUS

Asperges

Cooked green asparagus should be tender yet not limp, and a fresh, beautiful green. Fresh white asparagus, so prevalent in Europe, is rarely seen in

this country, but it is prepared and cooked in the same way as green asparagus. The French method of cooking asparagus is to peel it, tie it in bundles, plunge it into a very large kettle of rapidly boiling, salted water, boil it slowly until it is just tender; and to drain it immediately. Peeled asparagus cooks more quickly than unpeeled asparagus, retains its color and texture, and can be eaten usually all the way down to the butt. We have tested every asparagus cooking method we have heard of—peeled, unpeeled, boiled butts, steamed tips—and can say categorically that the freshest, greenest, and most appetizing asparagus is cooked by the French method.

SERVING SUGGESTIONS

Whole boiled asparagus, hot or cold, is served as a separate vegetable course either at the beginning of the meal, or in place of a salad. With hot asparagus serve a not too dry, chilled white wine such as a Graves, Barsac, Pouilly-Fumé, or Vouvray. No wine should accompany cold asparagus with a vinegar-based sauce, as the vinegar will spoil the taste of the wine.

CHOOSING ASPARAGUS

Select firm, crisp, stalks, moist at the cut end, and with tips which are compact and closed. Fat spears are just as tender as thin spears; as long as the asparagus must be peeled, the fat ones are easier to handle and less wasteful. Loose asparagus is preferable to asparagus in bundles, since you may examine each spear and choose ones all of a size. Plan on 6 to 10 fat spears per person, depending on your menu.

PREPARATION FOR COOKING

You will find that a vegetable peeler is not useful for this operation because it does not go deep enough. Asparagus is peeled not just to remove the skin, but to shave off enough of the tough outer flesh (particularly around the lower part of the spear) to make just about the whole cooked spear edible. Peeling is therefore economical.

Hold an asparagus spear with its butt end up. Peel off the outer skin with a sharp, small knife, going as deep as $\frac{1}{16}$ of an inch at the butt in order to expose the tender, moist flesh. Gradually make the cut shallower until you come up to the tender green portion near the tip. Shave off any scales which cling to the spear below the tip. Wash the peeled asparagus spears in a large basin of cold water. Drain.

Line up the tips evenly and tie the asparagus in bundles about 3½ inches

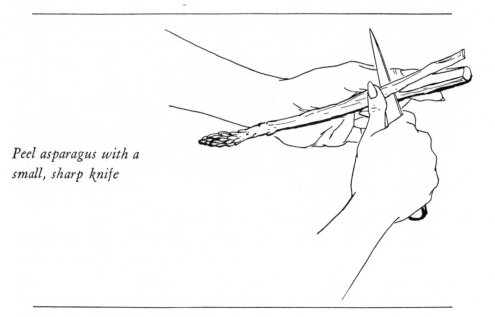

*Peel asparagus with a
small, sharp knife*

in diameter, one string near the tip, one near the butt. Leave one spear loose to be used as a cooking test later. Cut a bit off the butts if necessary, to make the spears all the same length.

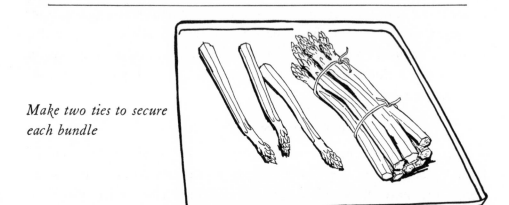

*Make two ties to secure
each bundle*

If not cooked immediately, set bunches upright in ½ inches of cold water. Cover the asparagus with a plastic bag and refrigerate.

✳ *ASPERGES AU NATUREL*

[Boiled Asparagus—Hot or Cold]

A large kettle or oval casse-   Kettle must be wide enough to hold the asparagus role containing 7 to 8 quarts rapidly boiling water (for 4 to 6 bundles of prepared asparagus spears)

1½ tsp salt per quart of water

bunches horizontally. Lay the asparagus bundles in the rapidly boiling salted water. Bring water to boil again as quickly as possible. When boil is reached, reduce heat and boil slowly, uncovered, for 12 to 15 minutes. The asparagus is done when a knife pierces the butt-end easily. The spears should bend a little, but should not be limp and droopy. Eat the loose spear as a test for doneness.

A serving platter covered with a folded white napkin (to absorb the asparagus liquid)

As soon as the asparagus is tender, lift it out of the water bundle by bundle with 2 forks, one slipped under each round of string. Hold up for a few seconds to drain, then place the bundle carefully on the napkin. Cut and remove the strings. Proceed quickly to the next bundle.

If the asparagus is not to be served immediately, it will keep warm for 20 to 30 minutes covered with a napkin. Set the platter on top of the kettle of hot asparagus cooking water. The asparagus will lose a bit of its texture as it waits because it will continue to exude moisture, but it will retain its taste and color.

Sauces to Serve with Hot Asparagus

Allow 3 to 4 tablespoons of sauce per person.

Sauce Hollandaise, page 79. You may beat 3 or 4 tablespoons of puréed cooked asparagus spears into the hollandaise if you wish.

Sauce Mousseline, hollandaise with cream, page 83

Sauce Maltaise, hollandaise with orange flavoring, delicious with asparagus, and makes a nice change, page 83

Sauce Crème, béchamel with cream and lemon juice, page 59

Beurre au Citron, lemon butter sauce, page 98

COLD ASPARAGUS

To serve cold asparagus, spread the cooked spears in one layer on a double thickness of clean toweling so the asparagus will cool rapidly. When thoroughly cold, arrange on a serving dish.

Sauces to Serve with Cold Asparagus

Allow 2 to 4 tablespoons of sauce per person.

Sauce Vinaigrette, French dressing, with herbs and mustard, page 94

Sauce Vinaigrette à la Crème, vinaigrette with cream and herbs, page 95

Sauce Ravigote, vinaigrette with herbs, shallots, and capers, page 95

Sauce Moutarde, mustard sauce with herbs, page 95

Sauce Alsacienne, soft-boiled egg mayonnaise with herbs, page 93

Mayonnaise, page 86. 2 to 3 tablespoons of green herbs, or 4 to 6 tablespoons of puréed cooked asparagus spears may be stirred into the mayonnaise if you wish.

ASPARAGUS TIPS

Pointes d'Asperges

Asparagus tips are the part of the spear from the tip as far down as the asparagus is green and still tender. Asparagus tips are served as a separate vegetable or as part of a vegetable garnish and go well with chicken breasts, veal scallops, brains, sweetbreads, scrambled eggs, and omelettes. They are also used in a sauce to fill tarts, tartlets, or artichoke hearts, or can be served as a cold vegetable or as part of a vegetable salad.

PREPARATION FOR COOKING

Choose thin asparagus spears ¼ to ⅜ of an inch in diameter. Hold each by its butt end and, moving your fingers up toward the tip, bend the spear until it snaps in two, usually at about the halfway point. (Set the butt ends aside; they may be peeled and cooked, and are good for soups or purées.) Scrape off all the scales below the tip and wash the asparagus. Cut the tips off so each is 1½ inches long and tie in bundles about 2 inches in diameter. Dice the remaining stalks.

✳ *POINTES D'ASPERGES AU BEURRE*

[Buttered Asparagus Tips]

For 4 to 6 people as a vegetable garnish

Blanching

2 lbs. asparagus tips prepared as directed in preceding paragraph 6 quarts rapidly boiling water 3 Tb salt	Drop the diced asparagus stalks in the boiling salted water and boil 5 minutes. Then add the asparagus bundles and boil slowly for 5 to 8 minutes more, or until just tender. Remove bundles carefully and drain; drain the diced stalks. (*) If you are cooking the asparagus in advance or wish to serve it cold, plunge for a minute or two in cold water to stop the cooking and set the color. Drain.

Braising in butter

Preheat oven to 325 degrees.

A covered baking dish or fireproof baking and serving dish 1 Tb softened butter Salt and pepper 4 Tb melted butter A round of waxed paper	Smear the baking dish with softened butter. Arrange the diced asparagus stalks in the bottom; season with salt, pepper, and part of the melted butter. Remove strings and arrange the asparagus tips over the stalks. Season with salt, pepper, and butter, and lay the waxed paper on top. Heat for a moment on top of the stove; cover the casserole and place in middle level of oven for 10 to 15 minutes or until asparagus is hot through. Serve immediately.

VARIATION: SAUCES

Sauces for hot and cold asparagus are listed on pages 437–8. If you are serving a hot sauce, you may wish only to blanch the asparagus tips and omit the braising-in-butter step in the preceding recipe.

FROZEN ASPARAGUS

Frozen asparagus will always be limp however you cook it; the following method is as good as any we have found. Allow the asparagus to thaw partially before cooking so the spears can be separated and will cook more evenly. If you are doing more than two boxes at a time, use two wide saucepans in order that the cooking water will boil away by the time the asparagus is done.

For each 10-ounce box of frozen asparagus, partially thawed:
½ cup water
⅛ tsp salt
1 Tb butter
A wide enameled saucepan or skillet
A cover
Pinch of pepper
More salt, if needed
A hot vegetable dish
Melted butter or one of the sauces listed on page 437

Bring the water, salt, and butter to the boil in the saucepan or skillet. Add the asparagus, cover, and boil slowly for 5 to 8 minutes or until asparagus is tender. Remove cover, raise heat, and quickly boil off any remaining liquid. Correct seasoning. Arrange in vegetable dish, pour on sauce or pass it separately, and serve as soon as possible.

TIMBALE D'ASPERGES

[Asparagus Mold]

This asparagus custard is served unmolded as a first course or luncheon dish, or may be served with roast or sautéed veal or chicken. The custard mixture may be prepared hours in advance of cooking, and the cooked mold may be kept warm for a considerable time or reheated. You can mold the custard in individual cups if you wish.

NOTE: Chopped, cooked Brussels sprouts, broccoli, cauliflower, spinach, or puréed green peas may be cooked in the same way; substitute 2½ to 3 cups of any of these vegetables for the asparagus.

For 6 people

Flavorless salad oil
A 6-cup soufflé mold
¼ cup stale, white bread crumbs

Preheat oven to 325 degrees. Oil the mold. Roll bread crumbs in it to cover the entire inner surface. Knock out excess crumbs.

½ cup finely minced onions
1 Tb butter

Cook the onions slowly in butter for about 10 minutes in a covered saucepan, not allowing them to color.

A 3-quart mixing bowl
Big pinch of white pepper

Scrape the onions into the mixing bowl. Stir in the seasonings, cheese, and bread crumbs. Beat in the

¼ tsp salt
Pinch of nutmeg
½ cup grated Swiss cheese
⅔ cup stale, white bread crumbs
5 eggs
1 cup milk brought to the boil with 4 Tb butter

eggs. In a thin stream of droplets, beat in the hot milk and butter.

3 lbs. boiled, fresh asparagus, or 3 cups cooked frozen asparagus, or canned asparagus
Salt and pepper

Cut the tender portion of the asparagus spears into ½-inch pieces. Fold the asparagus into the custard mixture. Correct seasoning.
(*) May be prepared ahead to this point.

A pan of boiling water large enough to hold the mold easily

Turn the custard into the prepared mold and set mold in a pan of boiling water. Place in lower third of preheated oven and bake for 35 to 40 minutes, regulating heat so water remains just below the simmer. Custard is done when a knife, plunged through the center, comes out clean.

A warm serving platter

Remove mold from water and allow to settle for 5 minutes. Run a knife around the edge of the custard and reverse on a warm serving platter. Surround with one of the sauces listed, and serve.
(*) If custard is not served immediately, do not unmold it, but leave in its pan of hot water, reheating the water from time to time, if necessary. Unmold when you are ready to serve.

Sauces for Asparagus Mold

Prepare 2½ to 3 cups of one of the following:
Sauce Chivry, béchamel with cream and green herbs, page 62
Sauce Mornay, béchamel with cheese, page 61
Sauce Mousseline, hollandaise with cream, page 83

GREEN BEANS

Haricots Verts

Green beans, snap beans, string beans, or whatever you wish to call them, are of many varieties: some are flat, others are round, still others are a mottled green rather than a uniform color. Most of those on the market today are stringless. Whichever you buy, look for beans which are clean, fresh-looking, firm, and which snap crisply and contain immature seeds. If possible, select beans all of the same circumference so they will cook evenly. The smaller around they are, the more they will approach tiny French beans; a diameter of not more than ¼ inch is most desirable.

Fresh beans take time to prepare for cooking, but have so much more flavor than frozen beans that they are well worth the trouble. The cooking itself is easy; however, beans demand attention if they are to be fresh-tasting, full of flavor, and green. Although their preliminary blanching may be taken care of hours in advance, the final touches should be done only at the last minute. It is fatal to their color, texture, and taste if they are overcooked, or if they are allowed to sit around over heat for more than a few minutes after they are ready to be eaten.

SERVING SUGGESTIONS

Green beans will go with just about any meat dish, or may constitute a separate vegetable course.

AMOUNT TO BUY

One pound of beans will serve 2 or 3 people depending on your menu.

PREPARATION FOR COOKING

Snap the tip of one end of a bean with your fingers and draw it down the length of one side of the bean to remove any possible string. Do the same thing with the other end, pulling it down the other side of the bean.

Beans of not much more than ¼ inch in diameter are cooked whole, and retain their maximum flavor. If they are large in circumference, you may slice them on the bias to make several 2½-inch lengths per bean; this or machine slicing is usually called Frenched beans though it is rarely done in France as it is seldom necessary. Sliced beans never have the flavor of whole beans.

Wash the beans rapidly in very hot water the moment before cooking.

HARICOTS VERTS BLANCHIS

[Blanched Green Beans—Preliminary Cooking]

Whatever recipe you choose for your beans, always give them a preliminary blanching in a very large kettle of rapidly boiling salted water. Depending on what you plan to do to them later, boil them either until tender or until almost tender, and drain immediately. This essential step in the French art of bean cookery always produces a fine, fresh, green bean of perfect texture and flavor.

For 6 to 8 people

3 lbs. green beans, trimmed and washed	A handful at a time, drop the beans into the rapidly boiling salted water. Bring the water back to the boil as quickly as possible, and boil the beans slowly, uncovered, for 10 to 15 minutes; test the beans frequently after 8 minutes by eating one. A well cooked bean should be tender, but still retain the slightest suggestion of crunchiness. Drain the beans as soon as they are done.
A large kettle containing at least 7 to 8 quarts of rapidly boiling water	
1½ tsp salt per quart of water	

For Immediate Serving

Turn the beans into a large, heavy-bottomed saucepan and toss them gently over moderately high heat by flipping the pan, not by stirring them. This will evaporate their moisture in 2 to 3 minutes. Then proceed with one of the following recipes.

For Later Serving or to Serve Cold

Run cold water over the beans for 3 to 4 minutes. This will stop the cooking immediately and the beans will retain color, taste, and texture. Drain, spread them out on a clean towel, and pat dry. The beans may then be set aside in a colander, or put in a covered bowl in the refrigerator where they will keep perfectly for 24 hours.

To Reheat: Depending on your recipe, either drop the beans in a large kettle of rapidly boiling, salted water, bring quickly again to the boil, then drain immediately. Or toss the beans in a tablespoon or two of hot butter or oil, season them, cover the pan, and let them warm thoroughly for 3 to 4 minutes over moderate heat. Then proceed with your recipe.

TWO RECIPES FOR BUTTERED GREEN BEANS

Buttered green beans go with almost anything, and particularly roast or broiled lamb, beef, chicken, veal, and liver. They may also be served as a separate course.

Haricots Verts à l'Anglaise

[Buttered Green Beans I]

For 6 to 8 people

3 lbs. hot, blanched green beans (preceding recipe)
A wide, heavy-bottomed, enameled saucepan or skillet
Salt and pepper
A hot serving dish
4 to 8 Tb butter, cut into pieces or formed into shells

Toss the hot beans in the saucepan or skillet over moderately high heat to evaporate their moisture. Toss briefly again with salt and pepper to taste. Turn them into the serving dish, distribute the butter over them, and serve at once.

Haricots Verts à la Maître d'Hôtel

[Buttered Green Beans II – with Lemon Juice and Parsley]

For 6 to 8 people

3 lbs. hot, blanched green beans (preceding master recipe)
A wide, heavy-bottomed, enameled saucepan or skillet
Salt and pepper
6 to 8 Tb softened butter cut into 4 pieces
2 to 3 tsp lemon juice
A hot vegetable dish
3 Tb minced parsley

Toss the hot beans in the saucepan or skillet over moderately high heat to evaporate their moisture. Toss briefly again with salt, pepper and a piece of butter. Add the rest of the butter gradually while tossing the beans; alternate with drops of lemon juice. Taste for seasoning. Turn into the vegetable dish, sprinkle with parsley, and serve immediately.

TWO RECIPES FOR GREEN BEANS IN CREAM

Serve creamed green beans with plain roast lamb, veal, or chicken, broiled or sautéed chicken, lamb chops, sautéed liver, or veal chops or scallops.

Haricots Verts à la Crème

[Creamed Green Beans I]

For 6 to 8 people

3 lbs. green beans, trimmed and washed A wide, heavy-bottomed, enameled saucepan or skillet Salt and pepper to taste 3 Tb softened butter 2 cups whipping cream A lid for the pan	Blanch the beans in 7 to 8 quarts of rapidly boiling salted water as described on page 443, but drain them 3 to 4 minutes before they are tender. Toss the beans in the pan over moderately high heat to evaporate their moisture. Then toss with the salt, pepper, and butter. Pour in the cream, cover the pan, and boil slowly for 5 minutes or so, until beans are tender and cream has reduced by half. Correct seasoning.
A hot vegetable dish 3 Tb fresh minced savory, tarragon, or parsley	Turn into hot vegetable dish, sprinkle with herbs, and serve at once.

Haricots Verts, Sauce Crème

[Creamed Green Beans II]

This is less rich than the pure cream treatment in the preceding recipe.

For 6 to 8 people

3 lbs. green beans, trimmed and washed A wide, heavy-bottomed, enameled saucepan or skillet	Blanch the beans in 7 to 8 quarts of boiling salted water as described on page 443, but drain them 3 to 4 minutes before they are tender. Toss the beans in the pan over moderately high heat to evaporate their moisture.
Salt and pepper to taste 3 Tb softened butter 3 Tb minced shallots or green onions A lid for the pan	Then toss them with the seasonings, butter, and minced shallots or onions. Cover the pan and let them cook slowly for 3 to 4 minutes.

3 cups boiling *sauce crème*
  (béchamel with cream)
  page 59
Salt and pepper
A hot vegetable dish
3 Tb fresh minced savory,
  tarragon, or parsley

Delicately fold the hot sauce into the beans. Cover pan and simmer slowly again for 3 to 4 minutes, or until beans are tender. Correct seasoning. Turn into a hot vegetable dish, sprinkle with herbs, and serve at once.

A GOOD ADDITION

½ to 1 lb. sliced mushrooms
  sautéed in butter

Fold the sautéed mushrooms into the beans with the sauce.

HARICOTS VERTS GRATINÉS, À LA MORNAY

[Green Beans *Gratinéed* with Cheese Sauce]

This is a good method for ahead-of-time preparation. Serve with the same meats suggested in the preceding recipes for green beans in cream.

For 6 to 8 people

3 lbs. green beans, trimmed
  and washed

Blanch the beans as described on page 443 until they are just tender. Drain, refresh in cold water, and dry in a towel.

3 cups *sauce mornay* (béchamel with cheese), page 61
A lightly buttered baking dish
Salt and pepper to taste
⅓ cup grated Swiss cheese
1 Tb butter cut into pea-sized dots

Spread a third of the sauce in the baking dish. Season the beans and arrange them over the sauce. Pour on the rest of the sauce. Sprinkle with cheese, dot with butter, and set aside uncovered.

Half an hour before serving time, bake in upper third of a preheated 375-degree oven until beans are well heated through and the sauce has browned lightly on top.

HARICOTS VERTS À LA PROVENÇALE

[Green Beans with Tomatoes, Garlic, and Herbs]

These full-flavored beans go wonderfully with roast lamb or beef, steaks, chops, or broiled chicken. Tossed with diced, sautéed ham, they can serve as a main-course luncheon or supper dish. Frozen beans react nicely to this treatment.

For 6 to 8 servings

2 cups thinly sliced onions
½ cup olive oil
An enameled saucepan or skillet large enough to hold the beans

Cook the onions slowly in the olive oil until they are tender and translucent but not browned, about 10 minutes.

4 to 6 large, firm, ripe, red tomatoes peeled, seeded, juiced, and chopped, page 505
2 to 4 cloves mashed garlic
A medium herb bouquet with cloves: 4 parsley sprigs, ½ bay leaf, ½ tsp thyme, and 2 cloves tied in cheesecloth
¾ cup liquid: juice from the tomatoes plus water or water only
Salt and pepper to taste

Add the ingredients at the left, and simmer for 30 minutes. Then remove the herb bouquet.

3 lbs. green beans
OR 3 boxes partially defrosted cut green beans added directly to the cooked tomato mixture
Salt and pepper
¼ cup chopped parsley, or a mixture of green herbs such as basil, savory, and tarragon plus parsley

While the tomatoes are cooking, blanch the beans in 7 to 8 quarts of boiling salted water as described on page 443, but drain them 3 to 4 minutes before they are tender. Toss them in the pan with the onions and tomatoes. Cover and simmer slowly for 8 to 10 minutes, tossing occasionally, until they are tender. Most of the liquid should have evaporated by this time; if not, uncover, raise heat, and boil it off rapidly, tossing the beans. Correct seasoning, toss in the herbs, and serve.

WAX OR YELLOW POD BEANS

Haricots Mange-tout — Haricots Beurre

Wax beans are trimmed and blanched in the same manner as green beans, and may be substituted for green beans in any of the preceding recipes. Here is a special recipe for large wax beans.

HARICOTS MANGE-TOUT À L'ÉTUVÉE

[Wax Beans Braised with Onions, Lettuce, and Cream]

For 6 to 8 people

3 lbs. large but tender wax beans

Trim and wash the beans according to directions on page 442, being sure all strings have been removed. Preheat oven to 350 degrees.

---

2 Tb softened butter
A covered fireproof casserole or baking dish
1½ cups diced onions
1 tsp salt
Big pinch of pepper
1 medium herb bouquet: 4 parsley sprigs, ½ bay leaf, and ¼ tsp thyme tied in cheesecloth
2 heads of Boston lettuce, shredded
8 Tb (¼ lb.) butter
1½ cups chicken stock or canned chicken broth
A round of waxed paper

Butter the casserole or baking dish heavily. Spread the onions in the bottom, arrange the beans over them, and season with salt and pepper. Bury the herb bouquet in their midst. Distribute the lettuce over the beans. Sliver the rest of the butter over the lettuce. Pour in the stock or broth. Set casserole over heat and bring liquid to the simmer. Place the round of paper over the vegetables, cover the casserole and set in lower third of oven. Regulate heat so liquid simmers regularly and has almost evaporated in 45 minutes. Remove herb bouquet.

---

2 cups light cream
Salt and pepper

Bring the cream to the boil and pour it into the casserole. Bake 30 minutes more. Correct seasoning.
(*) May be set aside, partially covered, and reheated at serving time.

---

3 Tb minced fresh savory, basil, tarragon, or parsley

Sprinkle with herbs just before bringing casserole to table.

FROZEN GREEN OR WAX BEANS

Frozen beans cook more evenly if they are partially thawed and not stuck all together in a solid block. When you are doing more than two packages, use two saucepans; if too many beans are cooked in one pan, the liquid will not evaporate by the time the beans are tender. Cut beans have more flavor than Frenched beans.

For each 10-ounce package of beans:

½ cup chicken stock, canned chicken broth, canned mushroom broth, or water

1 Tb minced shallots or green onions

¼ tsp salt

1 Tb butter

A heavy bottomed, enameled saucepan or skillet with cover

Bring the liquid, shallots or onions, salt, and butter to the boil in the saucepan. Add the partially thawed beans. Cover and boil slowly for 5 to 6 minutes, tossing occasionally, until the beans are just tender. Remove cover and rapidly boil off any remaining liquid. Correct seasoning.

The beans may now be used in any of the preceding green bean recipes. If they are to be simmered in cream or in a sauce, use half the amount of liquid for their preliminary cooking, and cook only until partially tender. They will finish cooking in the sauce.

If you wish to do the preliminary cooking in advance, spread the cooked beans out in one layer in a big cold saucepan or dish so they will cool rapidly.

If the beans are to be served cold, use olive oil rather than butter in the preceding recipe, and spread the beans out afterward in one layer to cool rapidly.

BRUSSELS SPROUTS

Choux de Bruxelles

Cooked Brussels sprouts should be bright green, fresh-tasting, and have the slightest suggestion of crunch at the core. Overcooked sprouts become yellowish, mushy, and develop the flavor of stale cabbage.

Choose firm, healthy, fresh, rounded heads all of the same size with bright green leaves. Soft-headed sprouts are overmature, tasteless, or unhealthy, and will cook into a pulp.

AMOUNT TO BUY

A 1-quart basket weighting about 1¼ pounds will serve 4 or 5 people as a vegetable garnish.

SERVING SUGGESTIONS

Buttered Brussels sprouts go well with roast duck, goose, turkey, beef, pork, liver, ham, and sausages. Creamed Brussels sprouts may be served with any of these, and also with roast chicken or veal.

PREPARATION FOR COOKING

Trim the base of each Brussels sprout with a small knife and pierce a cross in it for quick cooking. Remove any wilted or yellowish leaves. Discard any sprouts which are soft-headed, yellowish, or worm-eaten. Wash the trimmed vegetables quickly in a large basin of cold water and drain. Modern growing methods seem to have eliminated burrowing insects, so it is nowadays rarely necessary, as it used to be, to soak the vegetables for 10 to 15 minutes in salted water.

CHOUX DE BRUXELLES BLANCHIS

[Blanched Brussels Sprouts—Preliminary Cooking]

Brussels sprouts, whether they are to be served with melted butter and seasonings or are to be simmered or braised, always receive a blanching in a large kettle of boiling salted water. This preliminary may be accomplished hours before the final cooking is to take place.

---

1 to 2 quarts Brussels sprouts, trimmed and washed

A large kettle containing 7 to 8 quarts of rapidly boiling water

1½ tsp salt per quart of water

Drop the Brussels sprouts into the rapidly boiling salted water. Bring to the boil again as rapidly as possible.

Partially cooked

A skimmer
A colander

If the vegetables are to be partially cooked and finished off later as directed in most of the following recipes, boil them slowly, uncovered, for 6 to 8 minutes, or until almost tender. Immediately remove with a skimmer and drain in a colander.

Fully cooked

If they are to be fully cooked, and served at once with melted butter *à l'anglaise,* boil them slowly, uncovered, for a total of 10 to 12 minutes. They are done when a knife pierces the stem of a sprout easily; cut one in half and eat it, to be sure. Drain immediately.

AHEAD-OF-TIME BLANCHING

If the Brussels sprouts are not to be used at once, as soon as they have been drained spread them out in one layer, not touching one another, on a double thickness of clean toweling. This lets the air circulate around them and cool them quickly, so that they retain their color and texture. (You may plunge them into cold water instead, if you wish, but we think the one-layer cooling gives a better texture.) When the Brussels sprouts are thoroughly cold, they may be refrigerated and will keep perfectly for 24 hours. Complete the cooking as directed in any of the following recipes.

---

* *CHOUX DE BRUXELLES ÉTUVÉS AU BEURRE*

[Brussels Sprouts Braised in Butter]

Serve braised Brussels sprouts with roast turkey, pork, duck, or goose, steaks, chops, hamburgers, or sautéed liver. You may dress up braised Brussels sprouts with cream, cheese, or chestnuts, as suggested in the variations at the end of the recipe.

For 6 people

1½ **Tb softened butter**
A 2½-quart, fireproof, covered casserole or baking dish large enough to hold the Brussels sprouts in 1 or 2 layers

Preheat oven to 350 degrees, and smear the butter inside the casserole or baking dish.

1½ quarts blanched Brussels sprouts (partially cooked), page 450
Salt and pepper
2 to 4 Tb melted butter

Arrange the blanched Brussels sprouts heads up in the casserole or baking dish. Sprinkle lightly with salt and pepper, and with the melted butter.

A round of lightly buttered waxed paper

Lay the paper over the Brussels sprouts. Cover and heat on top of the stove until vegetables begin to sizzle, then place in middle level of preheated oven. Bake for about 20 minutes, or until the sprouts are tender and well impregnated with butter. Serve as soon as possible.

VARIATIONS

Choux de Bruxelles Étuvés à la Crème

[Creamed Brussels Sprouts]

Serve these with veal, chicken, or turkey.
For 6 people

1½ quarts Brussels sprouts
½ to ¾ cup boiling whipping cream
Salt and pepper
1 to 2 Tb butter cut into pea-sized dots

Braise the Brussels sprouts as in the preceding recipe, but use only 2 tablespoons of butter. After the casserole has been in the oven for 10 minutes, pour on the boiling cream and continue baking for 10 more minutes or until the vegetables are tender. They will have absorbed most of the cream. Correct seasoning, dot with butter, and serve as soon as possible.

Choux de Bruxelles aux Marrons

[Brussels Sprouts Braised with Chestnuts]

This recipe is particularly good with roast turkey, duck, or goose.
For 6 people

1½ quarts Brussels sprouts braised in butter
2 cups braised chestnuts, page 519

Follow the preceding master recipe for braising the Brussels sprouts, but add the braised chestnuts to the casserole to cook with them.

Choux de Bruxelles à la Mornay, Gratinés

[Brussels Sprouts Gratinéed with Cheese Sauce]

Serve these with roast chicken or veal, or as a luncheon or supper dish.
For 6 people

1½ quarts Brussels sprouts braised in butter

2 cups hot *sauce mornay* (*béchamel* with cheese), page 61

A lightly buttered baking dish about 9 inches in diameter and 2 inches deep

¼ cup grated Swiss cheese

1 Tb butter cut into pea-sized dots

Follow the preceding master recipe for braising the Brussel sprouts; you may use only 2 tablespoons of butter if you wish. Prepare the sauce, and spread one third of it in the baking dish when the sprouts are done. Arrange the Brussels sprouts over the sauce, spoon the rest of the sauce over them, and sprinkle with cheese and dots of butter. Set under a moderately hot broiler for 2 to 3 minutes to brown lightly, and serve at once.

Choux de Bruxelles à la Milanaise

[Brussels Sprouts Browned with Cheese]

These cheese-coated Brussels sprouts are good with steaks and chops.
For 6 people

1½ quarts Brussels sprouts braised in butter

½ cup grated Swiss cheese mixed with ½ cup grated Parmesan cheese

2 Tb melted butter

Follow the preceding master recipe for braising the Brussels sprouts, but when they have been in the oven 10 minutes, turn them into a bowl. Reset oven to 425 degrees. Sprinkle 2 to 3 tablespoons of cheese in the casserole or baking dish to coat the bottom and sides. Return the Brussels sprouts, spreading the rest of the cheese over each layer. Pour on the melted butter. Place uncovered in upper third of oven for 10 to 15 minutes, to brown the cheese nicely.

CHOUX DE BRUXELLES À LA CRÈME

[Brussels Sprouts Chopped and Simmered in Cream]

Serve this dish with steaks or chops, roast beef or lamb, pork, duck, or goose.
For 6 people

1½ quarts Brussels sprouts, trimmed and washed | Follow the recipe for blanched Brussels sprouts, page 450, but boil them for 5 minutes only. Drain. If you are not proceeding at once with the rest of this recipe, let them cool in one layer. Chop them roughly.

3 Tb butter
A 10-inch enameled skillet
¼ tsp salt
Big pinch of pepper | Heat the butter to bubbling in the skillet. Add the chopped Brussels sprouts and season with salt and pepper. Shake them over moderately high heat for several minutes to evaporate their moisture but not to brown them.

¾ cup whipping cream
Salt and pepper | Pour in the cream. Bring to the simmer. Cover the skillet and cook at a slow simmer for 8 to 10 minutes or until the vegetables have almost entirely absorbed the cream and are tender. Correct seasoning.

1 to 2 Tb softened butter
A hot vegetable dish
2 Tb minced parsley | Reheat to the simmer just before serving. Off heat, fold in the butter. Turn into a hot vegetable dish, sprinkle with parsley, and serve.

TIMBALE DE CHOUX DE BRUXELLES

[Brussels Sprouts Mold]

This is a purée of Brussels sprouts mixed with eggs, milk, cheese, and bread crumbs, cooked in a mold, then unmolded and served with a cream sauce. It makes an unusual luncheon dish, or a fine accompaniment to roast veal or chicken. Use the same method and ingredients as for the asparagus mold, page 440, substituting blanched, chopped Brussels sprouts for asparagus.

FROZEN BRUSSELS SPROUTS

This recipe is for fully-cooked Brussels sprouts. If you wish to substitute partially cooked frozen sprouts for fresh ones in any of the preceding recipes, use half the amount of water indicated here, and cook the sprouts until they are almost but not quite tender, 3 to 4 minutes. (When you are cooking more than two packages, use two saucepans; if too many vegetables are cooked in one pan, the liquid will not evaporate by the time they are tender.)

For each 10-ounce package frozen Brussels sprouts: | Allow the frozen Brussels sprouts to thaw just enough so that you can separate them. Boil the water with the

½ cup water
¼ tsp salt
1 Tb butter
Salt and pepper

salt and butter in a saucepan. Add the vegetables, cover, and boil slowly for 6 to 8 minutes or until the sprouts are tender. Uncover saucepan and rapidly boil off any remaining liquid. Correct seasoning.

(*) If not to be used immediately, spread them out in one layer in a large, cold saucepan or dish.

BROCCOLI

Choux Broccoli – Choux Asperges

Broccoli, for some reason, is rarely seen in France though it abounds next door in Italy. We shall therefore not give it full-dress treatment, though we think it a delicious and useful vegetable.

PREPARATION FOR COOKING

Fresh broccoli will cook much more rapidly and stay greener if you divide it into flowerets about 3 inches long and then peel the thin, green skin off the stalks. Peel the cut-off butt ends deeply enough to expose the whitish, tender flesh, and cut into bias lengths.

BLANCHING

Blanch the prepared broccoli in a large kettle of boiling, salted water; first put in the pieces of stem and boil 5 minutes, then add the flowerets. Because it is a fragile vegetable, broccoli is easier to handle if you place it in a vegetable rack which you may set into the boiling water, and lift out with the broccoli when it is done. If the broccoli is to be partially cooked then braised, or simmered in a sauce, boil the flowerets for about 5 minutes or until almost tender. Fully cooked broccoli that is to be served with melted butter or a sauce such as hollandaise requires 8 to 10 minutes of cooking, or until a knife pierces the stems easily. Drain immediately.

FROZEN BROCCOLI

Cook frozen broccoli in the same manner as frozen Brussels sprouts, page 454

SAUCES FOR PLAIN, BOILED BROCCOLI

Sauces for hot or cold broccoli are the same as those suggested for asparagus, pages 437–8

OTHER COOKING METHODS

Broccoli may be substituted for Brussels sprouts in any of the following recipes in the Brussels sprouts section:

Braised in Butter, page 451

Creamed, page 452

Gratinéed with Cheese Sauce, page 453

Browned with Swiss and Parmesan Cheese, page 453

Chopped and Simmered in Cream, page 453

Baked in a mold with eggs, milk, and cheese, then unmolded. See the master recipe for asparagus molds on page 440.

SERVING SUGGESTIONS

Hot or cold broccoli with a sauce such as hollandaise or vinaigrette may be served, like asparagus, as a separate vegetable course. Creamed broccoli goes with roast or broiled chicken, roast veal, or sautéed veal scallops. Broccoli with melted butter or browned with cheese goes with sautéed liver, steaks, chops, and broiled chicken.

CAULIFLOWER

Chou-fleur

Choose cauliflowers with hard, clean, white heads containing firm, compact, flower clusters. The leaves surrounding the head should be fresh, healthy, and green.

AMOUNT TO BUY

A trimmed cauliflower head about 8 inches across will serve 4 to 6 people as a vegetable garnish.

SERVING SUGGESTIONS

Cauliflower gratinéed or served with a sauce may constitute a separate vegetable course. All types of cauliflower dishes go with roast turkey, chicken, lamb, beef, pork, and with steaks or chops.

PREPARATION FOR COOKING

Cauliflower cooks more evenly if you divide it into flowerets; we therefore always advise that you do so. Pull the outside leaves off the cauliflower and cut the stem off close under the head. The smaller leaves and the peeled stem may be used for soup. Cut the flowerets off the central stalk, and peel the thin skin off their stems with a knife. Cut a slit in any stems larger than ¼ inch in diameter, so they will cook quickly. Peel the central stalk deeply enough to expose its tender flesh, and cut it in bias pieces. Wash the cauliflower rapidly in a large basin of cold water. Drain.

---

* CHOU-FLEUR BLANCHI

[Blanched Cauliflower – Preliminary Cooking]

1 or 2 heads of cauliflower, cut into flowerets

A large kettle containing 7 to 8 quarts of boiling water

1½ tsp salt per quart of water

A vegetable rack set in the kettle is useful

Optional: add 1 cup of milk to kettle for each 3 quarts of boiling water, to keep cauliflower white

Drop the washed cauliflower into the rapidly boiling water; use a vegetable rack if you have one. Bring back to the boil as quickly as possible. Boil slowly, uncovered, for 9 to 12 minutes. The cauliflower is done when a knife pierces the stems easily. Eat a piece to be sure. It should be tender but retain the merest suggestion of crunchiness at the core.

As soon as it is done, carefully remove the cauliflower with a skimmer or spoon and drain in a colander, or remove the rack with cauliflower in it.

Refreshing Blanched Cauliflower

When cooked cauliflower is not to be served immediately or is to be served cold, it should be refreshed in cold water as soon as it is blanched. This stops the cooking so that the cauliflower retains its fresh taste and texture. Plunge the colander or vegetable rack holding the hot cauliflower into a large basin of cold water for 2 to 3 minutes. Drain.

Reheating

If the refreshed cauliflower is to be served hot with melted butter or sauce, steam it in a covered colander over boiling water for 4 to 5 minutes until hot through. Then season with salt and pepper, and it is ready for saucing and serving.

How to Mold Cooked Cauliflower into its Original Shape

It is not necessary, of course, to mold the cooked flowerets back into the shape of a whole head, but it makes an attractive presentation.

Select a bowl slightly smaller than the width and depth of the cauliflower head before it was cut into flowerets. Set the bowl over simmering water to warm it. When the cauliflower heads have been blanched and drained, one by one place the longest flowerets in the bottom of the bowl, heads down and stems converging at the center of the bowl. Continue with the rest of the flowerets, arranging their heads around the sides of the bowl until it is filled. Place the cooked pieces of stem on top. Then turn a warm, round, serving dish upside down over the bowl. Reverse the bowl onto the dish and remove the bowl; the cauliflower will stand molded in approximately its original shape.

SAUCES FOR HOT CAULIFLOWER

Here is a list of sauces to serve with hot cauliflower; about 1 to 1½ cups are sufficient for an 8-inch head. If the cauliflower has been molded, spoon ⅓ of the sauce over the stems before reversing the bowl.

Beurre au Citron, lemon butter sauce, page 98

Beurre Noir, brown butter sauce, page 98. You may brown ¾ cup of fresh, white bread crumbs with the butter. Sieved hard-boiled egg yolks and chopped parsley mixed into the butter and breadcrumbs turn the cauliflower into *chou-fleur à la polonaise.*

Sauce Crème, béchamel with cream, page 59

Sauce Bâtarde, mock hollandaise, page 64

Sauce Hollandaise, page 79

Sauce Mousseline, hollandaise with cream, page 83

Sauce à la Crème

[Fresh Cream Sauce]

For an 8-inch cauliflower

---

2 cups whipping cream	Simmer the cream in the saucepan until reduced by
A small saucepan	half. Season to taste with salt, pepper, and drops of
Salt and white pepper	lemon juice. Set aside until ready to use, then reheat.

Lemon juice
2 Tb softened butter
A wire whip
Parsley sprigs

Remove from heat and beat in the butter half a tablespoon at a time and pour the sauce over the hot cauliflower. Decorate with parsley and serve.

CHOU-FLEUR À LA MORNAY, GRATINÉ

[Cauliflower *au gratin* with Cheese]

Cauliflower *au gratin* may be prepared for the oven well in advance of serving, and goes with all kinds of roasts, chops, and steaks. You may, if you wish, mold the cauliflower in a bowl before saucing it, page 458, so it will preserve its round shape.

For 4 to 6 people

An 8-inch cauliflower cut into flowerets

Following directions on page 457, blanch the cauliflower in 7 to 8 quarts of boiling, salted water for 9 to 12 minutes, refresh in cold water, and drain.

2½ cups *sauce mornay* (*béchamel* with cheese), page 61
A lightly buttered baking dish about 8 inches in diameter and 2 inches deep
Salt and pepper
2 Tb fine, dry, white bread crumbs mixed with 2 Tb grated Swiss cheese
2 Tb melted butter

Spread ⅓ of the sauce in the baking dish. Arrange the cauliflower over it and season with salt and pepper. Pour on the rest of the sauce and sprinkle the top with bread crumbs and cheese. Dribble on the melted butter.

(*) Set aside, covered loosely with waxed paper, until ready to bake.

About 30 minutes before serving time, place in upper third of a preheated 375-degree oven to warm through thoroughly and to brown lightly. Serve as soon as possible.

CHOU-FLEUR AUX TOMATES FRAÎCHES

[Cauliflower *Gratinéed* with Cheese and Tomatoes]

This dish is particularly good with steaks, chops, and hamburgers.

For 4 to 6 people

An 8-inch head of cauli-
flower, cut into flowerets

Following directions on page 457, blanch the cauliflower in boiling salted water for 9 to 12 minutes, refresh in cold water, and drain.

1 lb. firm, ripe, red tomatoes,
peeled, seeded, and juiced,
page 505 (makes 1½
cups of pulp)

Cut the tomato pulp into strips ½ inch wide.

A shallow 10-inch buttered
baking dish
¼ tsp salt
Big pinch of pepper
½ cup melted butter
¼ cup fine, dry, white
bread crumbs mixed with
½ cup grated Swiss and
Parmesan cheese

Arrange the cauliflower in the center of the dish.
Place the tomatoes around the edge of the dish. Season the vegetables with salt, pepper, and half the
melted butter. Spread the cheese and bread crumbs
over the vegetables, and pour on the rest of the melted
butter.
(*) Set aside until ready to bake.

About 30 minutes before serving time, place in upper
third of a preheated 375-degree oven to warm through
thoroughly and brown the cheese nicely. Serve as soon
as possible.

CHOU-FLEUR EN VERDURE

[Purée of Cauliflower and Water Cress with Cream]

Serve this delectable purée with roast veal, chicken, or turkey, broiled or
sautéed chicken, chicken breasts, or veal scallops.

For 4 to 6 people

An 8-inch head of cauli-
flower
A bunch of fresh water
cress about 3 inches in diameter across the stems
A kettle containing 7 to 8
quarts of rapidly boiling
water
1½ tsp salt per quart of water

Separate the cauliflower head into flowerets; peel off
and discard the tough skin of the central stalk and
chop the stalk. Cut off the bunch of water cress just
above the point where the stems join the leaves (stems
may be used for soup). Wash and drain the vegetables. Drop the cauliflower into the boiling, salted water and boil slowly for 6 minutes. Then add the wa-
tercress leaves and boil 4 to 5 minutes more, or until
cauliflower is just tender. Drain.

A food mill

A 3-quart mixing bowl

A rubber scraper

2 cups thick *béchamel* sauce page 57 (3½ Tb butter, 5 Tb flour, 2 cups boiling milk, salt, and pepper)

½ cup whipping cream

½ cup grated Swiss cheese

Salt and pepper

Purée the cauliflower and water cress through the food mill and place purée in mixing bowl. Fold in the béchamel sauce. By spoonfuls, fold in the cream but do not thin out the purée too much; it should just hold its shape when a bit is lifted on the scraper. Fold in the cheese, and season to taste with salt and pepper.

A lightly buttered baking dish 8 to 9 inches in diameter and 2 inches deep

2 Tb fine, dry, white bread crumbs mixed with 2 Tb grated Swiss cheese

2 Tb melted butter

Heap the purée in the baking dish. Sprinkle on the cheese and bread crumbs, then the melted butter. (*) Set aside until ready to bake.

About 30 minutes before serving, place in upper third of a preheated 375-degree oven to heat through thoroughly and brown the cheese and bread crumbs. Serve as soon as possible.

TIMBALE DE CHOU-FLEUR

[Cauliflower Mold]

This is a purée of cooked cauliflower mixed with eggs, bread crumbs, cheese, and milk. It is baked in a soufflé mold, unmolded, and surrounded with a sauce. Use the recipe for asparagus mold on page 440, substituting cauliflower for the asparagus. Other sauces to serve besides those suggested in the recipe are:

Coulis de Tomates, fresh tomato sauce with herbs, page 78

Sauce au Cari, béchamel with curry and onions, page 63

GREEN PEAS

Petits Pois

The tenderest, freshest, and sweetest peas have bright green pods that are rather velvety to the touch. The pods should be fairly well filled. A perfect raw pea will taste tender and sweet. As peas mature they become larger, harder, and less sweet; but even a quite tough pea will make good eating if it is cooked in the right way. Choose, if possible, pods of equal size with peas all at the same stage of development so they will cook evenly.

As we have not the space in this book to cover every aspect of pea cookery, we have felt it would be most useful to present one fundamental recipe each for the small tender pea, the large tender pea, the tough pea, peas *à la française,* and frozen and canned peas.

AMOUNT TO BUY

One pound of small, tender peas will usually furnish about 1 cup of shelled peas.

One pound of large peas will usually furnish about 1½ cups of shelled peas.

One cup of shelled peas will serve from 1 to 3 people depending on your menu. We have based our recipes on 2 people per cup.

SERVING SUGGESTIONS

Beautifully cooked peas make a delicious separate vegetable course, and they may accompany almost anything from eggs and roasts to stews.

THREE RECIPES FOR BUTTERED PEAS

Each of the three recipes here is designed for peas of a particular quality, from sweet and tender to rather tough. Pick the recipe which corresponds to the type of peas you are to cook.

Petits Pois Frais à l'Anglaise

[Buttered Peas I—for very tender, sweet, fresh, green peas]

Anyone who has eaten a plateful of small, tender, fresh, green peas in Italy or France in the springtime is not likely to forget the experience. These best-of-all peas are always cooked by blanching in a very large kettle of boiling salted water. They are served at once *à l'anglaise,* meaning they are merely seasoned, turned into a vegetable dish, and topped with pieces of butter. This simple and fundamental treatment preserves, unadulterated, their color, texture, and taste.

For 6 people

3 lbs. of very tender, sweet, young, fresh green peas (3 cups, shelled)

A large kettle containing 7 to 8 quarts of rapidly boiling water

1½ tsp salt per quart of water

Drop the shelled peas into the rapidly boiling salted water. Bring the water to the boil again as quickly as possible. Boil slowly, uncovered, for 4 to 8 minutes, testing the peas frequently by eating one. They will have more taste and be greener if they are drained at the point where they are tender but still retain a suggestion of texture. But this is a matter of personal taste, and they may be boiled a few more minutes if you wish.

A colander

A heavy-bottomed saucepan

Salt and pepper

½ to 1 Tb granulated sugar (depending on sweetness of peas)

A hot vegetable dish

6 Tb butter, formed into little shells or cut into pieces

Drain the peas immediately. Place in the saucepan with the seasonings and roll them gently over moderate heat for a moment or two to evaporate all their humidity. Correct seasoning. Turn the peas into a hot vegetable dish, arrange the butter over them, and serve at once.

Petits Pois Étuvés au Beurre

[Buttered Peas II—for large but tender fresh green peas]

This is for the larger pea, the kind you usually find at your market.

For 6 people

2 lbs. large but tender fresh green peas (3 cups, shelled)

A kettle containing 7 to 8 quarts of rapidly boiling water

1½ tsp salt per quart of water

A colander

Drop the peas in the boiling salted water and boil uncovered for 5 to 10 minutes or until the peas are almost but not quite tender. They will finish cooking later. Drain.

(*) If the peas are not to be served immediately, refresh them in cold water for 3 to 4 minutes to stop the cooking and to retain their color and texture. Drain.

A heavy-bottomed, 6- to 8-cup enameled saucepan

1 to 2 Tb granulated sugar (depending on the sweetness of the peas)

Roll the peas in the saucepan over moderate heat for a moment or two to evaporate their moisture. Then roll them with the sugar, salt, pepper, butter, and optional mint. When the peas are well coated with butter, cover and cook over very low heat for about 10

¼ tsp salt
Big pinch of pepper
6 Tb softened butter
Optional English touch: 1
     to 2 Tb minced fresh mint
     leaves
Salt and pepper
A hot vegetable dish

minutes, tossing occasionally, until they are tender. Correct seasoning, turn into a hot vegetable dish, and serve as soon as possible.

Petits Pois aux Oignons

[Buttered Peas with Onions]

12 to 18 small, white, peeled onions boiled in salted water until almost tender, OR 3 to 5 Tb minced shallots or green onions

Prepare the peas as in the preceding recipe, but add boiled onions or diced shallots or green onions to the saucepan with the peas and seasonings for the final, 10-minute cooking period.

Pois Frais en Braisage

[Buttered Peas III—for large, rather tough, fresh green peas]

This is for large, mature, end-of-season peas. They remain green after cooking, become tender, and have a fine flavor though they will look a bit wrinkled.

For 6 people

A heavy-bottomed, 2½-quart enameled saucepan
2 lbs. of large, mature, fresh peas (3 cups, shelled)
1 large head of Boston lettuce, shredded
½ tsp salt
2 Tb granulated sugar
4 Tb minced green onions
6 Tb softened butter

Place in the saucepan the peas and all the rest of the ingredients. Squeeze the peas with your hands rather roughly to bruise them slightly, and to mix them thoroughly with the butter, lettuce, onions, and seasonings. Add enough cold water to cover the peas by ¼ inch.

A hot vegetable dish

Cover the saucepan and set over moderately high heat. Boil rapidly for 20 to 30 minutes; test the peas frequently by eating one after 20 minutes, to see if they are tender. Add 2 to 3 tablespoons more water if it evaporates before the peas are done. When they are tender, uncover and quickly boil off any remaining liquid. Taste for seasoning. Turn into a hot vegetable dish, and serve.

(*) If not served immediately, set aside uncovered. Shortly before serving, add 2 to 3 tablespoons of water, cover, and boil slowly until the peas are well warmed through and the water has evaporated.

PETITS POIS FRAIS À LA FRANÇAISE

[Peas Braised with Lettuce and Onions—for medium sized, tender, fresh peas]

This dish is considered the glory of pea cookery; it should really be served as a separate course and eaten with a spoon. If you wish to have a wine with the peas, serve a chilled white that is not too dry, such as Traminer or Graves, or a chilled *rosé*.

For 4 to 6 people

1½ firm, fresh heads of Boston lettuce 7 to 8 inches in diameter
White string

Remove wilted leaves, trim the stems, and wash the lettuce heads carefully so they will not break apart. Cut into quarters. Wind several loops of string about each quarter to keep it in shape as much as possible during the cooking.

6 Tb butter
½ cup water
1½ Tb granulated sugar
½ tsp salt
⅛ tsp pepper
A heavy-bottomed, 3-quart, enameled saucepan
3 lbs. medium sized, tender, fresh green peas (3 cups, shelled)
8 parsley stems tied together with white string
12 green onion bulbs about 1 inch in diameter OR small white onions boiled for 5 minutes in salted water

Bring the butter, water, and seasonings to the boil in the saucepan. Then add the peas and toss to cover them with the liquid. Bury the parsley in their midst. Arrange the lettuce quarters over them and baste with the liquid. Pierce a cross in the root ends of the onions (for even cooking) and disperse them among the lettuce quarters.

A domed lid or a soup plate	So that the cooking steam will condense and fall back onto the peas, invert a lid over the saucepan and fill it with cold water or ice cubes; or use a soup plate. Bring the peas to the boil and boil slowly for 20 to 30 minutes or until tender. Several times during this period, remove the cover and toss the peas and vegetables to insure even cooking. As the water warms up and evaporates in the cover or soup plate, refill with ice cubes or cold water.
Salt and pepper	When the peas are tender their cooking liquid should have almost entirely evaporated. Correct seasoning.
2 Tb softened butter **A hot vegetable dish**	Discard the parsley and the lettuce strings. Just before serving, toss the peas and onions with the butter. Turn them into the vegetable dish, place the lettuce around the edge of the dish, and serve at once.

FROZEN PEAS

This method of cooking frozen peas gives them the character they often lack. Use two saucepans when you are cooking more than two 10-ounce boxes; if too many peas are cooked in one pan, the cooking liquid will not evaporate by the time the peas are done.

For each 10-ounce package of frozen peas: **1 Tb butter** **1 Tb minced shallots or green onions** **¼ tsp salt** **Pinch of pepper** **½ cup chicken stock or canned chicken or mushroom broth, or water**	Allow the peas to thaw enough so they can be separated. Bring the butter, shallots or green onions, seasonings, and liquid to the boil in a saucepan. Add the peas, cover, and boil slowly for 5 to 6 minutes or until the peas are tender. Uncover and rapidly boil off any remaining liquid. Correct seasoning.

CANNED PEAS

Here is a way to improve the flavor of canned peas.

For each No. 2 can of peas (1¼ lbs. or 2½ cups):	Turn the peas into a sieve and run cold water over them. Drain.
1½ Tb minced shallots or green onions 2 Tb butter Salt and pepper to taste 3 Tb stock or mushroom broth	Cook the shallots or onions in the butter for a moment. Add the peas and seasonings and toss them in the butter. Then add the stock or broth, cover the peas, and boil slowly for a few moments until the peas are warmed through. Uncover, raise heat, and rapidly boil off any remaining liquid.

SPINACH

Épinards

Spinach is an excellent vegetable when it is cooked properly. Except for the tenderest and freshest garden variety which may be simmered slowly in seasonings, butter, and its own juices, spinach is first blanched in a large kettle of boiling salted water; then all the water is pressed out of it, and it is simmered in butter and meat stock or cream. In addition to its role as a vegetable, it can serve as a bed for poached eggs, fish, or breasts of chicken. It is also used in various stuffings, and makes an excellent soufflé, tart, or mold.

SERVING SUGGESTIONS

Spinach goes with just about everything, eggs, fish, chicken, sweetbreads, ham, roasts, steaks, chops, sautés. Or it may constitute a separate vegetable course. The *gratins* may also serve as entrées, luncheon, or supper dishes. If it is a separate course, a dry white wine such as a Riesling goes with spinach braised in butter or in stock. Serve a less dry white wine, such as a Graves, with spinach braised in cream.

AMOUNT TO BUY

One pound of fresh spinach yields about 1 cup of cooked spinach, and we shall consider that enough for 2 people.

PREPARATION FOR COOKING

If the spinach is young and tender, the stems are usually removed at the base of the leaf. For more mature spinach, fold the leaf vertically, its underside up, in the fingers of one hand; grasp the stem in the other hand and rip it off toward the tip of the leaf, thus removing with the stem the tough tendrils which are attached to the underside of the leaf. Discard any wilted or yellow leaves. Whether or not it is claimed that the spinach is washed, plunge it into a large basin of cold water and pump it up and down for several minutes with your hands. Lift it out into a colander, leaving any sand in the bottom of the basin. Wash the spinach several times more, if necessary, until there is no sand to be seen in the bottom of the basin. Drain, and the spinach is ready for cooking.

ÉPINARDS BLANCHIS

[Blanched, Chopped Spinach—Preliminary Cooking]

For 3 cups of blanched, chopped spinach

3 lbs. fresh spinach	Prepare and wash the spinach as described in the preceding paragraph.
A large kettle containing at least 7 to 8 quarts of rapidly boiling water 1½ tsp salt per quart of water	A handful at a time, drop the spinach into the boiling salted water. Bring back to the boil as rapidly as possible and boil slowly, uncovered, for about 2 minutes, or until the spinach is almost tender. Test it by eating a piece.
A large colander	At once, set the colander, curved side down, into the kettle. Protecting your hands with a towel, hold the colander firmly clamped to the sides of the kettle as you tilt the kettle and pour out the water. Still with the colander in place, run cold water into the kettle for several minutes to refresh the spinach. This will preserve its color and texture. Remove colander and lift the spinach out of the water into the colander, thus leaving any possible bits of sand in the bottom of the kettle.

	A small amount at a time, squeeze the spinach in your hands to extract as much water as possible—last drops of water from each squeeze may be saved for soup.
A stainless steel chopping knife or a food mill	Chop the spinach with a big knife on a chopping board, or, if you want a fine purée, put it through a food mill. The spinach is now ready for further cooking and flavoring. (*) May be done several hours or a day in advance. Cover and refrigerate.

WARNING

Spinach quickly picks up an astringent and metallic taste if its final cooking is in iron or aluminum. For the following recipes, use only enamel, pyrex, earthenware, or stainless steel saucepans or baking dishes, and serve the spinach in enamel or porcelain, not silver.

* PURÉE D'ÉPINARDS SIMPLE

[Cooked Chopped Spinach—Purée of Spinach]

This is the last step in preparing spinach for use in soufflés, *quiches,* custards, *crêpes,* stuffings, or for final cooking in any of the following recipes. The directions on page 475 also bring frozen spinach to this point.

For 3 cups, or for 6 people

2 Tb butter A 2½-quart heavy-bottomed, enameled saucepan 3 cups blanched spinach, chopped or puréed (directions in preceding recipe) Salt and pepper Pinch of nutmeg	When the butter is bubbling in the saucepan over moderately high heat, stir in the spinach. Continue stirring for 2 to 3 minutes until all the moisture from the spinach has boiled off—the spinach will begin to adhere to the bottom of the pan. Season to taste, and the spinach is ready to use.

RECIPES FOR COOKED CHOPPED SPINACH

Épinards Étuvés au Beurre

[Spinach Braised in Butter—Buttered Spinach]

Serve this deliciously buttery spinach with steaks, chops, roasts, ham, or sautéed liver. Use it also in any recipe calling for a bed of buttered spinach.

For 6 people

3 cups cooked chopped spinach (the preceding recipe), in a heavy-bottomed enameled saucepan 4 Tb butter Salt and pepper to taste	After you have followed the directions in the preceding recipe (stirring the spinach over moderately high heat with butter and seasonings until its moisture has evaporated), stir in the 4 additional tablespoons of butter listed here. Cover the saucepan and cook very slowly for 10 to 15 minutes, stirring frequently, until the spinach has absorbed the butter and is very tender. Correct seasoning. (*) If not served immediately, set aside uncovered. Reheat when needed.
2 Tb softened butter A hot porcelain serving dish	Remove from heat, fold in the additional butter, and turn the spinach into the hot serving dish.

Épinards au Jambon

[Spinach with Ham]

½ cup finely diced ham, sautéed briefly in butter The preceding spinach braised in butter 12 *croûtons* (triangles of white bread sautéed in clarified butter), page 199	Stir the ham into the spinach 2 to 3 minutes before the end of the cooking. After arranging the spinach on its serving dish, place the *croûtons* around the edge of the dish.

* ### Épinards au Jus

[Spinach Braised in Stock]

* *Épinards à la Crème*

[Spinach Braised in Cream—Creamed Spinach]

This is an alternative to the preceding recipe for buttered spinach. Whether to use cream or stock for the braising depends on your judgment of which goes best with the rest of your menu. Creamed spinach would contrast well with sautéed ham, liver, brains, sweetbreads, chicken, or veal; spinach braised in stock would be preferable if you served any of these meats in a cream sauce. Spinach braised in stock or cream may also be gratinéed with cheese or be used as a filling for *crêpes* as suggested in the variations following the recipe.

For 6 people

3 cups cooked chopped spinach, page 469, in a heavy-bottomed enameled saucepan 1½ Tb flour, sifted to remove any lumps	After you have stirred the spinach over moderately high heat with butter and seasonings to evaporate its humidity, as directed in the recipe for cooked chopped spinach, lower heat to moderate. Sprinkle on the flour and stir for 2 minutes more to cook the flour.
1 cup brown stock, canned beef bouillon, or whipping cream Salt and pepper	Remove from heat and stir in two thirds of the stock, bouillon, or cream by spoonfuls. Bring to the simmer, cover, and cook very slowly for about 15 minutes. Stir frequently to prevent spinach from sticking to bottom of pan, and add more liquid by spoonfuls if spinach becomes too dry. Correct seasoning. (*) If not to be served immediately, set aside uncovered, and film top with a tablespoon of stock or cream. Reheat when needed.
1 to 2 Tb softened butter A hot porcelain serving dish Optional: 1 or 2 sieved or sliced hard-boiled eggs	Remove spinach from heat, fold in the butter, and turn into the serving dish. Decorate with optional egg.

VARIATIONS

Épinards Gratinés au Fromage

[Spinach *Gratinéed* with Cheese]

Serve this gratinéed spinach with steaks or chops, roast veal or chicken, or sautéed liver. It also goes well with broiled fish.

For 6 people

¾ cups grated Swiss cheese

3 cups spinach braised in stock (the preceding recipe)

A lightly buttered baking dish 8 inches in diameter and 1½ inches deep

2 Tb fine, dry, white bread crumbs

1½ Tb melted butter

Stir two thirds of the cheese into the spinach and turn it into the baking dish, heaping it into a slight dome. Mix the rest of the cheese with the bread crumbs and spread over the spinach. Sprinkle on the melted butter.

About 30 minutes before serving, place in upper third of a preheated, 375-degree oven to heat through thoroughly and brown the top lightly.

Canapés aux Épinards

[Spinach and Cheese Canapés]

Serve these canapés as a hot first course or luncheon dish, or make them smaller than directed here and serve as cocktail appetizers.

For 6 people

12 slices of white bread, 3½ by 2½ inches and ⅜ inch thick

¾ cup grated Swiss cheese

3 cups spinach braised in stock (the preceding master recipe)

2 Tb fine, dry, white bread crumbs

2 to 3 Tb melted butter

Cut off the crusts and sauté the bread in hot butter and oil in a skillet until lightly browned on each side. Stir two thirds of the cheese into the braised spinach and heap 2 or 3 tablespoons on each piece of sautéed bread. Sprinkle with the remaining grated cheese, the bread crumbs, and the melted butter.

Just before serving, run under a moderately hot broiler to heat through and brown lightly.

Épinards à la Mornay, Gratinés

[Spinach *Gratinéed* with Cheese Sauce]

Serve this gratinéed spinach with roasts, steaks, or chops, or as a hot first course or luncheon dish.

For 6 people

1½ cups *sauce mornay* (*béchamel* with cheese), page 61

A lightly buttered baking dish 8 inches in diameter and 1½ inches deep

3 cups spinach braised in stock or in cream, page 470–1

Optional: ½ lb. sliced mushrooms sautéed in butter, page 513

3 Tb grated Swiss cheese

1½ Tb melted butter

Spread a third of the sauce in the bottom of the baking dish. If you are using the optional mushrooms, fold them into the spinach. Heap the spinach in the dish over the sauce, and spoon the rest of the sauce over it. Sprinkle with the grated cheese and melted butter.

About 30 minutes before serving, place in upper third of a preheated, 375-degree oven to heat through thoroughly and brown lightly on top.

Épinards en Surprise

[Spinach Hidden under a Giant *Crêpe*]

This is an amusing presentation; the spinach is heaped in a serving dish and a large French pancake is spread over it, hiding it completely. Serve it as a main course luncheon or supper dish and, if you wish, mix a cup of sautéed, diced ham or mushrooms into the spinach.

For 6 people

½ cup grated Swiss cheese

3 cups spinach braised in stock or in cream, page 470–1

A hot, lightly buttered porcelain serving dish about 8 inches in diameter

A French pancake, *crêpe,* large enough to cover the spinach completely, page 191

Just before serving, stir the cheese into the hot, braised spinach and heap it in the serving dish. Then cover with the *crêpe.*

PETITES CRÊPES D'ÉPINARDS

[Spinach Pancakes]

Spinach pancakes may be folded in quarters to garnish a roast, steaks, or chops. Filled as suggested in the *Crêpe* section, pages 193 to 195, they may be served as a hot first course, or luncheon or supper dish.

For about 12 crêpes 6 inches in diameter

Ingredients for ½ the recipe for *crêpes*, page 191

1 cup blanched spinach, page 468

If you are making the *crêpe* batter in an electric blender, you may purée the blanched spinach at the same time. Otherwise, purée the spinach in a food mill and combine with the *crêpe* batter. Let batter rest for 2 hours before using. Cook spinach *crêpes* like ordinary *crêpes,* according to directions following those for the batter.

TIMBALE D'ÉPINARDS

[Spinach Mold]

This is a purée of spinach mixed with eggs, milk, cheese, and breadcrumbs, baked in a soufflé dish, unmolded, and surrounded with a sauce. Use the recipe for asparagus mold on page 440, substituting spinach purée, page 469, for asparagus. Other sauces besides those with the asparagus mold recipe are:

Sauce Tomate or *Coulis de Tomates,* tomato sauce, pages 76 to 78

Sauce Aurore, velouté or béchamel sauce with tomato flavoring, page 62

ÉPINARDS À LA BASQUAISE

[*Gratin* of Spinach and Sliced Potatoes with Anchovies]

Serve this with steaks, roast beef, roast lamb, or with broiled fish such as mackerel, fresh tuna, herring, or sardines.

For 6 people

½ cup grated Swiss cheese

3 cups spinach braised in stock, page 470

Stir the cheese into the braised spinach.

1 lb. "boiling" potatoes	Peel the potatoes and cut them into slices ⅛ inch thick. Boil them in salted water for 5 to 6 minutes, or until tender. Drain.
A lightly buttered baking dish 2 inches deep and 9 inches in diameter 2 Tb mashed anchovies (or 1 Tb anchovy paste) blended with 4 Tb softened butter and ⅛ tsp pepper	Spread half of the potatoes in the bottom of the baking dish. Cover with half of the anchovy mixture. Spread half of the spinach over the potatoes. Repeat with the remaining potatoes, anchovy mixture, and spinach.
⅓ cup grated Swiss cheese mixed with 3 Tb dry white bread crumbs 2 Tb melted butter	Spread the cheese and bread crumbs over the top of the spinach and pour on the melted butter.
	About 30 minutes before serving, place in upper third of a preheated, 375-degree oven to heat through thoroughly and brown the top nicely.

FROZEN SPINACH

Although it cannot have the lovely taste of fresh spinach, and there is almost more stem than leaf to it, frozen spinach does have its place. When it's given this preliminary treatment, you may use it in any of the preceding recipes. If you are cooking more than two packages at once, use two saucepans; when too much is in one saucepan, the liquid will not evaporate quickly enough and the spinach will overcook.

For each 10-ounce package of frozen spinach: A heavy, stainless steel chopping knife	Whether the frozen spinach is whole, chopped, or puréed, it will cook most successfully if you unwrap and defrost it just enough so you can slice it by bearing down on the block with a heavy knife. If the spinach is already chopped or puréed, cut the slices roughly into half-inch pieces. If the spinach is whole, chop the slices into small bits.
1½ Tb butter A heavy-bottomed, enam-	Melt the butter in the saucepan or skillet, then stir in the chopped spinach and seasonings. Cover and cook

eled saucepan or skillet
¼ tsp salt
Pinch of pepper
Small pinch of nutmeg

very slowly for a minute or two, until the spinach has thawed and released its juices. Uncover, raise heat, and stir for 2 to 3 minutes until all moisture has evaporated.

This may now be substituted for the cooked chopped spinach on page 469, and used in any of the recipes calling for it or blanched spinach.

CARROTS, ONIONS, AND TURNIPS

Carottes, Oignons, et Navets

Carrots, onions, and turnips *à la française* are all cooked in substantially the same manner, so we have grouped them together.

CARROTS

Carottes

Carrots develop their maximum flavor if they are cooked in a covered saucepan with a small amount of liquid, butter, and seasonings until the liquid has evaporated and the carrots are beginning to sauté in the butter.

SERVING SUGGESTIONS

Buttered or glazed carrots go well with all kinds of roasts, and combine with other vegetables to make many of the classic garnitures which may surround a meat platter. One of the more elaborate of these is *à la bouquetière* which includes glazed carrots and turnips, diced green beans, peas, cauliflower bouquets, and potato balls sautéed in butter. Creamed carrots are particularly good with veal and chicken.

AMOUNT TO BUY

One pound of carrots minus their tops will serve 3 or 4 people. A pound of raw carrots, sliced, diced, or quartered, makes about 3½ cups.

PREPARATION FOR COOKING

Trim off the stems and peel the carrots with a vegetable peeler. Depending on their size and the effect you wish, slice them horizontally, or halve or quarter them lengthwise, then cut the lengths into 2-inch pieces. These pieces may, if you wish, be trimmed into the form of long garlic cloves; in French this is termed *tourner en gousses* or *en olives*.

(For tough old carrots only: If you happen to have end-of-season carrots, quarter them lengthwise, then cut out and remove the woody central section, and use only the reddish outer portion which French recipes call *rouge de carotte*. Then before proceeding with any of the following recipes, blanch the carrots by boiling for 5 to 8 minutes in salted water.)

✻ CAROTTES ÉTUVÉES AU BEURRE

[Carrots Braised in Butter]

This is the basic recipe for cooked carrots; they may be served with a sprinkling of parsley, simmered in cream, mixed with other vegetables, or puréed.

For 6 people

A heavy-bottomed, 2-quart, enameled saucepan

1½ lbs. carrots, peeled, and sliced or quartered (about 5½ cups)

1 Tb granulated sugar (to develop their flavor)

1½ cups water

1½ Tb butter

½ tsp salt

Pinch of pepper

In the saucepan, bring the carrots to the boil with the sugar, water, butter, and salt. Cover and boil slowly for 30 to 40 minutes or until the carrots are tender and the liquid has evaporated. Correct seasoning.

(*) If they are not to be served at once, set aside uncovered and reheat when needed.

VARIATIONS

Carottes aux Fines Herbes

[Braised Carrots with Herbs]

1½ lbs. carrots braised in butter

2 Tb softened butter

2 Tb minced parsley, chervil and chives, or parsley only

A hot vegetable dish

Just before serving and off heat, toss the carrots with the butter and herbs. Turn into a hot vegetable dish.

Carottes à la Crème

[Creamed Carrots]

1 to 1½ cups whipping cream
1½ lbs. carrots braised in butter, page 477
Salt and pepper

Bring the cream to a boil in a saucepan and pour in enough to cover the carrots. Boil slowly, uncovered, for 15 to 20 minutes or until the cream has been almost entirely absorbed by the carrots. Correct seasoning.

2 Tb softened butter
2 Tb minced parsley, chervil and chives, or parsley only
A hot vegetable dish

Just before serving and off heat, gently toss the butter and herbs into the carrots. Turn into a hot vegetable dish.

Carottes à la Forestière

[Braised Carrots with Artichoke Bottoms and Mushrooms]

½ lb. quartered fresh mushrooms
1 Tb oil
1½ Tb butter
Salt and pepper

In a skillet, sauté the mushrooms in hot oil and butter for 4 to 5 minutes until very lightly browned. Season with salt and pepper.

2 Tb minced shallots or green onions
3 or 4 cooked fresh artichoke bottoms cut into quarters, page 431 (or cooked frozen artichoke hearts, page 434)
1½ lbs. carrots braised in butter, page 477

Stir the shallots or onions and the cooked fresh artichoke bottoms into the mushrooms and toss for 2 to 3 minutes over moderately high heat. (If you are using frozen artichoke hearts, cook them separately, then add them directly to the carrots.) Fold or toss the artichoke hearts and mushrooms into the carrots.

⅓ cup good brown stock or canned beef bouillon
Salt and pepper

Pour the stock or bouillon into the vegetables. Cover and boil slowly for 4 to 5 minutes until the stock has almost completely evaporated. Correct seasoning.

A hot vegetable dish	Turn into a hot vegetable dish and sprinkle with the
2 Tb minced parsley, cher- vil, and chives, or parsley only	herbs.

CAROTTES GLACÉES

[Glazed Carrots]

Glazed carrots receive the same type of cooking process as braised carrots; the only difference is that they are cooked in stock instead of water, and more butter and sugar are used so that the liquid reduces to a syrupy glaze in the bottom of the pan. Just before serving, the carrots are rolled about in the syrup so each piece is shiny with glaze.

For 6 people

1½ lbs. carrots, peeled, quartered and cut into 2-inch lengths (5½ cups)	Boil the carrots slowly in the covered saucepan with the stock or bouillon, sugar, pepper, and butter for 30 to 40 minutes until the carrots are tender and the liquid has reduced to a syrupy glaze. Correct seasoning.
A 2½-quart, heavy-bottomed, enameled saucepan with cover	
1½ cups good brown stock or canned beef bouillon	
2 Tb granulated sugar	
Pinch of pepper	
6 Tb butter	
Salt and pepper	

A hot vegetable dish	Reheat just before serving and roll the carrots gently
2 Tb very finely minced parsley	in the pan to coat them with syrup. Turn into a hot vegetable dish or arrange them around your roast, and sprinkle with parsley.

CAROTTES VICHY

[Carrots Vichy]

The recipe for carrots Vichy is exactly the same as that for the preceding glazed carrots except that in place of stock you would use bottled Vichy water (or plain bottled water with a pinch of soda). The assumption is that pure noncalcareous bottled water produces a more delicate carrot.

CAROTTES À LA CONCIERGE

[Casserole of Creamed Carrots with Onions and Garlic]

This hearty dish of carrots goes nicely with red meats, pork, sausages, or plain roast chicken. It can also constitute a meatless main-course dish.

For 6 people

1½ lbs. carrots, peeled and cut into ¼-inch slices (5½ cups) ½ lb. (1½ cups) sliced onions 4 Tb olive oil A 2½-quart, heavy-bottomed, enameled saucepan with cover	Cook the carrots, onions, and olive oil slowly in the covered saucepan, tossing occasionally, for about 30 minutes. The vegetables should be tender but not browned.
A large clove mashed garlic	Add the garlic for the last 5 minutes of cooking.
1 Tb flour	Toss the vegetables with the flour and cook 3 minutes more.
¾ cup boiling brown stock or canned beef bouillon ¾ cup boiling milk Salt and pepper to taste 1 tsp granulated sugar Pinch of nutmeg	Off heat, fold in the boiling stock or bouillon, then the milk, and finally the seasonings. Simmer uncovered for about 20 minutes or until the liquid has reduced to about a third of its volume and has thickened into a light cream. Correct seasoning.
2 egg yolks blended with 4 Tb whipping cream A rubber spatula A hot vegetable dish 2 Tb minced parsley	Off heat and just before serving, use the spatula to fold in the egg yolks and cream. Shake and swirl saucepan over low heat until the egg yolks have thickened but be careful not to bring them near the simmer or they may coagulate. Turn into a hot vegetable dish and sprinkle with parsley.

ONIONS

Oignons

It is hard to imagine a civilization without onions; in one form or another their flavor blends into almost everything in the meal except the dessert. We shall concentrate here on the small, whole, cooked, white onions which are so often called for as a vegetable garnish. When they are used in stews and fricassees it is generally advisable that they be cooked separately so you are sure they will be tender and retain their shape.

AMOUNT TO BUY

One pound of small onions will serve 3 or 4 people if they constitute a principal vegetable dish. If they are used as a garnish or in a mixture with other vegetables, count on 3 or 4 small onions per person.

PREPARATION FOR COOKING

The quickest, neatest, and least tearful way to peel small white onions is to drop them into a saucepan of rapidly boiling water and leave them for 5 to 10 seconds, just long enough for their skins to loosen. Drain. Run cold water over them. Trim off the top and bottom portions, removing only a little bit so as not to disturb the onion layers. Then slip off the outside skin and the first onion layer with your fingers. Pierce a cross in the root ends so that the onions will cook evenly without bursting.

If the onions are old and very strongly flavored, or if for digestive reasons you wish to make them milder, drop them into boiling, salted water and boil slowly for 5 minutes before proceeding with a recipe.

To remove onion flavor from your hands, wash them in cold water, rub them with salt, rinse again in cold water, then wash in soap and warm water.

---

* OIGNONS GLACÉS À BLANC

[White-braised Onions—Glazed Onions]

White-braised onions may be served as they are, or they may be simmered for a moment in a good cream sauce. Use them also as a garnish for fricassees or *blanquettes*.

For 18 to 24 peeled white onions about 1 inch in diameter:

A heavy-bottomed, enameled saucepan or skillet

Place the onions in the saucepan or skillet with the liquid, butter, seasonings, and herb bouquet. Cover and simmer very slowly, rolling the onions in the saucepan from time to time, for 40 to 50 minutes. The onions should not color, and should be perfectly

which will just hold the onions in one layer

½ cup white stock, canned chicken broth, dry white wine, or water

2 Tb butter

Salt and pepper to taste

A small herb bouquet: 2 parsley sprigs, ⅛ tsp thyme, and ⅓ bay leaf tied in cheesecloth

tender yet retain their shape. If all the liquid evaporates during the cooking, add more by spoonfuls as necessary. Remove herb bouquet.

(*) May be cooked several hours in advance, reheated, and served as in the following suggestions.

TO SERVE

Petits Oignons Persillés

[Parslied Onions]

These go particularly well with chicken, veal, or fish in cream sauce.

2 Tb softened butter
A warm vegetable dish
2 Tb minced parsley

Just before serving the onions, correct seasoning. Off heat, roll them with the softened butter. Turn into a warm vegetable dish and sprinkle with parsley.

Petits Oignons à la Crème

[Creamed Onions]

Serve creamed onions with roast veal, chicken, or turkey, chops, steaks, or hamburgers, sautéed veal, chicken, or liver.

(For 2 lbs. of white-braised onions, serving 6 people.)

2 cups *sauce crème* (*béchamel* with cream), page 59
Salt and pepper
1 to 2 Tb softened butter
2 Tb minced parsley
A hot vegetable dish

Fold the cream sauce into the braised onions and simmer for 5 minutes. Correct seasoning. Off heat, fold in the butter. Turn into a hot vegetable dish and sprinkle with parsley.

✳ *OIGNONS GLACÉS À BRUN*

[Brown-braised Onions]

Brown-braised onions are used whenever you wish a brown effect, such as in brown fricassees like *coq au vin* and *boeuf bourguignon,* or in a mixture with other vegetables.

For 18 to 24 peeled white onions about 1 inch in diameter:

1½ Tb butter

1½ Tb oil

A 9- to 10-inch enameled skillet

When the butter and oil are bubbling in the skillet, add the onions and sauté over moderate heat for about 10 minutes, rolling the onions about so they will brown as evenly as possible. Be careful not to break their skins. You cannot expect to brown them uniformly.

½ cup of brown stock, canned beef bouillon, dry white wine, red wine, or water

Salt and pepper to taste

A medium herb bouquet: 4 parsley sprigs, ½ bay leaf, and ¼ tsp thyme tied in cheesecloth

Then either braise them as follows:

Pour in the liquid, season to taste, and add the herb bouquet. Cover and simmer slowly for 40 to 50 minutes until the onions are perfectly tender but retain their shape, and the liquid has evaporated. Remove herb bouquet. Serve them as they are, or follow one of the suggestions at the end of the recipe.

Or bake them as follows:

Transfer the onions and their sautéing fat to a shallow baking dish or casserole just large enough to hold them in one layer. Set uncovered in upper third of a preheated 350-degree oven for 40 to 50 minutes, turning them over once or twice. They should be very tender, retain their shape, and be a nice golden brown. Remove herb bouquet. Serve them as they are or according to one of the following suggestions.

(✳) The onions may be cooked hours in advance, and reheated before serving.

TO SERVE

Petits Oignons Persillés

[Parslied Onions]

1 to 2 Tb softened butter	Roll the hot onions gently in the butter. Turn into a
A hot vegetable dish	hot vegetable dish or place them around your roast,
1 Tb minced parsley	and sprinkle with parsley.

Petits Oignons en Garniture

[Vegetable Mixtures]

Braised onions go nicely mixed with other vegetables such as glazed carrots, sautéed mushrooms, artichoke hearts, and sautéed potatoes.

CANNED ONIONS

All the brands of canned "small boiled onions" we have tried have tasted, to us, rather unpleasantly sweetish and overacidulated; they also need more cooking to make them tender. However they are so useful in an emergency that we offer the following treatment which improves them considerably.

For each No. 2 can of small boiled onions (1¼ lbs. or 2½ cups):	Drain the onions. Drop them into boiling water, bring back to the boil and boil 1 minute. Drain. This removes some of the canned taste. Then simmer them
2 Tb butter	slowly in a covered saucepan for 10 to 15 minutes with
¼ cup stock, canned beef bouillon, or mushroom broth	the butter, stock, seasonings, and herb bouquet until they are very tender and the liquid has evaporated.
Salt and pepper to taste	
A small herb bouquet: 2 parsley sprigs, ⅓ bay leaf, and ¼ tsp thyme tied in cheesecloth	

SOUBISE

[Braised Rice and Onions]

This is a savory mixture of sliced onions, rice, and butter cooked slowly together until they melt into a purée. The natural moisture of the onions is sufficient to cook the rice; no other liquid is needed. *Soubise* is particularly good with veal or chicken, or boiled leg of lamb *à l'anglaise*. It may be turned into a *sauce soubise* by puréeing it with a *sauce béchamel* or *velouté* and enriching it with cream.

For 6 people

Preheat oven to 300 degrees.

½ cup rice
4 quarts rapidly boiling water
1½ Tb salt

Drop the rice into the boiling salted water and boil for 5 minutes exactly. Drain immediately.

4 Tb butter
A 3-quart, fireproof casserole
2 lbs. (6 to 7 cups) thinly sliced yellow onions
½ tsp salt
⅛ tsp pepper
Salt and pepper

When the butter is foaming in the casserole, stir in the onions. As soon as they are well coated with butter, stir in the rice and seasonings. Cover and cook very slowly in the 300-degree oven for about 1 hour, stirring occasionally. The rice and onions should become very tender and will usually turn a light golden yellow. Correct seasoning.

(*) May be cooked several hours in advance and reheated later.

¼ cup whipping cream
¼ cup grated Swiss cheese
2 Tb softened butter
A hot vegetable dish
1 Tb minced parsley

Just before serving, stir in the cream and cheese, and then the butter. Taste again for seasoning. Turn into a hot vegetable dish and sprinkle with parsley.

TURNIPS

Navets

The turnip is a wonderful vegetable when given the treatment required to bring out its delicious qualities. It wants and needs to absorb butter or meat fats, which is why turnips are particularly succulent when finished off in a stew or a braised dish, or in the juices of roasting meat. In France rutabagas, or yellow turnips, are practically unheard of as food for humans, but they may be used interchangeably with white turnips.

SERVING SUGGESTIONS

The full flavor of turnips goes well with pork, sausages, ham, goose, and duck.

AMOUNT TO BUY

One pound of turnips without tops will serve 3 or 4 people. A pound of raw sliced or quartered turnips measures about 3½ cups.

PREPARATION FOR COOKING

Small, tender, early-crop turnips, usually sold in bunches with their tops attached, are trimmed, peeled, and set to cook with no preliminary blanching. The older and stronger winter turnips and rutabagas, always sold without tops, are peeled fairly deeply with a knife, and are cut into slices or quarters. Quarters may be trimmed into neat ovals the shape of large garlic cloves, called in French *tourner en gousses* or *en olives*. Any turnips which are woody or fibrous should be discarded.

PRELIMINARY BLANCHING

After peeling and cutting winter turnips or rutabagas, place them in a saucepan with salted water to cover them by 2 inches, bring to the boil and boil for 3 to 5 minutes or until they are partially tender. Drain them. This removes some of their overly strong taste. The following recipes are based on winter turnips; omit the blanching step if your turnips are young and tender.

✳ *NAVETS À L'ÉTUVÉE*

[Turnips Braised in Butter]

Braised turnips may be served by themselves or combined with other vegetables. Their final cooking may be done around a roast or in a braised dish or a fricassee.

For 6 people

2 lbs. turnips, peeled and quartered (7 to 8 cups)

A heavy-bottomed, 3-quart, enameled saucepan

2 Tb butter

1 to 1½ cups stock, canned beef or chicken bouillon, or water

Salt and pepper to taste

Blanch the turnips for 3 to 5 minutes in boiling salted water to cover. Drain, and place them in the saucepan with the butter and enough liquid barely to cover them. Season lightly. Cover and boil slowly for 20 to 30 minutes or until they are tender but retain their shape. If the liquid has not evaporated, uncover and boil it off. Correct seasoning.

(*) May be cooked several hours in advance of serving.

TO SERVE

Navets Persillés

[Parslied Turnips]

2 Tb softened butter

Optional: Drops of lemon juice to taste

2 Tb minced parsley

A hot vegetable dish

Just before serving, toss the hot turnips gently with the butter, optional lemon juice, and parsley. Turn into the vegetable dish.

VARIATION

Purée de Navets Parmentier

[Turnip and Potato Purée]

Serve this purée with roast turkey, duck, goose, ham, pork, or pork chops or sausages.

For 6 people

7 to 8 cups turnips braised in butter (the preceding master recipe)

2 cups warm mashed potatoes

4 Tb softened butter

Salt and pepper

A hot vegetable dish

2 Tb minced parsley

Purée the turnips and beat them into the mashed potatoes. Beat the purée in a saucepan over moderate heat to evaporate moisture and to heat thoroughly. Off heat and just before serving, beat in the butter. Season to taste with salt and pepper. Turn into a hot vegetable dish and sprinkle with parsley.

✳ *NAVETS GLACÉS À BRUN*

[Glazed Turnips]

Glazed turnips are used to garnish a roast, or may be served as a separate vegetable. It is essentially the same procedure as that for braised turnips, except they are browned before being simmered, and are cooked with sugar and more butter to reduce the liquid to a glaze.

For 6 people

2 lbs. turnips, peeled and quartered (7 to 8 cups)	Blanch the turnips for 3 to 5 minutes in boiling salted water to cover. Drain, and dry them in a towel.
A 10- to 12-inch enameled skillet 2 Tb butter and 2 Tb oil, or 4 Tb rendered fresh pork or goose fat 1 to 1½ cups stock or canned beef bouillon 2 Tb butter 3 Tb granulated sugar	Sauté the turnips in hot butter and oil, or in fat, for 3 to 4 minutes to brown them lightly. Pour in enough stock or bouillon barely to cover them. Add the butter and sugar. Cover and boil slowly for 20 to 30 minutes or until the turnips are tender but retain their shape. Correct seasoning.
	(✳) When cooked in advance, set aside uncovered. Before serving, add a tablespoon of water, if necessary, and reheat in covered saucepan.
A hot vegetable dish 2 Tb very finely minced parsley	If the liquid has not reduced to a syrupy glaze, uncover and boil it down rapidly. Gently toss the turnips to coat them with the glaze. Turn them into a hot vegetable dish or heap them around your roast, and sprinkle with parsley.

NAVETS À LA CHAMPENOISE

[Turnip Casserole]

People who disdain the turnip almost invariably revise their opinion after tasting this dish. It goes admirably with roast pork, beef, duck, goose, turkey, ham, or grilled sausages. (Yellow turnips or rutabagas do well here.)

For 6 to 8 people

2½ lbs. turnips, peeled and cut into quarters (8 to 9 cups)	Blanch the turnips for 3 to 5 minutes in boiling salted water to cover. Drain.

A ¼-lb. chunk of bacon	Remove the rind and cut the bacon into ¼-inch dice, making about ⅔ cup. Simmer for 10 minutes in a quart of water. Drain.
A 3-quart, fireproof casserole about 2 inches deep 1 Tb butter ⅔ cup finely diced onions	Sauté the bacon in the butter for several minutes until very lightly browned. Stir in the onions, cover, and cook slowly for 5 minutes without browning the onions.
1 Tb flour	Blend in the flour and cook slowly for 2 minutes.
¾ cup stock or canned beef bouillon ¼ tsp sugar Salt and pepper ¼ tsp sage	Off heat, blend in the stock or bouillon, seasonings to taste, and the sage. Simmer for a moment, then fold in the turnips. Cover and simmer slowly for 20 to 30 minutes or until the turnips are tender. If sauce is too liquid, uncover and boil slowly for several minutes until it has reduced and thickened. Correct seasoning. (*) May be cooked several hours in advance and reheated later.
2 Tb minced parsley	Sprinkle with parsley and serve.

BRAISED VEGETABLES
Légumes Braisées

LETTUCE, CELERY, ENDIVE, AND LEEKS
Laitues, Céleris, Endives, et Poireaux

The braising of lettuce, celery, endive, or leeks requires a relatively long, slow cooking, usually of an hour and a half or more, before the desired interchange of flavors between the vegetable and its braising medium can take place. It is this culinary osmosis which gives them the delicious flavor they should always have. Any one of these vegetables may be braised, set aside uncovered to cool, then covered and reheated several hours or even a day later.

LAITUES BRAISÉES

[Braised Lettuce]

Plain boiled lettuce is dreadfully uninteresting, but lettuce braised slowly in stock and herbs is a marvelous dish. It goes well with roast veal, roast beef, and roast chicken. It can also be combined with other vegetables such as grilled tomatoes and sautéed potatoes to garnish a meat platter.

Boston lettuce, chicory, and escarole are all equally good for braising. Count on one 6- to 8-inch head per person.

For 6 people

6 heads of lettuce, 6 to 8 inches in diameter	Trim the stems of the lettuce and remove wilted leaves. Two at a time, hold each head by its stem and plunge up and down gently in cold water to remove all traces of sand.
A large kettle containing 7 to 8 quarts of boiling water **1½ tsp salt per quart of water** **Salt and pepper**	Plunge three of the heads in the boiling salted water. Bring rapidly back to the boil and boil slowly, uncovered, for 3 to 5 minutes until the heads have wilted. Remove and plunge for 2 to 3 minutes in a large basin of cold water. Repeat with the remaining lettuce. A head at a time, squeeze gently but firmly in both hands to eliminate as much water as you can. Slice each head in half lengthwise. Sprinkle with salt and pepper. Fold in half crosswise and shape with your hands to make fat triangles.
	Preheat oven to 350 degrees.
6 thick slices of bacon **A 4-inch square of bacon rind**	Simmer the bacon and rind in a quart of water for 10 minutes. Drain, rinse in cold water, and dry.
A 12-inch, fireproof, covered casserole **½ cup sliced onions** **½ cup sliced carrots** **3 Tb butter**	In the casserole cook the onions and carrots slowly with the butter until tender but not browned. Push them to the sides of the casserole and arrange the lettuce triangles in the bottom, closely pressed against each other. Spread part of the vegetables over the lettuce, then the bacon and bacon rind.
About 2 cups good beef stock or canned beef bouillon, plus, if you wish, ½ cup dry white wine or dry white vermouth **A medium herb bouquet: 4 parsley sprigs, ¼ tsp**	Pour in enough liquid barely to cover the lettuce. Add the herb bouquet. Bring to the simmer on top of the stove. Place the buttered paper over the lettuce, cover the casserole, and set in lower third of preheated oven. Regulate heat so lettuce simmers slowly for 1½ hours.

thyme, and ½ bay leaf
tied in cheesecloth
A round of buttered paper

A lightly buttered serving
dish

Remove the lettuce to the serving dish and keep it warm. Quickly boil down the braising liquid until it has reduced to a syrup (about ½ cup).

2 Tb butter
2 to 3 Tb minced parsley

Off heat, swirl the butter into the sauce, then strain it over the lettuce, sprinkle with parsley and serve.
(*) If done in advance, do not sauce the lettuce until the last moment. Boil down the braising liquid and strain it into a saucepan. Reheat the lettuce by covering with buttered foil and setting it for about 15 minutes in a 350-degree oven. Just before serving, butter the sauce and pour it over the lettuce.

CÉLERIS BRAISÉS

[Braised Celery]

Except for slight differences at the beginning and at the end, celery is braised in the same way as lettuce, so we shall not give it a full recipe. Serve braised celery with chops, steaks, roast beef, turkey, goose, duck, pork, or lamb.

For 6 people

6 bunches of tender, practically stringless celery about 2 inches in diameter
A kettle containing 7 to 8 quarts boiling water
1½ tsp salt per quart of water
White string

Trim the roots, and cut off the tops to make each celery bunch 6 to 7 inches long. Wash thoroughly, using warm water if necessary: spread the stalks apart gently while running water all the way down to the root to remove all grit. Drop into the boiling, salted water and boil slowly for 15 minutes. Drain. Plunge for 2 to 3 minutes in a basin of cold water. Drain, and gently extract as much water as possible by pressing each bunch in a towel. Tie each with 2 or 3 loops of white string to keep the stalks in place while braising.

The same ingredients as for braised lettuce (preceding recipe)
A lightly buttered baking or serving dish

Following the method for the preceding braised lettuce, arrange the celery in a casserole or baking dish large enough to hold it in one layer. Cover with blanched bacon strips and cooked vegetables. Add the wine and enough stock just to cover the celery. Season lightly and add the herb bouquet. Cover, bring to the simmer, and bake for 1½ hours in a 350-degree oven. Then uncover the casserole, raise oven heat to 400 degrees, and bake 30 minutes more, basting 2 or 3 times, until the celery has browned lightly. Drain the celery, remove strings, cut bunches in half lengthwise, and arrange in dish. Cover and keep warm if to be served immediately.

---

1 Tb arrowroot (or potato starch or cornstarch) blended with 2 Tb Madeira, port, stock, or bouillon

Strain the braising liquid into a saucepan and boil it down rapidly until it has reduced to 1 cup. Off heat, beat in the starch mixture. Simmer for 3 to 4 minutes. Correct seasoning.

---

2 Tb softened butter
2 Tb minced parsley

Off heat and just before serving, beat the butter into the sauce. Pour it over the hot celery and sprinkle with parsley.

(*) May be cooked ahead; see preceding recipe for braised lettuce.

VARIATION

Cold Braised Celery

Degrease the braising liquid thoroughly before you reduce it. Omit the starch and the enrichment butter.

CÉLERI-RAVE BRAISÉ

[Braised Celeriac—Celery Root]

Celeriac, a delicious winter vegetable, is not nearly as common in American markets as it should be. Besides braising it in stock as in the following recipe, you may treat it exactly like the turnips on page 486, cooking it slowly in a small amount of liquid, butter, and seasonings, and serving it with butter and parsley, or puréed with mashed potatoes. Celeriac may accompany roast goose, duck, pork, ham, or turkey.

For 6 people

---

2 lbs. celeriac

Peel the celeriac and cut it into slices ½ inch thick; you will have 7 to 8 cups. Drop it into a saucepan with boiling salted water to cover, and boil slowly for 5 minutes. Drain.

Preheat oven to 350 degrees.

A ¼-lb chunk of bacon, rind removed

Cut the bacon into ¼-inch dice; you will have about ⅔ cup. Simmer 10 minutes in a quart of water. Drain.

⅔ cup minced onions
1 Tb butter
A 3-quart, fireproof casserole
1 to 1½ cups brown stock or canned beef bouillon
Optional: ½ cup dry white wine or dry white vermouth in place of ½ cup stock
Salt and pepper

Cook the onions, and bacon in butter slowly in the casserole for 10 minutes without browning. Arrange the celeriac in the casserole and spread the onions and bacon over it. Pour in enough liquid barely to cover the celeriac. Season lightly.

A round of buttered aluminum foil
A bulb baster
2 Tb minced parsley

Bring to the simmer on top of the stove. Cover loosely with the foil. Set in upper third of preheated oven and bake for about 1 hour, basting 2 or 3 times with a bulb baster. The celeriac is done when it is very tender, has browned lightly, and the liquid has almost evaporated. Serve sprinkled with parsley.

---

* *ENDIVES À LA FLAMANDE*

[Braised Belgian Endive]

It is too bad Belgian endive is so expensive in this country, as it is one of the better winter vegetables. The plain butter-braise is, in our opinion, the most delicious way of cooking endive. It emerges a beautiful light golden color and its characteristic flavor is enhanced by its slow absorption of the butter. Endive goes particularly well with veal.

For 6 people

Preheat oven to 325 degrees.

---

12 firm, medium-sized endives with tightly closed leaves

Trim the base of the endives. Discard any withered leaves. Wash one by one rapidly under running cold water. Drain.

5 Tb butter

A 2½- to 3-quart enameled
  casserole

¼ tsp salt

1 Tb lemon juice

¼ cup water

Smear 1½ tablespoons butter in the casserole. Lay the endives in it in two layers. Sprinkle each layer with salt and lemon juice, and dot with butter. Pour in the water. Cover and boil slowly for 10 minutes. Uncover and boil rapidly for about 10 minutes or until liquid is reduced to 2 or 3 tablespoons.

A round of buttered paper
EITHER:
  2 Tb minced parsley
  A hot vegetable dish
OR:
  A shallow baking dish
  2 Tb melted butter
  2 Tb minced parsley

Lay the paper over the endives, cover the casserole, and bake in middle level of preheated oven for 1 hour. Remove casserole cover but leave paper in place, and bake 30 minutes more or until endives are a nice golden yellow. *Either* arrange the endives in a hot vegetable dish or around your roast, and sprinkle with parsley, *or,* for a more golden effect, arrange them in a baking dish, baste with melted butter, and brown briefly under the broiler. Sprinkle with parsley just before serving.

VARIATION

Endives Gratinées

[Endives Gratinéed with Cheese]

Butter-braised endives are also good when sauced and browned under the broiler. For a main-course dish, wrap each endive in a thin slice of boiled ham before saucing. See also the *quiche aux endives* on page 152, and the *gratin d'endives* on page 156.

For 6 people

2 cups *sauce crème* or
  sauce mornay (béchamel
  with cream, page 59, or
  with cheese, page 61)

A shallow, lightly buttered
  baking dish

12 endives butter-braised as
  in the preceding recipe

2 to 3 Tb grated Swiss
  cheese

1 Tb butter cut into pea-
  sized dots

Spread a third of the sauce in the baking dish. Arrange the braised endives over it, and pour the rest of the sauce over them. Sprinkle with cheese and dot with butter.

Shortly before serving, set under a moderately hot broiler to reheat thoroughly and brown the cheese lightly.

---

* *POIREAUX BRAISÉS AU BEURRE*

[Braised Leeks]

Braised leeks are a fine accompaniment to roast beef, steaks, or turkey.
For 6 people

12 fine fresh leeks about 1½ inches in diameter A covered, fireproof casserole or baking dish, square or oval, and long enough to hold the trimmed leeks 3 to 4 cups water 6 Tb butter ½ Tb salt	Trim off the roots, remove any withered leaves, and slit the green part of the leeks lengthwise two ways. Wash thoroughly under running water, spreading leaves apart. Cut off a portion of the green tops to leave the leeks about 7 inches long. Lay the leeks in the casserole, making 2 or 3 layers. Pour in enough water to come two thirds the way up the layers of leeks. Add the butter and salt.
	Set over high heat and bring to the boil. Partially cover, leaving a $\frac{1}{16}$-inch space to allow steam to escape, and maintain liquid at a fairly fast boil. As leeks soften, water will just cover them. In 30 to 40 minutes, the white part of the leeks should be tender when pierced with a knife, and the liquid should have almost evaporated.
A shallow, fireproof baking and serving dish	Transfer the leeks to the baking dish, and pour the remaining cooking juices over them.
Aluminum foil 2 to 3 Tb chopped parsley	Half an hour before serving, cover loosely with aluminum foil and set in the middle level of a preheated, 325-degree oven for 20 to 30 minutes or until the leeks have taken on a light golden color. Sprinkle with parsley and serve. (*) After their baking, the leeks may be set aside uncovered, and reheated later.

VARIATIONS

Poireaux Gratinés au Fromage

[Leeks Browned with Cheese]

The preceding braised leeks	After the braised leeks have browned lightly in the
½ cup grated Swiss, or	oven, sprinkle them with the cheese or cheese and
Swiss and Parmesan	bread crumbs. Pour the butter over them. Run for 2
cheese, or mixture of	to 3 minutes under a moderately hot broiler to brown
cheese and bread crumbs	the cheese lightly.
3 Tb melted butter	

Poireaux à la Mornay, Gratinés

[Leeks Browned with Cheese Sauce]

The braised leeks in the pre-	After the braised leeks have browned very lightly in
ceding master recipe	the oven, pour the *sauce mornay* over them, sprinkle
2½ cups *sauce mornay*	on the cheese, dot with the butter. Run under a
béchamel with cheese),	moderately hot broiler for 2 to 3 minutes to brown
page 61	the top of the sauce lightly.
¼ cup grated Swiss cheese	
1 Tb butter cut into pea-	
sized dots	

RED CABBAGE AND SAUERKRAUT
Chou Rouge et Choucroute

Both braised red cabbage and braised sauerkraut need 4 to 5 hours of slow cooking for them to develop their full flavor. Once they have been set in the oven they need little or no attention, and are even better when cooked in advance and reheated the next day.

CHOU ROUGE À LA LIMOUSINE

[Braised Red Cabbage with Red Wine and Chestnuts]

Red cabbage braised in this fashion is a fine dish to serve with roast goose, duck, pork, venison, or wild boar. Or you may cook the meat in the casserole with the cabbage, see the recipe for duck on page 280. All red vegetables must cook with something acid to retain their color; thus the tart apples and red wine in the following recipe.

For 6 people

	Preheat oven to 325 degrees.
A ¼-lb. chunk of bacon	Remove the rind and cut the bacon into *lardons,* strips 1½ inches long and ¼ inch across. You will have about ⅔ cup. Simmer for 10 minutes in 1 quart of water. Drain.
½ cup thinly sliced carrots 1 cup sliced onions 3 Tb rendered fresh goose or pork fat, or butter A 5- to 6-quart, covered, fireproof casserole	Cook the bacon, carrots, and onions, in fat or butter slowly in the covered casserole for 10 minutes without browning.
2 lbs. (6 to 7 cups) red cabbage leaves cut into ½-inch slices	Stir in the cabbage leaves and when well covered with the fat and vegetables, cover and cook slowly for 10 minutes.
2 cups diced tart apples 2 cloves mashed garlic ¼ tsp ground bay leaf ⅛ tsp clove ⅛ tsp nutmeg ½ tsp salt ⅛ tsp pepper 2 cups good, young red wine (Bordeaux, Mâcon, or Chianti) 2 cups brown stock or canned beef bouillon	Stir in all the ingredients listed at the left. Bring to the simmer on top of the stove. Cover and place in middle level of preheated oven. Regulate heat so cabbage bubbles slowly for 3 to 3½ hours.
24 peeled chestnuts, page 518 Salt and pepper	Add the chestnuts to the cabbage, cover and return casserole to oven for 1 to 1½ hours more, or until the chestnuts are tender and all the liquid in the casserole has been absorbed by the cabbage. Taste carefully for seasoning, and serve as follows: (*) If not served immediately, set aside uncovered. Reheat slowly before serving.

4 or 5 sprigs of parsley A hot vegetable dish	Turn into a vegetable dish or heap around your meat, and decorate with parsley.

CHOUCROUTE BRAISÉE À L'ALSACIENNE
[Braised Sauerkraut]

In France before sauerkraut is braised with wine, stock, aromatic vegetables, and spices, it is always drained and soaked in cold water for 15 to 20 minutes to remove all but a suggestion of its preserving brine. If you have never cared much for the sour flavor of most sauerkraut dishes, this recipe may well change you into an enthusiast. Sauerkraut makes a most savory accompaniment to duck, goose, pheasant, pork, ham, or sausages any of which may even cook along with the sauerkraut and give it that much more flavor.

For 6 people

2 lbs. (about 5 cups) fresh sauerkraut (canned raw sauerkraut may be used, but it is never as good as the fresh)	Drain the sauerkraut (either fresh or canned) and soak it in a large basin of cold water for 15 to 20 minutes or more, changing the water three times. Taste the sauerkraut, and when as much of the briny flavor as you wish has been removed, drain it. Taking it by small handfuls, squeeze out as much water as you can. Pick it apart to separate the strands.
A ½-lb. chunk of bacon	Remove the rind and slice the bacon into ½-inch pieces about 2 inches long. Simmer it in 2 quarts of water for 10 minutes. Drain.
	Preheat oven to 325 degrees.
½ cup thinly sliced carrots 1 cup sliced onions 4 Tb rendered fresh goose or pork fat, or butter A 2½- to 3-quart, covered, fireproof casserole	Cook the bacon, carrots, and onions, in fat or butter slowly in the covered casserole for 10 minutes without browning. Stir in the sauerkraut and when it is well covered with the fat and vegetables, cover and cook slowly for 10 minutes more.
The following tied in washed cheesecloth: 4 sprigs of parsley 1 bay leaf 6 peppercorns	Bury the herb and spice packet in the sauerkraut. Pour in the wine, and enough stock or bouillon just to cover the sauerkraut. Season lightly with salt. Bring to the simmer on top of the stove. Lay on the round of buttered paper. Cover and set in middle

10 juniper berries (or add
¼ cup gin to the casse-
role)
1 cup dry white wine or ⅔
cup dry white vermouth
2 to 3 cups white stock,
brown stock, or canned
beef or chicken bouillon
Salt
A round of buttered paper

level of preheated oven. Regulate heat so sauerkraut bubbles slowly for 4½ to 5 hours, and until all the liquid has been absorbed by the sauerkraut. Taste carefully for seasoning.

(*) If not served immediately, set aside uncovered. Reheat slowly before serving.

TO SERVE

Choucroute Garnie

[Sauerkraut Garnished with Meat]

Braised sauerkraut may be used as a bed for sliced roast pork, pork chops, ham, or browned sausages, or with roast goose, duck, or pheasant. The dish is usually accompanied with boiled potatoes and either a chilled Alsatian wine such as Riesling or Traminer, a white domestic wine of the same type, or beer.

If you wish to cook your meats in the sauerkraut, brown them first in a skillet in hot fat; then bury them in the casserole while the sauerkraut is braising, timing the meats so they and the sauerkraut will be done together. See the recipe for duck braised in sauerkraut on page 280.

CUCUMBERS

Concombres

* CONCOMBRES AU BEURRE

[Baked Cucumbers]

If the natural moisture content is not withdrawn beforehand, cucumbers exude so much water as they are heated that you usually end up with a tasteless mush and swear never to attempt cooked cucumbers again. Blanching for 5 minutes before cooking will remove unwanted water, but also most of the cucumber flavor. A preliminary sojourn in salt draws out the water and also the bitterness, if they are of the bitter European type, yet leaves the flavor, which a little vinegar and a pinch of sugar accentuates. We have found the following method delicious, and suggest it for all cooked cucumber recipes. Baked cucumbers go with roast, broiled, or sautéed chicken, roast veal, veal chops or scallops, and sautéed brains or sweetbreads.

For 6 people

6 cucumbers about 8 inches long	Peel the cucumbers. Cut in half lengthwise; scoop out the seeds with a spoon. Cut into lengthwise strips about ⅜ inch wide. Cut the strips into 2-inch pieces.
2 Tb wine vinegar **1½ tsp salt** **⅛ tsp sugar** **A 2½-quart porcelain or stainless steel bowl**	Toss the cucumbers in a bowl with the vinegar, salt, and sugar. Let stand for at least 30 minutes or for several hours. Drain. Pat dry in a towel.
	Preheat oven to 375 degrees.
A baking dish 12 inches in diameter and 1½ inches deep **3 Tb melted butter** **½ tsp dill or basil** **3 to 4 Tb minced green onions** **⅛ tsp pepper**	Toss the cucumbers in the baking dish with the butter, herbs, onions, and pepper. Set uncovered in middle level of preheated oven for about 1 hour, tossing 2 or 3 times, until cucumbers are tender but still have a suggestion of crispness and texture. They will barely color during the cooking. (*) Set aside uncovered; reheat before serving as in the following suggestions.

TO SERVE

Concombres Persillés

[Parslied Cucumbers]

A hot vegetable dish **2 Tb minced parsley**	Turn the baked cucumbers into the vegetable dish, sprinkle with minced parsley, and serve.

Concombres à la Crème

[Creamed Cucumbers]

1 cup whipping cream **Salt and pepper** **1 Tb minced parsley**	Boil the cream in a small saucepan until it has reduced by half. Season with salt and pepper, fold into the hot, baked cucumbers, sprinkle with parsley, and serve.

Concombres aux Champignons et à la Crème

[Creamed Cucumbers with Mushrooms]

½ lb. fresh mushrooms
An enameled skillet
1 cup whipping cream
1 tsp cornstarch mixed with
     1 tsp water
Salt and pepper to taste
2 Tb minced parsley

Trim, wash, and quarter the mushrooms. Dry in a towel. Set them in the dry skillet and toss over moderately low heat for 5 minutes. Pour in the cream and cornstarch mixture; boil slowly for 5 minutes or so, until cream has reduced and thickened. Stir in salt and pepper, simmer a moment and check seasoning. Fold into the hot baked cucumbers, sprinkle with parsley, and serve.

Concombres à la Mornay

[Cucumbers with Cheese Sauce]

1½ cups *sauce mornay*
     (béchamel with grated
     cheese), page 61
2 to 3 Tb grated Swiss
     cheese
1 Tb butter cut into pea-
     sized dots

Fold the cheese sauce into the hot, baked cucumbers. Sprinkle with cheese, dot with butter, and run under a hot broiler for 2 to 3 minutes to brown top delicately.

EGGPLANT

Aubergines

Eggplants, like cucumbers, contain a considerable amount of water which must be removed before cooking; in their raw state they also have a bitter, puckery quality. The most satisfactory way to remove both moisture and bitterness yet retain flavor is to let them stand in salt for about half an hour.

AUBERGINES FARCIES DUXELLES

[Eggplant Stuffed with Mushrooms]

This excellent eggplant dish goes with roast lamb, lamb chops, or roast, sautéed, or broiled chicken. Or it may be a separate vegetable course. Preparation is somewhat long, as it is for many good things, but you may have the dish ready for the oven several hours or even the day before baking it.

For 6 people—12, if the eggplants are divided as they are served

3 eggplants about 6 inches long and 3 inches in diameter	Remove the green stem covering and cut the eggplants in half lengthwise. Cut striations an inch apart in the flesh, going down to within ¼ inch of the skin. Preheat broiler in time for paragraph three.
1 Tb salt 2 Tb olive oil	Sprinkle the flesh with salt and lay the eggplants flesh down on a towel for half an hour. Gently squeeze them to extract as much water as possible. Dry them, then dribble the oil over them.
A shallow roasting pan large large enough to hold eggplant halves in one layer	Place them flesh-side up in a roasting pan and pour ⅛ inch of water around them. Set them so their flesh is 4 to 5 inches from preheated, moderately hot broiler for 10 to 15 minutes, until tender, and lightly browned on top.
A 3-quart mixing bowl	Leaving the skin intact, remove all but ¼ inch of the eggplant meat with a spoon. Chop it and place it in a mixing bowl. NOTE: In the following stuffing, you may, if you wish, substitute for part of the mushrooms 1 cup of rice steamed in butter, page 531.
1 cup finely minced yellow onions 1½ Tb olive oil or butter A 9- to 10-inch enameled skillet Salt and pepper	Cook the onions slowly in the oil or butter in a skillet for about 10 minutes until very tender but not browned. Season lightly and add to the eggplant in the mixing bowl.
1 lb. finely minced fresh mushrooms 3 Tb butter 1 Tb olive oil Salt and pepper	Following the recipe for mushroom *duxelles* on page 515, twist the mushrooms, a handful at a time, in the corner of a towel to extract their juice. Sauté them in butter and oil until very lightly browned (5 to 6 minutes). Season and add to the mixing bowl.
1½ packages (4½ ounces) cream cheese 4 Tb minced parsley ½ tsp basil or ¼ tsp thyme	Mash the cheese with a fork, then beat it into the mixing bowl. Beat in the herbs, and taste carefully for seasoning.

Preheat oven to 375 degrees.

3 Tb grated Swiss cheese mixed with 3 Tb fine, dry, white bread crumbs 2 to 3 Tb melted butter	Fill the eggplant shells with the mixture. Top with cheese and bread crumbs, and baste each half with melted butter. (*) May be prepared ahead to this point.

About 40 minutes before serving, arrange in roasting pan and surround with ⅛ inch of water. Bake in upper third of preheated oven for 25 to 30 minutes to heat thoroughly and brown the cheese and bread crumbs.

RATATOUILLE

[Eggplant Casserole—with tomatoes, onions, peppers, and zucchini]

Ratatouille perfumes the kitchen with the essence of Provence and is certainly one of the great Mediterranean dishes. As it is strongly flavored it is best when it accompanies plain roast or broiled beef or lamb, *pot-au-feu* (boiled beef), or plain roast, broiled, or sautéed chicken. Equally good hot or cold, it also makes a fine accompaniment to cold meats, or may be served as a cold hors d'oeuvre.

A really good *ratatouille* is not one of the quicker dishes to make, as each element is cooked separately before it is arranged in the casserole to partake of a brief communal simmer. This recipe is the only one we know of which produces a *ratatouille* in which each vegetable retains its own shape and character. Happily a *ratatouille* may be cooked completely the day before it is to be served, and it seems to gain in flavor when reheated.

For 6 to 8 people

1 lb. eggplant 1 lb. zucchini A 3-quart, porcelain or stainless steel mixing bowl 1 tsp salt	Peel the eggplant and cut into lengthwise slices ⅜ inch thick, about 3 inches long, and 1 inch wide. Scrub the zucchini, slice off the two ends, and cut the zucchini into slices about the same size as the eggplant slices. Place the vegetables in a bowl and toss with the salt. Let stand for 30 minutes. Drain. Dry each slice in a towel.

A 10- to 12-inch enameled skillet 4 Tb olive oil, more if needed	One layer at a time, sauté the eggplant, and then the zucchini in hot olive oil for about a minute on each side to brown very lightly. Remove to a side dish.
½ lb. (about 1½ cups) thinly sliced yellow onions 2 (about 1 cup) sliced green bell peppers 2 to 3 Tb olive oil, if necessary 2 cloves mashed garlic Salt and pepper to taste	In the same skillet, cook the onions and peppers slowly in olive oil for about 10 minutes, or until tender but not browned. Stir in the garlic and season to taste.
1 lb. firm, ripe, red tomatoes, peeled, seeded, and juiced, page 505 (makes 1½ cups pulp) Salt and pepper	Slice the tomato pulp into ⅜-inch strips. Lay them over the onions and peppers. Season with salt and pepper. Cover the skillet and cook over low heat for 5 minutes, or until tomatoes have begun to render their juice. Uncover, baste the tomatoes with the juices, raise heat and boil for several minutes, until juice has almost entirely evaporated.
A 2½ quart fireproof casserole about 2½ inches deep 3 Tb minced parsley	Place a third of the tomato mixture in the bottom of the casserole and sprinkle over it 1 tablespoon of parsley. Arrange half of the eggplant and zucchini on top, then half the remaining tomatoes and parsley. Put in the rest of the eggplant and zucchini, and finish with the remaining tomatoes and parsley.
Salt and pepper	Cover the casserole and simmer over low heat for 10 minutes. Uncover, tip casserole and baste with the rendered juices. Correct seasoning, if necessary. Raise heat slightly and cook uncovered for about 15 minutes more, basting several times, until juices have evaporated leaving a spoonful or two of flavored olive oil. Be careful of your heat; do not let the vegetables scorch in the bottom of the casserole. (*) Set aside uncovered. Reheat slowly at serving time, or serve cold.

MOUSSAKA, a mold of eggplant and lamb, is in the Lamb section, page 349.

TOMATOES

Tomates

Many recipes calling for tomatoes direct that they be peeled, seeded, and juiced. This applies to tomato sauces, to the tomato *fondues* which are used in egg dishes, to various Basque or Provençal recipes, and to the diced tomato pulp which may be poached in a soup or a sauce. One pound or 4 or 5 medium tomatoes will yield about 1½ cups of pulp.

TO PEEL TOMATOES

Use firm, ripe, red tomatoes. Drop the tomatoes one or two at a time in boiling water to cover, and boil for exactly 10 seconds. Remove. Cut out the stem. Peel off the skin starting from the stem hole.

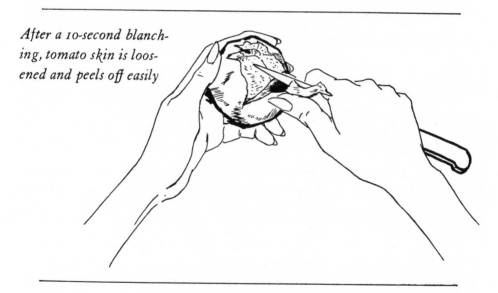

After a 10-second blanching, tomato skin is loosened and peels off easily

TO SEED AND JUICE TOMATOES
(*for illustration, see next page*)

Cut peeled or unpeeled tomatoes in half crosswise, not through the stem. Squeeze each half gently to extract the seeds and juices from the center of the tomato. If they are to receive a cold stuffing, sprinkle the interior with salt which will draw more juices out, then invert them in a colander.

*Gently press the juice and
seeds out of the tomato
half*

DICED, SLICED, OR CHOPPED TOMATO PULP

Chop, dice, or slice the peeled, seeded, and juiced tomato halves. Roughly chopped tomato pulp is *tomates concassées.*

TOMATES GRILLÉES AU FOUR

[Whole Baked Tomatoes]

These make an attractive decoration around a meat platter, or surrounding a dish of green beans. They should be baked only at the last minute if they are to retain their shape.

Preheat oven to 400 degrees.

Firm, ripe, red tomatoes, all of the same size and not more than 2 inches in diameter
Salt and pepper
Olive oil
An oiled roasting pan just large enough to hold the tomatoes easily

Wash and dry the tomatoes. Cut out the stems, leaving as small a hole as possible. Sprinkle salt and pepper into the stem hole. Brush the tomatoes with olive oil, then place them stem-end down in the roasting pan. Do not crowd them together.

Bake in the middle level of the preheated oven for about 10 minutes. Keep an eye on them; they are done when the skins break a little, but they should not be baked so long that they burst.

Salt and pepper
Minced, mixed green herbs or parsley

Baste them with the pan juices. Season lightly with salt and pepper, and sprinkle herbs or parsley over them. Serve as soon as possible.

---

* TOMATES À LA PROVENÇALE

[Tomatoes Stuffed with Bread Crumbs, Herbs, and Garlic]

One of the most savory ways of serving tomatoes is *à la provençale*. These tomatoes go well with many things—steaks, chops, roast beef, lamb, roast or broiled chicken, broiled mackerel, tuna, sardines, herring, or swordfish. They may also be a hot hors d'oeuvre, or accompany egg dishes.

For 6 people

Preheat oven to 400 degrees.

6 firm, ripe, red tomatoes about 3 inches in diameter
Salt and pepper

Remove the stems, and cut the tomatoes in half crosswise. Gently press out the juice and seeds. Sprinkle the halves lightly with salt and pepper.

1 to 2 cloves mashed garlic
3 Tb minced shallots or green onions
4 Tb minced fresh basil and parsley, or parsley only
⅛ tsp thyme
¼ tsp salt
Big pinch of pepper
¼ cup olive oil
½ cup crumbs from fresh white bread with body
A shallow, oiled roasting pan just large enough to hold the tomatoes easily in one layer

Blend all the ingredients to the left in a mixing bowl. Correct seasoning. Fill each tomato half with a spoonful or two of the mixture. Sprinkle with a few drops of olive oil. Arrange the tomatoes in the roasting pan; do not crowd them.

(*) May be prepared ahead to this point.

Shortly before you are ready to serve, place them in the upper third of the preheated oven and bake for

10 to 15 minutes, or until the tomatoes are tender but hold their shape, and the bread crumb filling has browned lightly.

VARIATION

Tomates Farcies Duxelles

[Tomatoes Stuffed with Mushrooms]

Follow the preceding recipe, but use the mushroom filling described in the recipe for stuffed mushrooms on page 516.

CULTIVATED MUSHROOMS
Champignons de Couche – Champignons de Paris

Fresh, cultivated mushrooms are an essential element of French *cuisine* and appear not only as a vegetable or in a garnish, but as an important flavor factor in numerous dishes, sauces, and stuffings. Mushrooms should never be submitted to prolonged cooking or they will lose most of their taste and texture. Therefore if they are to go into a sauce they are usually cooked separately, then added to the sauce to simmer a moment and blend their flavor with the sauce.

CHOOSING MUSHROOMS

It is always advisable to buy mushrooms in bulk rather than in a package, so you can hand-pick each one. Some varieties of cultivated mushrooms are creamy white, others have brownish caps. The freshest of fresh mushrooms are closed on the underside of the cap so that you cannot see the gills. Caps and stems should be smooth, unblemished, fresh looking, and fresh smelling. As a mushroom ages in the market, the cap expands to expose the gills, the mushroom darkens, and begins to dry out.

If you are not going to use fresh mushrooms immediately, refrigerate them in a plastic bag and they will keep perfectly for two to three days.

PREPARATION FOR COOKING

Trim the base of the stems. If the gills are even partially exposed, break the stem off inside the cap so you will be able to wash out any sand which may have lodged in the gills.

Just before using them, drop the mushrooms in a large basin of cold water. Rapidly rub them between your hands for several seconds to dislodge dirt particles. Immediately lift them out into a colander. If there are more than a few grains of sand left in the bottom of the basin, wash the mushrooms again. Dry them in a towel.

HOW TO CUT MUSHROOMS

After they have been washed and dried, here are the various ways in which mushrooms may be cut.

To mince or dice

Place the mushrooms in a heap on the chopping board. Chop them with a big, sharp, straight-edged knife, holding an end of the blade in the fingers of each hand. Use rapid up and down movements, and repeatedly brush mush-

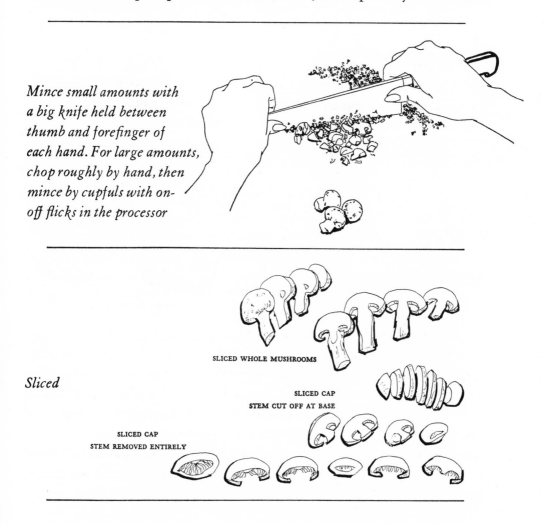

Mince small amounts with a big knife held between thumb and forefinger of each hand. For large amounts, chop roughly by hand, then mince by cupfuls with on-off flicks in the processor

SLICED WHOLE MUSHROOMS

Sliced

SLICED CAP
STEM CUT OFF AT BASE

SLICED CAP
STEM REMOVED ENTIRELY

rooms back into a heap with the knife. Chop until the pieces are less than ⅛ inch.

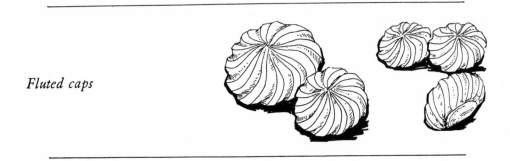

QUARTERED WHOLE
MUSHROOMS

Quartered

QUARTERED CAPS

QUARTERED STEMS

To flute mushroom caps

Fluted mushroom caps may be stewed or broiled, and are used as decorations. It takes a little practice to master the technique of fluting, but it is quite a nice professional touch to have at your command.

Fluted caps

Hold the mushroom, cap up, in the fingers of your left hand. Its blade pointing away from you, hold a very sharp, small knife rigidly in your right hand. Rest the thumb of your right hand on the mushroom cap to act as a guide. Then rotate the cap toward you against the blade of the knife starting at the crown, thus removing a very shallow strip, or flute, down one half of the cap. Note that the knife remains stationary; the mushroom cuts itself as it rotates against the blade. It is your left hand, controlling the mushroom's movement, which determines the depth and direction of the cut. Continue in the same manner all around the cap.

Starting at crown, rotate mushroom toward you against rigidly held knife blade

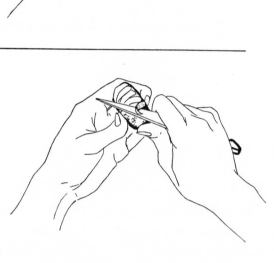

Left hand guides mushroom against knife blade and regulates cut

CHAMPIGNONS À BLANC

[Stewed Mushrooms]

When mushrooms are used in white sauces, or in a garniture in which they must remain white, they are cooked this way.

¼ lb. fresh mushrooms
⅓ cup water
⅛ tsp salt
½ Tb lemon juice (which helps keep mushrooms white)
1 Tb butter
A 4- to 6-cup enameled saucepan

Trim and wash the mushrooms; cut as directed in your recipe, or as shown in the preceding illustrations. Bring the water, salt, lemon juice, and butter to the boil in the saucepan. Add the mushrooms and toss to cover them with the liquid. Cover and boil moderately fast, tossing frequently, for 5 minutes. Set aside until ready to use.

FUMET DE CHAMPIGNONS

[Mushroom Essence]

Mushroom essence is the reduction or boiling down of the cooking juice from stewed mushrooms or canned mushrooms. It is used as a concentrated mushroom flavoring for sauces.

Drain the preceding stewed mushrooms. Rapidly boil down their cooking liquid in a small saucepan until it has reduced almost to a syrup.

(*) If not used immediately, refrigerate or freeze it.

CHAMPIGNONS GRILLÉS

[Broiled Mushroom Caps]

Broiled mushroom caps are used as a garniture, usually on steaks. They may also be served as a separate vegetable, or as a hot hors d'oeuvre on toast.

Fresh mushrooms of whatever size you wish	Preheat broiler to moderately hot. Separate the mushroom caps from the stems. Wash and dry the caps. Stems may be minced and turned into a *duxelles,* page 515.
Melted butter A shallow, buttered baking dish Salt and pepper	Paint the mushroom caps with melted butter. Arrange them hollow-side up in the baking dish. Sprinkle lightly with salt and pepper. Place 4 to 5 inches from heat, and broil rather slowly for 5 minutes. Turn the caps, and broil 5 minutes more or until the caps are tender and lightly browned.
Optional: *Beurre Maître d'Hôtel* (butter mixed with lemon juice, parsley, and seasonings), page 102 OR: *Beurre pour Escargots* (butter mixed with herbs, shallots, and garlic), page 103	The caps may then, if you wish, be filled with parsley butter into which you may also incorporate finely minced shallots with or without a bit of mashed garlic. Spread the butter in the caps, filling them by about a third.
	Just before serving, heat them for a moment or two under the broiler until the butter is bubbling.

* CHAMPIGNONS SAUTÉS AU BEURRE
[Sautéed Mushrooms]

Use these mushrooms either as a vegetable alone or in a combination with other vegetables, or as an integral part of such dishes as *coq au vin, boeuf bourguignon, poulet en cocotte.* Successfully sautéed mushrooms are lightly browned and exude none of their juice while they are being cooked; to achieve this the mushrooms must be dry, the butter very hot, and the mushrooms must not be crowded in the pan. If you sauté too many at once they steam rather than fry; their juices escape and they do not brown. So if you are preparing a large amount, or if your heat source is feeble, sauté the mushrooms in several batches.

A 10-inch enameled skillet 2 Tb butter 1 Tb oil ½ lb. fresh mushrooms, washed, well dried, left whole if small, sliced or quartered if large	Place the skillet over high heat with the butter and oil. As soon as you see that the butter foam has begun to subside, indicating it is hot enough, add the mushrooms. Toss and shake the pan for 4 to 5 minutes. During their sauté the mushrooms will at first absorb the fat. In 2 to 3 minutes the fat will reappear on their surface, and the mushrooms will begin to brown. As soon as they have browned lightly, remove from heat.
Optional: 1 to 2 Tb minced shallots or green onions Salt and pepper	Toss the shallots or green onions with the mushrooms. Sauté over moderate heat for 2 minutes. (*) Sautéed mushrooms may be cooked in advance, set aside, then reheated when needed. Season to taste just before serving.

VARIATIONS

Champignons Sautés à la Bordelaise
[Mushrooms Sautéed with Shallots, Garlic, and Herbs]

These may garnish a meat or vegetable platter.

½ lb. fresh mushrooms, whole if small, quartered if large 1 Tb oil 2 Tb butter	Sauté the mushrooms in oil and butter until lightly browned.

3 Tb minced shallots or green onions	Stir in the shallots or green onions, optional garlic, and bread crumbs, and toss over moderate heat for 2 to 3 minutes.
Optional: 1 small clove minced garlic	
3 Tb fine, white, dry bread crumbs	

Salt and pepper to taste	Just before serving, season to taste, and toss with the herbs.
3 Tb minced fresh parsley, chervil, chives, and tarragon, or parsley only	

Champignons Sautés à la Crème

[Creamed Mushrooms]

Creamed mushrooms may garnish canapés, little *vol-au-vents,* tartlet shells, artichoke bottoms, or may accompany such foods as omelettes, poached eggs, sweetbreads, or chicken.

½ lb. fresh mushrooms, whole if small, sliced, quartered, or minced if large	Sauté the mushrooms in hot butter and oil for 4 to 5 minutes, but do not allow them to brown any more than necessary. Add the shallots or onions and toss over moderate heat for 2 minutes.
2 Tb butter	
1 Tb oil	
2 Tb minced shallots or green onions	

1 tsp flour	Stir in the flour and cook slowly for 2 minutes more, stirring.

⅔ to 1 cup whipping cream	Off heat, blend in the cream and seasonings. Then boil down rapidly until the cream has reduced and thickened. Add the optional wine, and boil for a moment to evaporate its alcohol. Correct seasoning. (*) May be set aside and reheated later.
⅛ tsp salt	
Pinch of pepper	
Optional: 2 to 3 Tb Madeira	

1 to 2 Tb softened butter	Off heat and just before serving, fold in the butter.

Champignons Sautés, Sauce Madère

[Sautéed Mushrooms in Brown Madeira Sauce]

Another appetizing way of using mushrooms is in a brown Madeira sauce. You may smother a *filet mignon* with them, or fill tartlets, or combine the mushrooms with sautéed chicken livers and ham to fill a rice ring. If you do not have on hand one of the classic, flour-thickened, long simmered brown sauces, you may use a quick brown sauce made of very good bouillon thickened with arrowroot or cornstarch, as suggested in the recipe.

½ lb. mushrooms, sliced, quartered, or minced 2 Tb butter 1 Tb oil 1 Tb minced shallots or green onions	Sauté the mushrooms in butter and oil, adding minced shallots or green onions at the end. Remove to a side dish.
⅓ cup Madeira	Pour the Madeira into the sautéing skillet and boil it down rapidly until it has reduced by half.
1 cup brown sauce (the flour-thickened sauces Numbers I or II, pages 67 to 69, or the quick sauce, Number III, page 70)	Add the sauce and simmer for 2 to 3 minutes. Then stir in the sautéed mushrooms and simmer a moment more to blend flavors. Correct seasoning. (*) May be made ahead of time. Dot top of sauce with butter and set aside.
1 to 2 Tb butter	Reheat just before serving. Off heat, stir in the enrichment butter.

DUXELLES

[Mushroom *Duxelles*—Minced Mushrooms Sautéed in Butter]

Duxelles is a dry, mushroom flavoring for many kinds of stuffings and quick mushroom sauces; once made it will keep for several weeks under refrigeration or may be frozen. The juice is squeezed out of the raw minced mushroom so that the cooked *duxelles* will be as dry as possible; if the *duxelles* were wet it would dilute and soften a stuffing.

For about 1 cup

½ lb. finely minced fresh mushrooms, whole or just stems (about 2 cups)

A handful at a time, twist the mushrooms into a ball in the corner of a towel to extract as much juice as possible. (Juice may be saved to go into a sauce or soup.)

An 8-inch enameled skillet
2 Tb minced shallots or green onions
2 Tb butter
1 Tb oil

In the skillet, sauté the mushrooms and shallots or onions in butter and oil over moderately high heat, stirring frequently. After 6 to 8 minutes the mushroom pieces should begin to separate from each other and brown lightly.

Salt and pepper to taste
Optional: ¼ cup Madeira and ¼ cup brown stock or canned beef bouillon

Season to taste with salt and pepper. Add the optional wine and stock, and boil down rapidly until liquid has reduced to nothing.
(*) If not to be used immediately, allow to cool. Pack in a covered jar, and refrigerate or freeze.

CHAMPIGNONS FARCIS

[Stuffed Mushrooms]

Stuffed mushrooms make a good hot hors d'oeuvres or a garnish for a meat platter.

Preheat oven to 375 degrees.

12 fresh mushroom caps 2 to 3 inches in diameter, stems removed
2 to 3 Tb melted butter
A shallow, lightly buttered roasting pan
Salt and pepper

Brush the mushroom caps with melted butter. Place them, hollow-side up, in the roasting pan. Sprinkle lightly with salt and pepper.

3 Tb finely minced onions
2 Tb butter
1 Tb oil
3 Tb minced shallots or green onions
Stems from the mushroom caps, finely minced and squeezed in a towel to extract their juice

Sauté the onions in butter and oil for 3 to 4 minutes without browning. Then add the shallots or green onions and mushroom stems. Sauté as in the preceding *duxelles* recipe.

Optional: ¼ cup Madeira	Add the optional Madeira and boil it down rapidly until it has almost entirely evaporated.
3 Tb fine, white, dry bread crumbs ¼ cup grated Swiss cheese ¼ cup grated Parmesan cheese 4 Tb minced parsley ½ tsp tarragon Salt and pepper 2 to 3 Tb whipping cream	Off heat, mix in the bread crumbs, cheeses, parsley, tarragon, and seasonings. A spoonful at a time, blend in just enough cream to moisten the mixture but keep it sufficiently stiff to hold its shape in a spoon. Correct seasoning.
3 Tb grated Swiss cheese 2 Tb melted butter	Fill the mushroom caps with the stuffing. Top each with a pinch of cheese and drops of melted butter. (*) May be done ahead to this point.
	Bake in upper third of a preheated, 375-degree oven for 15 to 20 minutes, or until caps are tender and stuffing has browned lightly on top.

CANNED MUSHROOMS

Canned mushrooms will have more flavor in sauces or garnitures if you follow the procedure outlined here. (If they are to be browned, drain them, dry in a towel, and sauté quickly in butter and oil with minced shallots or onions.)

For 1 cup drained, canned mushrooms: 1 Tb minced shallots or green onions 2 Tb butter Salt and pepper Optional: 1 to 2 Tb port or Madeira	In a small enameled saucepan, cook the shallots or onions slowly in the butter for 2 minutes without browning. Add the mushrooms and seasonings, and toss them in the butter. Add the optional wine. Cover and cook slowly for 2 minutes. NOTE: The juice from the can may be boiled down in a saucepan until reduced to a third of its volume or less. Use as a sauce flavoring.

CHESTNUTS

Marrons

Fresh raw chestnuts are in season in the winter months. Choose heavy nuts with tight-fitting shells—indications that they are fresh and will have their maximum flavor.

SERVING SUGGESTIONS

Chestnuts have a traditional affinity for roast turkey, goose, venison, boar, wild duck, and pheasant; they also go with pork and with sausages. Chestnut purée is used as a starchy vegetable to accompany any of these meats. Whole braised chestnuts are often combined with other vegetables such as red cabbage, Brussels sprouts, mushrooms, onions, or carrots. Whole partially-cooked chestnuts go into stuffings, particularly sausage stuffings for goose and turkey.

AMOUNT TO BUY

One pound or 35 to 40 whole raw chestnuts will yield approximately 2½ cups of peeled chestnuts.

HOW TO PEEL CHESTNUTS

Chestnuts have an outside shell and a bitter inside skin, both of which must be removed before the chestnuts can be used. Peeling off the inside skin is a chore whatever method you adopt. To our mind, and we have tried them all, the following is the most satisfactory, especially if you want the chestnuts to remain whole.

With a small sharp knife, peel a ⅛-inch strip of shell off one side of each chestnut. Set chestnuts in a saucepan of cold water, bring to the boil and boil 1 minute; remove from heat. Then three at a time, with a slotted spoon, dip the chestnuts out of the water and peel off the shells and inner skins. (Set aside until later any recalcitrant chestnuts. Drop them all later into boiling water for a moment, then peel them one by one.) The whole peeling process must be a continuous operation and done while the chestnuts are still warm.

PURÉE DE MARRONS

[Chestnut Purée]
For 6 to 8 people

A 3-quart, heavy-bottomed saucepan
8 cups peeled chestnuts
2 stalks celery
A medium herb bouquet:
  4 parsley sprigs, ½ bay

Place in the saucepan the chestnuts, celery stalks, and herb bouquet. Pour in enough stock, or bouillon and water to cover the chestnuts by 1½ inches. Simmer very slowly and uncovered for 45 to 60 minutes, or until the chestnuts are cooked through. Do not overcook and allow them to become mushy. Drain im-

leaf, and ⅛ tsp thyme tied in cheesecloth

3 cups good brown stock or 2 cups canned beef bouillon and 1 cup water

A food mill

mediately; remove celery and herb bouquet. Purée the chestnuts in the food mill, then return them to the saucepan.

---

3 to 6 Tb softened butter, or butter and whipping cream

Salt and pepper

Pinch of sugar, if needed

Beat in the butter, or butter and cream. If purée is too thick, beat in spoonfuls of the cooking liquid. Season to taste with salt and pepper, and a pinch or two of sugar if you feel it necessary.

(*) If not to be used immediately, instead of beating in the butter, spread it over the surface of the purée. To reheat, cover and set over boiling water, beating occasionally.

MARRONS BRAISÉS

[Whole Braised Chestnuts]

Preheat oven to 325 degrees.

---

24 peeled chestnuts

A heavy, fireproof casserole or baking dish just large enough to hold the chestnuts in one layer

1 Tb arrowroot or cornstarch mixed to a paste with 2 Tb port, Madeira, or water

2 cups good brown stock or 1½ cups canned beef bouillon and ½ cup water

Water, if necessary

3 Tb butter

Place the chestnuts in the casserole or baking dish. Beat the starch mixture into the stock or bouillon and pour over the chestnuts. There should be enough liquid to cover them by ½ inch; add water, if necessary. Add the butter. Bring to the simmer, cover, then set in lower third of preheated oven. Regulate heat so liquid simmers very slowly for 45 to 60 minutes or until chestnuts are tender.

(*) If not to be served immediately, set aside uncovered. Cover and reheat slowly on top of stove before proceeding.

If liquid has not reduced to a syrupy glaze at the end of the cooking, drain it off and boil it down in a saucepan. Pour it back into the casserole and roll the chestnuts gently around in it to cover them with the glaze. Serve as follows:

Serve sprinkled with parsley, or combined with other vegetables as directed in whatever recipe you are using.

POTATOES
Pommes de Terre

Out of the vast store of French potato dishes, we have selected an unusual version of mashed potatoes, some excellent grated potato pancakes, a series of good regional recipes for scalloped potatoes, and one for potatoes sautéed in butter.

KIND OF POTATOES TO BUY

We shall not classify potato varieties by name. We shall merely specify baking potatoes when we mean the type of white potato such as Idaho which turns floury after cooking, and boiling potatoes when we are talking about the white potato which retains its shape. It is particularly important that you use the right kind of potato for such dishes as scalloped potatoes, for the potato must not disintegrate during cooking; in such cases we have used quotation marks in order to draw your attention to the necessity for using "boiling" potatoes.

PURÉE DE POMMES DE TERRE À L'AIL

[Garlic Mashed Potatoes]

Two whole heads of garlic will seem like a horrifying amount if you have not made this type of recipe before. But if less is used, you will regret it, for the long cooking of the garlic removes all of its harsh strength, leaving just a pleasant flavor. Garlic mashed potatoes go with roast lamb, pork, goose, or sausages. Although both garlic sauce and potatoes may be cooked in advance, they should be combined only at the last minute; the completed purée loses its nice consistency if it sits too long over heat, or if it is cooked and then reheated.

For 6 to 8 people

---

2 heads garlic, about 30 cloves	Separate the garlic cloves. Drop into boiling water, and boil 2 minutes. Drain. Peel.

A 3- to 4-cup, heavy-bot-
tomed saucepan with
cover
4 Tb butter

Cook the garlic slowly with the butter in the covered saucepan for about 20 minutes or until very tender but not browned.

2 Tb flour
1 cup boiling milk
¼ tsp salt
Pinch of pepper
A sieve and wooden spoon,
or an electric blender

Blend in the flour and stir over low heat until it froths with the butter for 2 minutes without browning. Off heat, beat in the boiling milk and seasonings. Boil, stirring, for 1 minute. Rub the sauce through a sieve or purée it in the electric blender. Simmer for 2 minutes more.

(*) May be done ahead of time. Dot top of sauce with bits of butter to keep a skin from forming. Reheat when needed.

2½ lbs. baking potatoes
A potato ricer
A 2½ quart enameled sauce-
pan
A wooden spatula or spoon
4 Tb softened butter
Salt and white pepper

Peel and quarter the potatoes. Drop in boiling salted water to cover, and boil until tender. Drain immediately and put through a potato ricer. Place the hot purée in the saucepan and beat with the spatula or spoon for several minutes over moderate heat to evaporate moisture. As soon as the purée begins to form a film in the bottom of the pan, remove from heat and beat in the butter a tablespoon at a time. Beat in salt and pepper to taste.

(*) If not used immediately, set aside uncovered. To reheat, cover and set over boiling water, beating frequently.

3 to 4 Tb whipping cream
4 Tb minced parsley
A hot, lightly buttered vegetable dish

Shortly before serving, beat the hot garlic sauce vigorously into the hot potatoes. Beat in the cream by spoonfuls but do not thin out the purée too much. Beat in the parsley. Correct seasoning. Turn into hot vegetable dish.

CRÊPES DE POMMES DE TERRE

[Grated Potato Pancakes]

These are excellent with roasts, steaks, or chops. As a bed for fried or poached eggs, they may be topped with a cheese or tomato sauce. Or roll them around a filling of mushrooms, chicken livers, or ham, top with a sauce, and brown under the broiler.

For 18 crêpes *about 3 inches in diameter, or 8* crêpes *made in individual 6-inch* crêpe *pans*

8 ounces cream cheese 3 Tb flour A 3-quart mixing bowl	Mash the cream cheese with the flour, in the mixing bowl.
2 eggs ½ tsp salt ⅛ tsp pepper	Mix in the eggs and seasonings and beat until smooth.
6 ounces (1¼ cups) Swiss cheese cut into ⅛-inch dice	Stir in the Swiss cheese.
2½ lbs. of baking potatoes (4 cups when grated) A vegetable grater	Peel the potatoes and rub them through the large holes of the grater. A small handful at a time, twist them into a ball in the corner of a towel to squeeze out as much of their water as you can. Stir the grated raw potatoes into the egg and cheese mixture.
3 to 6 Tb whipping cream Optional: ½ cup diced boiled ham, or ½ cup sautéed mushrooms, chicken livers, or onions 3 to 4 Tb fresh herbs, such as parsley, chives, chervil	Stir in the cream by spoonfuls to make a mixture the consistency of a thick, creamed cole slaw—not runny. Add optional ingredients. Taste carefully for seasoning.
A 10-inch skillet 1½ Tb butter, more as needed ½ Tb oil, more as needed A large spoon or ladle A hot platter	Set skillet over moderately high heat with the butter and oil. When you see the foam begin to subside, ladle 3 piles of batter into the skillet to form 3 *crêpes* approximately 3 inches in diameter and ⅜ inch thick. Regulate heat so *crêpes* are lightly browned on the bottom and bubble holes have appeared on the surface in about 3 minutes. Then turn and brown on the other sides for about 3 minutes. Transfer to platter

and keep warm in one layer while making the remaining *crêpes*.

(*) If not served immediately, arrange *crêpes* in one layer on a baking sheet. Set aside uncovered. Reheat for 4 to 5 minutes in a 400-degree oven.

---

* *GRATIN DAUPHINOIS*

[Scalloped Potatoes with Milk, Cheese, and a Pinch of Garlic]

There are as many "authenic" versions of *gratin dauphinois* as there are of *bouillabaisse*. Of them all, we prefer this one because it is fast, simple, and savory. It goes with roast or broiled chicken, turkey, and veal. With roast beef, pork, lamb, steaks, and chops you may prefer the *gratin savoyard* which follows, since it is cooked with stock rather than milk. Although some authorities on *le vrai gratin dauphinois* would violently disagree, you may omit the cheese. If you do so, add 2 more tablespoons of butter.

For 6 people

Preheat oven to 425 degrees.

2 lbs. "boiling" potatoes (6 to 7 cups when sliced)

Peel the potatoes and slice them ⅛ inch thick. Place in a basin of cold water. Drain when ready to use.

A fireproof baking-serving dish about 10 inches in diameter and 2 inches deep (if recipe is increased, dish must be wider but no deeper)
½ clove unpeeled garlic
4 Tb butter
1 tsp salt
⅛ tsp pepper
1 cup (4 ounces) grated Swiss cheese
1 cup boiling milk

Rub the baking dish with the cut garlic. Smear the inside of the dish with 1 tablespoon of the butter. Drain the potatoes and dry them in a towel. Spread half of them in the bottom of the dish. Divide over them half the salt, pepper, cheese, and butter. Arrange the remaining potatoes over the first layer, and season them. Spread on the rest of the cheese and divide the butter over it. Pour on the boiling milk. Set baking dish over heat and when simmering, set in upper third of preheated oven. Bake for 20 to 30 minutes or until potatoes are tender, milk has been absorbed, and the top is nicely browned. (As the oven is hot, and the dish shallow, the potatoes cook quickly.)

(*) May wait for half an hour, loosely covered, over simmering water. For a longer wait, stop initial cooking just before all milk has evaporated. Set aside uncovered. Shortly before serving, dot with 2 Tb butter, reheat on top of stove, and set in a 425-degree oven for 5 to 10 minutes to finish cooking.

VARIATIONS

Gratin Savoyard

[Scalloped Potatoes with Meat Stock and Cheese]
For 6 people

Ingredients for the preceding *gratin dauphinois* with the following exceptions:

1 cup brown stock or canned beef bouillon instead of milk

6 rather than 4 Tb butter

Follow the recipe for *gratin dauphinois,* but substitute stock for milk, and increase the butter proportions as indicated at the left.

Gratin Jurassien

[Scalloped Potatoes with Heavy Cream and Cheese]

Potatoes baked in heavy cream are mouth-watering with roast lamb or chicken, or turkey, veal, beef, or pork. An important point in this recipe is that you must never let the cream come quite to the simmer during the baking; thus it will not curdle.

For 6 people

Preheat oven to 300 degrees.

4 Tb butter

A 10-inch, fireproof dish 2 inches deep

2 lbs. "boiling" potatoes, sliced ⅛ inch thick (6 to 7 cups)

1 tsp salt

⅛ tsp pepper

1 cup grated Swiss cheese

1¼ cups whipping cream

Smear 1 tablespoon of the butter in the baking dish. Arrange layers of potatoes in it, seasoning each layer with salt, pepper, cheese, and dots of butter. End with a sprinkling of cheese and butter dots. Pour on the cream and bring slowly almost to the simmer on top of the stove. Then place in middle level of preheated oven and bake for 1 to 1¼ hours, regulating oven heat throughout baking so that cream never quite bubbles. The *gratin* is done when the potatoes are tender and have absorbed the cream, and the top is lightly browned.

Gratin de Pommes de Terre Crécy

[Scalloped Potatoes and Carrots with Cream]

This mixture of potatoes, carrots, and cream is delicious with veal or chicken. It is the same as the preceding *gratin jurassien* but the potatoes are interspersed with sliced, braised carrots prepared as follows:

2 cups carrots sliced ⅛ inch thick ½ Tb butter ¼ tsp salt 2 Tb finely minced shallots or green onions ¾ cup water A 4- to 6-cup, heavy-bottomed, enameled saucepan with cover	Boil the carrots slowly with the butter, salt, shallots or onions, and water in the covered saucepan for 20 to 30 minutes or until the liquid has evaporated and the carrots are tender. Then continue as for the preceding *gratin jurassien,* but alternate carrot slices with the potato slices.

Gratin de Pommes de Terre Provençal

[Scalloped Potatoes with Onions, Tomatoes, Anchovies, Herbs, and Garlic]

This casserole with its full-bodied Mediterranean flavor goes with roast lamb or beef, steaks, chops, or grilled mackerel, tuna, or swordfish. It is also good served cold. The potatoes need no other liquid than that rendered by the tomatoes as they cook together.

For 6 people

Preheat oven to 400 degrees.

2 cups thinly sliced onions 2 Tb olive oil A small saucepan 1½ lbs. tomatoes, peeled, seeded, and juiced, page 505 (4 to 5 tomatoes, 2¼ cups pulp) ¼ tsp salt	Cook the onions and olive oil slowly together in the saucepan until the onions are tender but not browned. Cut the tomato pulp into strips ⅜ inch wide. Fold the tomatoes and salt into the onions. Set aside.

6 canned anchovies packed in olive oil, drained

2 cloves mashed garlic

¼ tsp basil

¼ tsp thyme

⅛ tsp pepper

2 Tb olive oil (include as part of this the oil from the anchovy can)

In a small mixing bowl, mash the anchovies into a paste with the garlic, herbs, pepper, and oil.

An oiled baking dish about 10 inches in diameter and 2 inches deep

2 lbs. "boiling" potatoes sliced ⅛ inch thick (6 to 7 cups)

¼ cup grated Parmesan or Swiss cheese

1 tsp olive oil

Spread one quarter of the tomatoes and onions in the baking dish. Over them arrange half the potato slices, then half the anchovy mixture, then half the remaining tomatoes and onions. Spread over this the rest of the potatoes and the anchovy mixture; top with the last of the tomatoes and onions. Spread on the cheese, and sprinkle with olive oil.

Aluminum foil, if necessary

Place in middle level of preheated oven and bake for about 40 minutes, or until potatoes are tender and have absorbed all of the juice from the tomatoes. If the top browns too much during cooking, cover very loosely with a sheet of foil.

(*) Keep warm or reheat as for the *gratin dauphinois*, page 523.

---

* *POMMES DE TERRE SAUTÉES*
POMMES DE TERRE POUR GARNITURE
POMMES DE TERRE CHÂTEAU

[Potatoes Sautéed in Butter]

Although we rationed ourselves strictly on potato recipes, potatoes sautéed in butter appear as a garnishing suggestion in so many of the main-course dishes that we are including directions for doing them. The following recipe demands that the potatoes be sautéed raw, which produces a delectable result. But the cooking is rather exacting as raw potatoes will stick to the sautéing pan unless certain precautions are taken.

If you were living in France, you would buy smooth oval potatoes 2 to 2½ inches long, with yellowish flesh, *pommes de terre de Hollande.* You would peel them neatly, and sauté them whole. Elsewhere, choose small boiling potatoes or new potatoes. Peel them, and cut them into elongated olive shapes all the same size, 2 to 2½ inches long and 1 to 1¼ inches at their widest diameter. Cut them smoothly, so they will roll around easily and color evenly when they are sautéed. (You might save the cuttings for the good leek and potato soup, page 37.) Do not wash the potatoes; simply pat them thoroughly dry in a towel. If you peel them some time in advance of their cooking, roll them in a damp towel; dry them in a fresh towel just before sautéing.

For 4 to 6 people

2 lbs. (5 to 6 cups) "boiling" potatoes or new potatoes	Cut the potatoes according to the directions in the preceding paragraph. Remember they are not to be washed, merely well dried in a towel.
3 to 4 Tb clarified butter, page 15, or 2 Tb butter and 1 Tb oil, more if needed A 10- or 11-inch heavy skillet large enough to hold all the potatoes easily in one layer	Add enough clarified butter or the butter and oil to the skillet to film it by 1/16 inch and set over moderately high heat. When the clarified butter is very hot but not coloring, or when the butter foam in the butter and oil mixture begins to subside, put the potatoes into the skillet. Leave them for 2 minutes, regulating heat so butter is always very hot but not coloring. Then shake the skillet back and forth to roll the potatoes and to sear them on another side for 2 minutes. Continue thus for 4 to 5 minutes more until the potatoes are a pale golden color all over, indicating that a seared, protective film has formed over them, so that they will not stick to the pan.
¼ tsp salt	Then sprinkle the potatoes with salt and roll them again in the skillet.
A heavy, close-fitting lid for the skillet	Lower heat, cover the skillet, and cook the potatoes for about 15 minutes, shaking them every 3 to 4 minutes to prevent their sticking to the skillet, and to insure an even coloring.
	They are done when they yield slightly to the pressure of your finger, or when a knife pierces them easily;

they should be a nice, fairly even, golden brown color. Hold the cover slightly askew over the skillet, and pour out the sautéing fat.

(*) If not to be used immediately, set cover askew to allow for air circulation, and place skillet on an asbestos mat over very low heat. The potatoes can be kept thus for about half an hour. Reheat just to sizzling hot before serving.

---

2 to 3 Tb softened butter
2 to 3 Tb minced parsley, chives, or fresh tarragon, or a mixture of fresh green herbs
Big pinch of pepper
A hot vegetable dish

Then off heat, add the butter and herbs, sprinkle on the pepper, and roll the potatoes in the skillet so they glisten with herbs and butter. Arrange the potatoes around your meat platter, or turn them into a vegetable dish.

VARIATIONS

Pommes de Terre Parisiennes

[Potato Balls Sautéed in Butter]

Pommes de Terre Sautées en Dés

[Diced Potatoes Sautéed in Butter]

Use exactly the same system as that in the preceding recipe, but form the raw potatoes into balls with a potato-ball cutter, or cut them into ¼-inch dice.

RICE

Riz

Whatever method you use for rice the grains should emerge whole, tender, and separate. Although raw rice is not difficult to cook, many people are so afraid of it they dare to attempt only the precooked or parboiled varieties, thus limiting their scope of rice dishes and denying their skill as good cooks. Two factors contribute to the gumminess of badly cooked rice. One is overcooking. The other is failure to deal with the floury coating which clings to raw rice and becomes sticky and gluey unless the rice is washed or sautéed in butter or oil.

TYPES OF RICE

Although more than 40,000 varieties of rice exist, only a few of them are available commercially. *Long grain rice* is the one that cooks up the fluffiest for plain boiled or steamed rice, *risottos,* and salads. *Medium grain rice* is shorter and tenderer, good for puddings. *Short grain* and *glutinous rice,* which vary from rather sticky to very sticky indeed, are used mostly by Oriental cooks and commercial gravy makers. Remarks on parboiled and precooked as well as wild rice are on pages 534–5.

ENRICHED RICE

This means that certain minerals and vitamins have been added to replace those lost during milling. Since the enrichment is on the surface of the grains, it is soluble, and that means (unless you do not want the enrichments!) you should neither wash rice before cooking nor rinse it afterward. Most states now have laws that rice must be enriched—your box or package will so indicate. It seems to us that enriched rice cooks faster by 2 to 3 minutes than un-enriched rice. In other words, whereas it used to take 18 minutes for the cooking of braised rice or *risotto,* it now takes about 15 minutes.

AMOUNT TO BUY

One cup of raw rice makes about 3 cups of cooked rice, or enough for 4 to 6 people.

WARNING

Never stir cooked rice with anything but a wooden fork or chopsticks; lift and fluff the rice, being careful not to mash or break the grains.

---

* *RIZ À L'INDIENNE–RIZ À LA VAPEUR*

[Steamed Rice]

There are many ways to arrive at plain boiled or steamed rice, and most cooks choose one that best suits their temperaments. We find the following to be a foolproof system where the rice may be cooked hours ahead of time and reheated when needed.

For 4½ cups of cooked rice serving 6 people

1½ cups plain or enriched raw white rice

A heavy-bottomed 2-quart saucepan

3 cups water

1 tsp salt

Place the rice in the saucepan; stir in the water and salt. Bring to the boil over high heat, stir up once thoroughly, reduce heat to the simmer—very slight heat and bubbling—cover the pan and set timer for 12 minutes. Take a quick peek at the rice: the liquid should be almost absorbed. Fork up a few grains but don't stir it because stirring at this point could turn it sticky. Bite into it. It should be very slightly *al dente* —with the faintest crunch, but almost tender. Cover the pan and set off heat to let the rice finish cooking. (If not tender, sprinkle on droplets of water and cook a few minutes more; if liquid has not absorbed, uncover and boil it off, fluffing with a fork.)

The rice is now ready to serve, but if you are not ready to serve it, here are the alternatives:

Reheating cooked rice

Once cooked, rice may be allowed to cool; then cover it airtight and refrigerate it for a day or two before reheating it. To reheat, first fluff it lightly and steam it as follows:

3 thicknesses of well-washed cheesecloth

A colander set over a pan of simmering water

A cover

Steaming—à la vapeur. Fold the rice into the cheesecloth, set in the colander, cover it, and place over the simmering water. Steam it for several minutes until well heated through.

ALTERNATE METHODS: *Riz à l'anglaise* or *au beurre*

The frying pan: Sauté the cooked rice lightly in butter, tossing and turning and fluffing it with seasonings as it warms.

Double boiler: Turn it into a covered pan and set in a larger pan of simmering water. Fluff it with butter, salt, and pepper as it heats.

VARIATIONS AND SERVING SUGGESTIONS

You can do many things to vary the flavor of plain rice. For instance, use half chicken broth and half water rather than water alone for its initial cooking. Or add some white wine or dry white French vermouth to your water or broth. You may wish an herb flavoring, like a bay leaf, a big pinch of thyme or tarragon, or an herb bouquet; add the herbs right at the beginning of the cooking. A big pinch of curry or turmeric or saffron flowers gives color to rice served with lamb stew or curried dishes. And there are always onions and garlic: Simmer ⅓ cup or so of minced onions in a tablespoon of oil or butter or half a cup of chicken broth or wine; when tender, proceed in the usual way. Or add minced garlic to the rice at the beginning of the cooking, or whole peeled raw garlic cloves, which will cook along with the rice. Here are other ideas:

Riz Duxelles

[Buttered Rice with Mushrooms]

½ lb. finely diced fresh mushrooms
2 Tb butter
1 Tb oil
1 to 2 Tb minced shallots or green onions
Salt and pepper to taste
1 to 2 Tb more butter
2 to 3 Tb minced parsley

Following the procedure for *duxelles* on page 515, twist the mushrooms, a handful at a time, in the corner of a towel to extract their juice. Sauté the mushrooms in butter and oil for 6 to 8 minutes until very lightly browned. Stir in the shallots or onions and cook slowly for 2 minutes more. Mix in the hot, steamed rice with a fork and season to taste. Fluff in the rest of the butter and the parsley.

(*) May be set aside and reheated later.

RIZ A L'ORIENTALE

[Vegetarian Rice Bowl]

For 4 servings

4 cups hot steamed rice
1 cup minced onions cooked in butter and mixed herbs
1 cup diced eggplant sautéed in oil and garlic
⅓ cup chopped walnut meats
12 cherry tomatoes, halved
Salt and pepper
1 omelette, cut into strips
Chopped parsley

With the hot rice in a roomy saucepan, deftly fluff in the onions, eggplant, walnuts, and cherry tomatoes. Season carefully to taste, and turn into warm bowls. Decorate with the omelette strips, and sprinkle with parsley.

Pass chopsticks to your guests.

SALADES DE RIZ
[Rice Salads]

Cooked rice is a versatile base for many a salad combination, and it is always useful to have on hand for quick and attractive meals. Save up such treasures to combine with the rice as cooked peas or green beans, ham, chicken or other poultry tidbits, lamb, pork sausages, shrimp, crab, lobster—anything that you can dice up and, perhaps, marinate first in a tossing of oil, lemon, minced shallots or scallions, herbs, and seasonings. For instance:

For 4 servings

2 to 3 cups cooked rice
Good salad oil
Lemon juice or wine vinegar
Salt and pepper
4 scallions, thinly sliced, including tender green·
A handful of black olives, quartered lengthwise
½ cup ham, diced
½ cup each cooked carrots and beans, diced
1 small head shredded romaine
1 bunch broccoli spears, cooked

Toss the rice in a bowl with droplets of oil, lemon or vinegar, and salt and pepper to taste. (Be sure to use a wooden spoon and fork, and toss gently so as not to break the grains.) Toss in the rest of the ingredients except for the romaine and broccoli. Season carefully. Arrange the shredded romaine on plates or a serving dish, mound the rice salad on top, and decorate with the cooked broccoli, which you have seasoned nicely beforehand with salt, pepper, lemon, and oil. (Fresh herbs, such as basil, chives, chervil, and tarragon, are always welcome.)

RISOTTO–PILAF–PILAU
[*Risotto*—Braised Rice]

This is the standard French method for braised rice, meaning rice sautéed in fat and onions, then cooked in seasoned liquid. Whether the final dish is labeled *risotto,* pilaf, or pilau it is usually done in this manner regardless of the traditional techniques of other rice-eating nations. A good *risotto* is simple to make if you bear the following points in mind that apply to a plain *risotto* as well as to one which includes vegetables, chicken, or sea foods.

SAUTÉING

The rice must first be sautéed slowly in butter for 2 to 3 minutes until it turns a milky color. This cooks the rice-flour coating and prevents the rice from becoming sticky.

PROPORTIONS

Use the correct amount of liquid: 2 cups for each cup of raw rice.

HEAT

Regulate your heat so the liquid is entirely absorbed in 18 to 20 minutes. If the liquid is absorbed too quickly, the rice will not be tender. If it is absorbed too slowly, the rice becomes gummy, the grains disintegrate, and the flavor of the rice is impaired.

STIRRING

Do not stir the rice until all the liquid has been absorbed.

For 6 people

Preheat oven to 375 degrees.

¼ cup finely minced onions 4 Tb butter A 6-cup fireproof casserole about 8 inches in diameter with a tight-fitting cover	Cook the onions and butter slowly in the casserole for about 5 minutes until tender but not browned.
1½ cups clean, unwashed, raw rice	Blend the rice into the onions and butter and stir over moderate heat for several minutes, not letting the rice brown. The grains will at first become translucent, then will gradually turn a milky color.
3 cups boiling liquid, depending on what your *risotto* is to be served with: Chicken stock or canned chicken broth Brown stock or canned beef bouillon and water Mushroom broth and water White wine fish stock White wine or white vermouth, and water OR, water only Salt and pepper	As soon as the rice looks milky, pour in the boiling liquid. Add the herb bouquet, and salt and pepper to taste. Bring to the simmer, stir once, cover the casserole, and set in lower third of preheated oven. As soon as the liquid maintains itself at a very slow boil, in 4 to 5 minutes, reduce heat to 350 degrees; the boil should be regulated so the liquid has been absorbed by the rice in 14 to 15 minutes. Do not touch the rice during this time. Then uncover the casserole; tilt it and lift rice with a fork to see if all liquid at bottom of casserole has evaporated. If not, return to oven for 2 to 3 minutes more. Then remove the casserole from the oven. If you wish the rice to be slightly *al dente,* uncover it. If you wish it to become a little more tender, leave it covered for 10 minutes. Discard herb

A small herb bouquet: 2
parsley sprigs, ⅓ bay leaf,
and ⅛ tsp thyme tied in
cheesecloth

bouquet. Fluff the rice with a fork and correct seasoning.
(*) If not to be used immediately, keep warm over
barely simmering water. Or set aside, and reheat casserole over boiling water when needed.

VARIATION

Riz en Couronne

[Rice Ring]

This is how to make a ring of rice which is to be filled with creamed
shellfish, sautéed chicken livers with ham and mushrooms, buttered peas, or
whatever luscious sauced tidbits you wish.

For 6 people

Preheat oven to 350 degrees.

A 6-cup ring mold, smeared
with ½ Tb butter
The preceding *risotto*
A round of waxed paper
A lid to cover the mold
A pan of boiling water to
hold the mold

Turn the *risotto* into the buttered mold, patting down
the rice lightly; it should fill the mold exactly. Lay
the waxed paper over the *risotto*. Cover with the lid,
and set the mold in the pan of boiling water. Place in
lower third of preheated oven for 10 minutes.

A round serving platter,
heated and lightly but-
tered

Just before serving, turn platter upside down over
mold and reverse the two, to unmold the rice ring
onto the platter.
(*) If *risotto* is not to be served immediately, leave it
in its mold, covered, and over barely simmering
water.

PATENTED PARBOILED RICE

This is treated by a special steam process designed to harden the grains so
that they will not stick together when cooked. Use it like regular rice, but it
may call for a little more liquid and the timing may be a little longer than for
regular rice. It is a great invention, and the rice has excellent flavor.

PACKAGED PRECOOKED RICE

This is the type of rice which, according to the printed directions, you mix with salt and boiling water, then cover and let stand for 5 minutes. It can be made much more interesting if you add to it onions or shallots cooked in butter, and use a well seasoned boiling stock rather than boiling salted water.

WILD RICE

Wild rice has hardly been heard of in France, but you can cook it deliciously in the French manner by using a modified *risotto* technique.

For 6 to 8 people

Preheat oven to 350 degrees.

1½ cups wild rice
3 quarts boiling water
1½ Tb salt

Drop the rice in the boiling salted water and boil uncovered for 5 minutes. Drain thoroughly.

3 Tb each: finely minced carrots, onions, and celery
4 Tb butter
A 2½-quart fireproof casserole with cover
1½ cups brown stock or canned beef bouillon
1 bay leaf
¼ tsp thyme
Salt and pepper

While the rice is boiling, cook the minced vegetables slowly in the butter in the casserole for 5 to 6 minutes until tender but not browned. Then add the drained rice and stir over moderate heat for 2 minutes to impregnate it with the butter. Add the stock or bouillon, bay leaf, thyme, and seasonings to taste. Bring to the boil. Cover the casserole and set in lower third of preheated oven for 30 to 35 minutes or until the rice is tender and has absorbed all the liquid. Add a few drops more liquid if all has been absorbed before the rice is tender. The rice grains should emerge separate and lightly filmed with butter. Discard bay leaf. Fluff rice with a fork and correct seasoning.

(*) May be cooked in advance and reheated when needed.

CHAPTER NINE

COLD BUFFET

Préparations Froides

Cold vegetables, composed salads, aspics, molded mousses, *pâtés,* and *terrines,* any of these may be served as a first course for a dinner, or be the mainstay of a summer meal. And a collection of such dishes on a buffet table can be most inviting. Recipes for various salad dressings are in the Sauce chapter under vinaigrettes starting on page 94, and mayonnaise starting on page 87.

COLD VEGETABLES
Légumes Servis Froids

✳ *LÉGUMES À LA GRECQUE*

[Vegetables Cooked in Aromatic Broth]

Vegetables *à la Grecque,* a refreshing idea for any time of the year, are simmered in an aromatic *court bouillon* of water, oil, herbs, and seasonings. After the vegetables have been removed to a serving dish, the *court bouillon* is boiled down to concentrate its flavor, and is poured over the vegetables. When the vegetables are cold, serve as hors d'oeuvre, or combine them with other vegetables for a composed salad.

Court Bouillon
[The Aromatic Broth]
For 1 pound (about 4 cups) of vegetables

2 cups water

6 Tb olive oil

⅓ cup lemon juice

½ tsp salt

2 Tb minced shallot or green onions

The following (tied in cheesecloth if you wish):

   6 sprigs parsley including roots if available

   1 small celery stalk with leaves or ⅛ tsp celery seeds

   1 sprig fresh fennel or ⅛ tsp fennel seeds

   1 sprig fresh thyme or ⅛ tsp dried thyme

   12 peppercorns

   6 coriander seeds

A 2½-quart enameled or stainless steel saucepan with cover

Place all the ingredients to the left in the covered saucepan and simmer for 10 minutes.

Champignons à la Grecque

[Mushrooms *à la Grecque*]

1 lb. fresh mushrooms, button size if possible

1 cup of the preceding *court bouillon*, strained if you wish

Trim and wash the mushrooms. Leave whole if small, quarter if large. Add them to the simmering *court bouillon*, tossing them to cover with the liquid. Cover and simmer for 10 minutes.

A slotted spoon

A serving dish

Salt and pepper

Remove the mushrooms from the saucepan with the slotted spoon, and arrange them in a serving dish. Rapidly boil down the *court bouillon* until it has reduced almost to a syrup. Correct seasoning; strain it over the mushrooms.

(*) When cold, the mushrooms may be covered and refrigerated, and will keep for 2 to 3 days.

2 to 3 Tb minced parsley or mixed green herbs

Sprinkle with herbs just before serving.

VARIATIONS: OTHER VEGETABLES À LA GRECQUE

Any of the following vegetables may be prepared *à la Grecque*. In each case, make a *court bouillon* as directed in the preceding recipe, prepare and simmer the vegetables as indicated for each kind in the list, then drain and arrange on a serving dish. Boil down *court bouillon* until it has reduced almost to a syrup (less than ¼ cup usually). Pour over the vegetables and chill. Sprinkle on minced, fresh green herbs just before serving.

Fonds d'Artichauts à la Grecque

[Artichoke Bottoms *à la Grecque*]

Fresh artichoke bottoms

Before cooking, trim the artichoke bottoms as described on page 428. The choke is removed after cooking. Simmering time is from 30 to 40 minutes.

Frozen artichoke hearts

Before cooking, defrost the artichoke hearts enough so that they can be separated from each other. As they have been acidulated before freezing, use only 1 teaspoon of lemon juice in the *court bouillon*. Simmering time is about 10 minutes.

Céleri à la Grecque

[Celery *à la Grecque*]

Buy bunches labeled "celery hearts." Remove any tough outside stalks. Cut off the tops of the bunches to just below the main body of leaves. Halve or quarter the bunches lengthwise, wash thoroughly under running water, and arrange them in a baking dish. Pour on the simmering *court bouillon,* adding more water if necessary to cover the celery. Cover the dish, bring to the simmer, and bake in a preheated 350-degree oven for 30 to 40 minutes or until tender.

Concombres à la Grecque

[Cucumbers *à la Grecque*]

Peel, cut in half lengthwise, and scoop out the seeds with a spoon. Cut the halves into ½-inch strips, then into 2-inch pieces. Toss with ½ teaspoon of salt for each 4 cups of cucumber pieces, and let stand in a bowl for 20 minutes. Drain thoroughly, and proceed with the recipe. Simmering time is about 10 minutes.

Aubergines à la Grecque
[Eggplant à la Grecque]

Peel the eggplant, cut into serving pieces, and let stand for 20 minutes in ½ teaspoon of salt and 1 teaspoon of lemon juice for each 4 cups of eggplant pieces. Drain thoroughly and proceed with the recipe. Simmering time is about 10 minutes.

Endives à la Grecque
[Endive à la Grecque]

Fenouil à la Grecque
[Fennel à la Grecque]

Quarter or halve the endives or fennel lengthwise, wash under cold, running water, then proceed with the recipe. Simmering time is 30 to 40 minutes.

Poireaux à la Grecque
[Leeks à la Grecque]

Trim off the roots, make two lengthwise cuts in green part, remove a portion of the green tops to leave the leeks about 7 inches long. Wash thoroughly under cold, running water, being sure you get off all grit from each leaf. Arrange the leeks in a fireproof dish, pour on the simmering *court bouillon,* and add boiling water, if necessary, to cover the leeks. Cover the baking dish, bring to the simmer on top of the stove, then bake in a preheated, 350-degree oven for 30 to 40 minutes or until the leeks are tender. Drain off *court bouillon,* boil it down to ⅓ cup, pour over the leeks, and chill.

Oignons à la Grecque
[Onions à la Grecque]

Buy pearl onions, or small white onions about an inch in diameter. Drop them for 1 minute in boiling water to cover, drain and peel them, then pierce a cross in their root ends to insure even cooking. Proceed with the recipe. Simmering time is 30 to 40 minutes.

Poivrons à la Grecque

[Red or Green Bell Peppers à la Grecque]

Halve the peppers lengthwise, remove seeds and ribs, and slice or quarter the peppers. Proceed with the recipe. Simmering time is about 10 minutes.

CÉLERI-RAVE RÉMOULADE

[Celery Root in Mustard Sauce]

Celeriac or celery root prepared in this manner makes a typically French hors d'oeuvre. But raw celeriac can be tough, and we have suggested a preliminary steeping in salt and lemon before it is dressed. However, if you grate it fine, through a miniature French vegetable mill known as the julienne (available in many import shops, and inexpensive), you can dispense with the steep and move straight on to the dressing.

NOTE: *Céleri-rave rémoulade* has nothing to do with *sauce rémoulade,* a mayonnaise with pickles, capers, and other ingredients.

1 lb. celery root (3 to 3½ cups when cut)
A 2-quart mixing bowl
1½ tsp salt
1½ tsp lemon juice

Peel the celery root and cut it into julienne matchsticks as illustrated on page 28. Toss in a bowl with the salt and lemon juice, and let steep for 30 minutes. Rinse the pieces in cold water, drain, and dry them in a towel.

4 Tb strong Dijon-type prepared mustard
3 Tb boiling water
A wire whip
⅓ to ½ cup olive oil or salad oil
2 Tb wine vinegar
Salt and pepper

Warm the mixing bowl in hot water. Dry it. Add the mustard and beat in the boiling water by droplets with a wire whip. Then beat in the oil by droplets to make a thick creamy sauce. Beat in the vinegar by drops, and season to taste.

2 to 3 Tb chopped mixed green herbs or parsley

Fold the celery root into the sauce, and allow it to marinate for 2 to 3 hours or overnight. Decorate with herbs before serving.

POMMES DE TERRE À L'HUILE

[French Potato Salad—sliced potatoes in oil and vinegar dressing]

French potato salad is prepared while the boiled, sliced potatoes are still warm, so they will absorb the dressing. The salad may be eaten warm with grilled sausage, or cold. Mayonnaise may be folded into the potatoes if you wish. Be sure to use potatoes which may be boiled and sliced without crumbling.

For *about 6 cups*

2 lbs. "boiling" potatoes (8 to 10 medium potatoes) A 3-quart mixing bowl	Scrub the potatoes. Drop them in boiling salted water to cover, and boil until the potatoes are just tender when pierced with a small knife. Drain. As soon as they are cool enough to handle, peel, and cut them into slices about ⅛ inch thick. Place them in the mixing bowl.
4 Tb dry white wine, or 2 Tb dry white vermouth and 2 Tb stock or canned bouillon	Pour the wine or vermouth and stock or bouillon over the warm potato slices and toss very gently. Set aside for a few minutes until the potatoes have absorbed the liquids.
2 Tb wine vinegar, or 1 Tb vinegar and 1 Tb lemon juice 1 tsp prepared mustard ¼ tsp salt A small bowl and wire whip 6 Tb olive oil or salad oil Pepper Optional: 1 to 2 Tb minced shallots or green onions	Beat the vinegar or vinegar and lemon juice, mustard, and salt in the small bowl until the salt has dissolved. Then beat in the oil by droplets. Season to taste, and stir in the optional shallots or onions. Pour the dressing over the potatoes and toss gently to blend.
2 to 3 Tb chopped mixed green herbs or parsley	Serve them while still warm, or chill. Decorate with herbs before serving.

COMPOSED SALADS
Salades Composées

Here are three recipes and several suggestions for salad mixtures. Green vegetables will lose their fresh color if they sit in a vinaigrette for more than half an hour; therefore prepare each component of the salad in a separate dish. Just before serving, season each with dressing, and put together the salad in its serving bowl.

SALADE NIÇOISE

[Mediterranean Combination Salad]

Tuna, anchovies, tomatoes, potatoes, green beans, hard-boiled eggs, and lettuce are the usual elements for this appetizing combination, and you may arrange the salad in any manner you wish. Serve as an hors d'oeuvre or as a main-course summer salad.

For 6 to 8 people

---

3 cups cold, blanched, green beans, page 443 (see also directions for frozen beans, page 449)

3 or 4 quartered tomatoes

1 cup vinaigrette (French dressing) with herbs, page 94

1 head Boston lettuce, separated, washed, drained, and dried

A salad bowl

3 cups cold French potato salad (preceding recipe)

1 cup canned tuna chunks, drained

½ cup pitted black olives, preferably the dry Mediterranean type

2 or 3 hard-boiled eggs, cold, peeled, and quartered

6 to 12 canned anchovy filets, drained

2 to 3 Tb minced, fresh green herbs

Just before serving, season the beans and tomatoes with several spoonfuls of vinaigrette. Toss the lettuce leaves in the salad bowl with ¼ cup of vinaigrette, and place the leaves around the edge of the bowl. Arrange the potatoes in the bottom of the bowl. Decorate with the beans and tomatoes, interspersing them with a design of tuna chunks, olives, eggs, and anchovies. Pour the remaining dressing over the salad, sprinkle with herbs, and serve.

SALADE DE BOEUF À LA PARISIENNE

[Cold Beef and Potato Salad]

This is an attractive way to use cold boiled or braised beef as a main-course summer dish or on a cold buffet table. We shall not give proportions because they depend on how much meat you have.

Thinly sliced, cold, boiled or braised beef Vinaigrette (French dressing) with herbs, page 94 Thinly sliced rings of mild onion A serving platter French potato salad, page 541 Boston lettuce or water cress Quartered hard-boiled eggs Quartered tomatoes Optional: cold cooked green beans, broccoli or cauliflower; canned beets Minced fresh green herbs	In separate bowls, marinate the beef and the onion rings in vinaigrette for half an hour or longer. When ready to serve the salad, arrange the beef on the platter alternating the slices with onion rings. Decorate the platter with the rest of the ingredients, spoon a bit of vinaigrette over them, and sprinkle with herbs.

* SALADE À LA D'ARGENSON

[Rice or Potato and Beet Salad]

When rice or potatoes are marinated with beets in a vinaigrette for a sufficient amount of time, the whole mass becomes beet-colored. Then it can be tossed in an herbal mayonnaise, and all sorts of cooked vegetables, meat, or fish leftovers can be mixed into it to make a nourishing hors d'oeuvre, a main-course dish, or an attractive addition to a picnic.

For 1 quart or more

2 cups boiled rice *riz au blanc,* page 532, OR, 2 cups of warm boiled potatoes, peeled and diced	Toss the rice or potatoes, beets, and shallots or onions in a bowl with the vinaigrette. Season to taste. Cover, and refrigerate for at least 12, preferably 24, hours.

2 cups diced cooked or
canned beets
4 Tb minced shallots or
green onions
A 2-quart bowl
¾ cup vinaigrette (French
dressing), page 94

1½ to 2 cups mayonnaise
with green herbs, page
87, or the recipe follow-
ing it, for green mayon-
naise
Salt and pepper
1 cup, one or a mixture
of the following:
Cooked green peas, or
cooked and diced green
beans, cauliflower, broc-
coli, carrots, turnips, or
asparagus; diced cooked
beef, pork, poultry, or
fish; flaked canned tuna
or salmon; diced raw ap-
ples; grated raw carrots;
walnuts
A salad bowl
Decorate with any or all of
the following:
Green or black olives,
anchovies, sliced hard-
boiled eggs, water cress or
parsley sprigs

Shortly before serving, fold in the mayonnaise and
other ingredients. Season carefully. Arrange the salad
in the bowl and decorate with the suggestions listed.

ASPICS

Préparations Froides en Aspic

Cold chicken decorated with tarragon leaves and shimmering with jelly,
a molded aspic of chicken livers, or a *boeuf mode en gelée*—these are lovely
summer dishes, and fun to do if you enjoy decorating. You may be frightfully

elegant with your designs, or amusing, and, after a little experience, very professional.

DEFINITIONS: GELÉE, JELLY, ASPIC

Gelée is the French culinary term for beef, veal, chicken, or fish stock which stiffens when cold because it contains natural gelatin, or because gelatin has been added to it. Liquid or jelled, it is always spoken of as *gelée*. We shall refer to *gelée,* whether hot or cold, liquid or set, as jelly or jellied stock. Aspic, in French, usually refers not to the jelly, but to the whole decorated dish of various elements coated with or molded in jelly.

RECIPES FOR JELLY

Directions for homemade jellied stock are on page 112 in the Stocks and Aspic section. These stocks are almost always clarified, meaning that they are rendered clear and sparkling through a simmering with egg whites; directions for clarification are on page 111. Canned bouillons and consommés are turned into jelly by the addition of powdered gelatin, as described on page 113; following this are directions for wine flavorings.

HOW TO WORK WITH JELLY

Never fail to test out the jelly before you begin to work with it: Pour ½ inch of jelly into a small, chilled saucer, and refrigerate for about 10 minutes or until set. Then break it up with a fork and let it stand at room temperature; the pieces should hold their shape but not be rubbery. Further information and gelatin proportions are on page 113.

Allow yourself plenty of time and cracked ice, for the jelly must be given full opportunity to set; it cannot be hurried. A complicated decoration need not be completed in one continuous operation. Successive coats of jelly may be spooned over the dish whenever you have time, and the process may go on in spurts all one day and on into the next.

Coating Foods with Aspic Jellied stocks set very quickly once they are cold. To avoid continual warmings of the whole amount when you are to coat foods with successive layers of jelly, heat just what you will need at one time in a small saucepan. Stir over cracked ice until the liquid turns syrupy, indicating it is about to congeal. Then remove the pan immediately from its bed of ice, and spoon a layer of jelly over the chilled food. Refrigerate the platter for about 10 minutes to set the layer of jelly, and repeat the process two or three times until you have built up a coating of jelly almost ⅛ of an inch thick.

DECORATIVE ELEMENTS

CHOPPED JELLY   When you spoon jelly over foods arranged on a platter, you will usually need to fill up empty spaces or cover dribbles of jelly that have run off the edges of the food. Chopped jelly is an easy solution, and is made as follows: Pour a ½-inch layer of jelly into a plate or pan and chill until set. Then make narrow crosshatches through the jelly with a knife to cut it into small pieces ⅛ inch or less in size. Either force the jelly through a pastry bag to outline the food or to fill up the platter, or heap it into place with a spoon.

JELLY CUTOUTS   These make nice decorations around the edge of a platter. Chill a ¼-inch layer of jelly in a plate or pan, then cut it into squares, triangles, or diamonds, and it is ready to use.

DESIGNS AND COLORS   You can make fanciful decorations of curlicues, sprays, branches and flowers, or geometric patterns out of the ingredients listed below. Use them as follows: First spoon two or three layers of jelly over the chilled food; chill your decorative materials and cut them into various shapes. Then, holding them with two trussing needles or skewers, dip them into almost-set jelly and arrange them over the food. Refrigerate the platter of food to set the designs, then give a final coating or two of jelly to cover the decorations with a transparent film.

FOR BLACK: Use thin slices of truffle or black olives.

FOR RED: Use thin strips, dice, or dots of canned red pimiento. The pulp of peeled, seeded, and juiced tomatoes, page 505, may be diced or sliced, or twisted in the corner of a towel to make little balls.

FOR YELLOW: Use hard-boiled egg yolks, mashed with softened butter, and pushed through a pastry tube to make dots or fluted designs.

FOR ORANGE: Use cooked carrots sliced, diced, or cut into strips.

FOR GREEN: Use fresh or pickled tarragon leaves, dropped in boiling water for 30 seconds, refreshed in cold water, and dried on a towel. Cooked green peppers cut into strips or dice. The green tops of leeks or green onions simmered in water for several minutes until softened, refreshed in cold water, and dried; cut into thin strips, these can then be formed into curlicues, or made to look like branches of mimosa (use dots of "yellow" for the flowers).

FOR WHITE: Use hard-boiled egg white, thinly sliced and cut into strips, dice, or shapes.

OEUFS EN GELÉE

[Poached Eggs in Aspic]

Serve eggs in aspic as a first course or luncheon dish, or arrange them around a platter of cold meats, fish, or vegetables.

For 6 eggs

3 cups jelly (jellied stock, page 112, or canned consommé with gelatin, page 113) 6 round or oval molds of ½ cup capacity, preferably of metal as they are easier to unmold	Pour ⅛ inch of jelly in the bottom of each mold and refrigerate for about 10 minutes or until set.
12 tarragon leaves, fresh or preserved in vinegar	Drop the tarragon leaves into boiling water for 30 seconds. Refresh in cold water, drain, dry, and chill. Dip them in a bit of almost-set jelly, and arrange them in a cross over the jelly in the bottom of each mold. Chill for a few minutes to set the tarragon.
6 chilled poached eggs, page 116	Place an egg in each mold, its least attractive side up. Pour in almost-set jelly to cover the eggs. Chill for an hour or so, until the jelly is well set.
Chilled plates Lettuce leaves	At serving time, dip each mold for 3 to 4 seconds in hot water. Run a knife around the edge of the jelly, turn the mold upside down and, giving it a sharp knock on the bottom, unmold on a chilled serving plate over a bed of lettuce leaves.

OTHER DECORATIONS

Lay a thin slice of ham over the cross of tarragon leaves. Or make designs of truffle in the bottom of the mold, top with a slice of *foie gras,* then add the poached egg and the rest of the jelly.

✳ *FOIES DE VOLAILLE EN ASPIC*

[Chicken Livers in Aspic]

Chicken livers sautéed in butter, simmered in wine, then molded in aspic make a delicious hors d'oeuvre, and are most simple to do.

For six ½-cup molds

2½ cups jelly (jellied stock, page 112, or canned consommé with gelatin, page 113) 6 round or oval molds of ½ cup capacity, preferably of metal	Pour a ⅛-inch layer of jelly into the bottom of each mold and chill until set.
6 large, whole chicken livers	Look over the chicken livers, and cut out any blackish or greenish spots. Dry the livers thoroughly on paper towels.
An 8-inch enameled skillet 2 Tb butter 1 Tb oil 2 Tb finely minced shallots or green onions	Set the skillet over moderately high heat with the butter and oil. When you see that the butter foam has almost subsided, add the chicken livers. Stir and toss for 2 minutes to brown the livers very lightly. Add the shallots or onions and toss for 5 seconds more. Hold a cover askew over the skillet and drain out all the sautéing fat.
Big pinch of salt Pinch of pepper Pinch of allspice ½ cup Madeira or port, or ⅓ cup cognac	Sprinkle the seasonings over the livers; pour in the wine or cognac. Cover the skillet and simmer very slowly for 8 minutes, then remove the livers to a side dish. Rapidly boil down the cooking juices until reduced to a syrupy consistency. Remove from heat, roll the livers in the skillet to cover with the juices, and chill.
Optional: 6 slices of truffle Chilled plates or platter Lettuce leaves	Place a slice of optional truffle over the jelly layer in each mold, and arrange a chicken liver over it. Fill the molds with the remaining jelly, which should be syrupy and almost set. Chill for an hour or so. Unmold on chilled serving plates or a platter, over lettuce leaves.

VARIATION

Homard, Crabe, ou Crevettes en Aspic

[Lobster, Crab, or Shrimp in Aspic]

The preceding system may also be adapted for lobster, crab, or shrimp meat in aspic.

POULET EN GELÉE À L'ESTRAGON

[Chicken Tarragon in Aspic]

Also for: turkey, game hens, squab pigeons, guinea hen, and pheasant.

Chicken in tarragon jelly is one of the simplest and best of the cold poultry dishes. The chicken may be poached by complete immersion in tarragon-flavored stock which is then clarified and turned into jelly, or you may follow the simpler version here.

For 6 people

Cooking the chicken

A 3-lb. ready-to-cook roasting chicken

⅛ tsp salt, ½ Tb butter, and 3 sprigs fresh tarragon or ½ tsp dried tarragon for inside the chicken

2 Tb butter and 1 Tb oil for browning the chicken

A heavy, covered, fireproof casserole

¼ tsp salt

3 sprigs fresh tarragon or ½ tsp dried tarragon for the casserole

Following the procedure for casserole-roasted chicken with tarragon, page 249, season the cavity with salt, butter, and tarragon. Truss and butter the chicken, then brown it on all sides in hot butter and oil in a casserole. Salt the chicken, add the tarragon, cover the casserole, and roast in a preheated 325-degree oven for 1 hour and 10 to 20 minutes. Remove the chicken, and let it cool to room temperature. Then chill it.

The tarragon jelly

2 or 3 sprigs fresh tarragon or 1 tsp dried tarragon

4 cups jelly (jellied stock made from brown chicken

Stir the tarragon into the jelly; bring to the simmer, cover, and let steep over very low heat for 10 minutes.

stock, page 112, or canned
consommé with gelatin,
page 113)
An enameled saucepan

---

4 to 5 Tb Madeira or port
A chilled saucer

Remove from heat, and stir in the wine by spoonfuls, tasting, until you have achieved the flavor you wish. Strain through a very fine sieve or several thicknesses of washed cheesecloth. Test a bit of it in a chilled saucer in the refrigerator, to be sure it will jell to the right consistency.

Decorating the chicken

An oval serving platter about 16 inches long

Pour a ⅛-inch layer of jelly into the platter, and chill in the refrigerator until set.

Carve the chicken and arrange it over the layer of jelly. Return the platter to the refrigerator.

A small saucepan
A bowl of cracked ice

Pour a cupful of jelly into the saucepan and stir over ice until it has become syrupy. Immediately remove from the ice, and spoon the almost-set jelly over the chicken; this first layer will not adhere very well. Chill the chicken for 10 minutes, and spoon another layer of almost-set jelly over it. Repeat.

---

20 to 30 fresh tarragon leaves or tarragon leaves preserved in vinegar
2 trussing needles or skewers, or a small, pointed knife (for picking up tarragon leaves)
A saucer of almost-set jelly

Drop the tarragon leaves in boiling water for 10 seconds. Refresh in ice water, and dry. Dip each leaf in the almost-set jelly, and arrange in a decorative pattern over the chicken. Chill. Then spoon on a final layer of almost-set jelly.

A pan or platter

Pour the remaining jelly into the pan or platter and chill until set. Chop the jelly into ⅛-inch pieces and distribute it around the chicken.

Refrigerate. Unless the weather is very warm, remove the chicken from the refrigerator half an hour before serving; it will have more flavor if it is not too cold.

* SUPRÊMES DE VOLAILLE EN CHAUD-FROID, BLANCHE NEIGE

[Breast of Chicken in *Chaud-froid*]

Here is a decorative, delicious, and easy-to-execute aspic which lends it-self to numerous variations as suggested at the end of the recipe. The cold cream sauce for this, which congeals into an aspic covering over the chicken breasts, looks like the classic *sauce chaud-froid*—flour-based, jellied *velouté* with cream. The sauce *chaud-froid blanche neige* used here is purely a reduc-tion of tarragon-flavored stock and cream in which gelatin has been dissolved; it is much lighter and nicer in texture than the classic sauce, we think. Serve chicken breasts in *chaud-froid* as a luncheon dish, or as part of a cold buffet.

For 6 people

6 *suprêmes* (the skinless and boneless breast-halves from 3 frying chickens)
A serving platter
Waxed paper

Poach the chicken breasts in butter as described at the beginning of the recipe, *suprêmes de volaille à blanc,* page 268. Drain them, and let them cool to room tem-perature. Arrange them in a serving platter, cover with waxed paper, and chill.

1¼ cups whipping cream
1½ cups excellent white chicken stock, page 237, OR, canned chicken broth simmered for 20 minutes with ¼ cup thinly sliced carrots, ¼ cup thinly sliced onions, and a pinch of thyme
1 sprig fresh tarragon or ¼ tsp dried tarragon
Salt and white pepper

Simmer the cream, chicken stock or broth, and tarra-gon slowly in the saucepan for about 10 minutes, until the mixture has reduced to 2 cups. Correct seasoning, and strain.

1 Tb (1 envelope) gelatin
3 Tb dry white vermouth

Soften the gelatin in the vermouth for a few minutes. Then beat it into the cream mixture and stir over low heat until the gelatin has dissolved completely. Cool, or stir over cracked ice, until the sauce has thickened slightly and is just about to congeal.

Spoon a layer of sauce over the chilled chicken breasts, and refrigerate until the sauce has set. Repeat with

successive coats of almost-set sauce until all but enough
for a final layer has been used.

A handful of fresh tarragon leaves or tarragon leaves preserved in vinegar; OR, thinly sliced or finely diced truffle Water cress or parsley	Drop the tarragon leaves in boiling water for 30 seconds, refresh in ice water, and dry. Immediately after coating the chicken with the final layer of sauce, decorate with the tarragon leaves or truffles. Surround the edge of the platter with water cress, or sprigs of parsley, and refrigerate again until serving time.

AN ELABORATION

After the tarragon leaves or slices of truffle have set, the chicken breasts may be given one or two coats of almost-set jelly, as in the preceding recipe for chicken tarragon, and the platter may be decorated with chopped jelly or jelly cutouts.

VARIATIONS

Suprêmes de Volaille en Chaud-froid à l'Écossaise

[Breast of Chicken in *Chaud-froid* with Diced Vegetables]

Ingredients for the master recipe ⅓ cup each: finely diced carrots, celery, and onions cooked until tender in 1½ Tb butter 1 or 2 finely minced truffles, or ¼ cup diced mushrooms cooked in butter	Proceed as for the master recipe, but stir the cooked carrots, celery, and onions into the chicken stock and cream mixture as it is reducing. Mix in the truffles or mushrooms, then the gelatin called for in the recipe, and continue as directed. With this sauce, the chicken breasts need no other decoration.

Suprêmes et Mousse de Volaille en Chaud-froid

[Breasts of Chicken and Mousse of Chicken in *Chaud-froid*]

When you wish to make something wonderful for an elaborate buffet, such as a wedding breakfast, here is a good idea. Directions for chopped jelly,

jelly cutouts, and other decorative elements are at the beginning of this section on aspics. We shall not note the number of servings for this recipe, as it is designed primarily to give you an indication of how to go about such a dish.

Ingredients for chicken breasts in *chaud-froid* **(the master recipe)**

Cook and chill the chicken breasts and prepare the *chaud-froid* sauce as directed in the master recipe. The chicken breasts may be cut in halves or in thirds, if you wish.

A mousse of chicken, page 560, or of chicken livers, page 559
A chilled serving platter
Sufficient jelly for glazing and for other decorations (jellied stock, page 112, or consommé with gelatin, page 113)

Unmold the mousse on the platter and pour around it a ⅛-inch layer of almost-set jelly. Chill.

Place the chilled chicken breasts on a rack set over a tray, and coat the breasts with several layers of *chaud-froid* sauce, chilling between each layer. Decorate with truffles, tarragon leaves, or whatever else you wish; then chill and glaze with coats of almost-set jelly. With two knives lift each breast off the rack and arrange on the platter around the mousse. Decorate platter with chopped jelly or jelly cutouts. Chill until shortly before serving time.

Crabe ou Homard en Chaud-froid, Blanche Neige

[Crab or Lobster in *Chaud-froid*]

Crab or lobster in *chaud-froid* follows the general method of chicken breasts in *chaud-froid,* and makes a decorative cold first course or summer luncheon dish. Directions for steaming live lobster (which also apply to crab) are at the beginning of the lobster *Thermidor* recipe on page 221; boil down the steaming-liquid afterward, and use it in place of the fish stock called for in the following recipe.

For an hors d'oeuvre serving 6 people

2 cups cooked lobster or crab meat

3 Tb butter

An enameled skillet

2 Tb minced shallots or green onions

⅛ tsp dry mustard

Pinch Cayenne pepper

Salt and pepper

3 Tb cognac

Dice or flake the shellfish meat. Heat the butter to bubbling in the skillet, then stir in the shallots or onions and shellfish meat, and cook slowly for 2 minutes. Stir in the mustard and Cayenne pepper, and season to taste. Then pour in the cognac, and boil rapidly for a minute or two, shaking the skillet, until the cognac has reduced almost completely. Chill.

1¼ cups whipping cream

1¼ cups white-wine fish stock (shellfish steaming-liquid, or the white-wine stock on page 114, or the emergency stock following it)

1 sprig fresh tarragon or ¼ tsp dried tarragon

1 Tb (1 envelope) gelatin softened in 3 Tb dry white vermouth

Following the recipe for breast of chicken in *chaud-froid*, page 551, simmer the cream and stock together with the tarragon until reduced to 2 cups. Dissolve the gelatin completely in the hot sauce, strain, correct seasoning, and cool until the sauce is almost set.

6 crab, lobster, or scallop shells, or porcelain or glass shells of about ½ cup capacity

Crab or lobster claws, scalloped shellfish meat, truffle slices, or blanched tarragon leaves (enough to decorate the shells)

Optional: 1 cup almost-set jellied stock, page 112–13

Fold 1⅓ cups of the almost-set sauce into the chilled shellfish meat. Arrange the mixture in the shells, and coat with the remaining sauce. Decorate with shellfish claws, shellfish meat, truffle slices, or tarragon leaves. Then, if you wish, chill, and coat with a layer of jellied stock. Chill until shortly before serving time.

VOLAILLES EN ESCABÈCHE

[Cold Fowl in Lemon Jelly]

For: chicken, pigeon, mature pheasant and partridge, and for game hens.

The Paris restaurateur from whom we borrowed this recipe makes a specialty of *escabèche* in the late fall when partridge are no longer young, and have turned from *perdreau* to *perdrix*. The birds are slowly simmered in wine, stock, olive oil, vinegar, aromatic vegetables, herbs, garlic, and slices of lemon. They are cooled in this liquid which, because of the pectin in the lemon and the gelatin in the poultry bones, turns into a very light jelly. If you want a stiffer jelly, you can add powdered gelatin to the liquid after the birds are cooked. *Escabèche,* which is Spanish in origin, is usually associated with fish, but it is also extremely successful for elderly poultry as the lemon and vinegar help to tenderize the flesh. Simmering times for various birds are as follows:

> Cut-up frying chicken, 1 hour
> Cut-up roasting chicken, 1½ hours
> Cut-up stewing chicken, 2½ hours or more
> Whole Cornish game hen or pigeon weighing about 1¼ pounds, 1½ hours
> Mature, whole partridge, 2 to 2½ hours
> Mature, cut-up pheasant, 2 to 2½ hours

For 1 cut-up, 4-lb. stewing chicken (or 1 cut-up, 4-lb. pheasant, or 2 whole game hens or partridges, simmered according to the preceding time-table)

½ cup each: thinly sliced onions, carrots and celery
6 cloves peeled garlic
A 2-quart saucepan
½ cup olive oil

Place the vegetables and garlic in the saucepan and cook slowly with the olive oil for 10 minutes without browning.

½ cup dry white wine or ⅓ cup dry white vermouth
⅓ cup wine vinegar
½ lemon cut into ⅛-inch slices
½ cup thinly sliced green or red bell peppers
¼ tsp thyme
¼ tsp rosemary
½ bay leaf
2 parsley sprigs
5 peppercorns
2 cups white stock or canned chicken broth
Salt

Stir in all the ingredients at the left and simmer for 10 minutes. Taste for seasoning, and salt lightly if necessary.

A cut-up stewing chicken, plus the neck, heart, and peeled gizzard
A heavy, covered, fireproof casserole just large enough to hold the chicken
A slotted spoon

Place the neck, heart, and gizzard in the bottom of the casserole. Arrange the dark meat over them. With a slotted spoon, distribute half the cooked vegetables and lemon slices over the dark meat. Then put in the white meat, cover with the rest of the vegetables, and pour on the cooking broth. Add water if necessary, so chicken is just covered with liquid.

Bring to the simmer on top of the stove, cover, and simmer very slowly either on the stove or in a preheated 300-degree oven for 2½ hours, or until the chicken is very tender but the meat does not fall from the bones. Uncover, and allow the chicken to cool in the stock for half an hour. Remove any loose bones.

A serving dish deep enough to hold chicken and sauce
Salt and pepper

Arrange the chicken in a deep serving dish. Dip out the vegetables and lemon slices and distribute them on and around the chicken. Skim the fat and oil off the cooking stock and boil the stock down rapidly if necessary until it has reduced to 2 cups. Correct seasoning, and strain over the chicken. Allow the dish to cool to room temperature, then cover and refrigerate. When chilled, the sauce will thicken into the consistency of a jellied soup.

BOEUF MODE EN GELÉE

[Cold Braised Beef in Aspic]

The braised beef on page 309 can be turned into a splendid cold dish with very little trouble. If you are going to make the traditional recipe, the proceedings must be started at least the day before you are to serve; the beef needs 24 hours of marination, 5 hours for browning and braising, and 4 to 6 hours for chilling in jelly. Once made, it may be covered and kept under refrigeration for 2 to 3 days. A light red wine and French bread would go very well with it.

For 10 to 12 people

Ingredients for the marination and braising of a 5-lb.

Marinate and braise the beef, and braise the carrots and onions according to the recipe, but omit the final

piece of boneless beef, page 309, including the braised carrots and onions

sauce-thickening step. Remove the meat to a carving board.

---

2 Tb (2 envelopes) gelatin
3 cups cold brown stock or canned consommé
Salt and pepper
¼ cup port or brandy
A chilled saucer

Degrease the braising liquid thoroughly, then boil it down until it has reduced to 3½ to 4 cups. Soften the gelatin in the cold stock or consommé, pour it into the braising liquid and stir over low heat until the gelatin has dissolved completely. Correct seasoning carefully. Pour in the port or brandy and strain. The liquid has now become a jelly; test a bit of it in a chilled saucer as described on page 114.

For a simple arrangement in a mold

A rectangular mold, *terrine,* or baking dish large enough to hold the sliced meat and vegetables

Slice the beef into serving pieces and arrange in the mold, interspersing the slices with the braised carrots and onions. Pour in the jelly, which need not be cold. Chill for 4 to 6 hours, or until well set.

A chilled serving platter
Water cress, parsley, or leaves of Boston lettuce

When ready to serve, dip the mold in hot water for several seconds. Run a knife around the edge of the aspic. Turn platter over mold, reverse, and give a sharp jerk to unmold aspic on platter. Decorate platter with water cress, parsley, or lettuce.

For a more elaborate arrangement on a platter

Cut the beef into serving pieces and chill. Chill the braised onions and carrots.

An oval serving platter

Pour ⅛ inch of the jelly into the serving platter and chill until set. Then arrange the chilled meat and vegetables on the layer of jelly.

A small saucepan set in a bowl of cracked ice

Pour 2 cups of jelly into the saucepan and stir over cracked ice until the jelly is syrupy, and on the point of setting. Spoon a layer over the meat and vegetables. Chill for 10 minutes. Repeat with 2 or 3 more layers of almost-set jelly, chilling the meat between each. Chill the remaining jelly, chop into ⅛-inch pieces, and arrange it around the platter.

MOLDED MOUSSES

Mousses Froides — Mousselines

A beautifully flavored and molded creation glittering in aspic is always impressive as a first course, as a luncheon dish, or on a cold buffet table. All of the following are purées of chicken liver, poultry, ham, or fish mixed with wine and seasonings and, in all but one recipe, jellied stock. Softened butter or lightly whipped cream is combined with them to give body and what the French call *moelleux* or a velvety texture. An electric blender is a great time-saver. If you do not have one, pass meat twice through the finest blade of the meat grinder (fish may be puréed in a food mill) then beat in the liquids.

The first recipe in this section may be packed into a decorative bowl and served just as it is; the rest must be molded. If they are molded plain, without a jelly lining in the mold, they should be glazed with jelly after they are unmolded, or with a type of *chaud-froid* sauce such as the one described for the fish mousse on page 563. They may then be decorated with truffles, tarragon leaves, jelly cutouts, or, if it is a fish mousse, with designs of shellfish meat.

HOW TO "CHEMISER UN MOULE" OR LINE A MOLD WITH JELLY

A mold lined with jelly is one which contains a fairly stiff coating of jellied stock about ⅛ inch thick all over its inside surface. The mousse is packed into the lined mold, and chilled. When unmolded, the mousse is encased in a shell of jelly. The jelly should be made from clarified stock so it will be clear, glistening, and transparent. Recipes for stock, clarification, homemade jellied stock, and jellies made from canned consommé begin on page 106.

You can roll a mold over cracked ice with spoonfuls of jellied stock until an adequate layer of jelly has been built up inside the mold, or you can use the following method which we find easier.

4 cups clarified jelly (jellied stock, page 112, or consommé with gelatin, page 113) A bowl of cracked ice	The jelly should be fairly stiff; be sure to test it as directed in the recipe for jellies before you line your mold. Chill the jelly over cracked ice until syrupy and almost set.
A 4-cup mold, preferably of metal as it is easier to unmold	Then pour the almost-set jelly into the mold and place the mold in cracked ice. Watch it carefully, and as soon as a ⅛-inch layer of jelly has set around the

edges of the mold, pour out the unset jelly. If there
is too thick a layer of jelly in the bottom of the mold,
scoop it out with a spoon dipped in hot water.

Chill the mold for about 20 minutes until the jelly lining is stiff. Then pack the cold mousse into the mold
as directed in whatever recipe you are following.

DECORATIONS

If you wish to decorate the bottom of a mold, begin by pouring into it a
1/16-inch layer of jelly and chill until firm. Choose any of the decorative suggestions on page 546, or sliced poultry meat, ham, tongue, shrimp, or lobster;
cut into shapes and chill. Dip into almost-set jelly, and arrange on the jelly in
the bottom of the mold. Chill until set, then proceed to line the mold with
jelly as described in the preceding directions.

HOW TO UNMOLD AN ASPIC

Dip the mold in very hot water for 3 to 4 seconds (a nonmetal mold will
require a few seconds longer). Quickly wipe it dry. Invert a chilled serving
platter over it, and turn upside down. Give it a sharp downward jerk to dislodge it from the mold to the platter.

Another method is to invert the mold on a chilled platter, and surround
the mold with a towel wrung out in very hot water. As soon as the aspic drops,
remove the mold.

MOUSSE DE FOIES DE VOLAILLE

[Chicken Liver Mousse]

The following mousse may be packed into a decorative jar and used as
a spread for cocktail appetizers, or molded in aspic for an hors d'oeuvre. It is
easy to make in an electric blender; if you do not have one, purée the liver in
a meat grinder or food mill.

For about 2 cups

---

1 lb. or about 2 cups chicken livers	Look the livers over and remove any greenish or blackish spots. Cut the livers into 1/2-inch pieces.

2 Tb minced shallots or green onions 2 Tb butter A skillet An electric blender	Sauté with the shallots or green onions in hot butter for 2 to 3 minutes, until the livers are just stiffened, but still rosy inside. Scrape into the blender jar.
⅓ cup Madeira or cognac	Pour the wine or cognac into the sauté pan and boil it down rapidly until it has reduced to 3 tablespoons. Scrape it into the blender jar.
¼ cup whipping cream ½ tsp salt ⅛ tsp allspice ⅛ tsp pepper Pinch of thyme	Add the cream and seasonings to the blender jar. Cover and blend at top speed for several seconds until the liver is a smooth paste.
½ cup (4 ounces) melted butter	Then add the melted butter and blend several seconds more.
A fairly fine-meshed sieve A wooden spoon Salt and pepper	Force the mixture through the sieve and taste carefully for seasoning.
A decorative bowl or jar Waxed paper	Pack into the bowl or jar, cover with waxed paper, and chill for 2 to 3 hours. Or chill until almost set, then pack into a mold lined with jelly as described on page 558; chill for several hours before unmolding.

* MOUSSELINE DE VOLAILLE

[Mousse of Chicken, Turkey, Duck, or Game]

This is an excellent way to use up cold fowl, and you may mix several kinds together if you wish. *Foie gras,* liver pâté, or chicken livers, a good stock, wine, and careful seasoning give character to the blandness of the meat. If you do not have an electric blender, purée the ingredients with a meat grinder.

For about 6 cups serving 8 to 10 people

3 Tb minced shallots or green onions 1 Tb butter A 4-cup saucepan 2 cups well flavored poultry stock or white stock;	Cook the shallots or onions slowly with the butter in the saucepan for 2 minutes without browning. Add the stock and the gelatin mixture, and simmer for 1 minute. Pour into the blender jar.

OR, canned chicken broth simmered for 20 minutes with ¼ cup of thinly sliced carrots, celery, and onions, and an herb bouquet, then strained

2 Tb (2 envelopes) gelatin softened in ¼ cup dry white wine or vermouth

An electric blender

2 tightly packed cups chopped, cooked chicken, turkey, duck, or game-bird meat

⅓ cup *foie gras* (goose liver), or liver paste; OR ½ cup chicken livers lightly sautéed in butter

A 3-quart mixing bowl

Add the poultry meat and *foie gras,* liver paste, or sautéed livers to the blender. Cover and blend at top speed for a minute or two until the ingredients are puréed. Pour into the bowl.

2 to 3 Tb cognac or Madeira

Salt and pepper

Pinch of nutmeg

Beat in the cognac or wine to taste, and overseason slightly as the cream, which comes later, will mask the flavor a bit. Cover and chill until almost set, stirring occasionally.

¾ cup chilled whipping cream

A chilled bowl

A chilled wire whip

Optional: 1 or 2 minced truffles

A 6-cup mold, lightly oiled OR an 8-cup mold lined with jelly, page 558

Following directions on page 580, beat the cream until it has doubled in volume and holds its shape softly. Fold the cream and optional truffles into the cold chicken mixture. Pack into the mold. Cover with waxed paper and chill for several hours before unmolding.

VARIATIONS

Mousse de Jambon

[Ham Mousse]

Use the same recipe and ingredients as for the preceding chicken mousse, but substitute 2⅓ cups of lean, chopped, boiled ham for the chicken and *foie gras;* a tablespoon of tomato paste may be added for color. Either 1 or 2 diced truffles or ½ cup minced mushrooms sautéed in butter may be folded into the mousse with the cream.

Mousse de Saumon

[Salmon Mousse]

Use the same recipe and ingredients as for the master recipe, chicken mousse, but with 2⅓ cups of cooked or canned salmon instead of chicken and *foie gras,* and use a white-wine fish stock, page 114 or 115, instead of white stock.

---

* *MOUSSELINE DE POISSON, BLANCHE NEIGE*

[Fish Mousse—with shellfish and *chaud-froid* sauce]

This is a handsome cold dish for a first course or luncheon, and looks well on a cold buffet table. It is important, however, that you season the mixture with care, and use an excellent stock for your jelly, or the flavor of the mousse will not be interesting. Instead of molding the mousse, you may heap it into individual serving shells, then sauce and decorate them as suggested in the recipe.

If you do not have an electric blender, purée the cooked fish in a food mill.

For about 6 cups serving 8 to 10 people

3¼ cups very good white-wine fish stock, page 114 or 115
(note that 1¼ cups are to be reserved for sauce at end of recipe)
¾ cup skinless and boneless sole or flounder *filets*
A small herb bouquet: 2 parsley sprigs, ⅓ bay leaf, and ⅛ tsp thyme tied in cheesecloth
A 2½-quart enameled saucepan

Place 2 cups of the fish stock with the fish and herb bouquet in the saucepan. Bring slowly almost to the simmer, cover, and poach the fish at just below the simmer for about 8 minutes, or until just tender when pierced with a fork.

An electric blender A slotted spoon	Remove the fish to the blender jar with a slotted spoon. Discard herb bouquet.
½ lb. diced fresh mush-rooms	Add the mushrooms to the fish stock in the saucepan. Boil slowly for 8 minutes. Strain, set mushrooms aside, and return liquid to saucepan.
2 Tb (2 envelopes) gelatin softened in 4 Tb dry white vermouth Salt and white pepper A 2½-quart mixing bowl	Stir the gelatin mixture into the liquid in the saucepan and simmer a moment to dissolve the gelatin com-pletely. Pour into the blender jar with the fish. Cover and blend at top speed for a minute or two until puréed. Taste very carefully for seasoning. Pour into a bowl, stir in the mushrooms, and chill. Stir occa-sionally until cold and almost set.
¾ cup chilled whipping cream, lightly beaten, page 580 A 6-cup, lightly oiled ring mold A chilled serving platter	Fold the whipped cream into the cold fish mixture, and turn into the oiled mold. Cover with waxed pa-per and chill for several hours to set. When ready to decorate, unmold the mousse on the platter and cover with the following sauce.

Sauce chaud-froid, blanche neige (2 cups)

The remaining fish stock from first paragraph (1¼ cups) 1¼ cups whipping cream ¼ tsp tarragon 1 Tb (1 envelope) gelatin softened in 3 Tb dry white vermouth Salt and white pepper A bowl of cracked ice	Simmer the stock, cream, and tarragon in a saucepan until reduced to 2 cups. Stir in the gelatin mixture and simmer a moment to dissolve it completely. Cor-rect seasoning, and strain. Stir over cracked ice until the sauce thickens lightly and is about to set.
1½ cups cooked shrimp, lobster, or crab meat warmed in ¼ cup dry white wine or vermouth, seasoned with salt and pepper, then chilled Thin slices of truffle or any of the decorative sugges-tions on page 546	Fold ½ cup of the sauce into the chilled shellfish, and place in the center of the mousse. Coat the mousse and shellfish with several spoonfuls of sauce. Chill for 10 minutes, and repeat with layers of almost-set sauce. Immediately after the last application of sauce, decorate the mousse with truffles or whatever else you have chosen. Chill until serving time.

VARIATION

Mousseline de Crustacés, Blanche Neige

[Shellfish Mousse]

Substitute cooked shellfish meat for the sole or flounder in the preceding recipe, but omit the simmering of fish in stock, paragraph one.

PÂTÉS AND TERRINES
Pâtés et Terrines

The memory of a good French *pâté* can haunt you for years. Fortunately they are easy to make, and you can even develop your own special *pâté maison*. Do not expect a top-notch mixture to be inexpensive, however, for it will contain ground pork, pork fat, and usually veal, as well as cognac, port, or Madeira, spices, strips or cubes of other meats, game, or liver, and often truffles. If the mixture is cooked and served cold in its baking dish it is called either a *terrine* or a *pâté*. If it is molded in a pastry crust, it is a *pâté en croûte*. A boned chicken, turkey, or duck filled with the same type of mixture is a galantine. *Pâtés* and *terrines* will keep for about 10 days under refrigeration; they are fine to have on hand for cold impromptu meals, since all you need to serve with them are a salad and French bread.

Wines to serve with *pâtés* include the dry whites such as Chablis or Mâcon, *rosés,* or one of the light regional red wines such as Beaujolais or Chinon, or a good domestic wine of the same general types.

A NOTE ON PORK FAT

Fresh pork fat is an essential ingredient for the type of meat mixture which goes into a *pâté*. Blended with the meats, it prevents them from being dry and gives them a lighter texture. Cut into thin sheets, *bardes de lard,* it is used to line the inside of the baking dish. The best type is fat back—*lard gras*. This comes from the back of the pig next to the skin. It is firm and does not disintegrate as easily as fat from other parts of the animal. Fresh fat back is unfortunately difficult to find in America outside of areas catering to special clienteles. Alternatives are fat salt pork simmered for 10 minutes in water to freshen it and remove the salt, or fat trimmed from fresh ham, or from around a fresh pork loin. Thick strips of fat bacon, simmered for 10 minutes in water to remove the smoky taste, may be used to line a baking dish.

BAKING DISHES

Pâtés may be cooked in almost any kind of a baking dish from a special rectangular or oval mold called a *terrine,* to a soufflé dish, casserole, or bread pan. The best materials are glazed pottery, porcelain, enameled iron, or pyrex. Cover the meat mixture with aluminum foil, and the dish with a heavy lid; old recipes call for a cover held in place with a thick band of flour and water paste.

STORAGE

Pâtés, terrines, and galantines may be frozen, but they will never again have their original texture. Once you have compared the two, you will always recognize the somewhat damp quality of thawed *pâté.* If a *pâté* is to be kept for 10 days or more under refrigeration, it should be unmolded after it has been chilled and the meat jelly wiped off its surface. It then may be wrapped airtight in waxed paper and foil, or returned to its *terrine* and covered with melted pork fat.

ASPIC

(Recipes for aspics are on pages 112 to 115; instructions for lining and decorating molds start on page 558.)

To serve a *pâté* in aspic unmold the *pâté* after it has been chilled, and scrape off the layer of pork fat surrounding it. Line the bottom of a slightly larger mold with a ⅛-inch layer of jellied stock and chill until set. Place the *pâté* in the mold, and pour almost-set jellied stock around and over it. Chill. Unmold on a chilled platter.

Another system is to slice the chilled *pâté,* arrange it on a platter lined with jellied stock, and then glaze the slices with jelly as for the *boeuf mode en gelée* on page 556.

FARCE POUR PÂTÉS, TERRINES, ET GALANTINES

[Pork and Veal Stuffing]

This good general-purpose meat mixture we shall refer to as a stuffing, for that is a translation of the French generic term *farce.* It can be used as the basis for any type of *pâté, terrine,* or galantine you wish. Mixed with chestnuts, it can also serve as a filling for roast goose or turkey. The pork gives flavor, the veal gives lightness. The proportions may be changed according to your own ideas, and sautéed liver, ground poultry, or game may be beaten into it. Minced truffles are always a good addition, and you can include such things as pistachios, or strips or cubes of pork fat, tongue, or ham to give a pattern to the meat when it is sliced.

For about 4 cups

½ cup very finely minced onions
2 Tb butter
A large mixing bowl

Cook the onions slowly with the butter in a small skillet for 8 to 10 minutes until they are tender and translucent but not browned. Scrape them into the mixing bowl.

½ cup port, Madeira, or cognac

Pour the wine into the skillet and boil it down until reduced by half. Scrape it into the mixing bowl.

¾ lb. (about 1½ cups) each, lean pork and lean veal and ½ lb. (1 cup) fresh pork fat, all finely ground together
2 lightly beaten eggs
1½ tsp salt
⅛ tsp pepper
Big pinch of allspice
½ tsp thyme
Optional: 1 clove mashed garlic
A wooden spoon

Add all the ingredients to the left, and beat vigorously with a wooden spoon until the mixture has lightened in texture and is thoroughly blended. Sauté a small spoonful and taste. Then beat in whatever additions you feel are necessary. It should be perfectly flavored. If not to be used immediately, cover and refrigerate.

---

* *TERRINE DE PORC, VEAU, ET JAMBON*

[Pork and Veal *Pâté* with Ham]

A pork and veal *pâté* with decorative strips of veal and ham buried in its slices is the most classic of all *pâté* mixtures; the three elements blend themselves in a very savory manner.

For about 7 cups

Marinating the veal strips

½ lb. lean veal from the round or *filet* cut into strips ¼ inch thick

Optional: 2 or 3 canned truffles cut into ¼-inch dice, and juice from can

A bowl

3 Tb cognac

Big pinch of salt and pepper

Pinch of thyme

Pinch of allspice

1 Tb finely minced shallots or green onions

Marinate the veal and optional truffles and their juice in a bowl with the cognac and seasonings while preparing the other ingredients. Before using, drain the strips, and reserve the marinade.

Molding the pâté

Preheat oven to 350 degrees.

An 8-cup rectangular or oval *terrine,* baking dish, casserole, or loaf pan

Sheets of fresh pork fat back ⅛ inch thick, or blanched fat salt pork, or blanched fat bacon, page 15

4 cups of the preceding pork and veal stuffing

½ lb. lean boiled ham cut into strips ¼ inch thick

1 bay leaf

A sheet of pork fat or strips of blanched bacon to cover the *pâté*

Line the bottom and sides of the *terrine* with the pork fat or bacon. Beat marinade into stuffing; divide stuffing into three parts. Dip your hands in cold water, and arrange the first third of the stuffing in the bottom of the *terrine.* Cover with half the strips of marinated veal alternating with half the strips of ham. If using diced truffles, place a row down the center. Cover with the second third of the stuffing, and a final layer of veal and ham strips, and optional truffles. Spread on the last of the meat stuffing. Lay the bay leaf on top, and cover with a sheet of pork fat or bacon strips.

Baking the pâté

Aluminum foil

A heavy lid for the terrine

A pan of boiling water

Enclose the top of the *terrine* with aluminum foil, cover, and set in the pan of boiling water. The water should come about halfway up the outside of the *terrine;* add boiling water during cooking, as necessary. Set in lower third of preheated oven and bake for about 1½ hours depending on the shape of the *terrine;*

a long loaf shape will cook faster than a round or oval shape. The *pâté* is done when it has shrunk slightly from the sides of the *terrine,* and the surrounding fat and juices are clear yellow with no traces of rosy color.

Cooling and chilling

Take the *terrine* from the water and set it on a plate. Remove lid, and on top of the foil covering the *pâté* put a piece of wood, a pan, or a casserole which will just fit into the *terrine.* On or in it, place a 3- to 4-lb. weight or parts of a meat grinder; this will pack the *pâté* into the *terrine* so there will be no air spaces in the meat. Allow the *pâté* to cool at room temperature for several hours or overnight. Then chill it, still weighted down.

Serving

Serve the *pâté* from its *terrine,* slicing down through it with a knife. Or unmold it and serve on a platter, or decorate in aspic as suggested on page 565.

VARIATIONS

Pâté de Veau et Porc avec Gibier

[Game *Pâté*]

For rabbit, hare, partridge, pheasant, duck, and other game

---

1 lb. (about 2 cups) boneless, skinless, raw game
Ingredients for the preceding pork and veal *pâté,* minus the veal strips and ham strips

Following the preceding recipe, cut the game meat into strips ¼ inch wide, and marinate them in cognac and seasonings. Grind the smaller pieces and beat them into the stuffing mixture; then proceed with the recipe.

Pâté de Veau et Porc avec Foie

[Pork and Veal *Pâté* with Liver]

Ingredients for the pork and veal *pâté* in the preceding master recipe, minus the veal strips and ham strips

Follow the master recipe, but after cooking the onions for the meat stuffing, cut the liver into ¼-inch pieces and sauté with the onions for 2 to 3 minutes until the liver is slightly stiffened but still rosy inside. Scrape

1 lb. (about 2 cups) liver: chicken, calf, lamb, pork, or beef   into the mixing bowl, and proceed with the recipe. (The cognac and other ingredients listed in the recipe as a marinade may be beaten into your meat stuffing, if you wish.)

A NOTE ON GALANTINES

The boned and stuffed duck in the following recipe would be a *galantine de canard* rather than a *canard en croûte* if it were stuffed then wrapped in a damp towel, poached in meat stock, cooled with a weight over it, chilled, and glazed with jellied stock. The same system may be used also for large roasting chickens, capons, and turkeys.

PÂTÉ EN CROÛTE

[*Pâté* Baked in a Crust]

Canard en Croûte

The recipe we have chosen to illustrate *pâté en croûte* is boned duck stuffed, reformed, surrounded with decorated pastry, and baked. The same method may be used for any of the *pâté* mixtures previously described, and they do not have to be enclosed in duck skin. You may simply heap the mixture into a loaf on an oval of pastry and enclose it with a second oval. Or you may line a spring mold with pastry, pack the mixture into it, and cover with more pastry. All *pâtés en croûte,* in other words, follow the same general out-line for forming and baking.

HOW TO BONE A DUCK, TURKEY, OR CHICKEN

You may think that boning a fowl is an impossible feat if you have never seen it done or thought of attempting it. Although the procedure may take 45 minutes the first time because of fright, it can be accomplished in not much more than 20 on your second or third try. The object is to remove the flesh with the skin from the carcass bones without piercing the skin except at the back where the bird is slit open, and at the natural openings at the vent and neck. The skin is to serve as a container for the *pâté*. Laid flat on a board, the *pâté* mixture is heaped onto it, then the skin is folded over the *pâté* mixture and sewed in place. When baked in a *terrine* and unmolded, or baked in a crust, the sutures are on the bottom, and the *pâté* appears to be enclosed in an unbroken, browned casing—which is the skin. It is always an impressive sight. The important thing to remember is that the cutting edge of your knife must always face the bone, never the flesh, thus you cannot pierce the skin.

To begin with, cut a deep slit down the back of the bird from the neck to the tail, to expose the backbone. With a small, sharp knife, its edge always cutting against the bone, scrape and cut the flesh from the carcass bones down one side of the bird, pulling the flesh away from the carcass with your fingers as you cut. When you come to the ball joints connecting the wings and the second joints to the carcass, sever them, and continue down the carcass until you reach just the ridge of the breast where skin and bone meet. Then stop. You must be careful here, as the skin is thin and easily slit. Repeat the same operation on the other side of the bird. By the time you have completed half of this, the carcass frame, dangling legs, wings, and skin will appear to be an unrecognizable mass of confusion and you will wonder how in the world any sense can be made of it all. But just continue cutting against the bone, and not slitting any skin, and all will come out as it should. When you finally arrive at the ridge of the breastbone on this opposite side, stop again. Then lift the carcass frame and cut very closely against the ridge of the breastbone to free the carcass, but not to slit the thin skin covering the breastbone. Chop off the wings at the elbows, to leave just the upper wing bones attached.

Then arrange this mass of skin and flesh on a board, flesh side up. You will now see, protruding from the flesh, the pair of ball joints of the wings and of the two second joints. Scrape the meat from the bones of the wings and pull out the bones. Repeat for the second joints, severing them from the ball joints of the drumsticks; the drumstick bones may be left in place if you wish. Discard any bits of fat adhering to the flesh, and the bird is ready to become a *pâté* or a galantine.

PÂTÉ DE CANARD EN CROÛTE

[Boned Stuffed Duck Baked in a Pastry Crust]
For 12 people

Stuffing the duck

A 5-lb. ready-to-cook roaster duckling **½ tsp salt** **⅛ tsp pepper** **Pinch of allspice** **2 Tb cognac** **2 Tb port** **Optional: 2 or 3 diced canned truffles and their juice**	Bone the duck as described in the preceding paragraphs, and lay the boned bird skin-side down on a board. Slice off the thickest layers of breast and thigh meat, and cut into cubes about ⅜ inch across. Place the cubes back on the duck, season, and sprinkle with cognac and port. Add the optional truffles and their juice. Roll up the duck, place it in a bowl, and refrigerate.
4 cups pork and veal stuffing, page 565	Prepare the meat stuffing and mix into it the cubed duck meat, optional truffles, and marinade.
A trussing needle **White string**	Spread the boned duck on a board, skin-side down. Heap the stuffing in the center and shape it into a

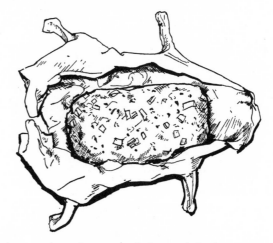

*Boned duck
with stuffing*

NOTE: *In this and following drawings, wings bones and drumsticks have not been removed.*

Duck skin folded
around stuffing

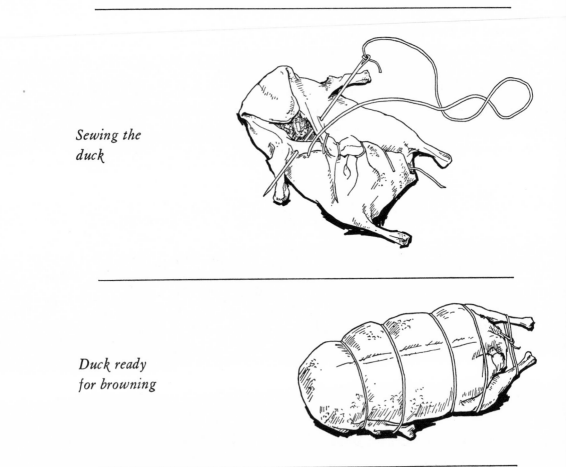

loaf. Bring the duck skin up over the loaf to enclose
it completely. Sew it in place with a trussing needle

Sewing the
duck

Duck ready
for browning

and white string. Make 3 or 4 ties around the circumference of the duck to give it a cylindrical shape.

---

3 Tb cooking oil
A large skillet

Heat the oil in the skillet until it is almost smoking. Then brown the duck slowly on all sides. Remove, and allow it to cool. The trussing strings remain on the duck to hold its shape while baking.

Forming the crust

6 cups (1¼ lbs.) all-purpose
    flour
¼ cup (2 ounces) vegetable
    shortening
½ cup (4 ounces) butter
1½ tsp salt
¼ tsp sugar
2 eggs
About ⅔ cup cold water

Following directions on page 139, prepare a chilled pastry dough with the ingredients at the left.

Preheat oven to 400 degrees.

A greased baking sheet
A pastry brush

Roll two thirds of the pastry dough into an oval ⅛ inch thick. Lay it on the baking sheet. Place the duck

---

*Duck in bottom
pastry oval*

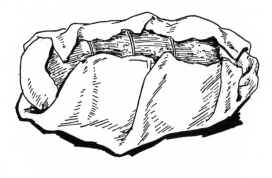

---

1 egg beaten with 1 tsp cold
    water in a small bowl

on the oval, breast up. Bring the pastry up around the duck, patting it into place. Roll out the rest of the dough ⅛ inch thick and cut it into an oval to fit over the top of the duck. Paint the edges of the bottom pastry oval with a pastry brush dipped in beaten egg,

*Pressing pastry
ovals together*

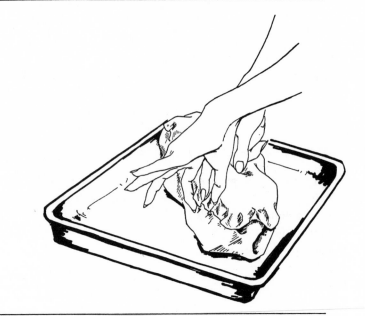

and press the top oval in place. Flute or pinch the
edges together to seal them.

Make circles or ovals with a 1½-inch cooky cutter in the remaining pastry, and press
fan-shaped lines into them with the back of a knife.

Pastry cut-outs

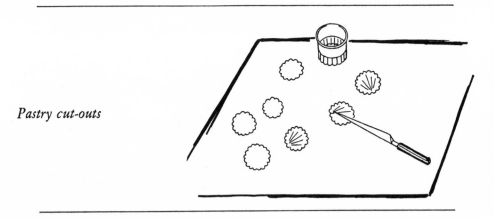

Paint the top pastry oval with beaten egg, and press the pastry cutouts over it in a
decorative design. Paint with beaten egg.

Make a ⅛-inch hole in the center of the pastry and insert a brown paper or foil
funnel; this will allow cooking steam to escape. Insert a meat thermometer into the
hole through the funnel, and down through the duck skin into the *pâté*.

The duck is ready for the oven

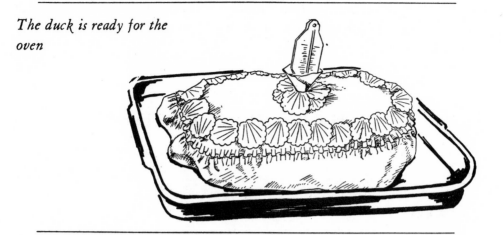

Baking the pâté

Place the duck in the middle position of the preheated oven, and turn the heat down to 350 degrees. Bake for about 2 hours, or to a thermometer reading of 180 degrees.

Remove from oven and allow to cool for several hours; the crust will soften if the *pâté* is refrigerated too soon. Then chill.

TO SERVE

A little preliminary work in the kitchen will enable you to present your duck with the elegance and drama it deserves. Before bringing it to the table, then, cut around the crust just under the seam of the top pastry oval; lift the oval off carefully so as not to break it. The duck will have shrunk from the crust during its baking, so you can lift it out of the bottom crust. Remove the circular trussing strings from around the duck, then cut and pull out the sewing strings underneath the duck.

If carving is to take place at the table, put the duck back into the bottom crust and replace the top pastry oval. The carver will then decide whether to remove the duck from the crust and carve it as suggested farther on, or whether to cut right down through the crust and through the duck, making crosswise slices of duck with crust.

If the duck is to be carved before serving, follow either of the two methods in the next paragraph, then reconstruct the duck in its bottom crust, and replace the top pastry oval.

To carve the duck after removing it from the crust, either make crosswise slices as though you were cutting a sausage, or make a deep incision the length of the breast, and cut lengthwise slices angled toward the center of the duck on each side.

OTHER COLD DISHES

Here is a list of cold dishes which are described as hot elsewhere in the book.

Eggs

Oeufs brouillés pipérade, scrambled eggs garnished with a *pipérade* (the cooked green peppers, onions, and tomatoes used for *omelette pipérade* on page 137). The *pipérade* is mixed into the eggs after they have been scrambled; the eggs are chilled, and used to fill tomato cases.

Fish

Thon à la provençale, tuna or swordfish baked with tomatoes, wine, and herbs, page 219

Poultry

Poulet grillé à la diable, broiled chicken with herbs, mustard, and bread crumbs, page 265

Poulet sauté and *poulet sauté aux herbes de Provence,* either of these two recipes for sautéed chicken beginning on page 254, without the sauce

Poulet poêlé à l'estragon, casserole-roasted chicken with tarragon, page 249. This is one of the best ways to cook a whole chicken that is to be served cold.

Canard à l'orange, duck with orange, page 276, or with the other fruits suggested in the recipes following it. The sauce is made according to the directions in the recipe but, instead of thickening the sauce with arrowroot, dissolve gelatin in it (1 tablespoon or 1 envelope for each 2 cups), and glaze the duck as in the recipe for *poulet en gelée à l'estragon,* page 549.

Beef

Daube de boeuf, casserole of beef with wine, herbs, and vegetables, page 322.

Lamb

Moussaka, lamb and eggplant baked in a mold lined with eggplant skins, then unmolded, page 349. This makes a handsome cold dish, and is an excellent way to use up cold roast lamb.

Pork and Veal

Veau poêlé or *rôti de porc poêlé,* casserole-roasted veal with herbs, page 353, or pork, page 380. Both of these are good cold, and if you wish to dress them up, slice the meat and spread each slice with *beurre Montpellier* (green herb mayonnaise with butter, anchovies, pickles, and capers, page 90), reform the roast, and spread with a covering of the mayonnaise. Chill before serving.

Veau Sylvie or porc Sylvie, veal marinated in wine then stuffed with ham and cheese before roasting, page 357, or pork treated in the same manner, page 385.

Ham

Jambon braisé au Madère, ham braised in Madeira wine, page 393. See also the recipes following it, for ham braised with mushroom stuffing, and ham in a pastry crust. All of these are good cold, and a pleasant change from plain cold, baked or boiled ham.

Sweetbreads and Brains

Ris de veau braisés or *cervelles braisés,* braised sweetbreads, page 409, or brains, page 415. Either may be dressed with vinaigrette and herbs and used as a cold meat dish, or as part of a combination salad.

Artichokes

Artichauts au naturel or *fonds d'artichauts à blanc,* cold boiled artichokes, page 424, or cooked artichoke bottoms, page 430. Either of these may be served with vinaigrette or mayonnaise. You may fill cold, cooked artichoke bottoms with vegetables, meat, poultry, or fish in mayonnaise; you could also fill them with one of the aspics or mousses described in this chapter.

Eggplant

Aubergines farcies duxelles, eggplant cases stuffed with mushrooms, page 501. These go well with cold, roast lamb.

Ratatouille, eggplant casserole with tomatoes, onions, and zucchini, page 503. This dish is just as good cold as it is hot, and is especially recommended with cold roast lamb, beef, pork, chicken, and fish. A bit of leftover *ratatouille* may be passed through a food mill with hard-boiled egg yolks to make a filling for stuffed eggs or stuffed tomatoes.

Celery and Leeks

Céleris braisés and *poireaux braisés,* braised celery, page 491, braised leeks, page 495. Either of these may be part of a cold vegetable combination, or be served with cold meats.

Potatoes

Gratin de pommes de terre provençale, potato and tomato casserole with anchovies, page 525. Serve this with cold meats or fish.

Rice Salads

Cooked rice as a base for many salads and impromptu meals; ideas and one full recipe, page 532.

CHAPTER TEN

DESSERTS AND CAKES

Entremets et Gâteaux

FUNDAMENTAL TECHNIQUES AND INFORMATION

ONE OR SEVERAL of the following processes will be a part of almost any dessert or cake recipe you encounter. Some can be accomplished by machine, others are better performed by hand. None is difficult, but all contribute to the success of your dish and must be done precisely.

EGG WHITES

Innumerable desserts, as well as soufflés and all the spongecakes, call for stiffly beaten egg whites. Successful cooking of any of these dishes is usually dependent on how voluminous and stiff you have beaten the egg whites, and how carefully you have folded them into the rest of the ingredients. As they are so important, we shall continually put in little reminders and warnings about them. Directions and illustrations for egg whites begin on page 159, in the Entrée chapter. You will note that in all the recipes for beaten egg whites in this chapter a tablespoon of sugar is whipped into them near the end of the beating; this gives them an added bit of stiffness and body. You will also note that egg whites may be folded into either a hot or a cold sauce or batter; unlike whipped cream, which liquefies when it comes in contact with hot ingredients, egg whites are actually given a boost.

BEATING EGGS AND SUGAR TO FORM THE RIBBON

Whenever egg yolks and sugar are beaten together the recipe will say to continue beating "until the mixture is pale yellow and forms the ribbon." This prepares the egg yolks so that they can be heated without turning granular. To accomplish it, add the sugar gradually to the egg yolks in a mixing bowl while beating with a wire whip or an electric beater; continue beating for 2 to 3 minutes. The mixture will turn a pale, creamy yellow, and thicken enough so that when a bit is lifted in the beater, it will fall back into the bowl forming a slowly dissolving ribbon on the surface of the mixture. Do not beat beyond this point or the egg yolks may become granular.

WHIPPED CREAM

As used in French cooking, whipped cream should double in volume, and be light, smooth, and free from granules. Much the same principles apply to it as to the beating of egg whites, in that you must incorporate as much air as possible. The stationary electric beater never produces as smooth and light a cream as could be wished; the electric blender is not recommended at all. For success every time, beat your chilled heavy cream with a large balloon whip or hand-held electric beater in a large metal bowl set in another, larger bowl containing a tray of ice cubes and water to cover them. It will take you 4 to 5 minutes to whip cream until the beater leaves light traces on the surface, and worth every minute to achieve an unbelievably beautiful and tender texture.

Warning

If whipped cream is to be folded into other ingredients, be sure the other ingredients are cold; otherwise the cream will lose its stiffness and thin out.

A note on French cream

Although French *crème fraîche* and American whipping cream both contain approximately the same amount of butter fat, the consistency of French cream is thicker because it is slightly fermented. It must be thinned before whipping by the addition of 1 part of cold milk, iced water, or shaved ice for every 3 parts of cream.

Crème Chantilly

[Lightly Beaten Cream]

This is lightly beaten cream, which is usually specified for such desserts as Bavarian cream, and for dessert sauces.

For about 2 cups

½ pint (1 cup) chilled whipping cream
A 3-quart metal bowl set
   over a bowl with ice cubes
   and water to cover them
A large balloon whip or a
   portable electric beater

Pour the cream into the bowl set over ice, and beat it
slowly until it begins to foam, while circulating the
beater all around the bowl and lifting the cream as
you whip it. Gradually increase the beating speed to
moderate and continue until the beater leaves light
traces on the surface of the cream. A bit of cream
lifted and dropped on the surface will softly retain its
shape.

Stiffly beaten cream

For desserts which require more body, continue beating a few seconds
more until the cream is a little bit stiffer and forms soft peaks. Do not beat beyond this stage or the cream will become granular, and then begin to turn into
butter.

Storing whipped cream

Once cream is whipped, it will keep for several hours under refrigeration.
As it usually exudes a bit of liquid, it is a good idea to turn it into a fine-meshed
sieve and place the sieve over a bowl. This allows any seeping liquid to drop
out of the cream.

Flavored whipped cream

Before serving, fold in 2 tablespoons of sifted powdered sugar and a
tablespoon or two of brandy, rum, or sweet liqueur, or a teaspoon or two of
vanilla extract.

CREAMING BUTTER AND SUGAR

Numerous dessert and cake recipes direct that butter and sugar be
creamed together; this may be accomplished either by machine or by hand.

Electric Beater Use the pastry-blender attachment if you have one;
you may use the regular beater, but the blades will become clogged. Cut the
butter into ½-inch pieces. Warm the large mixing bowl in hot water. Dry it,
add the butter and sugar, and beat at a moderate speed for several minutes.
The mixture is ready to be used when it is light, fluffy, and a pale ivory color.

Hand Beating If the butter has been left at room temperature for an
hour to soften, simply beat the butter and sugar together in a bowl for several
minutes until they form a light, fluffy mass. For cold, hard butter, use the following system: Cut the butter into ½-inch pieces and place it with the sugar
in a mixing bowl set over barely simmering water. Beat with a wooden spoon
for several seconds until the butter softens. Then set the bowl in a basin of

cold water and beat for a minute or two until the mixture is light, fluffy, and a pale ivory color.

MELTED CHOCOLATE

Because baking chocolate burns easily, it needs special treatment. We find it best to break the chocolate into small pieces (or use chocolate drops: 2 ounces make ⅓ cup). Place the chocolate in a small covered saucepan by itself, or with the liquid specified in your recipe; set the pan in another, larger pan of simmering water, and at once remove the larger pan from heat. In 4 to 5 minutes your chocolate will be perfectly melted and smooth. Keep it in the warm water until ready to use.

ALMONDS

Whole, slivered, and powdered almonds have many uses in French pastries and desserts. Luckily you can buy blanched almonds in airtight cans at almost any American market, and although you do not often see powdered almonds, they pulverize easily in the blender or processor. You will note that all the recipes which use almonds also call for a bit of almond extract to bring out the almond taste. This is not necessary in France, as one or two bitter almonds are always included. But as the oil of bitter almonds is poisonous when taken in too large a quantity, it can only be bought with a doctor's prescription in this country. But be careful with almond extract. It is strong; a few drops or a quarter teaspoon are usually sufficient.

Measurements Four ounces of whole, broken, or powdered almonds are equivalent to about ¾ cup or 125 grams.

Blanched Almonds Drop shelled almonds into boiling water and boil 1 minute. Drain. Squeeze each almond between the thumb and forefinger, and the almond will slip out of its skin. Spread the blanched almonds in a roasting pan and dry them out for 5 minutes in a 350-degree oven.

Pulverized Almonds These are most easily done in the blender or processor, and should always be ground ½ cup at a time for the blender (1 cup for the processor) with several tablespoons of sugar to prevent them from becoming oily and lumpy, which would make them impossible to combine with other dry ingredients.

Toasted or Grilled Almonds Spread whole, slivered, or powdered almonds in a roasting pan and set in a 350-degree oven for about 10 minutes. Stir them up frequently and keep an eye on them so they do not burn. They should emerge an even, light, toasty brown.

Pralin

[Caramelized Almonds]

This delicious ingredient is quickly made and can be stored for weeks in a screw-topped jar. It is used in desserts and sauces, as a sprinkling for ice cream, and as a flavoring for cake icings and fillings. In France, *pralin* is also made with hazel nuts or a mixture of hazel nuts and almonds.

For about 1 cup

½ cup slivered or powdered almonds	Toast the almonds in a 350-degree oven as previously described.
½ cup granulated sugar 2 Tb water An oiled marble slab or large baking sheet	Boil the sugar and water in a small saucepan until the sugar caramelizes (see directions for caramel farther on). Immediately stir in the toasted almonds. Bring just to the boil, then pour onto the marble or baking sheet. When cold, in about 10 minutes, break the hardened mass into pieces. Pulverize in the electric blender, pound to a coarse powder in a mortar, or put it through a meat grinder.

Pulverized Macaroons

Pulverized stale macaroons may be substituted for *pralin*. Break macaroons into small pieces, spread them in a roasting pan, and set in a 200-degree oven for about an hour. Remove when they are fairly dry and lightly browned; they will crisp up as they cool. When crisped, pulverize them in the electric blender, pound in a mortar, or put them through a meat grinder. Store in a screw-topped jar where they will keep for weeks.

Caramel

[Caramel]

Caramel is sugar syrup cooked until it turns a light, nut brown. It is used as a flavoring or coloring, or for coating a mold.

For about ½ cup

⅔ cup granulated sugar or crushed sugar lumps
⅓ cup water
A small, heavy saucepan (with cover)

until sugar has dissolved completely and liquid is perfectly clear. Cover the pan (steam condensing on cover will wash any crystals off sides of pan). Boil without stirring until syrup is thick and turns a light nutty brown (keep peeking).

Remove from heat just before desired color is reached because syrup will continue to darken (or plunge pan into cold water). Caramel may be reheated.

Caramel Syrup

Pour ⅓ cup of water into the preceding caramel and simmer, stirring, until the caramel has dissolved.

HOW TO LINE A MOLD WITH CARAMEL
Un Moule Caramelisé
[A Caramel-lined Mold]

Custard desserts are often baked in a mold lined with caramel so that the dessert will be covered with a brown glaze when unmolded. You may make the caramel directly in the mold when you are using a metal one such as the *charlotte* illustrated for soufflés on page 162. If you are using porcelain, make the caramel separately. Metal takes a caramel lining more evenly than porcelain, and the dessert is usually easier to unmold. We therefore suggest you buy metal molds if you plan to do many desserts of this type. After unmolding the dessert, you will be directed by your recipe to add a little liquid to the mold and simmer it to dissolve the remaining caramel; set the mold over an asbestos mat, if you are using fireproof porcelain, or omit this step.

For a 6-cup metal mold

½ cup granulated sugar or crushed sugar lumps
2 Tb water
A pan of cold water
A plate

Boil the sugar and water in the mold over moderate heat, swirling the mold frequently, until the syrup caramelizes. At once, dip the mold in the cold water for 2 to 3 seconds to cool it very slightly. Then tilt the mold in all directions to film the bottom and sides with caramel. When the caramel has ceased to run, turn the mold upside down over a plate. This is now a caramelized mold.

For a fireproof porcelain mold (or cup-custard molds or ramekins)

Make the caramel in a saucepan. While it is cooking, warm the porcelain mold in a pan of hot water; remove it as soon as the caramel is done. Pour in the caramel and tilt the mold in all directions to film its bottom and sides. When the caramel has ceased to run, reverse the mold on a plate.

Charlotte Malakoff

HOW TO LINE A MOLD WITH LADYFINGERS

Some of the grand desserts such as the *charlotte Malakoff,* page 605, the *diplomate,* page 612, and the *charlotte Chantilly,* page 608, call for a mold lined with ladyfingers. Any kind of a cylindrical mold or dish will do for the operation, but the dessert will be more spectacular if your mold is the *charlotte* type 3½ to 4 inches deep, like that illustrated in the Soufflé section on page 162. Some recipes direct that the ladyfingers be dipped first in diluted liqueur; others do not. The procedure for lining the mold is the same in either case.

Warning

Do not attempt any dessert calling for a mold lined with ladyfingers unless you have ladyfingers of premium quality—dry and tender, not spongy and limp. Inferior ladyfingers, unfortunately the only kind usually available in bakeries, will debase an otherwise remarkable dessert. The recipe for homemade ladyfingers is on page 666.

Lining the bottom
of the mold

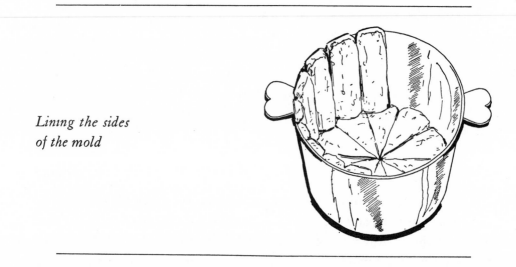

Cut the ladyfingers into a design of wedges to fit the bottom of the mold exactly. Lay them in the mold, their curved sides down.

Lining the sides
of the mold

Place a row of ladyfingers upright and pressed together, their curved sides against the sides of the mold. If your mold slants outward, you may have to trim the edges of the ladyfingers to make them slightly wedge-shaped.

The mold is now ready for filling, as directed in your recipe.

HOW TO UNMOLD A DESSERT

Many other desserts in this chapter, besides those with ladyfingers in the preceding paragraphs, are formed or baked in a mold, and are unmolded for serving. The easiest way to unmold them is: place a serving dish upside down over the mold and reverse the two quickly so the dish rests over a flat surface, give a sharp, downward jerk to dislodge the dessert, then remove the mold.

Vanilla

We have specified vanilla extract in all of the dessert and cake recipes. If you prefer to use the bean, steep it for 20 minutes in whatever hot liquid you are using. Sugar with a mild vanilla flavor is made by burying a vanilla bean for a week or so in a screw-topped jar with 1 pound of granulated sugar. For a strong flavor, pulverize ½ ounce or 2 whole vanilla beans in a mortar with ¼ pound or about ¾ cup of sugar lumps, then pass through a very fine-meshed sieve. If you use an electric blender for this, allow the pulverized mixture to stand in a closed jar for a week or so before sieving it.

Glazed Orange or Lemon Peel

This provides a nice decoration and is easy to make.
For about ½ cup

---

5 lemons or 3 bright-skinned oranges A vegetable peeler 1 quart of simmering water	Remove the colored part of the lemon or orange skin with a vegetable peeler. Cut into julienne strips 1½ inches long and 1/16 inch wide. Simmer in water for 10 to 12 minutes or until just tender when bitten. Drain. Refresh in cold water. Dry on paper towels.
1 cup granulated sugar ⅓ cup water A candy thermometer, if possible 1 tsp vanilla extract	Boil the sugar and water in a small saucepan to the thread stage (230 degrees). Remove from heat. Stir in the drained peel and the vanilla. Let the peel stand in the syrup for at least 30 minutes. Drain when ready to use. Under refrigeration, the peel will keep in the syrup for several weeks.

Flour

Be sure to measure your flour correctly. This is especially important for cakes. All recipes are based on the flour-measuring method described on page 17.

SWEET SAUCES AND FILLINGS

Sauces Sucrées et Crèmes

Crème anglaise, a light custard sauce, and *crème pâtissière,* a thick custard filling, are fundamental to French desserts and pastries. Both are quick to do, and should definitely be in anyone's repertoire.

CRÈME ANGLAISE

[Light Custard Sauce]

This sauce is a blend of egg yolks, sugar, and milk stirred over heat until it thickens into a light cream. If it comes near the simmer, the yolks will scramble. Although it can be omitted, a very small amount of starch in the sauce acts as a safeguard just in case the heat becomes too much for the egg yolks. Some recipes direct that the sauce be cooked in a double boiler; this is slow work and quite unnecessary if you concentrate on what you are doing, and use a heavy-bottomed saucepan. A candy thermometer is a useful guide.

Vanilla is the basic flavoring for *crème anglaise;* others are added to the vanilla if you wish, such as coffee, liqueurs, or chocolate. The sauce is served either warm or chilled, depending on your dessert. Less rich than cream, *crème anglaise* is used on fruit desserts, molded creams, puddings, ice cream, or accompanies any dessert where it could be substituted for cream. With additional egg yolks and with heavy cream, it becomes the custard used for ice creams. Also with more egg yolks, plus gelatin, whipped cream, and flavoring, it is ready to be a Bavarian cream.

For about 2 cups

½ cup granulated sugar
4 egg yolks
A 3-quart mixing bowl
A wire whip or electric
  beater

Gradually beat the sugar into the egg yolks and continue beating for 2 to 3 minutes until the mixture is pale yellow and forms the ribbon, page 579.

Optional: 1 tsp cornstarch
  or potato starch

Beat in the optional starch.

1¾ cup boiling milk

While beating the yolk mixture, very gradually pour on the boiling milk in a thin stream of droplets so that the yolks are slowly warmed.

A clean, heavy-bottomed enameled or stainless steel saucepan
A wooden spatula or spoon
Optional but recommended: a candy thermometer

Pour the mixture into the saucepan and set over moderate heat, stirring slowly and continuously with a wooden spatula or spoon, and reaching all over the bottom and sides of the pan, until the sauce thickens just enough to coat the spoon with a light, creamy layer. Do not let the custard come anywhere near the simmer. Maximum temperature is 165 degrees on the candy thermometer (170 if you have used starch). Then beat the sauce off heat for a minute or two to cool it. Strain it through a fine sieve, and beat in one of the flavorings at the left.

Flavorings

1 Tb vanilla extract
OR, 1 tsp vanilla extract and 1 Tb rum, kirsch, cognac, orange liqueur, or instant coffee
OR, 2 or 3 ounces or squares of semisweet baking chocolate melted in the boiling milk, and 1 tsp vanilla extract stirred into the finished sauce

To serve hot: Keep the sauce over warm but not hot water. If you wish, beat in 1 to 2 tablespoons of unsalted butter just before serving.

To serve cold: Set the saucepan in a pan of cold water, and stir frequently until cool. Then cover and chill.

Crème Brûlée

Crème brûlée originated in England, it appears, at Christ's College in Cambridge. Make the basic cream exactly like the preceding *crème anglaise,* but use half the amount of sugar, and whipping cream instead of milk. Chill in a serving dish. Rather than glazing the top of the cream with brown sugar, try spreading a ⅛-inch layer of *pralin,* page 583, over the cream. This would then be a *crème anglaise pralinée,* and is good as a dessert either by itself or served with strawberries.

CRÈME PÂTISSIÈRE

[Custard Filling]

This custard is also made of egg yolks, sugar, and milk, but unlike *crème anglaise,* it contains flour so it may be brought to the boil, and is much thicker. The proportions of flour vary according to the use of the filling; the following recipe is designed as a base for fruit tarts. With the addition of beaten egg whites it becomes a *crème Saint-Honoré* and may be used as a filling for cream puffs, or may be mixed with fruit to make a quick dessert like the *plombières* on page 594.

For about 2½ cups

1 cup granulated sugar
5 egg yolks
A 3-quart mixing bowl
A wire whip or electric beater

Gradually beat the sugar into the egg yolks and continue beating for 2 to 3 minutes until the mixture is pale yellow and forms the ribbon, page 579.

½ cup flour (scooped and leveled, see page 17)

Beat in the flour.

2 cups boiling milk

Beating the yolk mixture, gradually pour on the boiling milk in a thin stream of droplets.

A clean, heavy-bottomed 2½-quart, enameled saucepan
A wire whip

Pour into saucepan and set over moderately high heat. Stir with wire whip, reaching all over bottom of pan. As sauce comes to the boil it will get lumpy, but will smooth out as you beat it. When boil is reached, beat over moderately low heat for 2 to 3 minutes to cook the flour. Be careful custard does not scorch in bottom of pan.

1 Tb butter
Flavorings
1½ Tb vanilla extract

Remove from heat and beat in the butter, then one of the flavorings at the left. If the custard is not used immediately, clean it off the sides of the pan, and dot top

OR, 2 tsp vanilla extract and 2 to 3 Tb rum, kirsch, cognac, orange liqueur, or instant coffee

OR, 3 ounces or squares of semisweet baking chocolate melted with 2 Tb rum or coffee and 2 tsp vanilla extract

OR, ½ cup pulverized almonds, page 582, or pulverized macaroons, page 583, ¼ tsp almond extract, and 2 tsp vanilla extract

of custard with softened butter to prevent a skin from forming over the surface. *Crème pâtissière* will keep for a week under refrigeration, or may be frozen.

CRÈME SAINT-HONORÉ

[Custard Filling with Beaten Egg Whites]

A *crème pâtissière* with the addition of stiffly beaten egg whites is used as a filling for tarts and cream puffs, and as a dessert cream. It is flavored with chocolate, liqueurs, grated orange peel, *pralin,* or whatever your recipe calls for.

For 5 to 6 cups

2½ cups *crème pâtissière*
8 egg whites
Big pinch of salt
2 Tb granulated sugar

Make the *crème pâtissière* as directed in the preceding recipe. Beat in the flavorings you have chosen. Beat the egg whites and salt together until soft peaks are formed; sprinkle on the sugar and continue beating until stiff peaks are formed, page 159. Stir one quarter of the egg whites into the hot custard, fold in the rest. If the cream is to be served cold, chill it in the refrigerator.

FRANGIPANE

[Almond Custard Filling]

This is a very thick type of *crème pâtissière* with crushed macaroons or powdered almonds. Use it as a filling for *crêpes* or tarts. Any leftover *frangipane* may be mixed with an equal amount of *crème pâtissière* and used as a filling.

For about 2 cups

A wire whip or electric beater
1 egg
1 egg yolk
A 3-quart mixing bowl
¾ cup granulated sugar
⅓ cup flour (scooped and leveled, see page 17)
1 cup boiling milk

Beat the egg and egg yolk in the mixing bowl, gradually adding the sugar, until mixture is pale yellow and forms the ribbon, page 579. Beat in the flour. Then beat in the boiling milk in a thin stream of droplets.

A clean, heavy-bottomed, 2½-quart, enameled saucepan
A wire whip
A wooden spoon

Pour into saucepan and set over moderate heat. Stir slowly with the whip, reaching all over the bottom of the pan. When mixture begins to coagulate into lumps, beat it vigorously until it smooths and thickens into a stiff paste. Then over moderately low heat, beat it with a wooden spoon for 2 to 3 minutes to cook the flour thoroughly. Be careful the custard does not scorch on the bottom of the pan.

3 Tb butter
2 tsp vanilla extract
¼ tsp almond extract
½ cup pulverized macaroons, page 583, or pulverized almonds, page 582
Optional: 2 to 3 Tb kirsch

Off heat, beat in the butter, then the flavorings, macaroons or almonds, and optional kirsch. If not used immediately, clean custard off sides of pan and dot top with softened butter to prevent a skin from forming on the surface. *Frangipane* will keep for a week under refrigeration, or may be frozen.

FRUIT SAUCES

Fruit sauces are made from purées of fresh or frozen fruits, or from fruit jams and jellies. They are used with ice creams, custard desserts, and various puddings.

Sauce aux Fraises

[Fresh Strawberry Sauce]

Sauce aux Framboises

[Fresh Raspberry Sauce]
For about 2 cups

1 quart fresh strawberries or raspberries

Hull, wash, drain, and sieve the fruit. Add sugar to taste. Either whip for 2 to 3 minutes in a blender, or

A sieve and wooden spoon

¾ to 1¼ cups sugar (instant or very finely granulated if possible)

An electric blender or an electric beater

2 to 3 Tb kirsch, cognac, or lemon juice

beat for 10 minutes with an electric beater. The sugar should dissolve completely; the purée will be quite thick. Beat in kirsch, cognac, or lemon juice to taste.

Made with frozen berries

Thaw the berries and drain them thoroughly. Force them through a sieve, and beat in some of their syrup to thin out the purée. Flavor with kirsch, cognac, or lemon juice.

Made with jam, preserves, or jelly (about 1 cup)

½ cup orange marmalade and ½ cup apricot preserves

OR, ½ cup strawberry or raspberry jam and ½ cup red currant jelly

2 to 3 Tb kirsch or cognac

A sieve and wooden spoon

Stir the mixture in a saucepan over moderate heat until melted. Simmer for a moment with the liqueur, then force through a sieve.

STRAINED APRICOT PRESERVES

Before using apricot preserves (or jam) in a recipe, stir it over heat, if necessary, until it has melted, then rub it through a sieve to leave the bits of skin behind. If not used immediately, it will keep almost indefinitely in its original container.

GLAZES

Either apricot preserves or red currant jelly contains enough pectin so that when boiled to between 225 and 228 degrees it will stiffen slightly as it cools and not be sticky to the touch. You may then use it as a glaze, paint it over the top of a tart to give brilliance and glitter, spread it over a cake to act as a simple icing, or paint it inside a baked pastry shell to provide a light waterproofing before the filling goes in.

Abricot

[For Apricot Glaze]

Gelée de Groseilles

[For Red Currant Glaze]

For about ½ cup red currant or apricot glaze

½ cup apricot preserves, forced through a sieve OR, ½ cup red currant jelly

2 Tb granulated sugar

A small saucepan

A wooden spatula or spoon

Optional: a candy thermometer

Stir the strained apricot preserves or currant jelly with the sugar over moderately high heat for 2 to 3 minutes until thick enough to coat the spoon with a light film, and the last drops are sticky as they fall from the spoon (225 to 228 degrees on a candy thermometer). Do not boil beyond this point or the glaze will become brittle when it cools.

Apply the glaze while it is still warm. Unused glaze will keep indefinitely in a screw-topped jar; reheat again before using.

CUSTARDS, MOUSSES, AND MOLDS

Crèmes et Mousses

* *CRÈME PLOMBIÈRES PRALINÉE*

[Caramel Almond Cream—a cold dessert]

A *crème plombières* is a custard filling into which beaten egg whites and a flavoring or fresh fruits are folded. It is spooned over ladyfingers or sponge-cake, then chilled. For the few minutes it takes to assemble, *crème plombières* makes a surprisingly attractive dessert.

For 6 servings

6 squares of stale sponge-cake or ladyfingers, about 1½ inches across and ½ inch thick

A 2-quart serving bowl about 4 inches deep or 6 dessert cups

2 Tb rum mixed with 2 Tb coffee

If the squares of cake or ladyfingers are not stale, dry them out for about an hour in a 200-degree oven. Arrange the pieces in the serving bowl, or place one in each dessert cup. Sprinkle with the rum and coffee.

4 egg yolks
⅓ cup granulated sugar
3 Tb flour
2½ cups boiling milk
1 Tb vanilla extract, or 2 tsp vanilla and 3 Tb rum
1 Tb butter

Following the procedure for *crème pâtissière*, page 590, beat the egg yolks and sugar in a mixing bowl until they are pale yellow and form the ribbon. Beat in the flour. Then beat in the boiling milk by droplets. Pour into a clean saucepan and, stirring with a wire whip, boil slowly for 2 minutes. Remove from heat and beat in the vanilla or rum, then the butter.

4 egg whites
Pinch of salt
1 Tb granulated sugar
3 Tb *pralin* (caramelized almonds), page 583, or the pulverized macaroons, on page 582

Beat the egg whites and salt until soft peaks are formed; sprinkle on the sugar and beat until stiff peaks are formed, page 159. Fold the egg whites and the *pralin* or macaroons into the hot *crème pâtissière*.

2 Tb *pralin* or pulverized macaroons

Spoon the cream into the serving bowl or dessert cups and chill for 2 to 3 hours, or until serving time. Just before serving, sprinkle with the rest of the *pralin* or macaroons.

VARIATIONS

Crème Plombières au Chocolat

[Chocolate Cream]

Use the ingredients and method in the master recipe, but substitute chocolate for all or part of the *pralin* as follows:

3 ounces or squares of semisweet baking chocolate melted with 3 Tb rum or strong coffee, and 2 tsp vanilla extract

Beat the smooth melted chocolate into 2½ cups of hot *crème pâtissière*. Then fold in the beaten egg whites.

1 ounce grated or shaved semisweet baking chocolate

Just before serving, sprinkle chocolate over the cream.

Crème Plombières aux Fruits

[*Plombières* with Fresh Strawberries or Raspberries]

Use the ingredients and method in the master recipe, but substitute fresh strawberries or raspberries for the *pralin*. Instead of soaking the cake in rum, use kirsch or cognac diluted with water; and use kirsch or cognac plus vanilla for flavoring the cream.

You may substitute defrosted frozen fruits for fresh fruits here, but they look rather limp, especially when used for a decoration on top.

1 cup sliced fresh strawberries or whole raspberries 2 Tb instant sugar (very finely granulated)	Sprinkle fruit with sugar and let stand for 10 minutes, or until ready to use. Fold into the cream with the egg whites.
12 to 18 whole strawberries or 1 cup raspberries 2 Tb instant sugar	Sprinkle the berries with sugar, let stand for 10 minutes. Arrange over dessert just before serving.

Crème Plombières à l'Ananas

[*Plombières* with Pineapple]

Follow the ingredients and method in the master recipe, but substitute pineapple for the *pralin.* And instead of soaking the cake in rum, use kirsch or cognac diluted with water; use kirsch or cognac, plus vanilla for flavoring the cream.

1 cup (1 No. 8Z can) crushed pineapple in heavy syrup	Drain the pineapple. Boil ⅓ cup of the syrup in a small saucepan for 5 minutes. Add the crushed pineapple and boil for 5 minutes. Drain. Stir 2 tablespoons of the syrup into the *crème pâtissière.* Fold in the egg whites and all but ¼ cup of the pineapple. Reserve remaining pineapple to decorate dessert just before serving.

✳ BAVAROIS À L'ORANGE

[Orange Bavarian Cream—a cold desert]

Bavarian cream is a mold of *crème anglaise* (custard sauce) with gelatin, beaten egg whites, lightly beaten cream, and a flavoring. It is unmolded after it has been chilled, and makes a dessert as beautiful to see as it is to eat. When properly made, it has a most lovely, light, creamy, velvety quality and ranks as one of the best of the molded desserts.

We were curious to try out some recipes for Bavarian cream which claimed to produce masterpieces in seconds, so we experimented with the electric blender, raw egg yolks, cracked ice, and so forth. We also ran various changes of our own, such as substituting frozen fruits or ice cream for cracked ice. Though the molded results looked handsome, their flavor and consistency were disappointing. We have concluded that this particular masterpiece cannot be achieved in seconds; a cooked custard, well-dissolved gelatin, stiffly beaten egg whites, properly whipped cream, perfect flavoring, and then the right blending of one element into another at the right time seem to be the requisites for a true Bavarian cream. The classical method below is certainly far from difficult, and the whole dessert may be prepared the day, or even two days, before serving.

Orange Bavarian cream is our favorite. Other flavorings are suggested at the end of the recipe.

For 8 to 10 people

The orange flavoring

2 large, fine, bright-skinned oranges 2 large sugar lumps A 4-quart mixing bowl	Wash and dry the oranges. One at a time, rub the sugar lumps over them until all sides of each lump are impregnated with orange oil. Mash the sugar lumps in the mixing bowl. Grate the orange part of the skins into the bowl.
A measuring cup A strainer 1½ Tb (1½ packages) gelatin	Squeeze the juice of the oranges into the cup, to make ½ to ¾ cup of strained juice. Sprinkle the gelatin over the orange juice and set aside to soften.

The custard sauce

7 egg yolks A wire whip or electric beater 1 cup granulated sugar 2 tsp cornstarch	Following the procedure for *crème anglaise,* page 588, add the egg yolks to the orange sugar in the mixing bowl. Gradually beat in the granulated sugar and continue beating for 2 to 3 minutes until mixture is pale yellow and forms the ribbon. Beat in the cornstarch.
1½ cups boiling milk A 2-quart enameled saucepan A wooden spoon Optional: a candy thermometer	Beat the milk in a thin stream of droplets into the egg yolk mixture. Pour into saucepan and set over moderate heat. Stir with wooden spoon until mixture thickens enough to coat the spoon lightly (170 degrees). Do not overheat or egg yolks will scramble. Remove from heat and immediately add the orange

juice and gelatin mixture, beating for a moment or two until gelatin has dissolved completely. Rinse out the mixing bowl and pour in the custard.

The egg whites

5 egg whites
Pinch of salt
1 Tb granulated sugar
A rubber spatula
A bowl with a tray of ice cubes and water to cover them

Beat the egg whites and salt until soft peaks are formed; sprinkle on the sugar and beat until stiff peaks are formed, page 159. Using the rubber spatula, fold the egg whites into the hot custard. Set over the ice. Fold delicately with spatula frequently while mixture is cooling, to keep it from separating. When cold and almost but not quite set, proceed with recipe.

The whipped cream and final flavoring

½ cup chilled whipping cream
A 3-quart metal bowl
A balloon whip
2 Tb orange liqueur
An 8-cup cylindrical mold or ring mold, preferably of metal as unmolding is easier

Beat cream over the preceding bowl of ice until cream has doubled in volume and beater leaves faint traces on the surface (page 580). Fold the whipped cream and orange liqueur into the custard.

Lightly oiled waxed paper

Rinse mold in cold water and shake out excess. Turn the Bavarian cream into the mold. Cover with the waxed paper. Chill for 3 to 4 hours or overnight.

Unmolding and serving

A long, thin knife
A chilled serving platter

Remove waxed paper. Dip mold in very hot water for 1 second (a second or two longer for a porcelain mold) run knife around the edge of the cream, and reverse on a chilled serving platter. (May be unmolded and refrigerated several hours before serving.)

Peeled orange segments sprinkled with orange liqueur and sugar

Serve surrounded with the orange segments.

VARIATIONS

Bavarois au Chocolat

[Chocolate Bavarian Cream]

Use the same method and ingredients as for the master recipe for Bavarian cream, but omit the orange flavoring and make the following changes.

5 egg yolks instead of 7	Fewer egg yolks are needed for the custard when chocolate is used.
½ cup strong coffee **2 tsp vanilla extract**	Soften the gelatin in coffee and vanilla rather than in orange juice.
3 ounces or squares semi-sweet baking chocolate	Grate the chocolate into the 1½ cups of milk destined for the custard sauce. Heat slowly to the simmer, beating with a wire whip to blend the chocolate smoothly. Proceed with the custard sauce, beating in the coffee and gelatin at the end. Fold in the beaten egg whites and refrigerate, folding occasionally, until cool but not set.
2 Tb dark rum or orange liqueur	Rum is a more usual flavoring with chocolate, but orange liqueur may be used if you wish. Fold it in with the whipped cream, and fill the mold.
2 to 3 cups _crème anglaise_ (custard sauce), page 588, or _crème Chantilly_ (lightly whipped cream), page 580	Serve chocolate Bavarian cream with _crème anglaise_ or with _crème Chantilly_.

Bavarois Praliné

[Almond Bavarian Cream]

Use the same ingredients and method as for the master recipe for Bavarian cream, page 596, but omit the orange flavoring and substitute the following.

½ cup cold strong coffee	Soften the gelatin in coffee rather than in orange juice.

½ cup *pralin* (caramelized almonds), page 583, or pulverized macaroons, page 583

Fold the *pralin* or macaroons into the custard with the beaten egg whites. Chill, folding occasionally, until cool but not set.

1 Tb vanilla extract and ¼ tsp almond extract OR 1 tsp vanilla extract, ¼ tsp almond extract, and 2 Tb dark rum

Fold the flavoring into the custard with the whipped cream.

2 Tb *pralin* or pulverized macaroons
2 to 3 cups *crème anglaise* (custard sauce), page 588, or *crème Chantilly* (lightly whipped cream), page 580

Sprinkle the top of the Bavarian cream with *pralin* or macaroons just before serving. No sauce is necessary, but you may serve with it *crème anglaise* or *crème Chantilly*.

Bavarois aux Fruits

[Strawberry or Raspberry Bavarian Cream—and other fruits]

This recipe calls for raspberries or strawberries. Other fruit purées may be substituted, such as apricot, peach, or caramelized pears. Use the method and ingredients in the master recipe for Bavarian cream, page 596, but omit the orange flavoring and make the following changes.

5 egg yolks instead of 7

The fruit purée gives body to the custard, so fewer egg yolks are needed.

½ cup strawberry or raspberry juice, or orange juice

If you are using frozen berries, dissolve the gelatin in ½ cup of the juice. Otherwise use orange juice.

1 pint fresh strawberries or raspberries OR, 1 lb. frozen berries, thawed and well drained

Force the fruit through a sieve and measure out ¾ to 1 cup of purée. (Any leftover purée may go into your sauce.) Fold measured purée into the custard along with the whipped cream.

2 to 3 cups strawberry or raspberry sauce
OR, 1 pint fresh straw-

Serve this Bavarian cream with strawberry or raspberry sauce, or surround the dessert with fresh berries.

berries or raspberries,
hulled and sprinkled with
sugar

Cold Soufflés

Many of the recipes you will see for cold soufflés are not cold soufflés at all, but Bavarian creams. They look like soufflés because they appear to have risen several inches up beyond the rim of the mold. This effect is achieved by surrounding the mold with a paper collar which holds the cream in place until set; the paper is removed just before serving time. You may mold any of the preceding Bavarian creams this way, as well as the chocolate mousse on page 604, or the almond-cream filling for the *charlottes Malakoff* starting on page 605. Two recipes for actual cold soufflés are the rum and macaroon soufflé on page 620, and the caramel and almond soufflé on page 622.

RIZ À L'IMPÉRATRICE

[Bavarian Cream with Rice and Fruits—a cold dessert]

Riz à l'Impératrice is one of the grand old standbys of the classic French *cuisine,* and has no relation, fortunately, to the dreadful rice puddings of one's youth. It is velvet to the tongue, and is always accompanied by a decorative fruit sauce.

For 8 to 10 people

Preheat oven to 300 degrees.

¾ cup (4 ounces) finely diced glacéed fruits of various colors, such as cherries, angelica, orange peel
4 Tb kirsch or cognac
1⅓ Tb (1⅓ packages) gelatin

Mix the fruits in a small bowl with the kirsch or cognac. Sprinkle on the gelatin and set aside until needed.

½ cup (4 ounces) white rice
4 quarts boiling water

Sprinkle the rice into the boiling water and boil 5 minutes. Drain thoroughly.

1⅔ cups boiling milk
⅓ cup granulated sugar
2 Tb butter
A 1-quart covered, fireproof
    casserole
1 tsp vanilla extract
A round of buttered waxed
    paper

Bring milk, sugar, and butter to boil in the casserole.
Stir in the rice and vanilla. Bring to simmer on top
of the stove. Lay paper over the rice, cover casserole,
and set in preheated oven to cook very slowly for 35
to 40 minutes, until the milk has been absorbed and
the rice is very tender.

5 egg yolks
A 3- to 4-quart mixing bowl
A wire whip or an electric
    beater
¾ cup granulated sugar
1 tsp cornstarch
1½ cups boiling milk
A heavy-bottomed enameled
    saucepan
A wooden spoon
1 tsp vanilla extract
3 Tb apricot preserves forced
    through a sieve
A bowl with a tray of ice
    cubes and water to cover
    them
Flavorless cooking oil
A 6-cup cylindrical mold
    about 3½ inches deep, or a
    ring mold
A round of oiled waxed
    paper

Meanwhile, following the procedure for *crème anglaise,* page 588, place egg yolks in mixing bowl.
Gradually beat in the sugar and continue beating until mixture is pale yellow and forms the ribbon. Beat
in the cornstarch, then the boiling milk by droplets.
Pour into saucepan and stir over moderate heat until
custard coats the spoon lightly (170 degrees). Do not
bring near the simmer or egg yolks will curdle. Remove from heat and immediately stir in the glacéed
fruits and gelatin mixture, stirring until gelatin has
thoroughly dissolved. Add the vanilla and apricot preserves. Stir the rice into the custard, a spoonful at a
time if rice is hot. Fold delicately over the bowl of
ice cubes and water until cold but not set.

Lightly oil the inside of the mold and line the bottom
with oiled waxed paper.

1 cup chilled whipping
    cream
A 3-quart metal bowl
A balloon whip
A round of oiled waxed
    paper

When the rice custard has cooled, beat the cream over
the bowl of ice cubes and water until doubled in volume and beater leaves light traces on the surface (page
580). Fold into the rice custard, turn into the mold,
and cover with oiled waxed paper. Refrigerate for 4
hours or overnight.

2 cups strawberry or rasp-
    berry sauce, page 592
A chilled serving platter
Optional: ⅓ cup glacéed

Remove waxed paper. Dip mold in very hot water for
1 second (a few seconds more if mold is not of metal).
Run a knife around the custard, and unmold on
chilled serving platter. Surround with the sauce.

fruits, diced or cut into fancy shapes, and steeped in 1 Tb kirsch or cognac

(NOTE: After dessert has been unmolded, you may decorate it with glacéed fruits.)

MOUSSE À L'ORANGE

[Orange Mousse—a frozen dessert]

A becoming way to serve this delicate mousse is in the scooped-out halves of oranges.

For 6 people

3 Tb orange liqueur
A 1-quart measuring cup
3 or 4 bright-skinned oranges
½ lemon
Orange juice

Pour the liqueur into the measuring cup. Grate the colored part of the skins of 3 oranges and the ½ lemon into the cup. Strain in enough orange juice so liquid measures 2 cups.

6 egg yolks
½ cup granulated sugar
A 3-quart mixing bowl
A wire whip or electric beater
2 tsp cornstarch
A 2½-quart, heavy-bottomed enameled saucepan
A wooden spoon
Optional: a candy thermometer

Beat the egg yolks and sugar in a mixing bowl until mixture is pale yellow and forms the ribbon, page 579. Beat in the cornstarch and the orange juice mixture. Pour into the saucepan and stir over moderate heat with wooden spoon until mixture heats through and thickens, but does not come to the simmer, or a temperature of more than 170 degrees. It should coat the spoon lightly. Remove from heat and beat a moment to stop the cooking.

6 egg whites
Pinch of salt
1 Tb granulated sugar
A bowl with a tray of ice cubes and water to cover them

Beat the egg whites and salt in a separate bowl until soft peaks are formed; sprinkle in the sugar and beat until stiff peaks are formed, page 159. Fold the egg whites into the hot orange mixture, and fold over the bowl of ice until thoroughly chilled so the custard will not separate.

½ cup chilled whipping cream
6 orange-shell cups, or dessert cups, or a serving bowl

Beat the cream until stiff, page 580, and fold into the chilled mousse. Turn into orange-shell cups, dessert cups, or bowl. Cover and freeze for several hours or overnight.

Decorations:

Glazed orange peel, page 587, angelica cut into leaf shapes, mint leaves, or whipped cream

Decorate the desert just before serving.

MOUSSELINE AU CHOCOLAT
MAYONNAISE AU CHOCOLAT
FONDANT AU CHOCOLAT

[Chocolate Mousse—a cold dessert]

Among all the recipes for chocolate mousse this is one of the best, we think; it uses egg yolks, sugar, and butter, and instead of cream, beaten egg whites. The orange flavoring suggested here is delicious with chocolate. An interchangeable version is *charlotte Malakoff* on page 607, made of butter, chocolate, and powdered almonds. Either may be unmolded after chilling, or served in a bowl, or in dessert cups, or in little covered pots. (*Note:* When served in *pots,* this dessert is sometimes erroneously called *pots de crème au chocolat*. French dessert *crèmes* are custards, such as those on pages 610–11.)

For about 5 cups serving 6 to 8 people

A 3-quart porcelain or stainless steel mixing bowl
A wire whip or electric beater
4 egg yolks
¾ cup instant sugar (very finely granulated)
¼ cup orange liqueur
A pan of not-quite-simmering water
A basin of cold water

Beat the egg yolks and sugar together until mixture is thick, pale yellow, and falls back upon itself forming a slowly dissolving ribbon. Beat in the orange liqueur. Then set mixing bowl over the not-quite-simmering water and continue beating for 3 to 4 minutes until the mixture is foamy and too hot for your finger. Then beat over cold water for 3 to 4 minutes until the mixture is cool and again forms the ribbon. It will have the consistency of mayonnaise.

6 ounces or squares semisweet baking chocolate
4 Tb strong coffee
A small saucepan
6 ounces or 1½ sticks softened unsalted butter

Melt chocolate with coffee over hot water. Remove from heat and beat in the butter a bit at a time, to make a smooth cream. Beat the chocolate into the egg yolks and sugar, then beat in the optional orange peel.

Optional: ¼ cup finely
diced, glazed orange peel,
page 587

4 egg whites | Beat the egg whites and salt until soft peaks are
Pinch of salt | formed; sprinkle on the sugar and beat until stiff
1 Tb granulated sugar | peaks are formed, page 159. Stir one fourth of the
egg whites into the chocolate mixture. Fold in the
rest.

Turn into serving dish, dessert cups, or *petits pots*. Refrigerate for at least 2 hours or overnight.

2 cups vanilla-flavored | Pass the sauce or whipped cream separately.
crème anglaise (custard
sauce), page 588, or lightly
whipped cream sweetened
with powdered sugar,
page 580

Molded Mousse

Turn the preceding mousse into a lightly oiled, 6-cup ring mold. Cover
with oiled, waxed paper. Chill for 3 to 4 hours until well set. Remove paper,
dip mold for 1 second in very hot water, and unmold on a chilled serving dish.
Fill center of mousse with *crème anglaise* or lightly whipped cream.

Or use the following *charlotte Malakoff system,* lining a cylindrical mold
with ladyfingers dipped in orange liqueur.

* *CHARLOTTE MALAKOFF AUX FRAISES*

[Almond Cream with Fresh Strawberries—a cold dessert]

This delectable almond cream is relatively quick to assemble if you have
ladyfingers on hand—but they must be of excellent quality, not the soggy,
baking-powder variety. If you cannot buy them, or have not the time to make
them, omit the ladyfingers altogether and turn the almond cream into a ring
mold as described in the preceding paragraph, or into a serving dish, or into
individual dessert cups. Although the dessert cannot then be called a *charlotte*

Malakoff, it will still be delicious, and can be nicely decorated with fresh strawberries.

For 8 to 10 people

Preparing strawberries and lining mold

1 quart fresh strawberries **A cake rack**	Hull the strawberries. Wash them quickly if necessary, and set on cake rack to drain thoroughly.
A 2-quart cylindrical mold, **about 4 inches high and 7** **inches in diameter** **A round of waxed paper**	Line the bottom of the unbuttered mold with the round of unbuttered waxed paper.
⅓ cup orange liqueur **⅔ cup water** **A soup plate** **24 single ladyfingers, 4** **inches long and about 2** **inches wide, page 666** **A cake rack**	Pour orange liqueur and water into soup plate. Dip in the ladyfingers, one by one, and drain on rack. Line sides of mold with ladyfingers as described on page 585. Reserve the remaining dipped ladyfingers.

The almond cream

A 4-quart mixing bowl **An electric beater or wire** **whip** **½ lb. softened unsalted butter** **1 cup sugar (preferably the** **very finely granulated** **"instant" type)** **½ cup orange liqueur** **¼ tsp almond extract** **1⅓ cups pulverized almonds, page 582**	Cream butter and sugar together for 3 to 4 minutes, until pale and fluffy, page 581. Beat in orange liqueur and almond extract. Continue beating for several minutes until sugar is completely dissolved. Beat in the almonds.
2 cups chilled whipping **cream** **A chilled bowl** **A chilled beater**	Whip the cream until the beater, drawn across the top of the cream, leaves light traces, page 580. Fold the cream into the almond and butter mixture.

Molding and serving

A round of buttered waxed **paper**	Turn a third of the almond cream into the lined mold. Arrange over it a layer of strawberries, heads down.

A saucer which will just fit into the mold

A 1-lb. weight, or pieces of a meat grinder

Cover them with a layer of ladyfingers. Repeat with another layer each of almond cream, strawberries, and ladyfingers. Fill the mold with the rest of the almond cream and a layer of ladyfingers if there are any left. Trim off ladyfingers around edge of mold, and press the trimmed-off bits into the top of the cream. Cover mold with the waxed paper, set saucer over the paper, and place the weight on it. Refrigerate for 6 hours or overnight. The butter must be chilled firm, so the dessert will not collapse when unmolded.

A chilled serving platter

The remaining strawberries, more if needed

2 cups *crème Chantilly* (lightly whipped cream), page 580, or strawberry sauce, page 592

Remove waxed paper. Run a knife around the inside of the mold, and reverse dessert on a chilled serving platter. Peel waxed paper from top, and refrigerate dessert until serving time. Decorate with strawberries and accompany with whipped cream or strawberry sauce.

VARIATIONS

Use the same method and proportions as in the preceding master recipe for *charlotte Malakoff*, but make the following changes for these variations:

Charlotte Malakoff aux Framboises

[Almond Cream with Raspberries]

Substitute fresh raspberries for strawberries in the preceding recipe.

Charlotte Malakoff au Chocolat

[Almond Cream with Chocolate]

Ingredients for the master recipe but without the strawberries

4 ounces or squares of semi-sweet chocolate melted in ¼ cup strong coffee

¼ rather than ½ cup orange

Following the master recipe, line the mold with ladyfingers dipped in diluted orange liqueur. Make the almond cream as directed, but fold the melted chocolate into it, and only ¼ cup of orange liqueur. Cool before folding in the whipped cream, and complete the recipe. Serve with whipped cream or custard sauce.

liqueur for the almond
cream
2 cups *crème Chantilly*
(lightly whipped cream),
page 580, or *crème an-
glaise* (custard sauce),
page 588

Charlotte Basque

[Almond Custard with Chocolate]

This is lighter than the *charlotte Malakoff* because the base is a custard
and no whipped cream is folded into it.

For 8 to 10 people

4 cups *crème anglaise* (cus-tard sauce), page 588, flavored with chocolate	Prepare a chocolate-flavored custard sauce and beat over cold water, or refrigerate, until almost cold.
½ lb. unsalted butter 1⅓ cups pulverized al-monds, page 582 ½ tsp almond extract 2 to 3 Tb rum, kirsch, co-gnac, or orange liqueur A 2-quart mold lined with ladyfingers, and extra ladyfingers as described in master recipe 2 cups *crème Chantilly* (lightly whipped cream), page 580	Cream the butter and almonds together in a mixing bowl. Gradually beat in the cool custard sauce. Beat in the almond extract, and rum or liqueur to taste. Turn into lined mold, alternating with layers of lady-fingers, and chill until set. Serve with lightly whipped cream.

CHARLOTTE CHANTILLY, AUX FRAISES
CHARLOTTE CHANTILLY, AUX FRAMBOISES

[Strawberry or Raspberry Cream—a cold dessert]

Here is another handsome molded dessert; this one is also relatively
quick to execute. But unless the egg yolks are well thickened, and then chilled
before the cream is folded in, the dessert will collapse rather quickly. If you

do not wish to serve it unmolded, turn the cream into a serving bowl or into dessert cups. You may use frozen fruit instead of fresh, but be sure the fruit is well thawed and most thoroughly drained, otherwise the purée will be too liquid.

For 8 to 10 people

A round of waxed paper

A 2-quart cylindrical mold about 4 inches high and 7 inches in diameter, lined with ladyfingers, page 585

Place the round of waxed paper in the bottom of the unbuttered mold. Then line the sides of the mold (not the bottom) with upright ladyfingers as described in the directions.

1½ pints fresh strawberries or raspberries

Hull, wash, and drain the berries. Force them through a sieve and into a bowl. Measure out 1¼ cups of purée. Chill.

A wire whip or electric beater

A 3-quart stainless steel mixing bowl

⅔ cup instant sugar (very finely granulated)

8 egg yolks

A pan of not-quite-simmering water

A bowl with a tray of ice cubes and water to cover them

Beat the sugar into the egg yolks and continue beating until mixture is pale yellow and falls back on itself forming a slowly dissolving ribbon. Then place the mixing bowl over the not-quite-simmering water and beat until mixture has thickened into a cream and becomes uncomfortably hot for your finger. Set bowl in ice water and beat until mixture is cold and falls back upon itself forming a slowly dissolving ribbon on the surface; fold with a spatula until chilled.

2½ cups chilled heavy whipping cream

A 4-quart metal bowl

A chilled beater

When the egg yolk mixture has chilled, beat the cream until it has doubled in volume and forms stiff (rather than soft) peaks.

Extra ladyfingers, if needed

A round of waxed paper

Fold the chilled strawberry or raspberry purée into the chilled egg yolk mixture, then fold in the whipped cream. Turn into the mold. Place ladyfingers over the cream to fill the mold almost completely. Trim off any protruding ladyfingers around the edges of the mold. Cover with waxed paper and refrigerate for at least 6 hours or overnight.

A chilled serving dish

1 to 3 cups fresh strawberries or raspberries

Just before serving, remove waxed paper, run a knife around the edge of the mold, and reverse dessert onto a chilled serving dish. Remove waxed paper. Decorate the top of the dessert with fresh berries and, if you wish, place more berries around the dessert.

* *CRÈME RENVERSÉE AU CARAMEL*

[Caramel Custard, Unmolded—warm or cold]

French custards are usually unmolded, and therefore call for more eggs and egg yolks than custards served directly from their baking dishes.

For a 1-quart mold serving 4 to 6 people

The custard mixture

Preheat oven to 350 degrees.

A 1-quart, fireproof, cylindrical mold lined with caramel, page 584
2½ cups milk
Optional: 1 vanilla bean

Line the mold with caramel as directed. Bring the milk with the optional vanilla bean to just below the simmer in a saucepan, cover, and let the bean steep in the milk while you prepare the rest of the custard ingredients.

½ cup granulated sugar
3 eggs
3 egg yolks
A 3-quart mixing bowl
A wire whip
1 tsp vanilla extract, if you have not used a bean
A fine-meshed sieve

Gradually beat the sugar into the eggs and egg yolks in the bowl until well mixed, light, and foamy. Continue beating while pouring on the hot milk in a thin stream of droplets. Stir in vanilla extract, if you have not used a vanilla bean. Strain the mixture through a sieve into the caramel-lined mold.

Baking the custard

Set mold in a pan and pour enough boiling water around mold to come halfway up its sides. Place in bottom third of preheated oven, close oven door, and wait for temperature to return to 350; in 5 minutes, turn oven down to 325. Water in pan should always be almost-but-not-quite simmering—too much heat and the custard will be grainy. Bake for about 40 minutes: a trussing needle or straw should come out clean when plunged 1 inch from edge of mold, but center of custard should still tremble slightly—over-long cooking makes a tough rather than tender custard.

Unmolding and serving

If you wish to serve the custard warm, set mold in a pan of cold water for about 10 minutes to firm it up; otherwise chill in the refrigerator. To unmold, run a knife between custard and edge of mold, place a serving dish upside down over the mold, quickly reverse the two, and remove the mold from the custard. If you wish, simmer 2 to 3 tablespoons of water in the mold to dissolve the remaining caramel; strain around the custard.

VARIATIONS

To serve individual unmolded custards, use the custard mixture in the preceding master recipe, and mold the custards as follows:

Petits Pots de Crème

[Cup Custards, Unmolded]

1 quart caramel custard mixture, the preceding recipe
8 caramel-lined, ⅔ cup ramekins, page 585
A pan to hold the ramekins

Divide the custard mixture among the ramekins and pour boiling water into the pan to come halfway up; set in lower third level of a preheated 350-degree oven. In 5 minutes, turn oven down to 325 and bake 20 to 25 minutes longer or until a skewer or straw comes out clean when plunged one-eighth inch from edge of molds; centers should still tremble. Remove from oven, remove molds from water, and let cool. Unmold when ready to serve.

Crème Sainte-Anne au Caramel

[Macaroon Cup Custards, Unmolded]

1 Tb butter
8 caramel-lined ramekins, ⅔-cup capacity, page 585
1 cup pulverized macaroons, page 583
1 quart caramel custard mixture, the master recipe

Butter the insides of the caramel-lined ramekins and sprinkle 2 tablespoons of pulverized macaroons in each. Fill with the custard mixture and bake as in the preceding directions for cup custards. You may wish to garnish them when unmolded with one of the suggestions at the left.

Optional garnishings

Crème anglaise (custard sauce), page 588
OR, strawberry or raspberry sauce, page 592
OR, fresh or canned peach halves, coated with caramel syrup, page 584

DIPLOMATE
POUDING DE CABINET

[Custard with Glacéed Fruits, Unmolded—a warm or cold dessert]

This delicious and most classical of French desserts does not take too long to prepare, and can be baked the day before your dinner party. The custard is baked in a mold lined with ladyfingers which must be of best quality, tender and dry, not spongy.

For 8 people

⅓ cup small, seedless raisins
A saucepan of boiling water
A small bowl
⅔ cup finely diced, mixed, glacéed fruits, such as cherries, angelica, apricots, pineapple
3 Tb dark rum or kirsch

Drop the raisins into the boiling water and let stand for five minutes. Drain, and place in the bowl. Stir in the glacéed fruits, the rum or kirsch, and let stand until ready to use.

A round of buttered waxed paper
A 6-cup cylindrical mold about 3½ inches high

Place the buttered paper in the bottom of the mold.

⅓ cup dark rum or kirsch
⅔ cup water
A soup plate
About 40 single ladyfingers, 3½ inches long and 2 inches wide (recipe for homemade ladyfingers is on page 666)
A cake rack

Pour the rum or kirsch and water into the soup plate. One by one, dip 20 to 25 ladyfingers (or enough to line the mold) into the liquid. Drain on cake rack. Following directions on page 585, line the bottom and the sides of the mold with the dipped ladyfingers.

2 eggs
3 egg yolks
½ cup granulated sugar
A 3-quart mixing bowl
A wire whip
2 cups milk, brought to the boil with the grated rind of 1 orange

Beat the eggs, egg yolks, and sugar in a mixing bowl until light and foamy. Gradually beat in the boiling milk. Strain in the kirsch or rum from the glacéed fruits.

Preheat oven to 350 degrees.

½ cup apricot preserves forced through a sieve

Spoon a ladleful of custard into the prepared mold. Over it sprinkle a small handful of the glacéed fruits, then 2 to 3 tablespoons of apricot preserves. Cover with 2 or 3 ladyfingers, and spoon a bit of custard over them. Wait for a moment for the ladyfingers to absorb the custard, then continue with layers of fruit, apricot preserve, ladyfingers, and custard until the mold is filled. Trim off protruding ladyfingers around edge of mold.

A pan of boiling water

Set mold in a pan of boiling water, and place in bottom third of oven. Immediately reduce heat to 325 degrees. Bake for 50 to 60 minutes, making sure water in pan never comes to the simmer. When center of custard has risen very slightly and a needle or knife plunged to the bottom of the mold comes out clean, custard is done. Remove from pan of water and let cool. (May be served slightly warm, or chilled.)

A serving platter
2 cups strawberry sauce, page 592

Run a knife around the edge of the custard and reverse on a serving platter. Remove round of paper, and surround the dessert with the sauce.

SWEET SOUFFLÉS

Soufflés Sucrés

Many people consider the desert soufflé to be the epitome and triumph of the art of French cookery, a glorious and exciting finish to a great meal. Although sweet soufflés are lighter and airier than entrée soufflés, the general idea is the same: a flavored sauce base into which stiffly beaten egg whites are incorporated. All the points discussed in the Entrée chapter regarding soufflés, pages 157 to 163, apply also to sweet soufflés; these include soufflé molds, placement in the oven, testing, and serving. The discussion in that section on how to beat egg whites is of particular importance. Though you will get a soufflé of some sort no matter what you do, you will achieve magnificence only if your egg whites are beaten so they mount smoothly and stiffly to about seven times their original volume, and are then folded carefully into the sauce base so that their maximum volume is retained.

THE SAUCE BASE OR BOUILLIE

Of the three standard methods for making a soufflé base, the béchamel with its cooked *roux,* the *crème pâtissière* with its cooked egg yolks, and the *bouillie* used in the following recipes, we prefer the *bouillie* for lightness. A *bouillie* is milk, sugar, and flour or starch, boiled for a few seconds until thickened. After it has cooled slightly, egg yolks, butter, and flavoring are beaten in, then beaten egg whites are incorporated. Some people prefer a *bouillie* with flour; others use potato starch, rice starch, or cornstarch. You may take your choice except for the chocolate soufflé which requires starch. Although you can make a soufflé without starch or flour, as in the lemon soufflé tart on page 645, you will find that it lacks something in texture and tenderness.

SOUFFLÉ MOLDS

Be sure to read the illustrated section on soufflé molds, page 162 in the Entrée chapter.

TIMING

The following recipes for hot soufflés are based on a 6-cup mold, and, except for the chocolate soufflé, take 30 to 35 minutes to bake. Since you may fill your mold, cover it with an empty kettle, and let it wait about an hour before baking, you can time it quite accurately to coincide with dessert if you are also able to estimate the general eating-speed for the rest of the meal. In any case, no guest who knows a soufflé is in the oven should mind waiting a few minutes for dessert.

Soufflés made in a 3-cup mold take 15 to 20 minutes to bake; those in an 8-cup mold, 40 to 45 minutes. Molds larger than 8-cup capacity are difficult to time, and the soufflé is so large it may not rise satisfactorily.

✳ *SOUFFLÉ À LA VANILLE*

[Vanilla Soufflé]

All of the sweet soufflés with the exception of chocolate may be made according to the following vanilla soufflé formula. A fairly quick operator can make any of them ready for the oven in 20 minutes.

For 4 people

Preparing the soufflé mold

Preheat oven to 400 degrees.

½ Tb softened butter
A 6-cup mold, preferably
one 3½ inches deep like
the *charlotte*. See illustrations on page 162
Granulated sugar

Measure out your ingredients. Butter the entire inner
surface of the mold. Roll granulated sugar around in
it to coat the sides and bottom evenly. Knock out
excess sugar.

The bouillie sauce base

A wire whip
3 Tb sifted all-purpose flour
A 2½-quart enameled saucepan
¾ cup milk
⅓ cup granulated sugar

Beat the flour in the saucepan with a bit of the milk
until well blended. Beat in the rest of the milk, and
the sugar. Stir over moderately high heat until mixture thickens and comes to the boil. Boil, stirring, for
30 seconds. Sauce will be very thick. Remove from
heat and beat for 2 minutes to cool slightly.

4 eggs
A bowl for beating egg
whites
A wire whip

Separate one egg, dropping the white into the bowl,
and the yolk into the center of the sauce. At once beat
the yolk into the sauce with the wire whip. Continue
with the rest of the eggs, one by one.

2 Tb softened butter
A rubber scraper

Beat in half the butter. Clean sauce off sides of pan
with rubber scraper. Dot top of sauce with the rest of
the butter to prevent a skin from forming on the
surface.
(*) If made in advance, beat over gentle heat only
until sauce is barely warm to your finger, not hot.
Then proceed with recipe.

The egg whites

5 egg whites (4 left over
from the yolks and 1 ex-
tra white)
Pinch of salt
1 Tb granulated sugar

Beat the egg whites and salt together until soft peaks
are formed. Sprinkle on the sugar and beat until stiff
peaks are formed. (Directions for beating egg whites
are on page 159.)

The flavoring

2 Tb vanilla extract
(Or see Vanilla, page
587, if you prefer the
bean)

Beat the vanilla into the sauce base. Stir in a fourth
of the beaten egg whites. Delicately fold in the rest.
(Illustrated directions for folding are on page 161.)

Filling the mold

Turn the soufflé mixture into the prepared mold, leaving a space of at least 1¼ inches between the top of the soufflé and the rim of the mold. If the mold is too full, the soufflé will spill over as it rises.

(*) If soufflé is not to be cooked immediately, set an empty kettle upside down over the mold. Filled mold can now wait for about an hour before baking.

Baking the soufflé

Powdered sugar in a shaker

Place the mold in the middle level of the preheated oven, and immediately turn down to 375 degrees. In 20 minutes, when the soufflé has begun to puff and brown, quickly sprinkle the top with powdered sugar. After a total of 30 to 35 minutes of baking, the top of the soufflé should be nicely browned, and a trussing needle, straw, or long, thin knife, plunged into the soufflé through the side of the puff, should come out clean.

Serve immediately.

VARIATIONS

All of the following variations are based on the preceding master recipe, using the same method and ingredients except for changes in flavor.

Soufflé à l'Orange

[Orange Soufflé with Cointreau, Curaçao, Grand Marnier, Etc.]

1 bright-skinned orange
2 large sugar lumps

Use the master soufflé formula. Before making the *bouillie* sauce base, rub the sugar lumps over the orange to extract the oil. Mash the sugar lumps, grate the orange part of the peel, add to the saucepan with the granulated sugar, and proceed with the sauce base.

2 tsp vanilla extract instead of 2 Tb
3 to 4 Tb orange liqueur

Beat the vanilla and the orange liqueur into the sauce base just before incorporating the beaten egg whites. Complete the recipe.

Soufflé Rothschild

[Soufflé with Glacéed Fruits and Kirsch]

⅔ cup diced, mixed glacéed fruits ¼ cup kirsch	Let the glacéed fruits stand in the kirsch for half an hour.
2 tsp vanilla extract instead of 2 Tb	Using the master soufflé formula, prepare the *bouillie* sauce base. Just before incorporating the beaten egg whites, drain the fruits and beat their kirsch maceration into the sauce base with the vanilla.
	Turn a third of the soufflé mixture into the prepared mold. Sprinkle half of the glacéed fruits on top. Cover with half the remaining soufflé mixture, then with the rest of the fruits, and finally the last of the soufflé mixture.

Soufflé au Café

[Coffee Soufflé]

	Use the master soufflé formula on page 614, but before making the *bouillie* sauce base:
3 Tb coffee beans OR, 1 Tb instant coffee	*Either* bring ½ cup of the milk to the boil with coffee beans, cover and steep for 5 minutes, then strain into the milk and flour paste, beating thoroughly; *or* beat instant coffee into ½ cup of boiling milk.
1 Tb vanilla extract rather than 2 Tb	Then proceed with the recipe, beating the vanilla into the sauce base before incorporating the beaten egg whites.

Soufflé Praliné

Soufflé aux Macarons

[Soufflé with Caramelized Almonds or Macaroons]

Use the master soufflé formula on page 614.

1 Tb vanilla extract rather   Stir the vanilla and the *pralin* or macaroons into the
  than 2 Tb   *bouillie* sauce base just before incorporating the beaten
½ cup *pralin,* page 583, or   egg whites.
  the pulverized macaroons,
  page 583

Soufflé aux Amandes

[Almond Soufflé]

Almonds may be added to any soufflé, and are especially good with
coffee, orange, or chocolate, as well as with vanilla.

Use the master soufflé formula on page 614.

2 Tb vanilla extract   Stir the vanilla and almond extracts and almonds into
¼ tsp almond extract   the *bouillie* sauce base just before incorporating the
½ cup pulverized toasted al- beaten egg whites.
  monds, page 582

Soufflé Panaché

[Half-and-half Soufflé]

For two kinds of soufflé cooked in the same mold, use vanilla, and coffee,
pralin, or orange. Chocolate will not do, as it cooks in a different manner.

The *bouillie* sauce base,   Divide the sauce base into the two bowls.
  master recipe, page 615
2 two-quart bowls

5 egg whites   Beat the egg whites and salt together until soft peaks
Pinch of salt   are formed; sprinkle on the sugar and beat until stiff
1 Tb granulated sugar   peaks are formed.

1 Tb vanilla extract   Beat the vanilla flavoring into one bowl, and fold in
                              half the beaten egg whites.

½ tsp vanilla extract   Beat the vanilla extract and coffee into the other bowl,
2 tsp instant coffee mixed   and fold in the remaining egg whites.
  with 1 Tb boiling water

A 6-cup soufflé mold prepared as in the master recipe

½ cup pulverized macaroons, page 583, moistened with 2 Tb orange liqueur

Turn half the vanilla soufflé mixture into the prepared mold. Sprinkle with a third of the macaroons and liqueur mixture. Spread half of the coffee soufflé over this, then sprinkle on more macaroons. Continue with the remaining vanilla soufflé, macaroons, and the last of the coffee soufflé.

Bake for 30 to 35 minutes in a preheated, 375-degree oven as for the master recipe.

SOUFFLÉ AU CHOCOLAT

[Chocolate Soufflé]

Chocolate needs special treatment for soufflés because it is heavy. Although the formula in our first edition produced a dramatic puff, it was far too fragile. In this new version, you fold the chocolate mixture into a meringue—that is, rather than adding the sugar to the sauce base, you whip it into the egg whites, thereby firming them up. Just this simple change in method gives the soufflé staying power so that instead of collapsing rather rapidly into a pudding, it stays up and retains its primal soufflé character.

For 6 to 8 people

Preheat oven to 425 degrees.

7 ounces or squares of semisweet or sweet baking chocolate

⅓ cup strong coffee

A small saucepan with cover set in a larger pan of almost simmering water

Place the chocolate and coffee in the small pan, cover, and set in the larger pan of almost simmering water. Remove from heat and let the chocolate melt while you proceed with the recipe.

½ Tb softened butter

A 2- to 2½-quart soufflé dish or straight-sided baking dish 7½ to 8 inches in diameter

Smear the inside of the dish with the butter. Surround with a collar of buttered aluminum foil (double thickness) to reach 3 inches above the rim of the dish. Set out all the rest of the ingredients called for.

⅓ cup all-purpose flour

A 2-quart saucepan

A wire whip

2 cups milk

3 Tb butter

Measure the flour into the saucepan. Start whisking in the milk by dribbles at first to make a perfectly smooth cream; rapidly whisk in the rest. Add the butter, and stir over moderate heat until boiling; boil, stirring, for 2 minutes. Remove from heat and beat 1 minute or so to cool slightly.

4 egg yolks
1 Tb pure vanilla extract

One by one, whisk the egg yolks into the hot sauce, then the smoothly melted chocolate, and finally the vanilla.

(*) If you are not continuing within 5 to 10 minutes, lay a sheet of plastic wrap directly on top of the sauce to prevent a skin from forming.

6 egg whites (¾ cup)
⅛ tsp salt
½ cup sugar

Beat the egg whites and salt in a separate bowl until soft peaks are formed. Then, by sprinkles, beat in the sugar and continue until stiff shining peaks are formed (page 159).

Scrape the chocolate mixture into the side of the egg white bowl; delicately fold them together. Turn the soufflé mixture into the prepared mold and set on a rack in the lower level of the preheated oven. Turn thermostat down to 375 degrees.

Powdered sugar in a sieve or shaker
Serving suggestions: 2 cups of sweetened whipped cream, *crème anglaise* (page 588), or vanilla ice cream

In 35 to 40 minutes, when soufflé is well risen and the top has cracked, rapidly sprinkle the surface with powdered sugar; continue baking another 5 to 10 minutes. Soufflé is still creamy at the center when a skewer plunged down through a surface crack comes out slightly coated. It is fully done and will stand up well (if that is how you like it) when the skewer comes out clean. Serve at once with one of the suggestions listed.

(*) When turned into its baking dish, the soufflé may be covered loosely with a sheet of foil and set in a draft-free part of the kitchen for an hour or more before being baked.

SOUFFLÉ DÉMOULÉ AUX MACARONS

[Rum and Macaroon Soufflé, Unmolded—a cold dessert]

For 6 to 8 people

Preheat oven to 350 degrees.

1 tsp butter An 8-cup fireproof, cylindrical mold lined with caramel, page 584	Butter the inside of the caramel-lined mold.
A wire whip or electric beater 1½ cups (8 ounces) pulverized macaroons, page 583 ¼ cup dark rum A 3-quart mixing bowl ¾ cup milk brought to the boil with ¼ cup granulated sugar	Beat the macaroons and rum together in the mixing bowl while pouring on the hot milk and sugar, and continue beating for 1 minute.
4 egg yolks	One by one, beat in the egg yolks until blended with the macaroons.
4 egg whites Pinch of salt 1 Tb granulated sugar	Beat the egg whites and salt in a separate bowl until soft peaks are formed; sprinkle on the sugar and beat until stiff peaks are formed, page 159.
A rubber spatula	Fold the egg whites into the macaroon mixture, being sure the mixture, which is very liquid, is thoroughly but delicately blended with the egg whites. Turn into prepared mold which will be filled by about two thirds.
A pan containing enough boiling water to come halfway up outside of mold	Place mold in pan of boiling water; set in lower third of preheated, 350-degree oven for 15 minutes. Then reduce heat to 325 degrees and continue baking about 35 minutes more. Soufflé will rise about to the top of the mold. It is done when it shows a faint line of shrinkage from the sides of the mold.
A serving dish 3 cups chilled, coffee-flavored *crème anglaise* (custard sauce), page 588	Refrigerate for 3 to 4 hours. The soufflé will sink down as it cools, and shrink more from the mold. When chilled, reverse on the serving dish. Simmer 2 tablespoons of water in the mold to dissolve the remaining caramel; allow to cool for a moment, then pour the caramel syrup over the soufflé. Surround with the sauce, and serve.

ÎLE FLOTTANTE

[Caramel Almond Soufflé, Unmolded—a cold dessert]

French floating island can be either a layered cake covered with whipped cream and surrounded by custard sauce, or a meringue. We have chosen the meringue because it is light, delicious, and so very easy to do in the electric mixer. The addition of *pralin* gives texture and flavor as well as providing a ready-made sauce, allowing you to dispense with the traditional *crème anglaise* if you wish. (Those little mounds of egg white floating on custard may be English floating islands, but are French *oeufs à la neige*.)

For 6 to 8 people

A heavily buttered, 2-quart baking dish or charlotte mold 3½ to 4 inches deep
2 to 3 Tb sugar

Preheat oven to 250 degrees. Roll sugar in the buttered mold, knock out excess, and set mold aside.

An electric mixer with 2½- to 3-quart bowl
8 egg whites (1 cup) at room temperature
⅛ tsp salt
¼ tsp cream of tartar
1 cup instant or very finely granulated sugar
1 tsp vanilla extract
1 cup *pralin* (caramelized almonds), page 583
A rubber spatula

Beat egg whites at moderate speed until they are frothy, then beat in the salt and cream of tartar. Gradually increase speed to fast and when egg whites form soft peaks start beating in the sugar, 2 tablespoons at a time. Continue beating until egg whites form stiff peaks. Beat in the vanilla. Remove bowl from stand and fold in the *pralin* ¼ cup at a time with the rubber spatula.

Spread lightly in dish, which it will overfill by ¼ inch or so; smooth exposed sides and top with spatula. Bake in lower third of preheated, 250-degree oven for about 25 minutes, until meringue has colored slightly and risen about ½ inch. (It should be cooked enough so that meringue can hold its shape for unmolding; its rise indicates this.) Let cool for 30 minutes, then refrigerate for at least an hour so that it will settle.

A serving plate
2 Tb *pralin*
Optional: 2 cups chilled *crème anglaise* (custard sauce, page 588) in a sauce bowl

Set cover or plate askew over mold and drain accumulated caramel liquid into a small bowl. Unmold dessert onto serving plate. Sprinkle top with *pralin*, and pour the caramel around. Pass optional custard sauce separately.

FRUIT DESSERTS

Entremets aux Fruits

CHARLOTTE AUX POMMES

[Apple Charlotte, Unmolded—a hot or cold dessert]

This extremely good dessert is a thick, rum- and apricot-flavored apple purée piled into a cylindrical mold which has been lined with butter-soaked strips of white bread. It is baked in a very hot oven until the bread is golden brown, and is then unmolded. For the sake of drama, the mold should be 3½ to 4 inches high. Be sure to pick the right cooking apples and that your purée is very thick indeed, or the dessert will collapse when unmolded.

For 6 to 8 people

6 lbs. firm nonjuicy cooking apples (Golden Delicious are always reliable)

A heavy-bottomed stainless or enameled pan 12 inches across

A wooden spoon

Quarter, peel, and core the apples. Slice them roughly into ⅛-inch pieces. You should have about 4 quarts. Place in pan, cover, and cook over very low heat for about 20 minutes, stirring occasionally, until tender.

½ cup apricot preserves, forced through a sieve

1 cup granulated sugar

2 tsp vanilla extract

¼ cup dark rum

3 Tb butter

Uncover and beat in the apricot preserves, sugar, vanilla, rum, and butter. Raise heat and boil, stirring almost continuously until water content has all but evaporated—20 minutes or more. The purée should be a very thick and fairly stiff paste which holds itself in a solid mass in the spoon.

Preheat oven to 425 degrees.

10 to 12 slices of homemade-type white bread, 4 inches square and ¼ inch thick

A 6-cup, fireproof, cylindrical mold about 3½ inches high

1 cup clarified butter, page 15

Remove crusts. Cut a square and 4 semicircles of bread to fit the bottom of the mold exactly. Sauté to a very light golden color in 3 or 4 tablespoons of the clarified butter. Fit them into the bottom of the mold. Cut the rest of the bread into strips 1¼ inches wide. Dip in clarified butter and fit them, overlapping each other, around the inner circumference of the mold. Trim off protruding ends.

Pack the apple purée into the mold, allowing it to form a dome about ¾ inch high in the middle. (It will sink as it cools.) Cover with 4 or 5 butter-dipped bread strips. Pour any remaining clarified butter over the ends of the bread around the edges of the mold.

A pan
A serving platter

Set in a pan (to catch butter drippings) and bake in middle level of preheated oven for about 30 minutes. Slip a knife between bread and sides of mold; if bread is golden brown, the charlotte is done. Remove from oven and cool for 15 minutes. Reverse the mold on a serving platter and lift the mold up a few inches to see if the sides of the dessert will hold. If there is any suggestion of collapse, lower the mold over the dessert again; it will firm up as it cools. Test after 5 minutes or so, until the mold can safely be removed.

½ cup apricot preserves, forced through a sieve
3 Tb dark rum
2 Tb granulated sugar
Optional: 2 cups *crème anglaise* (custard sauce), page 588, or 2 cups lightly whipped cream flavored with rum and powdered sugar, page 580

Boil the apricot, rum, and sugar until thick and sticky. Spread it over the charlotte. Serve the dessert hot, warm, or cold, with the optional sauce or cream.

POMMES NORMANDE EN BELLE VUE

[Applesauce Caramel Mold—a warm or cold dessert]

This is a much lighter dessert than the apple charlotte, and also much easier to prepare.

For 6 people

4 lbs. crisp cooking or eating apples
A heavy-bottomed enameled pan (saucepan, casserole, or skillet) about 10 inches in diameter

Peel and core the apples. Slice them roughly into ⅛-inch pieces. You should have about 10 cups. Place them in the pan; cover and cook over very low heat for about 20 minutes, stirring occasionally, until tender.

A wooden spoon

Preheat oven to 400 degrees.

¼ tsp cinnamon
The grated peel of 1 lemon
½ cup granulated sugar

Beat the cinnamon, lemon peel, and sugar into the apples. Raise heat and boil, stirring, for 5 minutes or so, until the apples have reduced to a thick purée which will hold its shape in the spoon. You should have about 4 cups of applesauce.

¼ cup rum, cognac, or excellent apple brandy
4 Tb butter
4 eggs
1 egg white

Remove from heat and stir in the rum or brandy, then the butter. One by one, beat in the eggs, then the egg white.

A 6-cup, fireproof, cylindrical mold lined with caramel, page 584
A lid or a plate
A deep saucepan or kettle
Boiling water

Turn the apple mixture into the caramel-lined mold. Cover with lid or plate, and set in the saucepan or kettle. Pour boiling water around the outside of the mold to come up to the level of the apple mixture. Place in lower third of preheated oven. Regulate oven heat to maintain water almost at the simmer. The dessert is done in 1 to 1½ hours, when it begins to shrink from the sides of the mold and the top, all except for a small area in the very center, is set.

A serving dish

To serve warm, remove the mold from the saucepan or kettle and allow the dessert to cool for 20 minutes. Then reverse it on a serving dish. To serve cold, chill the dessert 4 to 5 hours or overnight. Then run a knife around the edge of the dessert and reverse on a serving dish; in a few minutes it will dislodge itself from the mold.

---

4 Tb rum, cognac, or apple brandy
2 cups lightly whipped cream flavored with powdered sugar and rum or brandy, or 2 cups *crème anglaise* (custard sauce), page 588

Simmer the rum or brandy in the mold to dissolve any remaining caramel, and strain over the dessert. Surround the dessert with the whipped cream or sauce.

POUDING ALSACIEN

[*Gratin* of Sautéed Apples—a cold dessert]

This simple apple dessert is always better if prepared the day before it is eaten, as a good 24 hours are needed for a slow blending of flavors.

For 6 to 8 people

2½ lbs. firm cooking apples (Golden Delicious)	Quarter, core, and peel the apples. Cut into ¼-inch lengthwise slices. You should have about 7 cups.
4 to 5 Tb butter A 10- to 12-inch skillet A lightly buttered baking dish, 8 to 9 inches in diameter and 2 inches deep	Sauté the apples, one layer at a time, in hot butter until they are very lightly browned on both sides and tender, but retain their shape. As they are done, place them in the baking dish.
¾ cup plum jam, forced through a sieve 2 Tb rum A rubber spatula	Melt the plum jam in the skillet with the rum. Delicately fold into the apples, and smooth the apples in the dish.
	Preheat oven to 325 degrees.
4 Tb butter ½ cup granulated sugar 3 egg yolks 1 Tb all-purpose flour ½ tsp cinnamon 1 cup fresh whole wheat or rye bread crumbs	Cream the butter and sugar together in a mixing bowl until light and fluffy, page 581. Beat in the egg yolks, then the flour and cinnamon, and finally the bread crumbs.
2 egg whites Pinch of salt ½ Tb granulated sugar	Beat the egg whites and salt until soft peaks are formed; sprinkle on the sugar and beat until stiff peaks are formed (page 159). Fold the egg whites into the bread-crumb mixture and spread evenly over the apples.
Powdered sugar in a shaker	Bake in middle level of preheated oven for 20 to 25 minutes, or until top has puffed slightly and has just

begun to color. Sprinkle liberally with powdered sugar and continue baking another 20 to 25 minutes; the top should be a nice golden brown under the sugar.

Allow to cool, then chill, preferably for 24 hours.

ASPIC DE POMMES

[Rum-Flavored Apple *Aspic,* Unmolded—a cold dessert]

Because the apples for this simple dessert are boiled in a heavy sugar syrup, they jell when chilled and can be unmolded on a serving dish. It makes a pretty effect with its decoration of glacéed fruits. Once made, the *aspic* may be kept molded or unmolded under refrigeration for at least 10 days.

For 6 to 8 people

3 lbs. cooking apples	Quarter, core, and peel the apples. Cut into lengthwise slices ⅜ inch thick. You should have about 8 cups.
A heavy 12-inch enameled skillet **¾ cup water** **3 cups sugar** **1 Tb lemon juice**	Bring water, sugar, and lemon juice to the boil, stirring until sugar has dissolved. Add the apples and boil over moderately high heat, stirring frequently to keep them from sticking and burning, for about 20 minutes. They should become an almost transparent mass.
A 1-quart cylindrical mold **1 tsp tasteless salad oil** **A round of waxed paper**	While the apples are cooking, rub inside of mold with oil; oil the waxed paper and set in the bottom of the mold.
4 ounces (about ¾ cup) glacéed fruits, such as red and green cherries, angelica, orange peel	Make a decorative design in the bottom of the mold with half the fruit. Dice the rest and add it to boil with the apples for 2 to 3 minutes at the end of the cooking.
3 Tb dark rum	When apples are done, remove from heat and stir in the rum. Spoon into the mold and chill for 4 to 6 hours, or until set. Serve as follows:

A chilled serving dish

2 cups *crème anglaise* (custard sauce), page 588

Surround the mold with a hot towel for 10 to 15 seconds. Run a knife around edge of mold, and reverse the aspic onto a chilled serving dish. Surround with the sauce and serve.

POMMES À LA SÉVILLANE

[Apples Braised in Butter, Orange Sauce—a hot or cold dessert]

For 6 people

Preheat oven to 325 degrees.

6 unblemished Golden Delicious apples

A mixing bowl containing 2 quarts water and 2 Tb lemon juice

One by one, peel and core the apples, and drop into the acidulated water.

A covered fireproof baking dish just large enough to hold the apples easily in one layer

4 Tb butter

¾ cup granulated sugar

½ cup dry white wine or dry white vermouth

½ cup water

2 Tb cognac

A round of buttered waxed paper

Smear inside of baking dish with half the butter. Drain the apples and place them upright in the dish. Sprinkle with sugar and place a teaspoon of butter in the center of each apple. Pour the wine, water, and cognac around the apples. Lay the round of buttered paper on top. Bring just to the simmer on top of the stove. Cover and bake in lower third of preheated oven for 25 to 35 minutes; it is important that you maintain the liquid at the merest simmer to prevent the apples from bursting. When a knife pierces them easily, they are done. Be careful not to overcook them.

2 or 3 brightly colored oranges

A vegetable peeler

While apples are cooking, remove the orange part of the skin with vegetable peeler. Cut into strips 2 inches long and ⅛ inch wide. Simmer 10 to 12 minutes in water until tender. Drain, rinse in cold water, and dry.

6 canapés (rounds of white bread sautéed in clarified butter), page 199

A serving dish

A slotted spoon

Also while the apples are baking, prepare the canapés, and arrange on serving dish. When apples are done, place a drained apple on each canapé.

½ cup red currant jelly 3 Tb cognac	Beat the jelly into the apple cooking liquid and boil down quickly over high heat until thick enough to coat a spoon lightly. Stir in the cognac and the cooked orange peel, and simmer a moment. Spoon the sauce and orange peel over the apples.
1½ to 2 cups heavy cream or *crème anglaise* (custard sauce) page 588	Serve them hot, warm, or cold, and pass the cream or sauce separately.

ORANGES GLACÉES

[Glazed Oranges—a cold dessert]

This recipe calls for whole, peeled oranges, placed in a bowl, then glazed with syrup and decorated with glazed orange peel. If you prefer sliced oranges, allow one to a serving, slice them crosswise, re-form the oranges horizontally in the serving dish, and glaze them.

For 6 people

6 large, brightly colored navel oranges A vegetable peeler	Remove the orange part of the skins with a vegetable peeler and cut into strips ⅛ inch wide and 2 inches long. Simmer in water for 10 to 12 minutes or until tender. Drain, rinse in cold water, and dry on paper towels.
A serving dish 2 inches deep	Cut the white part of the peel neatly off the oranges to expose their flesh. Cut a bit off one end of each, so it will stand up. Arrange oranges in the serving dish, with the flattened ends on the bottom.
2 cups granulated sugar ⅔ cup water A small saucepan Optional: a candy thermometer Optional: green-colored glacéed fruit cut into leaf shapes	Boil the sugar and water in the saucepan to the firm ball stage (244 degrees). Immediately drop the blanched orange peel into the syrup and boil a moment or two until syrup has thickened again. Spoon peel and syrup over oranges and chill until serving time.

PÊCHES CARDINAL

[Compote of Fresh Peaches with Raspberry Purée—a cold dessert]

This is an especially nice dessert when both peaches and raspberries are in season. Though the taste is not quite as good, you can substitute fresh apricots or pears for the peaches, or use canned fruit. Frozen raspberries do not make as thick a sauce as fresh ones, but are good anyway.

For 10 people

6 cups water
2¼ cups granulated sugar
2 Tb vanilla extract or a vanilla bean
A 12-inch saucepan

Simmer the water, sugar, and vanilla extract or bean in the saucepan and stir until sugar has dissolved.

10 firm, ripe, unblemished, fresh peaches about 2½ inches in diameter
A slotted spoon
A cake rack
A serving dish 2 inches deep

Add the unpeeled peaches to the simmering syrup. Bring again to the simmer, then maintain at just below the simmer for 8 minutes. Remove pan from heat and let peaches cool in syrup for 20 minutes. (Syrup may be used again for poaching other fruits.) Drain peaches on rack; peel while still warm, and arrange in serving dish. Chill.

1 quart fresh raspberries, and 1¼ cups granulated sugar
OR, 1½ lbs. frozen raspberries, thawed and well drained, and ⅔ cup sugar
An electric blender (or electric beater)

Force the raspberries through a sieve and place the purée in the jar of an electric blender along with the sugar. Cover and blend at top speed for 2 to 3 minutes, or until purée is thick and sugar has dissolved completely. Chill. (Or beat purée and sugar for about 10 minutes with an electric beater.)

Optional: fresh mint leaves

When both purée and peaches are chilled, pour the purée over the peaches and return to refrigerator until serving time. Decorate with optional fresh mint leaves.

POIRES AU GRATIN

[Pears Baked with Macaroons—a hot or cold dessert]

For 6 people

Preheat oven to 400 degrees.

2 lbs. fresh ripe pears or drained canned pears A baking dish about 2 inches high and 8 inches in diameter, smeared with 2 Tb butter	Peel, quarter, and core the pears. Cut into lengthwise slices about ⅜ inch thick. Arrange in overlapping layers in the baking dish.
4 Tb dry white wine or dry white vermouth, or canned pear juice ¼ cup apricot preserves, forced through a sieve	Beat the wine or pear juice and apricot preserves together and pour over the pears.
½ cup pulverized macaroons, page 583 3 Tb butter cut into pea-sized dots	Sprinkle on the macaroons and distribute the butter over them.
	Bake in middle portion of preheated oven for 20 to 30 minutes, or until top has browned lightly. Serve hot, warm, or cold.

FLAN DES ISLES

[Pineapple Custard, Unmolded—a cold dessert]

For 6 to 8 people

2½ cups drained, canned, crushed pineapple, and 1⅔ cups syrup from the pineapple (or about 30 ounces: a No. 2½ and a No. 1 can) A 6-to 8-cup saucepan	Boil the pineapple syrup for 5 minutes in the saucepan. Add the pineapple, bring again to the boil, and boil slowly 5 minutes more.
A wire whip 1 Tb flour	Beat flour and lemon juice in the mixing bowl until blended, then beat in the kirsch or cognac, and the

3 Tb lemon juice
A 3-quart mixing bowl
¼ cup kirsch or cognac
5 eggs

eggs. Gradually beat in the hot pineapple mixture in a thin stream of droplets.

A 6-cup, fireproof, cylindrical mold lined with caramel, page 584
A deep saucepan
Boiling water

Pour the pineapple custard into the caramel-lined mold, and set mold in a deep saucepan. Pour boiling water around the outside of the mold to come up to the level of the custard. Bring to the simmer on top of the stove, and maintain water barely at the simmer, always on top of the stove, for 1¼ to 1½ hours. Custard is done when it begins to shrink from the sides of the mold. A little circle in the center of the custard will remain creamy.

Remove mold from water, let cool, then chill for 3 to 4 hours or overnight.

A serving platter
3 Tb kirsch or cognac
2 cups chilled *crème an-
   glaise* (custard sauce),
   page 588

Reverse on a serving platter. Simmer kirsch or cognac in mold to dissolve remaining caramel. Strain it into the chilled *crème anglaise,* and pour the sauce around the custard.

DESSERT TARTS
Tartes Sucrées

French dessert tarts, like French entrée tarts and *quiches,* are open faced and stand supported only by their pastry shells. They should be beautiful to look at, especially the fruit tarts which lend themselves to glittering arrangements of rosettes and overlapping circles.

THE PASTRY

The pastry for dessert tart shells is molded and baked in a *flan* ring or a false-bottomed cake pan so that the shell may be unmolded. You may use either sweet short paste, which is ordinary short paste with sugar added, or *pâte sablée,* sugar crust, which, besides flour and butter, contains eggs and usually more sugar. We give proportions for both here, and refer you to the illustrated directions in the Entrée chapter for their molding and baking.

FLOUR

Be sure to read the illustrated directions on how to measure flour, on page 17. All our recipes are based on this method; other measuring systems can give different results. The small proportion of vegetable shortening included with the butter in each pastry recipe gives a less brittle crust when you are using all-purpose flour. If you have pastry flour or French flour, you may use all butter, increasing it by the amount indicated for vegetable shortening.

Pâte Brisée Sucrée

[Sweet Short Paste]

Sweet short paste is made exactly like regular short paste except that sugar is mixed into the flour before you begin.

AMOUNTS NEEDED

For an 8- to 9-inch shell, proportions for 1½ cups flour
For a 10- to 11-inch shell, proportions for 2 cups flour

Proportions for 1 cup flour

⅔ cup flour (scooped and leveled, see page 17)
A mixing bowl
1 Tb granulated sugar
⅛ tsp salt
5½ Tb fat: 4 Tb chilled butter and 1½ Tb chilled vegetable shortening
2½ to 3 Tb cold water

Place the flour in the bowl, mix in the sugar and salt, then proceed to make the dough and mold the shell either by hand or in the food processor as described on pages 140–5.

Pâte Sablée

[Sugar Crust]

Sugar crusts are particularly good with fresh fruit tarts, like the strawberry tart on page 640. They are more delicate than sweet short paste shells because of their eggs and additional sugar. The more sugar you mix in, the more difficult it is to roll and mold the pastry because it is sticky and breaks easily; the larger proportion of sugar, however, makes a delicious crust, actually a cooky dough.

By hand or by food processor. The following directions are for making the pastry by hand. Food processor directions are the same as for regular short paste dough, page 140.

For a 9- to 10-inch shell

1⅓ cups flour (scooped and leveled, page 17)

3 to 7 Tb granulated sugar (see remarks in preceding paragraph)

⅛ tsp double-action baking powder

7 Tb fat: 5 Tb chilled butter and 2 Tb chilled vegetable shortening

A 3-quart mixing bowl

1 egg beaten with 1 tsp water

½ tsp vanilla extract

A pastry board

Waxed paper

Place the flour, sugar, butter, vegetable shortening, and baking powder in the mixing bowl. Rub the fat and dry ingredients together rapidly with the tips of your fingers until the fat is broken into bits the size of small oatmeal flakes. Blend in the egg and vanilla, and knead the dough rapidly into a ball. Place on a pastry board and with the heel of your hand, not the palm, rapidly press the pastry by two-spoonful bits down on the board and away from you in a firm, quick smear of about 6 inches. (This final blending of fat and flour is illustrated on page 141.) The dough will be quite sticky if you have used the full amount of sugar. Form again into a ball, wrap in waxed paper, and chill for several hours until firm.

Mold the pastry in a *flan* ring or false-bottomed cake pan as described and illustrated on page 143. Work rapidly if you have used the full amount of sugar, as the dough softens quickly.

FULLY and PARTIALLY BAKED PASTRY SHELLS

Sweet Short Paste Shells

Sweet short paste shells, made from the formula in the first of the two preceding recipes, are baked exactly like regular short paste shells, directions for which are on page 146. You will note in these directions that shells may be fully or partially baked. Partial baking is for shells which are filled and baked again; this preliminary cooking sets the dough, and is a safeguard against soggy bottom crusts. A fully baked shell may be used for fresh fruit tarts, and and is an alternative to the sugar crust shell.

Sugar Crust Shells

Sugar crusts are usually fully baked, and must be watched while in the oven as they burn easily if the full sugar proportions have been used. Because the dough is collapsible until it has firmed in the oven, it is essential that the dough be held in place against the sides of the mold by a lining of foil and beans or a bean-filled mold, as illustrated in the directions for molding on page 145.

Bake the sugar crust shell in the middle level of a preheated, 375-degree oven for 5 to 6 minutes until the dough is set. Then remove the lining, prick the bottom of the pastry with a fork in several places, and bake for 8 to 10 minutes more. The shell is done when it has shrunk slightly from the mold and begins to brown very lightly. Immediately remove the mold from the shell and slip the shell onto a rack. It will become crusty as it cools.

LEFTOVER PASTRY DOUGH and SUGAR COOKIES

Leftover dough, securely wrapped, will keep for several days in the refrigerator or may be frozen. Or use it for sugar cookies in the following recipe:

Galettes Sablées

[Sugar Cookies]

Leftovers from either or both of the 2 preceding pastries
A 1¼ inch cooky cutter
Granulated sugar
A baking sheet
Optional: cinnamon
1 egg beaten in a small bowl with 1 tsp water
A pastry brush
A cake rack

Roll out the dough to a thickness of ¼ inch, and cut into rounds 1¼ inches in diameter. Spread a ¼-inch layer of granulated sugar on your pastry board, lay a round of dough over it, and heap sugar on top. Roll the round into a sugar-coated oval about 2½ inches long and place on the ungreased baking sheet. When all the cookies have been formed, sprinkle them with cinnamon if you wish. Paint tops with beaten egg. Bake in middle level of a preheated, 375-degree oven for 10 to 15 minutes, until lightly browned. Cool on a rack.

TARTE AUX POMMES

[Apple Tart—warm or cold]

The classic French apple tart consists of a thick, well-flavored applesauce spread in a partially cooked pastry shell. Over it thinly sliced apples are placed

Apple Tart

in an overlapping design of circles. After baking, it is coated with apricot glaze.

For 8 people

A 10-inch partially cooked pastry shell set on a baking sheet, page 634

Use the sweet short paste on page 633 for your pastry shell.

---

4 lbs. firm cooking apples (Golden Delicious)
1 tsp lemon juice
2 Tb granulated sugar
A 2-quart mixing bowl

Quarter, core, and peel the apples. Cut enough to make 3 cups into even ⅛-inch lengthwise slices and toss them in a bowl with the lemon juice and sugar. Reserve them for the top of the tart.

A 10-inch heavy-bottomed pan: enameled saucepan, skillet, or casserole
A wooden spoon
⅓ cup apricot preserves, forced through a sieve
¼ cup Calvados (apple brandy), rum, or cognac; or 1 Tb vanilla extract
⅔ cup granulated sugar
3 Tb butter
Optional: ½ tsp cinnamon, and/or the grated rind of 1 lemon or orange

Cut the rest of the apples into rough slices. You should have about 8 cups. Place in the pan and cook, covered, over low heat for about 20 minutes, stirring occasionally, until tender. Then beat in the ingredients at the left. Raise heat and boil, stirring, until applesauce is thick enough to hold in a mass in the spoon.

Preheat oven to 375 degrees.

Spread the applesauce in the pastry shell. Cover with a neat, closely overlapping layer of sliced apples arranged in a spiral, concentric circles, or as illustrated at the beginning of this recipe.

A cake rack or serving dish
½ cup apricot glaze, page 593
2 cups heavy cream, or *crème fraîche*, page 16

Bake in upper third of preheated oven for about 30 minutes, or until the sliced apples have browned lightly and are tender. Slide tart onto the rack or serving dish and spoon or paint over it a light coating of apricot glaze. Serve warm or cold, and pass with it, if you wish, a bowl of cream.

✳ *TARTE NORMANDE AUX POMMES*

[Custard Apple Tart—to be served hot]

While this creamy apple tart may be eaten cold, it is at its best when hot or warm. It can be reheated.

For 6 people

An 8-inch partially baked pastry shell placed on a baking sheet, page 634

Use the sweet short paste on page 633 for the pastry shell. Preheat oven to 375 degrees.

1 lb. firm cooking apples (Golden Delicious)
⅓ cup granulated sugar
½ tsp cinnamon

Quarter, core, and peel the apples. Cut into ⅛-inch lengthwise slices. You should have about 3 cups. Toss them in a bowl with the sugar and cinnamon, then arrange them in the pastry shell. Bake in upper third of preheated oven for about 20 minutes, or until they start to color and are almost tender. Remove from oven and let cool while preparing the custard.

1 egg
⅓ cup granulated sugar
¼ cup sifted flour
½ cup whipping cream
3 Tb Calvados (apple brandy) or cognac

Beat the egg and sugar together in a mixing bowl until mixture is thick, pale yellow, and falls back on itself forming a slowly dissolving ribbon. Beat in the flour, then the cream, and finally the brandy. Pour the mixture over the apples. It should come almost to the top of the pastry shell.

Powdered sugar in a shaker

Return to oven for 10 minutes, or until cream begins to puff. Sprinkle heavily with powdered sugar and

	return to oven for 15 to 20 minutes more. Tart is done when top has browned and a needle or knife plunged into the custard comes out clean.
A cake rack or serving dish	Slide tart onto a rack or serving dish, and keep warm until ready to serve.

VARIATION

Tarte aux Poires

[Pear Tart]

Using the same method and proportions, substitute sliced pears for the apples.

LA TARTE DES DEMOISELLES TATIN

[Upside-down Apple Tart—hot or cold]

This is an especially good tart if your apples are full of flavor. It is cooked in a baking dish with the pastry on top of the apples. When done, it is reversed onto a serving dish and presents a lovely mass of caramelized apples.

For 8 people

4 lbs. firm cooking apples (Golden Delicious) **⅓ cup granulated sugar** **Optional: 1 tsp cinnamon**	Quarter, core, and peel the apples. Cut into lengthwise slices ⅛ inch thick. Toss in a bowl with the sugar and optional cinnamon. You should have about 10 cups of apples.
2 Tb softened butter **A baking dish 9 to 10 inches in diameter and 2 to 2½ inches deep (pyrex is practical, as you can see when the tart is done)** **½ cup granulated sugar** **6 Tb melted butter**	Butter the baking dish heavily especially on the bottom. Sprinkle half the sugar in the bottom of the dish and arrange a third of the apples over it. Sprinkle with a third of the melted butter. Repeat with a layer of half the remaining apples and butter, then a final layer of apples and butter. Sprinkle the rest of the sugar over the apples.
	Preheat oven to 375 degrees.
Chilled sweet short paste (proportions for 1 cup of flour), page 633	Roll out the pastry to a thickness of ⅛ inch. Cut it into a circle the size of the top of the baking dish. Place it over the apples, allowing its edges to fall

against the inside edge of the dish. Cut 4 or 5 holes about ⅛ inch long in the top of the pastry to allow cooking steam to escape.

Aluminum foil, if needed

Bake in lower third of preheated oven for 45 to 60 minutes. If pastry begins to brown too much, cover lightly with aluminum foil. Tart is done when you tilt the dish and see that a thick brown syrup rather than a light liquid exudes from the apples between the crust and the edge of the dish.

A fireproof serving dish
Powdered sugar, if needed

Immediately unmold the tart onto serving dish. If the apples are not a light caramel brown, which is often the case, sprinkle rather heavily with powdered sugar and run under a moderately hot broiler for several minutes to caramelize the surface lightly.

---

2 cups heavy cream, or
crème fraîche, page 16

Keep warm until serving time, and accompany with a bowl of cream. (May also be served cold, but we prefer it warm.)

---

* _TARTE AUX ABRICOTS_
TARTE AUX PÊCHES

[Fresh Apricot or Peach Tart—warm or cold]

For 6 people

An 8-inch partially cooked pastry shell placed on a baking sheet, page 634

For the shell use the sweet short paste on page 633.

---

8 to 10 fresh apricots or 3 or 4 freestone peaches
Boiling water

Drop the fruit in boiling water for 10 to 15 seconds. Peel, halve, and remove pits. Slice the fruit if you wish.

Preheat oven to 375 degrees.

⅔ cup granulated sugar
2 Tb butter cut into pea-sized dots

Sprinkle 3 tablespoons of sugar in the bottom of the pastry shell. If the fruit is sliced, arrange it over the sugar in a closely overlapping layer of concentric circles. If it is halved, place the halves, domed side up, closely together in the shell. Spread on the rest of the sugar. Dot with the butter.

Bake in middle level of preheated oven for 30 to 40 minutes, or until fruit has colored lightly and the juices have become syrupy.

¼ cup slivered almonds
½ cup apricot glaze, page 593

Slip the tart onto a rack. Decorate with the slivered almonds, and spread on the apricot glaze.

Serve warm or cold.

VARIATIONS

Use the same system with plums, pears, or canned fruit. A nice combination is slices of canned apricots alternating with slices of banana.

Tartes Flambées Any of these tarts may be flamed with liqueurs as they are brought to the table, as described in the recipe for cherry tart, page 643.

✴ TARTE AUX FRAISES

[Fresh Strawberry Tart—cold]

Fresh fruit tarts are easy to make, pretty to look at, and refreshing to eat. They consist of a fully baked tart shell which is lined with liqueur-flavored

Fresh Strawberry Tart

crème pâtissière (custard filling). The fresh fruit is arranged over the filling and topped with apricot or red currant glaze. Other suggestions follow this recipe.

For 8 people

A 10-inch fully baked pastry shell, page 634	Use either the sweet short paste, or the sugar crust for your tart shell. Recipes begin on page 633.
1 quart large, ripe, handsome strawberries **A cake rack**	Hull the strawberries. If necessary to wash them, do so very quickly, and drain them on a rack.
1 cup red currant jelly **2 Tb granulated sugar** **2 Tb kirsch or cognac** **Optional: a candy thermometer** **A pastry brush**	Boil the currant jelly, sugar, and liqueur in a small saucepan until last drops from spoon are sticky (228 degrees). Paint the interior of the shell with a thin coating of the glaze and allow to set for 5 minutes. This will give the shell a light waterproofing. Reserve the rest of the glaze for the strawberries. Warm it briefly if it has hardened.
1½ to 2 cups chilled *crème pâtissière* (custard filling), page 590, with 2 to 3 Tb kirsch or cognac	Spread a ½-inch layer of *crème pâtissière* in the bottom of the pastry shell.
	Arrange a design of strawberries over the cream. Put the largest strawberry in the center, and graduate down in size, placing the berries closely together, their stem ends in the cream. Spoon or paint over them a thin coating of the glaze, and the tart is ready to serve. (*) Because of the glazed waterproofing in the bottom of the shell, the filled tart may wait an hour or so.

VARIATIONS

Using the same method as that for the preceding strawberry tart, substitute a layer of peeled and seeded grapes, sliced bananas, raspberries, or poached

Mixed Fruit Tart

or canned peaches, apricots, plums, or pears. Follow the above illustration for design.

TARTE AUX POIRES À LA BOURDALOUE

[Pear and Almond Tart—tepid or cold]

For 6 people

1½ to 2 lbs. firm, ripe, un-blemished pears	Peel and halve the pears. Neatly stem and core them with a grapefruit knife. Drop each half, as it is pre-

Pear Tart

2 cups cold water and 1 Tb lemon juice in a mixing bowl	pared, into the acidulated water to keep it from discoloring.
2 cups red Bordeaux wine 2 Tb lemon juice ¾ cup granulated sugar	Bring the wine, lemon juice, sugar, and cinnamon to the boil in the saucepan. Drain the pears, and drop into the boiling syrup; bring liquid to just below the

1 stick or ½ tsp cinnamon

A 3-quart enameled sauce-
pan

A slotted spoon

A rack

Optional: a candy ther-
mometer

¼ cup red currant jelly in a
small saucepan

A wooden spoon

A 10-inch fully cooked
sugar-crust shell, page 633

2½ cups chilled *frangipane*
(almond custard), page
591, with 2 Tb kirsch

Optional: ¼ cup slivered almonds

simmer for 8 to 10 minutes or until pears are tender
when pierced with a knife. Do not overcook; they
must hold their shape. Remove saucepan from heat
and let pears cool in the syrup for 20 minutes. Drain
the pears on a rack.

Rapidly boil down the syrup to the thread stage (230
degrees). Measure out ¼ cup of syrup and simmer it
with the red currant jelly until jelly has dissolved and
the syrup coats the spoon with a light glaze.

Paint the inside of the shell with a thin layer of the
pear and jelly glaze.

Spread the *frangipane* in the pastry shell. Cut the
pears into crosswise or lengthwise slices and arrange
them over the custard.

Decorate with the optional almonds. Spoon a light
coating of the glaze over the top of the tart.

TARTE AUX CERISES, FLAMBÉE

[Cherry Tart *Flambée*]

For a spectacular entrance, sprinkle sugar over a cooked fruit tart, caramelize it briefly under the broiler, pour on liqueur, and ignite it as you enter
the dining room. The following recipe is for cherries; you may use the same
technique for the apricot or peach tart on page 639, and for the variations
following it.

The cherries

You may use canned Bing cherries or defrosted frozen cherries instead
of fresh for this recipe. In this case, omit the first step in the directions, drain the
cherries thoroughly, and let them stand for at least half an hour with 3 tablespoons of kirsch or cognac and as much sugar as you feel they need. Drain
them again just before using, and beat their kirsch or cognac into the cream
filling.

For 6 people

3 cups fresh black cherries

1 cup red Bordeaux wine

Wash and pit the cherries. Bring the wine, lemon
juice, and sugar to the boil. Drop in the cherries, and

2 Tb lemon juice
6 Tb granulated sugar
A 2-quart enameled saucepan

bring the liquid to just below the simmer for 5 to 6 minutes or until cherries are tender, but retain their shape. Allow cherries to cool in the syrup for 20 to 30 minutes. Drain.

An 8-inch, fully cooked pastry shell, page 634, set in a fireproof serving dish

Use either of the sweet pastry recipes beginning on page 633. If you wish to fill the tart shell some time before serving, paint the interior with a thin coating of red currant glaze, page 594.

1½ cups cold *crème pâtissière* (custard filling), page 590, or *frangipane* (almond custard), page 591, with 2 Tb kirsch or cognac

Fold the drained cherries into the custard, and spread the mixture in the tart shell.

Preheat broiler to moderately hot.

3 Tb granulated sugar
¼ cup kirsch or cognac, warmed in a small saucepan

Immediately before serving, sprinkle the sugar over the surface of the tart and run it under the broiler for 2 to 3 minutes to caramelize the sugar lightly; be careful it does not burn. Just before entering the dining room, pour the warm liqueur over the hot caramelized surface. Avert your face and ignite the liqueur with a lighted match; bring the flaming tart to the table.

TARTE À L'ANANAS

[Pineapple Tart]

For 6 people

1 No. 2 can of sliced pineapple, pineapple wedges, or crushed pineapple (1½ cups fruit and about ¾ cup syrup)

Drain the pineapple. Boil the canned pineapple syrup for 5 minutes in a saucepan. Add the pineapple and boil for 5 minutes more. Drain the pineapple, and allow it to cool.

½ cup red currant jelly
2 Tb kirsch or cognac
Optional: a candy thermometer

Boil the pineapple syrup with the jelly and liqueur until it reduces to a glaze (last drops are sticky when dropped from a spoon, 228 degrees).

A pastry brush

An 8-inch, fully cooked, sugar-crust shell, page 633

1½ to 2 cups chilled *crème pâtissière* (custard filling), page 590, with 2 to 3 Tb kirsch or cognac

Paint the interior of the shell with a coating of the pineapple glaze. Spread the *crème pâtissière* in the pastry shell.

Optional: ¼ cup diced red and green glacéed fruit and ¼ cup slivered almonds

When the pineapple is cold, arrange it over the filling. Decorate with the optional glacéed fruits and almonds. Spoon a light coating of pineapple glaze over the top.

TARTE AU CITRON
TARTE AUX LIMETTES

[Lemon or Lime Soufflé Tart—hot]

This delicious, light tart is really a soufflé. The same filling is also attractive in little tart shells served for afternoon tea. Speaking of these, see also the lemon butter filling on page 676.

For 8 people

A 10-inch, cooked, sugar-crust shell placed on a baking sheet, page 633 (use only 3 Tb sugar in the pastry)

When you bake the shell let it barely color so it will not brown too much when it goes again into the oven.

Preheat oven to 325 degrees.

A wire whip or electric beater

A 3- to 4-quart stainless steel bowl

½ cup granulated sugar

4 egg yolks

Gradually beat the sugar into the egg yolks and continue beating until mixture is thick, pale yellow, and falls back on itself forming a slowly dissolving ribbon. Beat in the rind and juice. Set bowl over not-quite-simmering water and stir with wooden spoon until mixture is too hot for your finger (165 degrees), and

The grated rind of 1 lemon
or 2 limes
3 Tb lemon juice or lime
juice
A pan of not-quite-simmering water
A wooden spoon
Optional: a candy ther-
mometer

thickens enough to coat the spoon lightly. Be careful
not to overheat it and scramble the egg yolks.

---

4 egg whites
A pinch of salt
¼ cup granulated sugar

Beat the egg whites and salt until soft peaks are
formed; sprinkle on the sugar and continue beating
until stiff peaks are formed (page 159). Fold the egg
whites delicately into the warm lemon or lime mixture and turn into the tart shell.

Powdered sugar in shaker

Bake for about 30 minutes in middle level of preheated
oven. When tart has begun to puff and color, sprinkle
with powdered sugar. It is done when top is lightly
brown, and a needle or knife plunged into the center
comes out clean.

If you cannot serve it immediately, leave in turned-off
hot oven with the door ajar. It will sink slightly as it
cools. (May be served hot, warm, or cold but we think
it is best hot.)

TARTE AU CITRON ET AUX AMANDES

[Lemon and Almond Tart—cold]

For 6 people

An 8-inch, cooked, sugar-
crust shell placed on a
baking sheet, page 633
(use only 3 Tb sugar in
the pastry)

When you bake the shell, let it barely color so it will
not brown too much when it goes again into the oven.

---

3 lemons
A vegetable peeler

Remove the yellow part of the lemon skin with a vegetable peeler; cut into julienne strips ⅟₁₆ inch wide
and 2½ inches long. Simmer 10 to 12 minutes in water. Drain thoroughly.

2 cups granulated sugar
⅔ cup water
1 tsp vanilla extract
A small saucepan
Optional: a candy ther-
    mometer

Boil the sugar and ⅔ cup of water to the thread stage (230 degrees); add the vanilla and lemon peel. Let stand for 30 minutes.

Preheat oven to 325 degrees.

An electric beater or wire
    whip
2 eggs
½ cup granulated sugar
A 3-quart mixing bowl

Beat the eggs and sugar in a mixing bowl for 4 to 5 minutes, or until mixture is thick, pale yellow and falls back on itself forming a slowly dissolving ribbon.

¾ cup (4 ounces) pulverized
    almonds, page 582
¼ tsp almond extract
The grated rind and
    strained juice of 1½
    lemons
A rack

Beat in the almonds, almond extract, lemon rind, and lemon juice. Pour this almond cream into the pastry shell and bake in middle level of preheated oven for about 25 minutes. Tart is done when cream has puffed, browned very lightly, and a needle or knife plunged into the cream comes out clean. Slide tart onto rack.

Drain the strips of lemon peel and strew them over the tart. Boil their syrup down until it is a glaze (last drops are sticky when fall from spoon, 228 degrees), and spoon a thin coating over the top of the tart. This tart is usually served cold, but may be eaten warm if you wish.

---

* *TARTE AU FROMAGE FRAIS*

[Cream Cheese Tart—hot or cold]

This is really a *quiche*, and very simple indeed to make.
For 6 people

An 8-inch partially baked
    pastry shell placed on a
    baking sheet, page 634

Use the recipe for sweet short paste on page 633.

Preheat oven to 375 degrees.

½ lb. (1 cup) cream cheese
4 ounces (1 stick) softened
   unsalted butter
⅔ cup granulated sugar
A 3-quart mixing bowl
A wooden spoon or electric
   beater
2 eggs
Big pinch of nutmeg

Cream the cheese, butter, and sugar together in a mixing bowl. Beat in the eggs and nutmeg. Turn into pastry shell and bake in upper third of preheated oven for 25 to 30 minutes. Tart is done when it has puffed and browned, and a needle or knife plunged into the center comes out clean.

Tart will sink slightly as it cools. It may be served hot and puffed, or warm, or cold. It may also be reheated, but will not puff again.

VARIATION

Tarte au Fromage Frais et aux Pruneaux

[Cream Cheese and Prune Tart]

½ cup "tenderized" prunes
½ cup (about 3 ounces)
   pulverized almonds, page
   582
¼ tsp almond extract

Soften prunes for 5 minutes in hot water. Drain, remove pits, and dice the prunes. Stir prunes, almonds, and almond extract into tart mixture after the eggs have been beaten in.

DESSERT CRÊPES
Crêpes Sucrées

Dessert *crêpes*, especially if they are for *crêpes Suzette*, should be as thin and delicate as possible. There are numerous varying recipes for making them; some use egg yolks, others use whole eggs, and still others specify cream rather than milk. The lightness of *crêpes* made from the following recipe can be attributed to the use of milk diluted with water. If you wish a heavier *crêpe*, use all milk, or light cream. The batter for dessert *crêpes*, like that for entrée *crêpes*, must rest at least 2 hours before using.

METHOD FOR COOKING CRÊPES

The procedure for cooking *crêpes* is described and illustrated in the Entrée chapter on page 191. You may wish to sauté them in clarified butter, page 15, rather than in oil and butter. As dessert *crêpes* are fragile, you will probably find it best to lift them with your fingers to turn and cook them on the other side.

Crêpes may be made several hours before serving time. Pile them in a dish, cover with waxed paper and a plate to keep them from drying out.

CRÊPES FINES SUCRÉES

[Light Batter—for *crêpes Suzette*]

(If you do not have an electric blender proceed as follows: Gradually work the egg yolks into the flour with a wooden spoon, beat in the liquids by droplets, then strain the batter through a fine sieve.)

For 10 to 12 crêpes *6 inches in diameter, or 16 to 18* crêpes *4 to 5 inches in diameter*

¾ cup milk
¾ cup cold water
3 egg yolks
1 Tb granulated sugar
3 Tb orange liqueur, rum, or brandy
1 cup flour (scooped and leveled, page 17)
5 Tb melted butter
An electric blender
A rubber scraper

Place the ingredients in the blender jar in the order in which they are listed. Cover and blend at top speed for 1 minute. If bits of flour adhere to sides of jar, dislodge with a rubber scraper and blend 3 seconds more. Cover and refrigerate for at least 2 hours or overnight.

CRÊPES À LA LEVURE

[Yeast Batter—for stuffed *crêpes*]

The addition of yeast makes a more tender and slightly thicker *crêpe*.

Ingredients for the preceding *crêpe* batter
1½ tsp fresh or dry yeast

Warm ¼ cup of the milk to blood temperature (about 90 degrees) and allow the yeast to dissolve in it. Add it to the rest of the ingredients in the blender and proceed with the recipe.

Cover the batter with a towel and let it stand at room temperature for about 2 hours, or until the yeast has worked and the batter looks bubbly on top. Use immediately, or the yeast will overferment.

CRÊPES SOUFFLÉES

[Raised Batter—for stuffed *crêpes*]

Beaten egg whites folded into the batter makes the *crêpes* puff slightly.

Ingredients for one of the preceding *crêpe* batters, either plain or with yeast **3 egg whites** **Pinch of salt**	After the batter has rested for 2 hours, and just before you wish to make your *crêpes,* beat the egg whites and salt until stiff. Fold half into the batter, fold in the other half, then make the *crêpes.*

CRÊPES SUZETTE

[*Crêpes* with Orange Butter, *Flambées*]

Every chef has his own recipe for *crêpes Suzette;* of the many we have tried, we find this one especially good. Obviously if you plan to perform in public with a chafing dish, it is a good idea to practice on your family until you become adept at folding and flaming. *Crêpes* 4 to 5 inches in diameter are a convenient size, and three of these per person is the usual serving.

For 6 people

The orange butter (in a food processor, or by hand and electric mixer)

For the processor: ½ cup granulated sugar **By hand: 4 large sugar lumps and ¼ cup sugar** **2 bright-skinned oranges** **A vegetable peeler** **A rubber spatula** **½ lb. unsalted butter** **½ to ⅔ cup strained orange juice** **3 Tb orange liqueur**	*For the processor* (steel blade), place the ½ cup of sugar in the container along with the orange part of the peel (stripped from the fruit). Process for a minute or so, scraping down sides of bowl with a rubber spatula as necessary, until peel and sugar are finely blended. Cut the butter into pieces, and process until smooth and almost fluffy. By droplets, cream in ½ cup of the orange juice, then the orange liqueur, plus droplets more of the juice if the mixture will take it and still remain creamy. Cover and refrigerate. *By hand and electric mixer,* first rub the sugar lumps over the oranges until all sides have absorbed the oil from the skin. Mash the lumps on a board, add the orange part of the peel from the fruit, and the ¼ cup of sugar. Chop until very finely minced. Scrape into a bowl and cream in the butter with an electric

mixer, then ½ cup of orange juice, the liqueur, and more juice if possible. Cover and refrigerate.

The chafing dish finish

18 cooked *crêpes* 4 to 5 inches in diameter	Use the recipe for *crêpes fines sucrées*, page 649.
A chafing dish set over an alcohol flame	Place the orange butter in the chafing dish and heat until it is bubbling.
A spoon and fork	Dip both sides of a *crêpe* in the butter. Its best-looking side out, fold it in half and in half again, to form a wedge. Place it at the edge of the chafing dish. Rapidly continue with the rest of the *crêpes* until all have been dipped, folded, and arranged.
2 Tb granulated sugar ⅓ cup orange liqueur ⅓ cup cognac	Sprinkle the *crêpes* with the sugar. Pour over them the orange liqueur and cognac. Avert your face and ignite the liqueur with a lighted match. Shake the chafing dish gently back and forth while spooning the flaming liqueur over the *crêpes* until the fire dies down. Serve.

CRÊPES FOURRÉES ET FLAMBÉES

[*Crêpes* with Orange-almond Butter, *Flambées*]

These *crêpes* are stuffed with orange-flavored almond butter, and may be flamed in a chafing dish, or brought flaming to the table as suggested here.

For 6 to 8 people

The orange-almond butter

½ cup pulverized almonds, page 582, or pulverized macaroons, page 583 ¼ tsp almond extract The orange butter in the preceding recipe	Beat the almonds or macaroons and almond extract into the orange butter.

Filling the crêpes

18 cooked *crêpes* 4 to 5 inches in diameter	Use any of the 3 *crêpe* recipes starting on page 649. Spread the butter on the less good side of each

A lightly buttered baking dish suitable for serving	cooked *crêpe,* and fold into wedge shapes, or roll them, to enclose the butter filling. Arrange in the baking dish. (*) If not to be heated immediately, cover with waxed paper and refrigerate.

Flaming the crêpes

3 Tb granulated sugar	Shortly before serving time, sprinkle with sugar and set in a preheated, 375-degree oven for 10 to 15 minutes until dish is very hot and *crêpes* are beginning to caramelize on top.
⅓ cup orange liqueur and ⅓ cup cognac warmed in a small saucepan A long-handled serving spoon	Just before entering the dining room, pour the warm orange liqueur and cognac over the hot *crêpes.* Avert your face, ignite *crêpes* with a lighted match, and bring them blazing to the table. The server tilts the dish and spoons the flaming liqueur over the *crêpes* until the fire dies down.

CRÊPES FOURRÉES, FRANGIPANE

[*Crêpes* with Almond Cream]

This is a much lighter filling than the preceding orange-almond butter. It may be set aflame if you wish, or served with chocolate as suggested in the recipe.

For 6 people

12 cooked *crêpes* 6 inches in diameter	Use any of the three recipes for *crêpes* beginning on page 649.
1½ cups *frangipane* (almond custard), page 591 A lightly buttered baking-serving dish 2 ounces or squares of semi-sweet baking chocolate 2 Tb melted butter 1 Tb granulated sugar	Spread 2 tablespoons of *frangipane* on the less-good side of each *crêpe.* Fold the *crêpes* into wedge shapes, or roll them, to enclose the filling, and arrange in the baking dish. Grate the chocolate over the *crêpes,* sprinkle on the melted butter, then the sugar.
	About 20 minutes before serving, set in a preheated 350-degree oven until the chocolate has melted. Serve hot or warm.

GÂTEAU DE CRÊPES À LA NORMANDE

[Mound of *Crêpes* with Apples, *Flambé*]

Instead of stuffing each *crêpe* separately, you can pile them one upon the other with a layer of filling between each, as in this recipe.

For 6 to 8 people

2 lbs. crisp cooking or eating apples

A heavy-bottomed, 3-quart pan: saucepan, casserole, or skillet

A wooden spoon

½ cup granulated sugar, more if needed

Quarter, core, and peel the apples. Chop them roughly. You should have about 5 cups. Cook in a covered pan over low heat for about 20 minutes, stirring occasionally, until apples are tender. Uncover, add sugar, raise heat and boil, stirring, for 5 minutes or more. Applesauce should reduce and be thick enough to hold itself in a fairly solid mass in the spoon. Add more sugar while the apples are cooking if you feel it necessary.

2 Tb whipping cream

¼ tsp almond extract

2 Tb Calvados (apple brandy), cognac, or dark rum

Stir the cream, almond extract, and brandy or rum into the applesauce.

10 to 12 cooked *crêpes* 6 inches in diameter

Use the raised batter recipe for *crêpes soufflées* on page 650.

A lightly buttered baking-serving dish

½ cup (3 ounces) pulverized almonds, page 582, or pulverized macaroons, page 583

2 Tb slivered almonds or pulverized macaroons

2 Tb melted butter

2 Tb granulated sugar

Center a *crêpe* in the bottom of the dish. Spread a layer of apples over it and sprinkle with a scant tablespoon of almonds or macaroons. Continue with layers of *crêpe*, apples, and almonds, ending with a *crêpe*. This will look like a many-layered cake. Sprinkle the almonds or macaroons over the last *crêpe*. Pour on the butter and sprinkle with the sugar.

About 30 minutes before serving, place in the upper third of a preheated, 375-degree oven to heat through thoroughly. The sugar on top of the mound should almost begin to caramelize. Serve as follows:

½ cup Calvados (apple brandy), cognac, or dark rum, warmed in a small saucepan

A long-handled serving spoon

Just before entering the dining room, pour the warm brandy or rum over the hot mound of *crêpes*. Avert your face, set liqueur aflame with a lighted match, and bring the blazing dessert to the table. The server should spoon the flaming liqueur over the dessert until the fire subsides, then cut portions from the mound as from a cake.

OTHER FILLINGS FOR CRÊPES

Here are some other ideas following the general method in any of the preceding recipes. Flame the *crêpes* or not, as you wish.

Fresh Fruits

Let strawberries, raspberries, or sliced bananas stand in a bowl with a sprinkling of sugar and kirsch, orange liqueur, or cognac for an hour, then use as a filling.

Stewed Fruits

Any of the following may be folded into an equal amount of *crème pâtissière* (custard filling), page 590, and then used for stuffed *crêpes* or a mound of *crêpes:*

Apples, peeled, sliced, sautéed in butter, then sprinkled with sugar and cinnamon

Pears, peeled, poached in red-wine syrup, as in *tarte aux poires à la Bourdaloue,* page 642, then diced and sprinkled with crumbled macaroons

Peaches, apricots, or plums poached in syrup, using the system for poaching peaches in *pêches cardinal,* page 630, then drained, peeled, and diced

Pineapple (crushed, canned pineapple), drained, the syrup boiled for 5 minutes, then the pineapple boiled in the syrup for 5 minutes more and drained

Jams, Preserves, and Jellies

These simple fillings make a delicious dessert when the *crêpes* are flamed with liqueur. To prepare them, mix a little kirsch, cognac, or orange liqueur into red currant jelly, or raspberry, strawberry, apricot, or cherry jam or preserves. Stir in also, if you wish, some crumbled macaroons. Spread the filling on the *crêpes,* roll, fold them, or pile them into a mound in a fireproof dish.

Sprinkle with melted butter and granulated sugar, and set in a preheated, 375-degree oven until thoroughly heated. Flame with warmed liqueur just as you bring them to the table.

FRUIT FLANS
Clafoutis

∗ *CLAFOUTI*

[Cherry *Flan*]

The *clafouti* (also spelled with a final "s" in both singular and plural) which is traditional in the *Limousin* during the cherry season is peasant cooking for family meals, and about as simple a dessert to make as you can imagine: a pancake batter poured over fruit in a fireproof dish, then baked in the oven. It looks like a tart, and is usually eaten warm.

(If you have no electric blender, work the eggs into the flour with a wooden spoon, gradually beat in the liquids, then strain the batter through a fine sieve.)

For 6 to 8 people

Preheat oven to 350 degrees.

---

3 cups pitted black cherries

Use fresh, black, sweet cherries in season. Otherwise use drained, canned, pitted Bing cherries, or frozen sweet cherries, thawed and drained.

1¼ cups milk
⅓ cup granulated sugar
3 eggs
1 Tb vanilla extract
⅛ tsp salt
½ cup flour (scooped and leveled, page 17)
An electric blender

Place the ingredients at left in your blender jar in the order in which they are listed. Cover and blend at top speed for 1 minute.

A 7- to 8-cup lightly buttered, fireproof baking dish or pyrex pie plate about 1½ inches deep

Pour a ¼-inch layer of batter in the baking dish or pie plate. Set over moderate heat for a minute or two until a film of batter has set in the bottom of the dish. Remove from heat. Spread the cherries over the bat-

An asbestos mat, if necessary
⅓ cup granulated sugar

ter and sprinkle on the sugar. Pour on the rest of the batter and smooth the surface with the back of a spoon.

Powdered sugar in a shaker

Place in middle position of preheated oven and bake for about an hour. The *clafouti* is done when it has puffed and browned, and a needle or knife plunged into its center comes out clean. Sprinkle top of *clafouti* with powdered sugar just before bringing it to the table. (The *clafouti* need not be served hot, but should still be warm. It will sink down slightly as it cools.)

VARIATIONS

The *clafouti* in the preceding master recipe is the simple and classic version. Here are some variations:

Clafouti à la Liqueur
[Cherry *Flan* with Liqueur]

Ingredients for the preceding *clafouti*
¼ cup kirsch or cognac
⅓ cup granulated sugar

Follow the master recipe but first let the cherries stand for 1 hour in the kirsch or cognac and sugar. Substitute this liquid for part of the milk called for in the batter; omit the ⅓ sugar near the end of the recipe.

Clafouti aux Poires
[Pear *Flan*]

Ingredients for the master
   clafouti with changes as
   indicated
3 cups peeled, cored, and
   sliced ripe pears (1¼ to
   1½ lbs. pears)
¼ cup sweet white wine,
   kirsch, or cognac
⅓ cup granulated sugar

Follow the master recipe with these changes: Substitute pears for cherries, and let stand for 1 hour in wine, kirsch, or cognac and sugar. Substitute this liquid for part of the milk called for in the batter; omit the ⅓ cup of sugar near the end of the recipe.

Clafouti aux Pruneaux

[Plum *Flan*]

Ingredients for the master *clafouti* with changes as indicated

1 lb. firm, ripe plums

Boiling water

¼ cup orange liqueur, kirsch, or cognac

⅓ cup sugar

Follow the master recipe with these changes: Substitute plums for cherries, and drop in boiling water for exactly 10 seconds. Peel. Slice them or leave whole. Let stand with liqueur, kirsch, or cognac and sugar for 1 hour. Substitute this liquid for part of the milk called for in the batter; omit the ⅓ cup sugar near the end of the recipe.

Clafouti aux Pommes

[Apple *Flan*]

Ingredients for the master *clafouti* with changes as indicated

About 1¼ lbs. crisp eating or cooking apples

3 to 4 Tb butter

An enameled skillet

¼ cup Calvados (apple brandy), dark rum, or cognac

⅛ tsp cinnamon

⅓ cup sugar

Follow the master recipe with these changes: Substitute apples for cherries; peel, core, and cut them into lengthwise slices ¼ inch thick. You should have about 3 cups. Sauté to brown very lightly in hot butter, then let stand in the skillet for ½ hour with the brandy or rum, cinnamon, and sugar. Substitute this liquid for part of the milk called for in the batter; omit the ⅓ cup sugar near the end of the recipe.

Clafouti aux Mûres
Clafouti aux Myrtilles

[Blackberry or Blueberry *Flan*]

Ingredients for the master *clafouti* or the variation following it with changes as indicated

3 cups (about 1¼ lbs.) stemmed and washed blackberries or blueberries

Follow the master recipe or the variation after it with these changes: Substitute berries for cherries and, because berries are very juicy, increase the flour for your batter from ⅔ to 1¼ cups.

Clafouti à la Bourdaloue

[Cherry or Pear *Flan* with Almonds]

Ingredients for either of the 2 cherry *flans*, or for the pear *flan*
½ cup blanched almonds (can be bought in a can)
1 tsp almond extract

Follow the master recipe for cherry *flan*, or the variation after it, or the recipe for pear *flan*, but purée the almonds in the blender with the milk called for in your batter. Add the almond extract, and proceed with the recipe.

BABAS AND SAVARINS

Babas et Savarins

Babas and *savarins* always seem to delight guests, and they are not difficult to make if you have any feeling at all for doughs and baking. They may be cooked a day or two ahead. They freeze perfectly; all you need to do to make them ready to imbibe their syrup is to pop them from the freezer into a 300-degree oven, to warm through for about 5 minutes.

Whenever you are working with yeast doughs, do so in a warm place free from drafts; a sudden chill can cause the dough to fall. So that the dough will rise in one to two hours, cover it with a damp towel and set it where the temperature remains between 80 and 100 degrees. If you can control the heat and have a thermometer, put it in a plate-warming oven, or in a baking oven, heating briefly every once in a while to maintain the correct temperature. Or place the covered bowl on a pillow over the radiator. If you allow the dough to rise too much, or too long, or at too warm a temperature, it will develop a taste of overfermented yeast.

✳ PÂTE À BABA ET BABAS

[*Baba* Paste and *Babas*]

For about 12 babas

Mixing the paste

4 Tb butter

Melt the butter, and let it cool to tepid while you are preparing the other ingredients.

1 Tb dry active yeast
3 Tb tepid water
A 3-quart mixing bowl
A wire whip
2 Tb granulated sugar
⅛ tsp salt
2 "large" eggs

Blend the yeast and water in the bowl with a wire whip and let stand until yeast has dissolved completely. Beat in the sugar, salt, and eggs.

1⅓ cups flour (scooped and
   leveled, page 17)
A wooden spoon

(Be sure to measure your flour correctly to get a soft pliable dough.) Mix the flour and the cool melted butter into the yeast with a wooden spoon.

Kneading the paste

Then with the fingers of one hand held together and slightly cupped, knead the dough by lifting it, slapping it, and pulling it vigorously against the sides of the bowl for about 5 minutes. It will be very sticky at first, but will gradually detach itself from the bowl and from your hand. It has been worked to sufficient elasticity and body when you can grasp it in both hands, pull it to a length of 10 to 12 inches, and give it a full twist without breaking it. (NOTE: If you are doubling the recipe, you will have to remove the dough from the bowl and knead it by pulling and slapping it between your hands, like taffy.)

Preliminary rising in a bowl

1 tsp flour

Form it into a ball in the bottom of the bowl. Cut a cross an inch deep on top and sprinkle the ball with the flour. Cover the bowl with several thicknesses of damp towel and let it rise in a warm place, 80 to 100 degrees, for 1½ to 2 hours, or until the dough has doubled in bulk.

Again with the cupped fingers of one hand, gently deflate the dough by gathering it from the sides of the bowl to the center.

Final rising in molds

1 Tb softened butter
12 *baba,* popover, or muffin
   cups or muffin tins, about

Butter inside of cups. Lightly break off about a tablespoon of dough, enough to fill a third of a cup, and press it lightly into the bottom of the cup. Do not

Cylindrical Baba Mold, 2
Inches Deep and 2 Inches
in Diameter

**2 inches deep and 2 inches
   in diameter**

bother to even the top of the dough as it will smooth
out as it rises.

Place the cups, uncovered, again in a warm place and
allow to rise 1 to 2 hours more, or until the dough is
¼ inch over the rim of the cups.

Baking

As soon as the dough has risen this second time—and
do not delay or it may collapse—bake in the upper
third of a preheated, 375-degree oven for about 15
minutes. The *babas* should be nicely browned, and
slightly shrunk from the sides of the cups. Unmold
them onto a cake rack.

Babas au Rhum

[Rum *Babas*]

Both the *babas* and the rum syrup should be lukewarm but not hot before
this operation begins. If the *babas* are cold, heat them briefly in the oven; warm
the syrup if necessary. (NOTE: Some authorities use a stronger sugar syrup,
1½ cups of sugar to 2 of water. We prefer the lighter syrup given here.)

For 12 babas

The sugar syrup

**2 cups water
1 cup granulated sugar
A 1-quart saucepan
½ cup dark rum, more if
   needed (Jamaican rum is
   recommended)**

Bring the water and sugar to a boil. Remove from
heat and stir until sugar has dissolved. When the
sugar syrup has cooled to lukewarm, stir in the rum;
you may add a few tablespoons more if you feel it
necessary.

The babas imbibe the syrup

12 barely warm cooked *babas,* the preceding recipe

A dish 2 inches deep and just large enough to hold the *babas* easily

A skewer, trussing needle or sharp-pronged fork

Optional: a bulb baster

A cake rack set over a tray

Arrange the barely warm *babas* in the dish, their puffed tops up. Prick tops in several places, pour the lukewarm syrup over them, and let stand for ½ hour, basting frequently with syrup. They should imbibe enough syrup so they are moist and spongy but still hold their shape. Drain on rack for ½ hour.

TO SERVE

Babas au Rhum, Classique

[Rum *Babas*]

---

2 Tb dark rum

A pastry brush

½ cup apricot glaze, page 593

12 glacéed cherries

A serving dish or frilled paper cups

After the *babas* have drained, sprinkle the top of each with a few drops of rum. Paint them with the apricot glaze, and place a cherry on top of each. Arrange in a serving dish or in paper cups.

Babas aux Fruits

[Rum *Babas* with Fruit]

A serving dish

3 to 4 cups blueberries or fresh strawberries

Leftover *baba* syrup

2 to 3 cups *crème Chantilly,* (lightly whipped cream), page 580, flavored with rum and powdered sugar

Arrange the *babas* in the serving dish. Surround them with the berries which have stood for 10 to 15 minutes in leftover *baba* syrup. Pass the cream separately.

✳ *SAVARIN*

[*Savarin*]

Large Savarin *or Ring
Mold, 7 to 9 Inches in
Diameter. Small* Savarin
*Mold, 2¼ to 4 Inches in
Diameter*

The *savarin* uses the same paste or dough as the *baba*, but is baked in a ring mold, and its sugar syrup is flavored with kirsch rather than rum. The center is then filled with a cream or with fruits macerated in liqueur.

For 6 people

Filling the mold

1 Tb softened butter
**A 4- to 5-cup ring mold 2
 inches deep**
**The master recipe for *baba*
 paste, page 658**

Butter the ring mold. Make the *baba* paste as directed and let it rise in its bowl until doubled in bulk. Deflate it by pressing it rapidly in several places with the cupped fingers of one hand. Then break off a 2-tablespoon bit of the paste and press lightly into the bottom of the mold. Continue rapidly with the rest of the paste. The mold will be from a third to a half filled. Do not bother to smooth the surface of the paste; it will even out as it rises. Place uncovered in a warm place, 80 to 100 degrees, for 1 to 2 hours or until the paste has risen to fill the mold. Proceed at once to the following step.

Baking the savarin

Preheat oven to 375 degrees in time for this step.

Aluminum foil
A cake rack

Insert a cylinder of aluminum foil through the hole in the center of the mold; this will help the *savarin* rise evenly in the oven. Place in the middle level of the oven and bake for about 30 minutes. If top of *savarin* browns too much during baking, cover lightly with aluminum foil. The *savarin* is done when it is toasty brown and has begun to shrink a little from the sides of the mold. Remove from oven and let cool for 5 minutes. Reverse rack over mold, reverse the two, remove the mold. When savarin has cooled to tepid, proceed to the following step.

(*) It may be baked a day or two in advance, then heated briefly to tepid in a 300-degree oven.

The savarin imbibes the syrup

2 cups sugar syrup (rum *baba* recipe), page 660, but flavored with ½ cup kirsch rather than rum

A skewer, trussing needle, or sharp-pronged fork

A dish 2 inches deep and just large enough to hold the *savarin* easily

A bulb baster

A cake rack

A tray

While the *savarin* is baking, make the same sugar syrup as that for the *babas,* but perfume it with kirsch rather than rum. Let it cool to tepid. Prick the puffed side of the barely warm *savarin* and place it puffed-side down in the dish. Pour the tepid syrup over it and allow to stand for ½ hour, basting frequently with the syrup. The *savarin* should be moist and spongy, but still hold its shape. Then tilt the dish and pour out the remaining syrup (which may be reserved for flavoring fruits). Turn the rack upside down over the dish and reverse the dish onto the rack to unmold the *savarin*. Set rack on tray and let the *savarin* drain for about ½ hour.

A serving dish

The *savarin* is now resting puffed-side up on the rack; it is usually served puffed-side down. The safest way to get it from the rack to the serving dish is to turn the dish upside down over the *savarin* on the rack; then reverse the rack onto the dish.

1 Tb kirsch

Sprinkle the *savarin* with drops of kirsch before decorating and filling as directed in one of the following suggestions:

TO SERVE

Savarins are usually painted with a glaze into which are pressed designs of almonds and glacéed fruits, or fresh strawberries or raspberries. The center is filled with whipped cream, custard filling, or fruits. The following recipe gives the general procedure for glazing, decorating, and filling; other suggestions are listed after it.

Savarin Chantilly

[*Savarin* with Whipped Cream]

The preceding *savarin*
¾ **cup apricot glaze, page**
   593
A pastry brush
6 to 8 glacéed cherries
A piece of angelica
8 to 12 blanched almonds
2 cups *crème Chantilly*
   (lightly whipped cream),
   page 580, flavored with
   powdered   sugar   and
   kirsch

Paint the *savarin* with a light coating of apricot glaze. Cut the cherries in half, and the angelica into small diamond shapes. Press the fruits and almonds over the *savarin* in a decorative design and paint a bit of glaze over them. Fill the center of the *savarin* with the cream just before serving.

OTHER FILLINGS

Instead of whipped cream, you may use a custard or fruit filling. In the case of fruit fillings, decorate glazed *savarin* with the fruits you are using rather than with almonds and glacéed fruits. Between 1½ and 2 cups of custard filling are sufficient. If you are using fruits, you will probably want more; fill the center of the *savarin* with them, and heap the rest around the outside. The fruits are usually flavored with 3 to 4 Tb kirsch for 3 to 4 cups fruit, and several tablespoons of sugar, if necessary (or use leftover imbibing syrup).

Frangipane, custard filling with almonds or macaroons, flavored with vanilla and kirsch, page 591

Crème Saint-Honoré, crème pâtissière with beaten egg whites, flavored with vanilla and kirsch, page 591

Macédoine de Fruits, a mixture of cut-up fruits, such as cherries, pears, apricots, pineapple, either fresh, poached in syrup as for the *pêches cardinal* on page 630, or canned. Let stand for ½ hour in kirsch, and sugar if necessary, before using.

Fresh strawberries or raspberries, which have stood for ½ hour with sugar and kirsch

Cherries, poached in red wine syrup, as for the cherry tart on page 643

VARIATION

Petits Savarins

[Small *Savarins*]

Small *savarins* are baked in the small molds illustrated at the beginning of the *savarin* recipe; they range in diameter from 2¼ inches for tea parties to 3 or 4 inches for individual dessert servings.

MOLDING, BAKING, AND SYRUPING

Proceed exactly as for the large *savarin* on page 662, but omit the aluminum-foil funnel, and bake for only 10 to 15 minutes. Saturate them with kirsch-flavored syrup as directed for the large *savarin*. The proportions in the recipe will furnish about 12 small *savarins* 2¼ inches in diameter or about 6 *savarins* 3 inches in diameter.

TO SERVE

You may paint small *savarins* with apricot glaze, page 593, decorate with glacéed fruits cut into diamond shapes, and serve them as they are, or you may fill them. If you fill them and do not intend to serve them on dessert plates, it is best to set them on small rounds of baked sugar-crust dough, page 633. Paint the rounds first with the apricot glaze, then glaze and decorate the *savarins*. Use any of the fillings suggested for the large *savarin* in the preceding list.

LADYFINGERS

Biscuits à la Cuiller

Biscuits à la cuiller are among the oldest of the French *petits gâteaux secs*. Before pastry tubes were invented, the batter for ladyfingers was dropped onto baking sheets with a spoon, and this is how they acquired their French name.

Because store-bought ladyfingers are usually so dreadful in taste and texture that they cannot be used in good cooking, it is useful to know how to make your own. They can be made quickly when you become familiar with the process and will keep at least 10 days in an airtight container or freeze perfectly. With homemade ladyfingers on hand, you will find many of the spectacular desserts in the preceding pages not at all formidable. These include the *charlotte Chantilly* on page 608, the *charlotte Malakoff,* on page 605, and the *diplomate* on page 612. Then there are the easily assembled *plombières* on page 594, which consist of custard filling, beaten egg whites, and ladyfingers dipped in liqueur. To serve ladyfingers with afternoon tea, you may hold them together back to back with a bit of butter cream, page 680.

Batter for ladyfingers is of the sponge-cake type, with egg yolks and sugar beaten to a thick cream, then flour and stiffly beaten egg whites are folded in. You must be particularly careful to obtain a batter which will hold its shape; this means expert beating and folding. A batter that is too liquid will form flat rather than rounded ladyfingers. Be sure to read the illustrated directions on beating egg whites and folding which start on page 159.

BISCUITS À LA CUILLER

[Ladyfingers]

For 24 to 30 ladyfingers

Preheat oven to 300 degrees.

Two 12- by 24-inch baking sheets
1 Tb softened butter
Flour
A pastry bag with a round tube opening ½ inch in diameter
1½ cups powdered sugar in a sieve or a shaker

Prepare the baking sheets: butter lightly, dust with flour, and knock off excess flour. Assemble the pastry bag. Prepare the powdered sugar. Measure out all the rest of the ingredients listed in the recipe.

The batter

An electric beater or a wire whip
½ cup granulated sugar
3 egg yolks
1 tsp vanilla extract
A 3-quart mixing bowl

Gradually beat the sugar into the egg yolks, add the vanilla, and continue beating for several minutes until the mixture is thick, pale yellow, and forms the ribbon, page 579.

3 egg whites
Pinch of salt
1 Tb granulated sugar

Beat the egg whites and salt together in a separate bowl until soft peaks are formed. Sprinkle on the sugar and beat until stiff peaks are formed. (Directions are on page 159.)

A rubber spatula

½ cup all-purpose flour (scooped and leveled, page 17), turned into a flour sifter

Scoop one fourth of the egg whites over the top of the egg yolks and sugar mixture. Sift on one fourth of the flour, and delicately fold in until partially blended. Then add one third of the remaining egg whites, sift on one third of the remaining flour, fold until partially blended, and repeat with half of each, then the last of each. Do not attempt to blend the mixture too thoroughly or you will deflate the batter; it must remain light and puffy.

Forming the ladyfingers

Scoop batter into pastry bag. Squeeze out even lines onto the prepared baking sheets, making finger shapes 4 inches long and 1½ inches wide, spaced 1 inch apart. Sprinkle with a ⅟₁₆-inch layer of powdered sugar. To dislodge some of the excess sugar, hold baking sheet upside down and tap the back of it gently; the ladyfingers will not budge unless you are rough with them.

Baking the ladyfingers

Bake in middle and upper third levels of preheated oven for about 20 minutes. The ladyfingers are done when they are a very pale brown underneath their sugar coating. They should be slightly crusty outside, and tender but dry inside. If they are not baked enough, they will become soggy when they cool; overbaking makes them dry. As soon as they are done, remove from baking sheets with a spatula and cool on cake racks.

To serve

Ladyfingers may be served as they are, with tea or fruit desserts. Or you may make double ladyfingers by sticking the two flat sides together with apricot glaze, page 593, or one of the butter creams starting on page 680.

FIVE FRENCH CAKES
Cinq Gâteaux

Here are five unusually good and typically French cakes. They are all made in very much the same way, but as there are slight differences in mixing and in how each should look in the oven, we give full recipes for all five. After you have practiced with one or two, you will find that they all can be made very quickly; any one of them may be prepared for the oven in about 20 minutes. An electric beater is a help in mixing the batters but is far from essential, because a large wire whip does the work almost as quickly.

PRELIMINARY REMARKS

Before you begin the cake

Preheat the oven, prepare the cake pan as in the following directions, and measure out all your ingredients. Then your batter may be prepared and baked in one, continuous operation.

Preparing the cake pan

To prepare the pan for the cake batter, rub the entire inner surface with a thin film of softened butter. Then roll flour around in the pan to cover the sides and bottom; knock out excess flour by banging the pan, upside down, on a hard surface. A light dusting of flour should adhere all over the inner surface of the pan; this will make the cake easy to unmold (remove) after baking.

Flour

Measure flour as accurately as possible; this is essential in cakemaking. Be sure to read the illustrated directions for measuring flour on page 17.

Egg yolks, sugar, and butter

Directions for beating egg yolks and sugar until they "form the ribbon" are on page 579. Directions for creaming butter and sugar are on page 581.

Egg whites

You will note that no baking powder is used in any of the cakes; their lightness is due to the careful folding of perfectly beaten egg whites into the batter. As this is one of the most important aspects of successful cakemaking, be sure to read the illustrated directions on egg whites in the Entrée chapter starting on page 159.

Temperature

Oven temperature must be correct if the cake is to bake and rise as it should. Check your thermostat with an oven thermometer.

Unmolding

After the cake is done, your recipe will usually direct you to let it sit in its pan for a few minutes; it will settle, and shrink slightly from the sides of the pan. Unmold the cake as follows: Run a thin knife between the cake and the edge of the pan. Then, if you are using a one-piece pan, turn a cake rack upside down over the pan, reverse the two, and give a short, sharp, downward jerk to dislodge the cake onto the rack. For a false-bottomed pan, either use the same general system, or set the pan over a jar to release the rim from the false bottom; remove the cake from the false bottom to a rack with a spatula, or reverse the cake onto a rack. [Directions in recipes refer to a one-piece pan.]

Icings

A cake must be thoroughly cold before it is iced; if you ice a warm or even a tepid cake with butter cream, the icing will soften and usually dribble down the sides of the cake. Illustrated directions for filling and icing cakes are in the pair of recipes beginning on page 672.

Storage

After any of the following cakes has been baked and thoroughly cooled, but before it has been covered with icing, it may be stored for several days in an airtight container, or may be securely wrapped and frozen. Cakes iced with butter creams should be stored in the refrigerator.

BISCUIT AU BEURRE

[Butter Spongecake]

This fine, light spongecake may be served with a sprinkling of powdered sugar, and goes well with tea, or with fruits. It is also delicious as a strawberry shortcake. Or you may fill and decorate it as suggested at the end of the recipe.

For a 10-inch cake serving 10 to 12 people

	Preheat oven to 350 degrees.
A round cake pan, 10 inches in diameter and 2 inches deep	Butter and flour the cake pan, page 668. Measure out the ingredients.
4 Tb butter	Melt the butter and set aside to cool.
A 3-quart mixing bowl An electric beater or large wire whip ⅔ cup granulated sugar 4 egg yolks 2 tsp vanilla extract	Gradually beat the sugar into the egg yolks, add the vanilla, and continue beating for several minutes until mixture is thick, pale yellow, and forms the ribbon, page 579.
4 egg whites Pinch of salt 2 Tb granulated sugar A rubber spatula ¾ cup cake flour (scooped and leveled, page 17), turned into a flour sifter	Beat the egg whites and salt together in a separate bowl until soft peaks are formed; sprinkle on the sugar and beat until stiff peaks are formed. (Directions are on page 159.) Scoop one fourth of the egg whites over the top of the egg yolks and sugar mixture. Sift on one fourth of the flour, and delicately fold in until partially blended. Then add one third of the remaining egg whites, sift on one third of the remaining flour, fold until partially blended, and re-

peat with half of each, then the last of each and half of the tepid, melted butter. When partially blended, fold in the rest of the butter but omit the milky residue at the bottom of the pan. Do not overmix; the egg whites must retain as much volume as possible.

Turn into prepared cake pan, tilting pan to run batter to the rim all around. Set in middle level of preheated oven and bake for 30 to 35 minutes. Cake is done when it has puffed, is lightly brown, and has just begun to show a faint line of shrinkage from the edges of the pan.

A cake rack

Remove from oven and let stand in the pan for 6 to 8 minutes. It will sink slightly and shrink more from the edges of the pan. Run a knife around the edge of the pan, and reverse on cake rack, giving the pan a sharp little jerk to dislodge the cake. If cake is not to be iced, immediately reverse it so its puffed side is uppermost. Allow to cool for an hour or so.

TO SERVE

Sucre Glace

[Powdered Sugar]

Shake powdered sugar over the cake.

Glaçage à l'Abricot

[Apricot Glaze with Almonds or Glacéed Fruits]

A pastry brush
½ cup apricot glaze, page 593
1 cup pulverized almonds, page 582
¼ cup slivered almonds or glacéed fruits

Follow the general procedure for icing a cake illustrated on page 674: Brush crumbs off top and sides of cake, paint cake with apricot glaze. Brush almonds against the sides and decorate top with slivered almonds or with glacéed fruits cut into dice or fancy shapes.

Glaçage à la Crème ou au Chocolat

[Butter-cream or Chocolate Icing]

The spongecake may be iced, or filled and iced. Follow the recipe for orange-butter filling on page 672, or that for the orange butter-cream, page 674. Or, using the same procedure, follow one of the recipes for butter cream starting on page 680, or for the chocolate-butter icing on page 684.

GÂTEAU À L'ORANGE

[Orange Spongecake]

For a 9-inch cake serving 8 people

Preheat oven to 350 degrees.

A round cake pan 9 by 1½ inches

Butter and flour the cake pan, page 668. Measure out the ingredients.

A whip or electric beater
⅔ cup granulated sugar
4 egg yolks
A 3-quart mixing bowl
The grated rind of 1 orange
⅓ cup strained orange juice
Pinch of salt
¾ cup cake flour (scooped and leveled, page 17), turned into a sifter

Gradually beat the sugar into the egg yolks and continue beating until the mixture thickens to form the ribbon, page 579. Add the grated orange peel, orange juice, and salt. Beat for a moment or two until mixture is light and foamy. Then beat in the flour.

4 egg whites
Pinch of salt
1 Tb granulated sugar

Beat the egg whites and salt together in a separate bowl until soft peaks are formed. Sprinkle on the sugar and beat until stiff peaks are formed. (Directions are on page 159.) Stir one fourth of the egg whites into the batter, delicately fold in the rest.

Immediately turn into prepared cake pan and run the batter up to the rim all around. Bake in middle position of preheated oven for 30 to 35 minutes. Cake is done when it has puffed and browned, and shows a faint line of shrinkage from the edge of the mold.

A cake rack

Let cool for 6 to 8 minutes. Run a knife around the edge of the pan and reverse cake on a rack. If not to be iced, immediately reverse again, puffed side up. Allow to cool for an hour or two. When cake is cold, sprinkle it with powdered sugar, or fill and ice the cake according to one of the two following recipes:

DIRECTIONS FOR FILLING AND ICING A CAKE

Gâteau Fourré à la Crème d'Orange

[Spongecake with Orange-butter Filling]

This orange-butter filling may be used for cakes, or as a filling for tartlets or cookies. When softened butter is beaten into it, as described in the variation at the end of the recipe, it may also serve as an icing.

For about 2 cups, enough to fill a 9- to 10-inch cake

The orange-butter filling

6 Tb unsalted butter
1⅔ cups granulated sugar
2 eggs
2 egg yolks
The grated rind of 1 orange
¼ cup strained orange juice
1 Tb orange liqueur
A 6-cup enameled saucepan
A wire whip
Optional: a candy thermometer

Place all the ingredients at the left in the saucepan and beat with wire whip over low heat or not-quite-simmering water until mixture thickens like honey. When it is cooking properly, the bubbles that first appeared on its surface as it is heated will begin to subside, and if you look closely you will see a little whiff of steam rise; it will be too hot for your finger. You must heat it enough to thicken, but overheating will (of course) scramble the egg yolks.

A pan of cold water

Then set saucepan in cold water and beat for 3 to 4 minutes until filling is cool.

(*) May be refrigerated for 10 days, or may be frozen.

Filling the cake

A 9- to 10-inch cake: the preceding orange spongecake or the butter spongecake on page 669
A long, sharp, thin knife

Cut a tiny vertical wedge up the edge of the cake; this will guide you in re-forming it later. Slice the cake in half horizontally.

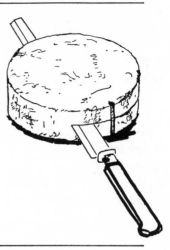

*Splitting the cake
in half*

A flexible blade-spatula

Using a spatula, spread enough orange-butter filling on the lower layer of the cake to make a ⅛-inch coating.

*Icing the
bottom layer*

*Replace top layer, lining
up with wedge*

Decorating the cake with apricot glaze and almonds

A pastry brush
⅔ cup apricot glaze, page 593
1 cup pulverized almonds, plain or toasted, page 582
A dish for the almonds
A cake platter
Optional: ¼ cup glazed orange peel, page 587

Brush off any crumbs, and paint the cake with a coating of apricot glaze. When the glaze has set slightly, brush the almonds against the sides of the cake; not more than one fourth of them will adhere, but you need a large amount for easy manipulation. Set the cake on the platter; decorate top with optional orange peel.

Hold cake over almonds and brush them against sides with free hand

VARIATIONS

Crème au Beurre à l'Orange

[Orange Butter-cream Icing]

For a richer filling, or for an icing, you may turn the preceding filling into a *crème au beurre,* which resembles the butter cream on page 683. In the following recipe, we have suggested that you use half the original orange-butter filling for inside the cake, and beat butter into the rest to make a butter-cream icing.

For 1 cup filling and 2 cups icing, enough for a 9- to 10-inch cake

---

2 cups orange-butter filling, the preceding recipe
A 3-quart mixing bowl
A wire whip or an electric beater
¼ lb. (1 stick) softened, unsalted butter, 2 to 3 Tb more if necessary

Use 1 cup of the filling to spread inside your cake as described in the preceding recipe. Re-form the cake. Place the rest of the filling in the mixing bowl and gradually beat in the softened butter. The mixture should thicken into a smooth, mayonnaiselike cream; if it looks grainy, beat in more butter a tablespoon at a time. Chill until firm but still of spreading consistency.

(NOTE: Be sure cake is thoroughly cold before you begin this operation.)

Icing the cake

A flexible blade-spatula
A cake platter
Optional: ¼ cup glazed orange peel, page 587

Brush crumbs off cake. Hold the cake in the palm of your hand as illustrated (or ice it on its serving platter). Spread on the icing with the spatula, starting at the top of the cake, and finishing with the sides. Set the cake on the platter. Decorate, if you wish, with pieces of glazed orange peel. Refrigerate the cake until ready to serve.

(*) Leftover butter cream may be refrigerated for about a week, or may be frozen. Before using, let warm at room temperature until it can be beaten into spreading consistency.

Spread icing on top of cake first, then smooth it around sides

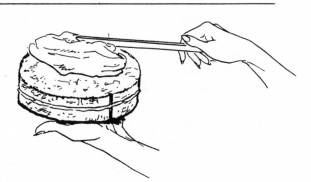

Crème au Citron

[Lemon-butter Filling]

Crème au Beurre au Citron

[Lemon Butter-cream Icing]

Use the same method and proportions as in either of the two preceding recipes, but substitute grated lemon rind and lemon juice for orange.

GÂTEAU À L'ORANGE ET AUX AMANDES

[Orange and Almond Spongecake]

This delicious cake may be served with a sprinkling of powdered sugar, with a glazing of apricot, or with a filling and icing.

For a 9-inch cake serving 8 people

Preheat oven to 350 degrees.

A round cake pan, 9 by 1½ inches

Butter and flour the cake pan, page 668. Measure out all the ingredients.

¼ lb. butter

Melt the butter and set aside.

A whip or electric beater
⅔ cup granulated sugar
3 egg yolks
A 3-quart mixing bowl
The grated rind of 1 orange
⅓ cup strained orange juice
¼ tsp almond extract
¾ cup (4 ounces) pulverized almonds, page 582
½ cup cake flour (scooped and leveled, page 17), turned into a sifter

Gradually beat the sugar into the egg yolks and continue beating until mixture is thick, pale yellow and forms the ribbon, page 579. Add the grated orange rind, orange juice, and almond extract. Beat for a moment or two until mixture is light and foamy. Then beat in the almonds, and finally the flour.

3 egg whites
Pinch of salt
1 Tb granulated sugar

Beat the egg whites and salt together in a separate bowl until soft peaks are formed; sprinkle on the sugar and beat until stiff peaks are formed. (Directions are on page 159.)

A rubber spatula	Using a rubber spatula, fold the cool, melted butter into the cake batter, omitting milky residue at bottom of butter pan. Stir one fourth of the egg whites into the batter, delicately fold in the rest.
	Immediately turn into prepared cake pan and run the batter up to the rim all around. Bake in middle level of preheated oven for 30 to 35 minutes. Cake is done when it has puffed, browned lightly, top is springy when pressed, and a needle plunged into the center of the cake comes out clean.
A cake rack	Remove from oven and let stand for about 10 minutes, until cake begins to shrink from sides of pan. Run a knife around the edge of the pan and reverse the cake onto the rack, giving it a small, sharp, downward jerk to dislodge it from the pan. If it is not to be iced, reverse the cake immediately so it will cool puffed-side up. Allow to cool for an hour or two.

TO SERVE

Serve with a sprinkling of powdered sugar, or with apricot glaze and almonds, page 674, or with the orange-butter filling or butter-cream icing described for the orange sponge cake and starting on page 672.

REINE DE SABA

[Chocolate and Almond Cake]

This extremely good chocolate cake is baked so that its center remains slightly underdone; overcooked, the cake loses its special creamy quality. It is covered with a chocolate-butter icing, and decorated with almonds. Because of its creamy center it needs no filling. It can be made in the same manner as the preceding cakes, starting out with a beating of egg yolks and sugar, then proceeding with the rest of the ingredients. But because the chocolate and the almonds make a batter so stiff it is difficult to fold in the egg whites, we have chosen another method, that of creaming together the butter and sugar, and then incorporating the remaining items.

For an 8-inch cake serving 6 to 8 people

Preheat oven to 350 degrees.

A round cake pan 8 inches in diameter and 1½ inches deep

4 ounces or squares semi-sweet chocolate melted with 2 Tb rum or coffee

Butter and flour the cake pan, page 668. Set the chocolate and rum or coffee in a small pan, cover, and place (off heat) in a larger pan of almost simmering water; let melt while you proceed with the recipe. Measure out the rest of the ingredients.

A 3-quart mixing bowl

A wooden spoon or an electric beater

¼ lb. or 1 stick softened butter

⅔ cup granulated sugar

Cream the butter and sugar together for several minutes until they form a pale yellow, fluffy mixture, page 581.

3 egg yolks

Beat in the egg yolks until well blended.

3 egg whites

Pinch of salt

1 Tb granulated sugar

Beat the egg whites and salt in a separate bowl until soft peaks are formed; sprinkle on the sugar and beat until stiff peaks are formed. (Directions are on page 159.)

A rubber spatula

⅓ cup pulverized almonds, page 582

¼ tsp almond extract

½ cup cake flour (scooped and leveled, page 17), turned into a sifter

With a rubber spatula, blend the melted chocolate into the butter and sugar mixture, then stir in the almonds, and almond extract. Immediately stir in one fourth of the beaten egg whites to lighten the batter. Delicately fold in a third of the remaining whites and when partially blended, sift on one third of the flour and continue folding. Alternate rapidly with more egg whites and more flour until all egg whites and flour are incorporated.

Turn the batter into the cake pan, pushing the batter up to its rim with a rubber spatula. Bake in middle level of preheated oven for about 25 minutes. Cake is done when it has puffed, and 2½ to 3 inches around the circumference are set so that a needle plunged into that area comes out clean; the center should move slightly if the pan is shaken, and a needle comes out oily.

A cake rack

Allow cake to cool in the pan for 10 minutes. Run a knife around the edge of the pan, and reverse cake on the rack. Allow it to cool for an hour or two; it must be thoroughly cold if it is to be iced.

TO SERVE

Use the chocolate-butter icing on page 684, and press a design of almonds over the icing.

LE MARQUIS

[Chocolate Spongecake]

For an 8-inch cake serving 6 to 8 people

	Preheat oven to 350 degrees.
A round cake pan 8 inches in diameter and 1½ inches deep	Butter and flour the cake pan, page 668. Measure out the ingredients.
3½ ounces of semisweet baking chocolate 2 Tb strong coffee A small covered pan A pan of simmering water A wooden spoon 3½ Tb softened butter	Place the chocolate and coffee in the small pan, cover, and set in the larger pan of simmering water. Remove pans from heat and let chocolate melt for 5 minutes or so while you proceed with the recipe. Then beat in the butter.
A wire whip or electric beater 3 egg yolks A 3-quart mixing bowl ½ cup granulated sugar	Beat the egg yolks in the mixing bowl, gradually adding the sugar, until mixture is thick, pale yellow and forms the ribbon, page 579.
3 egg whites Pinch of salt 1 Tb granulated sugar	Beat the egg whites and salt together in a separate bowl until soft peaks are formed; sprinkle on the sugar and beat until stiff peaks are formed. (Directions are on page 159.)
A rubber spatula ⅓ cup cake flour (scooped and leveled, page 17), turned into a sifter	Fold the tepid chocolate and butter into the batter, then fold in one fourth of the egg whites. When partially blended, sift on one fourth of the flour and continue folding, alternating rapidly with more egg whites and more flour until all egg whites and flour are incorporated.

Immediately turn batter into prepared pan and run it
up to the rim all around. Bake in middle level of preheated oven for 25 minutes, or until cake has puffed
¼ inch above rim and top has cracked. A skewer or
straw should come out clean when plunged 1½ inches
from edge, but should be slightly oily with a few
specks of chocolate clinging when plunged into the
middle area.

A cake rack

Let cool 10 minutes; cake will sink slightly. Run a
knife around inside of pan, and reverse onto a rack.
Let cool 2 hours before icing.

To serve

You may serve the cake with a sprinkling of powdered sugar, fill and
ice it with one of the following butter creams, or fill with butter cream and
cover with the chocolate-butter icing on page 684. Illustrated directions for
filling and icing a cake begin on page 672.

THREE BUTTER CREAMS

Trois Crèmes au Beurre

Butter creams consist of egg yolks, sugar, butter, and flavoring which are
beaten together into a creamy mass of spreading consistency. There are half
a dozen ways of arriving at them; one is the orange butter-cream on page 674.
Here are three more recipes. The first of these is quick and easy but always
slightly grainy, because the sugar never completely dissolves. The second is
made with sugar syrup in which egg yolks are poached before the butter is
beaten in; it makes a fairly firm cream good in hot weather. Custard sauce
and butter make up the third cream, which is lighter in texture than the other
two and better in cold weather than in hot. Any of these butter creams may
be used both as fillings and as icings.

AMOUNTS NEEDED

For both filling and icing a cake, you will need approximately the following amounts:

For an 8-inch cake, 1½ cups
For a 9-inch cake, 2 cups
For a 10-inch cake, 2½ cups

Butter creams may be refrigerated for several days, or frozen for several weeks. To use again, allow the cream to warm at room temperature until it can be beaten into spreading consistency. If it begins to separate or turn grainy, beat in a tablespoon or two of tepid, unsalted, melted butter.

FILLING AND ICING

Illustrated directions for filling and icing cakes are in the pair of recipes starting on page 672.

CRÈME AU BEURRE, MÉNAGÈRE

[Butter Cream I—with powdered sugar]

This should be made with an electric beater; it is heavy work by hand.
For about 1½ cups

A 2½-quart mixing bowl
2 egg yolks
⅔ cup sifted powdered sugar
2 Tb kirsch, rum, orange liqueur, or strong coffee, OR, 1 Tb vanilla extract, OR, 2 ounces (2 squares) melted, semisweet, baking chocolate
6 ounces (1½ sticks) softened, unsalted butter
An electric beater (or a wire whip)

Rinse the bowl in hot water, dry it, and place in it all the ingredients listed. Beat at a moderate speed for about 5 minutes to obtain a smooth cream. Chill until the cream is cold but still malleable, then fill and ice your cake.

CRÈME AU BEURRE, AU SUCRE CUIT

[Butter Cream II—with sugar syrup]

You may use either a wire whip or an electric beater for most of the steps in this recipe. We find, however, that a large balloon whip, such as that illustrated for beating egg whites on page 159, is the quickest and most effective instrument for the beating of egg yolks and sugar syrup step.

For about 2 cups

Preliminaries

A wooden spoon or an electric beater A 2½-quart mixing bowl ½ lb. (2 sticks) unsalted butter	Cream the butter until it is light and fluffy. (Directions are on page 100.) Set aside.
5 egg yolks, OR, 1 egg and 3 yolks A 2½-quart mixing bowl A large wire whip (or an electric beater)	Place the egg yolks (or egg and yolks) in the bowl and beat a few seconds to blend thoroughly. Set aside.

The sugar syrup

⅔ cup granulated sugar 3 Tb water A small, heavy saucepan Optional: a candy thermometer	Boil the sugar and water in the saucepan, shaking pan frequently, until the sugar has reached the soft ball stage (236 to 238 degrees on candy thermometer).

Beating the egg yolks with the syrup

	At once beat the boiling syrup in a stream of droplets into the egg yolks, using your wire whip (or electric beater).
A pan of not-quite-simmering water, large enough to hold the bowl A basin of cold water	Set the mixing bowl in the pan of not-quite-simmering water, on the stove, and continue beating the yolk and sugar mixture at a moderate speed, lifting in as much air as possible. In 4 to 5 minutes the mixture will be light, foamy, doubled in bulk, and feel very hot to your finger. When this stage is reached, set the bowl in cold water and continue beating for several minutes until mixture has cooled to tepid, and when a bit is lifted, it falls back forming a slowly dissolving ribbon on the surface of the mixture.

Combining with the butter

A wooden spatula or spoon, or an electric beater	Then beat the egg mixture by spoonfuls into the bowl of creamed butter. Beat in the flavoring. The *crème*

2 to 3 Tb kirsch, rum, orange liqueur, or strong coffee, OR, 1 Tb vanilla extract, OR, 2 ounces (2 squares) melted, semisweet, baking chocolate

2 to 4 Tb softened, unsalted butter, if needed

au beurre should be a smooth, homogeneous, creamy mass. If it looks grainy or has a tendency to separate, beat in softened butter by tablespoons. Chill until cold but still malleable, then fill and frost your cake.

CRÈME AU BEURRE, À L'ANGLAISE

[Butter Cream III—with custard base]

This final recipe is simpler to make than the preceding one with its sugar syrup and its poaching of egg yolks. The custard base here is that most familiar of custard sauces, *crème anglaise* which, when cooled, receives the butter.

For about 2½ cups

The crème anglaise (custard sauce)

A wire whip or electric beater

⅔ cup granulated sugar

4 egg yolks

A 2½-quart mixing bowl

½ cup boiling milk

A 1-quart, heavy-bottomed, enameled saucepan

A wooden spoon

Optional: a candy thermometer

A basin of cold water

A sieve

Following the general procedure in the master recipe for *crème anglaise* on page 588, gradually beat the sugar into the egg yolks in the bowl until mixture is thick, pale yellow, and forms the ribbon. Then beat in the boiling milk by droplets. Pour into saucepan and stir with wooden spoon over moderately low heat until mixture thickens enough to coat spoon with a light cream (165 degrees on candy thermometer). At once set saucepan in cold water and beat until custard has cooled to barely tepid. Rinse out mixing bowl and strain custard back into it.

Beating in the butter

A wire whip or electric beater

½ lb. (2 sticks) softened, unsalted butter, more if needed

2 to 3 Tb kirsch, rum, orange liqueur, or strong

Beat the softened butter into the barely tepid custard by spoonfuls, using whip or beater. Beat in the flavoring. If cream looks grainy or has a tendency to curdle, beat in more softened butter by tablespoons. Cream should be smooth, thick, and homogeneous. Chill until cold but still malleable, then fill and ice your cake.

coffee, OR, 1 Tb vanilla
extract OR, 2 ounces (2
squares) melted, semi-
sweet, baking chocolate

CHOCOLATE ICING

Glaçage au Chocolat

This simple chocolate icing is butter beaten into melted chocolate, and forms a tender coating over a white or chocolate cake, or over a thoroughly chilled butter-cream icing.

GLAÇAGE AU CHOCOLAT

[Chocolate-butter Icing]

For an 8-inch cake

2 ounces (2 squares) semisweet baking chocolate
2 Tb rum or coffee
A small covered pan
A larger pan of almost simmering water
5 to 6 Tb unsalted butter
A wooden spoon
A bowl with a tray of ice
cubes and water to cover
them
A small flexible-blade metal
spatula or a table knife

Place the chocolate and rum or coffee in the small pan, cover, and set in the larger pan of almost simmering water. Remove pans from heat and let chocolate melt for 5 minutes or so, until perfectly smooth. Lift chocolate pan out of the hot water, and beat in the butter a tablespoon at a time. Then beat over the ice and water until chocolate mixture has cooled to spreading consistency. At once spread it over your cake with spatula or knife.

INDEX

A NOTE ABOUT THE AUTHORS

Julia Child, a native of California and a Smith College graduate; Simone Beck, French-born and -educated; and Louisette Bertholle, half French and half American, educated in both countries, represented an even blending of the two backgrounds and were singularly equipped to write about French cooking for Americans. Mrs. Child studied at Paris's famous Cordon Bleu, and all three authors worked under various distinguished French chefs. In 1951 they started their own cooking school in Paris, L'Ecole des Trois Gourmandes, at the same time that this book was taking shape. Shortly after the appearance of *Mastering the Art of French Cooking* in 1961, Julia Child began appearing in the public television series *The French Chef,* which made her a national celebrity, earning her the Peabody Award in 1965 and an Emmy in 1966. Several public television programs and numerous cookbooks followed, including *Julia and Jacques Cooking at Home,* with Jacques Pépin, in 1999. *The Way to Cook,* her magnum opus, was published in 1989, and in 2000 she gave us *Julia's Kitchen Wisdom,* a distillation of her years of cooking experience. Julia Child died in 2004, and her memoir, *My Life in France,* was completed by Alex Prud'homme and published two years later.

THE TEXT OF THIS BOOK

IS SET IN GRANJON

THE TEXT OF THIS BOOK IS SET IN GRANJON, *a type named in compliment to Robert Granjon, type-cutter and printer— Antwerp, Lyons, Rome, Paris—active from 1523 to 1590. The boldest and most original designer of his time, he was one of the first to practice the trade of type-founder apart from that of printer.*

This type face was designed by George W. Jones, who based his drawings on a type used by Claude Garamond (1510–61) in his beautiful French books, and more closely resembles Garamond's own than do any of the various modern types that bear his name.

This book was composed by the Kingsport Press, Inc., Kingsport, Tennessee, and Maryland Linotype, Baltimore, Maryland, and printed by Kingsport Press, Inc.

Typography and binding design by

WARREN ⚹ CHAPPELL

Cover design: Adaptation by Naomi Osnos based on original design by Jay J. Smith Design Studio, Inc.